"The underlying message of *Nobody's Fool*? I get it—underneath our grandiose opinions of ourselves we're *all* pinheads and freaks! *Nobody's Fool* is boffo! The best graphic novel of the year!"
   —**R. Crumb**

"This is the book Bill Griffith was destined to make. The tale of Schlitzie the Pinhead is one of surprising triumph—an uplifting and heartfelt portrait of a simple man who finds joy in the strangest of lives. *Nobody's Fool* is a brilliant and fascinating work by a master storyteller. Bill Griffith is a comics treasure!"
   —**Derf Backderf**, *My Friend Dahmer* and *Trashed*

"Bill Griffith is amazing. While continuing to create one of the best daily comic strips, he has also produced a tour de force graphic novel. *Nobody's Fool* is wonderfully told with affectionate detail and exquisite pen lines—an obvious labor of love."
   —**Patrick McDonnell**, *Mutts* cartoonist

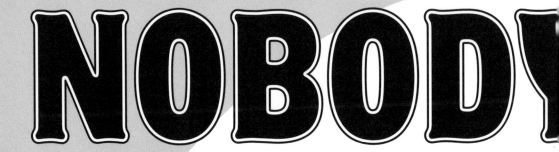

NOBODY

The Life and Times of Schlitzie the Pinhead

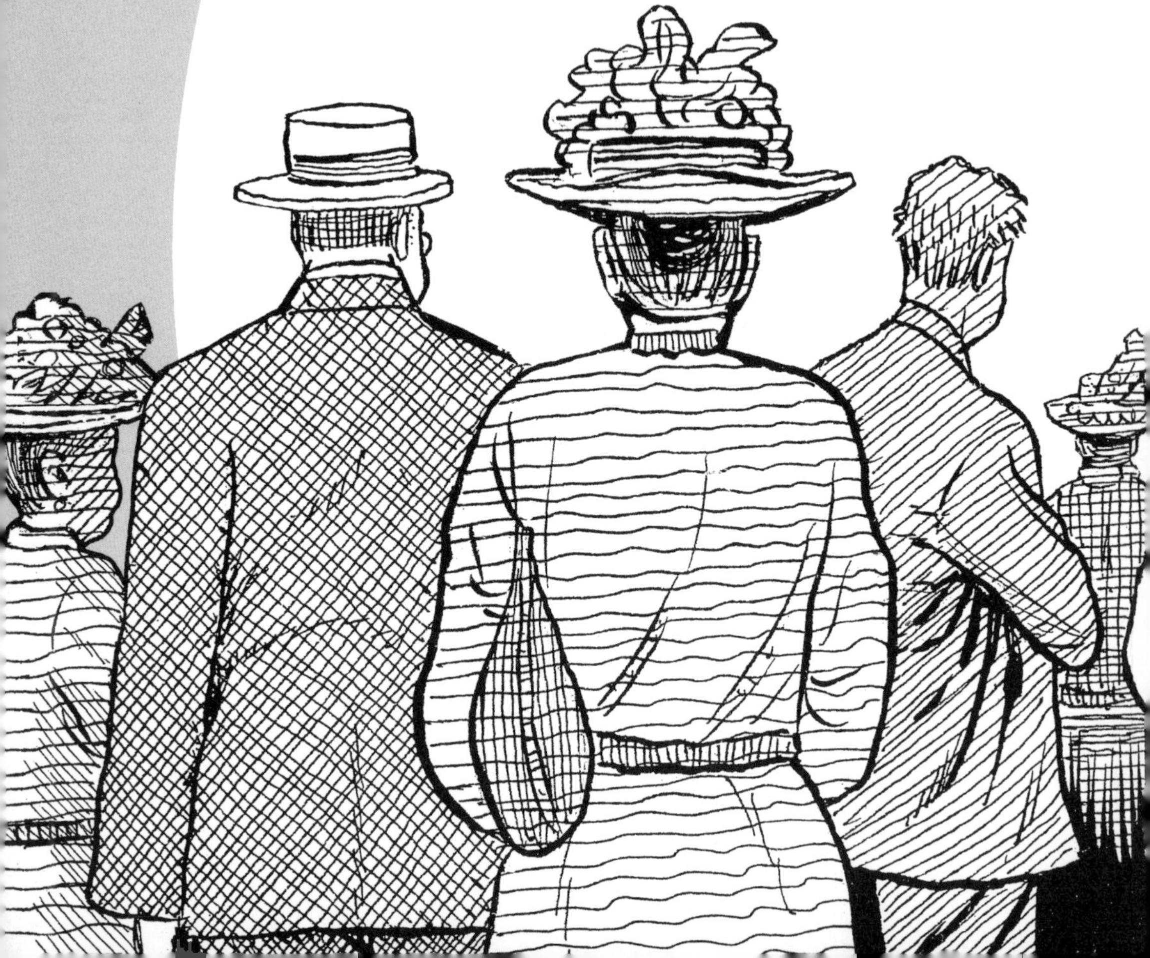

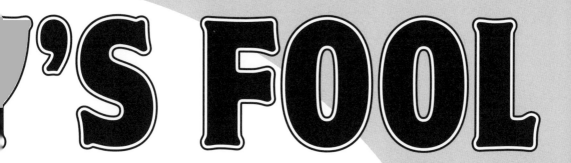

’S FOOL

Bill Griffith

Abrams ComicArts • New York

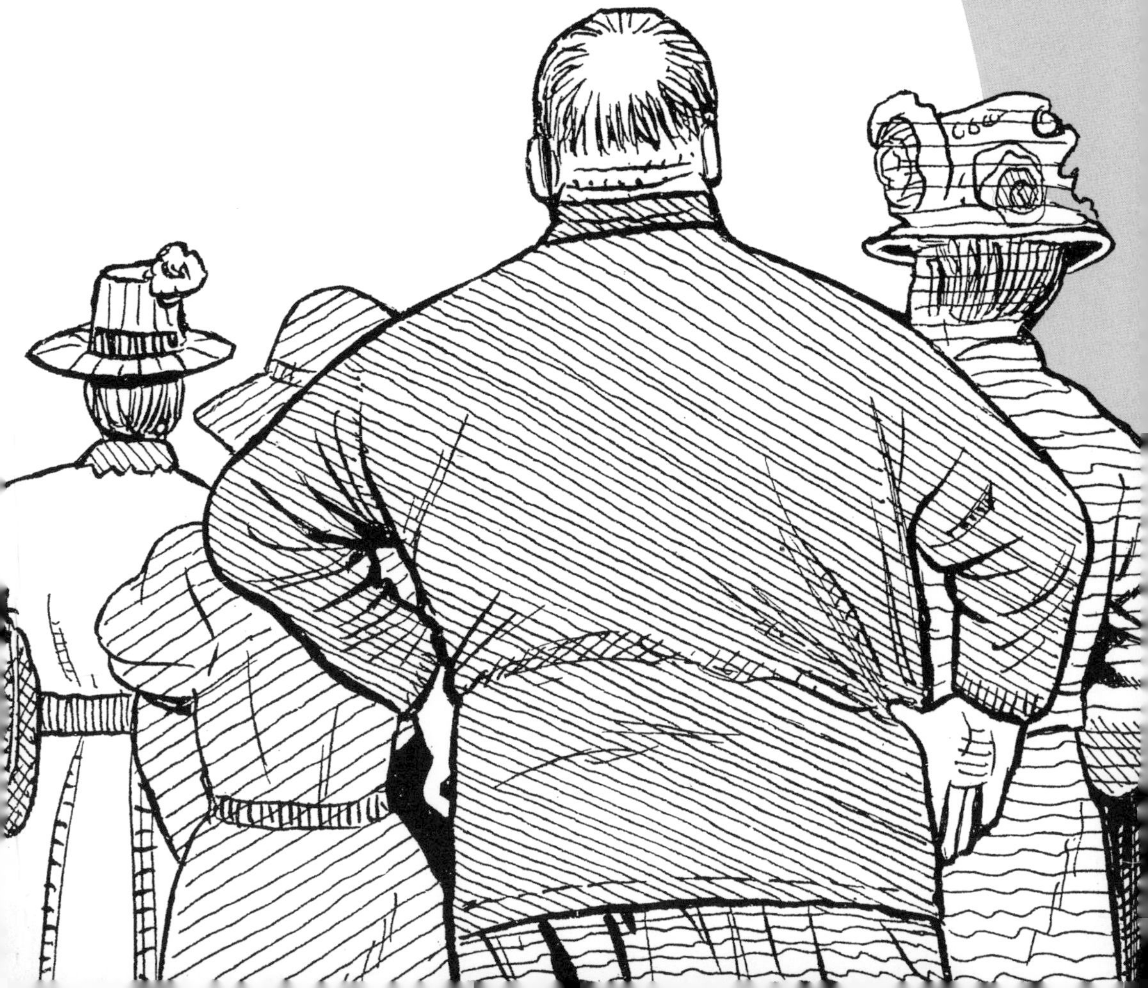

Editor: Charles Kochman
Art Director: Chad W. Beckerman
Designer: Bill Griffith
Design assistance: Liam Flanagan
Managing Editor: Evangelos Vasilakis
Production Manager: Alison Gervais

Library of Congress Cataloging-in-Publication Data

Names: Griffith, Bill, 1944- author.
Title: Nobody's fool: the life and times of Schlitzie the Pinhead /
written and illustrated by Bill Griffith.
Description: New York: Abrams ComicArts, 2019.
Identifiers: LCCN 2018025742 (print) | LCCN 2018043364 (ebook) |
ISBN 9781683354529 (All e-books) | ISBN 9781419735011 (hardback)
Subjects: LCSH: Schlitzie, 1901-1971—Comic books, strips, etc. | Circus
performers—United States—Biography—Comic books, strips, etc.
Sideshows—United States—History—20th century—Comic books,
strips, etc. | Freaks (Motion picture)—Comic books, strips, etc. | Graphic
novels. | BISAC: COMICS & GRAPHIC NOVELS / General. | COMICS
& GRAPHIC NOVELS / Literary.
Classification: LCC GV1811.S377 (ebook) | LCC GV1811.S377 G75
2019 (print) | DDC 791.3092 [B]—dc23

Printed and bound in China
10 9 8 7 6 5 4 3 2 1

Abrams ComicArts books are available at special discounts when
purchased in quantity for premiums and promotions as well as fundraising
or educational use. Special editions can also be created to specification.
For details, contact specialsales@abramsbooks.com or the address below.

Abrams ComicArts® is a registered trademark of Harry N. Abrams, Inc.

ABRAMS The Art of Books
195 Broadway, New York, NY 10007
abramsbooks.com

**To Wolf Krakowski,
who made Schlitzie come alive for me**

Grateful thanks to Diane Noomin, for
her indispensable overview and editing skills.

*Thanks also to Georgiana Goodwin and Chad W. Beckerman
for design advice; and to Charles Kochman,
for believing in the book and keeping all my dots
and dashes properly formatted.*

N obody's Fool: The Life and Times of Schlitzie the Pinhead has been fifty-six years in the making—ever since 1963, when I was an art student and first saw Tod Browning's 1932 film about the sideshow, *Freaks*.

My comic-strip character, Zippy the Pinhead, owes his origin to the same source. Although I derived the name *Zippy* from another famous sideshow pinhead, "Zip the What-Is-It?," Zippy's personality was based on Schlitzie's appearance in *Freaks*. Zippy made his comic book debut in *Real Pulp Comics* no. 1, March 1971.

My knowledge of the real-life Schlitzie was extremely limited back then. All I had to go on was an occasional viewing of *Freaks* on the midnight movie circuit and one souvenir postcard of Schlitzie, in the collection of a fellow cartoonist.

It wasn't until five or six years ago that I was able to put together a reliable time line of Schlitzie's life. Invaluable help came from interviews with Ward Hall, one of Schlitzie's last sideshow managers, and Wolf Krakowski, who worked in the same circus with Schlitzie in 1965. As I collected more information, this book started to take form.

Much of Schlitzie's life is undocumented. Nevertheless, people, places, and events depicted in this book are, for the most part, historically accurate. Details have been imagined or reconstructed when necessary.

Bill Griffith
Hadlyme, Connecticut
June 2018

On their faces was a strangely luminous smile.
I know now what it indicates—
they had met tragedy and fought it to a standstill;
they had taken a handicap
and turned it inside out,
making it work for them;
with courage and patience
they had built themselves a life.

—William Lindsay Gresham,
Monster Midway, 1953

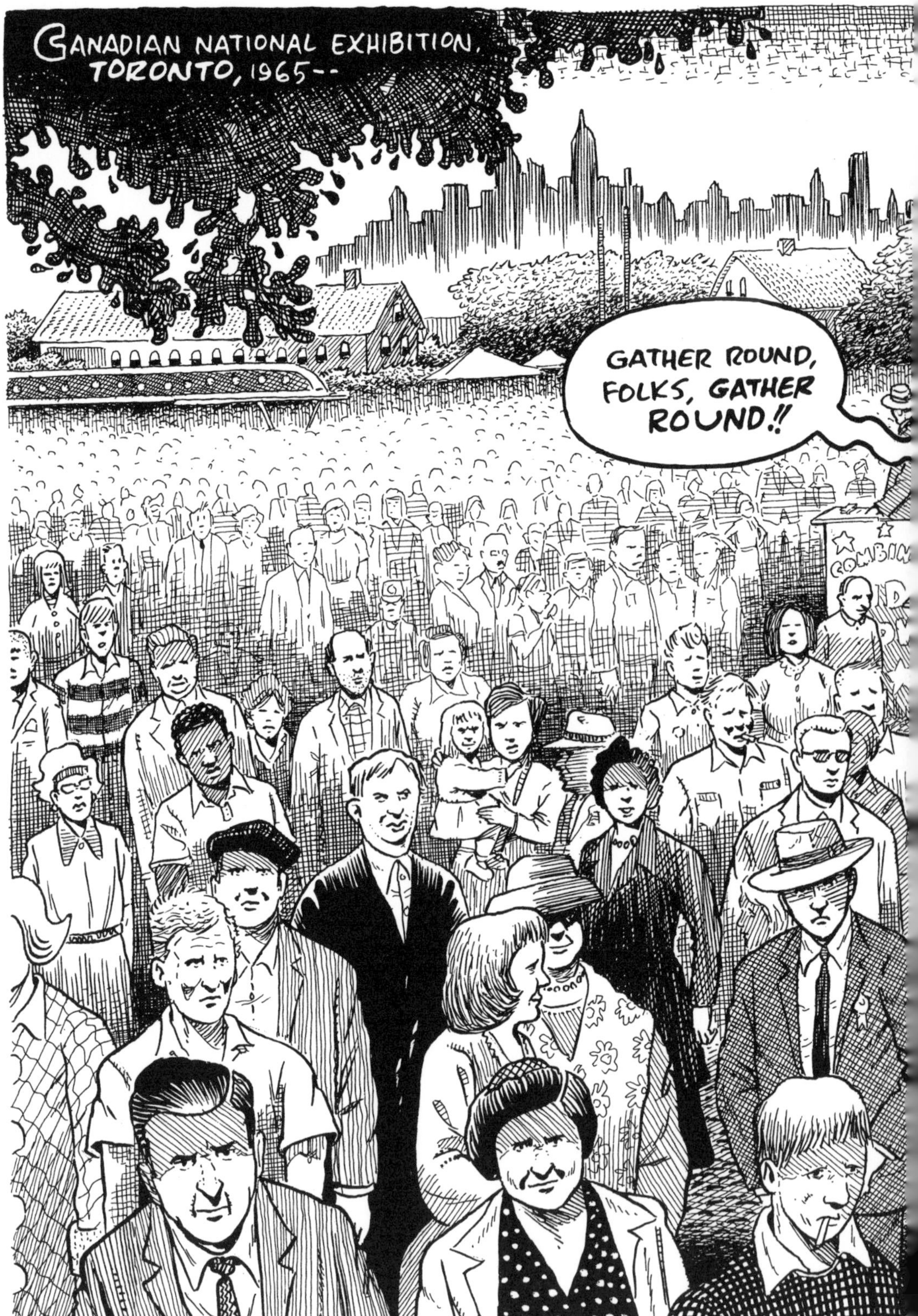
CANADIAN NATIONAL EXHIBITION, TORONTO, 1965--
GATHER ROUND, FOLKS, GATHER ROUND!!

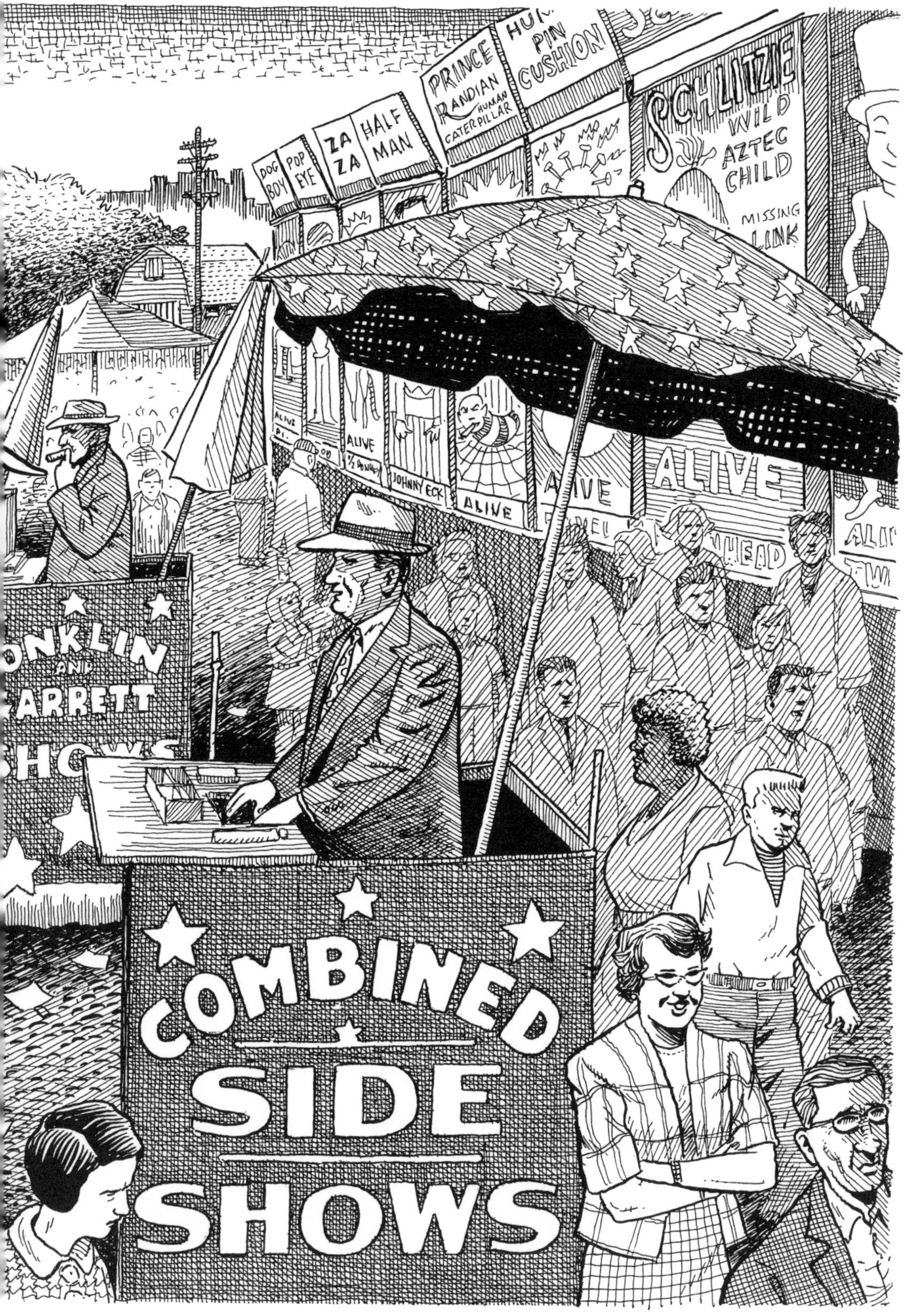
DOG BOY
POP EYE
ZA ZA
HALF MAN
PRINCE RANDIAN HUMAN CATERPILLAR
HUMAN PIN CUSHION
SCHLITZIE WILD AZTEC CHILD
MISSING LINK
ALIVE
1/2 DONKEY
JOHNNY ECK
ALIVE
ALIVE
ALIVE
ALIVE
ONKLIN AND ARRETT SHOWS
COMBINED SIDE SHOWS

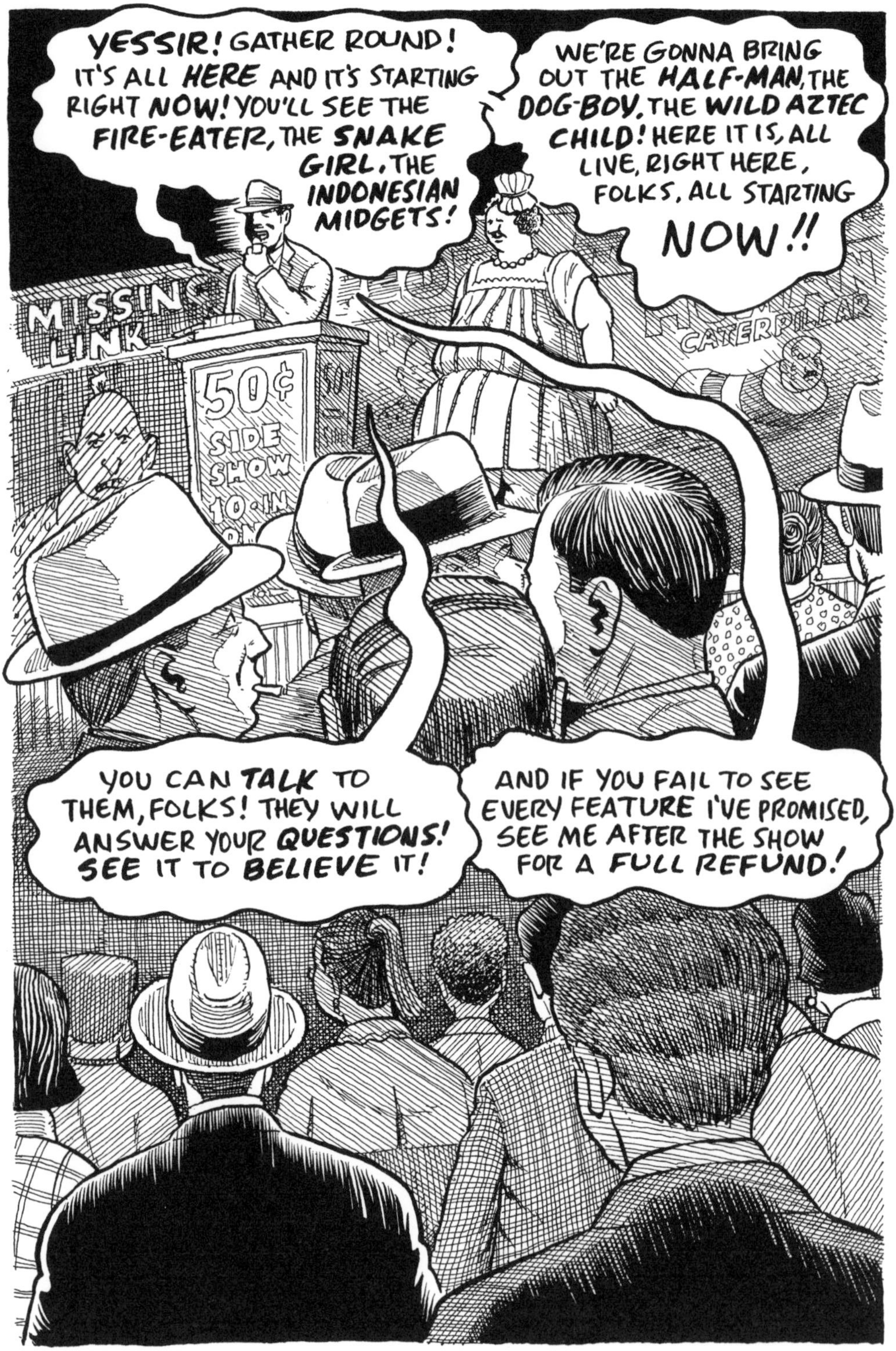
YESSIR! GATHER ROUND! IT'S ALL HERE AND IT'S STARTING RIGHT NOW! YOU'LL SEE THE FIRE-EATER, THE SNAKE GIRL, THE INDONESIAN MIDGETS!
WE'RE GONNA BRING OUT THE HALF-MAN, THE DOG-BOY, THE WILD AZTEC CHILD! HERE IT IS, ALL LIVE, RIGHT HERE, FOLKS, ALL STARTING NOW!!
MISSING LINK
50¢ SIDE SHOW
CATERPILLAR
YOU CAN TALK TO THEM, FOLKS! THEY WILL ANSWER YOUR QUESTIONS! SEE IT TO BELIEVE IT!
AND IF YOU FAIL TO SEE EVERY FEATURE I'VE PROMISED, SEE ME AFTER THE SHOW FOR A FULL REFUND!

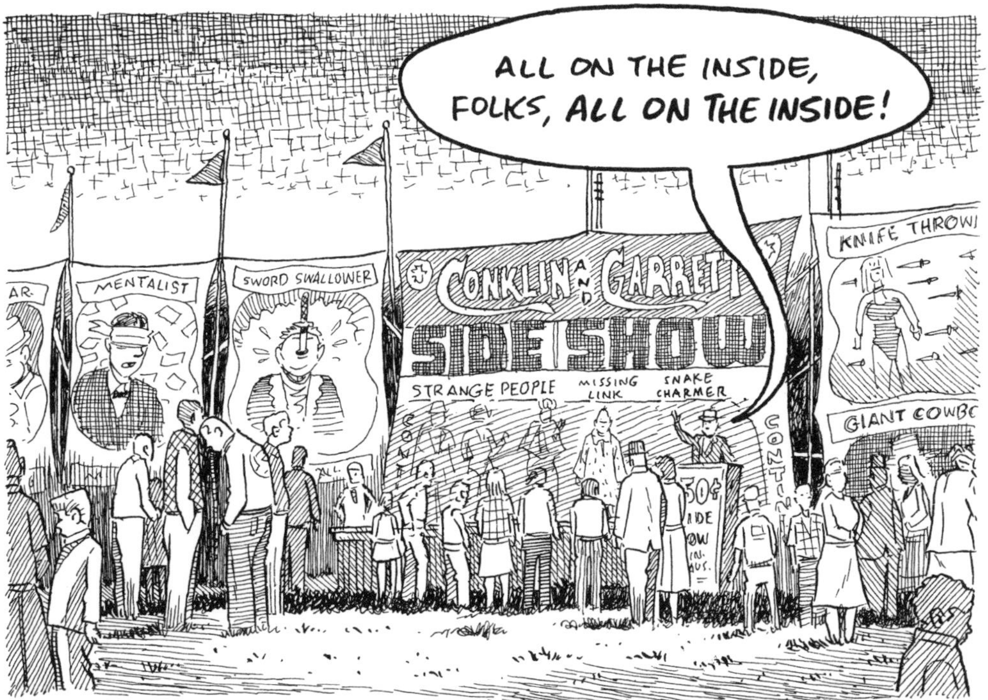
ALL ON THE INSIDE, FOLKS, ALL ON THE INSIDE!
MENTALIST
SWORD SWALLOWER
CONKLIN AND GARRETT
SIDE SHOW
STRANGE PEOPLE
MISSING LINK
SNAKE CHARMER
KNIFE THROWI
GIANT COWBO
50¢

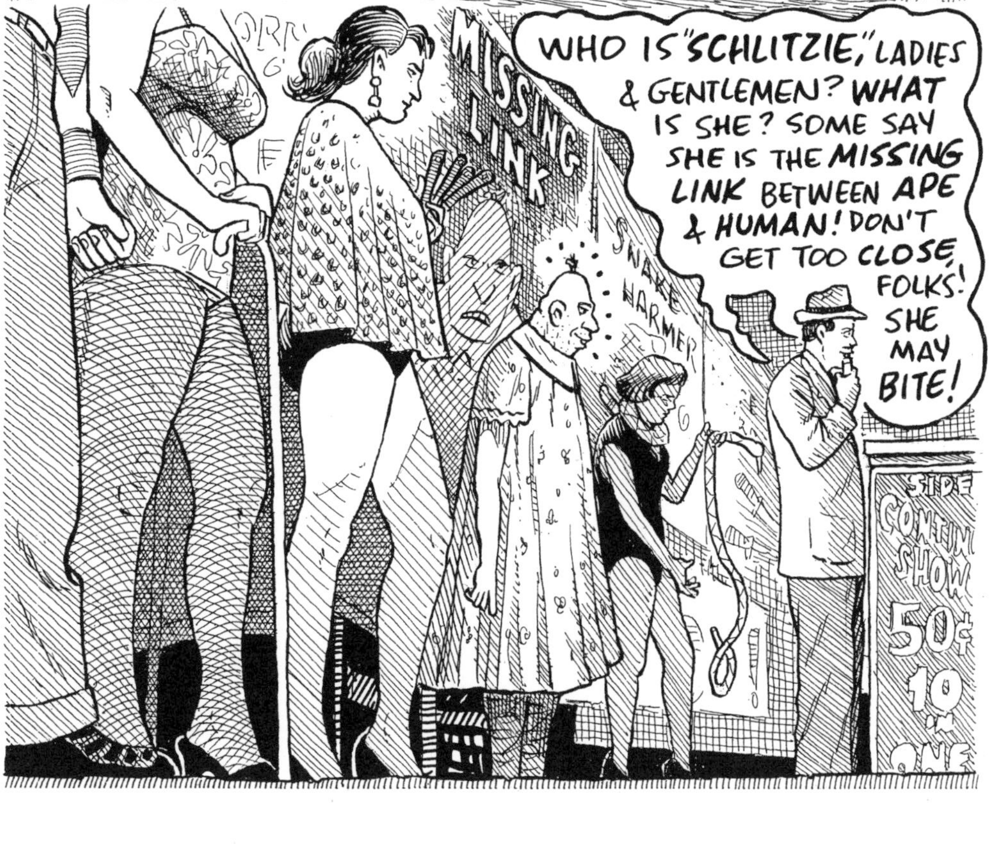
WHO IS "SCHLITZIE," LADIES & GENTLEMEN? WHAT IS SHE? SOME SAY SHE IS THE MISSING LINK BETWEEN APE & HUMAN! DON'T GET TOO CLOSE, FOLKS! SHE MAY BITE!
MISSING LINK
SNAKE CHARMER
50¢

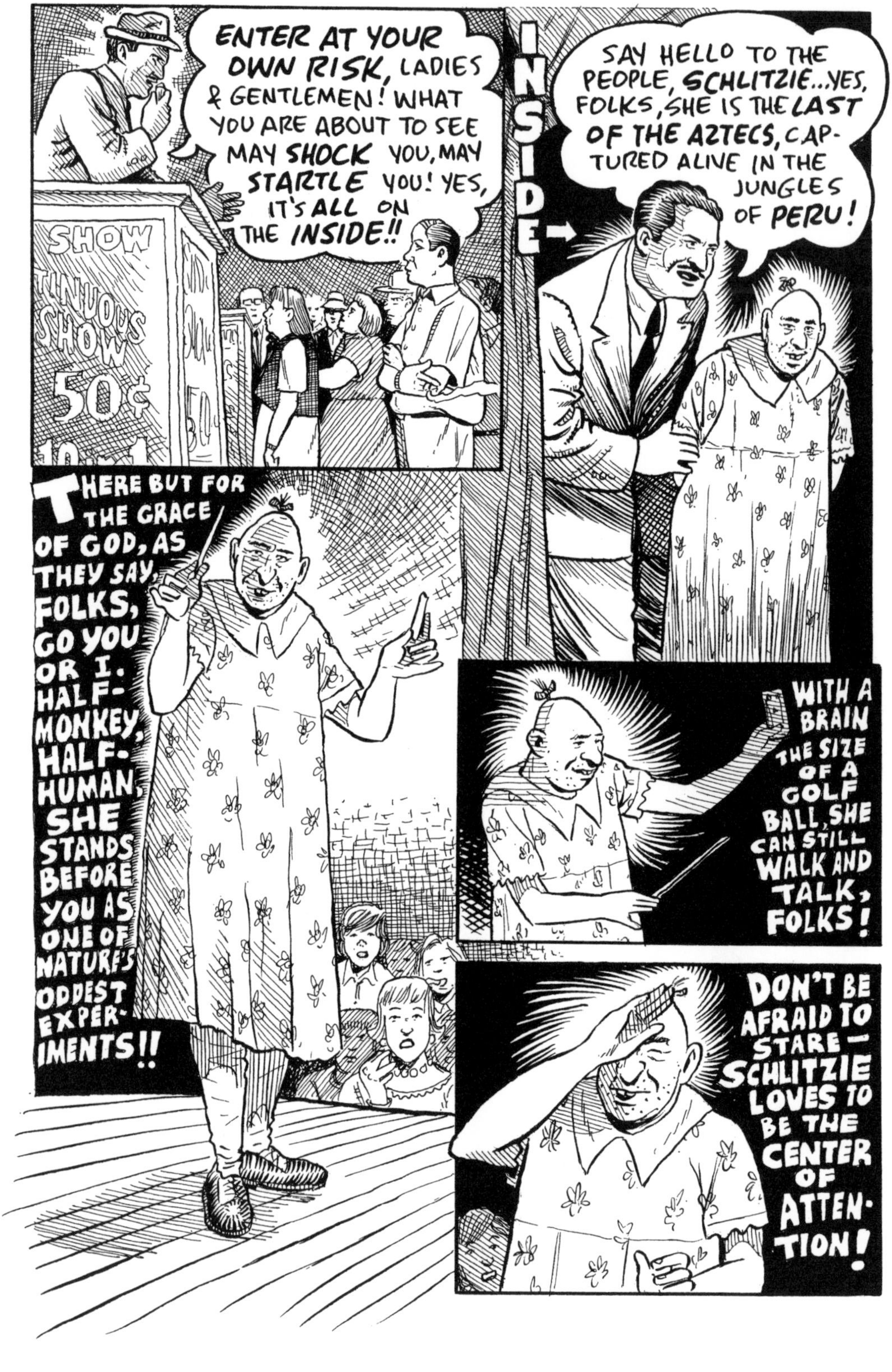
ENTER AT YOUR OWN RISK, LADIES & GENTLEMEN! WHAT YOU ARE ABOUT TO SEE MAY SHOCK YOU, MAY STARTLE YOU! YES, IT'S ALL ON THE INSIDE!!
SHOW
SHOW
50¢
INSIDE →
SAY HELLO TO THE PEOPLE, SCHLITZIE...YES, FOLKS, SHE IS THE LAST OF THE AZTECS, CAPTURED ALIVE IN THE JUNGLES OF PERU!
THERE BUT FOR THE GRACE OF GOD, AS THEY SAY, FOLKS, GO YOU OR I. HALF-MONKEY, HALF-HUMAN, SHE STANDS BEFORE YOU AS ONE OF NATURE'S ODDEST EXPERIMENTS!!
WITH A BRAIN THE SIZE OF A GOLF BALL, SHE CAN STILL WALK AND TALK, FOLKS!
DON'T BE AFRAID TO STARE— SCHLITZIE LOVES TO BE THE CENTER OF ATTENTION!

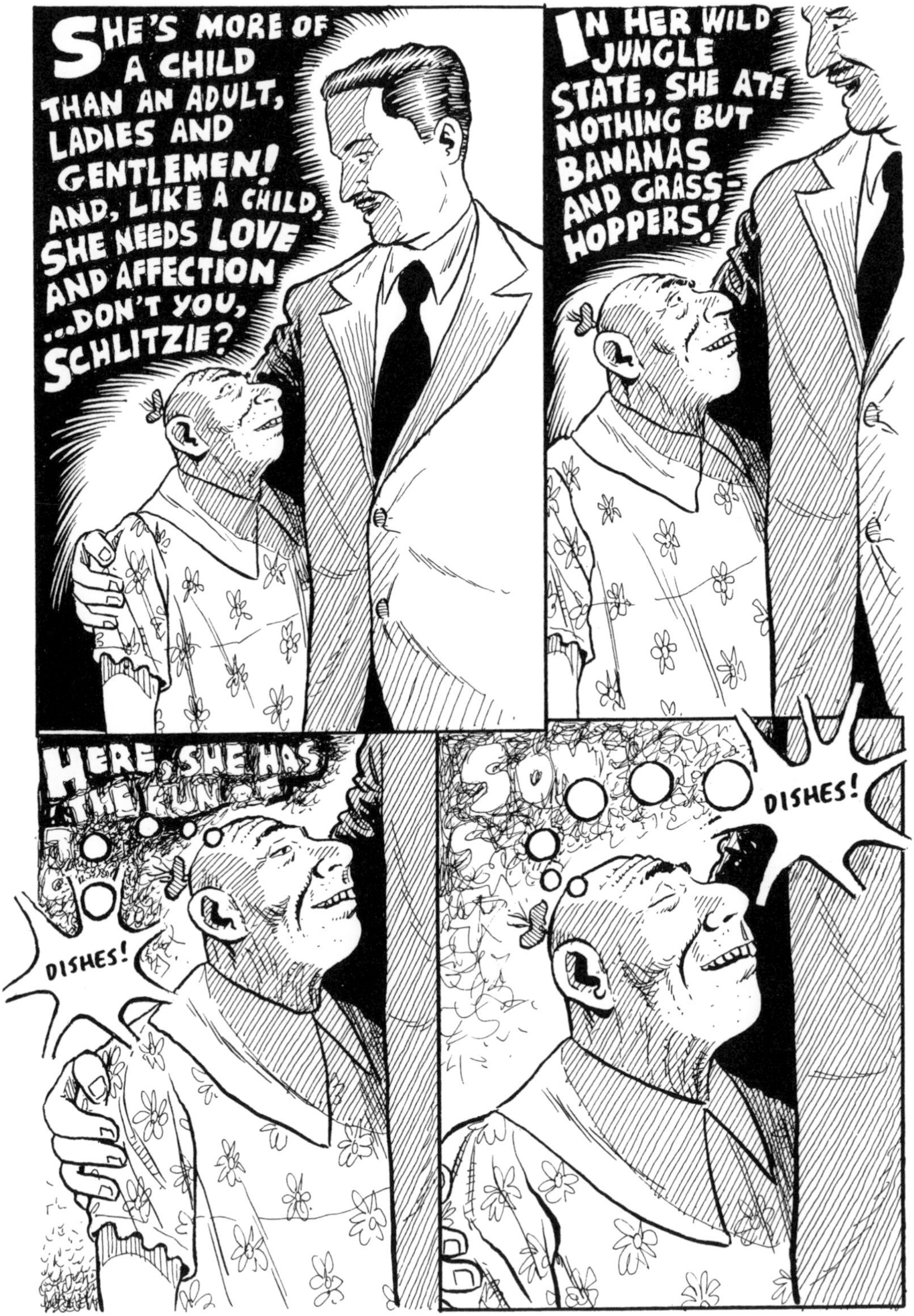
SHE'S MORE OF A CHILD THAN AN ADULT, LADIES AND GENTLEMEN! AND, LIKE A CHILD, SHE NEEDS LOVE AND AFFECTION ...DON'T YOU, SCHLITZIE?
IN HER WILD JUNGLE STATE, SHE ATE NOTHING BUT BANANAS AND GRASS-HOPPERS!
HERE, SHE HAS
DISHES!
DISHES!

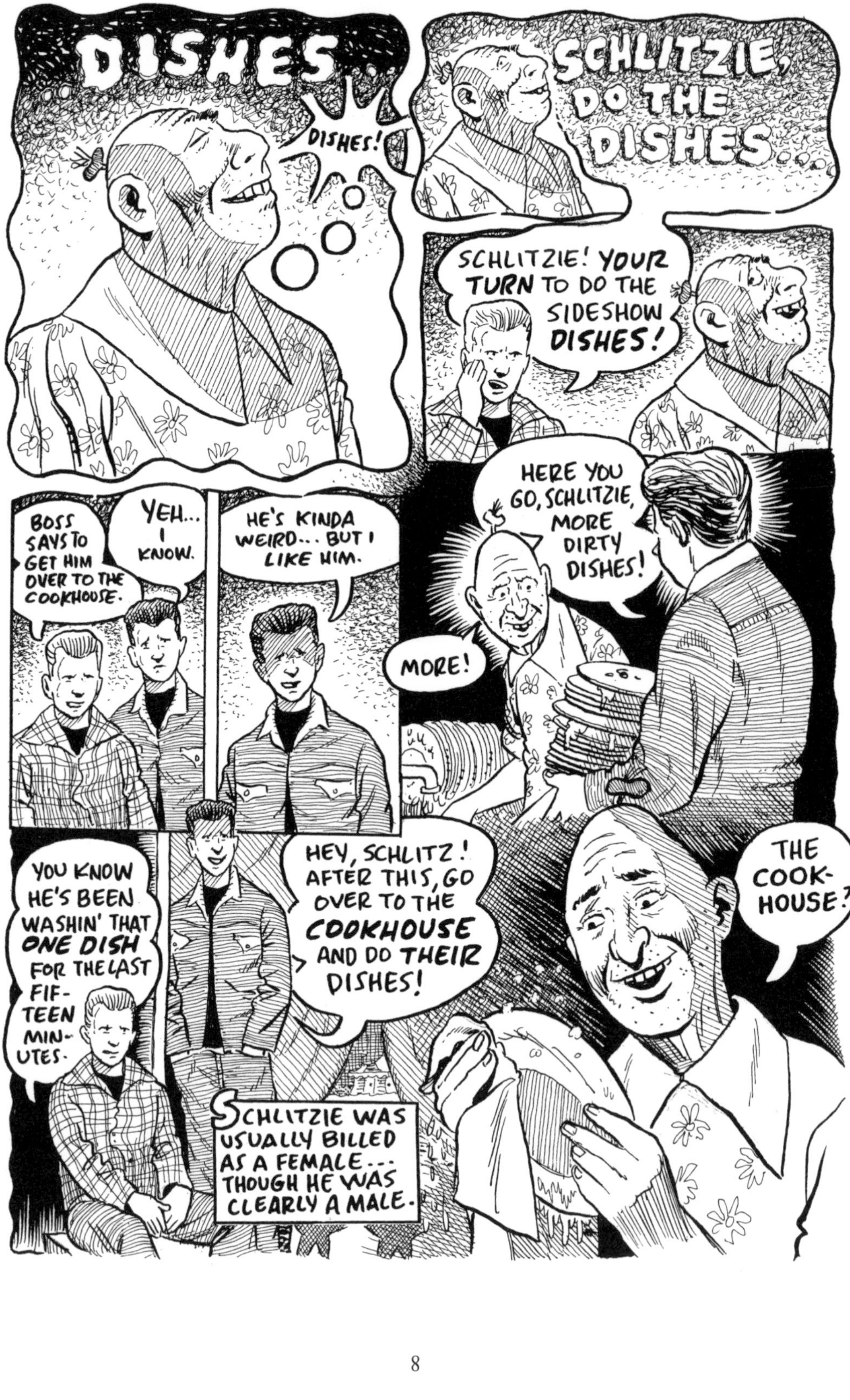
DISHES...
DISHES!
SCHLITZIE, DO THE DISHES...
SCHLITZIE! YOUR TURN TO DO THE SIDESHOW DISHES!
BOSS SAYS TO GET HIM OVER TO THE COOKHOUSE.
YEH... I KNOW.
HE'S KINDA WEIRD... BUT I LIKE HIM.
HERE YOU GO, SCHLITZIE, MORE DIRTY DISHES!
MORE!
YOU KNOW HE'S BEEN WASHIN' THAT ONE DISH FOR THE LAST FIF-TEEN MIN-UTES.
HEY, SCHLITZ! AFTER THIS, GO OVER TO THE COOKHOUSE AND DO THEIR DISHES!
THE COOK-HOUSE?
SCHLITZIE WAS USUALLY BILLED AS A FEMALE... THOUGH HE WAS CLEARLY A MALE.

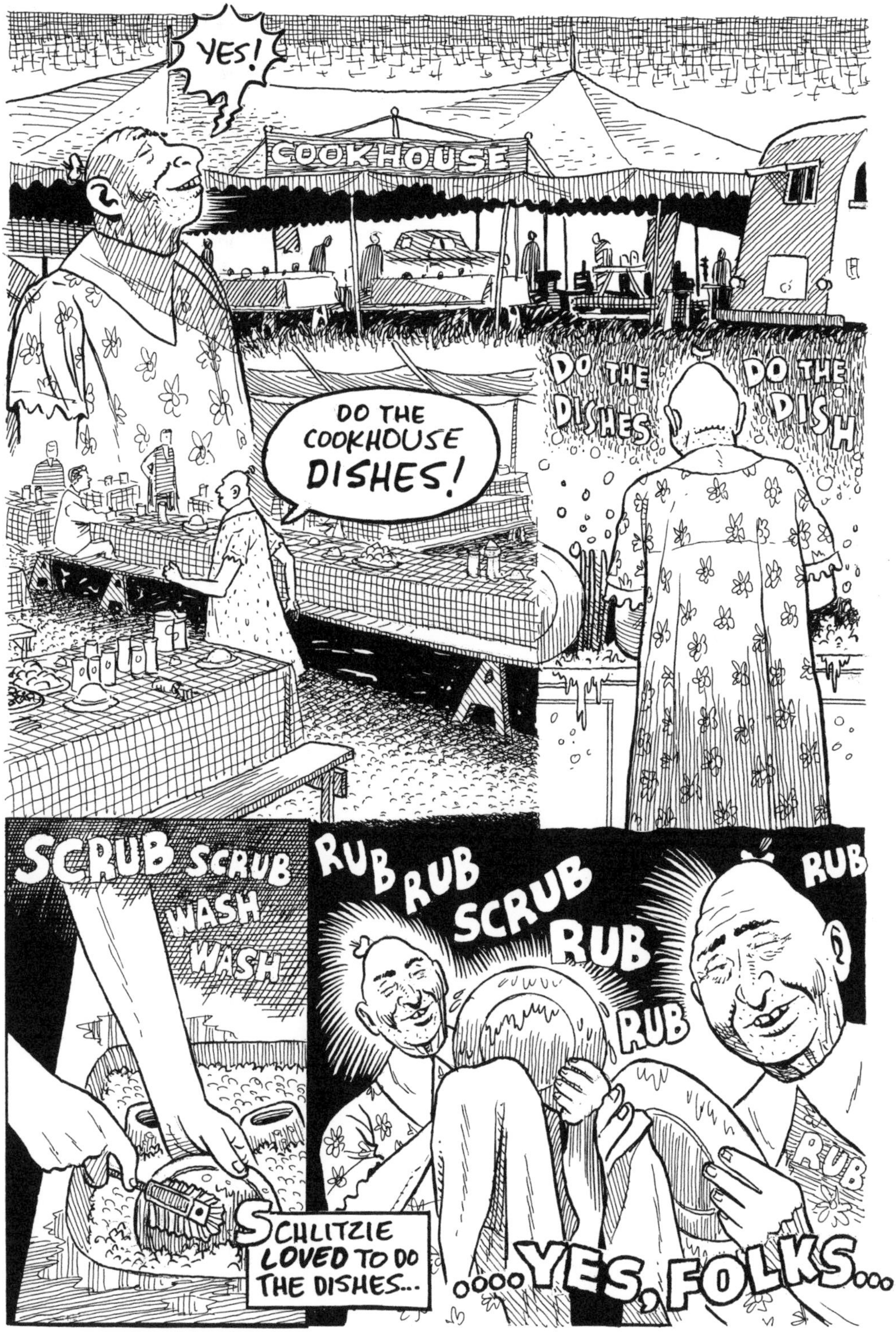
YES!
COOKHOUSE
DO THE COOKHOUSE DISHES!
DO THE DISHES
DO THE DISH
SCRUB SCRUB
WASH
WASH
SCHLITZIE LOVED TO DO THE DISHES...
RUB RUB
SCRUB
RUB
RUB
RUB
RUB
...YES, FOLKS...

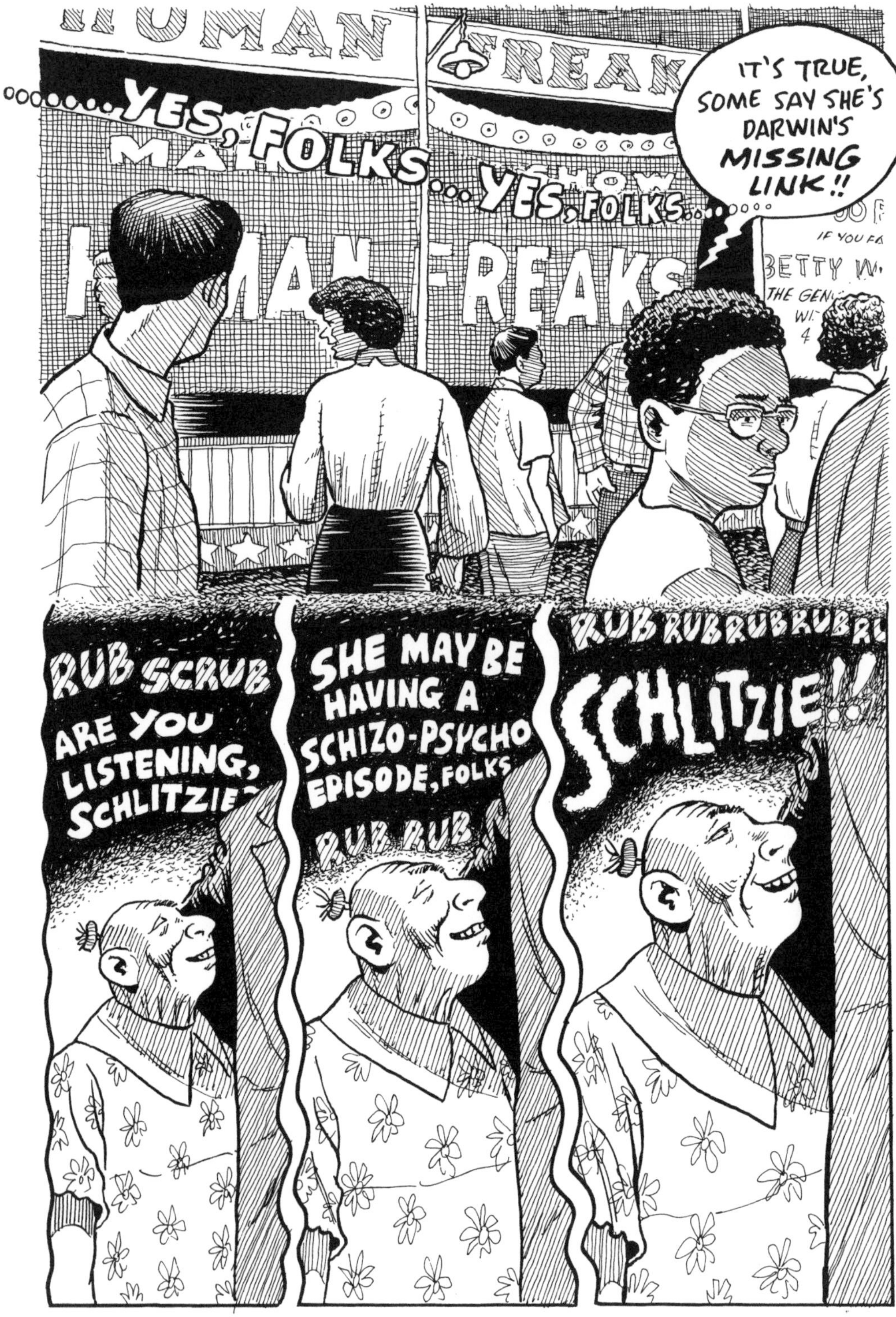
HUMAN FREAKS
oooooo...YES, FOLKS...YES, FOLKS...
IT'S TRUE, SOME SAY SHE'S DARWIN'S MISSING LINK!!
HUMAN FREAKS
BETTY W
THE GEN
RUB SCRUB
ARE YOU LISTENING, SCHLITZIE
SHE MAY BE HAVING A SCHIZO-PSYCHO EPISODE, FOLKS
RUB RUB
RUB RUB RUB RUB RUB
SCHLITZIE!!

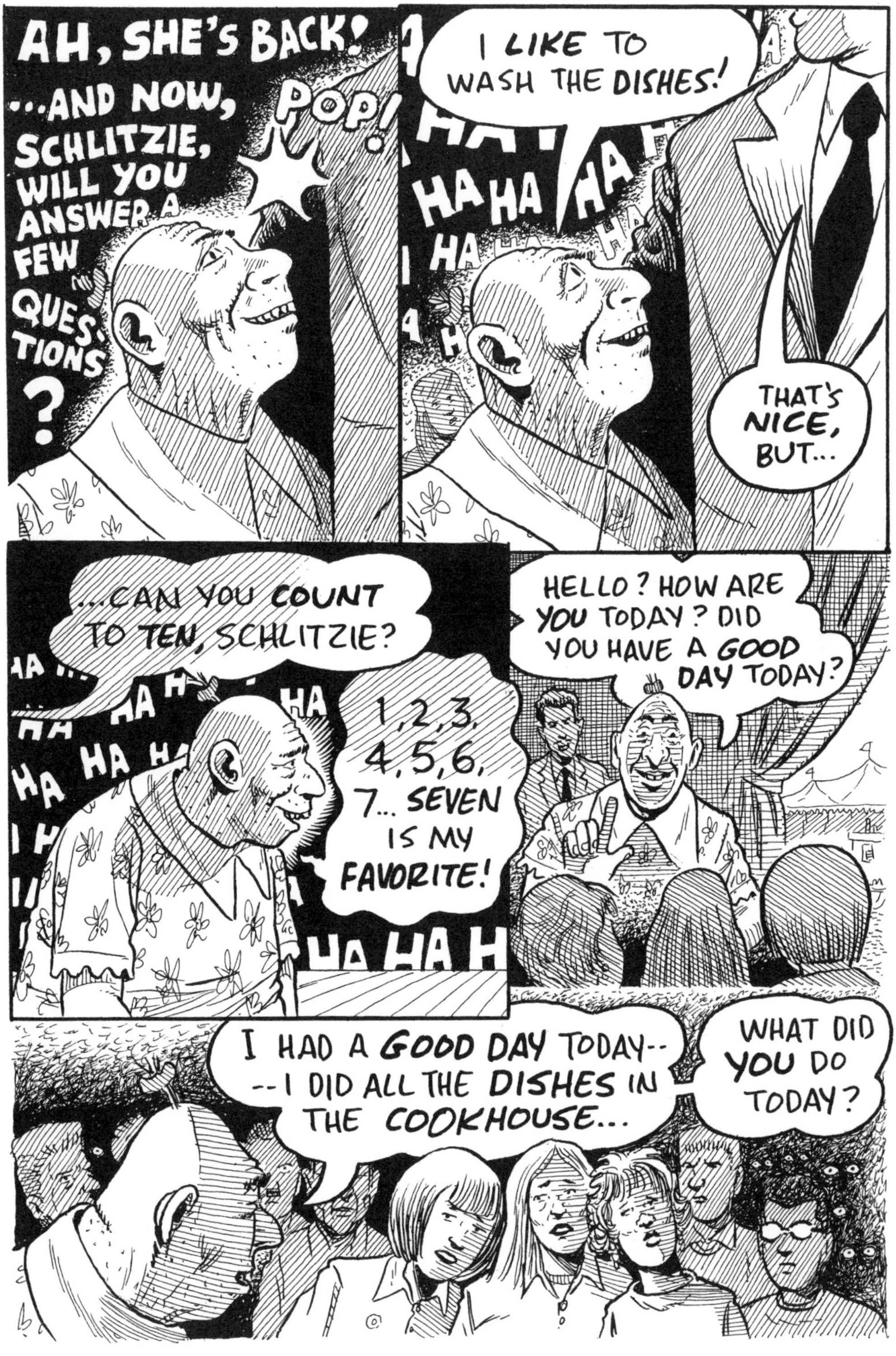
AH, SHE'S BACK!
...AND NOW, SCHLITZIE, WILL YOU ANSWER A FEW QUESTIONS?
POP!
I LIKE TO WASH THE DISHES!
HA HA HA HA
THAT'S NICE, BUT...
...CAN YOU COUNT TO TEN, SCHLITZIE?
HA HA HA
1,2,3, 4,5,6, 7... SEVEN IS MY FAVORITE!
HA HA H
HELLO? HOW ARE YOU TODAY? DID YOU HAVE A GOOD DAY TODAY?
I HAD A GOOD DAY TODAY-- --I DID ALL THE DISHES IN THE COOKHOUSE...
WHAT DID YOU DO TODAY?

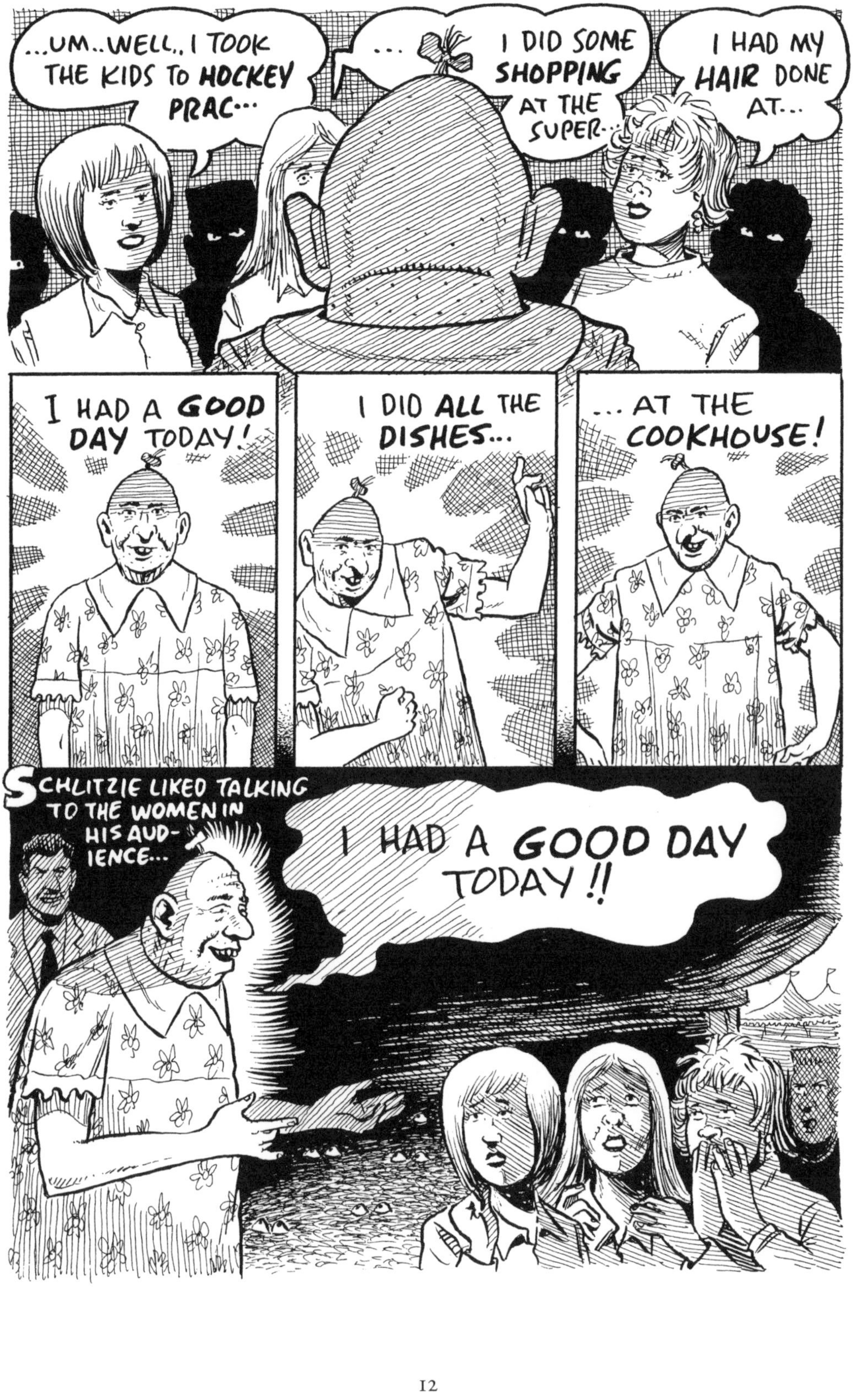
...UM..WELL.. I TOOK THE KIDS TO HOCKEY PRAC...
... I DID SOME SHOPPING AT THE SUPER...
I HAD MY HAIR DONE AT...
I HAD A GOOD DAY TODAY!
I DID ALL THE DISHES...
... AT THE COOKHOUSE!
SCHLITZIE LIKED TALKING TO THE WOMEN IN HIS AUD-IENCE...
I HAD A GOOD DAY TODAY !!

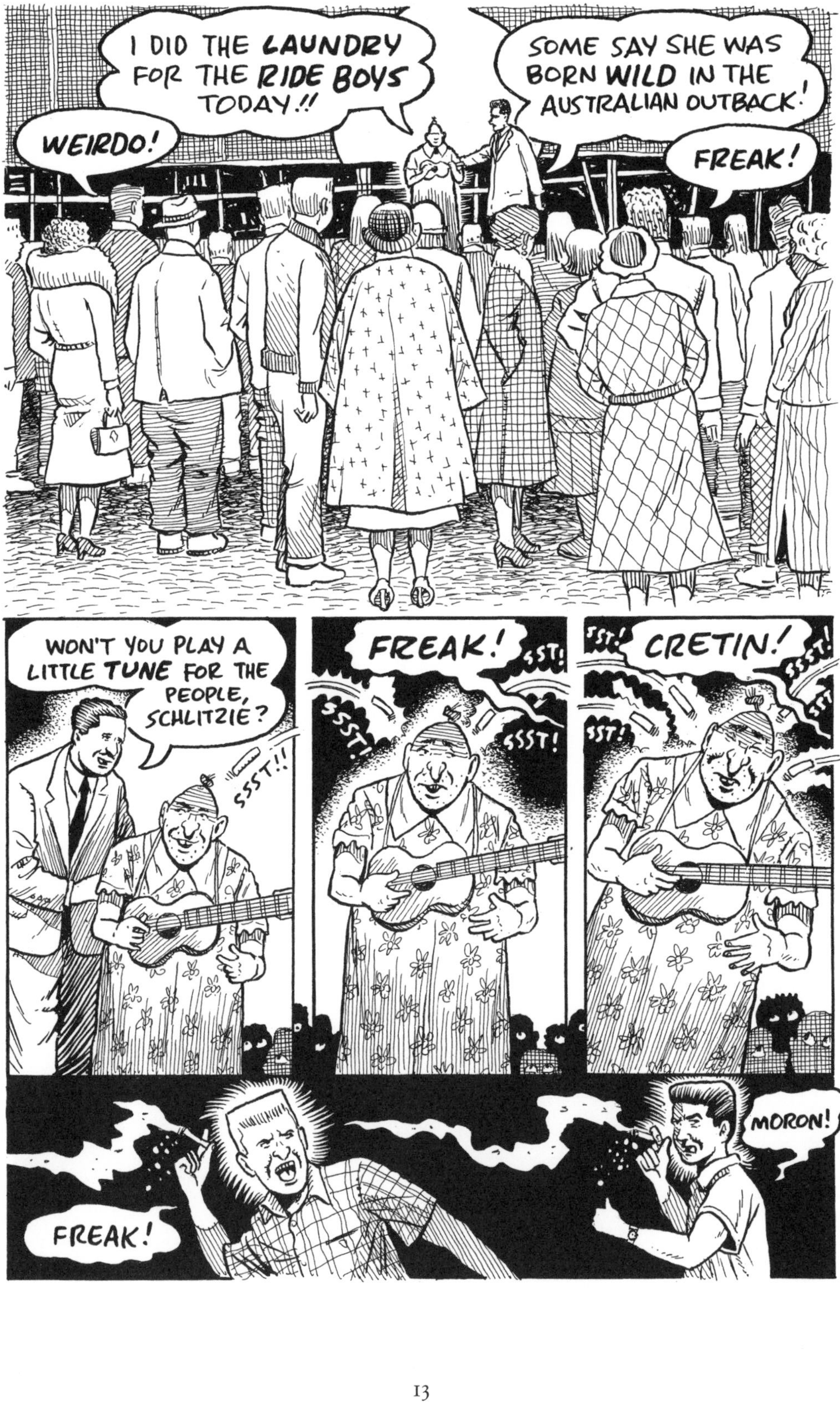
I DID THE LAUNDRY FOR THE RIDE BOYS TODAY!!
SOME SAY SHE WAS BORN WILD IN THE AUSTRALIAN OUTBACK!
WEIRDO!
FREAK!
WON'T YOU PLAY A LITTLE TUNE FOR THE PEOPLE, SCHLITZIE?
SSST!!
FREAK!
SSST!
SSSST!
SSST!
SST!
CRETIN!
SSST!
SST!
SST!
FREAK!
MORON!

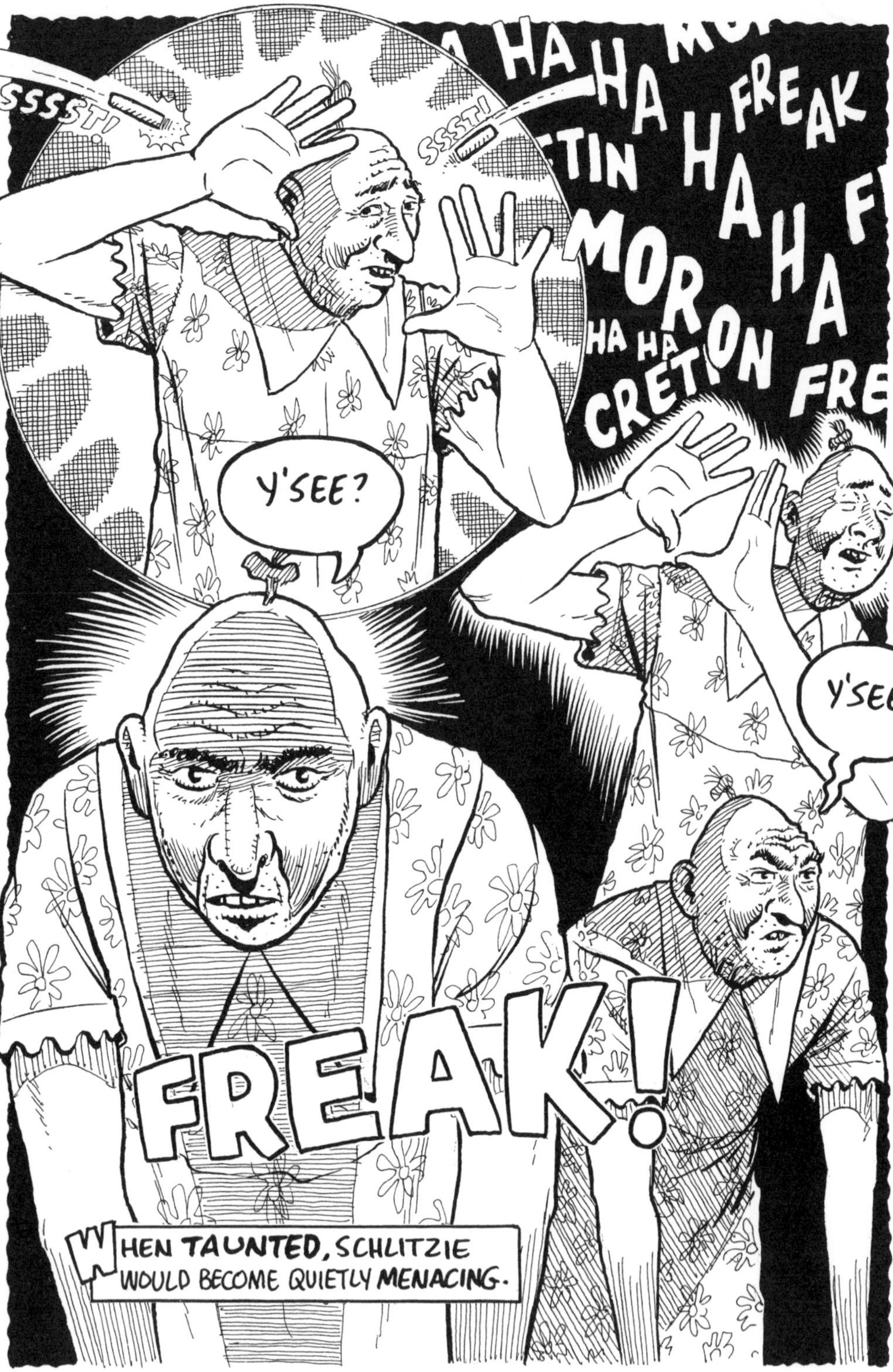
SSSST!
SSSST!
HA HA HA FREAK
ETIN HA HA F
MORON HA
HA HA
CRETIN FRE
Y'SEE?
Y'SEE?
FREAK!
WHEN TAUNTED, SCHLITZIE WOULD BECOME QUIETLY MENACING.

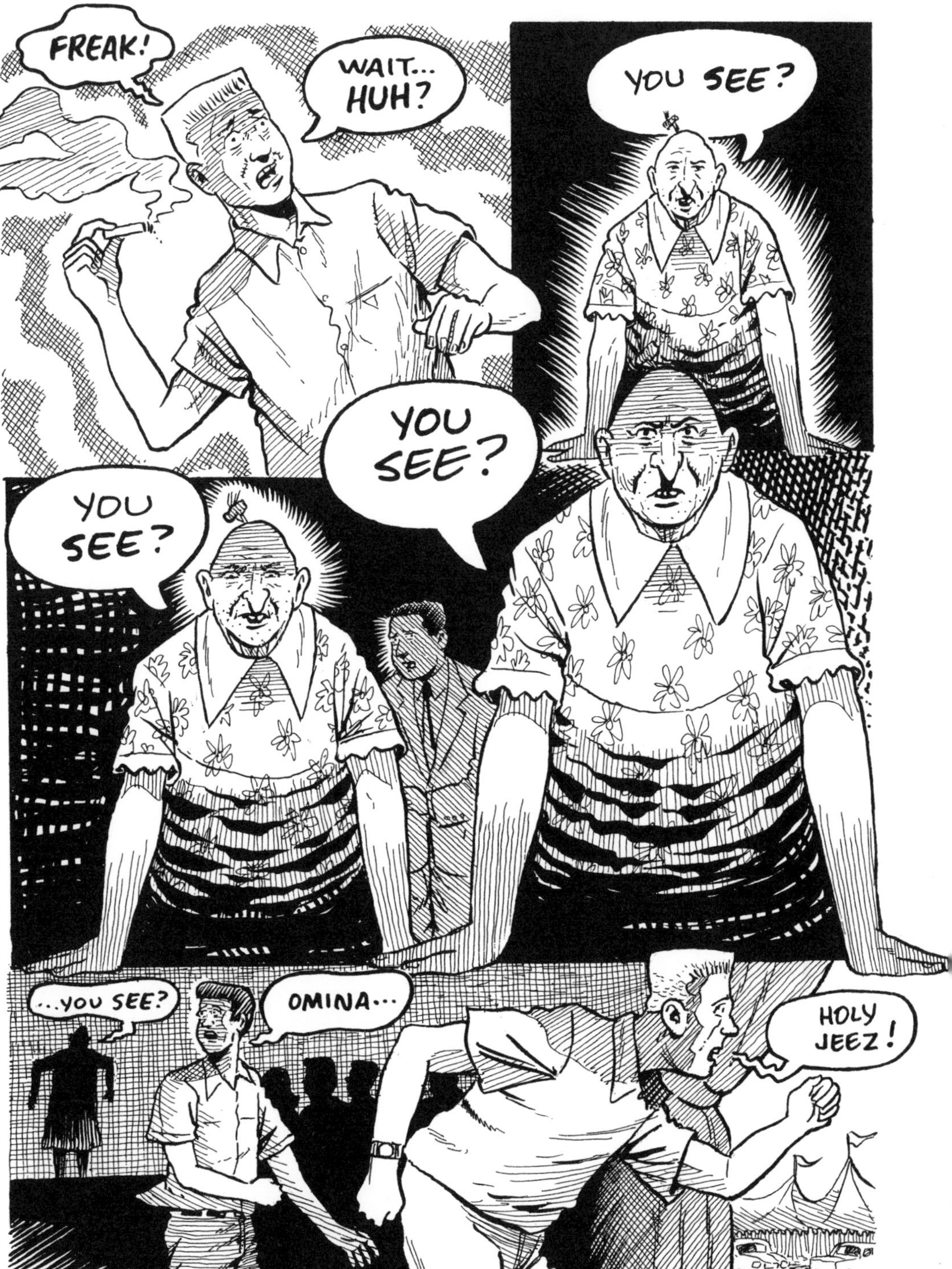
FREAK!
WAIT... HUH?
YOU SEE?
YOU SEE?
YOU SEE?
...YOU SEE?
OMINA...
HOLY JEEZ!

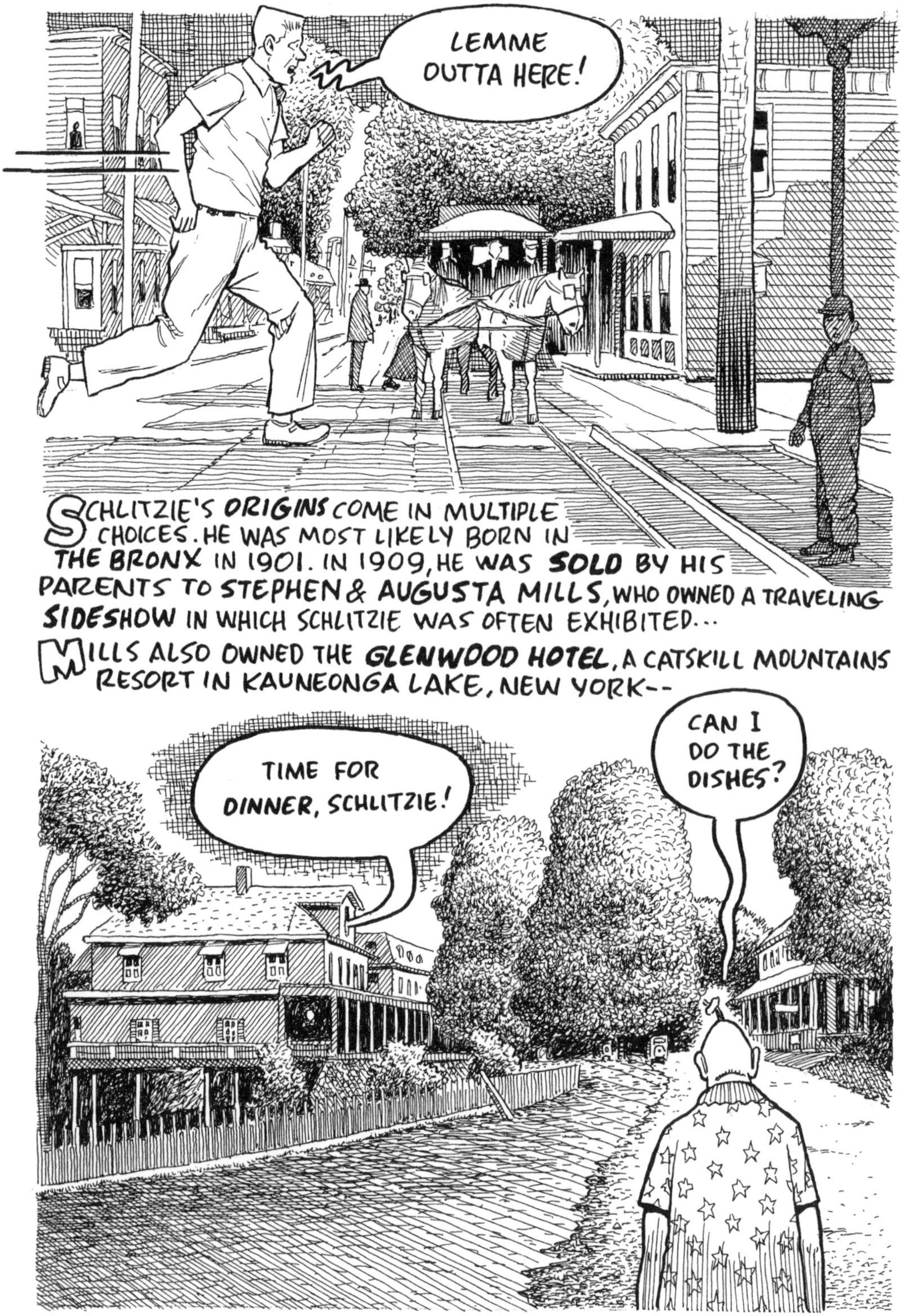
LEMME OUTTA HERE!
SCHLITZIE'S ORIGINS COME IN MULTIPLE CHOICES. HE WAS MOST LIKELY BORN IN THE BRONX IN 1901. IN 1909, HE WAS SOLD BY HIS PARENTS TO STEPHEN & AUGUSTA MILLS, WHO OWNED A TRAVELING SIDESHOW IN WHICH SCHLITZIE WAS OFTEN EXHIBITED...
MILLS ALSO OWNED THE GLENWOOD HOTEL, A CATSKILL MOUNTAINS RESORT IN KAUNEONGA LAKE, NEW YORK--
TIME FOR DINNER, SCHLITZIE!
CAN I DO THE DISHES?

ON 1922, SCHLITZIE MADE HIS FIRST **CONEY ISLAND** APPEARANCE-- HE WAS BILLED AS "**TIK-TAK**, THE AZTEC **CHILD**"...

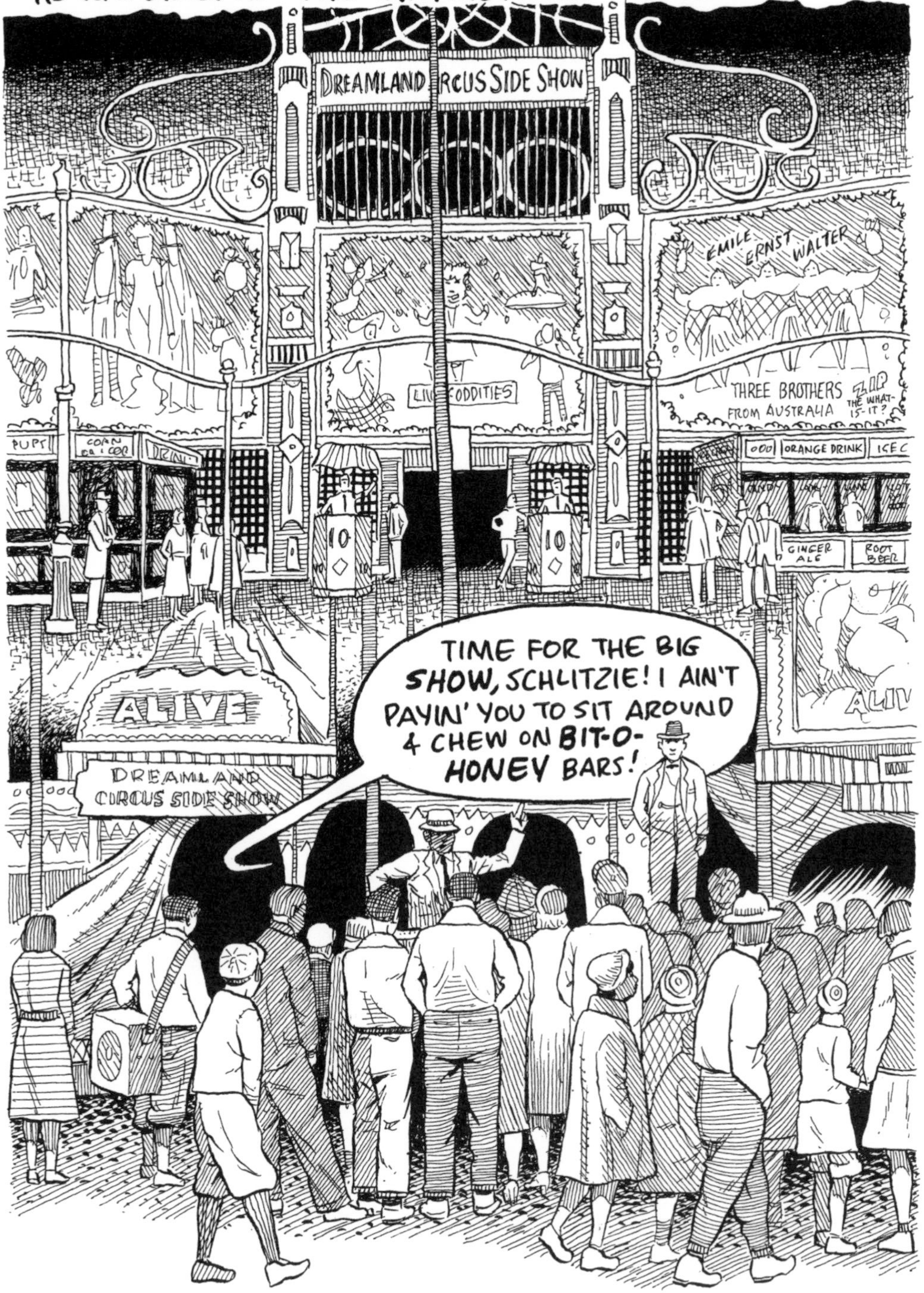
DREAMLAND RCUS SIDE SHOW
EMILE ERNST WALTER
THREE BROTHERS FROM AUSTRALIA
ZIP THE WHAT-IS-IT?
LIVE ODDITIES
ORANGE DRINK
GINGER ALE
ROOT BEER
ALIVE
DREAMLAND CIRCUS SIDE SHOW
TIME FOR THE BIG SHOW, SCHLITZIE! I AIN'T PAYIN' YOU TO SIT AROUND & CHEW ON BIT-O-HONEY BARS!

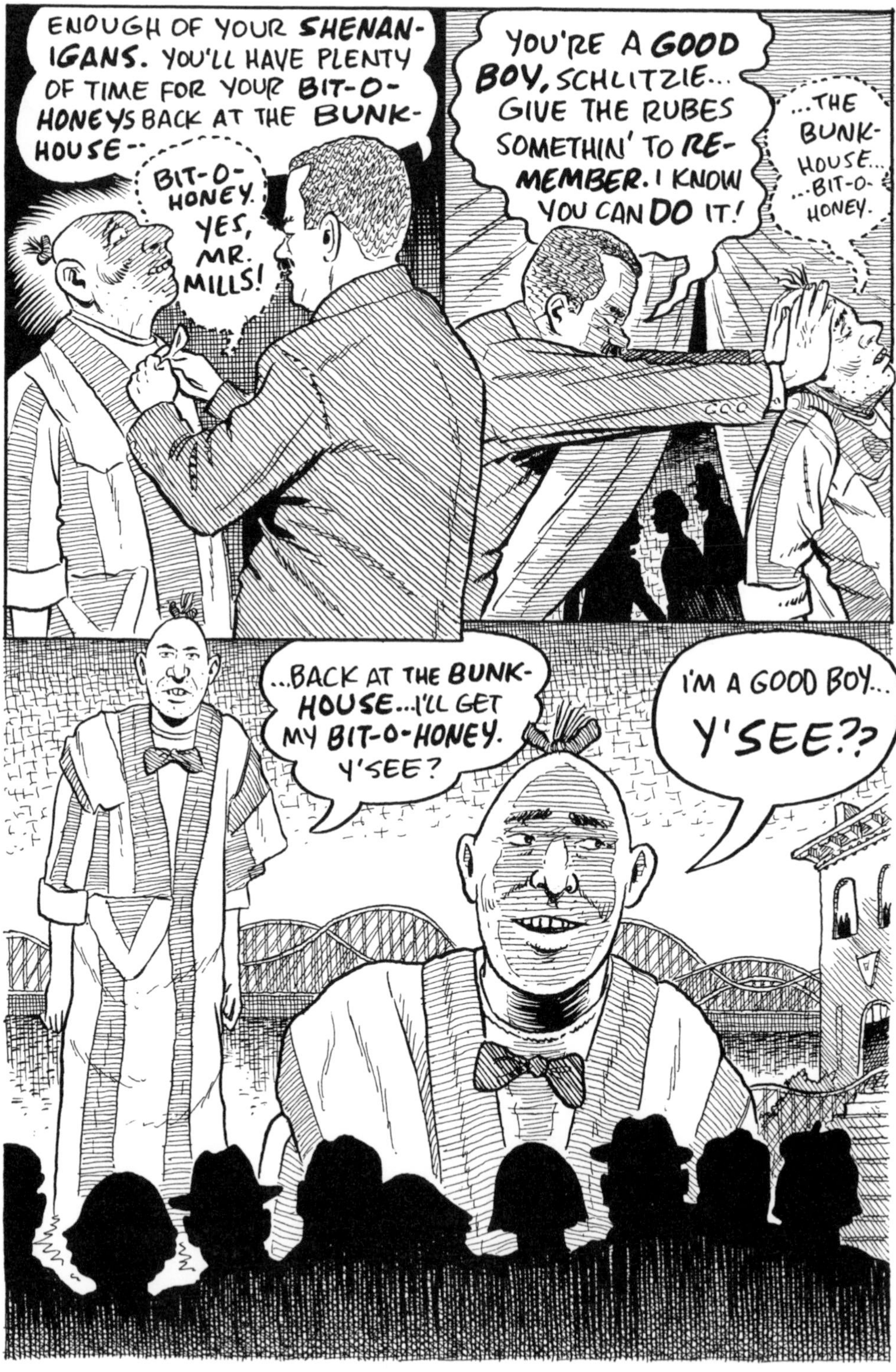
ENOUGH OF YOUR SHENANIGANS. YOU'LL HAVE PLENTY OF TIME FOR YOUR BIT-O-HONEYS BACK AT THE BUNKHOUSE--
BIT-O-HONEY. YES, MR. MILLS!
YOU'RE A GOOD BOY, SCHLITZIE... GIVE THE RUBES SOMETHIN' TO REMEMBER. I KNOW YOU CAN DO IT!
...THE BUNKHOUSE... ...BIT-O-HONEY.
...BACK AT THE BUNKHOUSE...I'LL GET MY BIT-O-HONEY. Y'SEE?
I'M A GOOD BOY... Y'SEE??

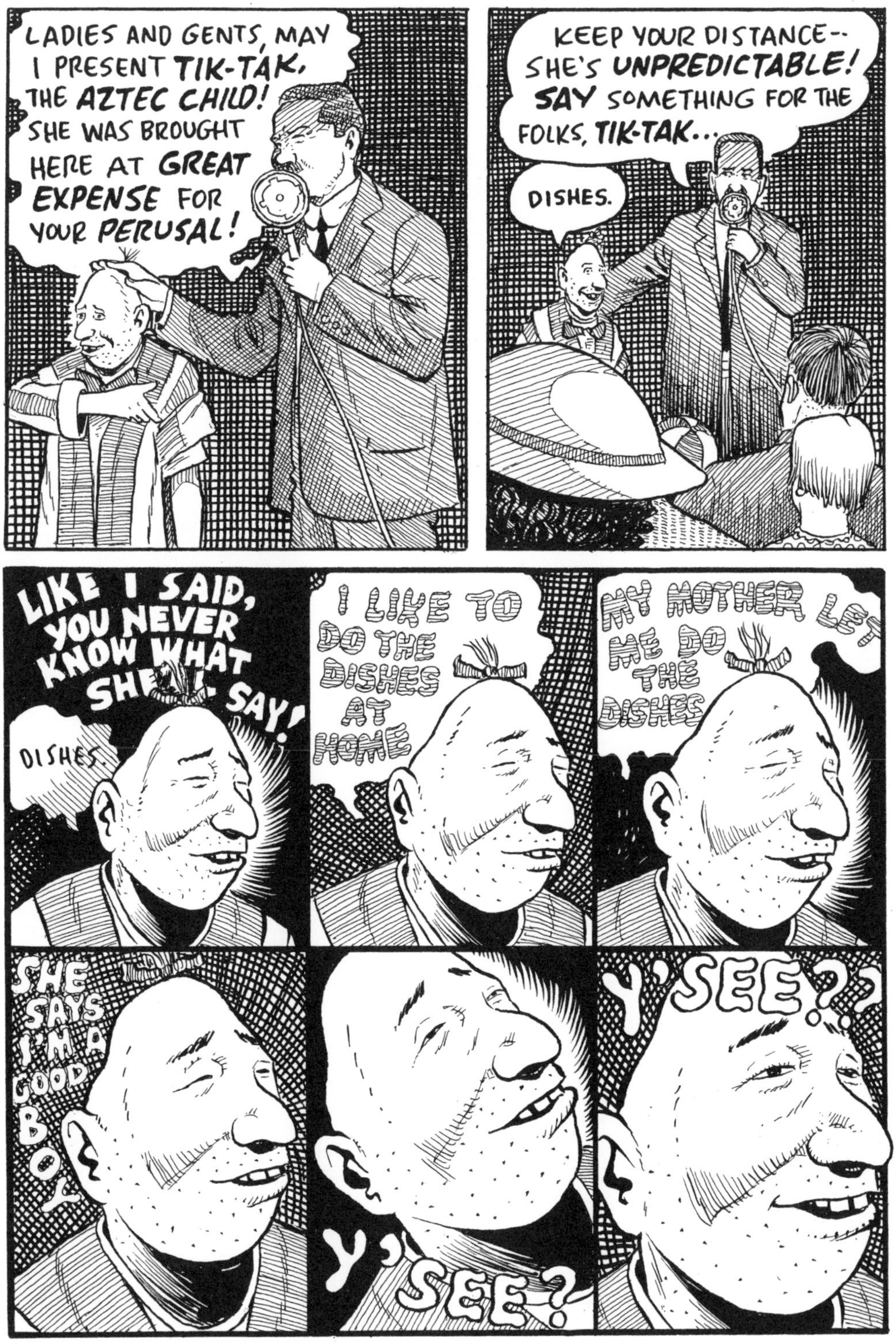

LADIES AND GENTS, MAY I PRESENT TIK-TAK, THE AZTEC CHILD! SHE WAS BROUGHT HERE AT GREAT EXPENSE FOR YOUR PERUSAL!
KEEP YOUR DISTANCE-- SHE'S UNPREDICTABLE! SAY SOMETHING FOR THE FOLKS, TIK-TAK...
DISHES.
LIKE I SAID, YOU NEVER KNOW WHAT SHE'LL SAY!
DISHES.
I LIKE TO DO THE DISHES AT HOME
MY MOTHER LET ME DO THE DISHES
SHE SAYS I'M A GOOD BOY
Y'SEE?
Y'SEE???

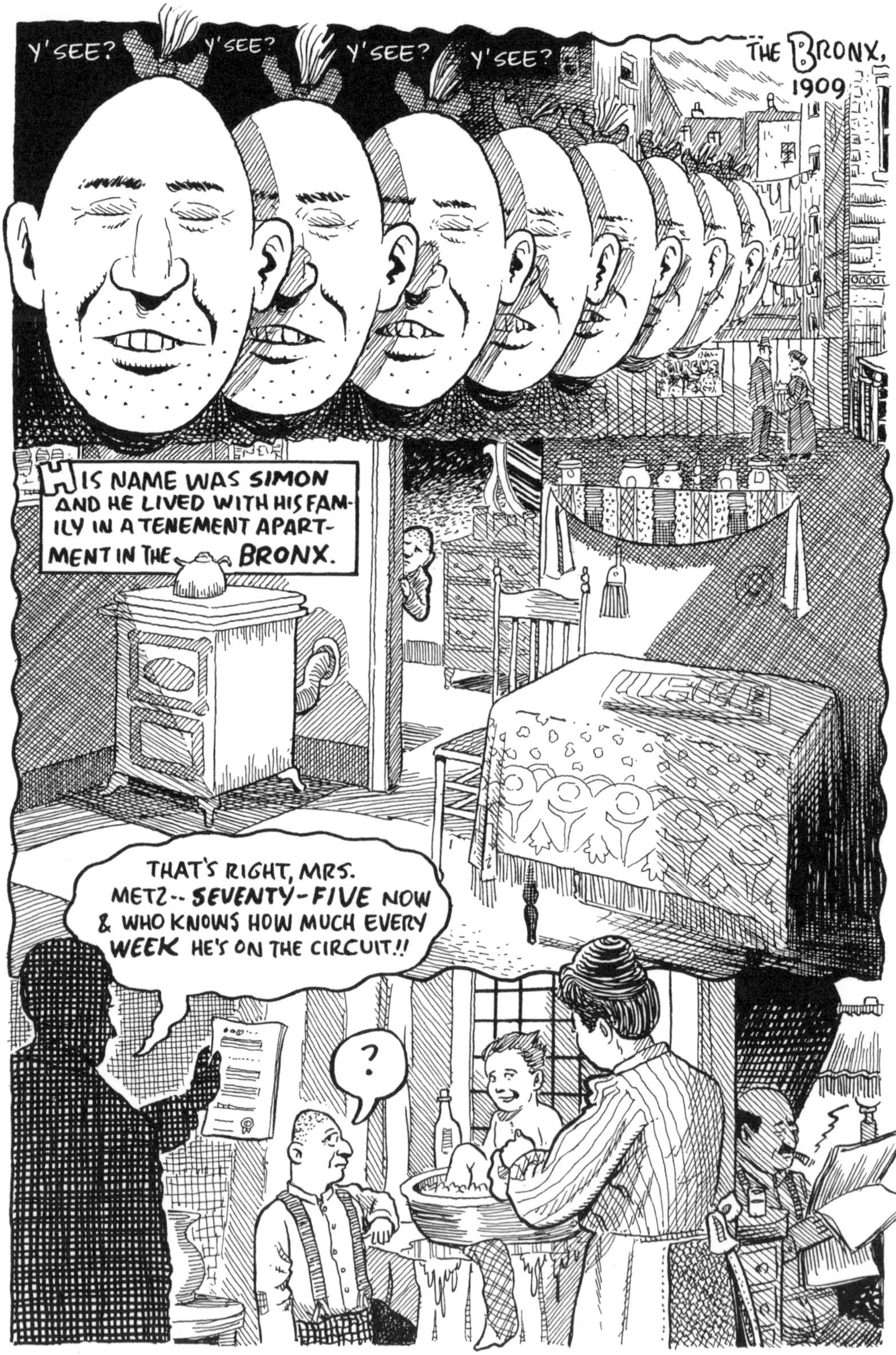
Y'SEE? Y'SEE? Y'SEE? Y'SEE?
THE BRONX, 1909
HIS NAME WAS SIMON AND HE LIVED WITH HIS FAMILY IN A TENEMENT APARTMENT IN THE BRONX.
THAT'S RIGHT, MRS. METZ-- SEVENTY-FIVE NOW & WHO KNOWS HOW MUCH EVERY WEEK HE'S ON THE CIRCUIT!!
?

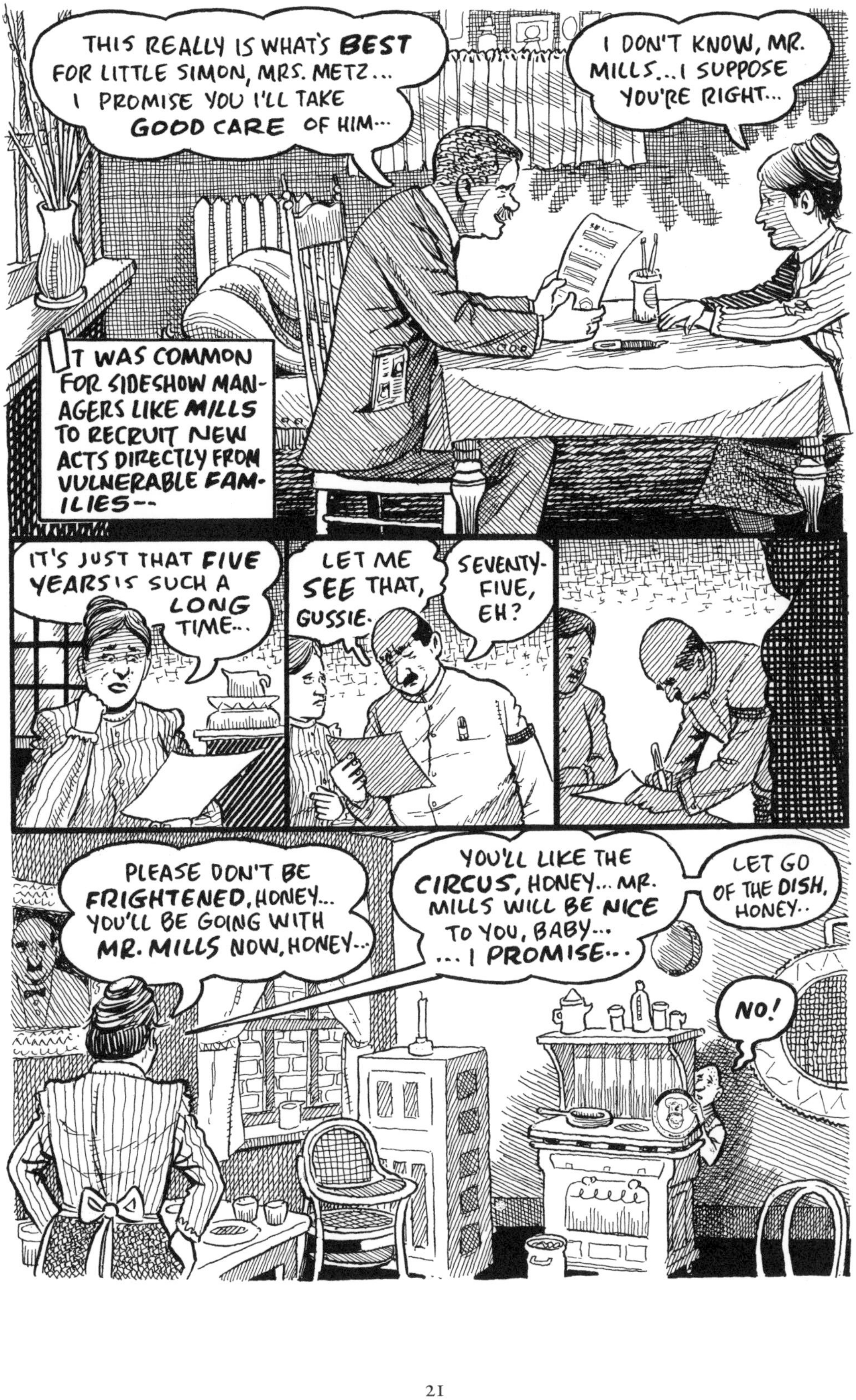
THIS REALLY IS WHAT'S BEST FOR LITTLE SIMON, MRS. METZ... I PROMISE YOU I'LL TAKE GOOD CARE OF HIM...
I DON'T KNOW, MR. MILLS...I SUPPOSE YOU'RE RIGHT...
IT WAS COMMON FOR SIDESHOW MANAGERS LIKE MILLS TO RECRUIT NEW ACTS DIRECTLY FROM VULNERABLE FAMILIES--
IT'S JUST THAT FIVE YEARS IS SUCH A LONG TIME...
LET ME SEE THAT, GUSSIE.
SEVENTY-FIVE, EH?
PLEASE DON'T BE FRIGHTENED, HONEY... YOU'LL BE GOING WITH MR. MILLS NOW, HONEY...
YOU'LL LIKE THE CIRCUS, HONEY... MR. MILLS WILL BE NICE TO YOU, BABY... ...I PROMISE...
LET GO OF THE DISH, HONEY..
NO!

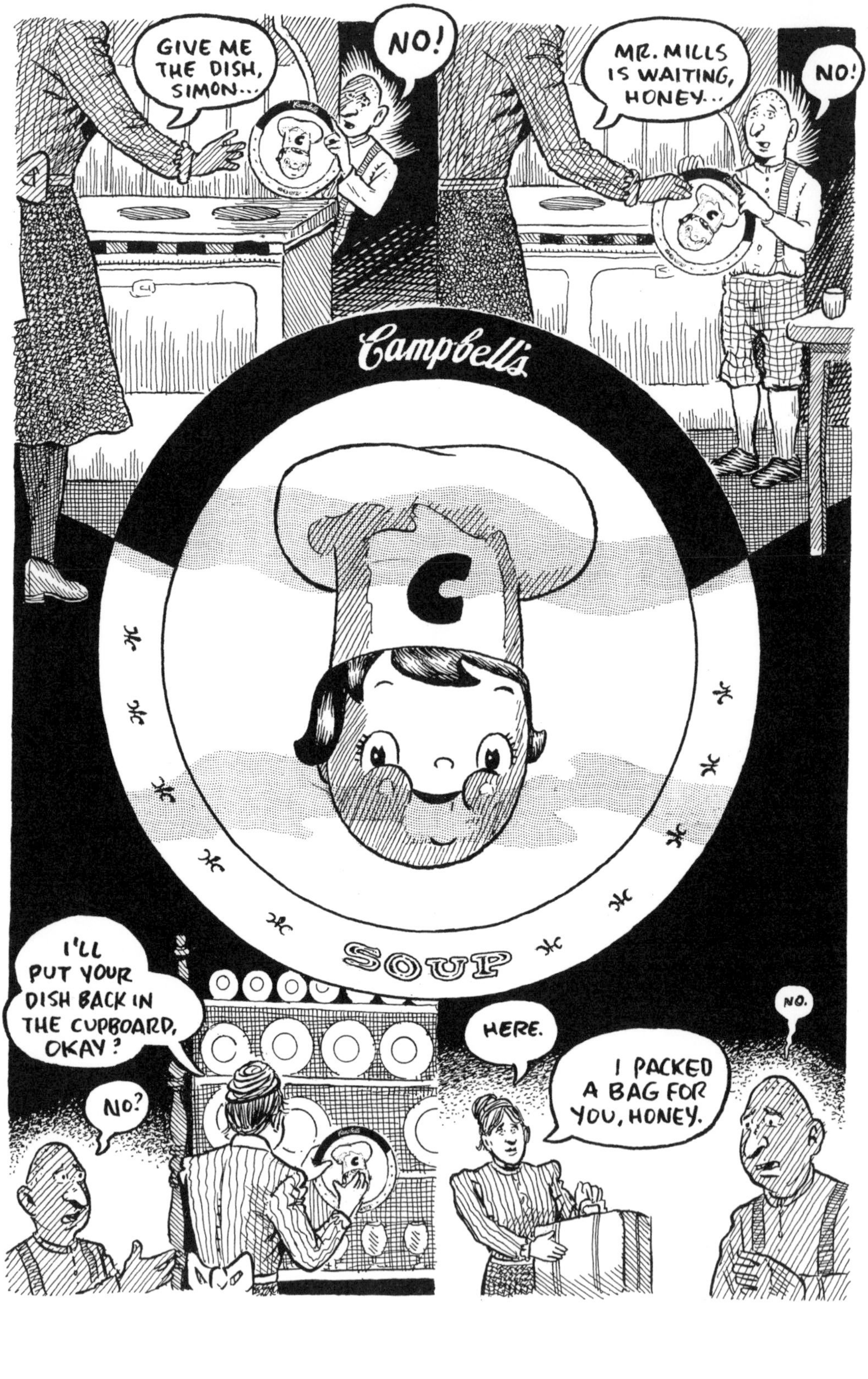
GIVE ME THE DISH, SIMON...
NO!
MR. MILLS IS WAITING, HONEY...
NO!
Campbell's
SOUP
I'LL PUT YOUR DISH BACK IN THE CUPBOARD, OKAY?
NO?
HERE.
I PACKED A BAG FOR YOU, HONEY.
NO.

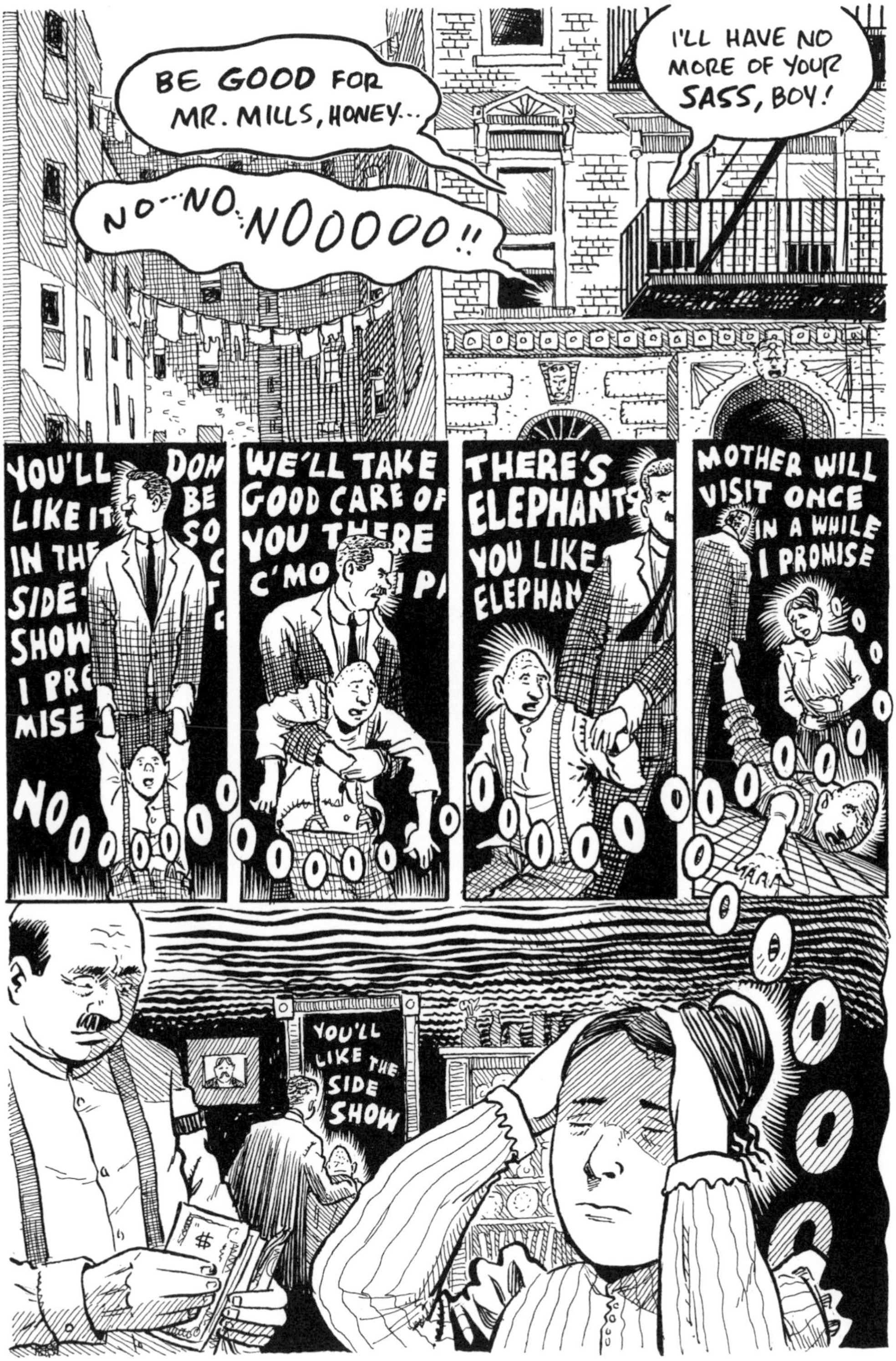
BE GOOD FOR MR. MILLS, HONEY...
I'LL HAVE NO MORE OF YOUR SASS, BOY!
NO...NO...NOOOOOO!!
YOU'LL LIKE IT IN THE SIDE-SHOW I PROMISE
NOOOOOO
WE'LL TAKE GOOD CARE OF YOU THERE
THERE'S ELEPHANTS YOU LIKE
MOTHER WILL VISIT ONCE IN A WHILE I PROMISE
YOU'LL LIKE THE SIDE SHOW

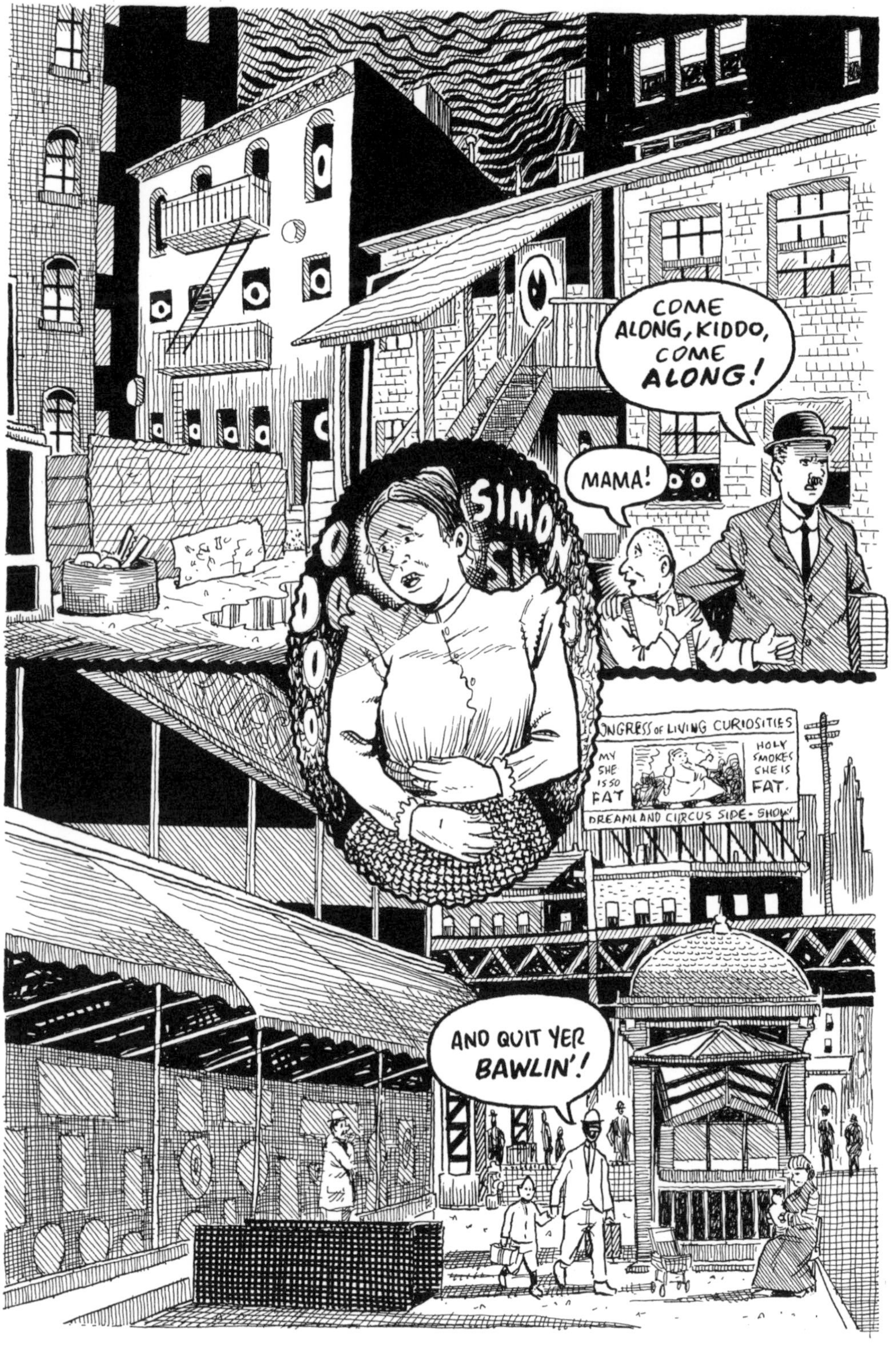
COME ALONG, KIDDO, COME ALONG!
MAMA!
SIMON
ONGRESS OF LIVING CURIOSITIES
MY SHE IS SO FAT
HOLY SMOKES SHE IS FAT.
DREAMLAND CIRCUS SIDE-SHOW
AND QUIT YER BAWLIN'!

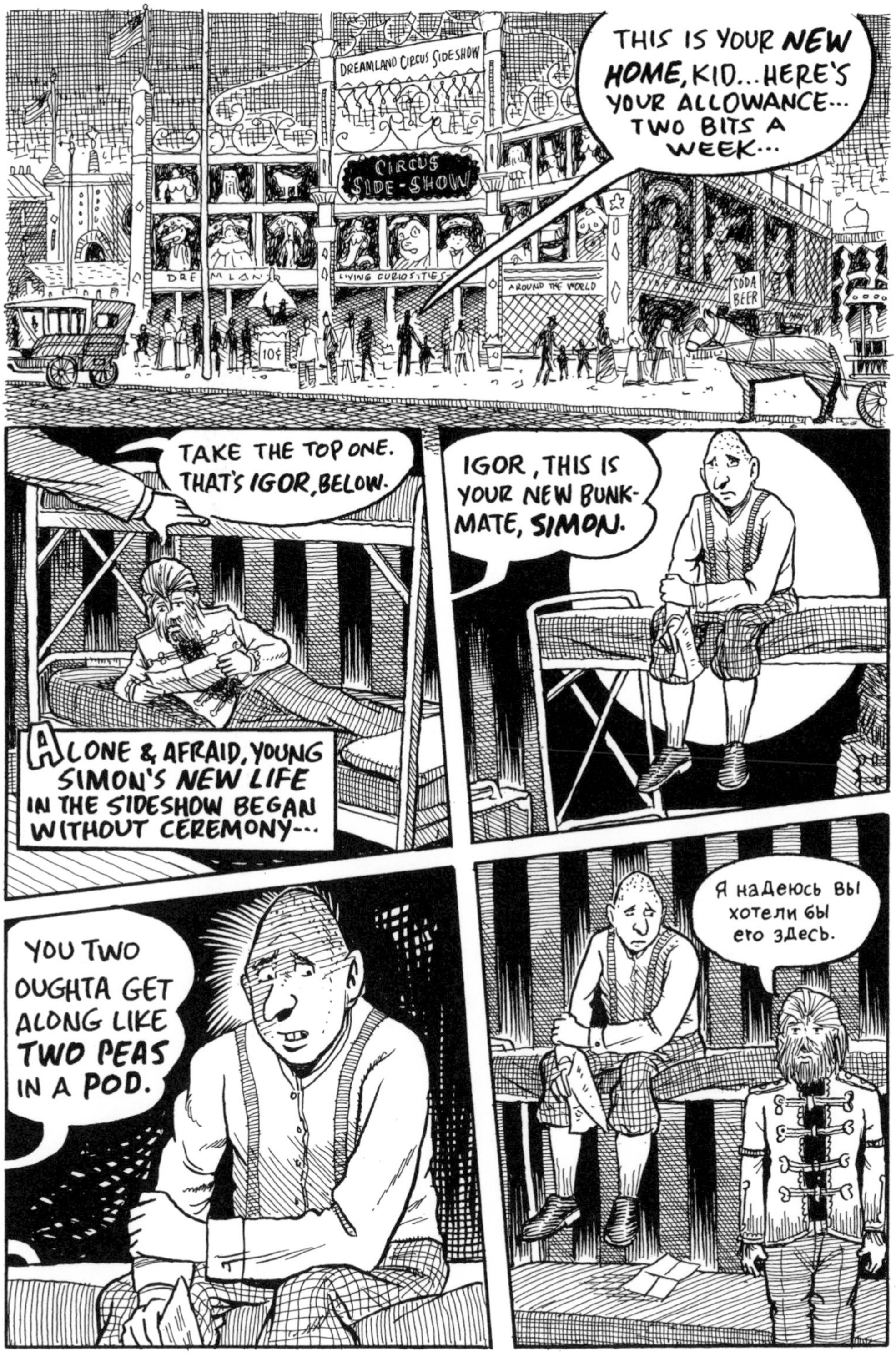
DREAMLAND CIRCUS SIDESHOW
CIRCUS SIDE-SHOW
LIVING CURIOSITIES
AROUND THE WORLD
SODA BEER
10¢
THIS IS YOUR NEW HOME, KID... HERE'S YOUR ALLOWANCE... TWO BITS A WEEK...
TAKE THE TOP ONE. THAT'S IGOR, BELOW.
ALONE & AFRAID, YOUNG SIMON'S NEW LIFE IN THE SIDESHOW BEGAN WITHOUT CEREMONY...
IGOR, THIS IS YOUR NEW BUNKMATE, SIMON.
YOU TWO OUGHTA GET ALONG LIKE TWO PEAS IN A POD.
Я надеюсь вы хотели бы его здесь.

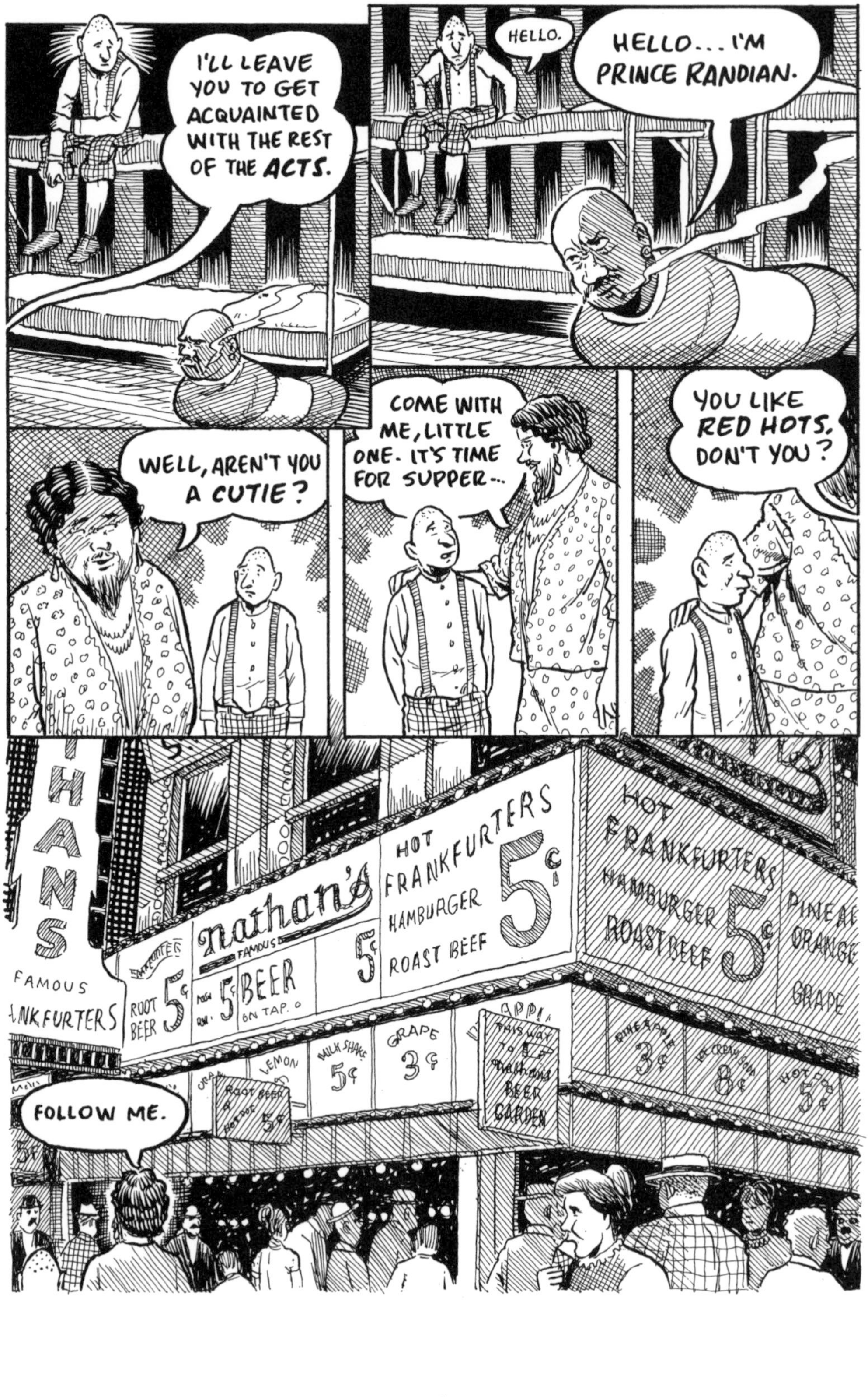
I'LL LEAVE YOU TO GET ACQUAINTED WITH THE REST OF THE ACTS.
HELLO.
HELLO... I'M PRINCE RANDIAN.
WELL, AREN'T YOU A CUTIE?
COME WITH ME, LITTLE ONE. IT'S TIME FOR SUPPER...
YOU LIKE RED HOTS, DON'T YOU?
nathan's FAMOUS
HOT FRANKFURTERS HAMBURGER ROAST BEEF 5¢
ROOT BEER 5¢
BEER ON TAP
FAMOUS
GRAPE 3¢
MILK SHAKE 5¢
LEMON
THIS WAY TO nathan's BEER GARDEN
FOLLOW ME.

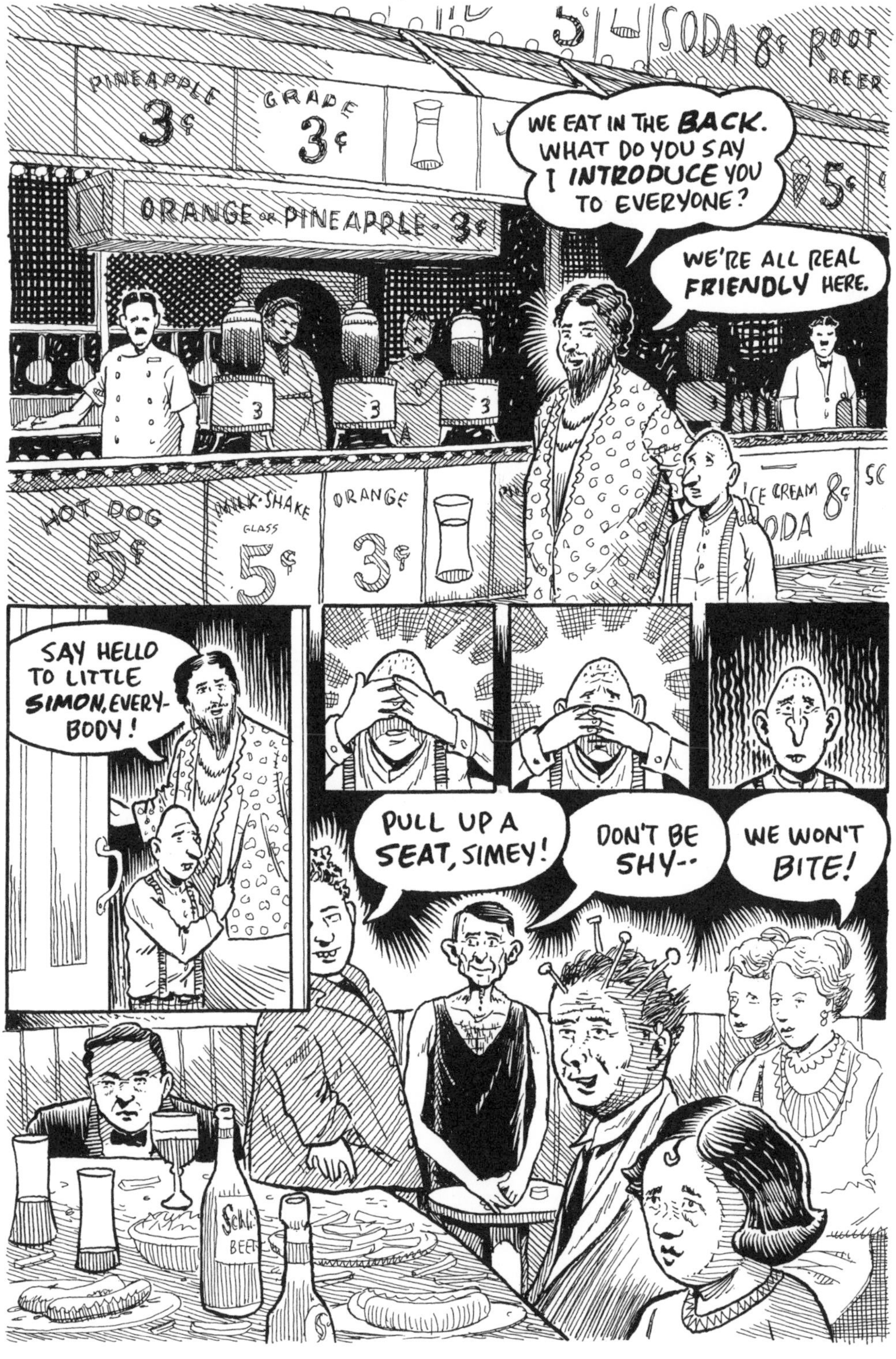
SODA 8¢ ROOT BEER
PINEAPPLE 3¢
GRAPE 3¢
ORANGE or PINEAPPLE 3¢
WE EAT IN THE **BACK**. WHAT DO YOU SAY I **INTRODUCE** YOU TO EVERYONE?
WE'RE ALL REAL **FRIENDLY** HERE.
HOT DOG 5¢
MILK SHAKE GLASS 5¢
ORANGE 3¢
ICE CREAM SODA 8¢
SAY HELLO TO LITTLE **SIMON**, EVERYBODY!
PULL UP A SEAT, SIMEY!
DON'T BE SHY--
WE WON'T BITE!

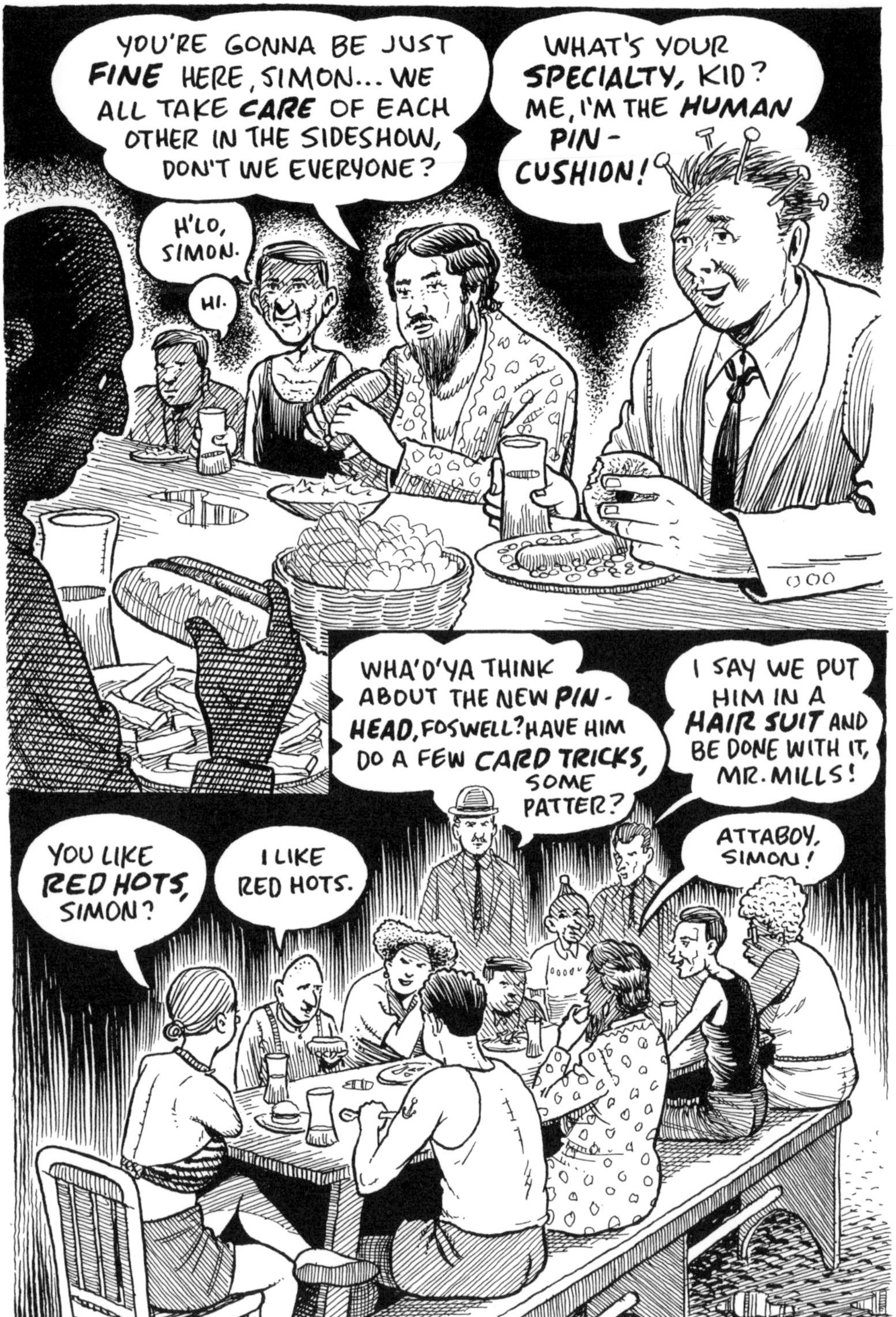
YOU'RE GONNA BE JUST FINE HERE, SIMON... WE ALL TAKE CARE OF EACH OTHER IN THE SIDESHOW, DON'T WE EVERYONE?
WHAT'S YOUR SPECIALTY, KID? ME, I'M THE HUMAN PIN-CUSHION!
H'LO, SIMON.
HI.
WHA'D'YA THINK ABOUT THE NEW PIN-HEAD, FOSWELL? HAVE HIM DO A FEW CARD TRICKS, SOME PATTER?
I SAY WE PUT HIM IN A HAIR SUIT AND BE DONE WITH IT, MR. MILLS!
YOU LIKE RED HOTS, SIMON?
I LIKE RED HOTS.
ATTABOY, SIMON!

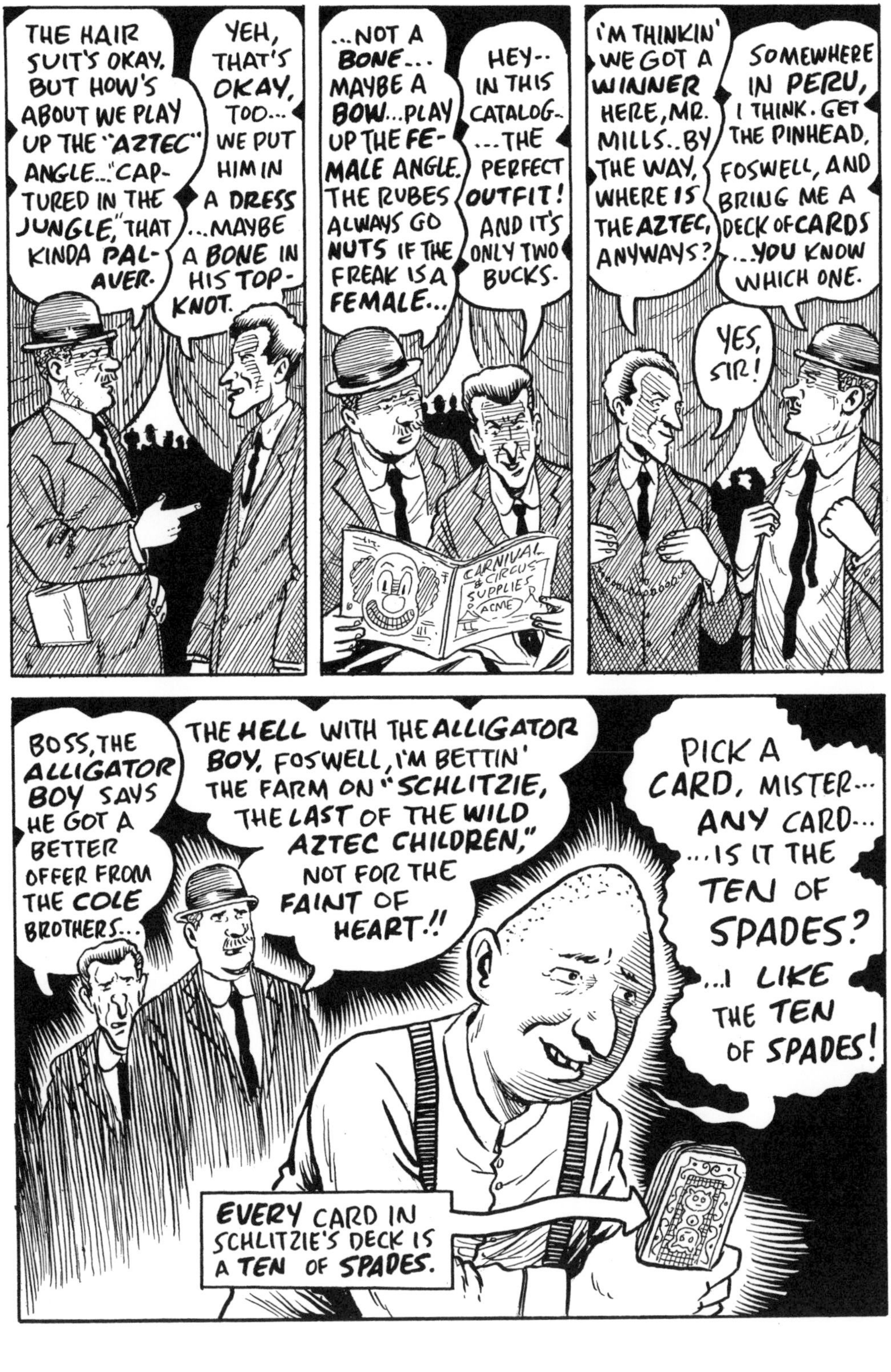
THE HAIR SUIT'S OKAY. BUT HOW'S ABOUT WE PLAY UP THE "AZTEC" ANGLE..."CAPTURED IN THE JUNGLE," THAT KINDA PALAVER.
YEH, THAT'S OKAY, TOO... WE PUT HIM IN A DRESS ...MAYBE A BONE IN HIS TOP-KNOT.
...NOT A BONE... MAYBE A BOW...PLAY UP THE FEMALE ANGLE. THE RUBES ALWAYS GO NUTS IF THE FREAK IS A FEMALE...
HEY-- IN THIS CATALOG-- ...THE PERFECT OUTFIT! AND IT'S ONLY TWO BUCKS.
CARNIVAL & CIRCUS SUPPLIES ACME
I'M THINKIN' WE GOT A WINNER HERE, MR. MILLS.. BY THE WAY, WHERE IS THE AZTEC, ANYWAYS?
SOMEWHERE IN PERU, I THINK. GET THE PINHEAD, FOSWELL, AND BRING ME A DECK OF CARDS ...YOU KNOW WHICH ONE.
YES, SIR!
BOSS, THE ALLIGATOR BOY SAYS HE GOT A BETTER OFFER FROM THE COLE BROTHERS...
THE HELL WITH THE ALLIGATOR BOY, FOSWELL, I'M BETTIN' THE FARM ON "SCHLITZIE, THE LAST OF THE WILD AZTEC CHILDREN," NOT FOR THE FAINT OF HEART!!
PICK A CARD, MISTER... ANY CARD... ...IS IT THE TEN OF SPADES? ...I LIKE THE TEN OF SPADES!
EVERY CARD IN SCHLITZIE'S DECK IS A TEN OF SPADES.

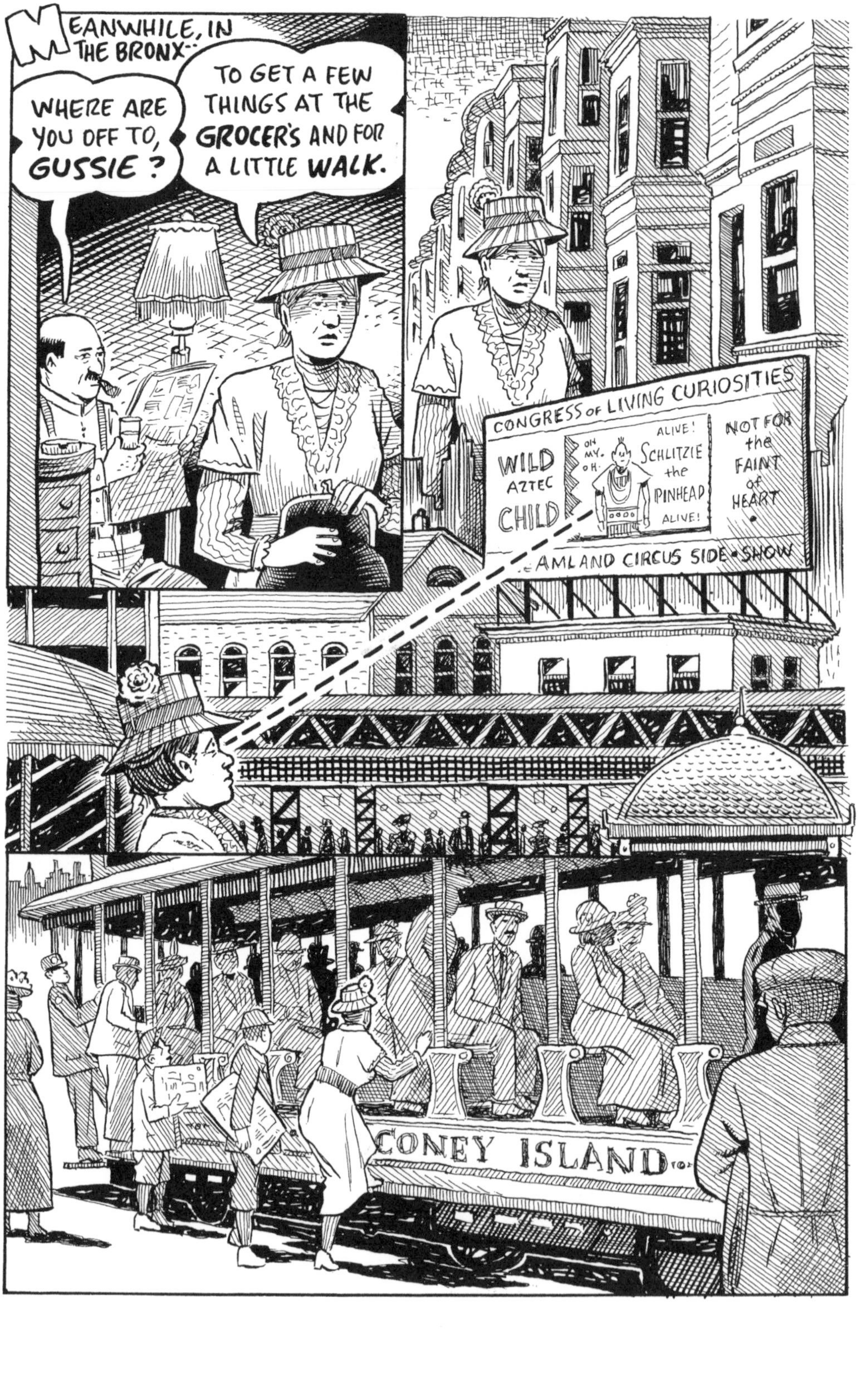
MEANWHILE, IN THE BRONX...
WHERE ARE YOU OFF TO, GUSSIE ?
TO GET A FEW THINGS AT THE GROCER'S AND FOR A LITTLE WALK.
CONGRESS of LIVING CURIOSITIES
WILD AZTEC CHILD
OH MY. OH.
ALIVE! SCHLITZIE the PINHEAD ALIVE!
NOT FOR the FAINT of HEART
AMLAND CIRCUS SIDE-SHOW
CONEY ISLAND

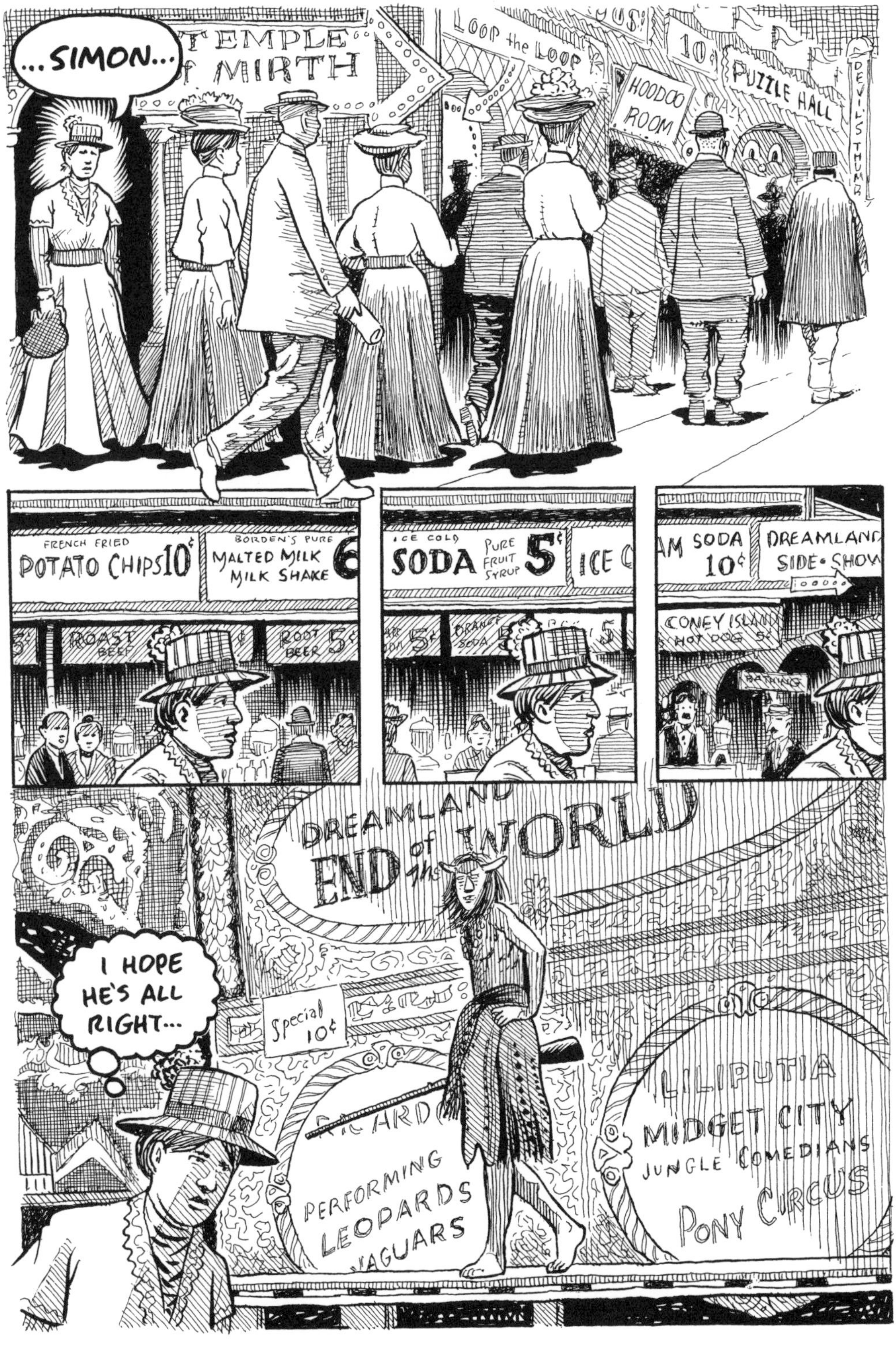
...SIMON...
TEMPLE of MIRTH
LOOP the LOOP
HOODOO ROOM
10¢
PUZZLE HALL
DEVIL'S THUMB
FRENCH FRIED POTATO CHIPS 10¢
BORDEN'S PURE MALTED MILK MILK SHAKE 6
ROAST BEEF
ROOT BEER 5¢
ICE COLD SODA PURE FRUIT SYRUP 5¢
ORANGE SODA
SODA 10¢
DREAMLAND SIDE-SHOW
CONEY ISLAND HOT DOG 5¢
BATHING
DREAMLAND END of the WORLD
Special 10¢
I HOPE HE'S ALL RIGHT...
PERFORMING LEOPARDS JAGUARS
LILIPUTIA MIDGET CITY JUNGLE COMEDIANS PONY CIRCUS

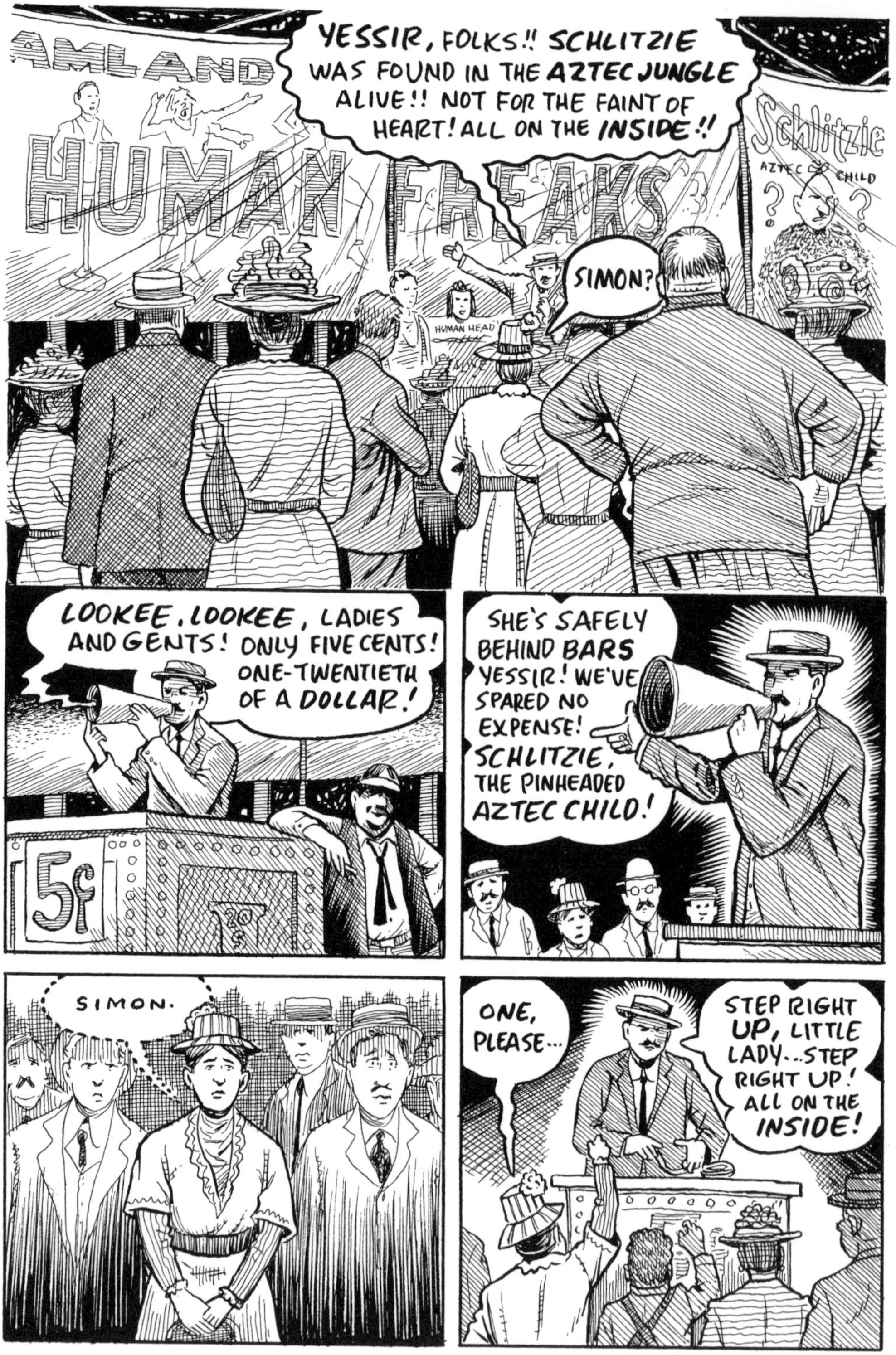
AMLAND
HUMAN FREAKS
YESSIR, FOLKS!! SCHLITZIE WAS FOUND IN THE AZTEC JUNGLE ALIVE!! NOT FOR THE FAINT OF HEART! ALL ON THE INSIDE!!
Schlitzie
AZTEC CHILD
HUMAN HEAD
SIMON?
LOOKEE, LOOKEE, LADIES AND GENTS! ONLY FIVE CENTS! ONE-TWENTIETH OF A DOLLAR!
5¢
SHE'S SAFELY BEHIND BARS YESSIR! WE'VE SPARED NO EXPENSE! SCHLITZIE, THE PINHEADED AZTEC CHILD!
SIMON.
ONE, PLEASE...
STEP RIGHT UP, LITTLE LADY...STEP RIGHT UP! ALL ON THE INSIDE!

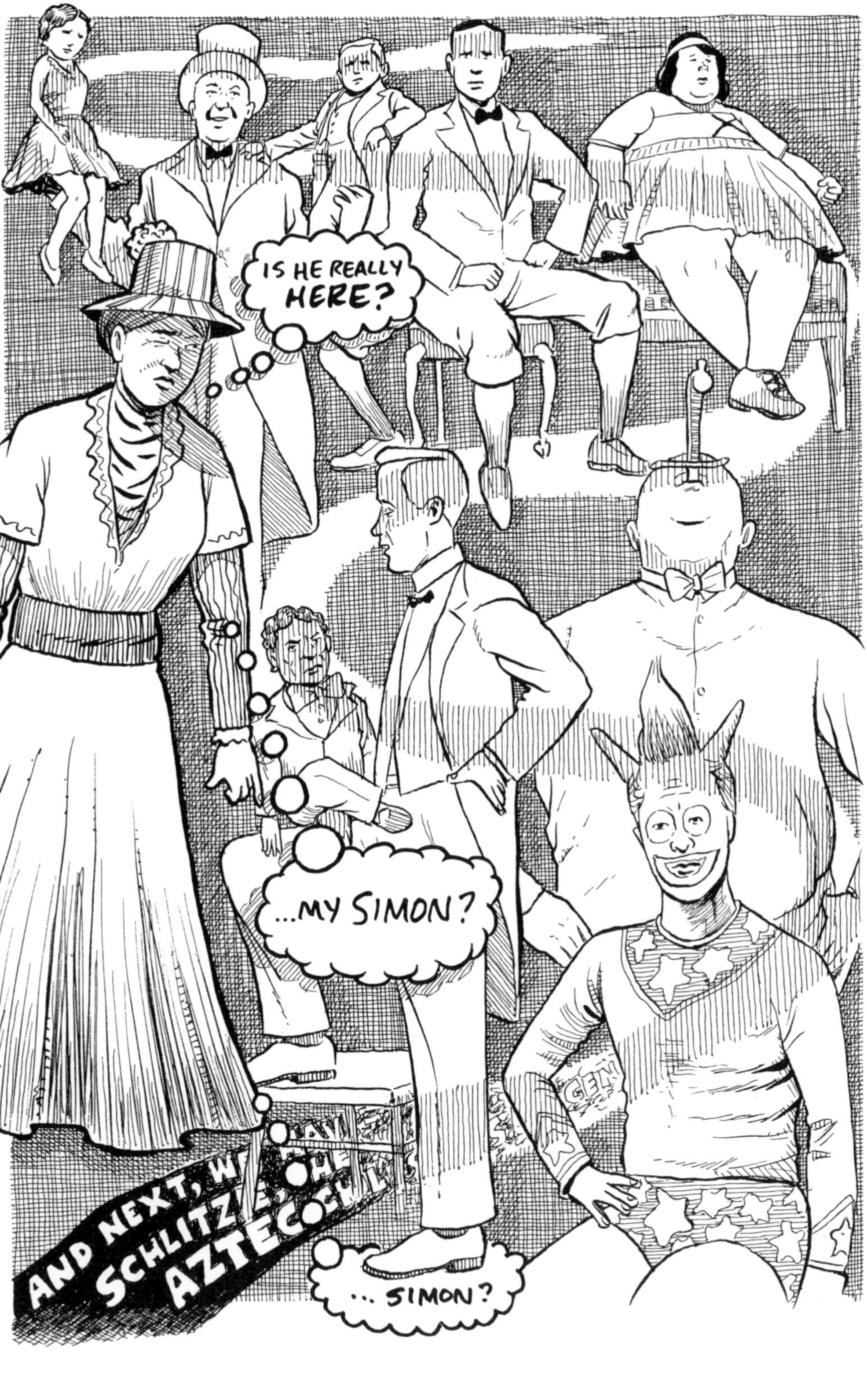
IS HE REALLY HERE?
...MY SIMON?
AND NEXT, W
SCHLITZ
AZTEC
... SIMON?

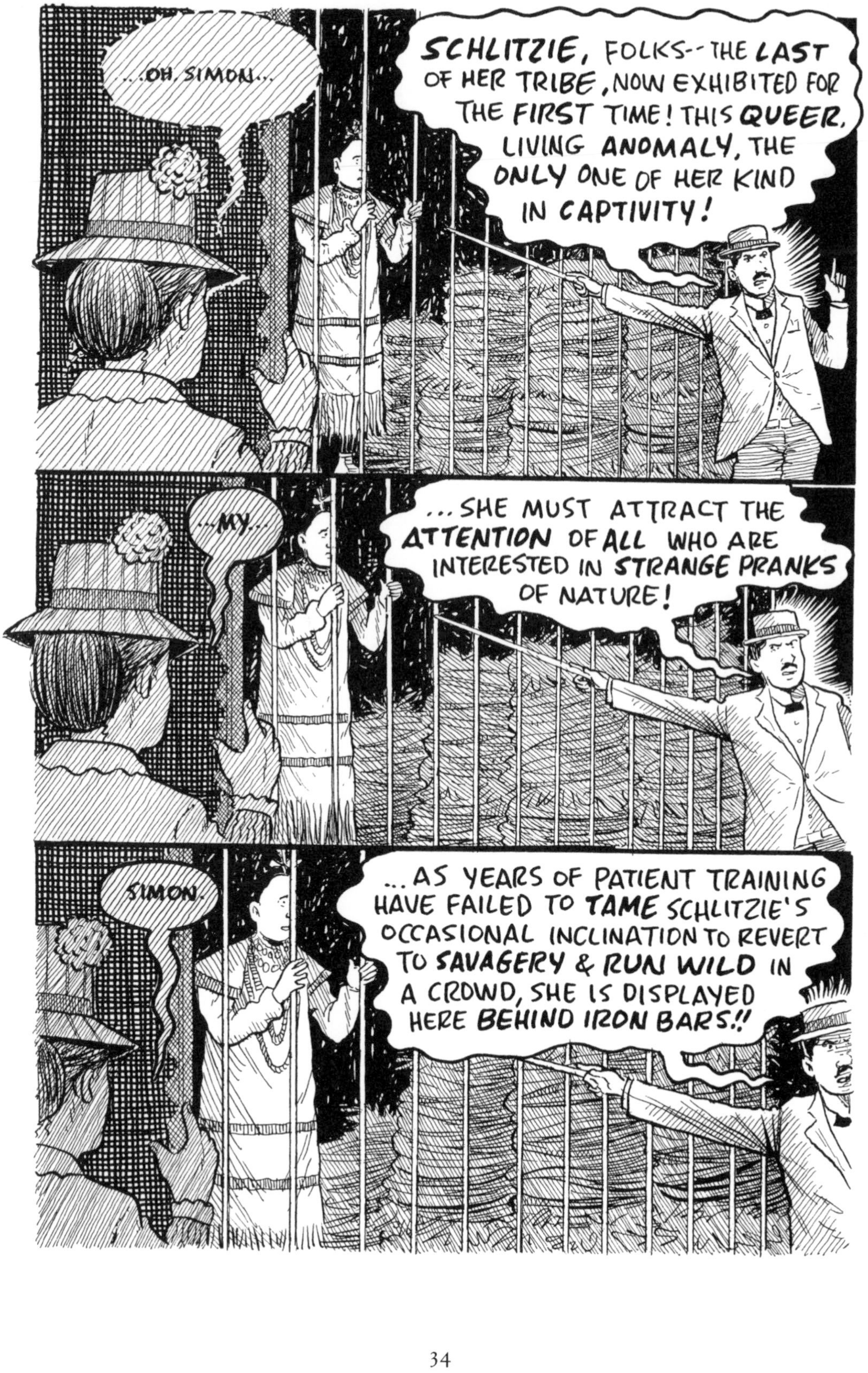
...OH, SIMON...
SCHLITZIE, FOLKS--THE LAST OF HER TRIBE, NOW EXHIBITED FOR THE FIRST TIME! THIS QUEER, LIVING ANOMALY, THE ONLY ONE OF HER KIND IN CAPTIVITY!
...MY...
...SHE MUST ATTRACT THE ATTENTION OF ALL WHO ARE INTERESTED IN STRANGE PRANKS OF NATURE!
SIMON.
...AS YEARS OF PATIENT TRAINING HAVE FAILED TO TAME SCHLITZIE'S OCCASIONAL INCLINATION TO REVERT TO SAVAGERY & RUN WILD IN A CROWD, SHE IS DISPLAYED HERE BEHIND IRON BARS!!

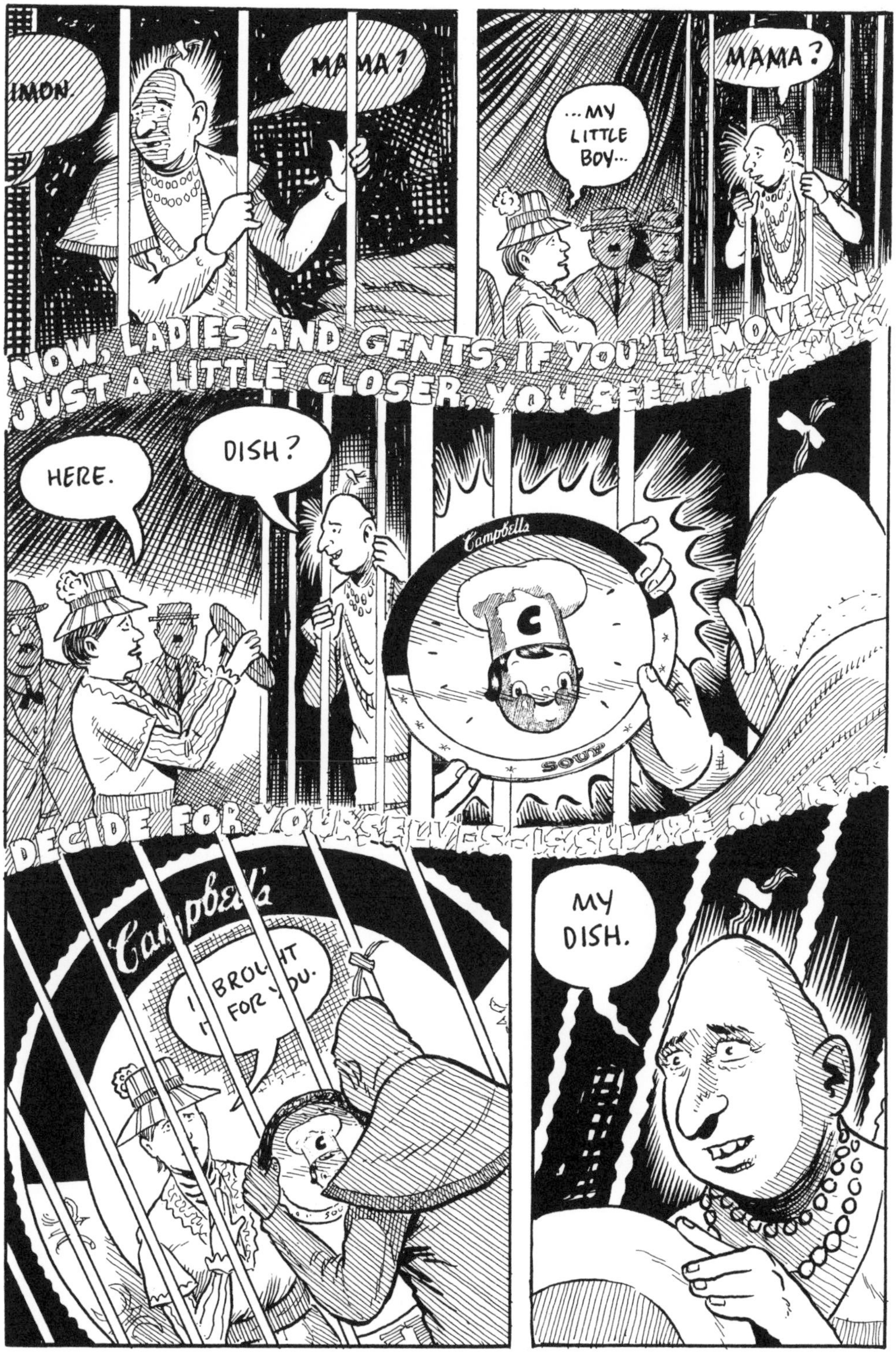
IMON.
MAMA?
...MY LITTLE BOY...
MAMA?
NOW, LADIES AND GENTS, IF YOU'LL MOVE IN
JUST A LITTLE CLOSER, YOU SEE
HERE.
DISH?
Campbell's
SOUP
DECIDE FOR YOU
Campbell's
I BROUGHT IT FOR YOU.
MY DISH.

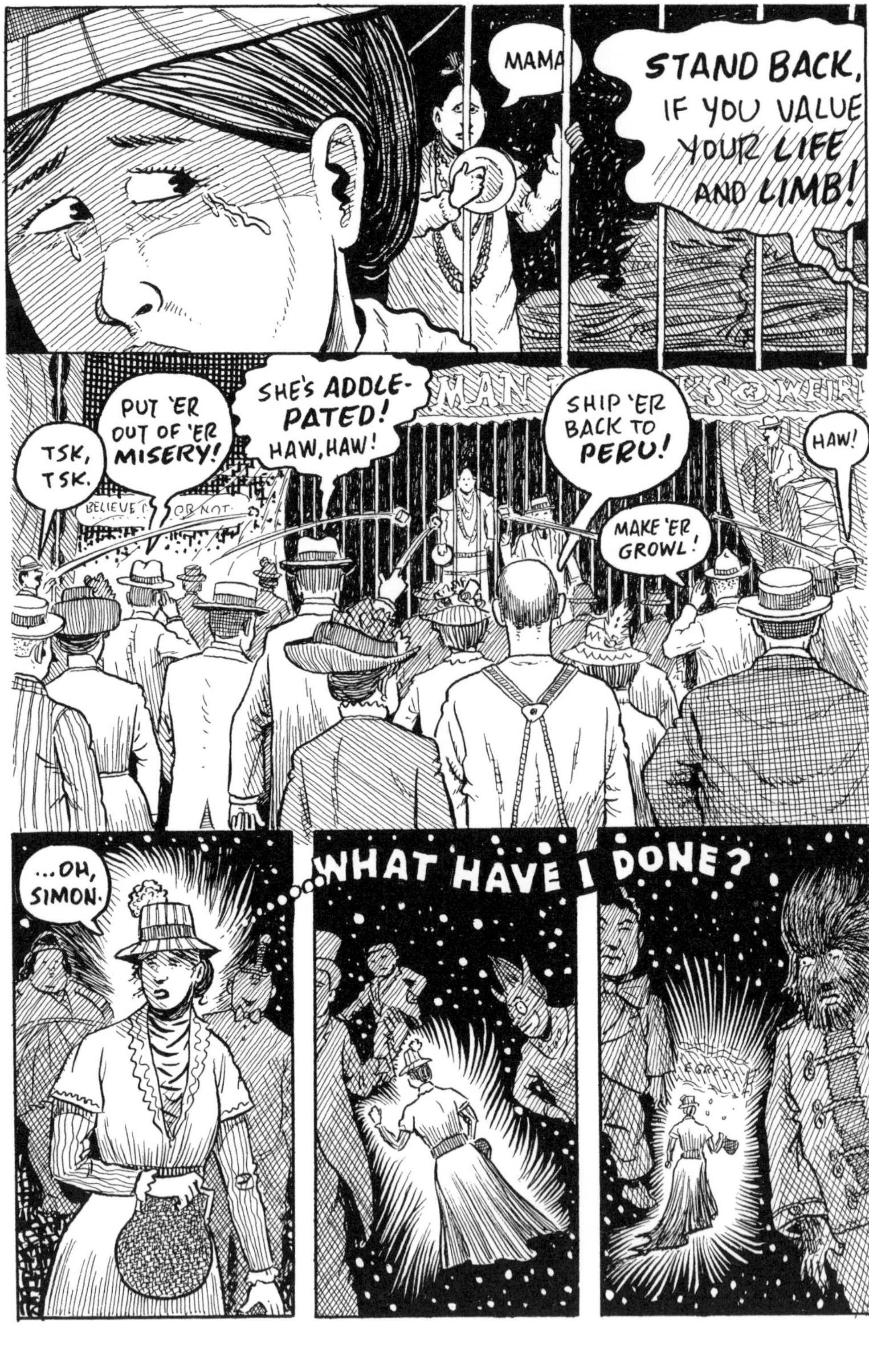
MAMA
STAND BACK, IF YOU VALUE YOUR LIFE AND LIMB!
TSK, TSK.
PUT 'ER OUT OF 'ER MISERY!
SHE'S ADDLE-PATED! HAW, HAW!
SHIP 'ER BACK TO PERU!
HAW!
MAKE 'ER GROWL!
...OH, SIMON.
WHAT HAVE I DONE?

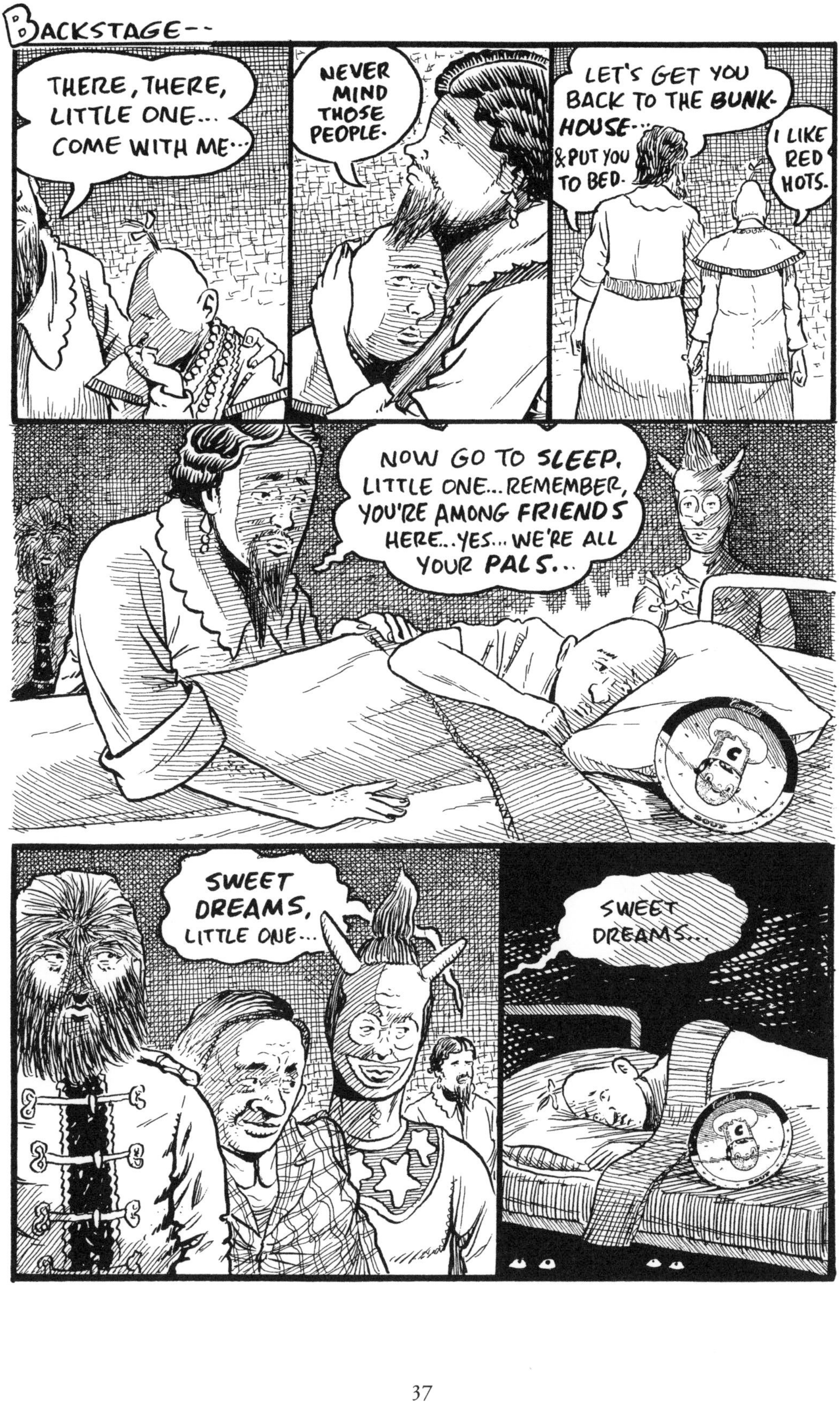
BACKSTAGE--
THERE, THERE, LITTLE ONE... COME WITH ME...
NEVER MIND THOSE PEOPLE.
LET'S GET YOU BACK TO THE BUNK-HOUSE... & PUT YOU TO BED.
I LIKE RED HOTS.
NOW GO TO SLEEP, LITTLE ONE... REMEMBER, YOU'RE AMONG FRIENDS HERE... YES... WE'RE ALL YOUR PALS...
SWEET DREAMS, LITTLE ONE...
SWEET DREAMS...

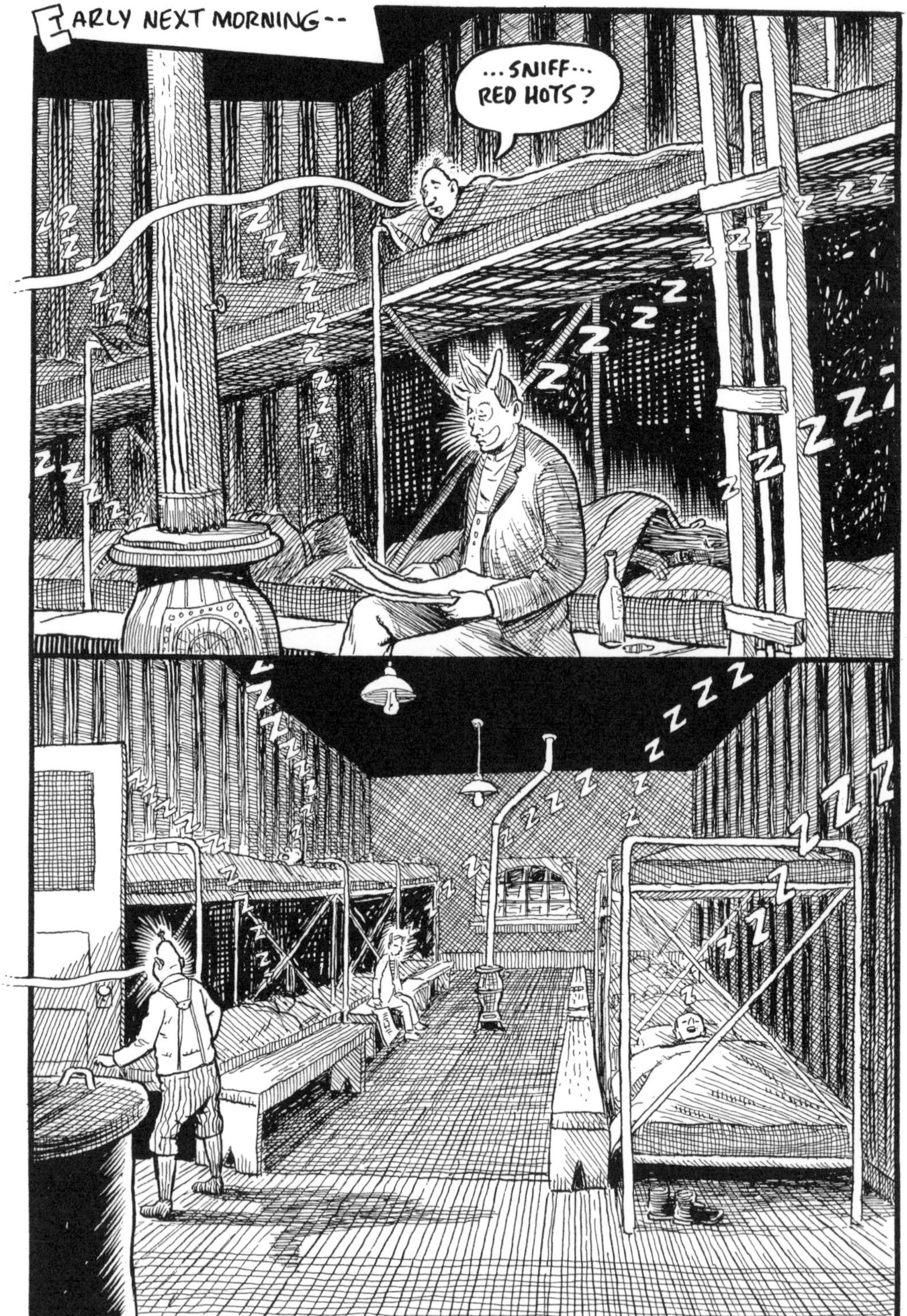
EARLY NEXT MORNING--
...SNIFF...
RED HOTS?

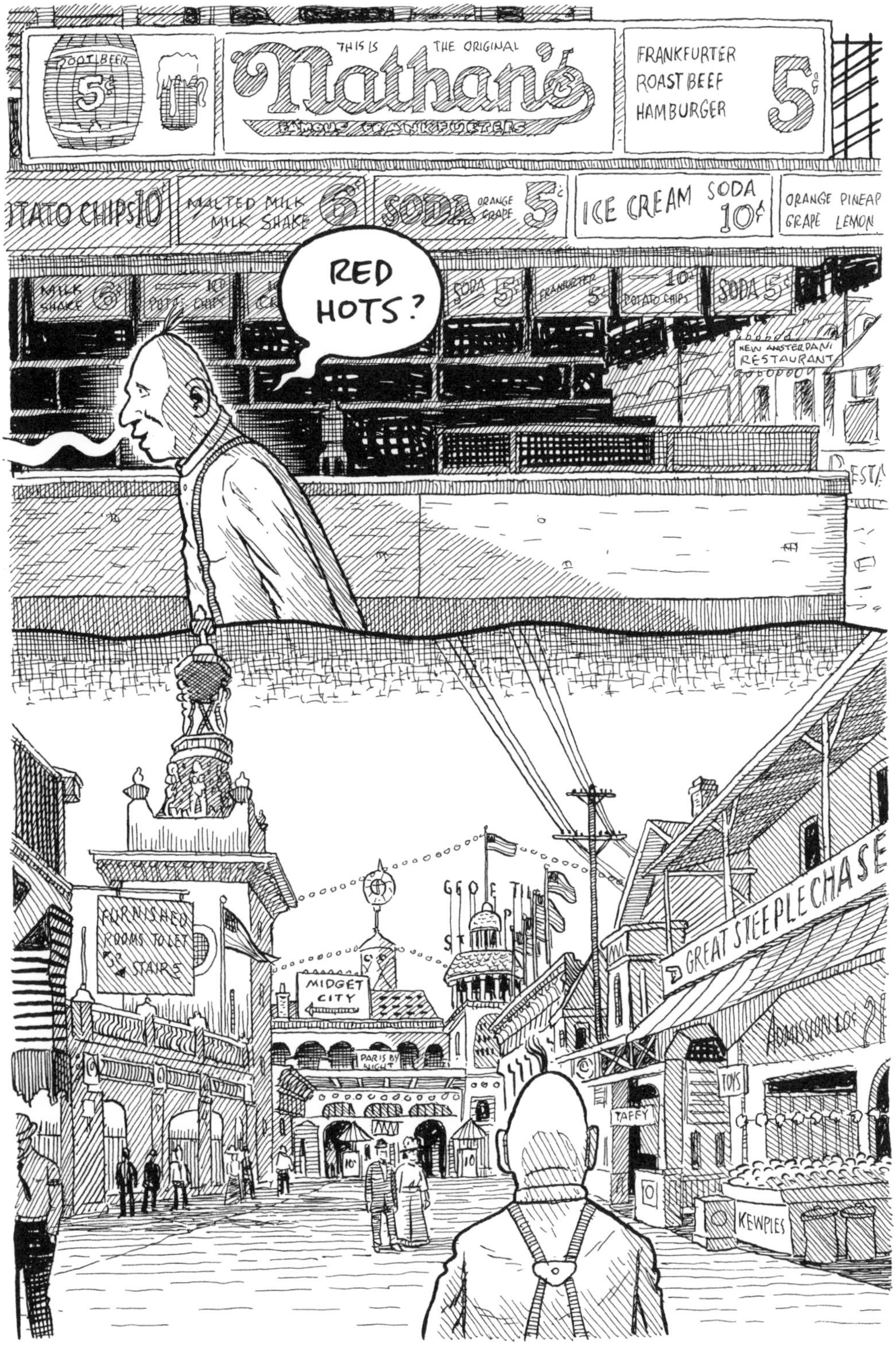
ROOT BEER 5¢
THIS IS THE ORIGINAL Nathan's FAMOUS FRANKFURTERS
FRANKFURTER
ROAST BEEF
HAMBURGER 5¢
MALTED MILK
MILK SHAKE 6¢
SODA ORANGE GRAPE 5¢
ICE CREAM SODA 10¢
ORANGE PINEAP
GRAPE LEMON
RED HOTS?
NEW AMSTERDAM RESTAURANT
FURNISHED ROOMS TO LET UP STAIRS
MIDGET CITY
PARIS BY NIGHT
GREAT STEEPLECHASE
TOYS
TAFFY
KEWPIES

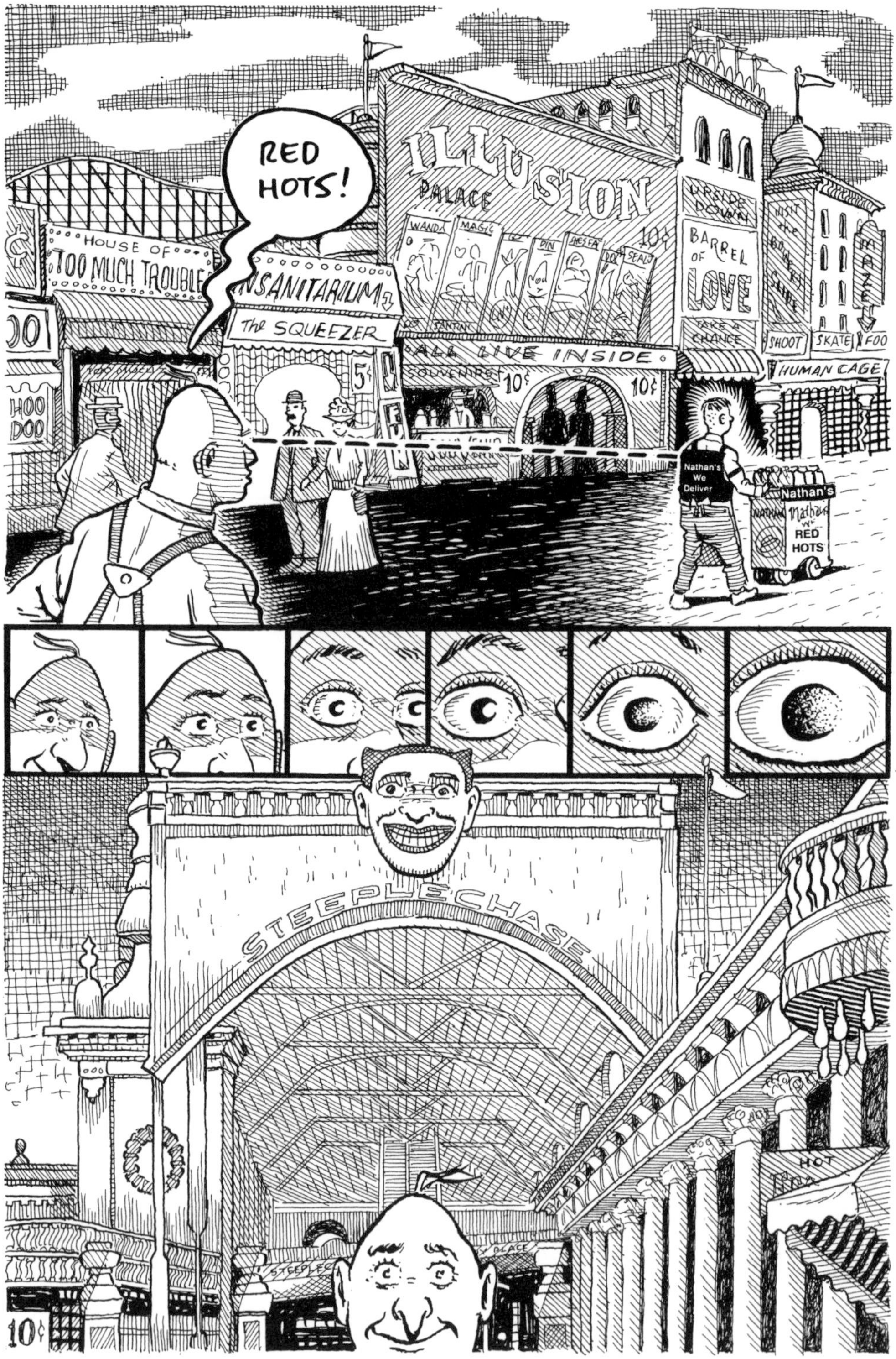
RED HOTS!
HOUSE OF TOO MUCH TROUBLE
INSANITARIUM
The SQUEEZER
5¢
ILLUSION PALACE
WANDA
MAGIC
ALL LIVE INSIDE
SOUVENIRS
10¢
10¢
10¢
UPSIDE DOWN
BARREL OF LOVE
TAKE A CHANCE
MAZE
SHOOT
SKATE
HUMAN CAGE
HOO DOO
Nathan's We Deliver
Nathan's
RED HOTS
STEEPLECHASE
10¢

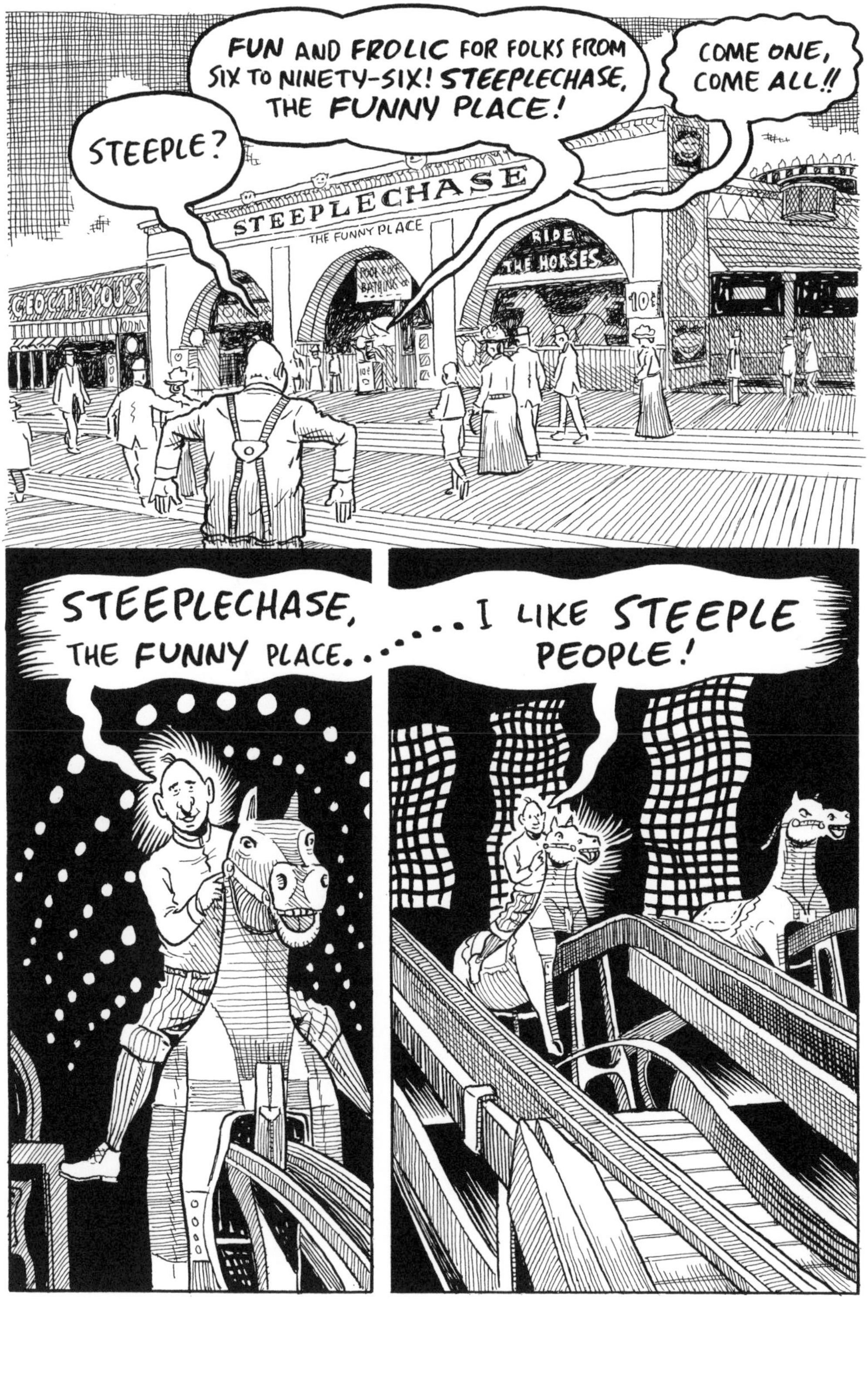
FUN AND FROLIC FOR FOLKS FROM SIX TO NINETY-SIX! STEEPLECHASE, THE FUNNY PLACE!
COME ONE, COME ALL!!
STEEPLE?
STEEPLECHASE
STEEPLECHASE
THE FUNNY PLACE
GEO. C. TILYOU'S
RIDE THE HORSES
10¢
STEEPLECHASE, THE FUNNY PLACE.......I LIKE STEEPLE PEOPLE!

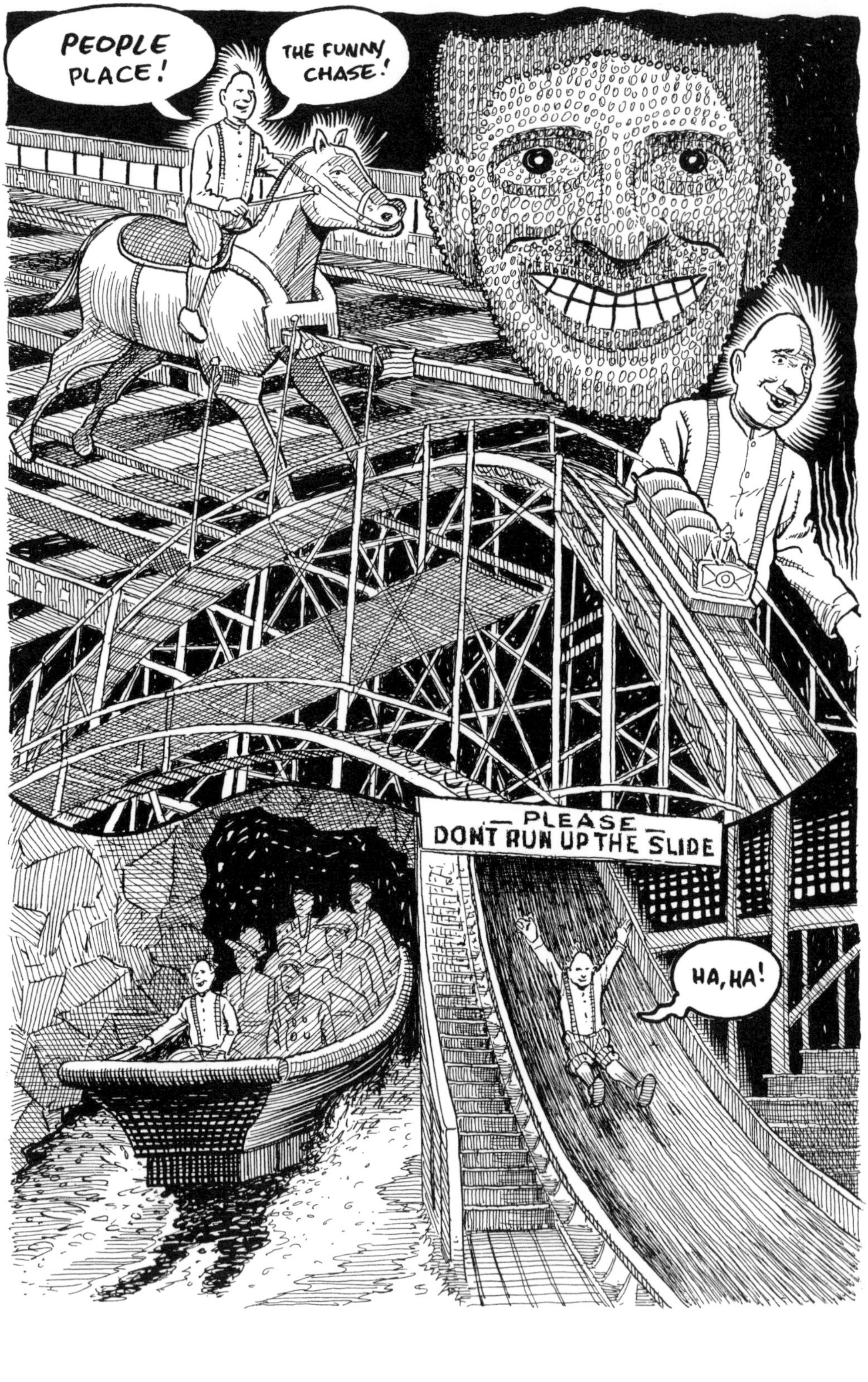
PEOPLE PLACE!
THE FUNNY CHASE!
PLEASE DONT RUN UP THE SLIDE
HA, HA!

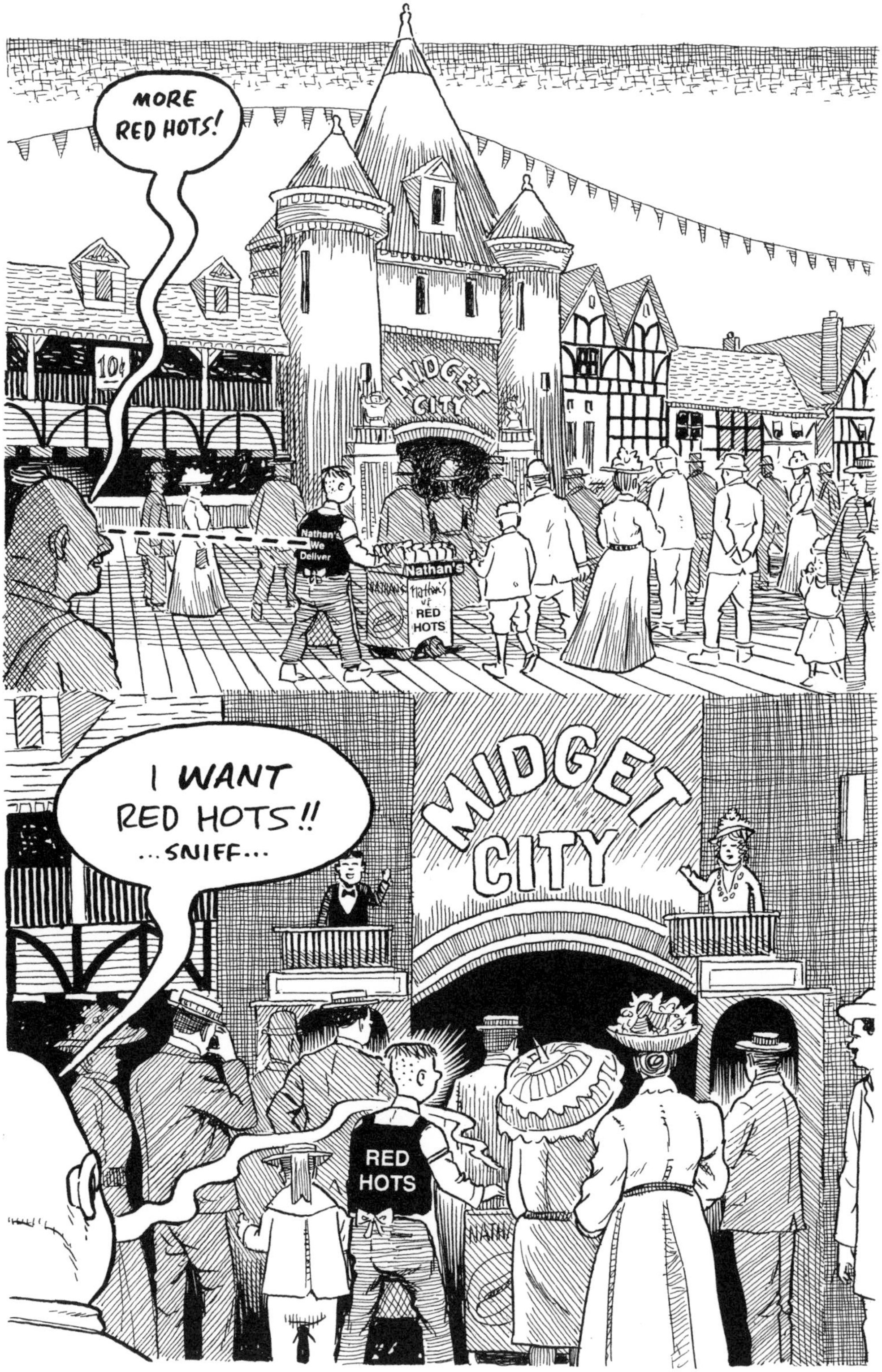
MORE RED HOTS!
10¢
MIDGET CITY
Nathan's We Deliver
Nathan's
RED HOTS
I WANT RED HOTS!! ...SNIFF...
MIDGET CITY
RED HOTS

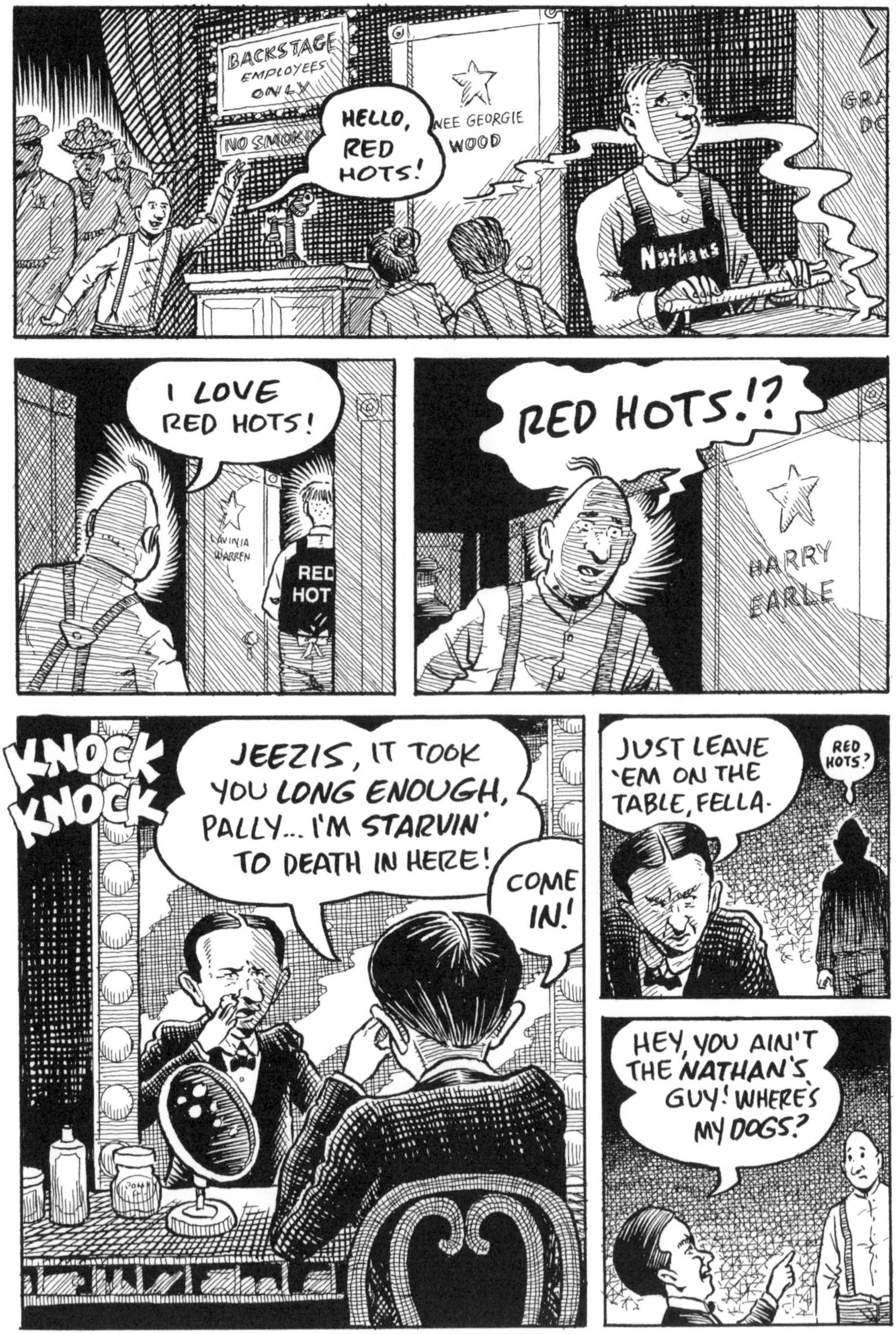
BACKSTAGE EMPLOYEES ONLY
NO SMOKIN
HELLO, RED HOTS!
WEE GEORGIE WOOD
Nathans
I LOVE RED HOTS!
LAVINIA WARREN
RED HOT
RED HOTS!?
HARRY EARLE
KNOCK KNOCK
JEEZIS, IT TOOK YOU LONG ENOUGH, PALLY... I'M STARVIN' TO DEATH IN HERE!
COME IN!
JUST LEAVE 'EM ON THE TABLE, FELLA.
RED HOTS?
HEY, YOU AIN'T THE NATHAN'S GUY! WHERE'S MY DOGS?

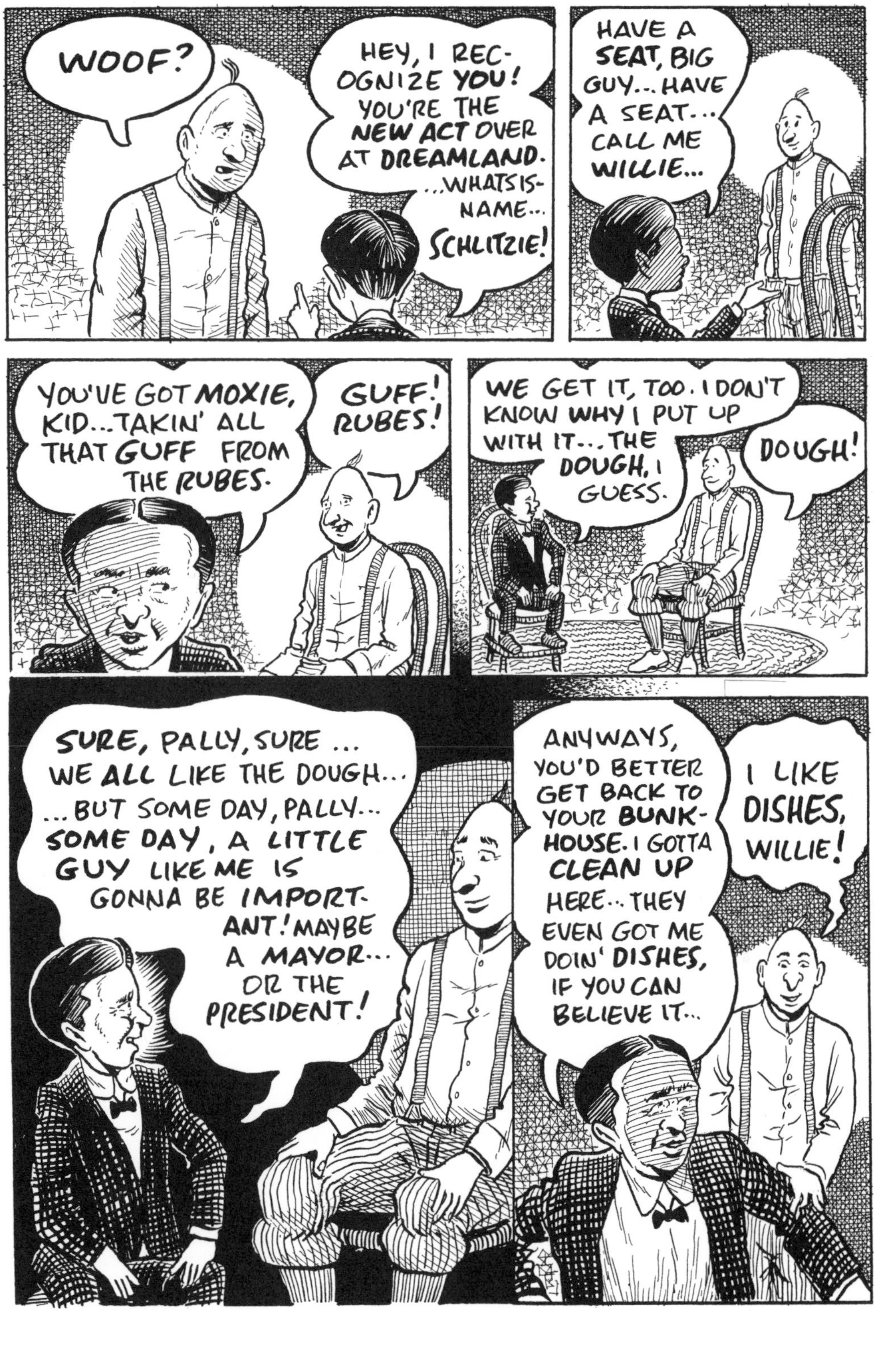
WOOF?
HEY, I REC-OGNIZE YOU! YOU'RE THE NEW ACT OVER AT DREAMLAND. ...WHATSIS-NAME... SCHLITZIE!
HAVE A SEAT, BIG GUY... HAVE A SEAT... CALL ME WILLIE...
YOU'VE GOT MOXIE, KID... TAKIN' ALL THAT GUFF FROM THE RUBES.
GUFF! RUBES!
WE GET IT, TOO. I DON'T KNOW WHY I PUT UP WITH IT... THE DOUGH, I GUESS.
DOUGH!
SURE, PALLY, SURE ... WE ALL LIKE THE DOUGH... ...BUT SOME DAY, PALLY... SOME DAY, A LITTLE GUY LIKE ME IS GONNA BE IMPORT-ANT! MAYBE A MAYOR... OR THE PRESIDENT!
ANYWAYS, YOU'D BETTER GET BACK TO YOUR BUNK-HOUSE. I GOTTA CLEAN UP HERE... THEY EVEN GOT ME DOIN' DISHES, IF YOU CAN BELIEVE IT...
I LIKE DISHES, WILLIE!

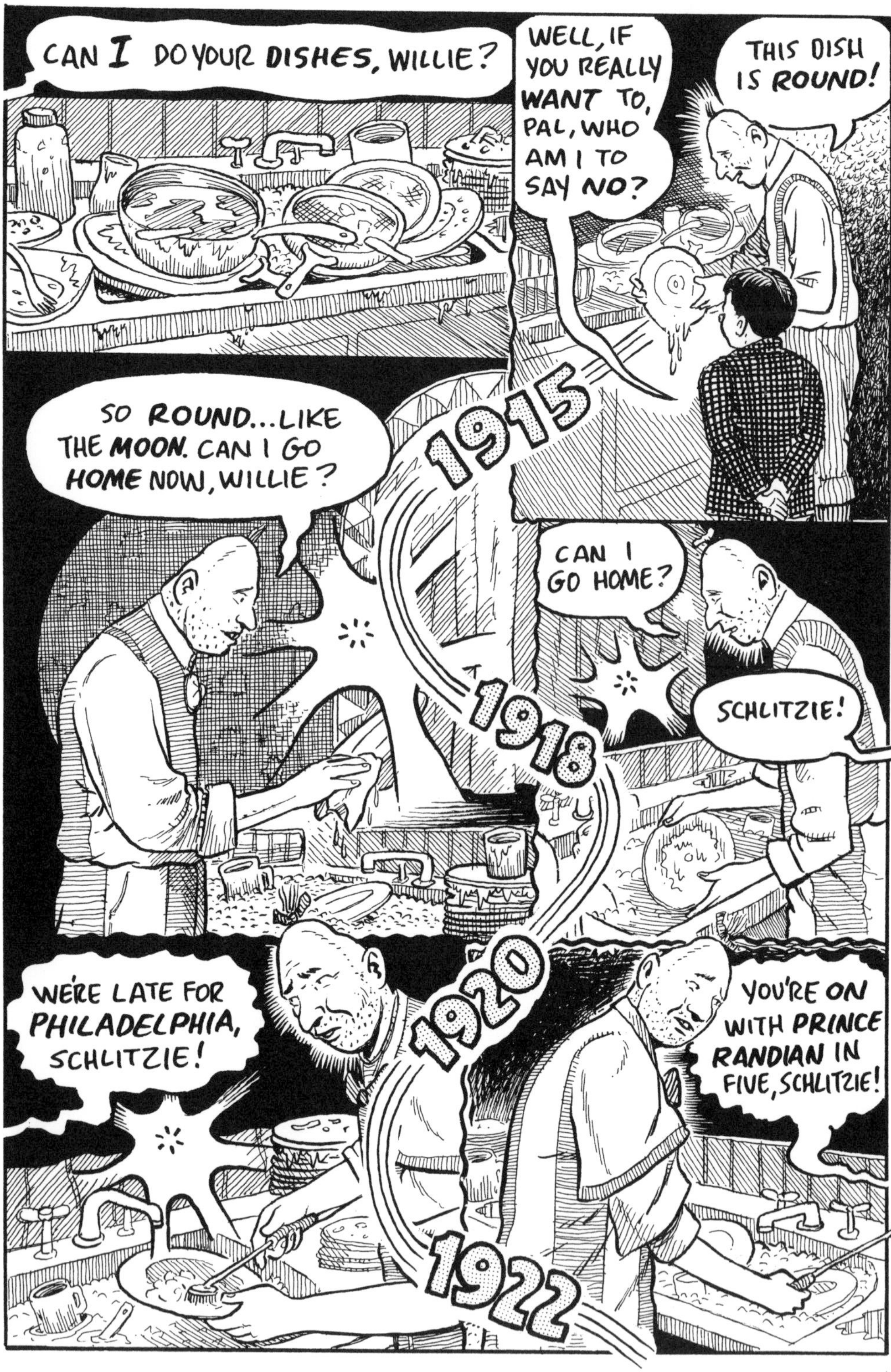
CAN I DO YOUR DISHES, WILLIE?
WELL, IF YOU REALLY WANT TO, PAL, WHO AM I TO SAY NO?
THIS DISH IS ROUND!
1915
SO ROUND...LIKE THE MOON. CAN I GO HOME NOW, WILLIE?
CAN I GO HOME?
1918
SCHLITZIE!
1920
WE'RE LATE FOR PHILADELPHIA, SCHLITZIE!
YOU'RE ON WITH PRINCE RANDIAN IN FIVE, SCHLITZIE!
1922

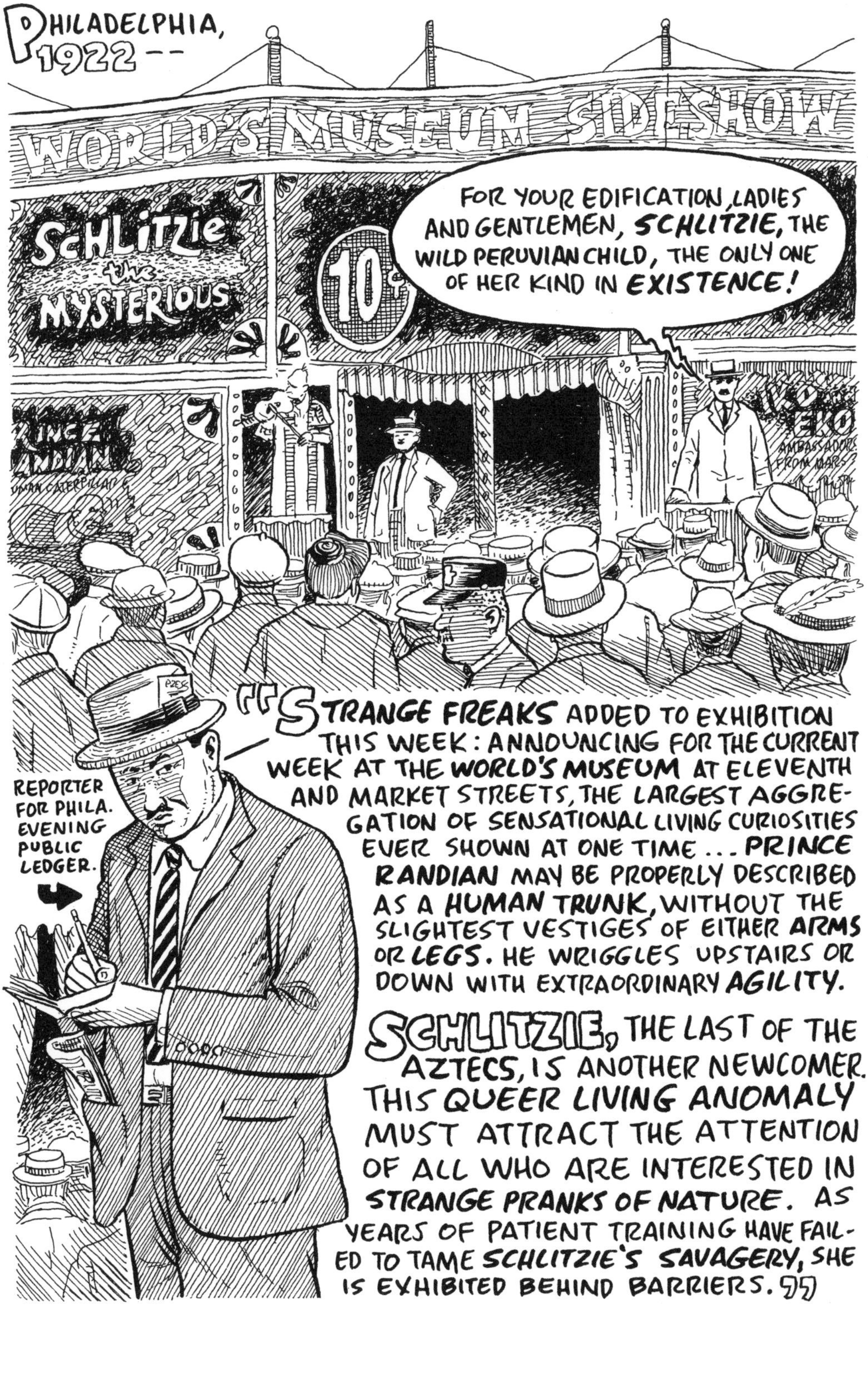
PHILADELPHIA, 1922 --
WORLD'S MUSEUM SIDESHOW
SCHLITZIE the MYSTERIOUS
10¢
FOR YOUR EDIFICATION, LADIES AND GENTLEMEN, SCHLITZIE, THE WILD PERUVIAN CHILD, THE ONLY ONE OF HER KIND IN EXISTENCE!
AMBASSADORS FROM MARS
REPORTER FOR PHILA. EVENING PUBLIC LEDGER.
"STRANGE FREAKS ADDED TO EXHIBITION THIS WEEK: ANNOUNCING FOR THE CURRENT WEEK AT THE WORLD'S MUSEUM AT ELEVENTH AND MARKET STREETS, THE LARGEST AGGREGATION OF SENSATIONAL LIVING CURIOSITIES EVER SHOWN AT ONE TIME ... PRINCE RANDIAN MAY BE PROPERLY DESCRIBED AS A HUMAN TRUNK, WITHOUT THE SLIGHTEST VESTIGES OF EITHER ARMS OR LEGS. HE WRIGGLES UPSTAIRS OR DOWN WITH EXTRAORDINARY AGILITY.
SCHLITZIE, THE LAST OF THE AZTECS, IS ANOTHER NEWCOMER. THIS QUEER LIVING ANOMALY MUST ATTRACT THE ATTENTION OF ALL WHO ARE INTERESTED IN STRANGE PRANKS OF NATURE. AS YEARS OF PATIENT TRAINING HAVE FAILED TO TAME SCHLITZIE'S SAVAGERY, SHE IS EXHIBITED BEHIND BARRIERS."

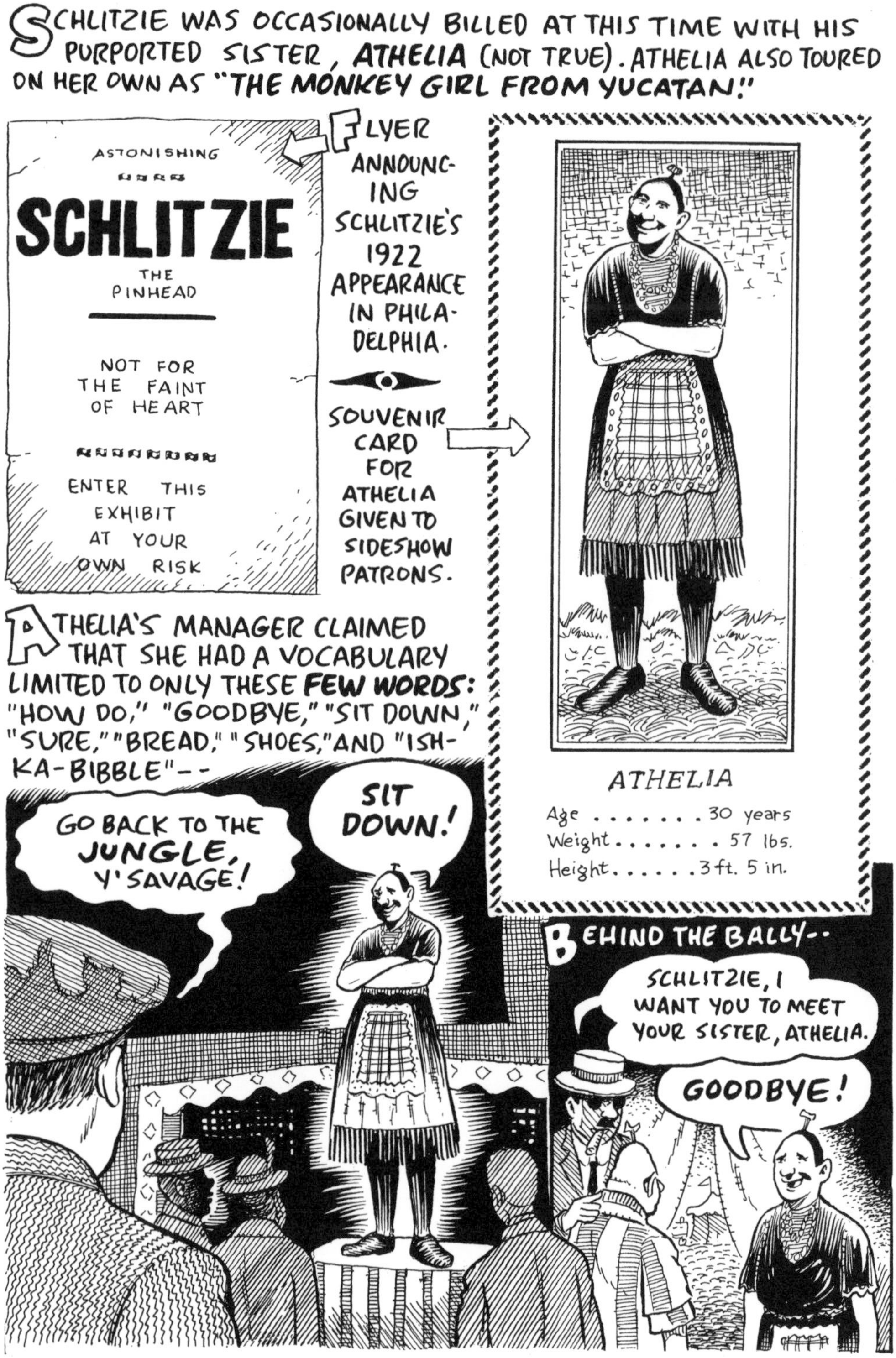
SCHLITZIE WAS OCCASIONALLY BILLED AT THIS TIME WITH HIS PURPORTED SISTER, ATHELIA (NOT TRUE). ATHELIA ALSO TOURED ON HER OWN AS "THE MONKEY GIRL FROM YUCATAN!"
ASTONISHING
SCHLITZIE
THE PINHEAD
NOT FOR THE FAINT OF HEART
ENTER THIS EXHIBIT AT YOUR OWN RISK
FLYER ANNOUNCING SCHLITZIE'S 1922 APPEARANCE IN PHILADELPHIA.
SOUVENIR CARD FOR ATHELIA GIVEN TO SIDESHOW PATRONS.
ATHELIA
Age . . . . 30 years
Weight . . . . 57 lbs.
Height . . . . . . 3 ft. 5 in.
ATHELIA'S MANAGER CLAIMED THAT SHE HAD A VOCABULARY LIMITED TO ONLY THESE FEW WORDS: "HOW DO," "GOODBYE," "SIT DOWN," "SURE," "BREAD," "SHOES," AND "ISHKA-BIBBLE"--
GO BACK TO THE JUNGLE, Y'SAVAGE!
SIT DOWN!
BEHIND THE BALLY--
SCHLITZIE, I WANT YOU TO MEET YOUR SISTER, ATHELIA.
GOODBYE!

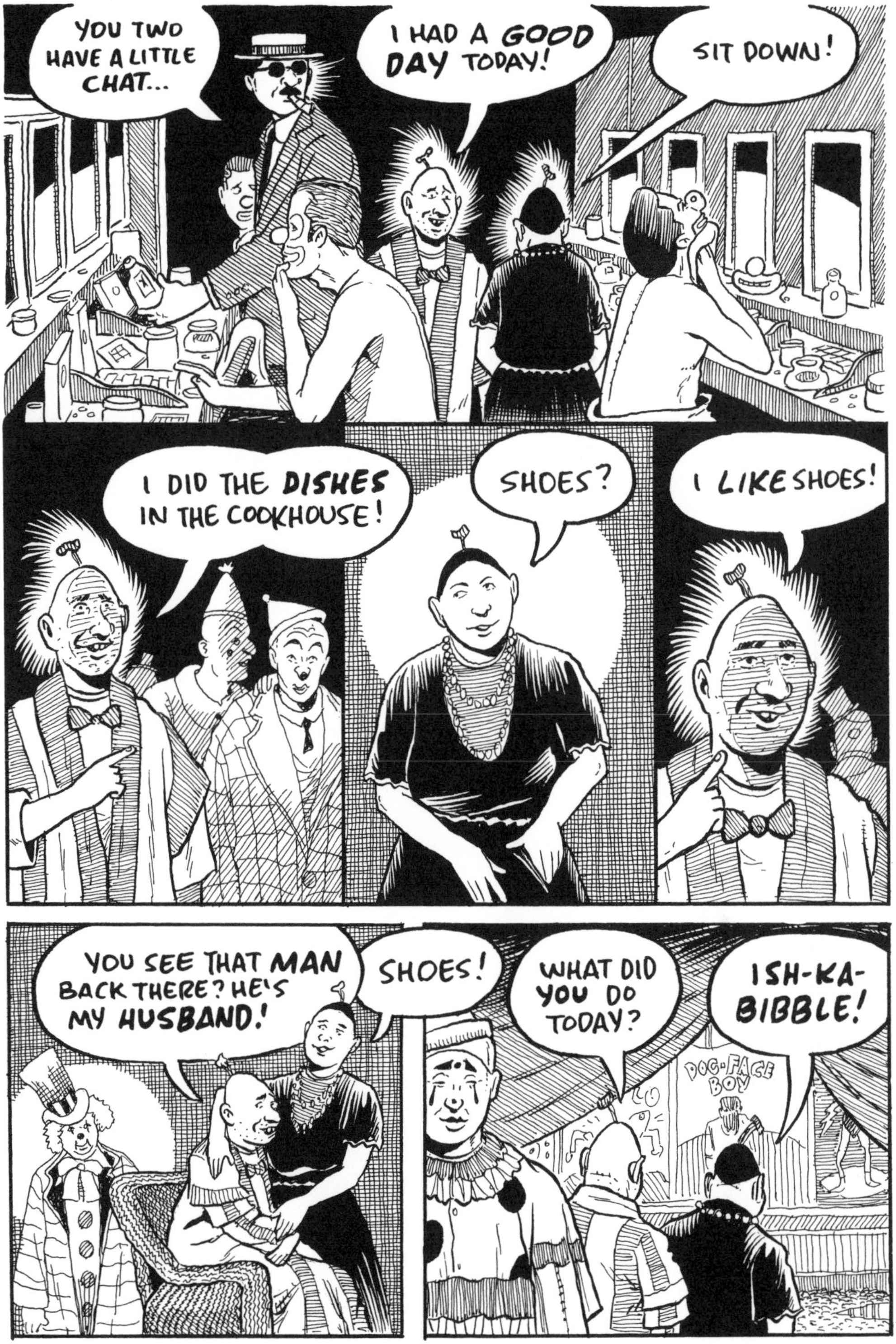
YOU TWO HAVE A LITTLE CHAT...
I HAD A GOOD DAY TODAY!
SIT DOWN!
I DID THE DISHES IN THE COOKHOUSE!
SHOES?
I LIKE SHOES!
YOU SEE THAT MAN BACK THERE? HE'S MY HUSBAND!
SHOES!
WHAT DID YOU DO TODAY?
ISH-KA-BIBBLE!
DOG-FACE BOY

SCHLITZIE WAS **"ON LOAN"** BY STEPHEN MILLS TO FELLOW SIDE-SHOW MANAGER **CHARLES ZERM** THROUGHOUT THE EARLY 1920s. THERE ARE UNCORROBORATED (AND CONFLICTING) ACCOUNTS OF SCHLITZIE'S EARLY YEARS; THE SIDESHOW, AFTER ALL, IS A WORLD WHERE THE TRUTH IS MALLEABLE & EXAGGERATION IS RAMPANT. HERE ARE A FEW SCHLITZIE **GENESIS** STORIES.

1 ON A RETURN TRIP FROM **CUBA** IN 1921, CHARLES & BERNICE ZERM INCLUDED SCHLITZIE ON THE PASSENGER LIST, STATING HE WAS BORN TO A SOCIALLY PROMINENT FAMILY IN **SAN ANTONIO, TEXAS.** HE WAS KEPT HIDDEN IN AN ATTIC UNTIL HE WAS ABOUT 25.

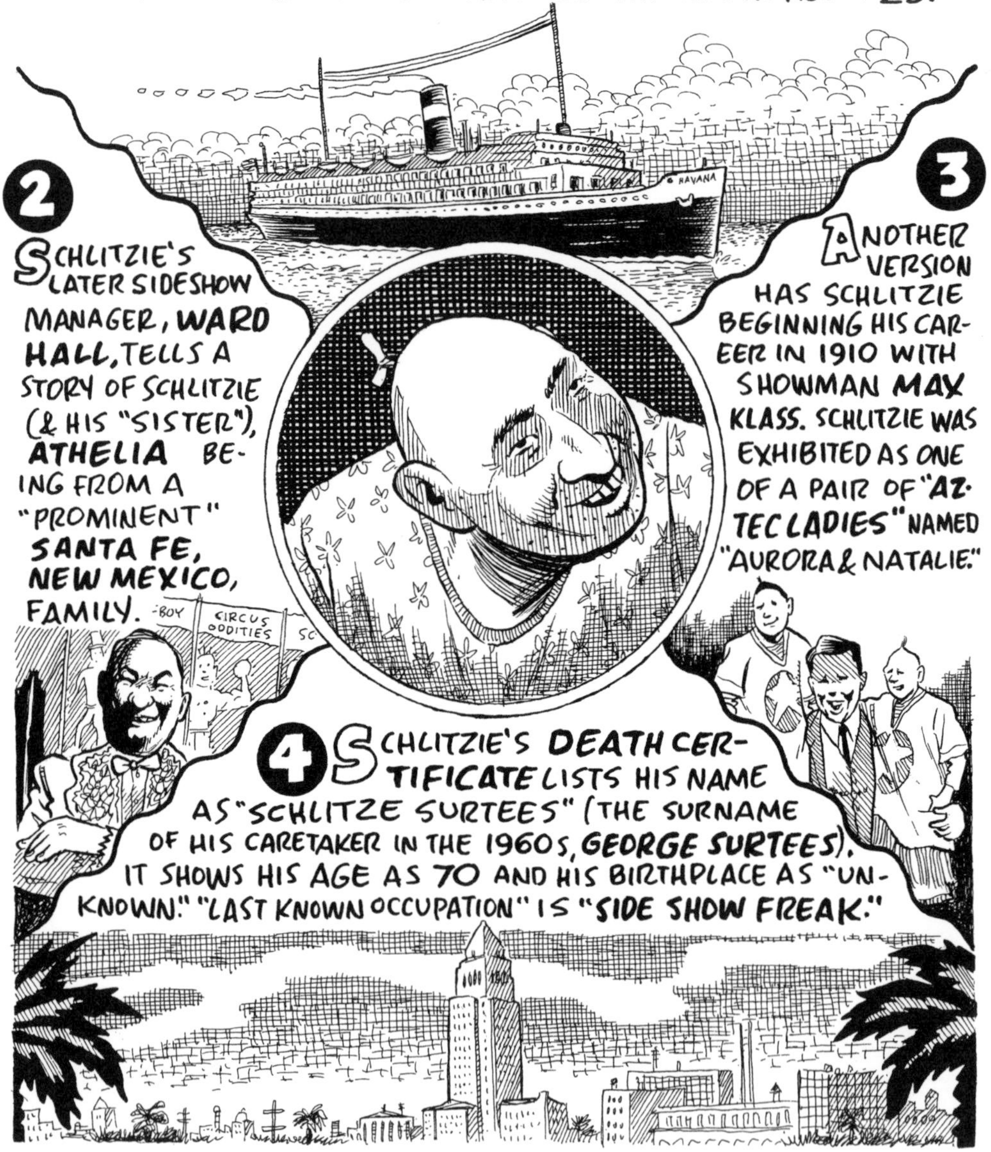
HAVANA
2 SCHLITZIE'S LATER SIDESHOW MANAGER, **WARD HALL,** TELLS A STORY OF SCHLITZIE (& HIS "SISTER"), **ATHELIA** BEING FROM A "PROMINENT" **SANTA FE, NEW MEXICO,** FAMILY.
BOY
CIRCUS ODDITIES
3 ANOTHER VERSION HAS SCHLITZIE BEGINNING HIS CAREER IN 1910 WITH SHOWMAN **MAX KLASS.** SCHLITZIE WAS EXHIBITED AS ONE OF A PAIR OF **"AZTEC LADIES"** NAMED "AURORA & NATALIE."
4 SCHLITZIE'S **DEATH CERTIFICATE** LISTS HIS NAME AS "SCHLITZE SURTEES" (THE SURNAME OF HIS CARETAKER IN THE 1960s, **GEORGE SURTEES**). IT SHOWS HIS AGE AS 70 AND HIS BIRTHPLACE AS "UNKNOWN." "LAST KNOWN OCCUPATION" IS **"SIDE SHOW FREAK."**

ONE OF THE MANY **MYTHS** ABOUT SCHLITZIE IS THE UNFOUNDED ASSERTION THAT HIS **NAME** WAS DERIVED FROM **SCHLITZ BEER**.

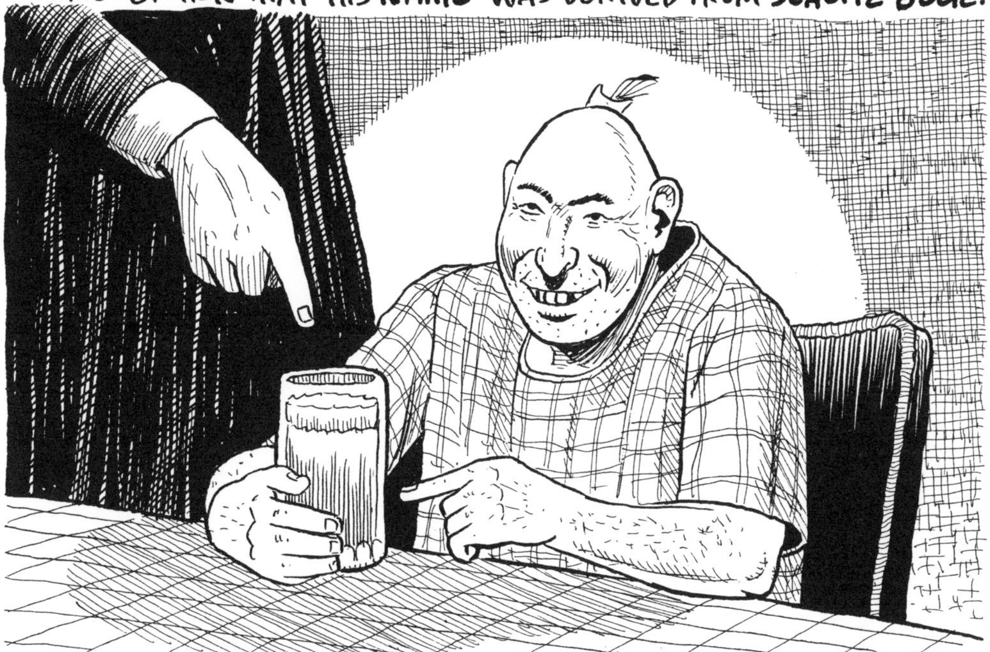

SCHLITZIE **WAS** FOND OF AN OCCASIONAL GLASS OF LAGER. **WARD HALL** SAID AS MUCH IN AN INTERVIEW WITH ME. "HE WOULD DRINK A LITTLE & GET A BIT TIPSY," HE SAID. "SO WE HAD TO BE CAREFUL ABOUT HOW MUCH HE WAS ALLOWED."

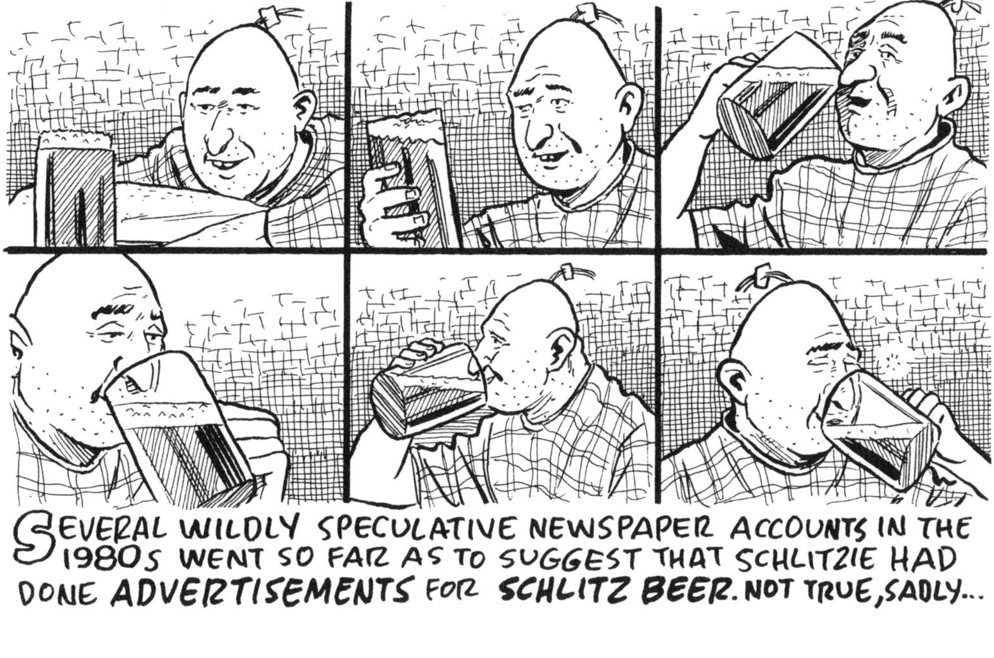

SEVERAL WILDLY SPECULATIVE NEWSPAPER ACCOUNTS IN THE 1980S WENT SO FAR AS TO SUGGEST THAT SCHLITZIE HAD DONE **ADVERTISEMENTS** FOR **SCHLITZ BEER**. NOT TRUE, SADLY...

SCHLITZIE WAS BILLED UNDER A VARIETY OF NAMES, CONCOCTED BY DIFFERENT SIDESHOW EXHIBITORS TO ACCENTUATE HIS "OTHERNESS."

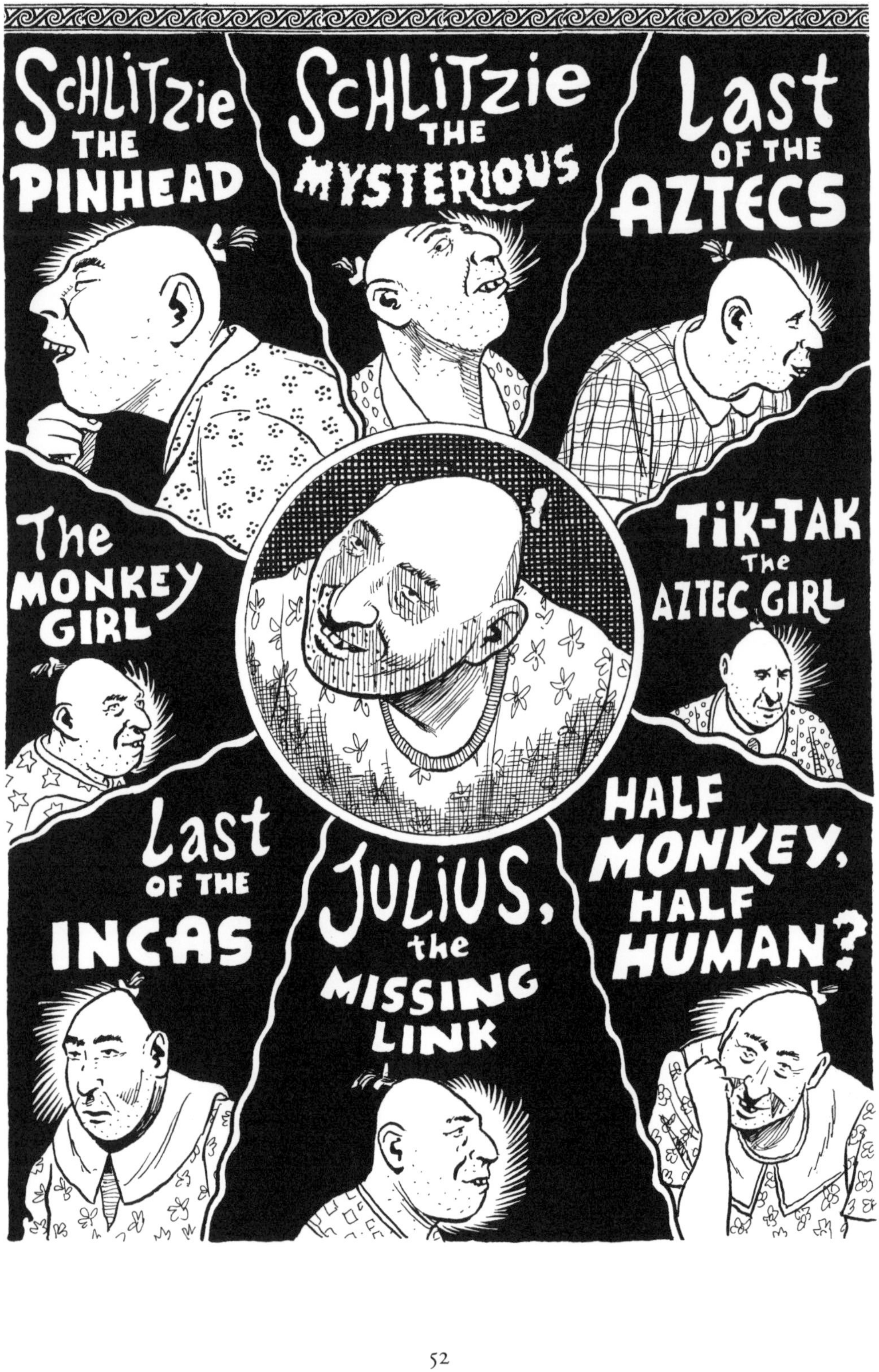
SCHLITZIE THE PINHEAD
SCHLITZIE THE MYSTERIOUS
LAST OF THE AZTECS
THE MONKEY GIRL
TIK-TAK THE AZTEC GIRL
LAST OF THE INCAS
JULIUS, THE MISSING LINK
HALF MONKEY, HALF HUMAN?

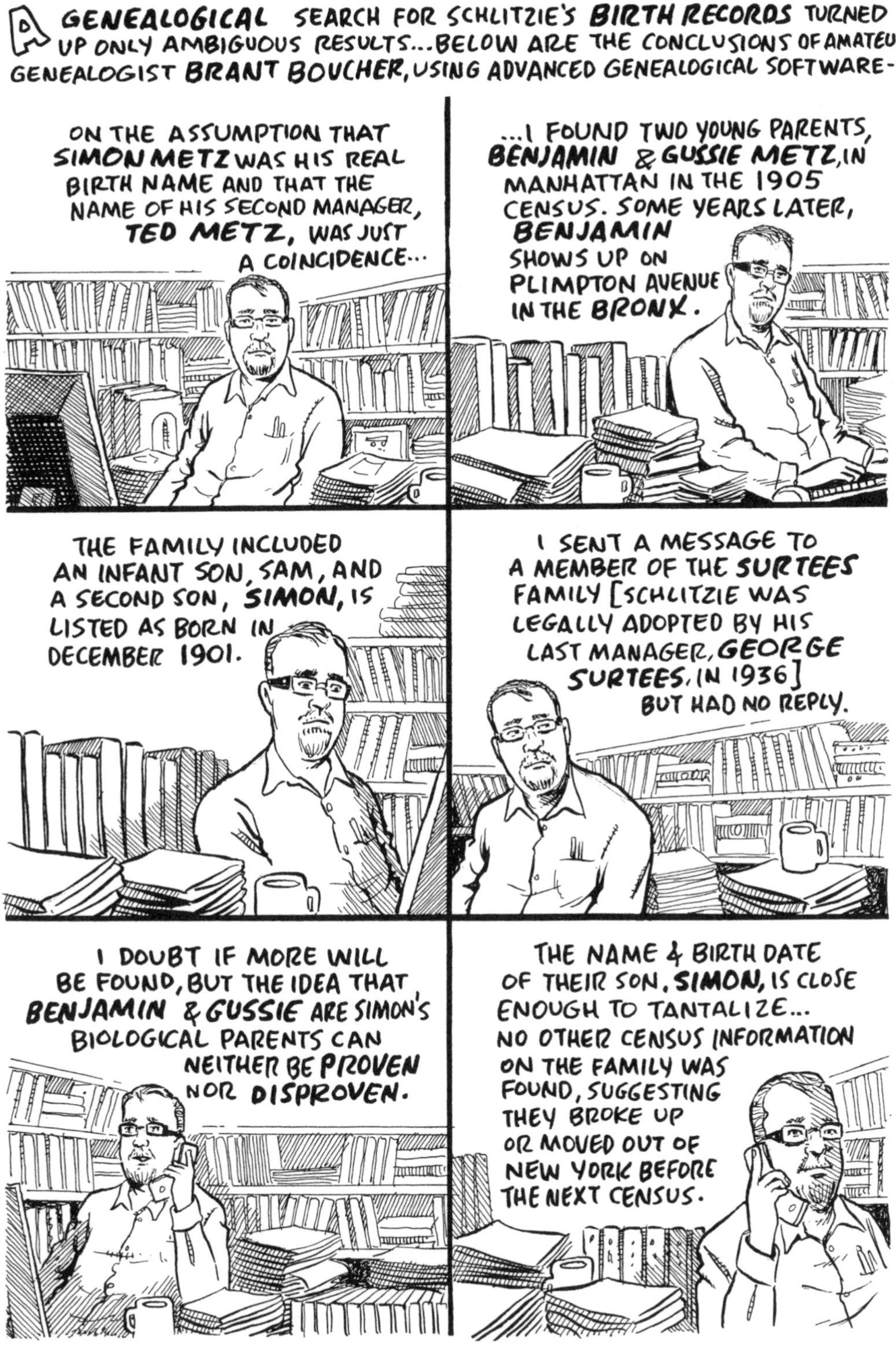
A GENEALOGICAL SEARCH FOR SCHLITZIE'S BIRTH RECORDS TURNED UP ONLY AMBIGUOUS RESULTS...BELOW ARE THE CONCLUSIONS OF AMATEUR GENEALOGIST BRANT BOUCHER, USING ADVANCED GENEALOGICAL SOFTWARE--
ON THE ASSUMPTION THAT SIMON METZ WAS HIS REAL BIRTH NAME AND THAT THE NAME OF HIS SECOND MANAGER, TED METZ, WAS JUST A COINCIDENCE...
...I FOUND TWO YOUNG PARENTS, BENJAMIN & GUSSIE METZ, IN MANHATTAN IN THE 1905 CENSUS. SOME YEARS LATER, BENJAMIN SHOWS UP ON PLIMPTON AVENUE IN THE BRONX.
THE FAMILY INCLUDED AN INFANT SON, SAM, AND A SECOND SON, SIMON, IS LISTED AS BORN IN DECEMBER 1901.
I SENT A MESSAGE TO A MEMBER OF THE SURTEES FAMILY [SCHLITZIE WAS LEGALLY ADOPTED BY HIS LAST MANAGER, GEORGE SURTEES, IN 1936] BUT HAD NO REPLY.
I DOUBT IF MORE WILL BE FOUND, BUT THE IDEA THAT BENJAMIN & GUSSIE ARE SIMON'S BIOLOGICAL PARENTS CAN NEITHER BE PROVEN NOR DISPROVEN.
THE NAME & BIRTH DATE OF THEIR SON, SIMON, IS CLOSE ENOUGH TO TANTALIZE... NO OTHER CENSUS INFORMATION ON THE FAMILY WAS FOUND, SUGGESTING THEY BROKE UP OR MOVED OUT OF NEW YORK BEFORE THE NEXT CENSUS.

UNLIKE MOST OTHER SIDESHOW PERFORMERS, MANAGING SCHLITZIE WAS A FULL-TIME RESPONSIBILITY FOR HIS "EMPLOYERS." HE WAS USUALLY ASSIGNED A **CARETAKER** WHO ATTENDED TO HIS NEEDS ON AND OFF THE SIDESHOW STAGE. THIS WOULD INCLUDE SCHLITZIE'S TRANSCONTINENTAL TRAIN RIDE FROM **NEW YORK** TO **LOS ANGELES** IN 1922 WITH CHARLES ZERM.

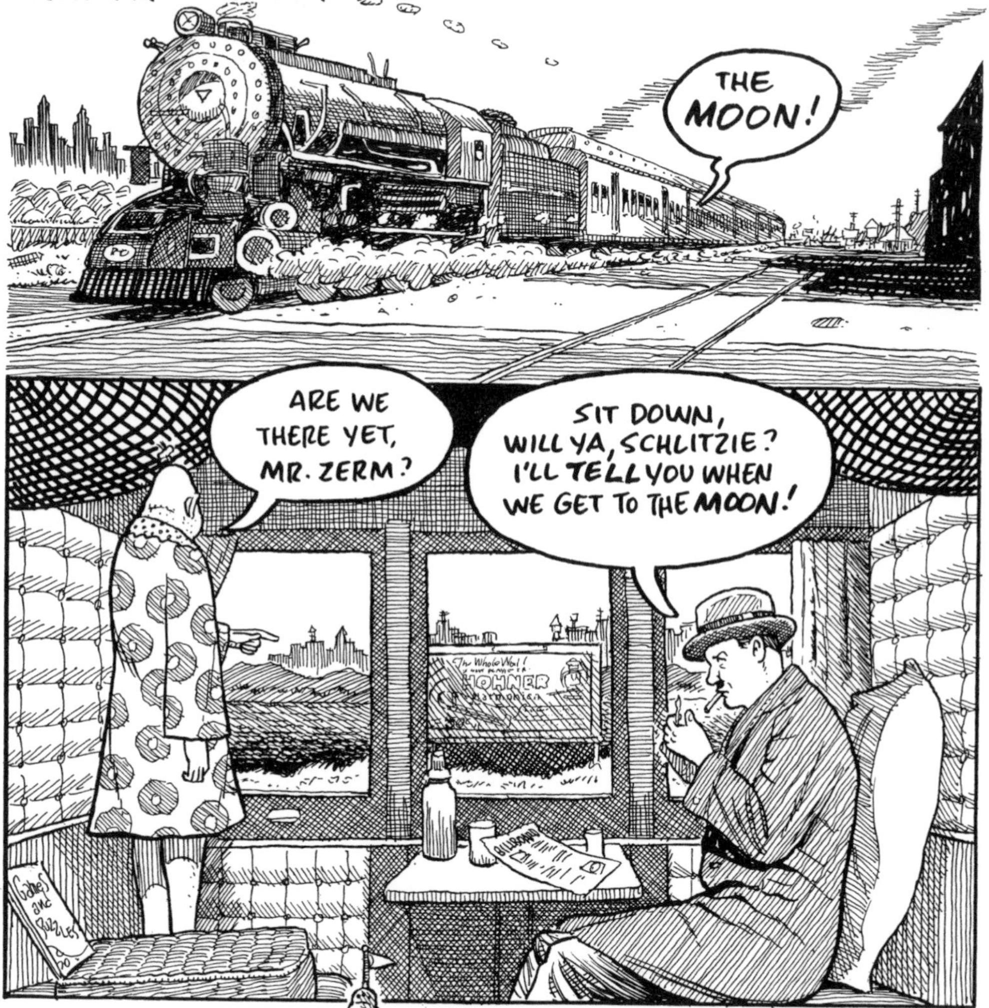
THE MOON!
ARE WE THERE YET, MR. ZERM?
SIT DOWN, WILL YA, SCHLITZIE? I'LL TELL YOU WHEN WE GET TO THE MOON!
HOHNER
Games and Puzzles

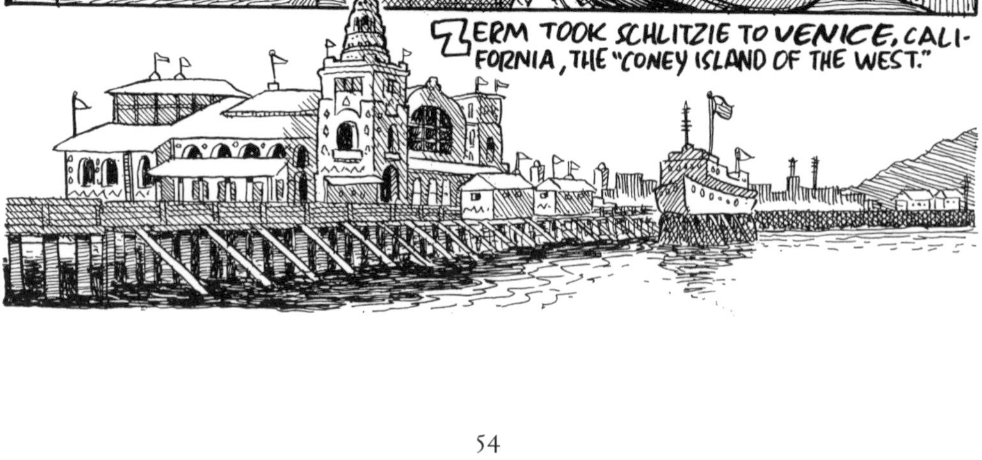
ZERM TOOK SCHLITZIE TO VENICE, CALIFORNIA, THE "CONEY ISLAND OF THE WEST."

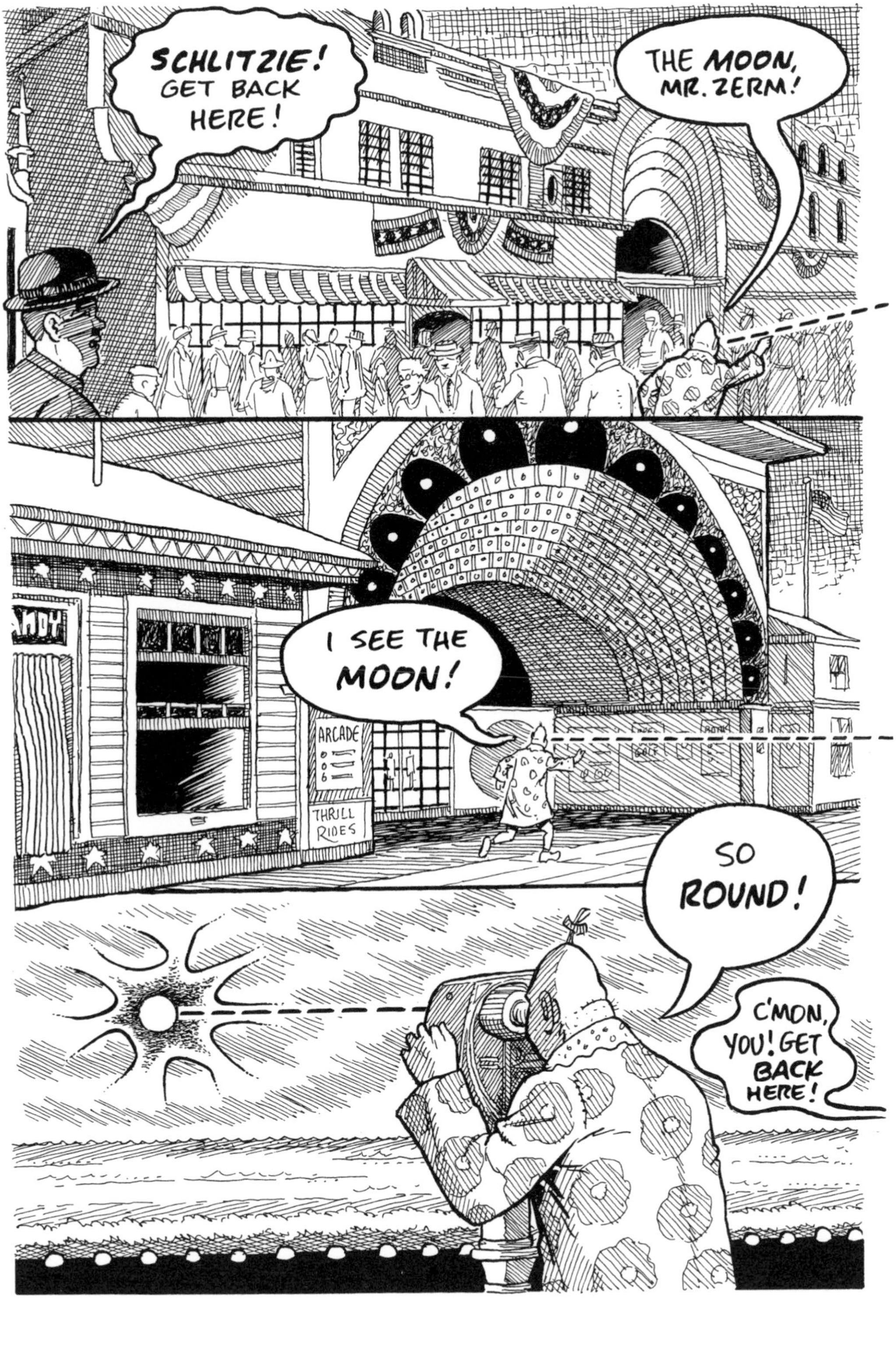
SCHLITZIE! GET BACK HERE!
THE MOON, MR. ZERM!
CANDY
I SEE THE MOON!
ARCADE
THRILL RIDES
SO ROUND!
C'MON, YOU! GET BACK HERE!

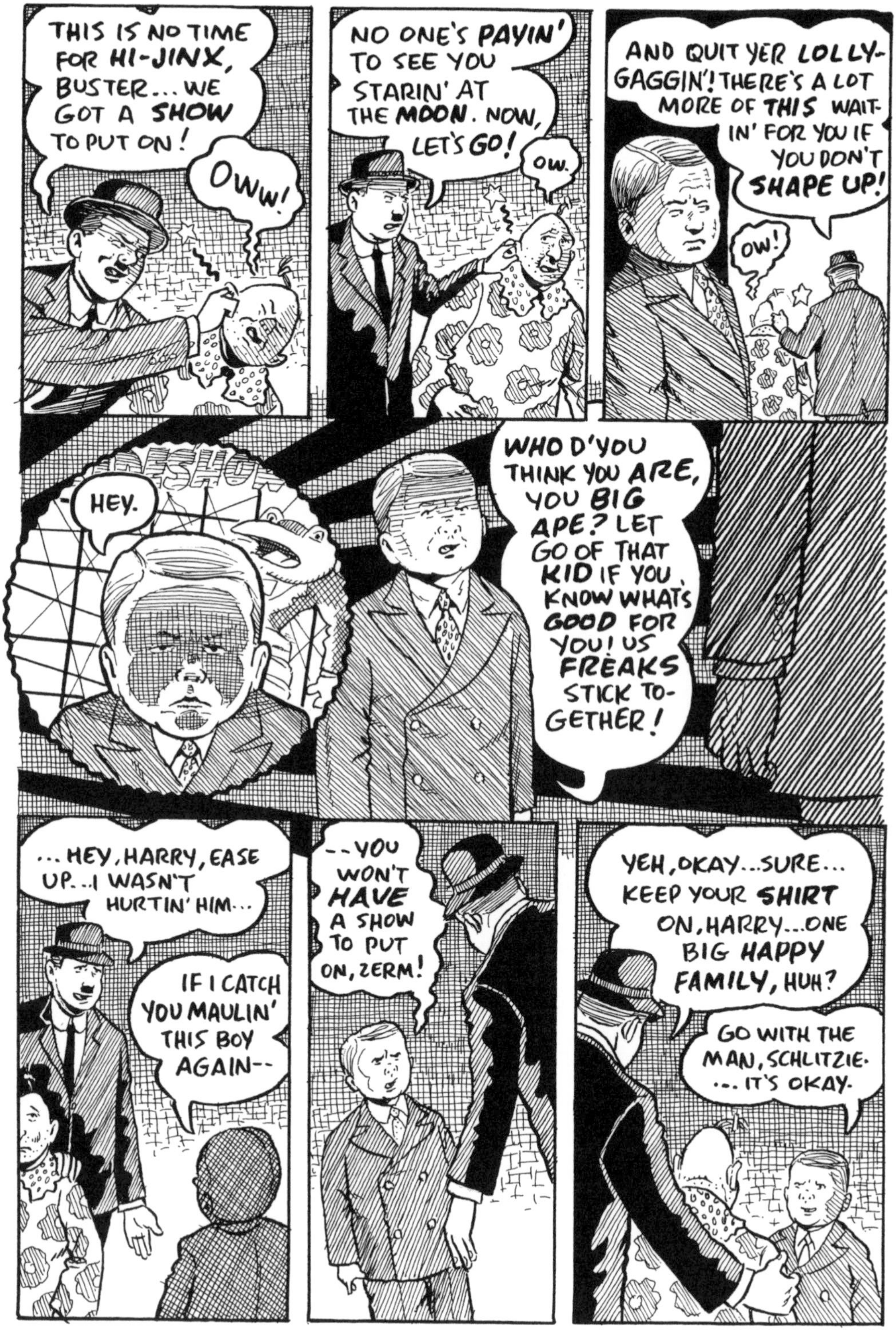
THIS IS NO TIME FOR HI-JINX, BUSTER... WE GOT A SHOW TO PUT ON!
OWW!
NO ONE'S PAYIN' TO SEE YOU STARIN' AT THE MOON. NOW, LET'S GO!
OW.
AND QUIT YER LOLLY-GAGGIN'! THERE'S A LOT MORE OF THIS WAIT-IN' FOR YOU IF YOU DON'T SHAPE UP!
OW!
HEY.
WHO D'YOU THINK YOU ARE, YOU BIG APE? LET GO OF THAT KID IF YOU KNOW WHAT'S GOOD FOR YOU! US FREAKS STICK TO-GETHER!
...HEY, HARRY, EASE UP...I WASN'T HURTIN' HIM...
IF I CATCH YOU MAULIN' THIS BOY AGAIN--
--YOU WON'T HAVE A SHOW TO PUT ON, ZERM!
YEH, OKAY...SURE... KEEP YOUR SHIRT ON, HARRY...ONE BIG HAPPY FAMILY, HUH?
GO WITH THE MAN, SCHLITZIE. ...IT'S OKAY.

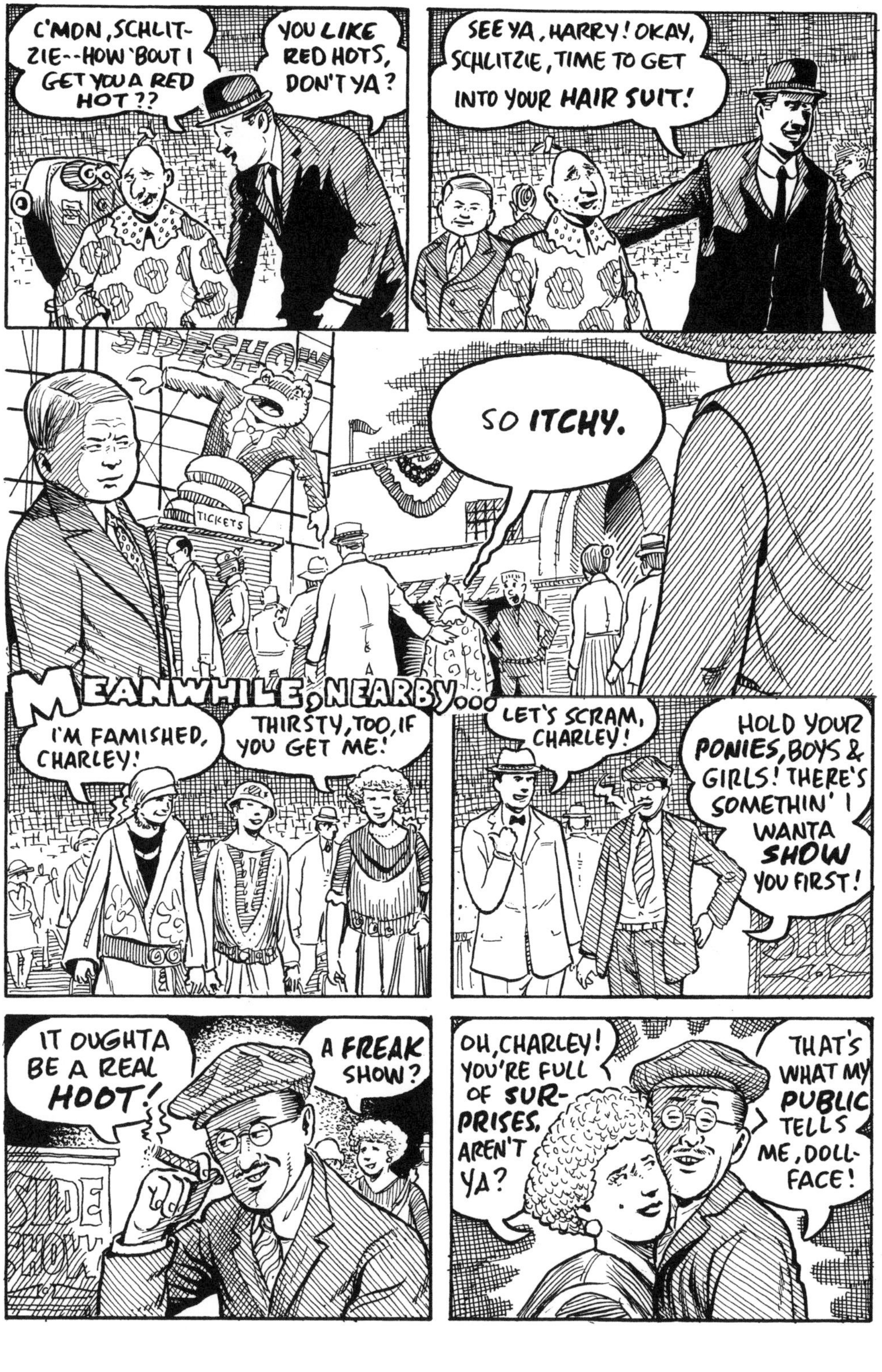

C'MON, SCHLITZIE--HOW 'BOUT I GET YOU A RED HOT??
YOU LIKE RED HOTS, DON'T YA?
SEE YA, HARRY! OKAY, SCHLITZIE, TIME TO GET INTO YOUR HAIR SUIT!
SIDESHOW
TICKETS
SO ITCHY.
MEANWHILE, NEARBY...
I'M FAMISHED, CHARLEY!
THIRSTY, TOO, IF YOU GET ME!
LET'S SCRAM, CHARLEY!
HOLD YOUR PONIES, BOYS & GIRLS! THERE'S SOMETHIN' I WANTA SHOW YOU FIRST!
IT OUGHTA BE A REAL HOOT!
A FREAK SHOW?
SIDE SHOW
OH, CHARLEY! YOU'RE FULL OF SURPRISES, AREN'T YA?
THAT'S WHAT MY PUBLIC TELLS ME, DOLL-FACE!

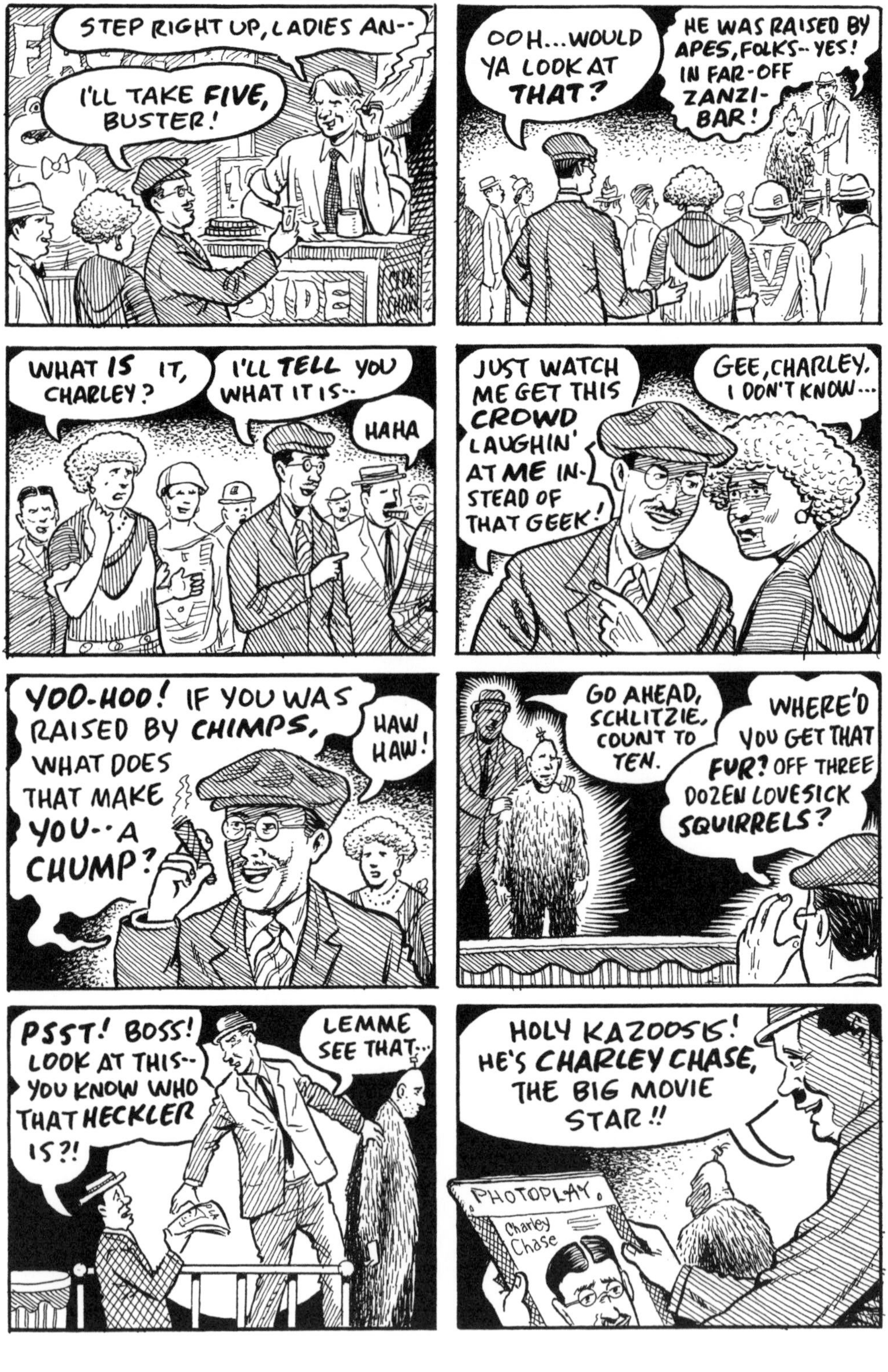
STEP RIGHT UP, LADIES AN--
I'LL TAKE FIVE, BUSTER!
OOH... WOULD YA LOOK AT THAT?
HE WAS RAISED BY APES, FOLKS-- YES! IN FAR-OFF ZANZIBAR!
WHAT IS IT, CHARLEY?
I'LL TELL YOU WHAT IT IS--
HAHA
JUST WATCH ME GET THIS CROWD LAUGHIN' AT ME INSTEAD OF THAT GEEK!
GEE, CHARLEY. I DON'T KNOW...
YOO-HOO! IF YOU WAS RAISED BY CHIMPS, WHAT DOES THAT MAKE YOU-- A CHUMP?
HAW HAW!
GO AHEAD, SCHLITZIE. COUNT TO TEN.
WHERE'D YOU GET THAT FUR? OFF THREE DOZEN LOVESICK SQUIRRELS?
PSST! BOSS! LOOK AT THIS-- YOU KNOW WHO THAT HECKLER IS?!
LEMME SEE THAT...
HOLY KAZOOSIS! HE'S CHARLEY CHASE, THE BIG MOVIE STAR!!
PHOTOPLAY
Charley Chase

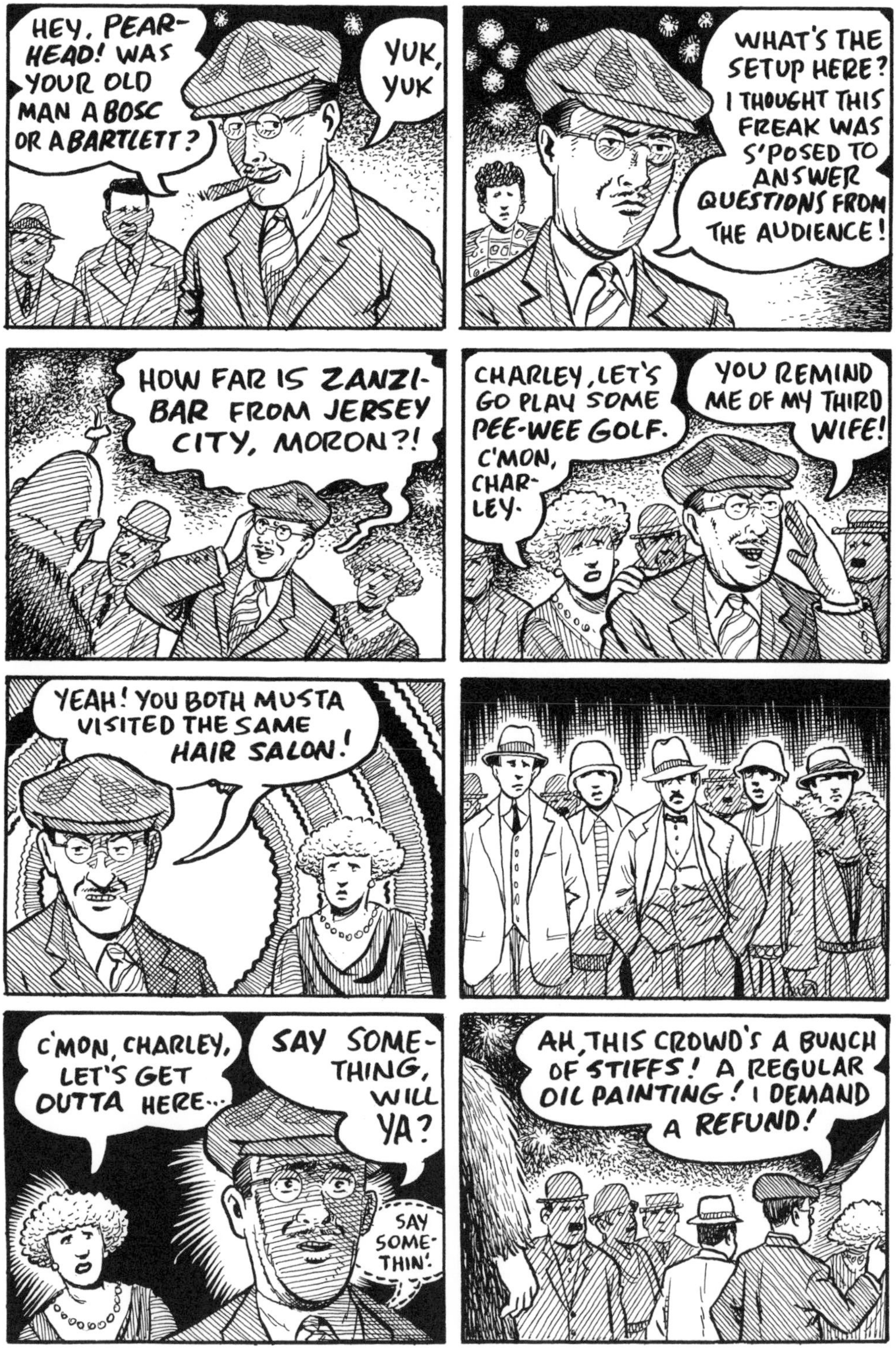
HEY, PEAR-HEAD! WAS YOUR OLD MAN A BOSC OR A BARTLETT?
YUK, YUK
WHAT'S THE SETUP HERE? I THOUGHT THIS FREAK WAS S'POSED TO ANSWER QUESTIONS FROM THE AUDIENCE!
HOW FAR IS ZANZIBAR FROM JERSEY CITY, MORON?!
CHARLEY, LET'S GO PLAY SOME PEE-WEE GOLF. C'MON, CHARLEY.
YOU REMIND ME OF MY THIRD WIFE!
YEAH! YOU BOTH MUSTA VISITED THE SAME HAIR SALON!
C'MON, CHARLEY, LET'S GET OUTTA HERE...
SAY SOMETHING, WILL YA?
SAY SOMETHIN'.
AH, THIS CROWD'S A BUNCH OF STIFFS! A REGULAR OIL PAINTING! I DEMAND A REFUND!

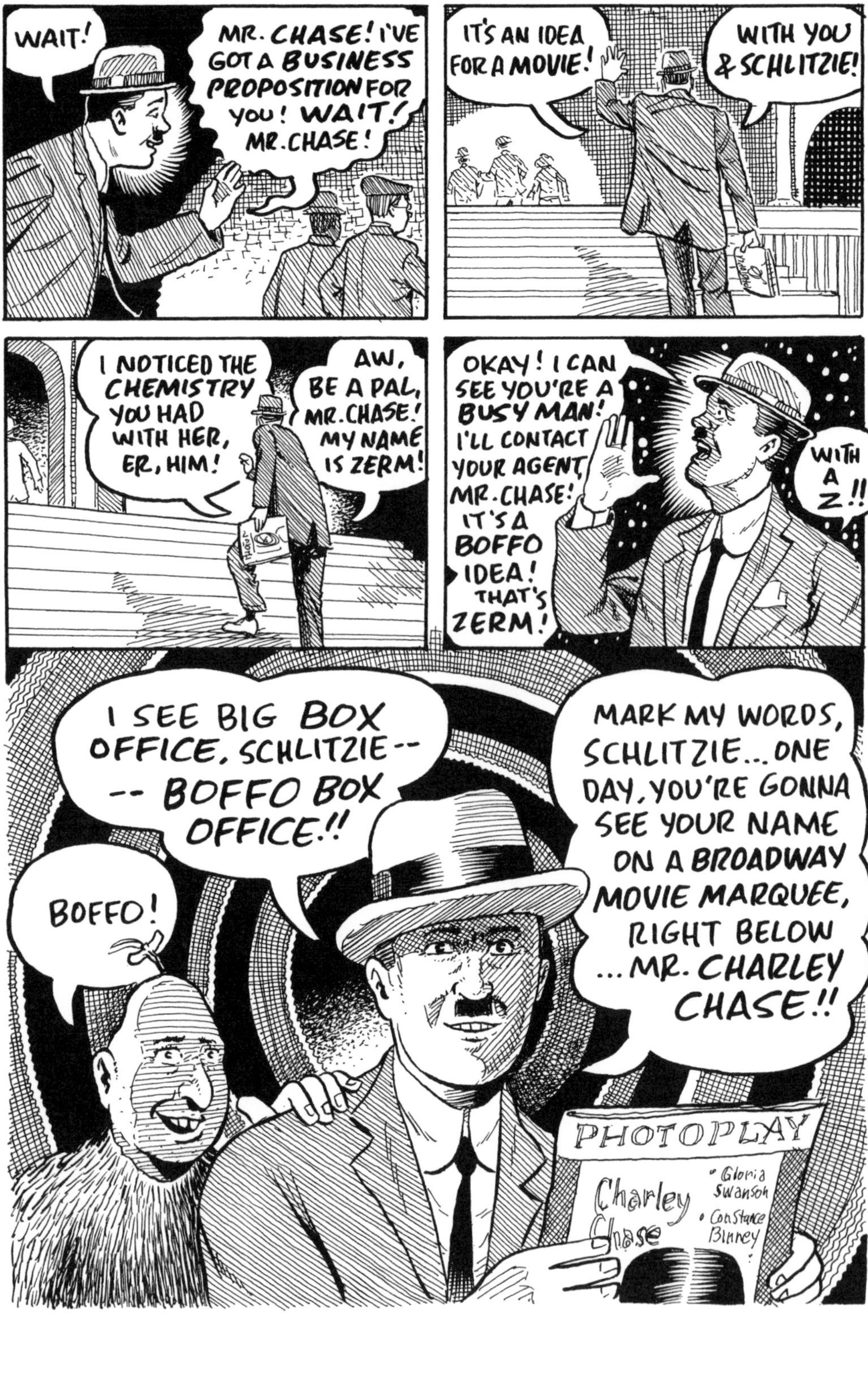
WAIT!
MR. CHASE! I'VE GOT A BUSINESS PROPOSITION FOR YOU! WAIT! MR. CHASE!
IT'S AN IDEA FOR A MOVIE!
WITH YOU & SCHLITZIE!
I NOTICED THE CHEMISTRY YOU HAD WITH HER, ER, HIM!
AW, BE A PAL, MR. CHASE! MY NAME IS ZERM!
OKAY! I CAN SEE YOU'RE A BUSY MAN! I'LL CONTACT YOUR AGENT, MR. CHASE! IT'S A BOFFO IDEA! THAT'S ZERM!
WITH A Z!!
I SEE BIG BOX OFFICE, SCHLITZIE-- --BOFFO BOX OFFICE!!
BOFFO!
MARK MY WORDS, SCHLITZIE... ONE DAY, YOU'RE GONNA SEE YOUR NAME ON A BROADWAY MOVIE MARQUEE, RIGHT BELOW ...MR. CHARLEY CHASE!!
PHOTOPLAY
Charley Chase
• Gloria Swanson
• Constance Binney

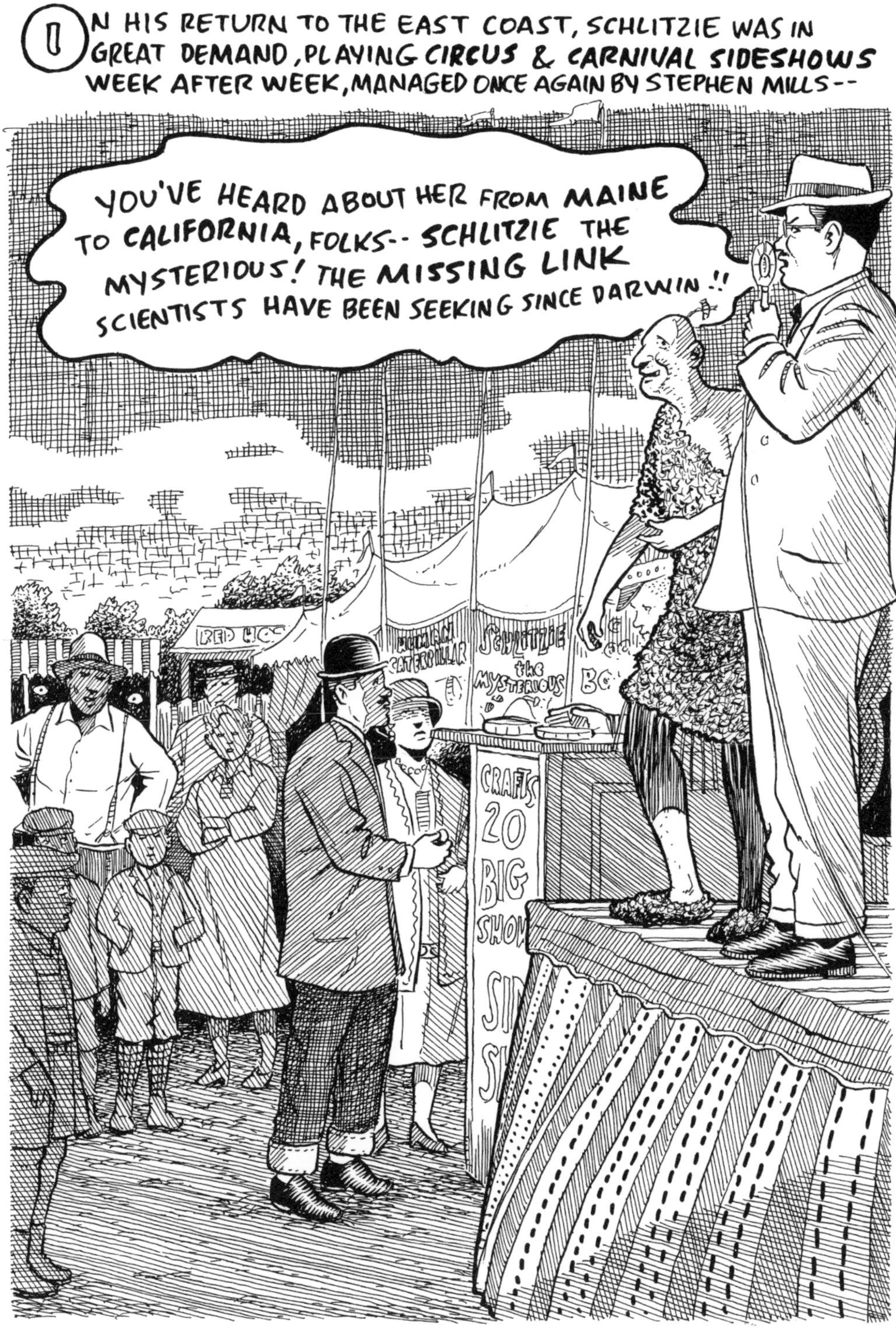
ON HIS RETURN TO THE EAST COAST, SCHLITZIE WAS IN GREAT DEMAND, PLAYING CIRCUS & CARNIVAL SIDESHOWS WEEK AFTER WEEK, MANAGED ONCE AGAIN BY STEPHEN MILLS--
YOU'VE HEARD ABOUT HER FROM MAINE TO CALIFORNIA, FOLKS-- SCHLITZIE THE MYSTERIOUS! THE MISSING LINK SCIENTISTS HAVE BEEN SEEKING SINCE DARWIN !!
HUMAN CATERPILLAR
SCHLITZIE the MYSTERIOUS
CRAFTS 20 BIG SHOW

THE CIRCUS WAS AT ITS COMMERCIAL PEAK IN THE 1920s, AND SCHLITZIE APPEARED IN ALL THE MAJOR VENUES, FROM THE RINGLING BROTHERS TO CLYDE BEATTY, TO MADISON SQUARE GARDEN. COMPETITION FROM MOVIES, VAUDEVILLE & RADIO BEGAN TO EAT AWAY AT ATTENDANCE, BUT THE SIDESHOWS STILL DREW ENORMOUS CROWDS--

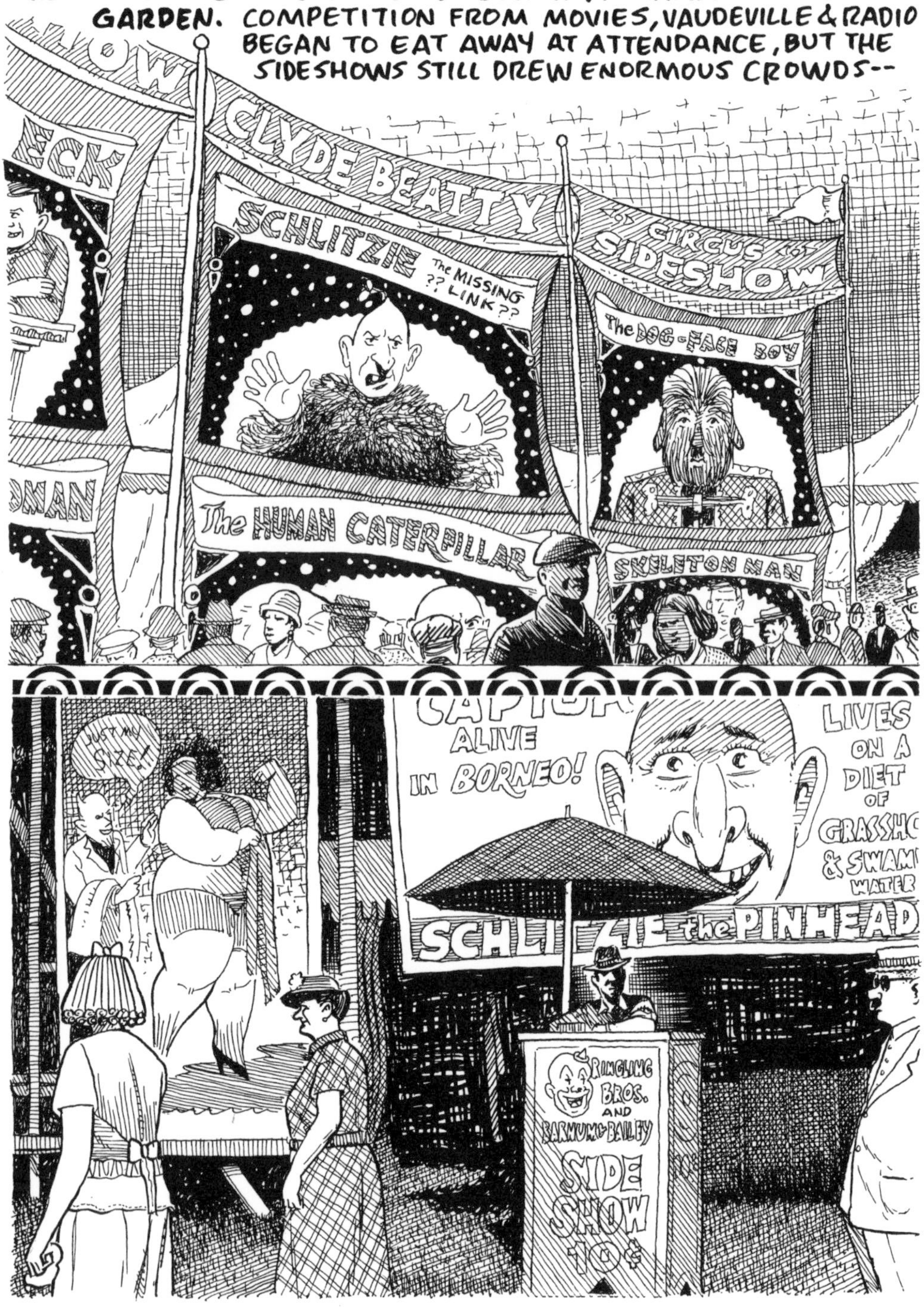
CLYDE BEATTY
CIRCUS SIDESHOW
SCHLITZIE The MISSING ?? LINK ??
The DOG-FACE BOY
The HUMAN CATERPILLAR
SKELITON MAN
JUST MY SIZE!
ALIVE IN BORNEO!
LIVES ON A DIET OF
SCHLITZIE the PINHEAD
RINGLING BROS. AND BARNUM & BAILEY
SIDE SHOW 10¢

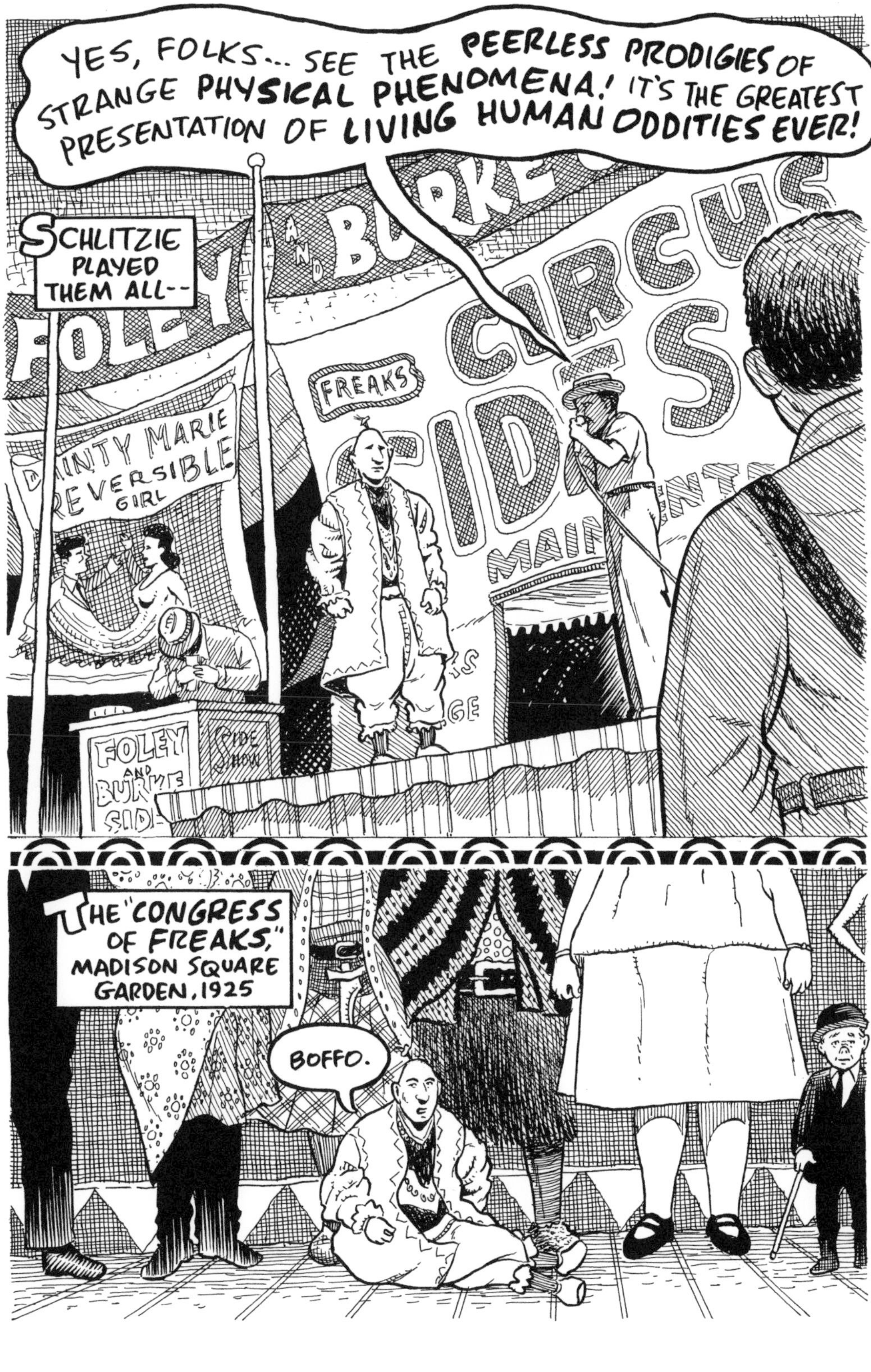
YES, FOLKS... SEE THE PEERLESS PRODIGIES OF STRANGE PHYSICAL PHENOMENA! IT'S THE GREATEST PRESENTATION OF LIVING HUMAN ODDITIES EVER!
SCHLITZIE PLAYED THEM ALL--
FOLEY AND BURKE CIRCUS
SIDE
FREAKS
DAINTY MARIE REVERSIBLE GIRL
FOLEY AND BURKE
SIDE SHOW
THE "CONGRESS OF FREAKS," MADISON SQUARE GARDEN, 1925
BOFFO.

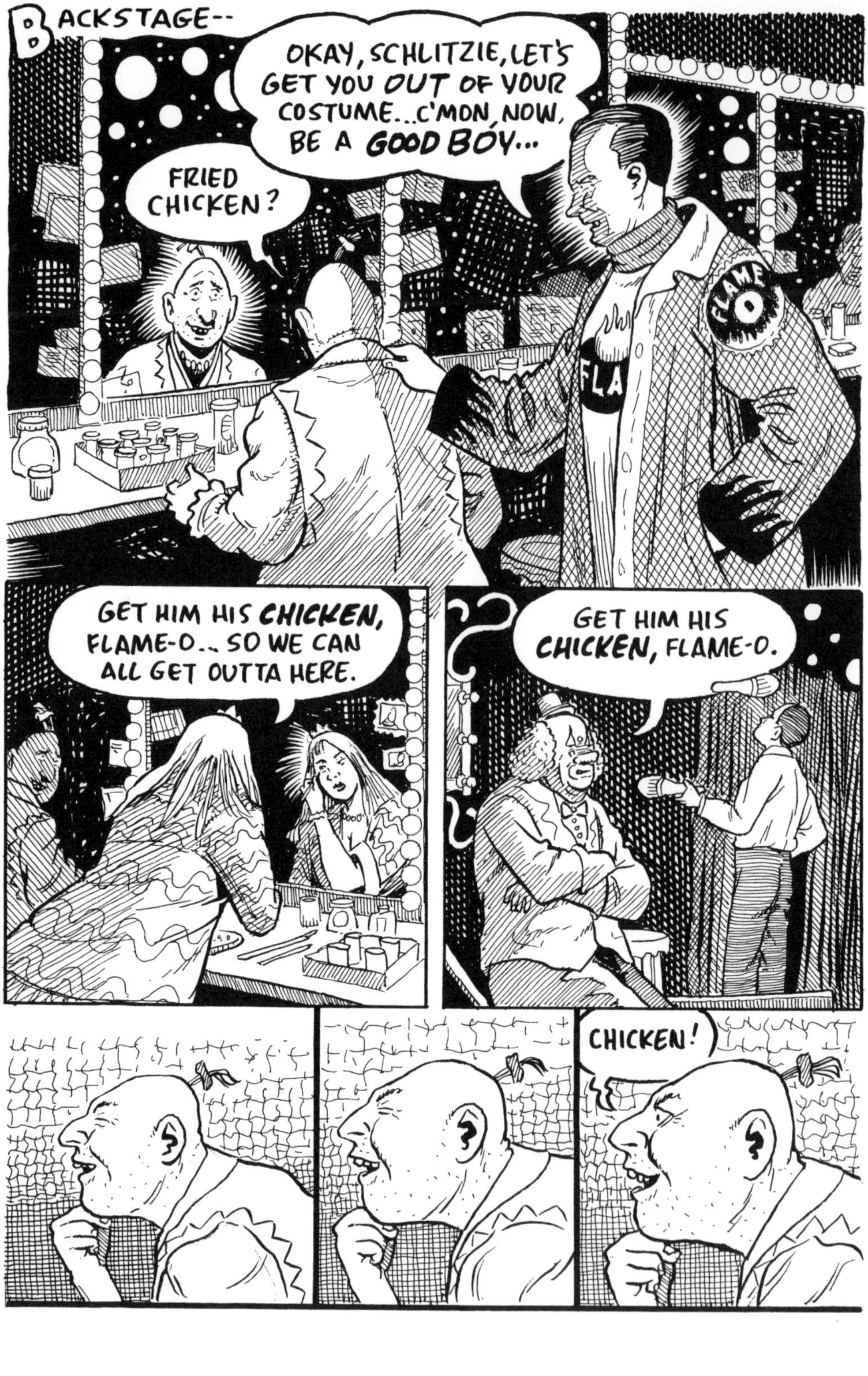
BACKSTAGE--
OKAY, SCHLITZIE, LET'S GET YOU OUT OF YOUR COSTUME...C'MON, NOW, BE A GOOD BOY...
FRIED CHICKEN?
FLA
FLAME-O
GET HIM HIS CHICKEN, FLAME-O... SO WE CAN ALL GET OUTTA HERE.
GET HIM HIS CHICKEN, FLAME-O.
CHICKEN!

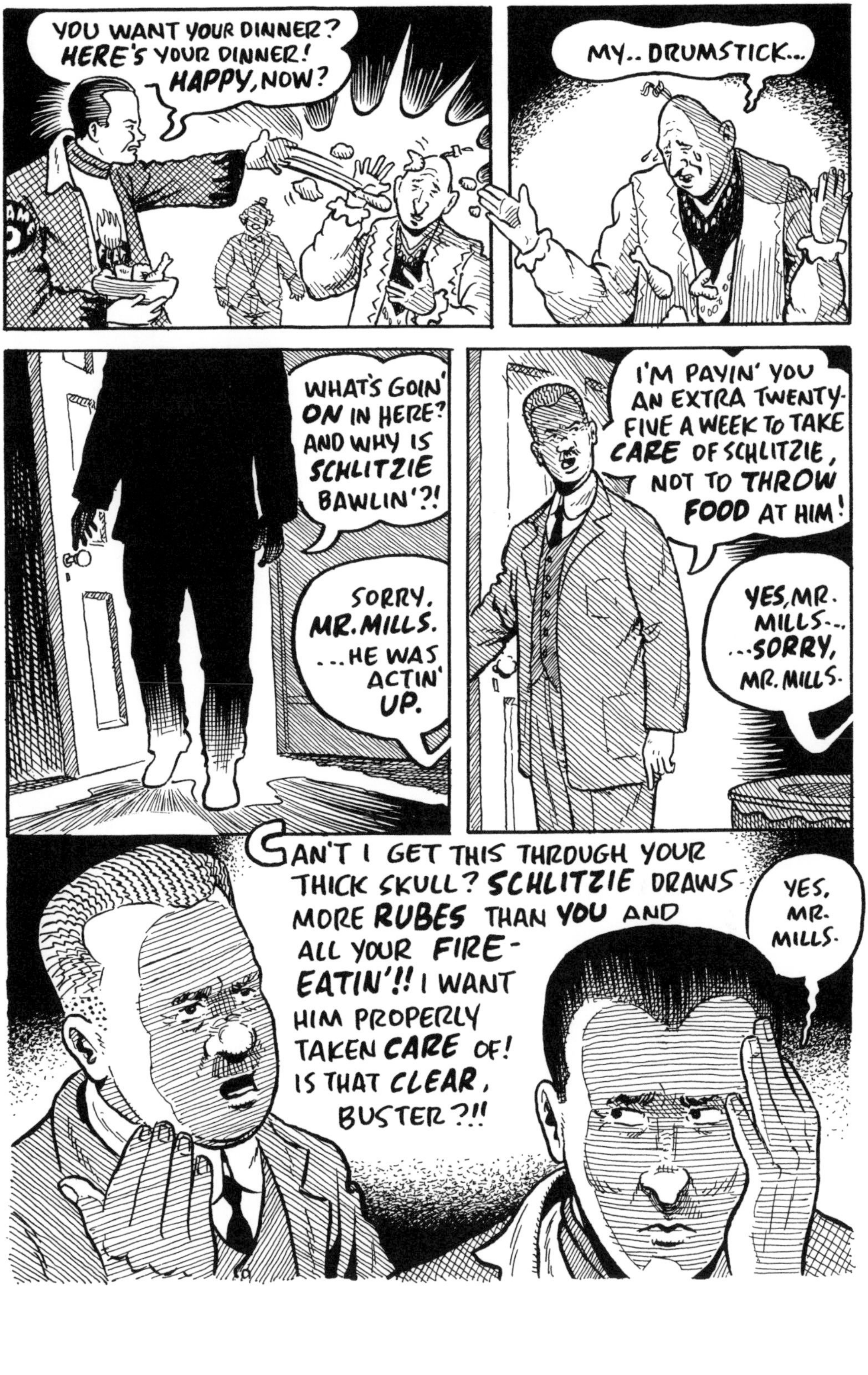
YOU WANT YOUR DINNER? HERE'S YOUR DINNER! HAPPY, NOW?
MY.. DRUMSTICK...
WHAT'S GOIN' ON IN HERE? AND WHY IS SCHLITZIE BAWLIN'?!
SORRY. MR. MILLS. ...HE WAS ACTIN' UP.
I'M PAYIN' YOU AN EXTRA TWENTY-FIVE A WEEK TO TAKE CARE OF SCHLITZIE, NOT TO THROW FOOD AT HIM!
YES, MR. MILLS... ...SORRY, MR. MILLS.
CAN'T I GET THIS THROUGH YOUR THICK SKULL? SCHLITZIE DRAWS MORE RUBES THAN YOU AND ALL YOUR FIRE-EATIN'!! I WANT HIM PROPERLY TAKEN CARE OF! IS THAT CLEAR, BUSTER?!!
YES, MR. MILLS.

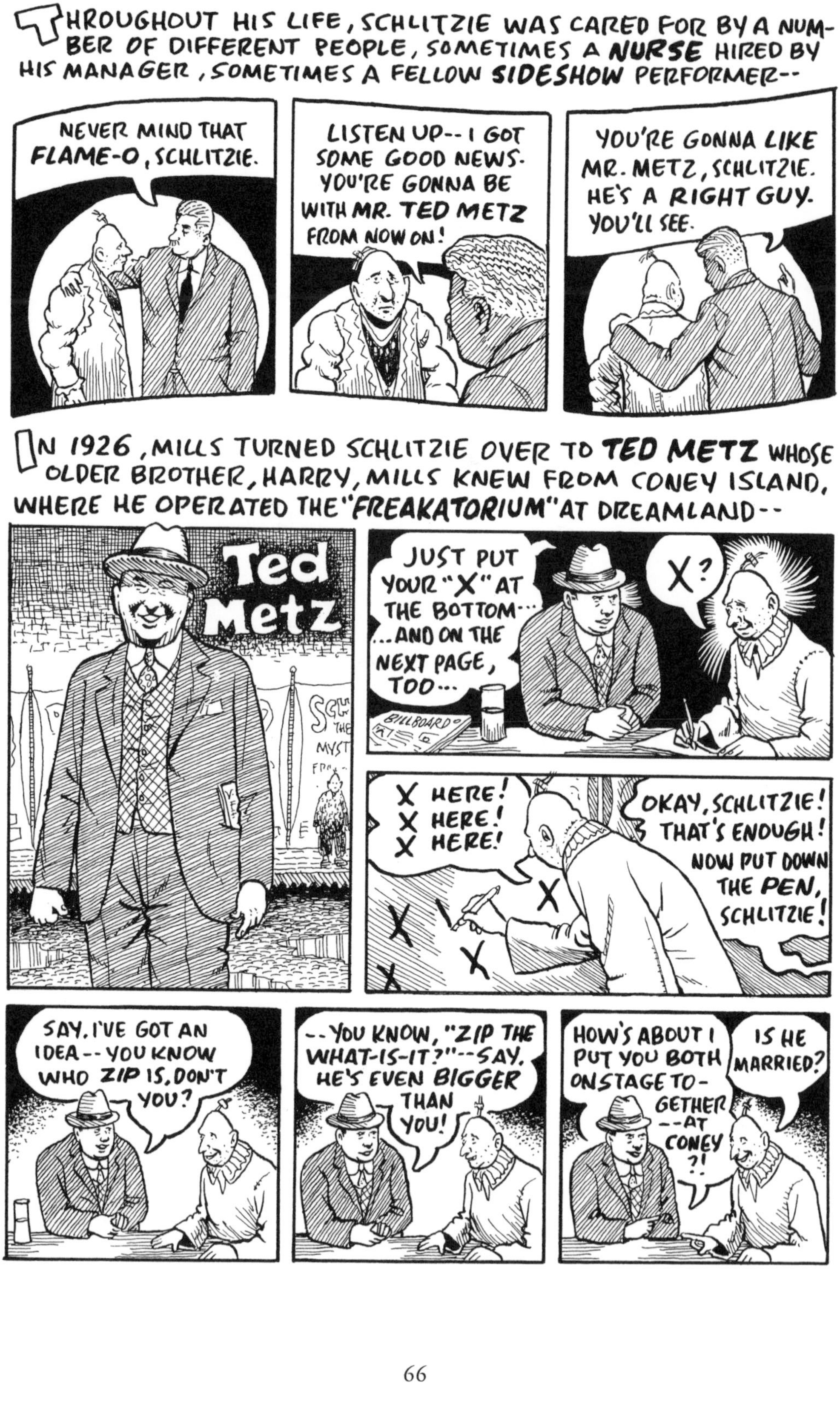
THROUGHOUT HIS LIFE, SCHLITZIE WAS CARED FOR BY A NUMBER OF DIFFERENT PEOPLE, SOMETIMES A NURSE HIRED BY HIS MANAGER, SOMETIMES A FELLOW SIDESHOW PERFORMER--
NEVER MIND THAT FLAME-O, SCHLITZIE.
LISTEN UP-- I GOT SOME GOOD NEWS. YOU'RE GONNA BE WITH MR. TED METZ FROM NOW ON!
YOU'RE GONNA LIKE MR. METZ, SCHLITZIE. HE'S A RIGHT GUY. YOU'LL SEE.
IN 1926, MILLS TURNED SCHLITZIE OVER TO TED METZ WHOSE OLDER BROTHER, HARRY, MILLS KNEW FROM CONEY ISLAND, WHERE HE OPERATED THE "FREAKATORIUM" AT DREAMLAND--
Ted Metz
JUST PUT YOUR "X" AT THE BOTTOM... ...AND ON THE NEXT PAGE, TOO...
X?
BILLBOARD
X HERE! X HERE! X HERE!
OKAY, SCHLITZIE! THAT'S ENOUGH! NOW PUT DOWN THE PEN, SCHLITZIE!
SAY, I'VE GOT AN IDEA-- YOU KNOW WHO ZIP IS, DON'T YOU?
--YOU KNOW, "ZIP THE WHAT-IS-IT?"--SAY, HE'S EVEN BIGGER THAN YOU!
HOW'S ABOUT I PUT YOU BOTH ONSTAGE TOGETHER --AT CONEY?!
IS HE MARRIED?

ZIP THE WHAT-IS-IT?, BORN WILLIAM HENRY JACKSON (OR JOHNSON) IN 1842 TO AN AFRICAN-AMERICAN FAMILY IN NEW JERSEY, WAS SO NAMED BY CHARLES DICKENS ON A VISIT TO P.T. BARNUM'S AMERICAN MUSEUM IN NEW YORK IN THE 1860s. ZIP WAS CALLED "THE DEAN OF FREAKS" & WORKED FOR THE RINGLING BROS. FOR MOST OF HIS CAREER.

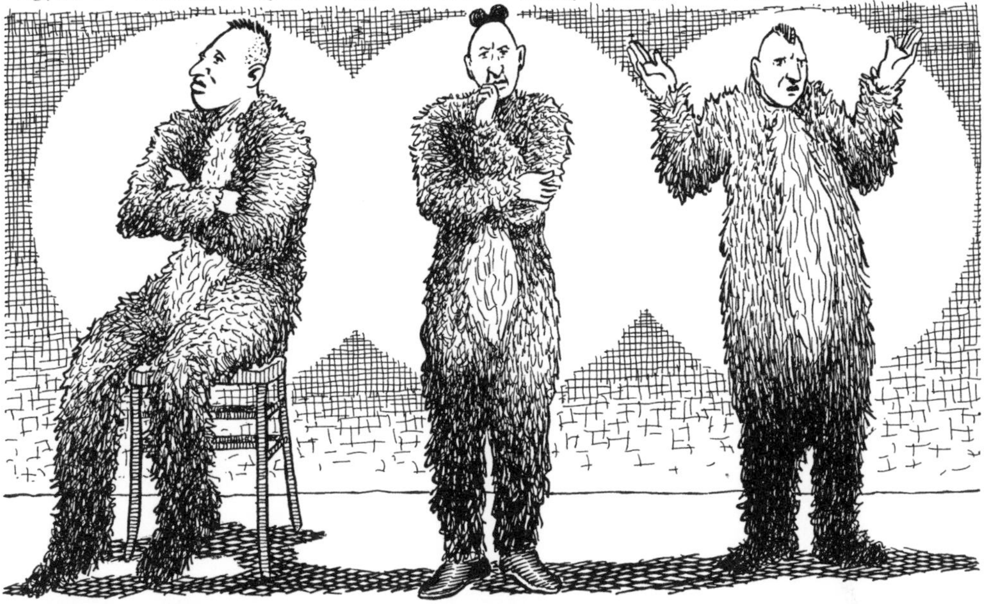

THERE'S ROOM FOR DOUBT AS TO ZIP'S "PINHEAD" CLAIM. FOR ONE THING, AS IS APPARENT IN THESE *POSES*, HE WAS "ACTING A PART." HIS SISTER, SARAH VAN DUYNE, IN A 1926 INTERVIEW, SAID THAT HER BROTHER WAS NOT MENTALLY HANDICAPPED & COULD "CONVERSE LIKE THE AVERAGE PERSON."

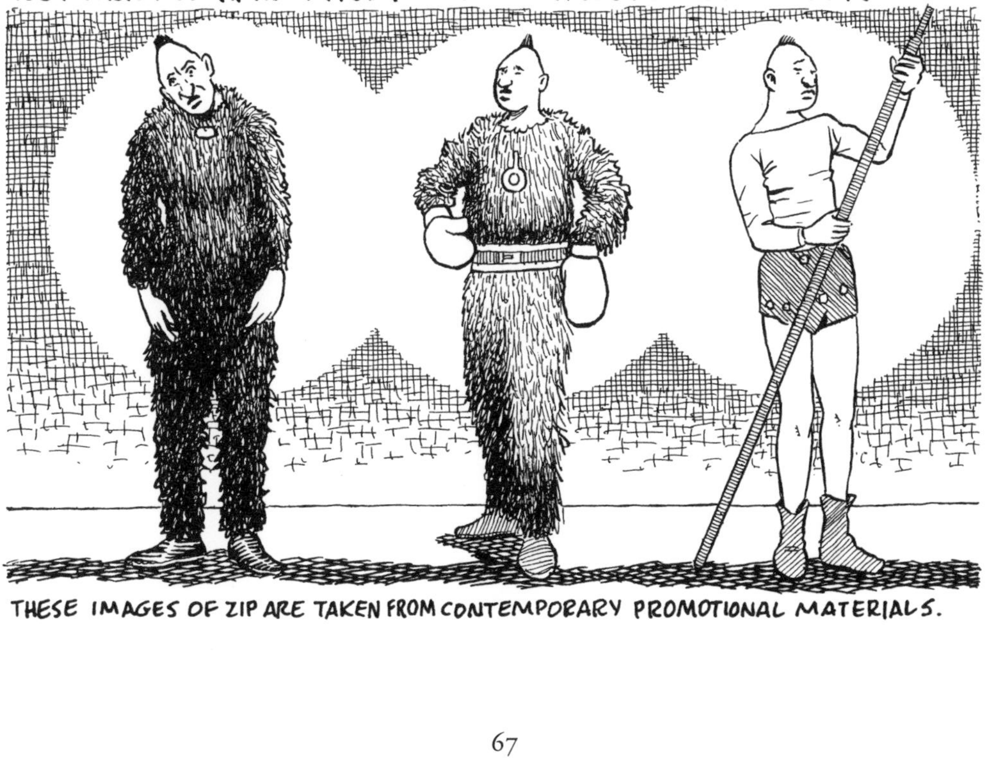

THESE IMAGES OF ZIP ARE TAKEN FROM CONTEMPORARY PROMOTIONAL MATERIALS.

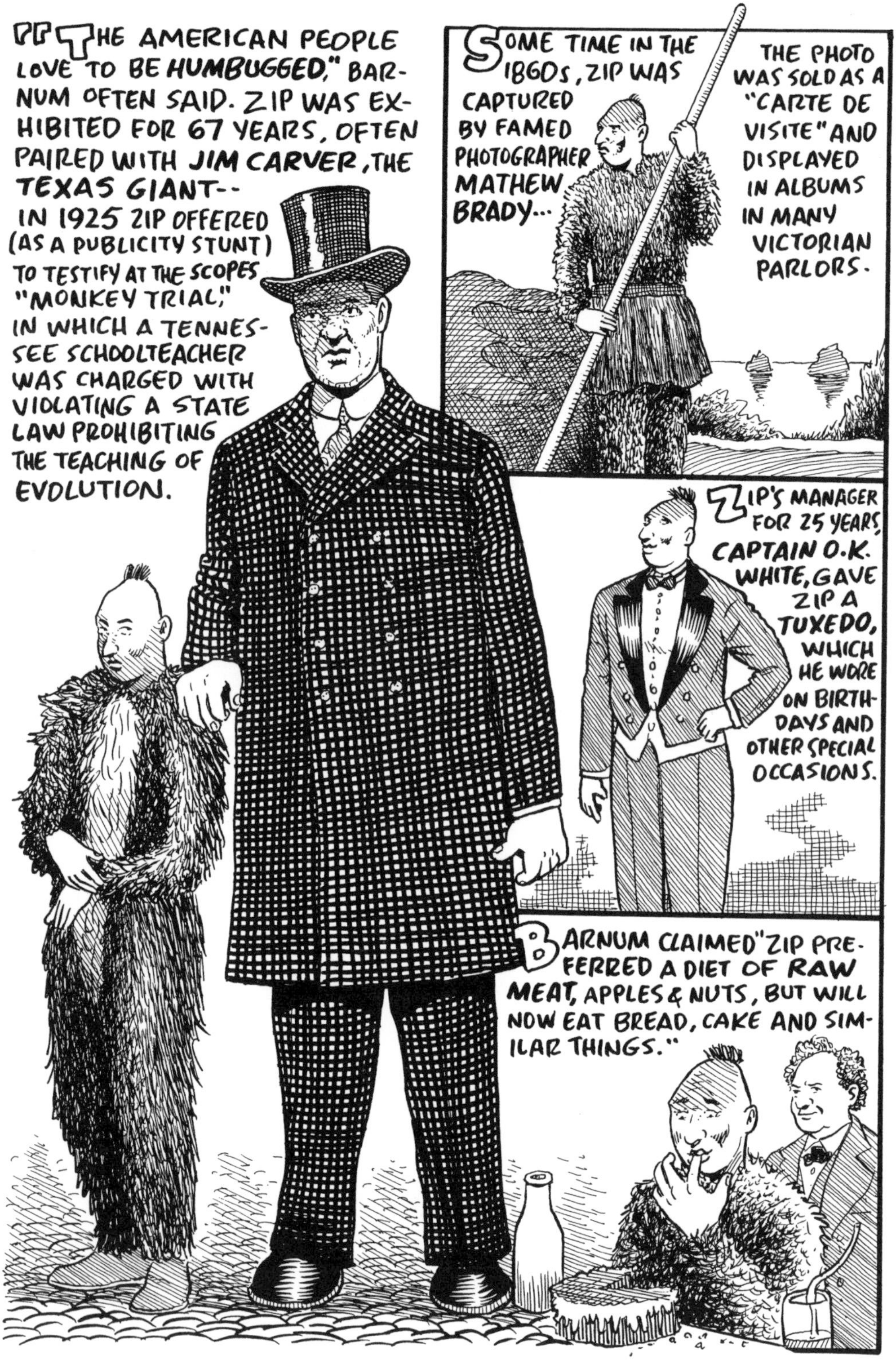
"THE AMERICAN PEOPLE LOVE TO BE HUMBUGGED," BARNUM OFTEN SAID. ZIP WAS EXHIBITED FOR 67 YEARS, OFTEN PAIRED WITH JIM CARVER, THE TEXAS GIANT--
IN 1925 ZIP OFFERED (AS A PUBLICITY STUNT) TO TESTIFY AT THE SCOPES "MONKEY TRIAL," IN WHICH A TENNESSEE SCHOOLTEACHER WAS CHARGED WITH VIOLATING A STATE LAW PROHIBITING THE TEACHING OF EVOLUTION.
SOME TIME IN THE 1860s, ZIP WAS CAPTURED BY FAMED PHOTOGRAPHER MATHEW BRADY...
THE PHOTO WAS SOLD AS A "CARTE DE VISITE" AND DISPLAYED IN ALBUMS IN MANY VICTORIAN PARLORS.
ZIP'S MANAGER FOR 25 YEARS, CAPTAIN O.K. WHITE, GAVE ZIP A TUXEDO, WHICH HE WORE ON BIRTHDAYS AND OTHER SPECIAL OCCASIONS.
BARNUM CLAIMED "ZIP PREFERRED A DIET OF RAW MEAT, APPLES & NUTS, BUT WILL NOW EAT BREAD, CAKE AND SIMILAR THINGS."

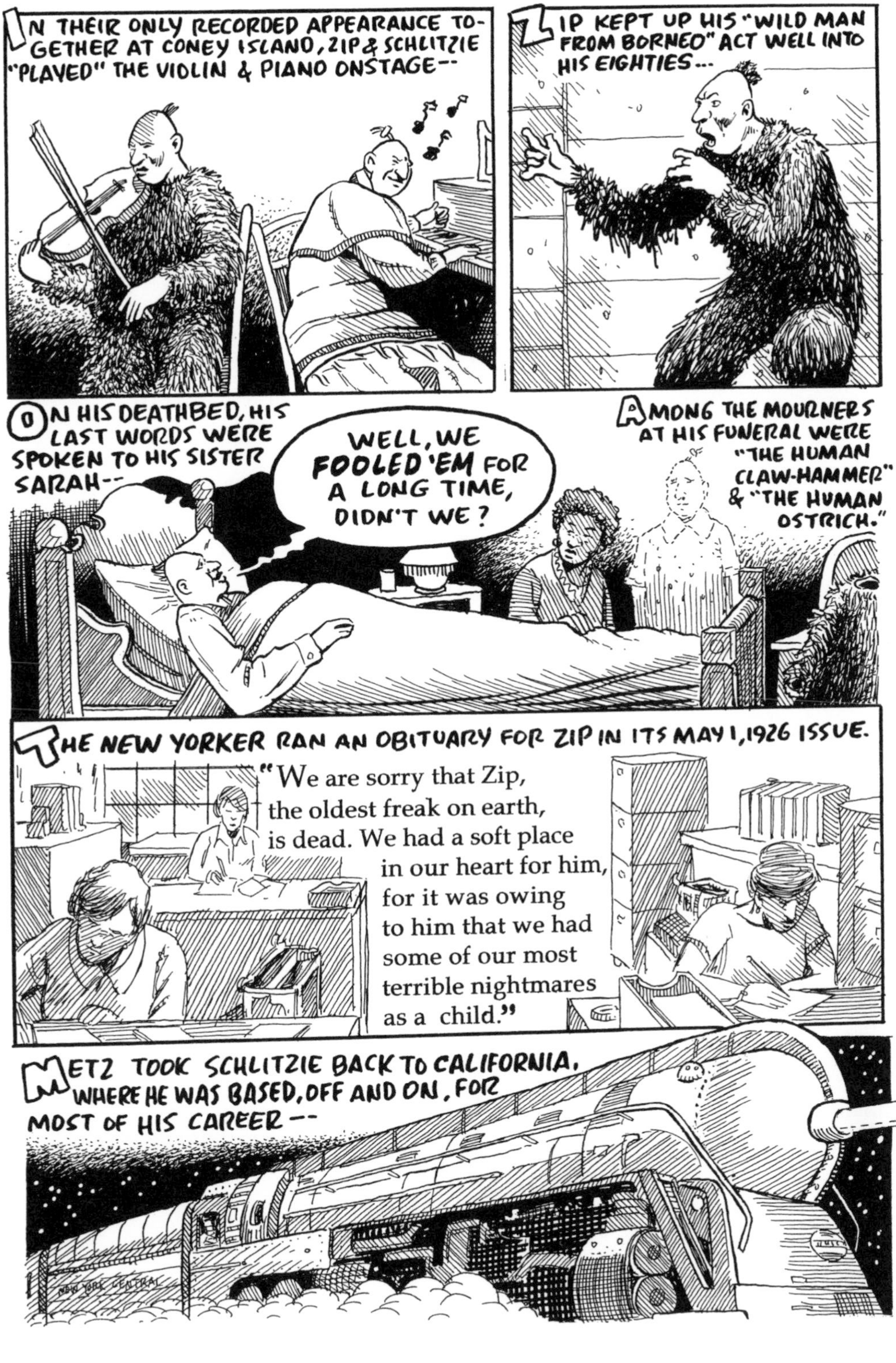
IN THEIR ONLY RECORDED APPEARANCE TOGETHER AT CONEY ISLAND, ZIP & SCHLITZIE "PLAYED" THE VIOLIN & PIANO ONSTAGE--
ZIP KEPT UP HIS "WILD MAN FROM BORNEO" ACT WELL INTO HIS EIGHTIES...
ON HIS DEATHBED, HIS LAST WORDS WERE SPOKEN TO HIS SISTER SARAH--
WELL, WE FOOLED 'EM FOR A LONG TIME, DIDN'T WE?
AMONG THE MOURNERS AT HIS FUNERAL WERE "THE HUMAN CLAW-HAMMER" & "THE HUMAN OSTRICH."
THE NEW YORKER RAN AN OBITUARY FOR ZIP IN ITS MAY 1, 1926 ISSUE.
"We are sorry that Zip, the oldest freak on earth, is dead. We had a soft place in our heart for him, for it was owing to him that we had some of our most terrible nightmares as a child."
METZ TOOK SCHLITZIE BACK TO CALIFORNIA, WHERE HE WAS BASED, OFF AND ON, FOR MOST OF HIS CAREER--
NEW YORK CENTRAL

NOW BILLED AS "**PRINCESS BIBI**" OR "**PRINCESS HA-HA**," SCHLITZIE APPEARED AT THE "**FREAKS OF THE WORLD**" SIDESHOW AT **PLAYLAND-AT-THE-BEACH** IN **SAN FRANCISCO** IN 1927--

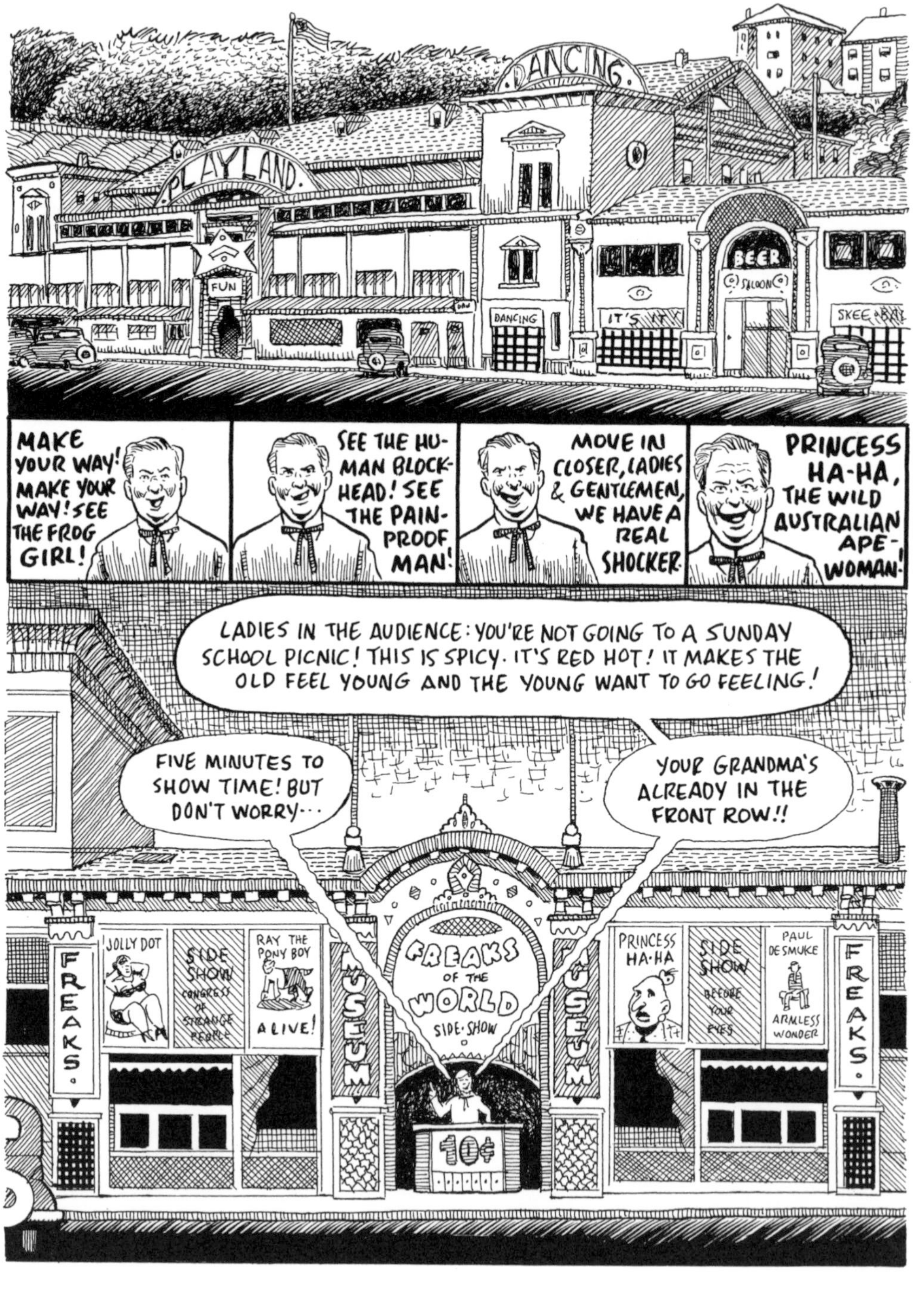

DANCING
PLAYLAND
FUN
DANCING
IT'S IT
BEER
SALOON
MAKE YOUR WAY! MAKE YOUR WAY! SEE THE FROG GIRL!
SEE THE HUMAN BLOCKHEAD! SEE THE PAIN-PROOF MAN!
MOVE IN CLOSER, LADIES & GENTLEMEN, WE HAVE A REAL SHOCKER.
PRINCESS HA-HA, THE WILD AUSTRALIAN APE-WOMAN!
LADIES IN THE AUDIENCE: YOU'RE NOT GOING TO A SUNDAY SCHOOL PICNIC! THIS IS SPICY. IT'S RED HOT! IT MAKES THE OLD FEEL YOUNG AND THE YOUNG WANT TO GO FEELING!
FIVE MINUTES TO SHOW TIME! BUT DON'T WORRY...
YOUR GRANDMA'S ALREADY IN THE FRONT ROW!!
FREAKS
JOLLY DOT
SIDE SHOW CONGRESS OF STRANGE PEOPLE
RAY THE PONY BOY ALIVE!
MUSEUM
FREAKS OF THE WORLD SIDE-SHOW
MUSEUM
PRINCESS HA-HA
SIDE SHOW BEFORE YOUR EYES
PAUL DESMUKE ARMLESS WONDER
FREAKS
10¢

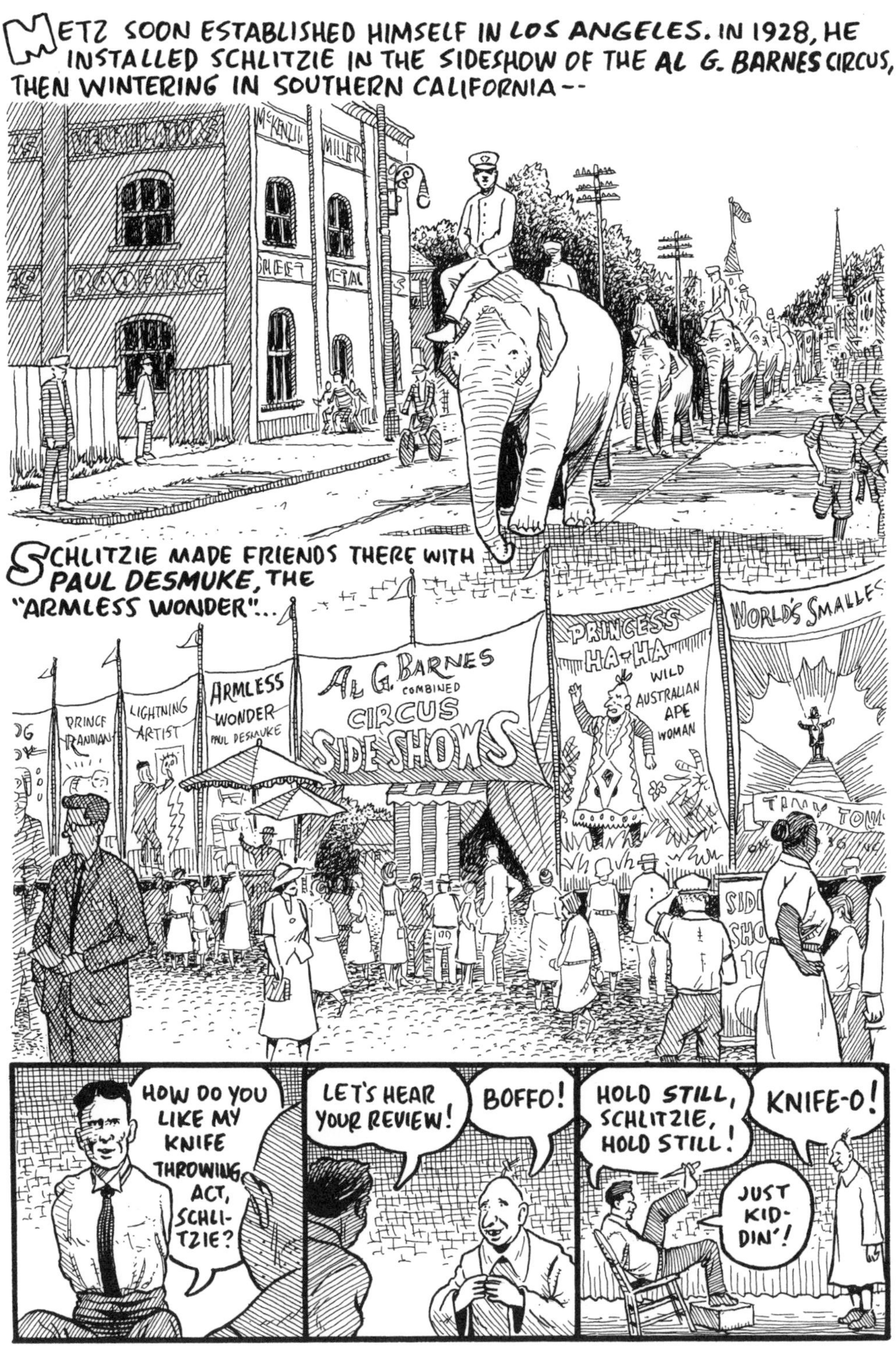
METZ SOON ESTABLISHED HIMSELF IN LOS ANGELES. IN 1928, HE INSTALLED SCHLITZIE IN THE SIDESHOW OF THE AL G. BARNES CIRCUS, THEN WINTERING IN SOUTHERN CALIFORNIA--
ROOFING
SHEET METAL
SCHLITZIE MADE FRIENDS THERE WITH PAUL DESMUKE, THE "ARMLESS WONDER"...
PRINCE RANDIAN
LIGHTNING ARTIST
ARMLESS WONDER PAUL DESMUKE
AL G. BARNES COMBINED CIRCUS SIDE SHOWS
PRINCESS HA-HA WILD AUSTRALIAN APE WOMAN
WORLD'S SMALLES
HOW DO YOU LIKE MY KNIFE THROWING ACT, SCHLI-TZIE?
LET'S HEAR YOUR REVIEW!
BOFFO!
HOLD STILL, SCHLITZIE, HOLD STILL!
KNIFE-O!
JUST KID-DIN'!

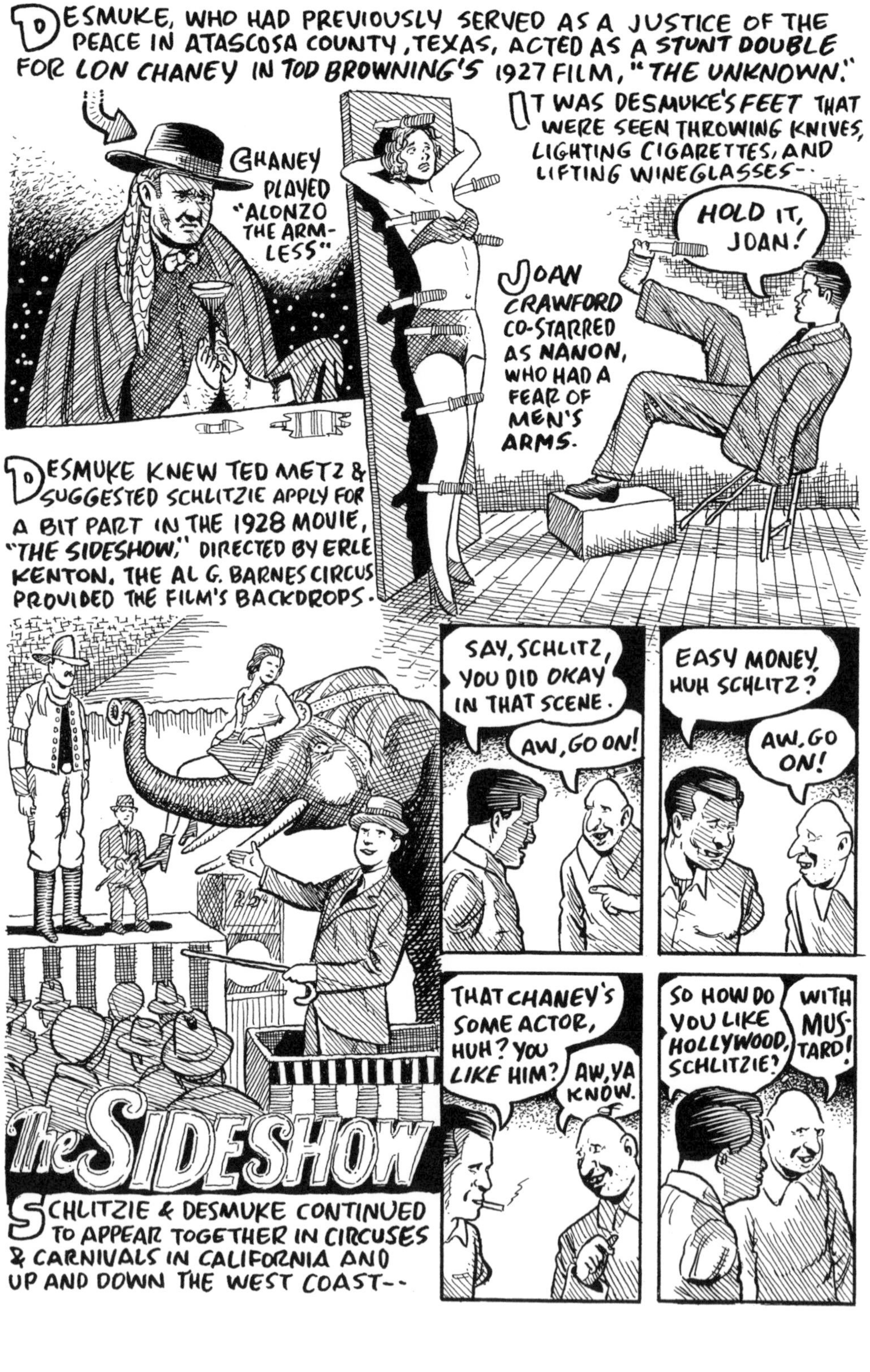
DESMUKE, WHO HAD PREVIOUSLY SERVED AS A JUSTICE OF THE PEACE IN ATASCOSA COUNTY, TEXAS, ACTED AS A STUNT DOUBLE FOR LON CHANEY IN TOD BROWNING'S 1927 FILM, "THE UNKNOWN."
CHANEY PLAYED "ALONZO THE ARM-LESS"
IT WAS DESMUKE'S FEET THAT WERE SEEN THROWING KNIVES, LIGHTING CIGARETTES, AND LIFTING WINEGLASSES--
HOLD IT, JOAN!
JOAN CRAWFORD CO-STARRED AS NANON, WHO HAD A FEAR OF MEN'S ARMS.
DESMUKE KNEW TED METZ & SUGGESTED SCHLITZIE APPLY FOR A BIT PART IN THE 1928 MOVIE, "THE SIDESHOW," DIRECTED BY ERLE KENTON. THE AL G. BARNES CIRCUS PROVIDED THE FILM'S BACKDROPS.
SAY, SCHLITZ, YOU DID OKAY IN THAT SCENE.
AW, GO ON!
EASY MONEY, HUH SCHLITZ?
AW, GO ON!
The SIDESHOW
SCHLITZIE & DESMUKE CONTINUED TO APPEAR TOGETHER IN CIRCUSES & CARNIVALS IN CALIFORNIA AND UP AND DOWN THE WEST COAST--
THAT CHANEY'S SOME ACTOR, HUH? YOU LIKE HIM?
AW, YA KNOW.
SO HOW DO YOU LIKE HOLLYWOOD, SCHLITZIE?
WITH MUS-TARD!

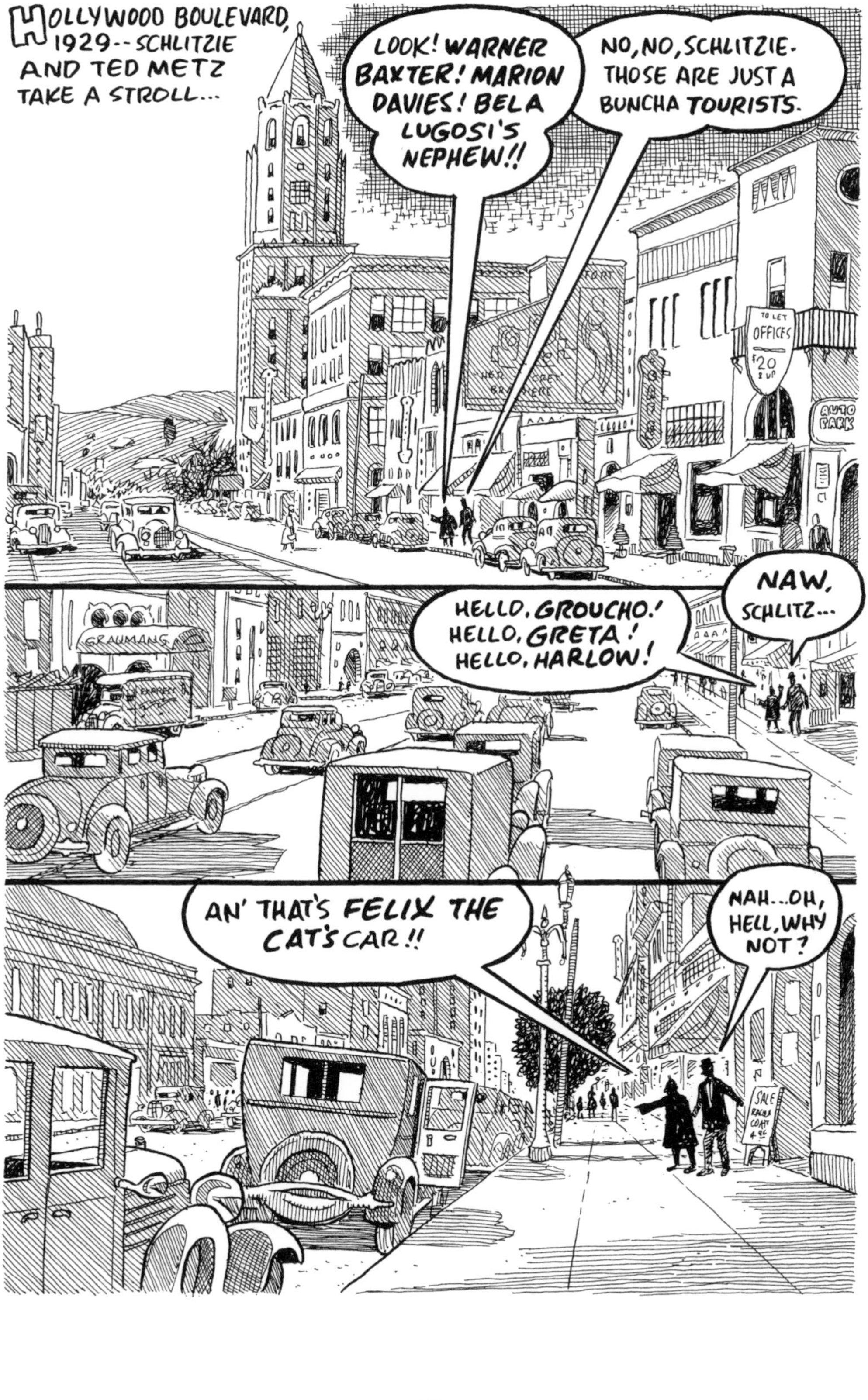
HOLLYWOOD BOULEVARD, 1929-- SCHLITZIE AND TED METZ TAKE A STROLL...
LOOK! WARNER BAXTER! MARION DAVIES! BELA LUGOSI'S NEPHEW!!
NO, NO, SCHLITZIE. THOSE ARE JUST A BUNCHA TOURISTS.
TO LET OFFICES $20 & UP
AUTO PARK
GRAUMANS
HELLO, GROUCHO! HELLO, GRETA! HELLO, HARLOW!
NAW, SCHLITZ...
AN' THAT'S FELIX THE CAT'S CAR!!
NAH...OH, HELL, WHY NOT?
SALE

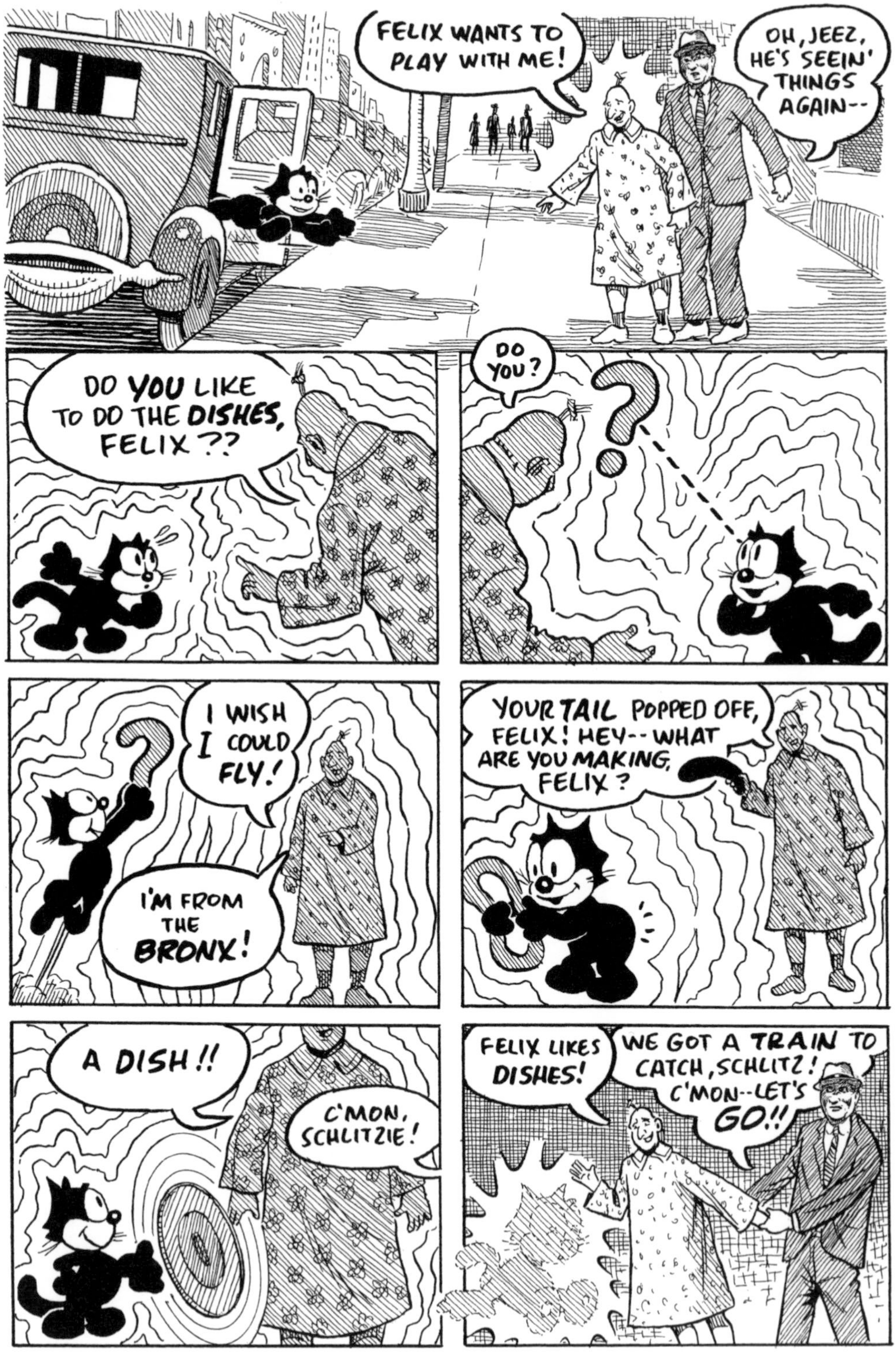

FELIX WANTS TO PLAY WITH ME!
OH, JEEZ, HE'S SEEIN' THINGS AGAIN--
DO YOU LIKE TO DO THE DISHES, FELIX??
DO YOU?
I WISH I COULD FLY!
I'M FROM THE BRONX!
YOUR TAIL POPPED OFF, FELIX! HEY-- WHAT ARE YOU MAKING, FELIX?
A DISH!!
C'MON, SCHLITZIE!
FELIX LIKES DISHES!
WE GOT A TRAIN TO CATCH, SCHLITZ! C'MON--LET'S GO!!

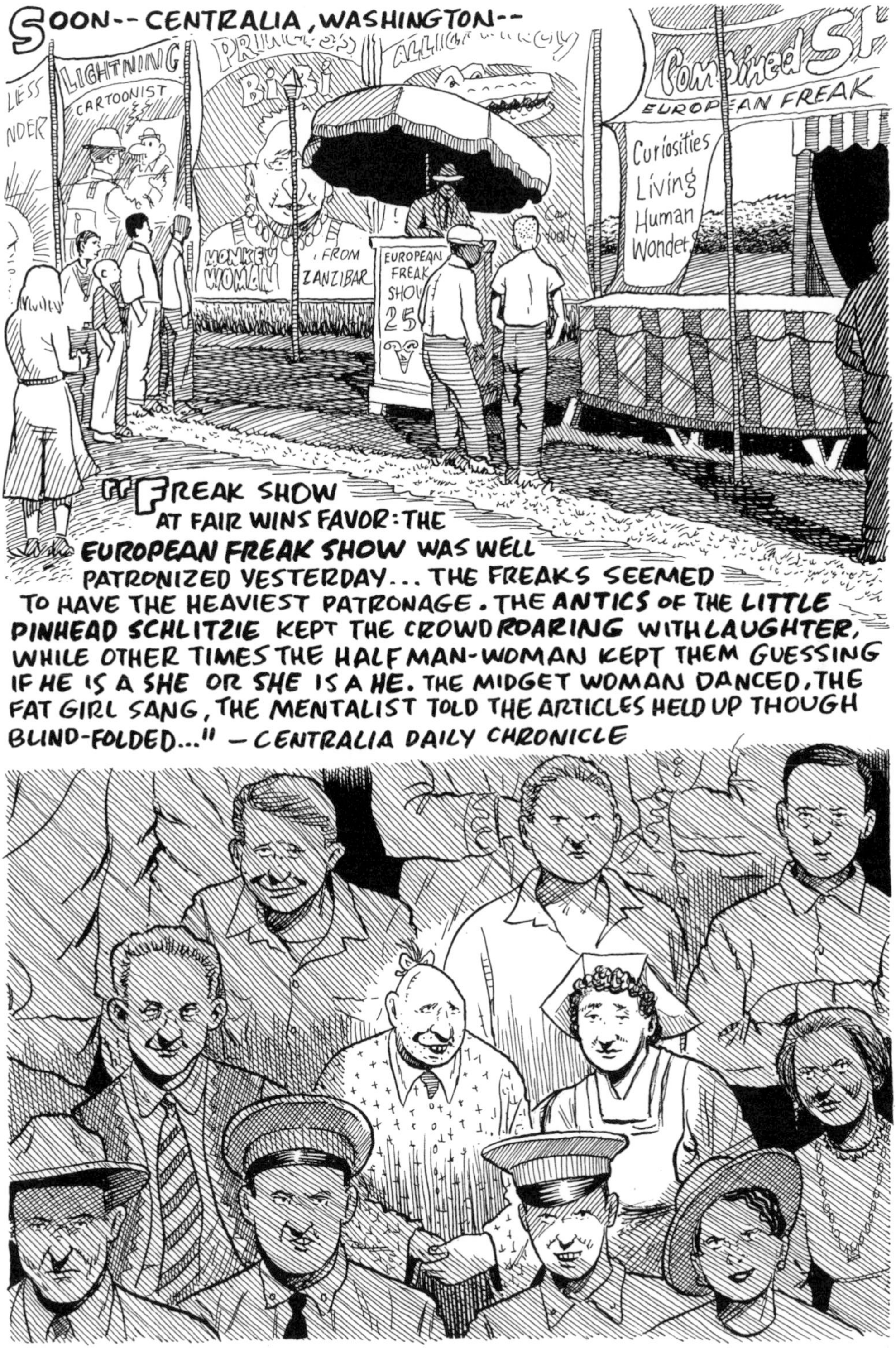
SOON--CENTRALIA, WASHINGTON--
LIGHTNING CARTOONIST
MONKEY WOMAN
FROM ZANZIBAR
EUROPEAN FREAK SHOW 25
EUROPEAN FREAK
Curiosities Living Human Wondet
"FREAK SHOW AT FAIR WINS FAVOR: THE EUROPEAN FREAK SHOW WAS WELL PATRONIZED YESTERDAY... THE FREAKS SEEMED TO HAVE THE HEAVIEST PATRONAGE. THE ANTICS OF THE LITTLE PINHEAD SCHLITZIE KEPT THE CROWD ROARING WITH LAUGHTER, WHILE OTHER TIMES THE HALF MAN-WOMAN KEPT THEM GUESSING IF HE IS A SHE OR SHE IS A HE. THE MIDGET WOMAN DANCED, THE FAT GIRL SANG, THE MENTALIST TOLD THE ARTICLES HELD UP THOUGH BLIND-FOLDED..." —CENTRALIA DAILY CHRONICLE

IN SOME VENUES, SCHLITZIE WAS LOOKED AFTER BY A **NURSE**, HIRED BY **METZ** FOR THE DURATION OF AN APPEARANCE--

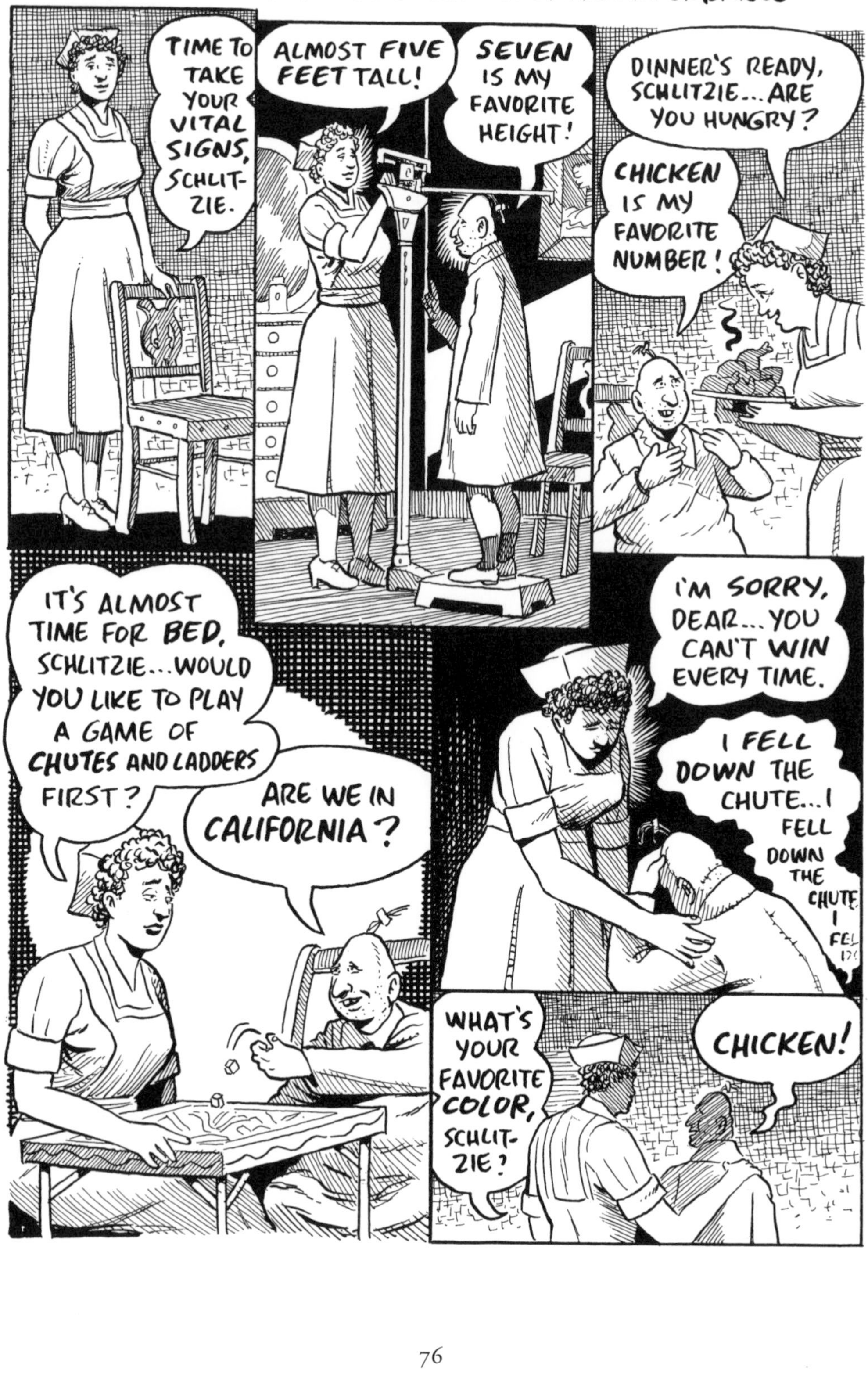

TIME TO TAKE YOUR VITAL SIGNS, SCHLITZIE.
ALMOST FIVE FEET TALL!
SEVEN IS MY FAVORITE HEIGHT!
DINNER'S READY, SCHLITZIE... ARE YOU HUNGRY?
CHICKEN IS MY FAVORITE NUMBER!
IT'S ALMOST TIME FOR BED, SCHLITZIE... WOULD YOU LIKE TO PLAY A GAME OF CHUTES AND LADDERS FIRST?
ARE WE IN CALIFORNIA?
I'M SORRY, DEAR... YOU CAN'T WIN EVERY TIME.
I FELL DOWN THE CHUTE... I FELL DOWN THE CHUTE I
WHAT'S YOUR FAVORITE COLOR, SCHLITZIE?
CHICKEN!

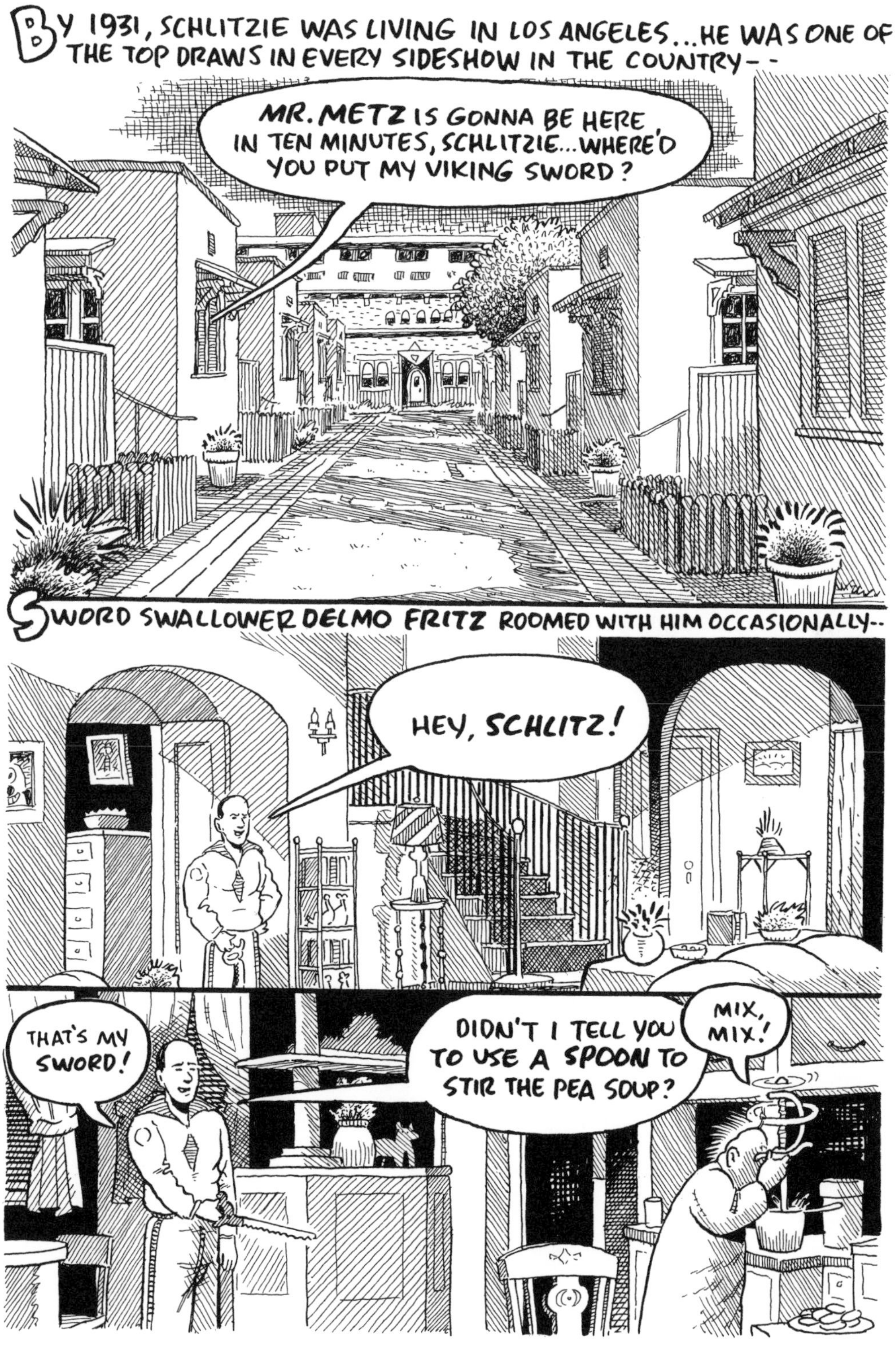
BY 1931, SCHLITZIE WAS LIVING IN LOS ANGELES... HE WAS ONE OF THE TOP DRAWS IN EVERY SIDESHOW IN THE COUNTRY--
MR. METZ IS GONNA BE HERE IN TEN MINUTES, SCHLITZIE... WHERE'D YOU PUT MY VIKING SWORD?
SWORD SWALLOWER DELMO FRITZ ROOMED WITH HIM OCCASIONALLY--
HEY, SCHLITZ!
THAT'S MY SWORD!
DIDN'T I TELL YOU TO USE A SPOON TO STIR THE PEA SOUP?
MIX, MIX!

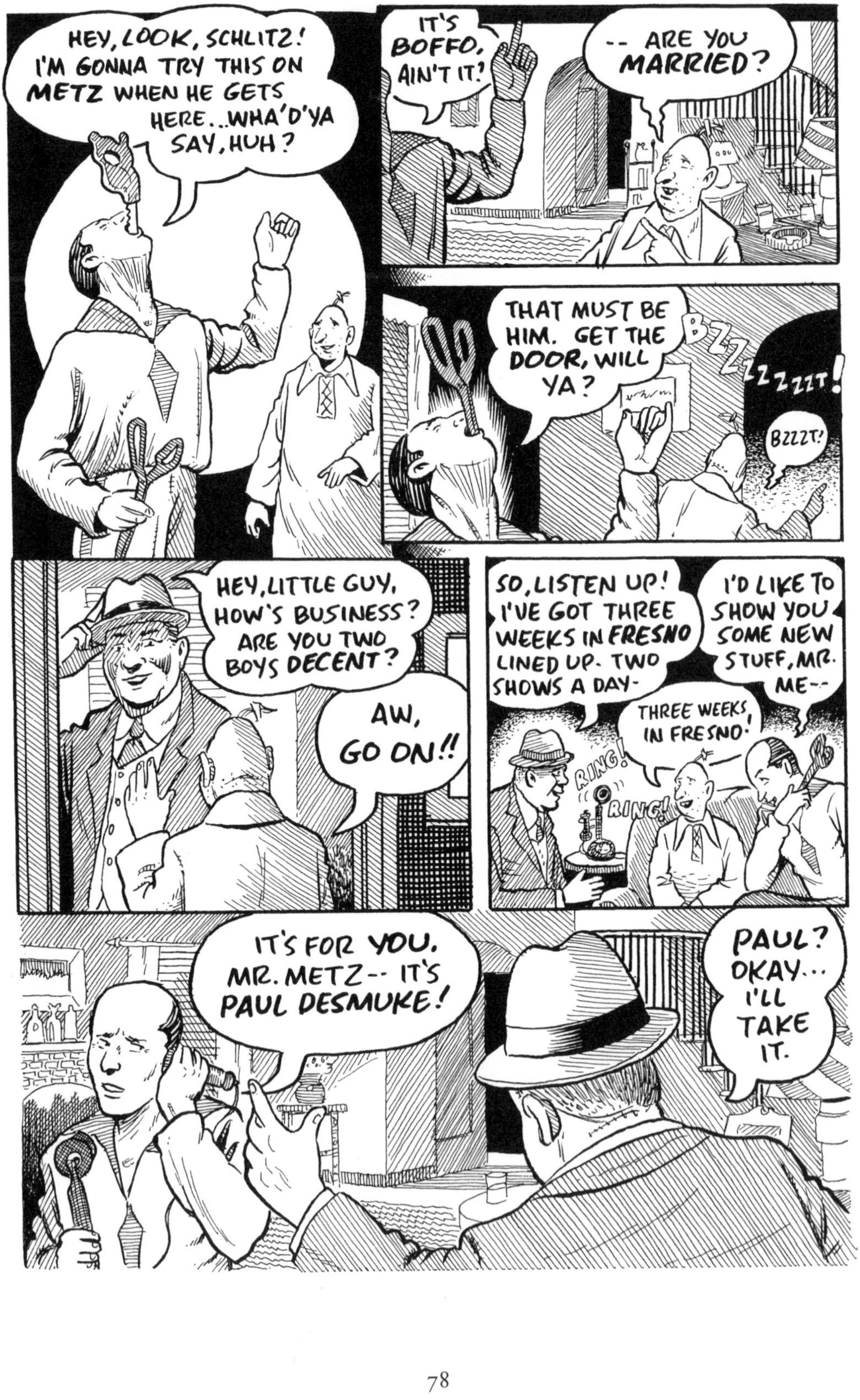
HEY, LOOK, SCHLITZ! I'M GONNA TRY THIS ON METZ WHEN HE GETS HERE...WHA'D'YA SAY, HUH?
IT'S BOFFO, AIN'T IT?
-- ARE YOU MARRIED?
THAT MUST BE HIM. GET THE DOOR, WILL YA?
BZZZZZZZT!
BZZZT!
HEY, LITTLE GUY, HOW'S BUSINESS? ARE YOU TWO BOYS DECENT?
AW, GO ON!!
SO, LISTEN UP! I'VE GOT THREE WEEKS IN FRESNO LINED UP. TWO SHOWS A DAY-
I'D LIKE TO SHOW YOU SOME NEW STUFF, MR. ME--
THREE WEEKS IN FRESNO!
RING!
RING!
IT'S FOR YOU, MR. METZ-- IT'S PAUL DESMUKE!
PAUL? OKAY... I'LL TAKE IT.

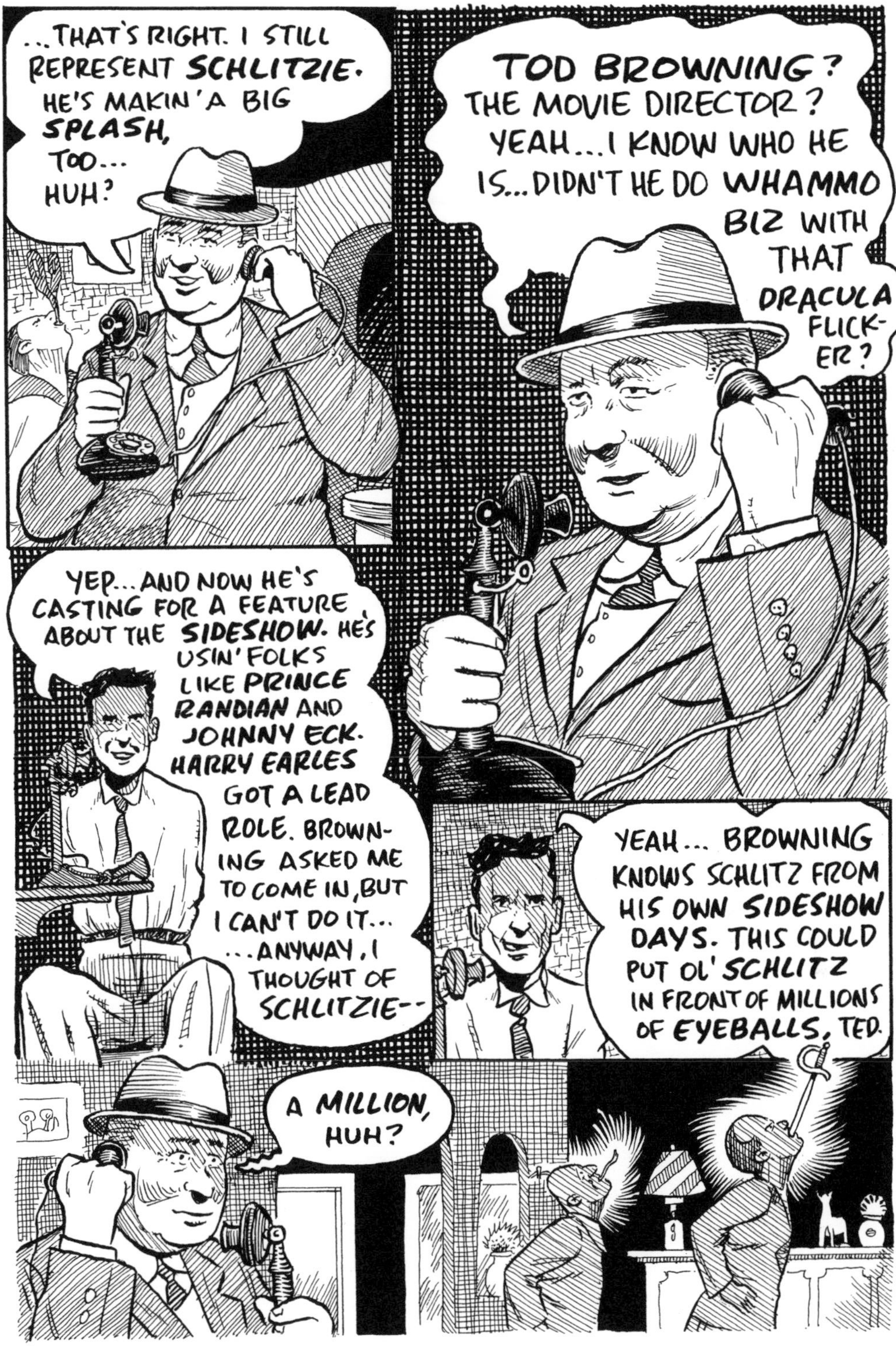
...THAT'S RIGHT. I STILL REPRESENT SCHLITZIE. HE'S MAKIN' A BIG SPLASH, TOO... HUH?
TOD BROWNING? THE MOVIE DIRECTOR? YEAH...I KNOW WHO HE IS...DIDN'T HE DO WHAMMO BIZ WITH THAT DRACULA FLICK-ER?
YEP...AND NOW HE'S CASTING FOR A FEATURE ABOUT THE SIDESHOW. HE'S USIN' FOLKS LIKE PRINCE RANDIAN AND JOHNNY ECK. HARRY EARLES GOT A LEAD ROLE. BROWN-ING ASKED ME TO COME IN, BUT I CAN'T DO IT... ...ANYWAY, I THOUGHT OF SCHLITZIE--
YEAH... BROWNING KNOWS SCHLITZ FROM HIS OWN SIDESHOW DAYS. THIS COULD PUT OL' SCHLITZ IN FRONT OF MILLIONS OF EYEBALLS, TED.
A MILLION, HUH?

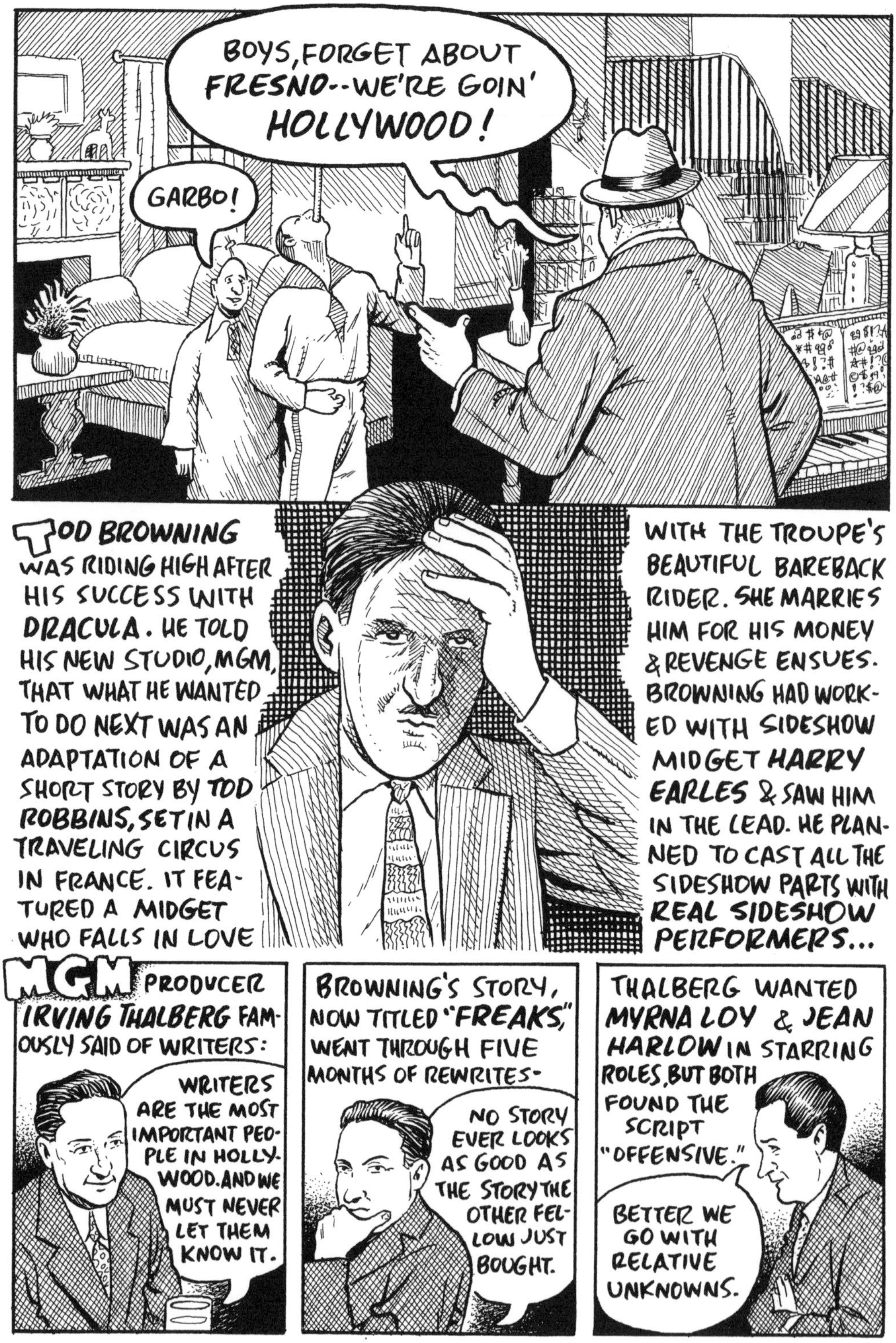
BOYS, FORGET ABOUT FRESNO--WE'RE GOIN' HOLLYWOOD!
GARBO!
TOD BROWNING WAS RIDING HIGH AFTER HIS SUCCESS WITH DRACULA. HE TOLD HIS NEW STUDIO, MGM, THAT WHAT HE WANTED TO DO NEXT WAS AN ADAPTATION OF A SHORT STORY BY TOD ROBBINS, SET IN A TRAVELING CIRCUS IN FRANCE. IT FEATURED A MIDGET WHO FALLS IN LOVE
WITH THE TROUPE'S BEAUTIFUL BAREBACK RIDER. SHE MARRIES HIM FOR HIS MONEY & REVENGE ENSUES. BROWNING HAD WORKED WITH SIDESHOW MIDGET HARRY EARLES & SAW HIM IN THE LEAD. HE PLANNED TO CAST ALL THE SIDESHOW PARTS WITH REAL SIDESHOW PERFORMERS...
MGM PRODUCER IRVING THALBERG FAMOUSLY SAID OF WRITERS:
WRITERS ARE THE MOST IMPORTANT PEOPLE IN HOLLYWOOD. AND WE MUST NEVER LET THEM KNOW IT.
BROWNING'S STORY, NOW TITLED "FREAKS," WENT THROUGH FIVE MONTHS OF REWRITES-
NO STORY EVER LOOKS AS GOOD AS THE STORY THE OTHER FELLOW JUST BOUGHT.
THALBERG WANTED MYRNA LOY & JEAN HARLOW IN STARRING ROLES, BUT BOTH FOUND THE SCRIPT "OFFENSIVE."
BETTER WE GO WITH RELATIVE UNKNOWNS.

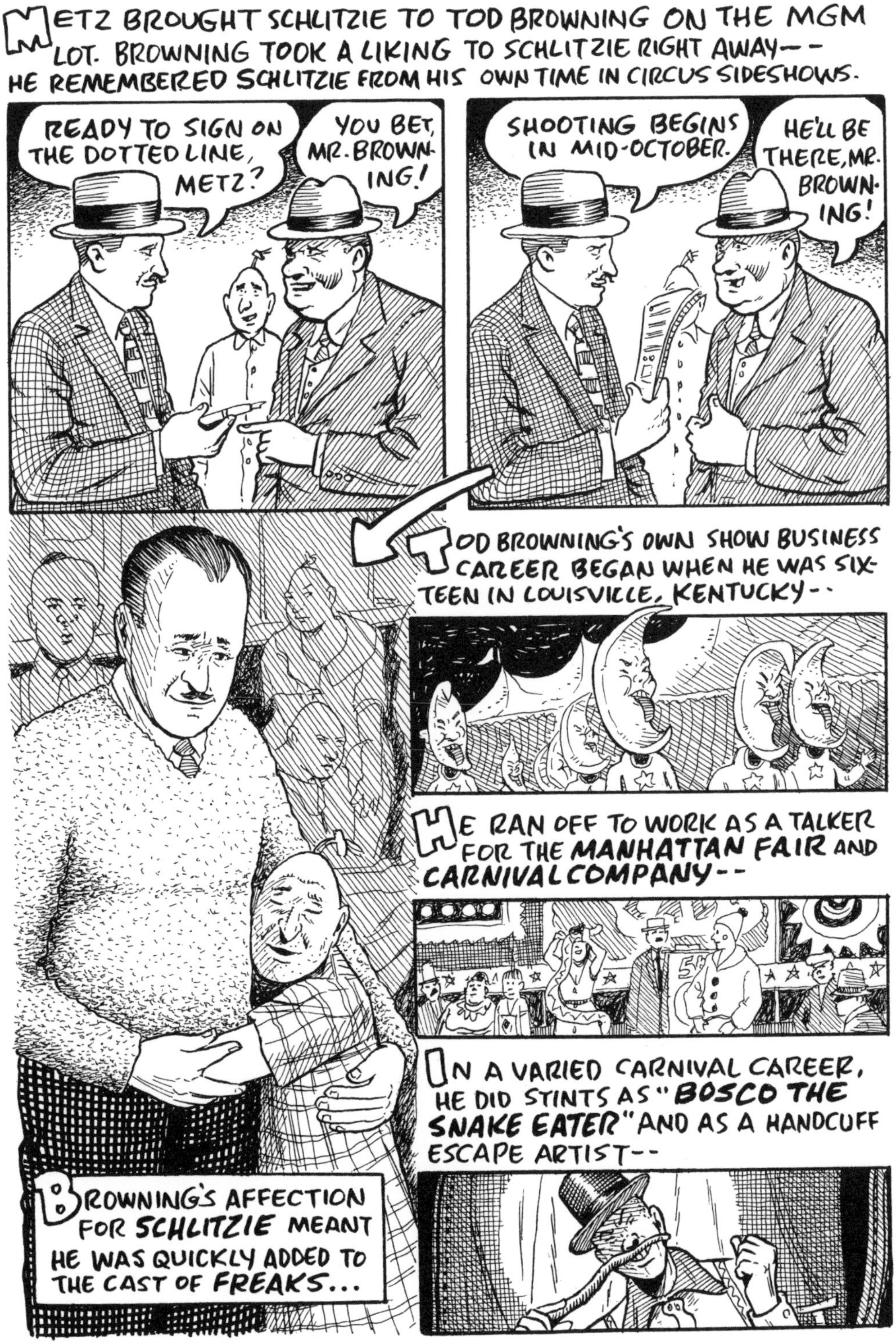
METZ BROUGHT SCHLITZIE TO TOD BROWNING ON THE MGM LOT. BROWNING TOOK A LIKING TO SCHLITZIE RIGHT AWAY-- HE REMEMBERED SCHLITZIE FROM HIS OWN TIME IN CIRCUS SIDESHOWS.
READY TO SIGN ON THE DOTTED LINE, METZ?
YOU BET, MR. BROWNING!
SHOOTING BEGINS IN MID-OCTOBER.
HE'LL BE THERE, MR. BROWNING!
TOD BROWNING'S OWN SHOW BUSINESS CAREER BEGAN WHEN HE WAS SIXTEEN IN LOUISVILLE, KENTUCKY--
HE RAN OFF TO WORK AS A TALKER FOR THE MANHATTAN FAIR AND CARNIVAL COMPANY--
IN A VARIED CARNIVAL CAREER, HE DID STINTS AS "BOSCO THE SNAKE EATER" AND AS A HANDCUFF ESCAPE ARTIST--
BROWNING'S AFFECTION FOR SCHLITZIE MEANT HE WAS QUICKLY ADDED TO THE CAST OF FREAKS...

BROWNING IS SAID TO HAVE ACTED AS THE FRONT MAN FOR THE "*WILD MAN FROM BORNEO*" (A WHITE MAN IN BLACKFACE), A *CIRCUS CLOWN* FOR THE *RINGLING BROS.* AND A "*HUMAN PRETZEL*" *CONTORTIONIST*...

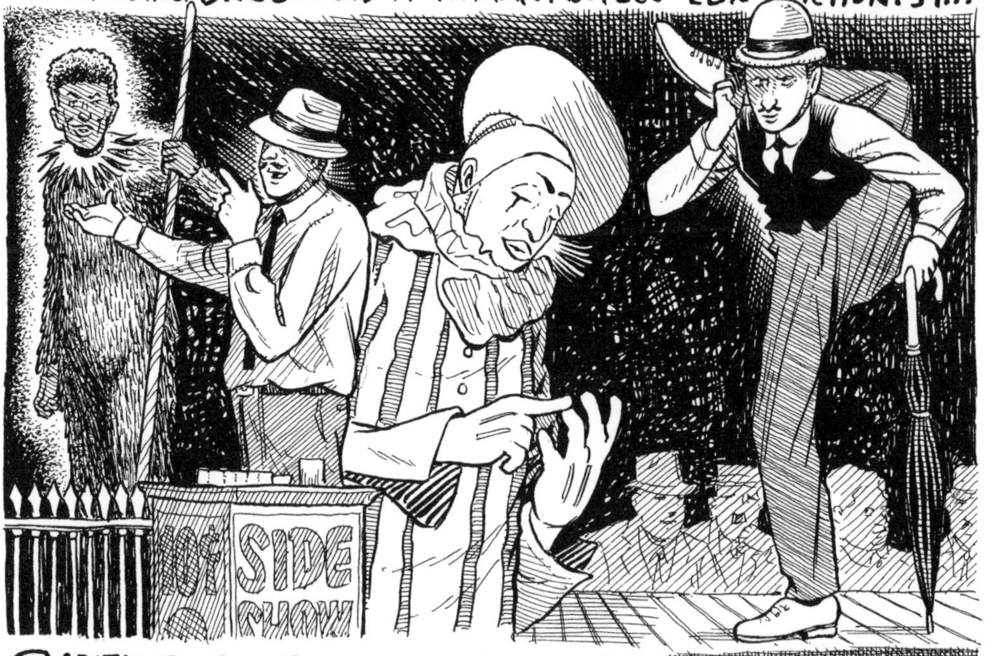
SIDE

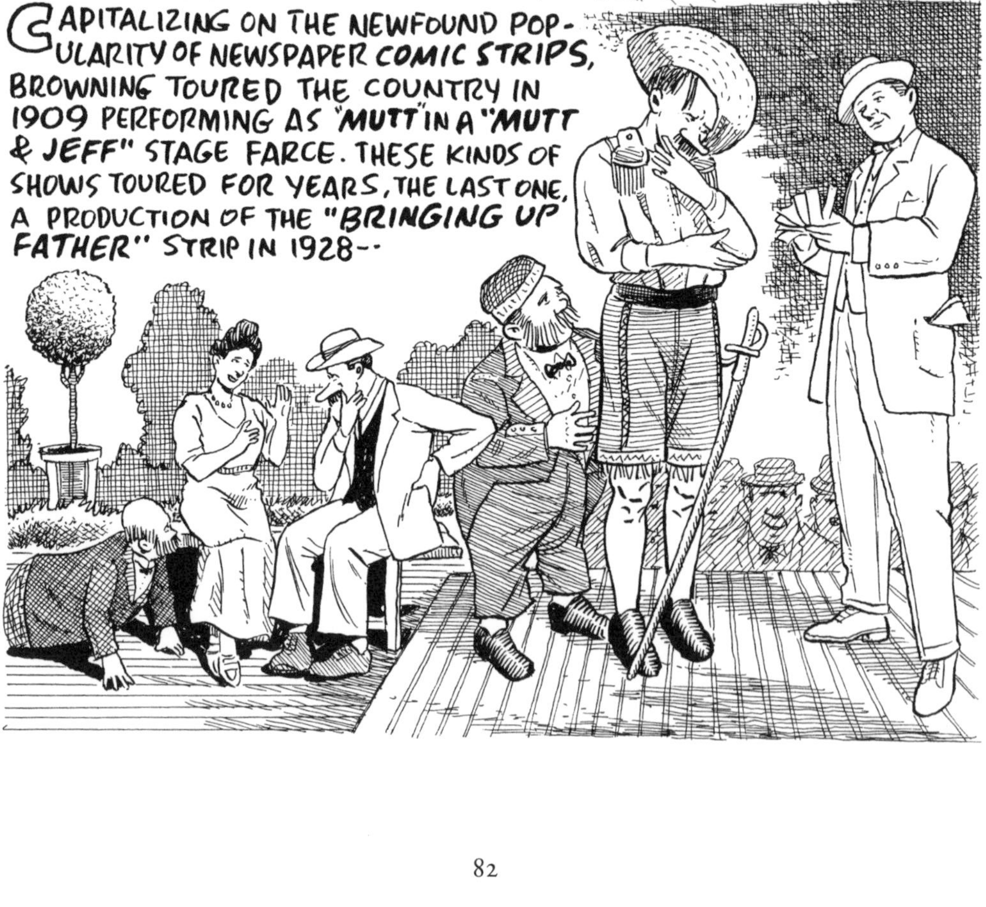
CAPITALIZING ON THE NEWFOUND POPULARITY OF NEWSPAPER *COMIC STRIPS*, BROWNING TOURED THE COUNTRY IN 1909 PERFORMING AS "*MUTT*" IN A "*MUTT & JEFF*" STAGE FARCE. THESE KINDS OF SHOWS TOURED FOR YEARS, THE LAST ONE, A PRODUCTION OF THE "*BRINGING UP FATHER*" STRIP IN 1928--

OF ALL THE NOVELTY ACTS OF HIS PRE-MOVIE CAREER, NONE WAS AS BIZARRE AS HIS "**HYPNOTIC LIVING CORPSE**" ROUTINE, IN WHICH, TO THE AMAZEMENT OF THE CARNIVAL CROWD, BROWNING WAS "**BURIED ALIVE**" IN A SHALLOW GRAVE FOR UP TO 48 HOURS. HE USED A TUBE TO BREATHE & TO RECEIVE **MALTED MILK PELLETS**--

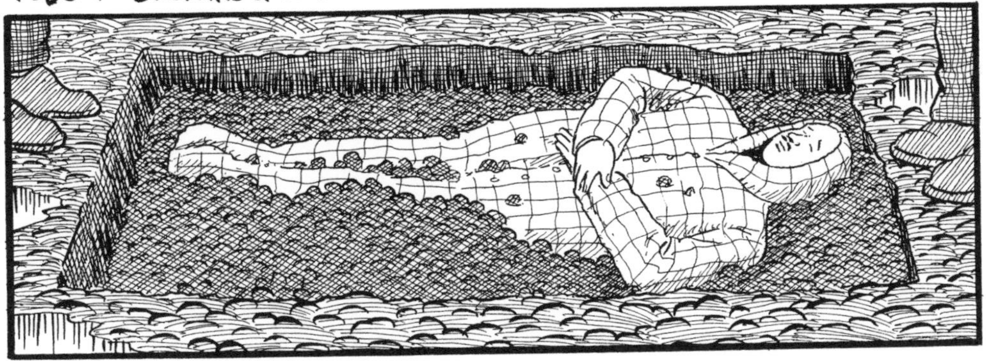

ACCORDING TO A LOCAL NEWS ACCOUNT, BROWNING "BECAME ACCUSTOMED TO THE PERFORMANCE & WAS ABLE TO ALMOST ENJOY THE CONFINEMENT."

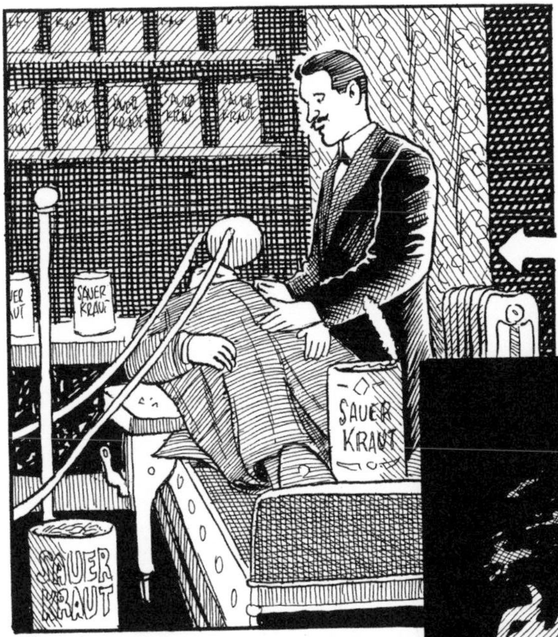
SAUER KRAUT
SAUER KRAUT
SAUER KRAUT

HIS FIRST WORK IN **FILM** WAS THE RESULT OF AN INTRODUCTION TO **D.W. GRIFFITH**, A FELLOW KENTUCKIAN. GRIFFITH GAVE BROWNING THE PART OF AN **UNDERTAKER** IN THE 1913 BIOGRAPH COMEDY "**SCENTING A TERRIBLE CRIME.**" BROWNING FOLLOWED GRIFFITH OUT TO **CALIFORNIA** IN 1915--

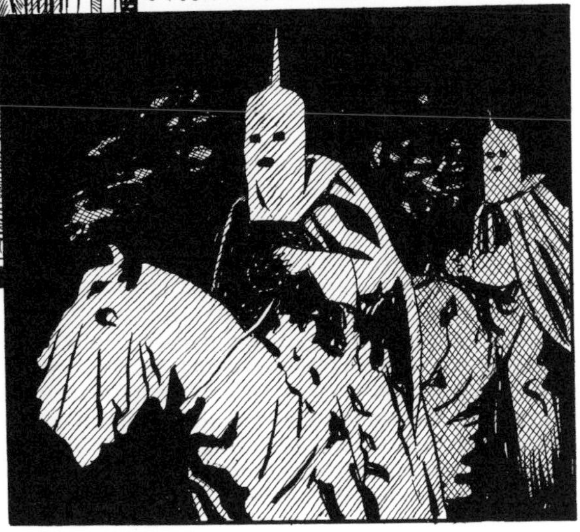

AN EARLY ASSIGNMENT FROM **GRIFFITH** WAS AS ONE OF MANY ASSISTANT DIRECTORS ON "**INTOLERANCE**," GRIFFITH'S RESPONSE TO THE CRITICISM LEVELED AT HIS EPIC, "**THE BIRTH OF A NATION.**"

IN A LONG CAREER MAKING COMEDIES & MELODRAMAS, BROWNING DIRECTED A STRING OF **LON CHANEY** HITS IN THE LATE 1920s, CULMINATING IN HIS BIGGEST BOX OFFICE SMASH, **DRACULA**, WITH **BELA LUGOSI**. ITS SUCCESS ALLOWED HIM TO FINALLY START PRODUCTION ON **FREAKS** IN 1931.

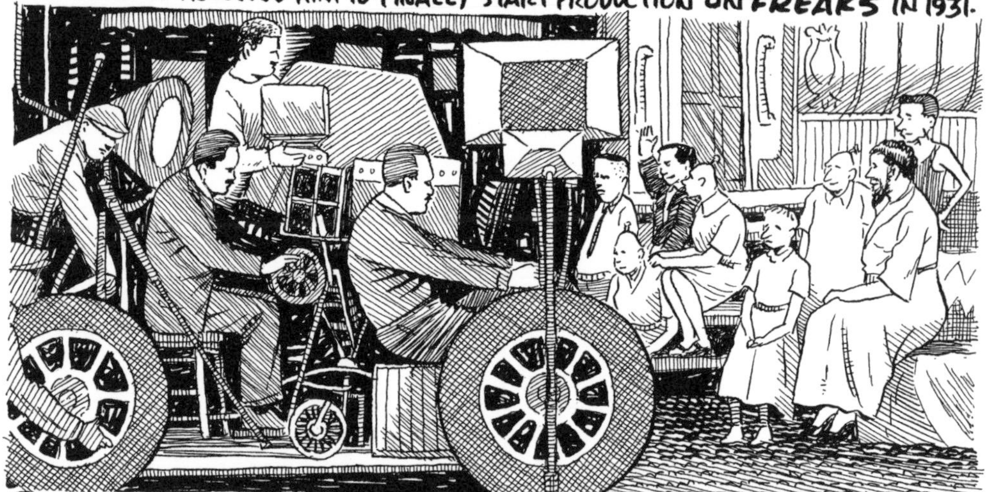

CASTING DIRECTOR BEN PIAZZA SPENT A MONTH COLLECTING PHOTOS & DOING SCREEN TESTS. BROWNING LOOKED THEM OVER & MADE HIS SELECTIONS.

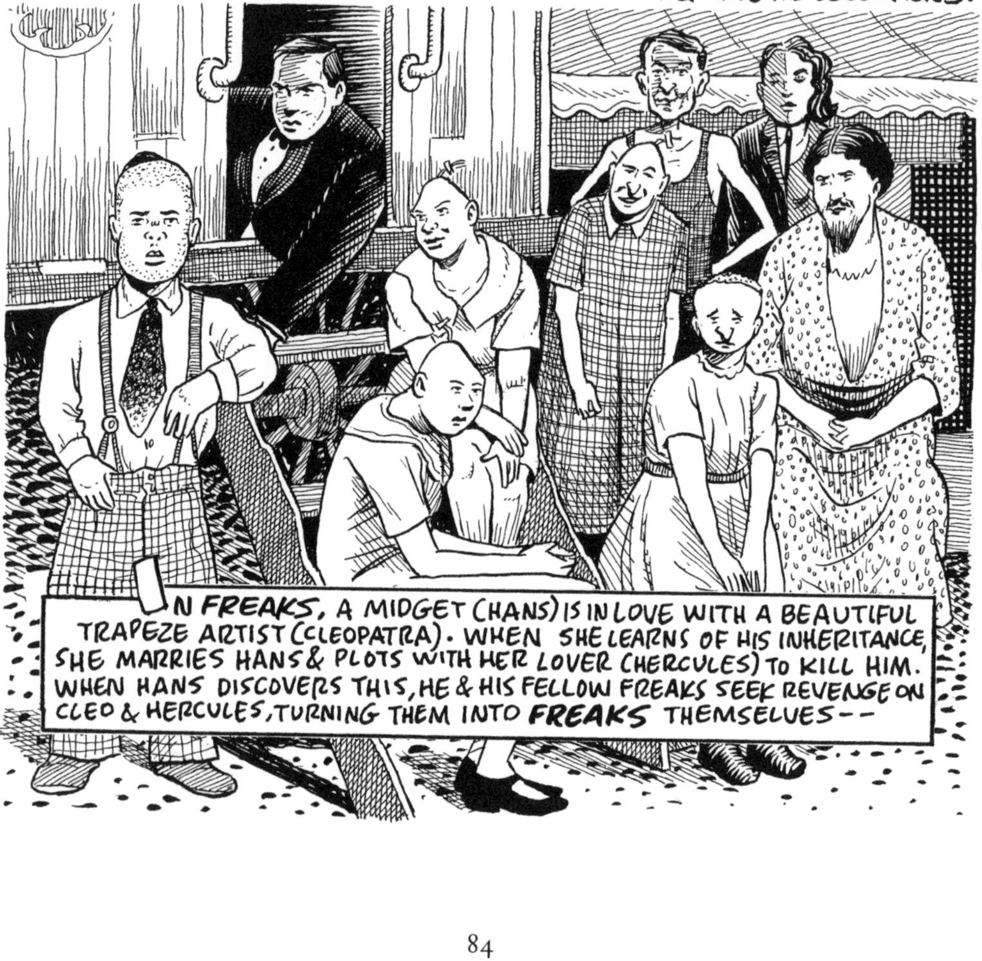
IN FREAKS, A MIDGET (HANS) IS IN LOVE WITH A BEAUTIFUL TRAPEZE ARTIST (CLEOPATRA). WHEN SHE LEARNS OF HIS INHERITANCE, SHE MARRIES HANS & PLOTS WITH HER LOVER (HERCULES) TO KILL HIM. WHEN HANS DISCOVERS THIS, HE & HIS FELLOW FREAKS SEEK REVENGE ON CLEO & HERCULES, TURNING THEM INTO FREAKS THEMSELVES--

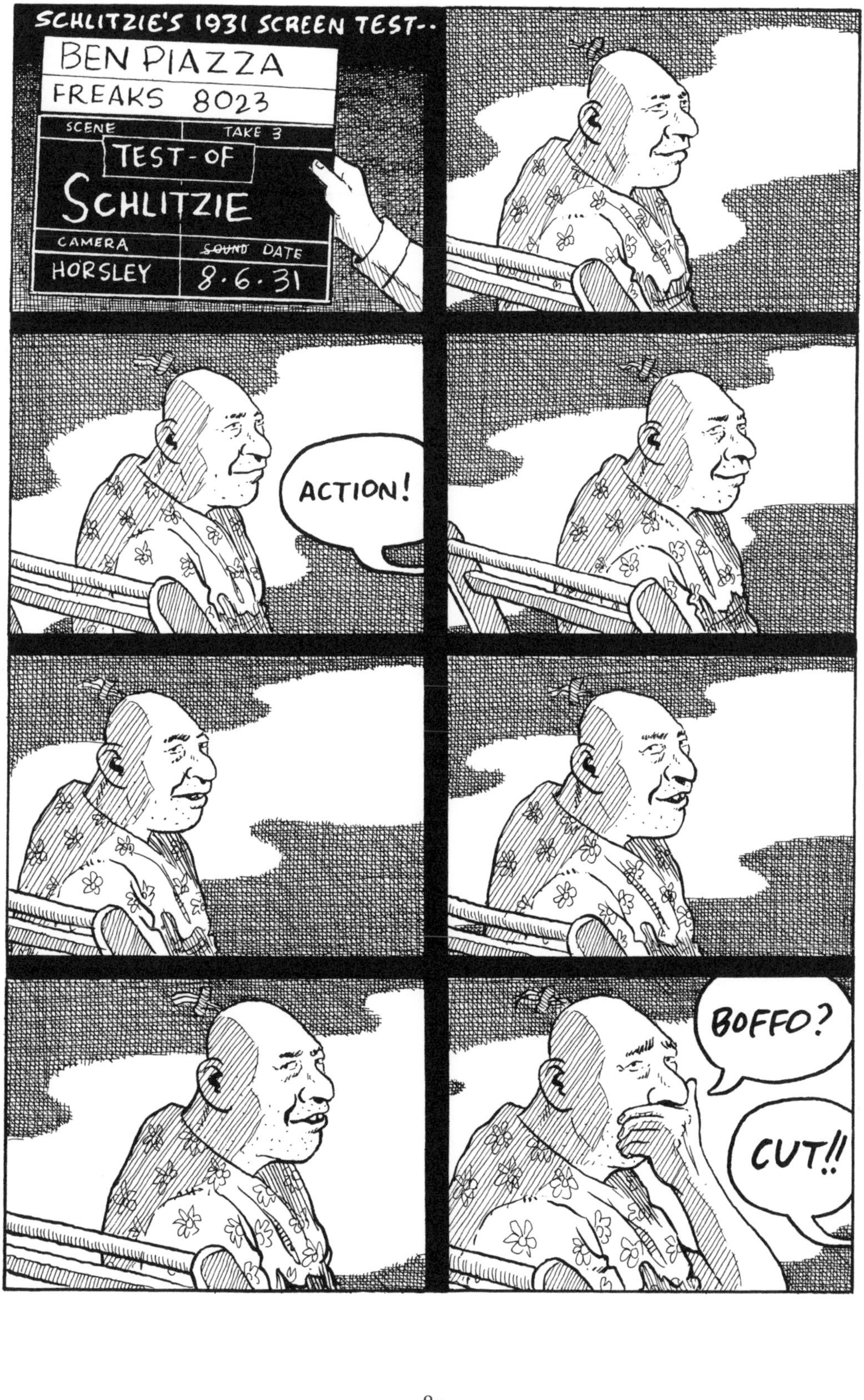
SCHLITZIE'S 1931 SCREEN TEST--
BEN PIAZZA
FREAKS 8023
SCENE
TAKE 3
TEST-OF
SCHLITZIE
CAMERA
SOUND DATE
HORSLEY
8·6·31
ACTION!
BOFFO?
CUT!!

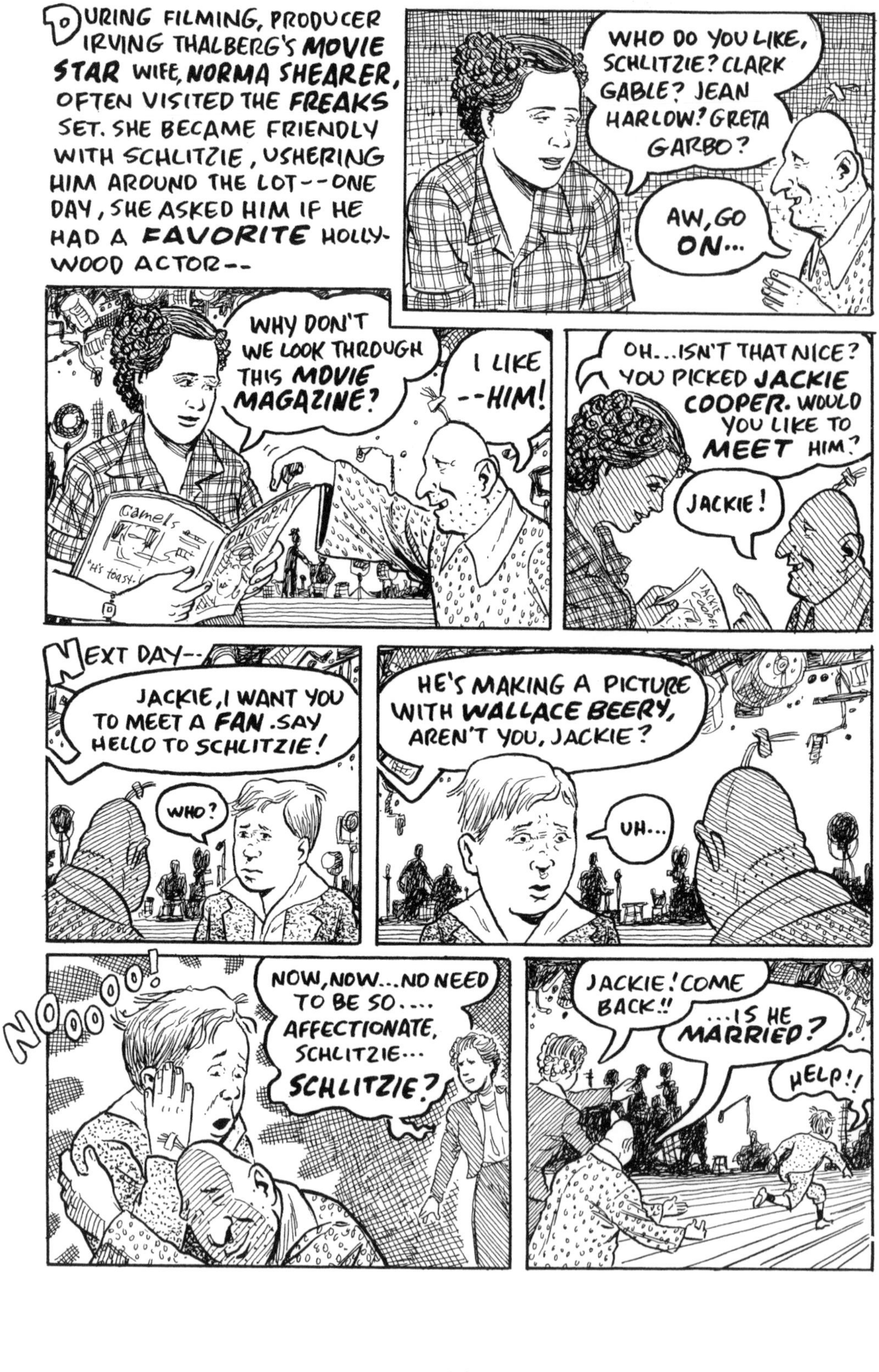
DURING FILMING, PRODUCER IRVING THALBERG'S MOVIE STAR WIFE, NORMA SHEARER, OFTEN VISITED THE FREAKS SET. SHE BECAME FRIENDLY WITH SCHLITZIE, USHERING HIM AROUND THE LOT--ONE DAY, SHE ASKED HIM IF HE HAD A FAVORITE HOLLY-WOOD ACTOR--
WHO DO YOU LIKE, SCHLITZIE? CLARK GABLE? JEAN HARLOW? GRETA GARBO?
AW, GO ON...
WHY DON'T WE LOOK THROUGH THIS MOVIE MAGAZINE?
I LIKE --HIM!
OH...ISN'T THAT NICE? YOU PICKED JACKIE COOPER. WOULD YOU LIKE TO MEET HIM?
JACKIE!
NEXT DAY--
JACKIE, I WANT YOU TO MEET A FAN. SAY HELLO TO SCHLITZIE!
WHO?
HE'S MAKING A PICTURE WITH WALLACE BEERY, AREN'T YOU, JACKIE?
UH...
NOOOOO!
NOW, NOW...NO NEED TO BE SO.... AFFECTIONATE, SCHLITZIE... SCHLITZIE?
JACKIE! COME BACK!!
...IS HE MARRIED?
HELP!!

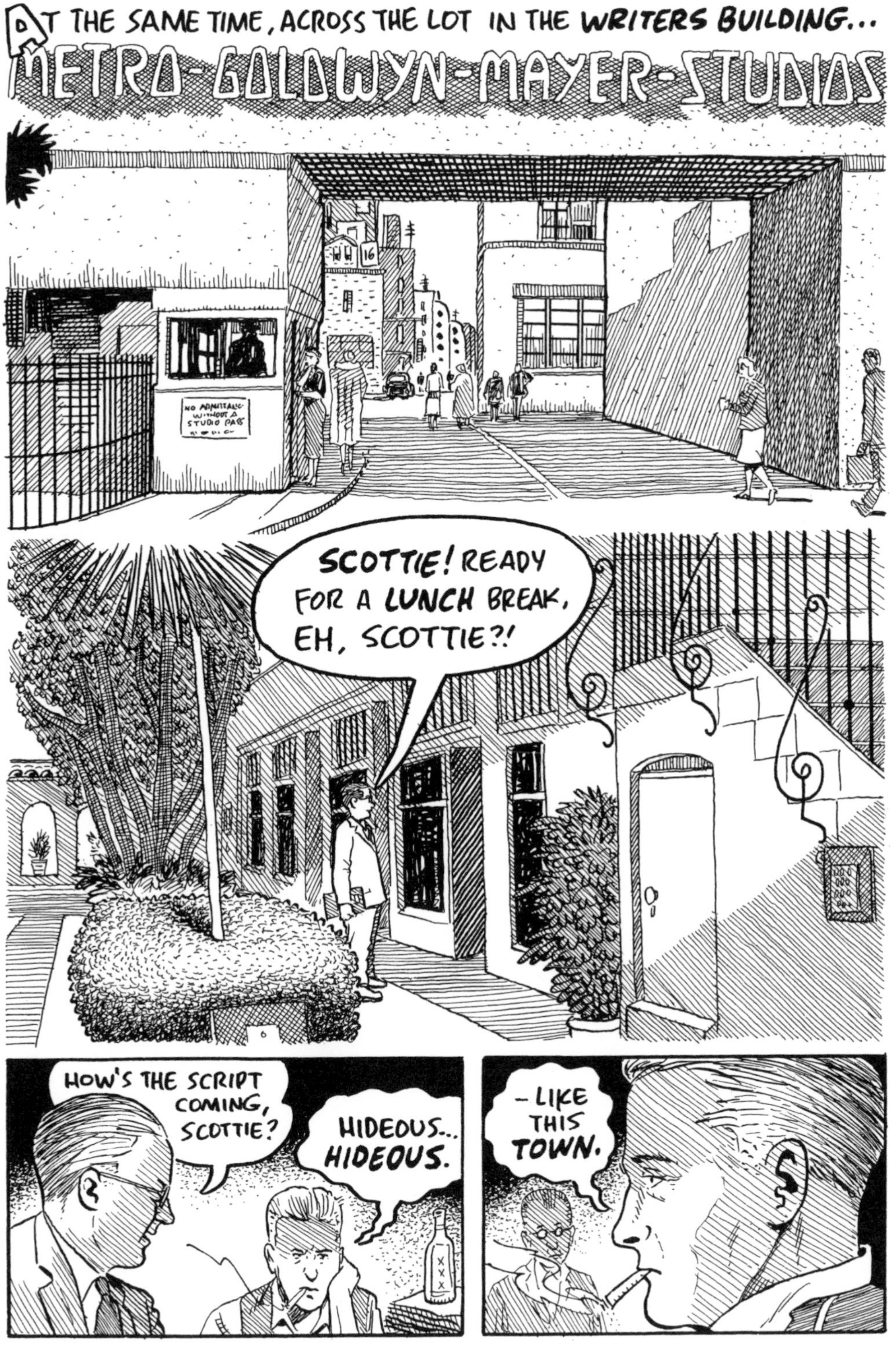
AT THE SAME TIME, ACROSS THE LOT IN THE WRITERS BUILDING...
METRO-GOLDWYN-MAYER-STUDIOS
NO ADMITTANCE WITHOUT A STUDIO PASS
SCOTTIE! READY FOR A LUNCH BREAK, EH, SCOTTIE?!
HOW'S THE SCRIPT COMING, SCOTTIE?
HIDEOUS... HIDEOUS.
-LIKE THIS TOWN.

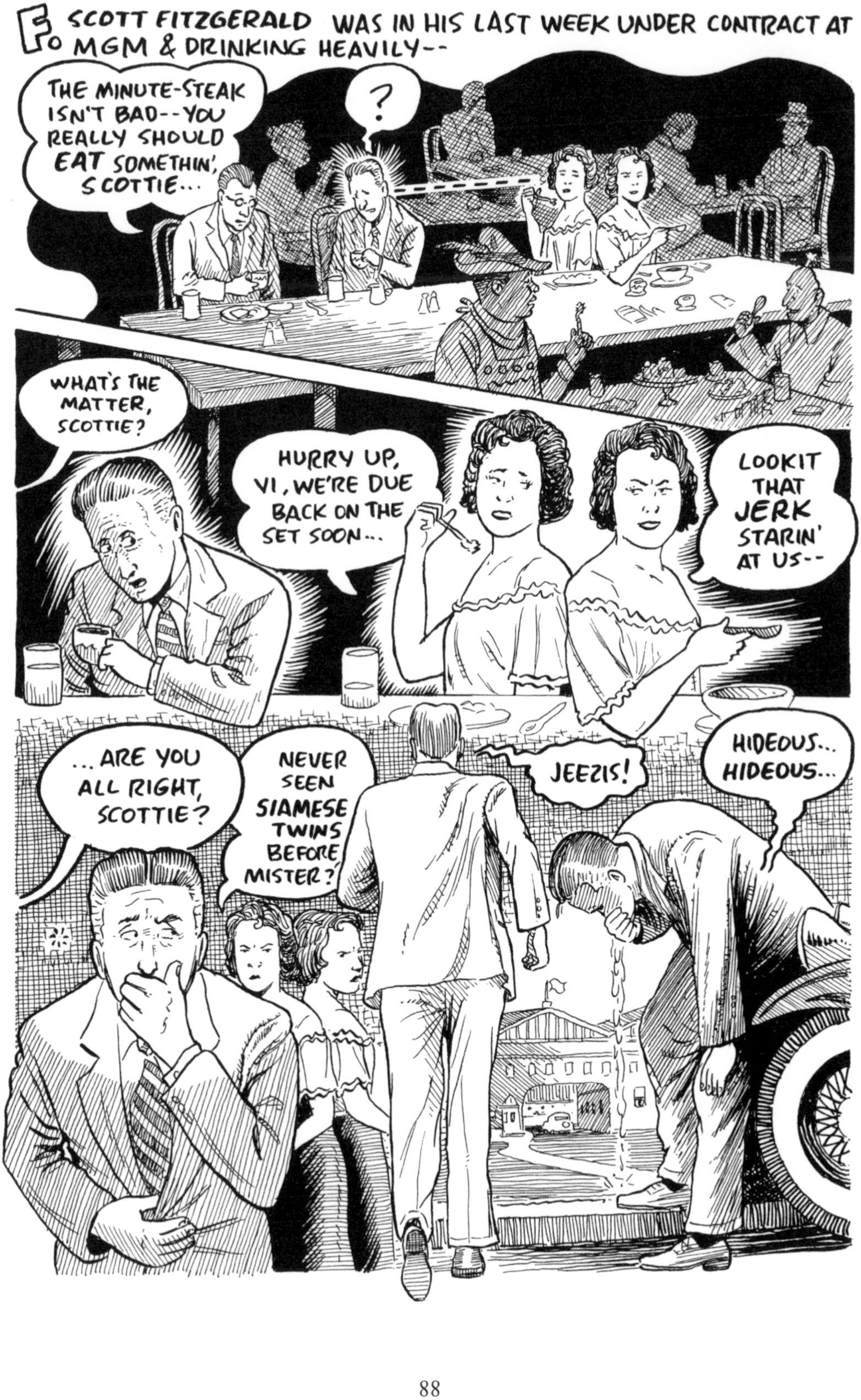
F. SCOTT FITZGERALD WAS IN HIS LAST WEEK UNDER CONTRACT AT MGM & DRINKING HEAVILY--
THE MINUTE-STEAK ISN'T BAD--YOU REALLY SHOULD EAT SOMETHIN', SCOTTIE...
?
WHAT'S THE MATTER, SCOTTIE?
HURRY UP, VI, WE'RE DUE BACK ON THE SET SOON...
LOOKIT THAT JERK STARIN' AT US--
...ARE YOU ALL RIGHT, SCOTTIE?
NEVER SEEN SIAMESE TWINS BEFORE, MISTER?
JEEZIS!
HIDEOUS... HIDEOUS...

FITZGERALD WASN'T ALONE IN HIS QUEASINESS AT SEEING THE FREAKS DINING ALONGSIDE THE OTHER EMPLOYEES & ACTORS IN THE MGM COMMISSARY... STUDIO HEAD **LOUIS B. MAYER** WALKED BY THE SET ONE DAY WHEN...

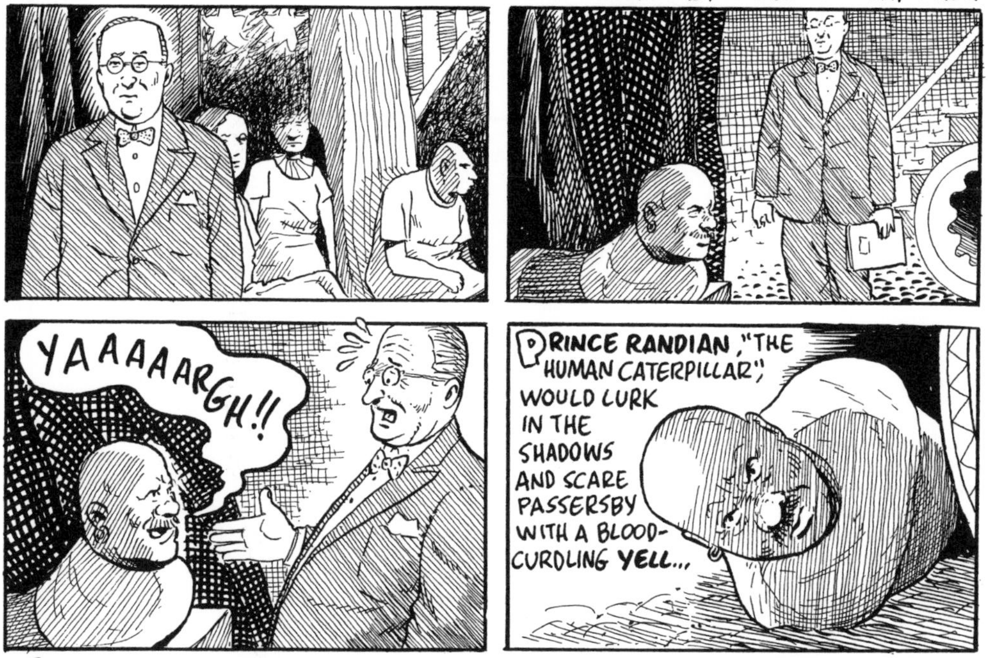
YAAAAARGH!!
PRINCE RANDIAN, "THE HUMAN CATERPILLAR", WOULD LURK IN THE SHADOWS AND SCARE PASSERSBY WITH A BLOOD-CURDLING **YELL**...

A COMPROMISE WAS REACHED: THE **MIDGETS & SIAMESE TWINS** WERE ALLOWED COMMISSARY PRIVILEGES BUT ALL OTHERS WERE SEATED AT AN **OUTSIDE** TABLE, AWAY FROM **OFFENDED SENSIBILITIES**--

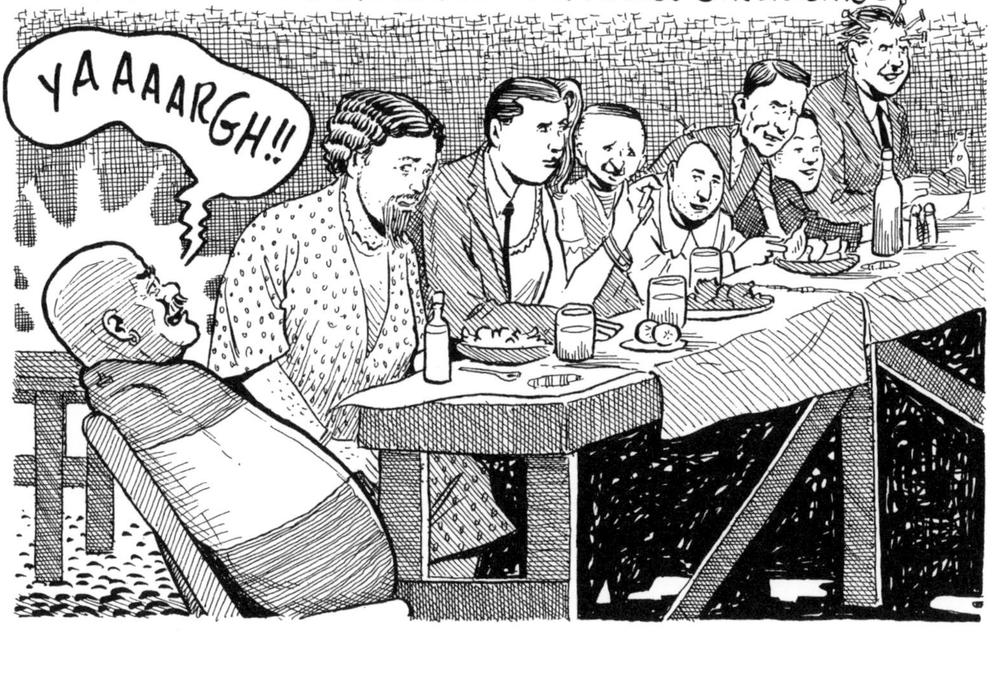
YAAAARGH!!

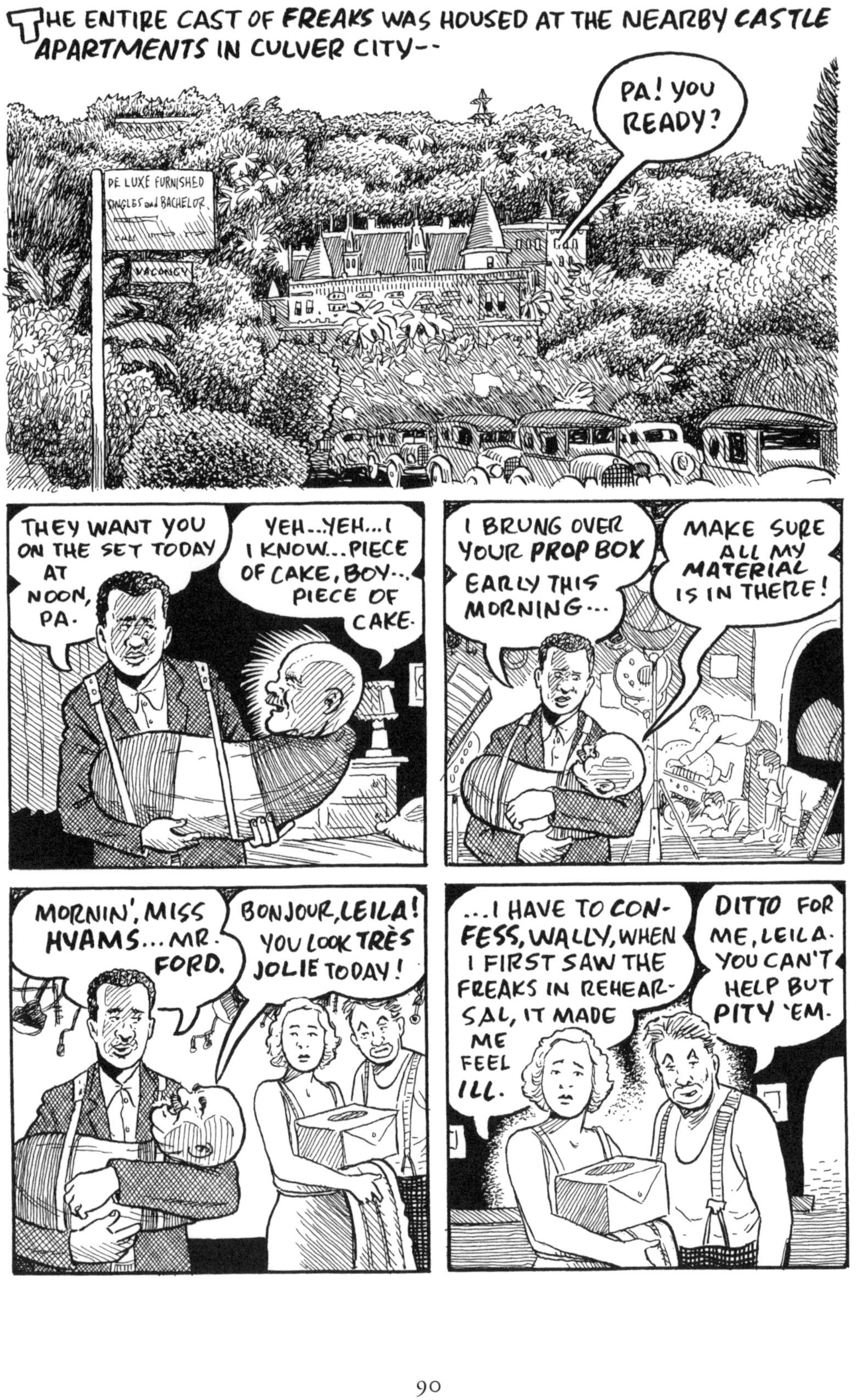
THE ENTIRE CAST OF FREAKS WAS HOUSED AT THE NEARBY CASTLE APARTMENTS IN CULVER CITY--
DE LUXE FURNISHED SINGLES and BACHELOR
PA! YOU READY?
THEY WANT YOU ON THE SET TODAY AT NOON, PA.
YEH...YEH...I I KNOW...PIECE OF CAKE, BOY... PIECE OF CAKE.
I BRUNG OVER YOUR PROP BOX EARLY THIS MORNING...
MAKE SURE ALL MY MATERIAL IS IN THERE!
MORNIN', MISS HYAMS... MR. FORD.
BONJOUR, LEILA! YOU LOOK TRÈS JOLIE TODAY!
...I HAVE TO CON-FESS, WALLY, WHEN I FIRST SAW THE FREAKS IN REHEAR-SAL, IT MADE ME FEEL ILL.
DITTO FOR ME, LEILA. YOU CAN'T HELP BUT PITY 'EM.

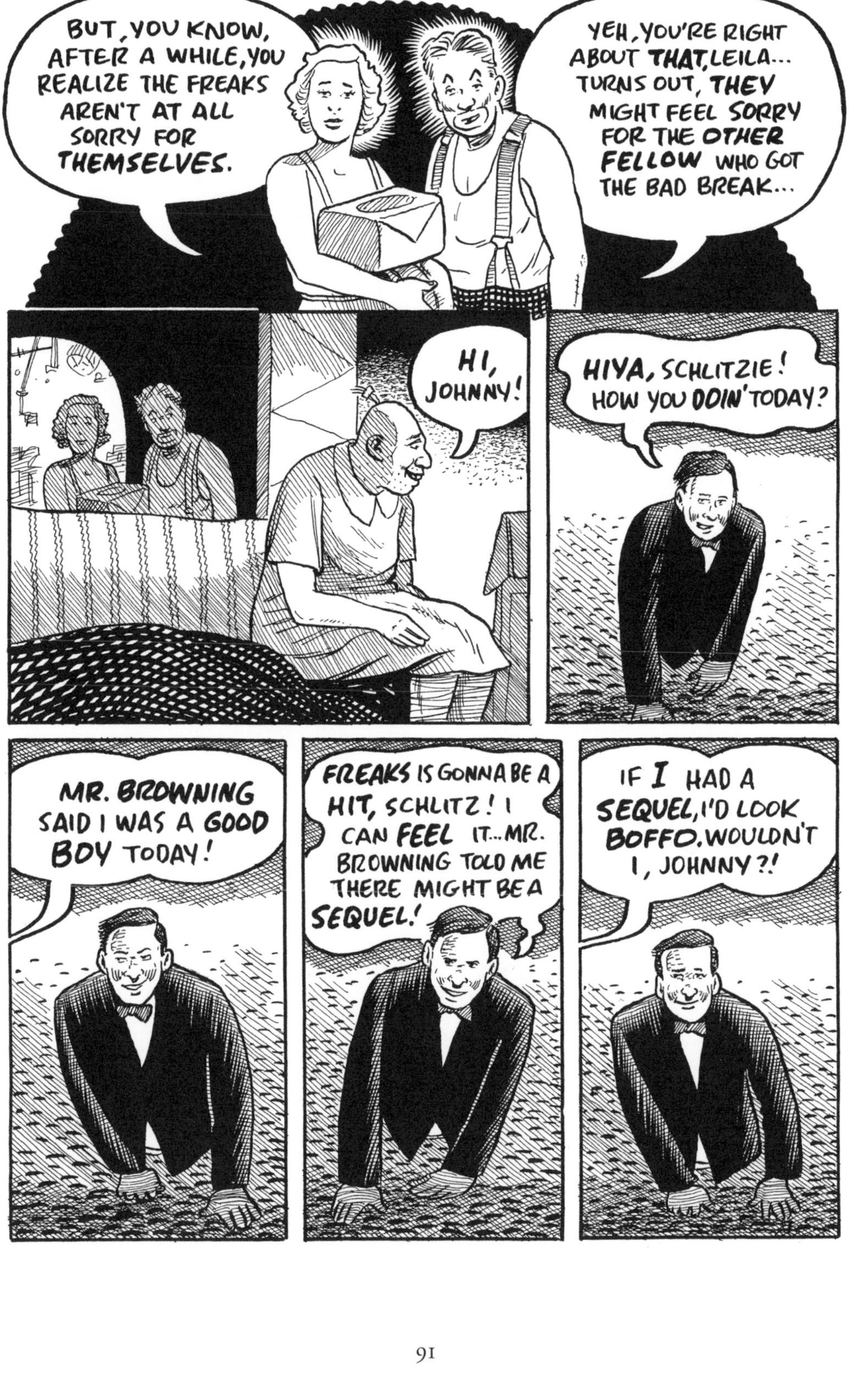
BUT, YOU KNOW, AFTER A WHILE, YOU REALIZE THE FREAKS AREN'T AT ALL SORRY FOR THEMSELVES.
YEH, YOU'RE RIGHT ABOUT THAT, LEILA... TURNS OUT, THEY MIGHT FEEL SORRY FOR THE OTHER FELLOW WHO GOT THE BAD BREAK...
HI, JOHNNY!
HIYA, SCHLITZIE! HOW YOU DOIN' TODAY?
MR. BROWNING SAID I WAS A GOOD BOY TODAY!
FREAKS IS GONNA BE A HIT, SCHLITZ! I CAN FEEL IT... MR. BROWNING TOLD ME THERE MIGHT BE A SEQUEL!
IF I HAD A SEQUEL, I'D LOOK BOFFO. WOULDN'T I, JOHNNY?!

"HALF-BOY" JOHNNY ECK WAS THE MOST STARSTRUCK MEMBER OF THE FREAKS CAST--

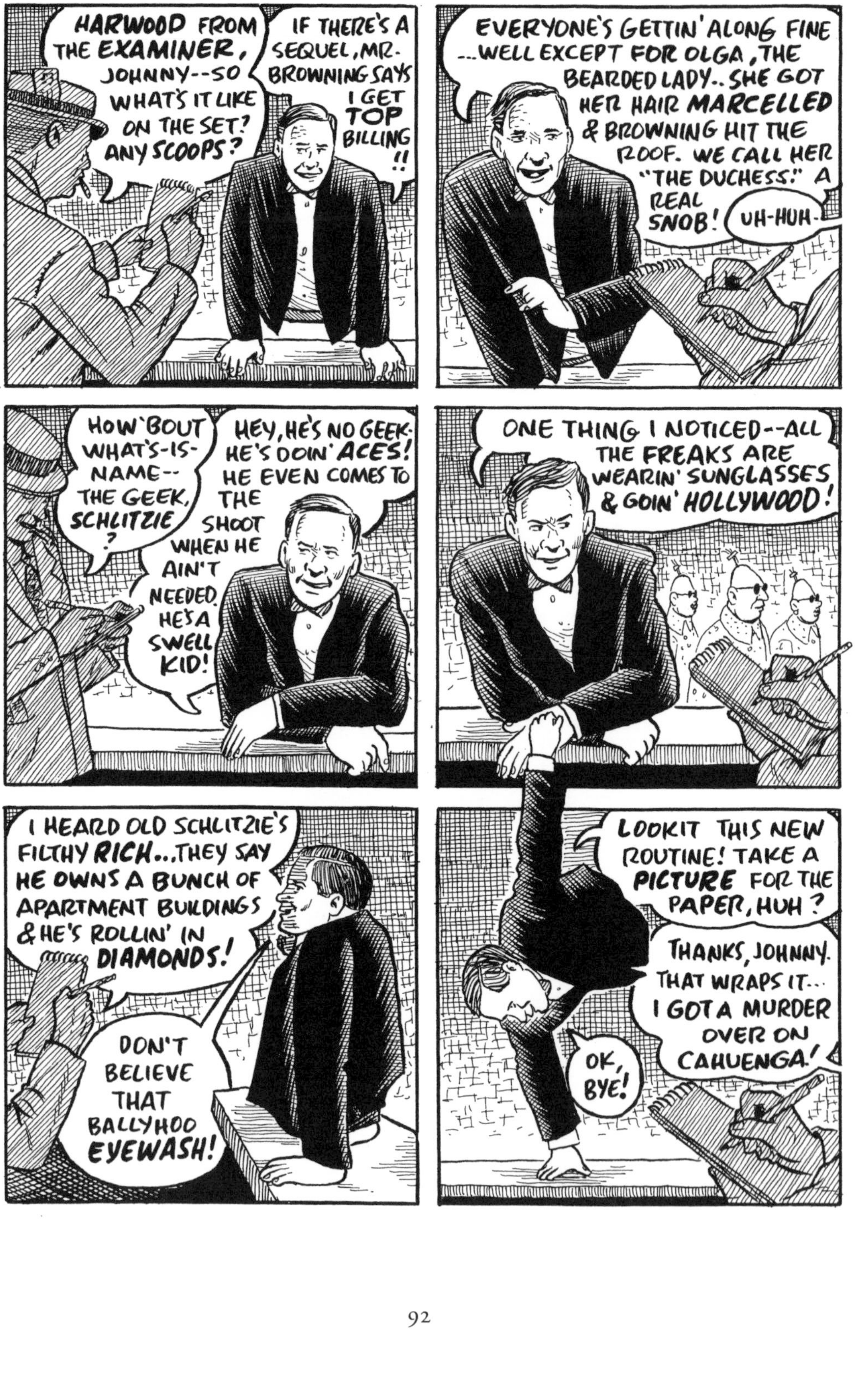
HARWOOD FROM THE EXAMINER, JOHNNY--SO WHAT'S IT LIKE ON THE SET? ANY SCOOPS?
IF THERE'S A SEQUEL, MR. BROWNING SAYS I GET TOP BILLING!!
EVERYONE'S GETTIN' ALONG FINE ...WELL EXCEPT FOR OLGA, THE BEARDED LADY.. SHE GOT HER HAIR MARCELLED & BROWNING HIT THE ROOF. WE CALL HER "THE DUCHESS." A REAL SNOB!
UH-HUH.
HOW 'BOUT WHAT'S-IS-NAME-- THE GEEK, SCHLITZIE?
HEY, HE'S NO GEEK-HE'S DOIN' ACES! HE EVEN COMES TO THE SHOOT WHEN HE AIN'T NEEDED. HE'S A SWELL KID!
ONE THING I NOTICED--ALL THE FREAKS ARE WEARIN' SUNGLASSES & GOIN' HOLLYWOOD!
I HEARD OLD SCHLITZIE'S FILTHY RICH...THEY SAY HE OWNS A BUNCH OF APARTMENT BUILDINGS & HE'S ROLLIN' IN DIAMONDS!
DON'T BELIEVE THAT BALLYHOO EYEWASH!
LOOKIT THIS NEW ROUTINE! TAKE A PICTURE FOR THE PAPER, HUH?
THANKS, JOHNNY. THAT WRAPS IT... I GOT A MURDER OVER ON CAHUENGA!
OK, BYE!

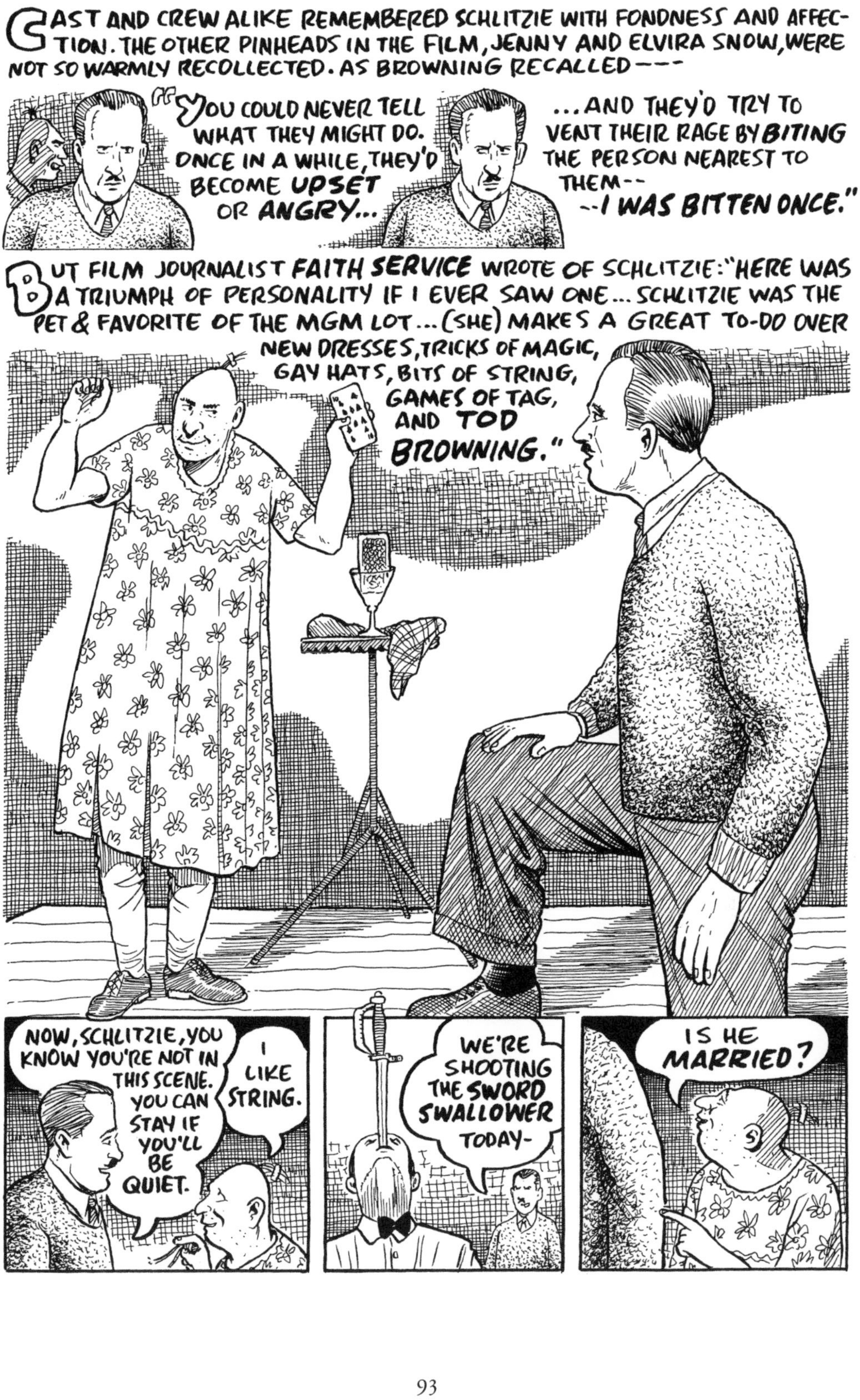
CAST AND CREW ALIKE REMEMBERED SCHLITZIE WITH FONDNESS AND AFFECTION. THE OTHER PINHEADS IN THE FILM, JENNY AND ELVIRA SNOW, WERE NOT SO WARMLY RECOLLECTED. AS BROWNING RECALLED---
"YOU COULD NEVER TELL WHAT THEY MIGHT DO. ONCE IN A WHILE, THEY'D BECOME UPSET OR ANGRY...
...AND THEY'D TRY TO VENT THEIR RAGE BY BITING THE PERSON NEAREST TO THEM--
--I WAS BITTEN ONCE."
BUT FILM JOURNALIST FAITH SERVICE WROTE OF SCHLITZIE: "HERE WAS A TRIUMPH OF PERSONALITY IF I EVER SAW ONE... SCHLITZIE WAS THE PET & FAVORITE OF THE MGM LOT... (SHE) MAKES A GREAT TO-DO OVER NEW DRESSES, TRICKS OF MAGIC, GAY HATS, BITS OF STRING, GAMES OF TAG, AND TOD BROWNING."
NOW, SCHLITZIE, YOU KNOW YOU'RE NOT IN THIS SCENE. YOU CAN STAY IF YOU'LL BE QUIET.
I LIKE STRING.
WE'RE SHOOTING THE SWORD SWALLOWER TODAY-
IS HE MARRIED?

ALL DURING THE FILMING OF **FREAKS**, BROWNING WAS ACUTELY AWARE THAT LOUIS B. MAYER WAS **NOT** A FAN OF THE PROJECT. THALBERG WAS FORCED TO DEFEND THE FILM AGAIN AND AGAIN. IN ADDITION, BROWNING WAS CONSTANTLY REMINDED THAT MGM EXPECTED HIM TO DELIVER A **HIT** LIKE HIS PREVIOUS BOX OFFICE SUCCESS, *Dracula*.

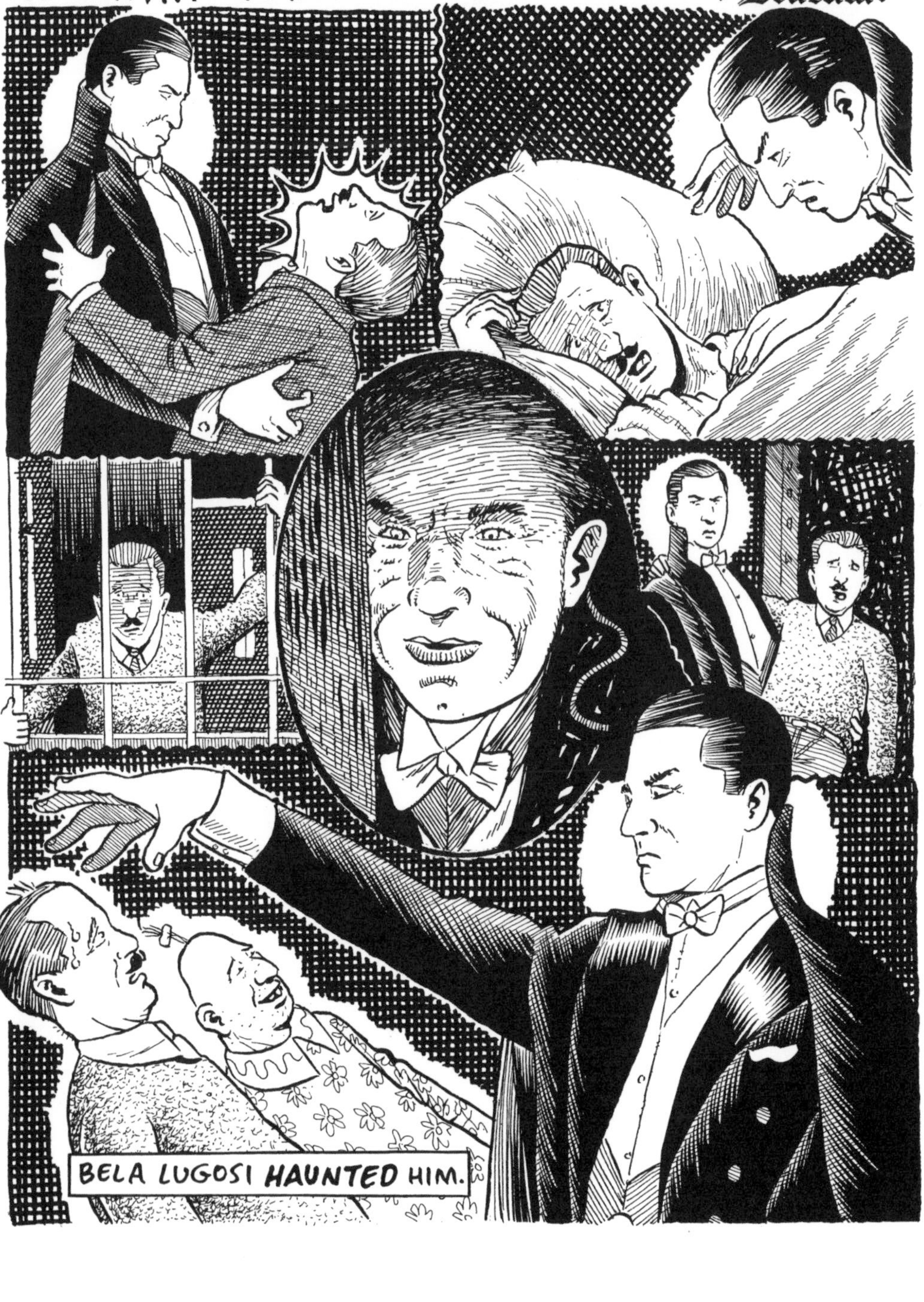
BELA LUGOSI HAUNTED HIM.

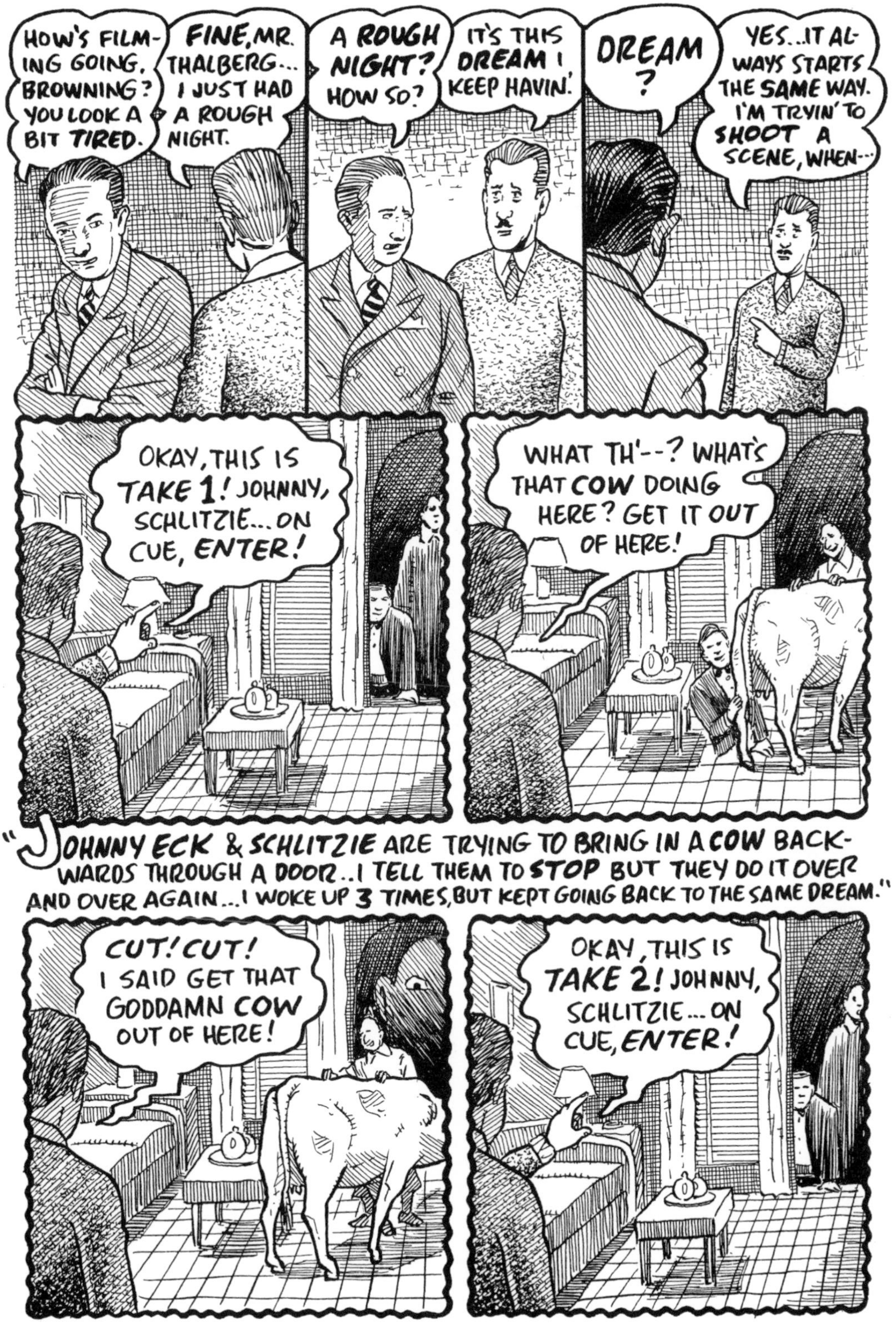
HOW'S FILMING GOING, BROWNING? YOU LOOK A BIT TIRED.
FINE, MR. THALBERG... I JUST HAD A ROUGH NIGHT.
A ROUGH NIGHT? HOW SO?
IT'S THIS DREAM I KEEP HAVIN'.
DREAM?
YES...IT ALWAYS STARTS THE SAME WAY. I'M TRYIN' TO SHOOT A SCENE, WHEN---
OKAY, THIS IS TAKE 1! JOHNNY, SCHLITZIE...ON CUE, ENTER!
WHAT TH'--? WHAT'S THAT COW DOING HERE? GET IT OUT OF HERE!
"JOHNNY ECK & SCHLITZIE ARE TRYING TO BRING IN A COW BACKWARDS THROUGH A DOOR..I TELL THEM TO STOP BUT THEY DO IT OVER AND OVER AGAIN...I WOKE UP 3 TIMES, BUT KEPT GOING BACK TO THE SAME DREAM."
CUT! CUT! I SAID GET THAT GODDAMN COW OUT OF HERE!
OKAY, THIS IS TAKE 2! JOHNNY, SCHLITZIE...ON CUE, ENTER!

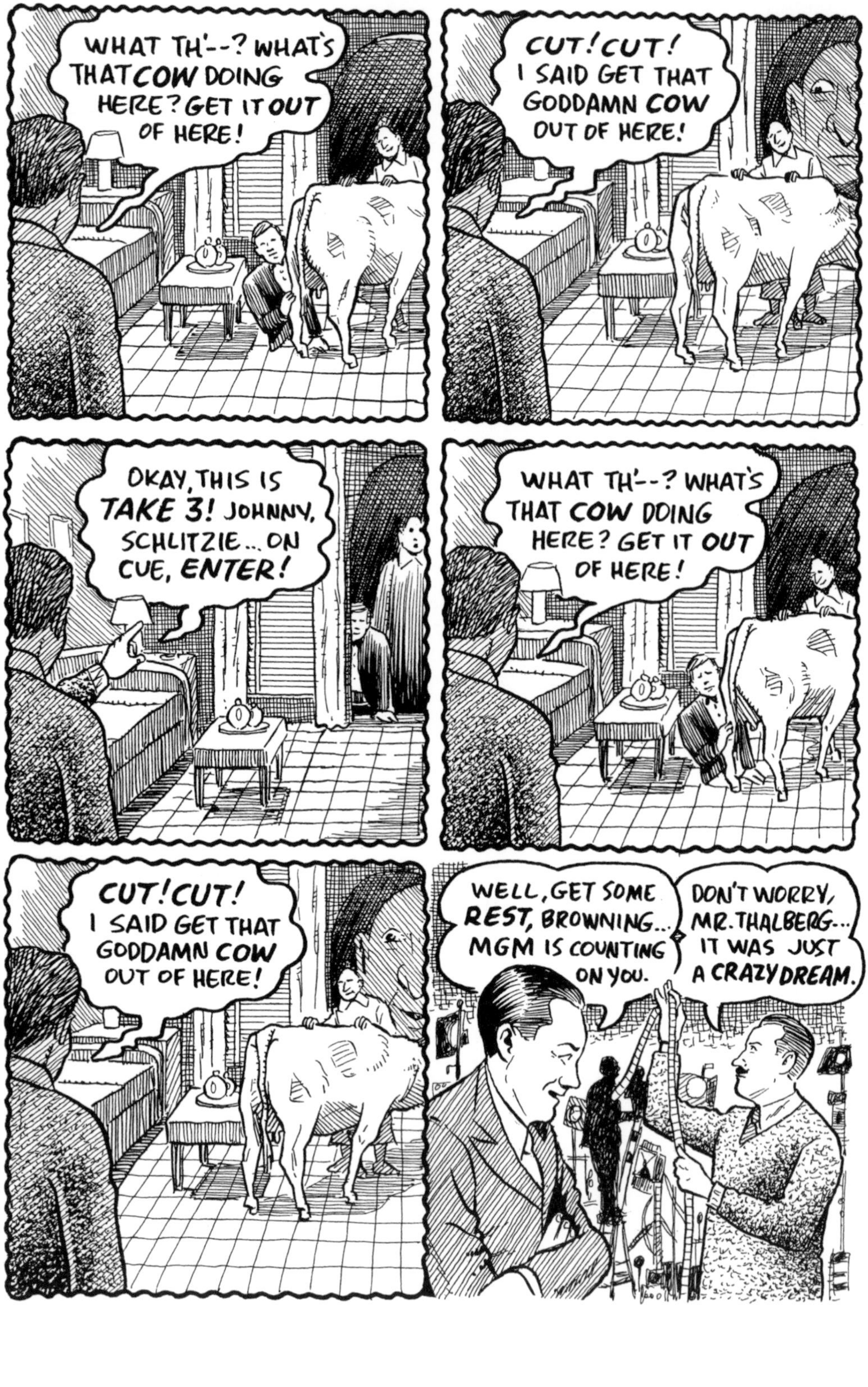
WHAT TH'--? WHAT'S THAT COW DOING HERE? GET IT OUT OF HERE!
CUT! CUT! I SAID GET THAT GODDAMN COW OUT OF HERE!
OKAY, THIS IS TAKE 3! JOHNNY, SCHLITZIE... ON CUE, ENTER!
WHAT TH'--? WHAT'S THAT COW DOING HERE? GET IT OUT OF HERE!
CUT! CUT! I SAID GET THAT GODDAMN COW OUT OF HERE!
WELL, GET SOME REST, BROWNING... MGM IS COUNTING ON YOU.
DON'T WORRY, MR. THALBERG... IT WAS JUST A CRAZY DREAM.

SCHLITZIE IS FEATURED IN TWO SCENES IN **FREAKS**, AS WELL AS IN SEVERAL WALK-ONS. IN THE **OPENING SEQUENCE**, HE'S SEEN DANCING HAND IN HAND WITH DWARF **ANGELO ROSSITTO**--

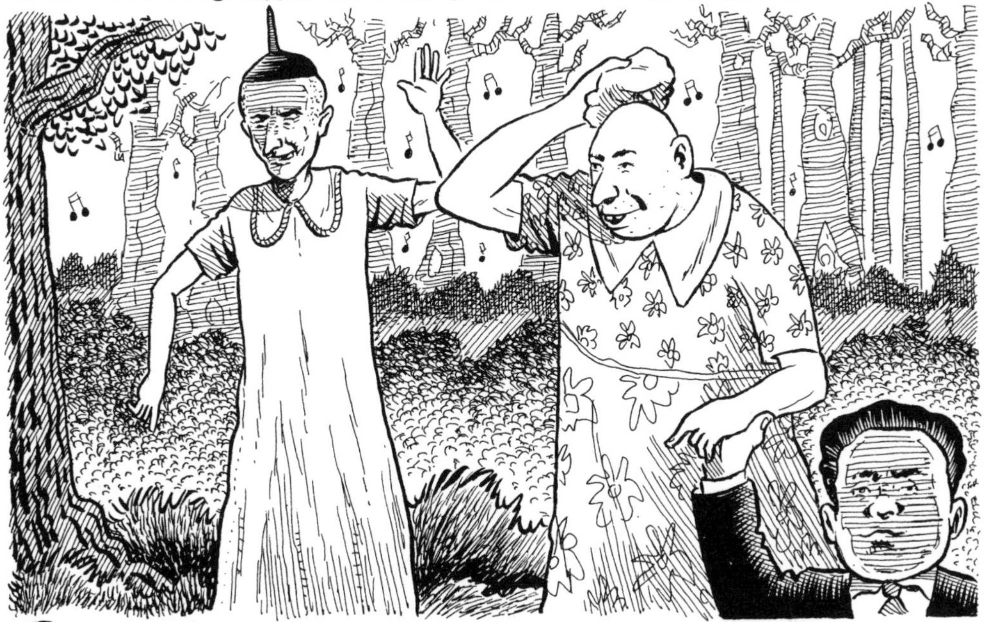

SCHLITZIE'S **BIG SCENE** COMES **26 MINUTES** INTO THE STORY. HE APPROACHES **PHROSO** THE CLOWN OUTSIDE A CIRCUS CARAVAN--

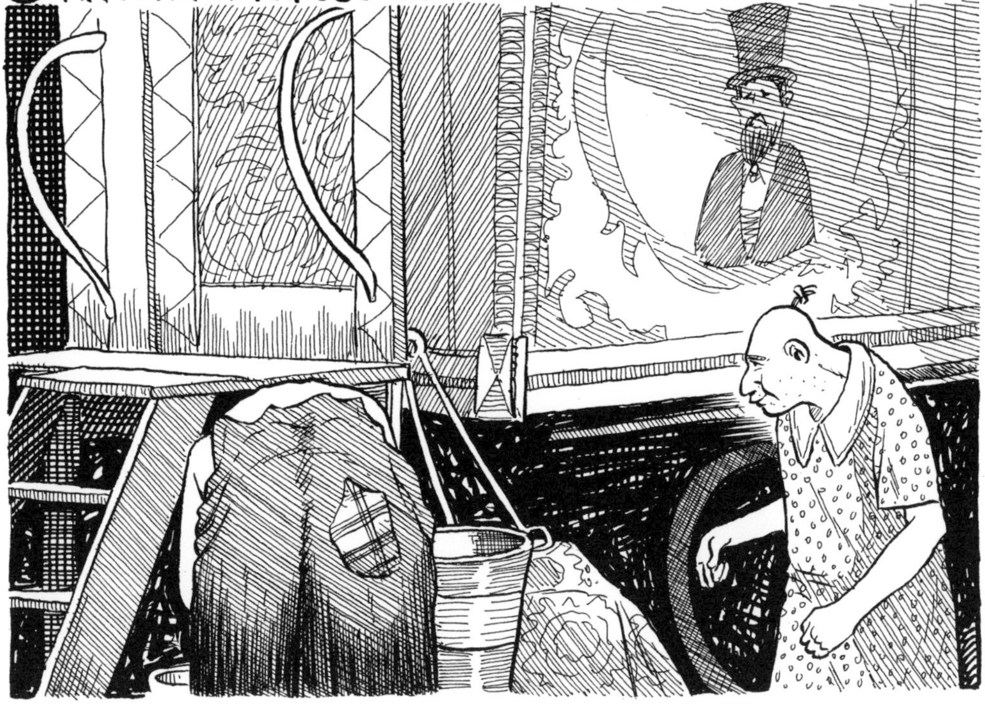

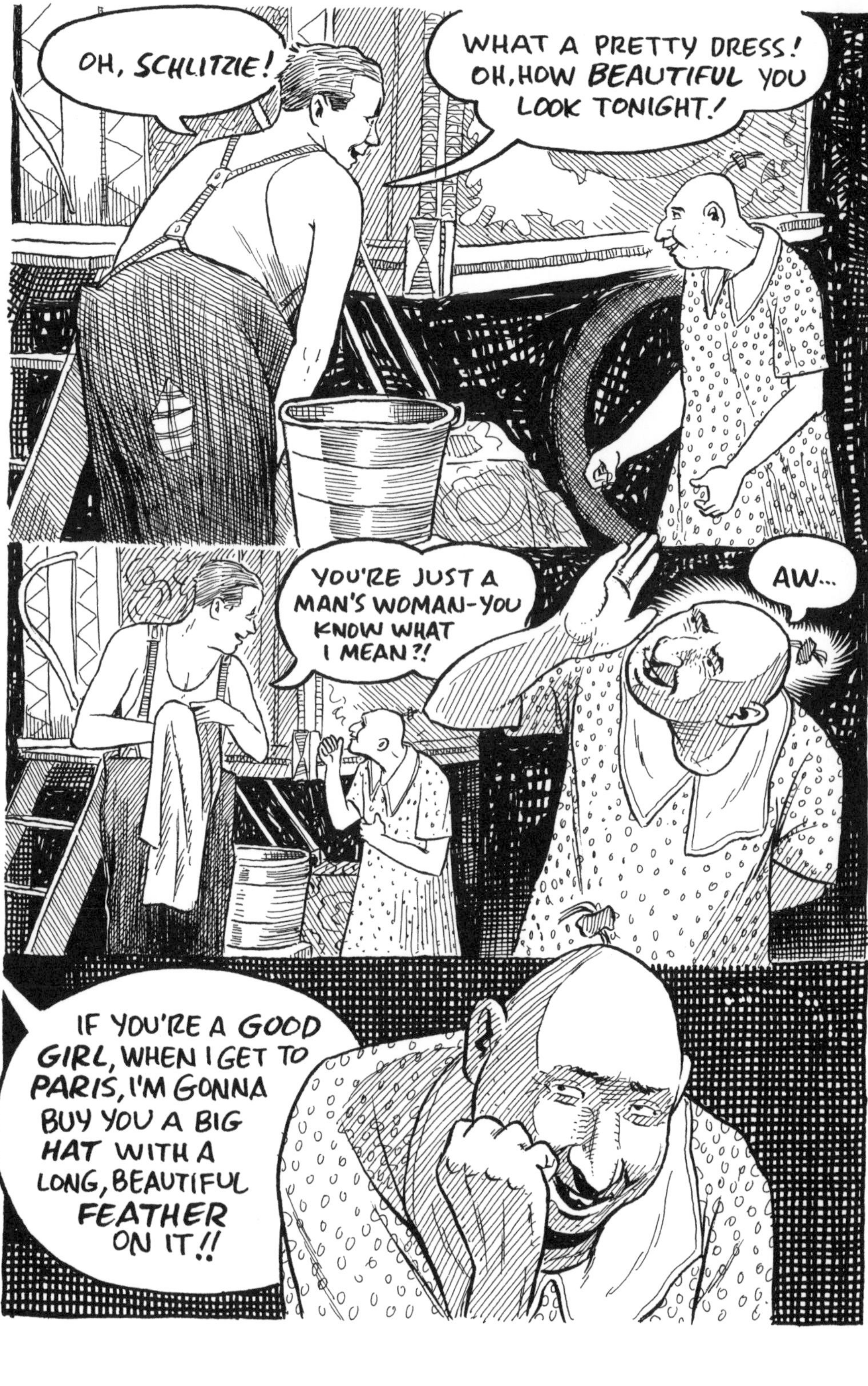
OH, SCHLITZIE!
WHAT A PRETTY DRESS! OH, HOW BEAUTIFUL YOU LOOK TONIGHT!
YOU'RE JUST A MAN'S WOMAN- YOU KNOW WHAT I MEAN?!
AW...
IF YOU'RE A GOOD GIRL, WHEN I GET TO PARIS, I'M GONNA BUY YOU A BIG HAT WITH A LONG, BEAUTIFUL FEATHER ON IT!!

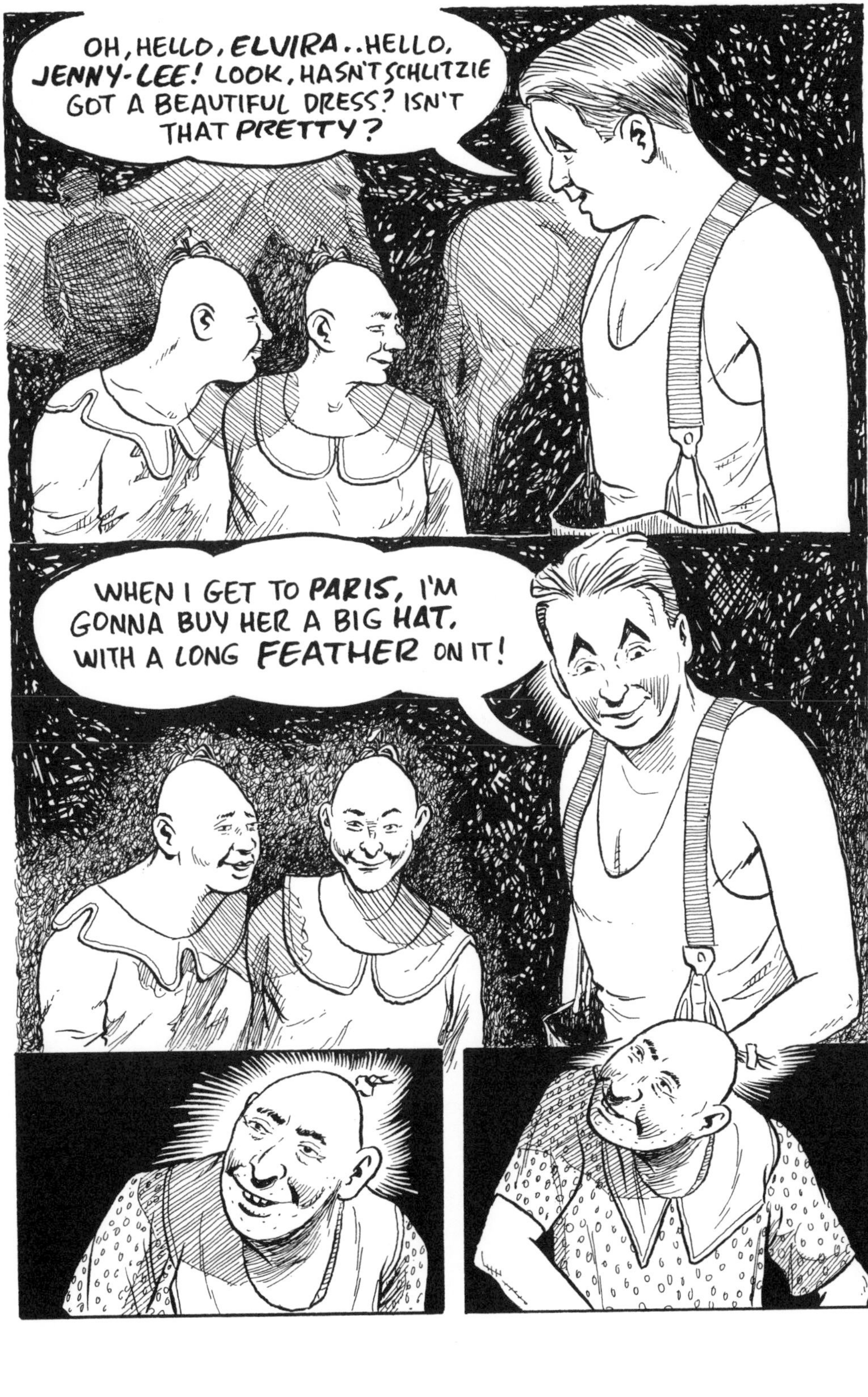
OH, HELLO, ELVIRA..HELLO, JENNY-LEE! LOOK, HASN'T SCHLITZIE GOT A BEAUTIFUL DRESS? ISN'T THAT PRETTY?
WHEN I GET TO PARIS, I'M GONNA BUY HER A BIG HAT, WITH A LONG FEATHER ON IT!

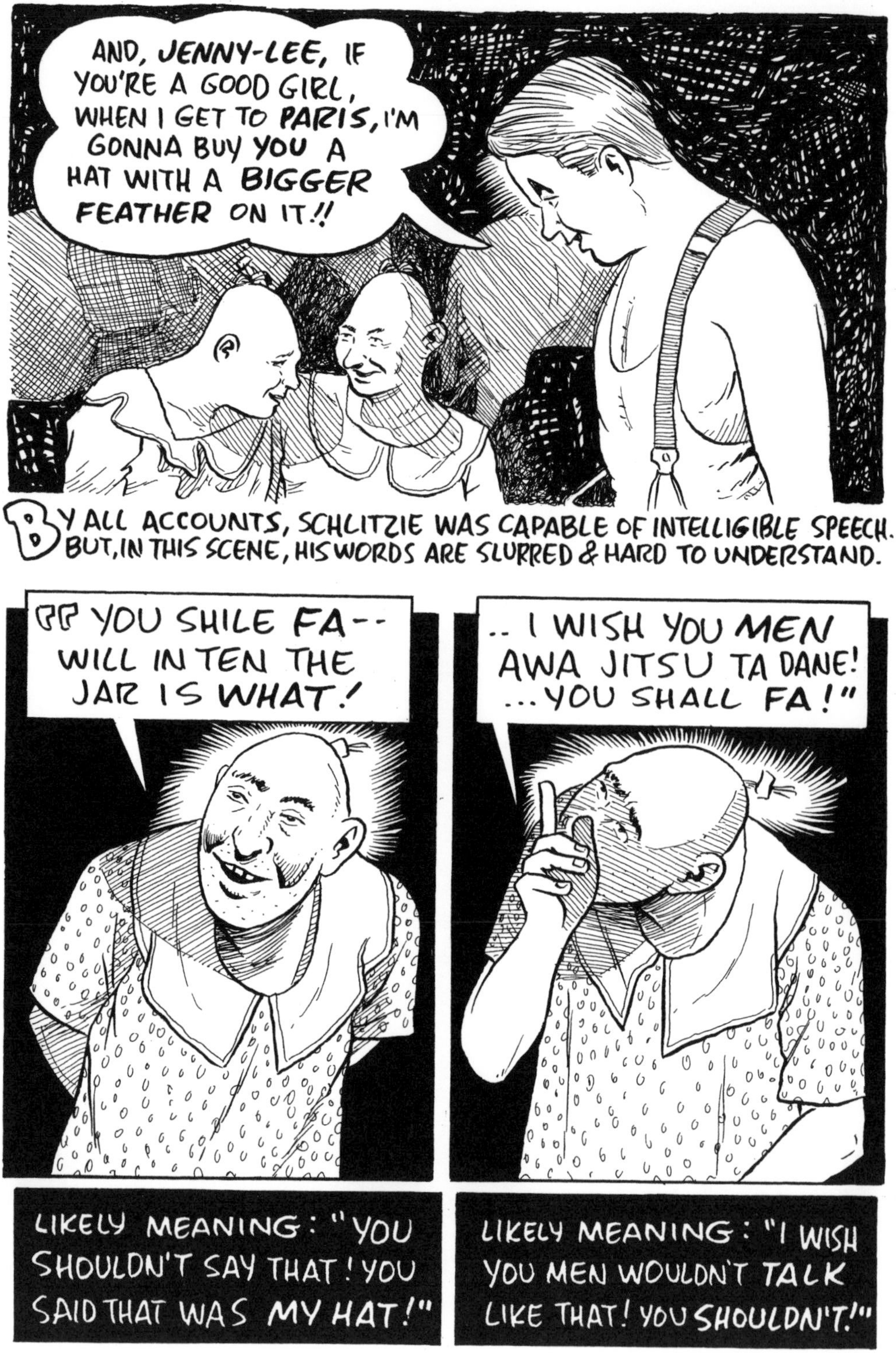
AND, JENNY-LEE, IF YOU'RE A GOOD GIRL, WHEN I GET TO PARIS, I'M GONNA BUY YOU A HAT WITH A BIGGER FEATHER ON IT!!
BY ALL ACCOUNTS, SCHLITZIE WAS CAPABLE OF INTELLIGIBLE SPEECH. BUT, IN THIS SCENE, HIS WORDS ARE SLURRED & HARD TO UNDERSTAND.
"YOU SHILE FA-- WILL IN TEN THE JAR IS WHAT!
.. I WISH YOU MEN AWA JITSU TA DANE! ...YOU SHALL FA!"
LIKELY MEANING: "YOU SHOULDN'T SAY THAT! YOU SAID THAT WAS MY HAT!"
LIKELY MEANING: "I WISH YOU MEN WOULDN'T TALK LIKE THAT! YOU SHOULDN'T!"

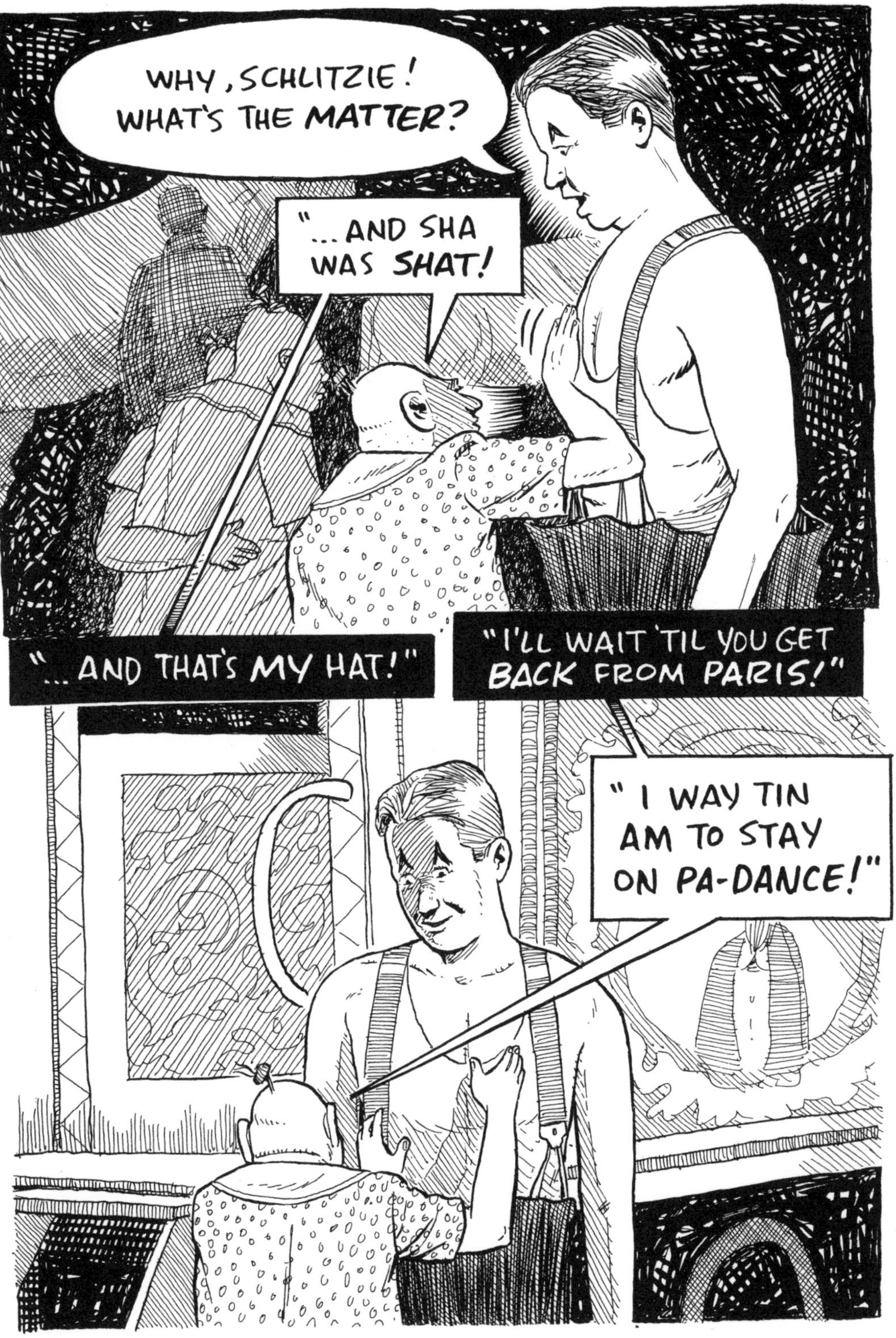
WHY, SCHLITZIE! WHAT'S THE MATTER?
"...AND SHA WAS SHAT!
"...AND THAT'S MY HAT!"
"I'LL WAIT 'TIL YOU GET BACK FROM PARIS!"
" I WAY TIN AM TO STAY ON PA-DANCE!"

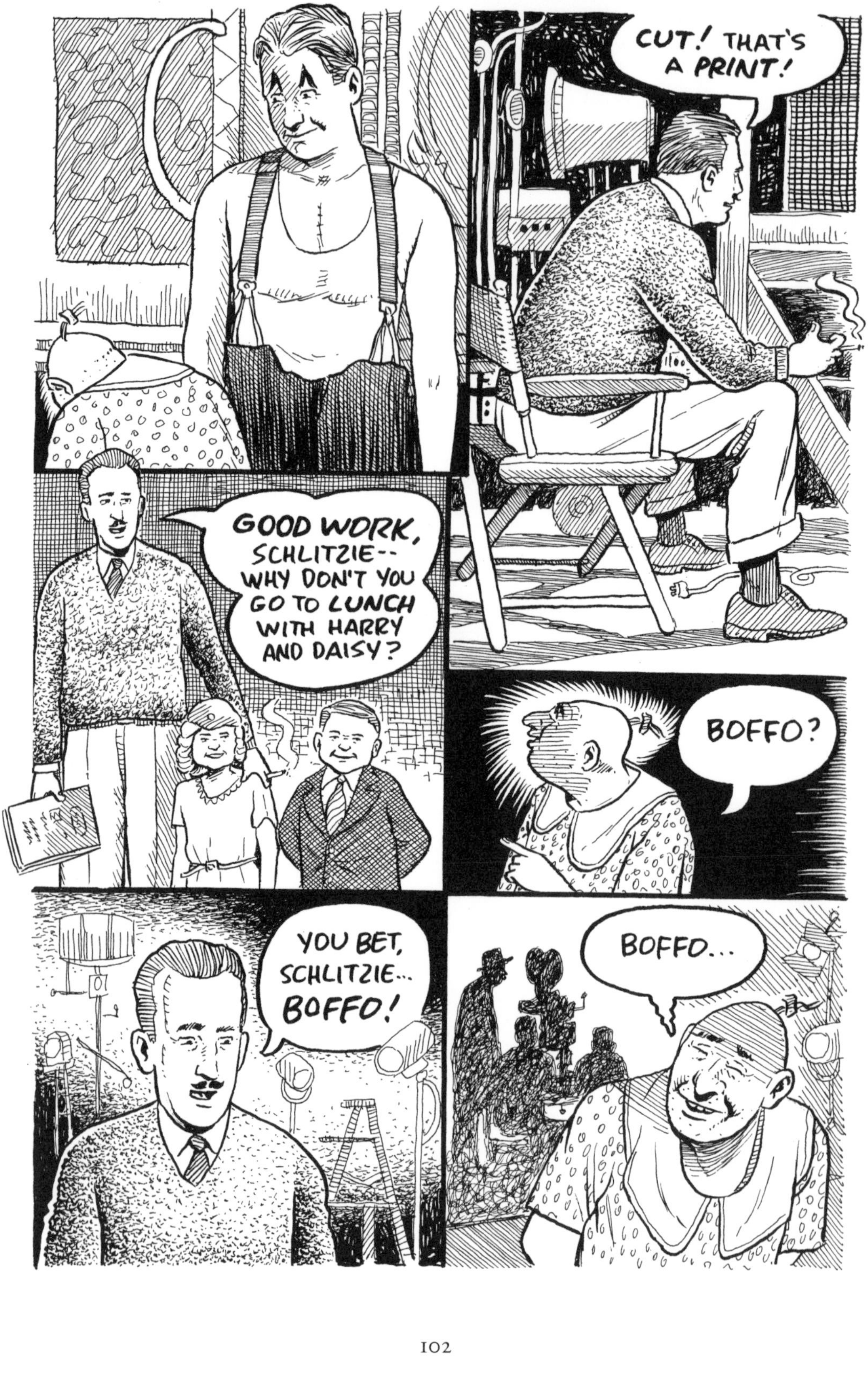
CUT! THAT'S A PRINT!
GOOD WORK, SCHLITZIE-- WHY DON'T YOU GO TO LUNCH WITH HARRY AND DAISY?
BOFFO?
YOU BET, SCHLITZIE... BOFFO!
BOFFO...

FREAKS COMPLETED FILMING JUST BEFORE CHRISTMAS 1931--

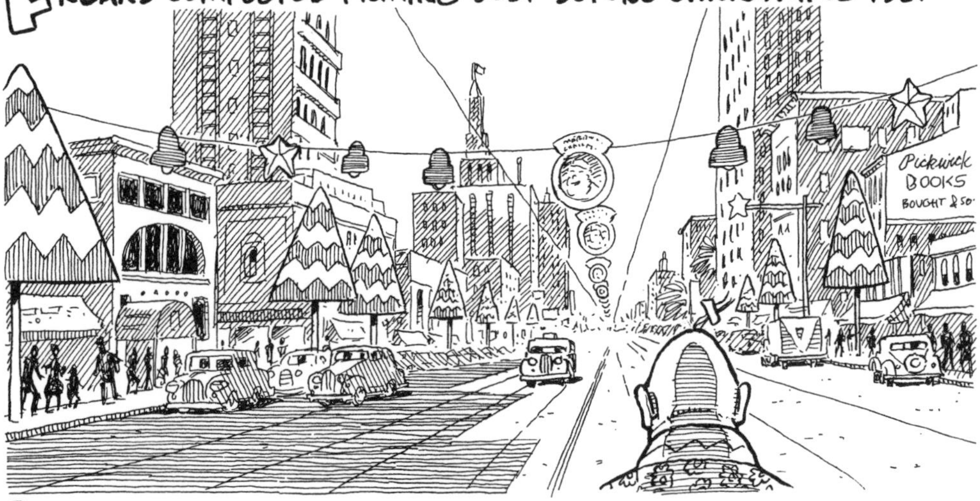
Pickwick
BOOKS

IN JANUARY 1932, THE MOVIE WAS SHOWN TO A PREVIEW AUDIENCE IN SAN DIEGO...THE THEATRE WAS OPTIMISTICALLY DECKED OUT--

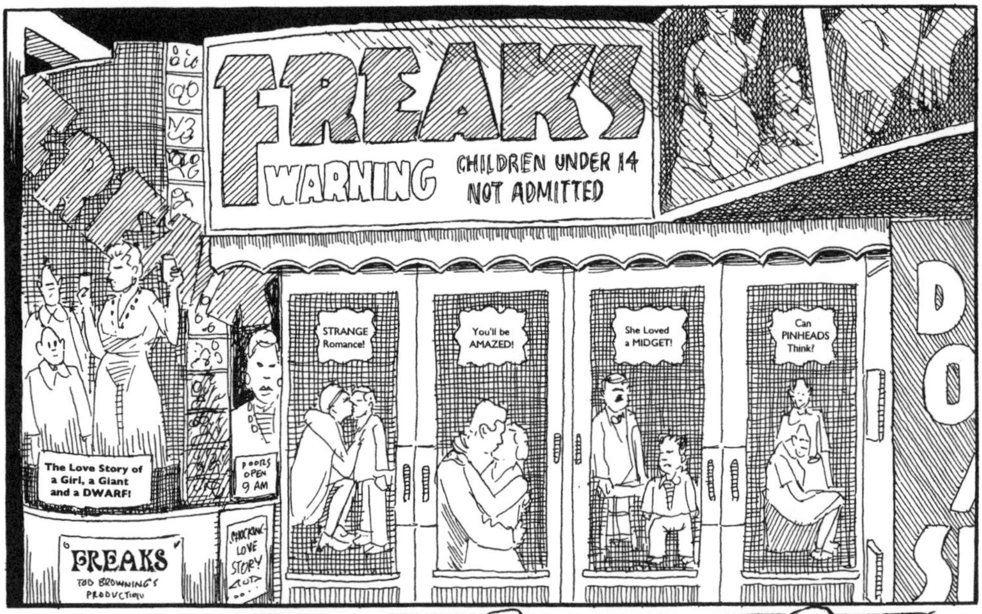
FREAKS
WARNING
CHILDREN UNDER 14 NOT ADMITTED
STRANGE Romance!
You'll be AMAZED!
She Loved a MIDGET!
Can PINHEADS Think?
The Love Story of a Girl, a Giant and a DWARF!
DOORS OPEN 9 AM
FREAKS
TOD BROWNING'S PRODUCTION

FREAKS ART DIRECTOR MERRILL PYE RECALLED THAT "HALFWAY THROUGH THE PREVIEW, A LOT OF PEOPLE GOT UP & RAN OUT. THEY DIDN'T WALK OUT. THEY RAN OUT."

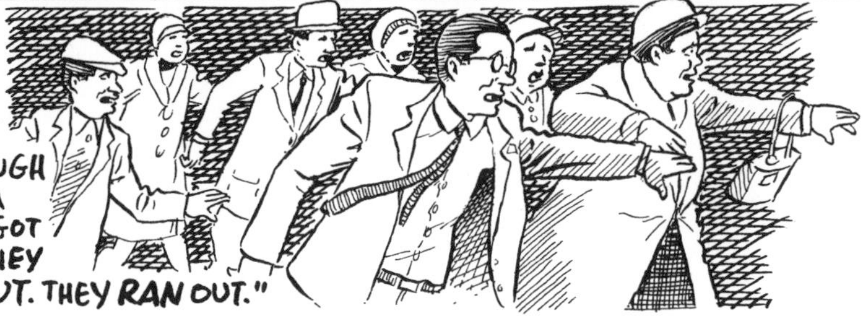

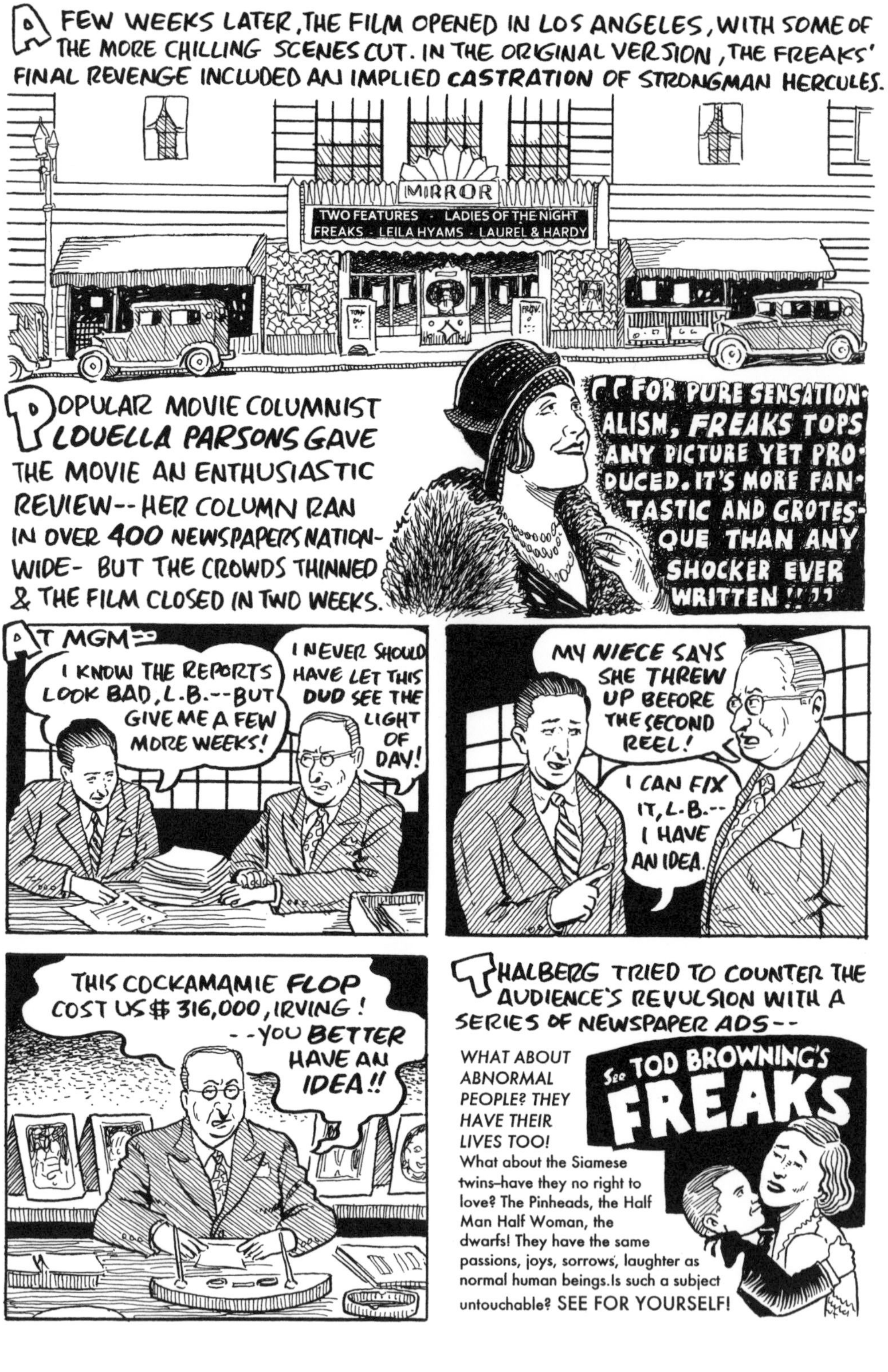
A FEW WEEKS LATER, THE FILM OPENED IN LOS ANGELES, WITH SOME OF THE MORE CHILLING SCENES CUT. IN THE ORIGINAL VERSION, THE FREAKS' FINAL REVENGE INCLUDED AN IMPLIED CASTRATION OF STRONGMAN HERCULES.
MIRROR
TWO FEATURES · LADIES OF THE NIGHT
FREAKS · LEILA HYAMS · LAUREL & HARDY
POPULAR MOVIE COLUMNIST LOUELLA PARSONS GAVE THE MOVIE AN ENTHUSIASTIC REVIEW-- HER COLUMN RAN IN OVER 400 NEWSPAPERS NATIONWIDE- BUT THE CROWDS THINNED & THE FILM CLOSED IN TWO WEEKS.
"FOR PURE SENSATIONALISM, FREAKS TOPS ANY PICTURE YET PRODUCED. IT'S MORE FANTASTIC AND GROTESQUE THAN ANY SHOCKER EVER WRITTEN!!"
AT MGM--
I KNOW THE REPORTS LOOK BAD, L.B.--BUT GIVE ME A FEW MORE WEEKS!
I NEVER SHOULD HAVE LET THIS DUD SEE THE LIGHT OF DAY!
MY NIECE SAYS SHE THREW UP BEFORE THE SECOND REEL!
I CAN FIX IT, L.B.-- I HAVE AN IDEA.
THIS COCKAMAMIE FLOP COST US $316,000, IRVING! --YOU BETTER HAVE AN IDEA!!
THALBERG TRIED TO COUNTER THE AUDIENCE'S REVULSION WITH A SERIES OF NEWSPAPER ADS--
WHAT ABOUT ABNORMAL PEOPLE? THEY HAVE THEIR LIVES TOO!
What about the Siamese twins–have they no right to love? The Pinheads, the Half Man Half Woman, the dwarfs! They have the same passions, joys, sorrows, laughter as normal human beings. Is such a subject untouchable? SEE FOR YOURSELF!
See TOD BROWNING'S
FREAKS

THE MGM PUBLICITY MACHINE CHURNED OUT DOZENS OF ATTENTION-GRABBING **NEWSPAPER & MAGAZINE ADS**... MANY EMPLOYED THE **EXAGGERATED CLAIMS & HYPERVENTILATING LANGUAGE** OF THE **SIDESHOW** WORLD, ALMOST SUGGESTING THAT THE **CIRCUS** HAD JUST ARRIVED AT YOUR LOCAL MOVIE THEATRE--

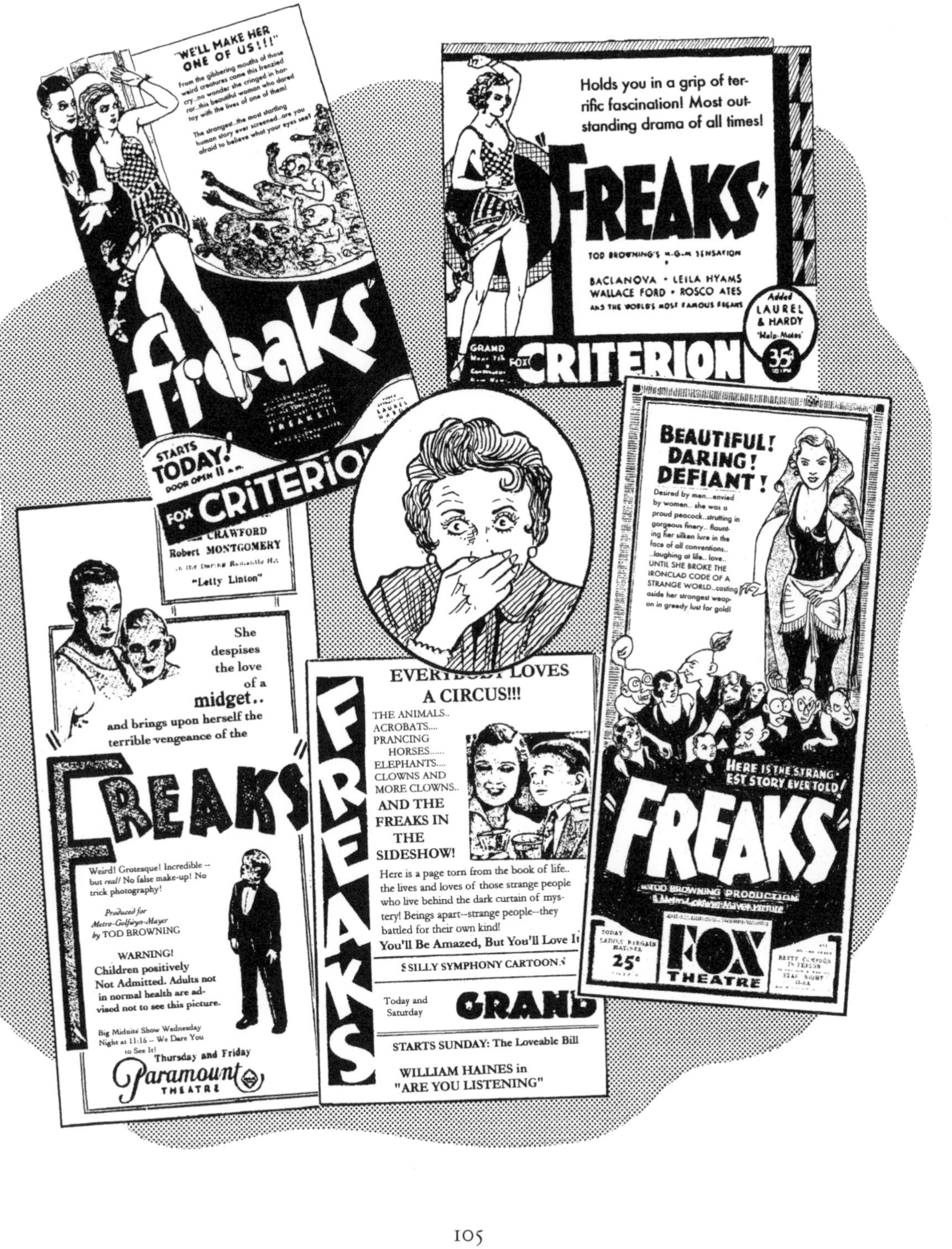

"WE'LL MAKE HER ONE OF US!!!"
From the gibbering mouths of those weird creatures came this frenzied cry...no wonder she cringed in horror...this beautiful woman who dared toy with the lives of one of them!
The strangest...the most startling human story ever screened...are you afraid to believe what your eyes see?
freaks
STARTS TODAY! DOOR OPEN 11 A.M.
FOX CRITERION
Robert MONTGOMERY
"Letty Linton"
Holds you in a grip of terrific fascination! Most outstanding drama of all times!
"FREAKS"
TOD BROWNING'S M-G-M SENSATION
BACLANOVA • LEILA HYAMS
WALLACE FORD • ROSCO ATES
AND THE WORLD'S MOST FAMOUS FREAKS
Added LAUREL & HARDY "Help-Mates"
GRAND
FOX CRITERION
35¢
BEAUTIFUL! DARING! DEFIANT!
Desired by men...envied by women.. she was a proud peacock...strutting in gorgeous finery.. flaunting her silken lure in the face of all conventions.. ..laughing at life.. love... UNTIL SHE BROKE THE IRONCLAD CODE OF A STRANGE WORLD...casting aside her strongest weapon in greedy lust for gold!
HERE IS THE STRANGEST STORY EVER TOLD!
"FREAKS"
A TOD BROWNING PRODUCTION
25¢
FOX THEATRE
She despises the love of a midget.. and brings upon herself the terrible vengeance of the
"FREAKS"
Weird! Grotesque! Incredible -- but real! No false make-up! No trick photography!
Produced for Metro-Goldwyn-Mayer by TOD BROWNING
WARNING! Children positively Not Admitted. Adults not in normal health are advised not to see this picture.
Big Midnite Show Wednesday Night at 11:15 -- We Dare You to See It!
Thursday and Friday
Paramount THEATRE
FREAKS
EVERYBODY LOVES A CIRCUS!!!
THE ANIMALS.. ACROBATS.... PRANCING HORSES...... ELEPHANTS.... CLOWNS AND MORE CLOWNS..
AND THE FREAKS IN THE SIDESHOW!
Here is a page torn from the book of life.. the lives and loves of those strange people who live behind the dark curtain of mystery! Beings apart--strange people--they battled for their own kind!
You'll Be Amazed, But You'll Love It
SILLY SYMPHONY CARTOON
Today and Saturday
GRAND
STARTS SUNDAY: The Loveable Bill
WILLIAM HAINES in "ARE YOU LISTENING"

BUT IN AN ERA WHEN MENTAL & PHYSICAL "ABNORMALITIES" WERE GENERALLY LOOKED UPON WITH LITTLE COMPASSION, THE PORTRAYAL OF ***REAL*** SIDESHOW PERFORMERS IN ***FREAKS*** GAVE OUTRAGED REVIEWERS PLENTY TO BE OUTRAGED ABOUT--THE ***BAD PRESS*** GRADUALLY ***SUNK*** THE FILM AT THE BOX OFFICE ACROSS THE COUNTRY--

"Unkind and brutal."
- Motion Picture Daily

•

"Freaks is loathsome, obscene, grotesque and bizarre."
- Atlanta Board of Review

•

"Freaks transcends the fascinatingly horrible, leaving the spectator appalled."
- The Atlanta Journal

•

"It took a weak mind to produce it and it takes a strong stomach to look at it."
- Kansas City Star

•

"The sadistically cruel plot savors nearly every perversion."
- **Boston Herald**

•

"Freaks failed to qualify in the sure-fire category and has been shown in most parts of the country with astonishingly variable results. In spots it has been a clean-up. In others it was merely misery."
- Variety

•

"(Browning) is fond of anything that happens underground or in the dark, especially a murder. He prefers lovers who are physically deformed."
-Time Magazine

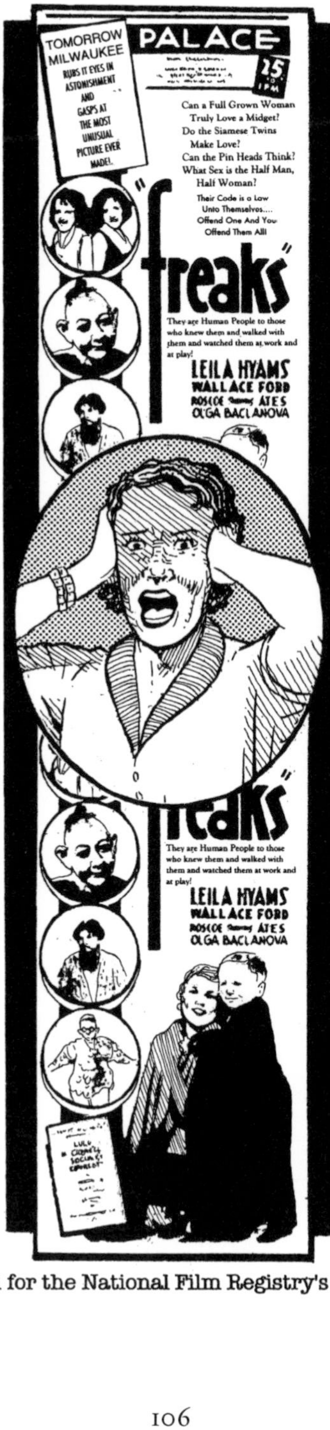

TOMORROW MILWAUKEE RUBS IT EYES IN ASTONISHMENT AND GASPS AT THE MOST UNUSUAL PICTURE EVER MADE!
PALACE
25
Can a Full Grown Woman Truly Love a Midget?
Do the Siamese Twins Make Love?
Can the Pin Heads Think?
What Sex is the Half Man, Half Woman?
Their Code is a Law Unto Themselves.... Offend One And You Offend Them All!
"freaks"
They are Human People to those who knew them and walked with them and watched them at work and at play!
LEILA HYAMS
WALLACE FORD
ROSCOE ATES
OLGA BACLANOVA
"freaks"
They are Human People to those who knew them and walked with them and watched them at work and at play!
LEILA HYAMS
WALLACE FORD
ROSCOE ATES
OLGA BACLANOVA

"M-G-M should change its famous motto--"Ars Gratia Artis"--'Art for Art's Sake'--to 'Muck for Money's Sake'".
- Rob Wagner's Script magazine

•

"I found it to be an interesting and entertaining picture, and I did not have nightmares, nor did I attempt to murder any of my relatives."
- Motion Picture Herald

•

"It is obviously an unhealthy and generally disagreeable work...Yet, in some strange way, the picture is not only exciting, but even occasionally touching."
- New York Herald-Tribune

•

" A picture not to be easily forgotten."
- New York Times

•

"Anyone who considers this entertainment should be placed in the pathological ward in some hospital. It is not fit to be shown anywhere."
- Harrison's Reports

In 1994, **Freaks** was selected for the National Film Registry's archive of cinematic treasures.

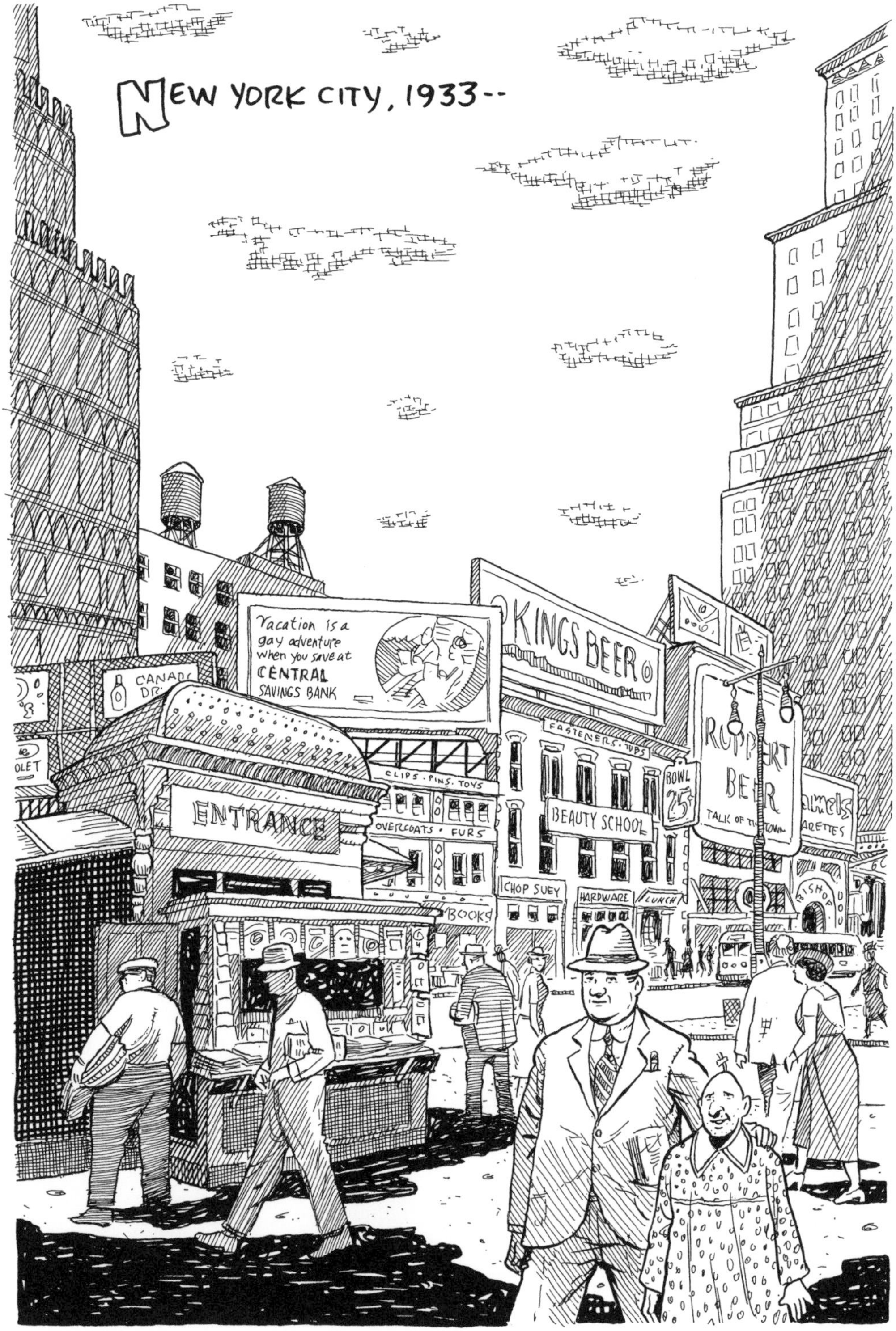
NEW YORK CITY, 1933--
Vacation is a gay adventure when you save at CENTRAL SAVINGS BANK
KINGS BEER
ENTRANCE
CLIPS · PINS · TOYS
OVERCOATS · FURS
FASTENERS · TUBS
BEAUTY SCHOOL
BOWL 25¢
CHOP SUEY
HARDWARE
LUNCH
BOOKS
BISHOP

BACK ON THE **SIDESHOW** CIRCUIT, SCHLITZIE TRAVELED THE USUAL VENUES, OFTEN APPEARING WITH **PRINCE RANDIAN** AND STILL MANAGED BY SHOWMAN **TED METZ**--

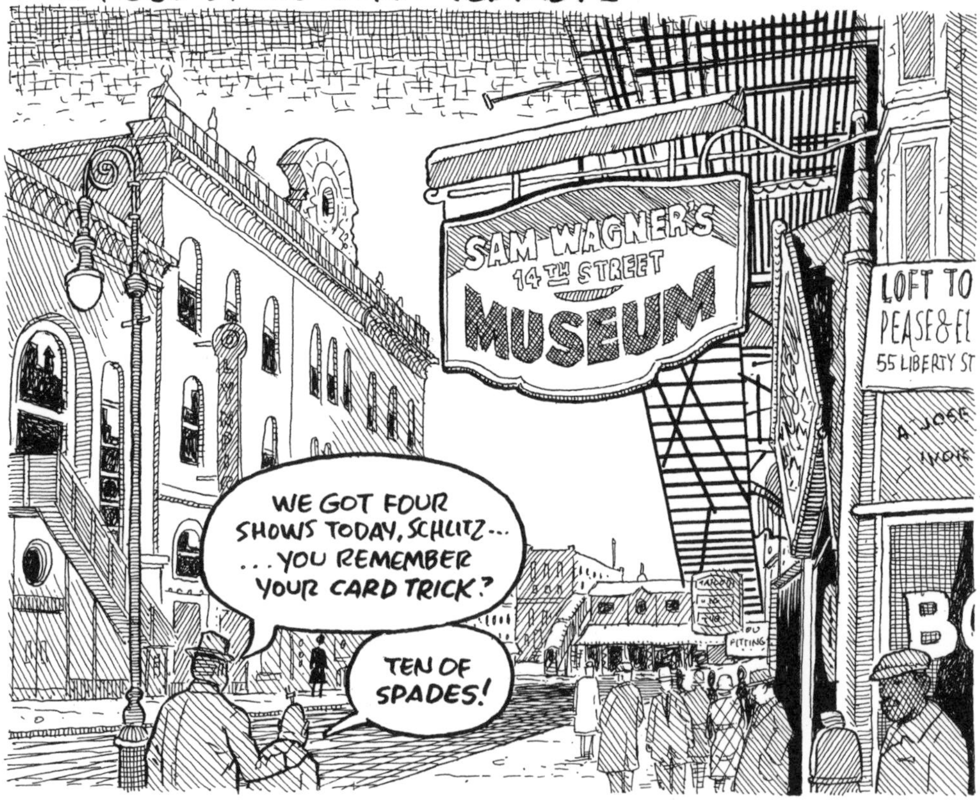
SAM WAGNER'S
14TH STREET
MUSEUM
WE GOT FOUR SHOWS TODAY, SCHLITZ... ...YOU REMEMBER YOUR CARD TRICK?
TEN OF SPADES!

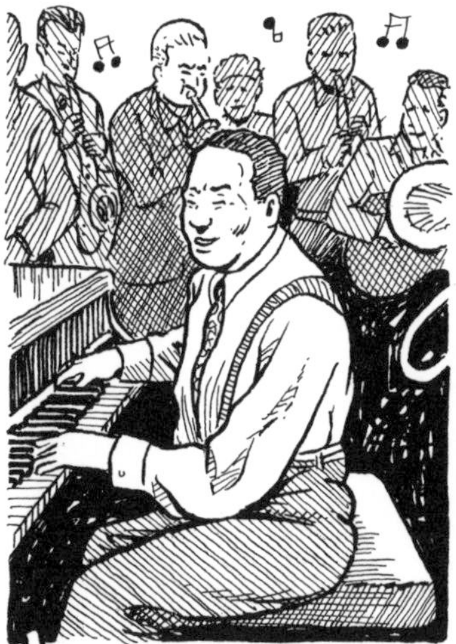

JAZZ BANDS SOMETIMES PLAYED ON STAGE BEFORE SIDESHOW PERFORMANCES.

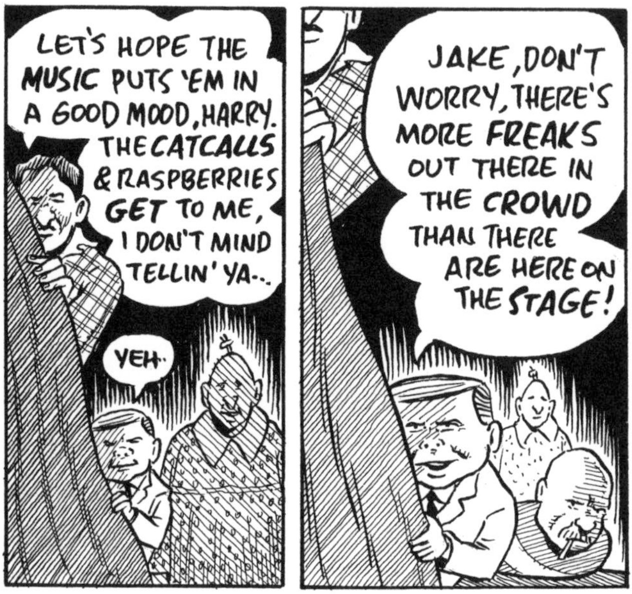
LET'S HOPE THE MUSIC PUTS 'EM IN A GOOD MOOD, HARRY. THE CATCALLS & RASPBERRIES GET TO ME, I DON'T MIND TELLIN' YA...
YEH.
JAKE, DON'T WORRY, THERE'S MORE FREAKS OUT THERE IN THE CROWD THAN THERE ARE HERE ON THE STAGE!

IN A TYPICAL YEAR, THE **SIDESHOW CIRCUIT** SCHLITZIE WOULD HAVE TRAVELED RANGED FROM CANADA, TO THE EASTERN U.S., TO SAN JUAN, PUERTO RICO, THEN TO MEXICO CITY, AND ON TO THE MIDWEST AND SOUTHERN U.S., TO THE WEST COAST, AND HAWAII--

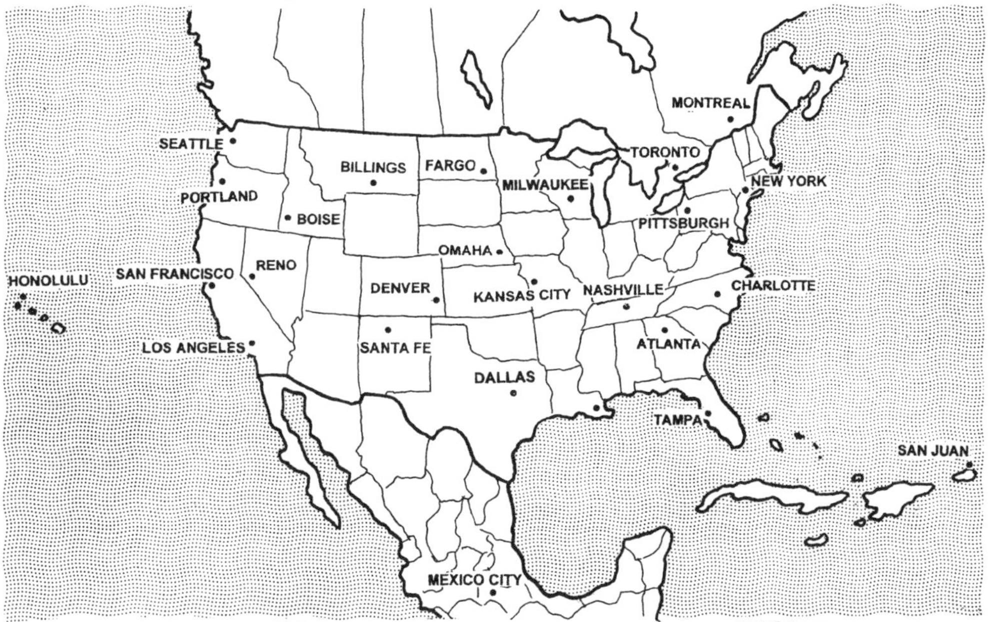

MONTREAL
SEATTLE
TORONTO
BILLINGS
FARGO
MILWAUKEE
NEW YORK
PORTLAND
BOISE
PITTSBURGH
OMAHA
RENO
HONOLULU
SAN FRANCISCO
DENVER
KANSAS CITY
NASHVILLE
CHARLOTTE
LOS ANGELES
SANTA FE
ATLANTA
DALLAS
TAMPA
SAN JUAN
MEXICO CITY

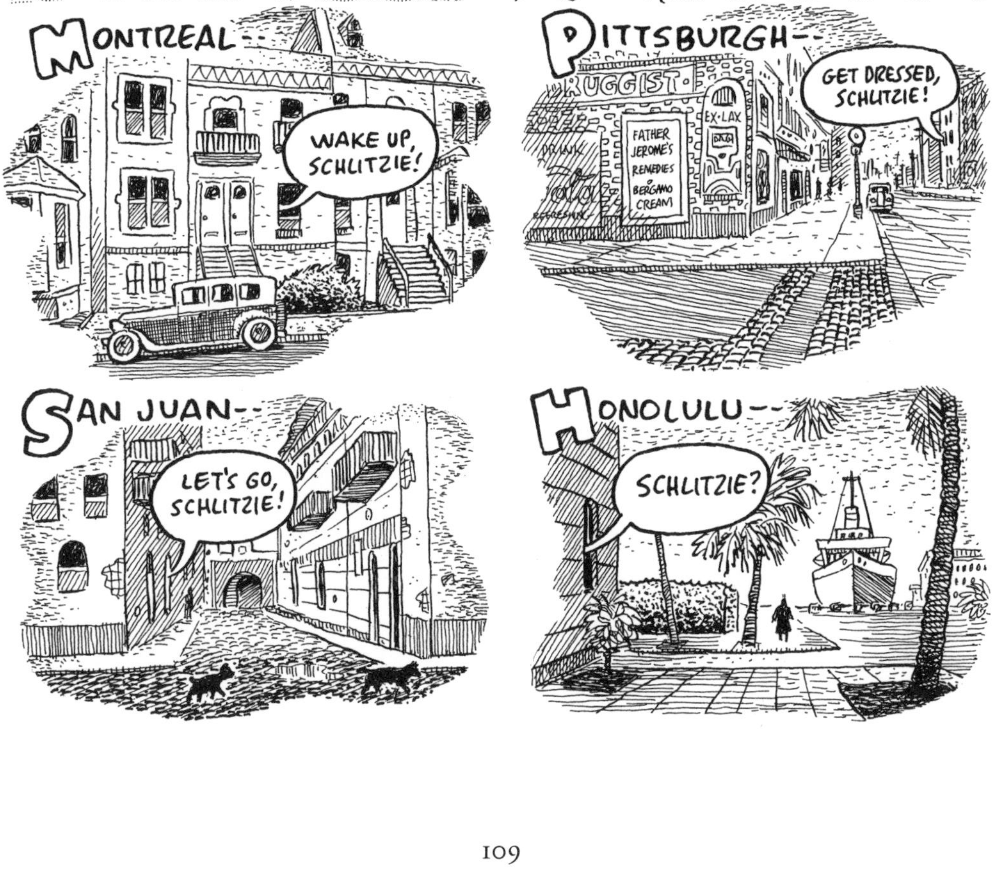

MONTREAL--
WAKE UP, SCHLITZIE!
PITTSBURGH--
RUGGIST
EX-LAX
FATHER JEROME'S REMEDIES
BERGAMO CREAM
GET DRESSED, SCHLITZIE!
SAN JUAN--
LET'S GO, SCHLITZIE!
HONOLULU--
SCHLITZIE?

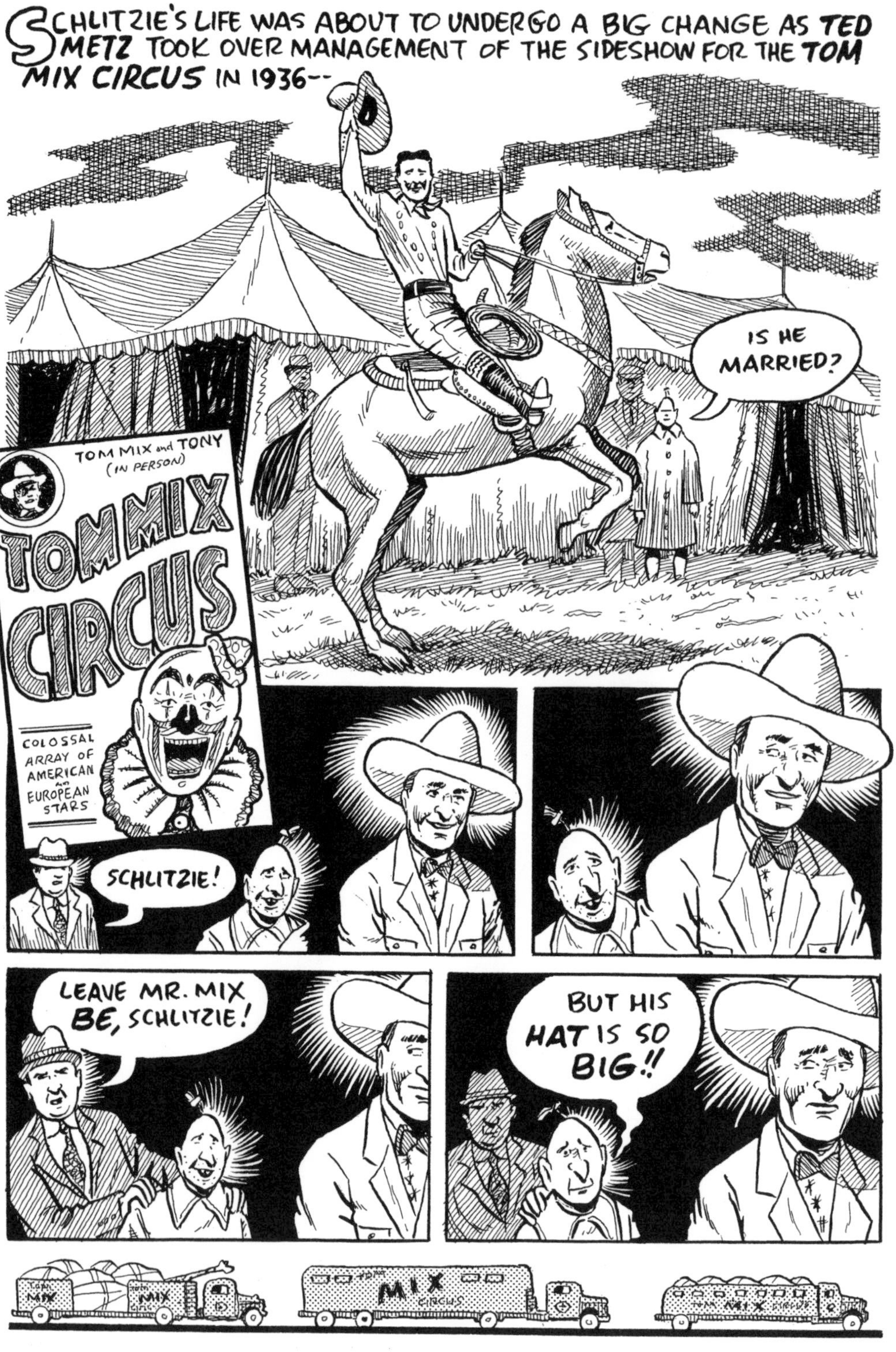
SCHLITZIE'S LIFE WAS ABOUT TO UNDERGO A BIG CHANGE AS TED METZ TOOK OVER MANAGEMENT OF THE SIDESHOW FOR THE TOM MIX CIRCUS IN 1936--
IS HE MARRIED?
TOM MIX and TONY (IN PERSON)
TOM MIX CIRCUS
COLOSSAL ARRAY OF AMERICAN AND EUROPEAN STARS
SCHLITZIE!
LEAVE MR. MIX BE, SCHLITZIE!
BUT HIS HAT IS SO BIG!!
MIX

DURING HIS YEARS WITH THE **TOM MIX CIRCUS**, SCHLITZIE PERFORMED ON THE SAME BILL WITH THE **CHIMPANZEE** ACT, **"SALLY & SAMMY"**, MANAGED AND TRAINED BY **GEORGE** AND **DODIE SURTEES**. ALSO IN THE **MIX** SIDESHOW WERE SNAKE CHARMER **EMILY MINTON**, MIND READER **FAY ASIA** & SWORD SWALLOWER, **LUCKY BALL**.

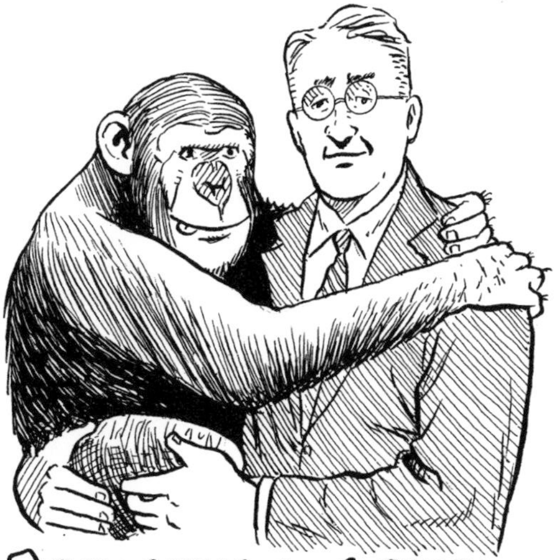

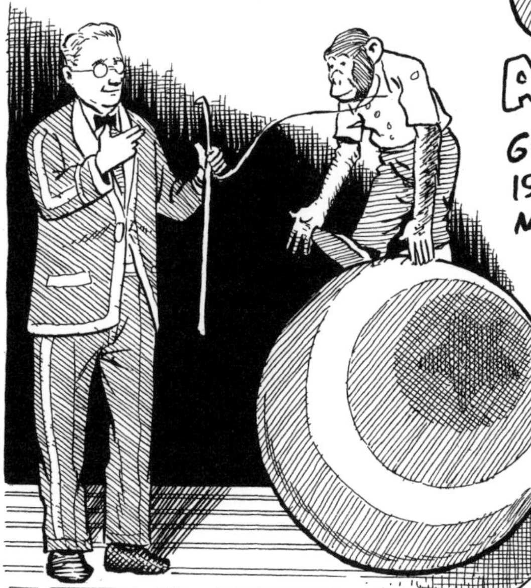

AT THIS TIME, THE **SURTEES** BECAME SCHLITZIE'S **LEGAL GUARDIANS**, ADOPTING HIM IN 1936 (SOME SOURCES SAY 1935). **METZ** OVERSAW THE SET-UP AND PERFORMANCES IN THE SIDESHOW, BUT THE **SURTEESES** EFFECTIVELY TOOK OVER AS SCHLITZIE'S NEW MANAGER--&"PARENTS."

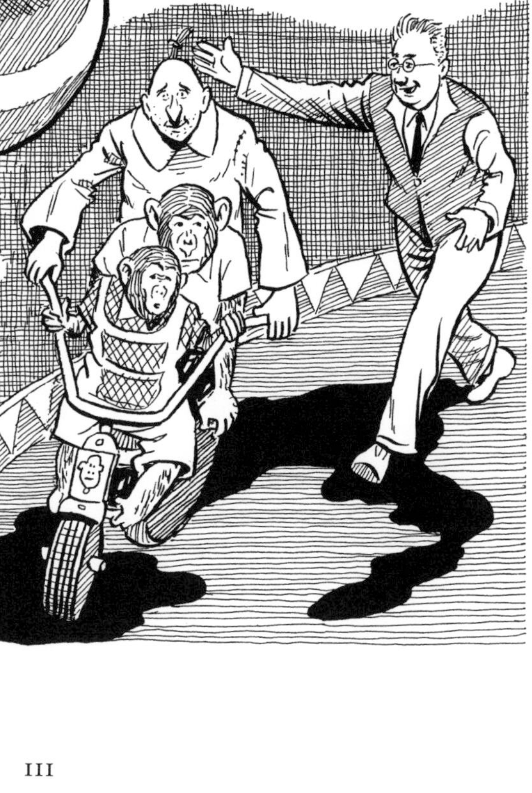

WHILE THERE'S NO DIRECT EVIDENCE THAT SCHLITZIE PERFORMED WITH **"SALLY & SAMMY,"** AT SOME POINT THEY WERE LIKELY ON STAGE TOGETHER AS THE **MIX CIRCUS** FOLLOWED A ROUTE FROM **TORONTO**, DOWN THROUGH **NEW ENGLAND**, ON TO **PHILADELPHIA**, **BALTIMORE**, **WASHINGTON, D.C.** & ACROSS THE **MIDWEST**, TO **CHICAGO**, **KANSAS CITY** &, FINALLY, TO **CALIFORNIA**.

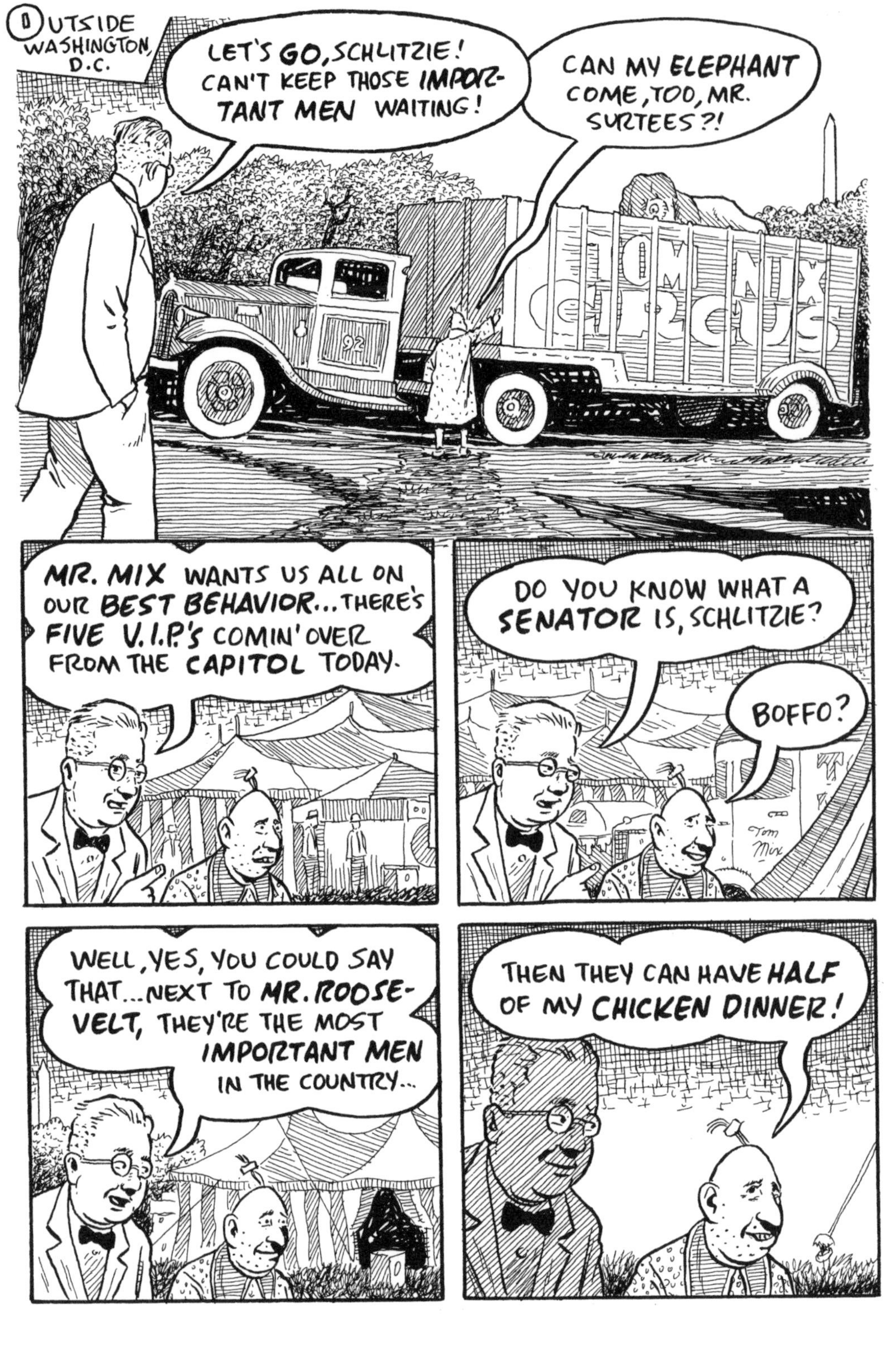
OUTSIDE WASHINGTON, D.C.
LET'S GO, SCHLITZIE! CAN'T KEEP THOSE IMPORTANT MEN WAITING!
CAN MY ELEPHANT COME, TOO, MR. SURTEES?!
TOM MIX CIRCUS
MR. MIX WANTS US ALL ON OUR BEST BEHAVIOR... THERE'S FIVE V.I.P.'S COMIN' OVER FROM THE CAPITOL TODAY.
DO YOU KNOW WHAT A SENATOR IS, SCHLITZIE?
BOFFO?
WELL, YES, YOU COULD SAY THAT... NEXT TO MR. ROOSEVELT, THEY'RE THE MOST IMPORTANT MEN IN THE COUNTRY...
THEN THEY CAN HAVE HALF OF MY CHICKEN DINNER!

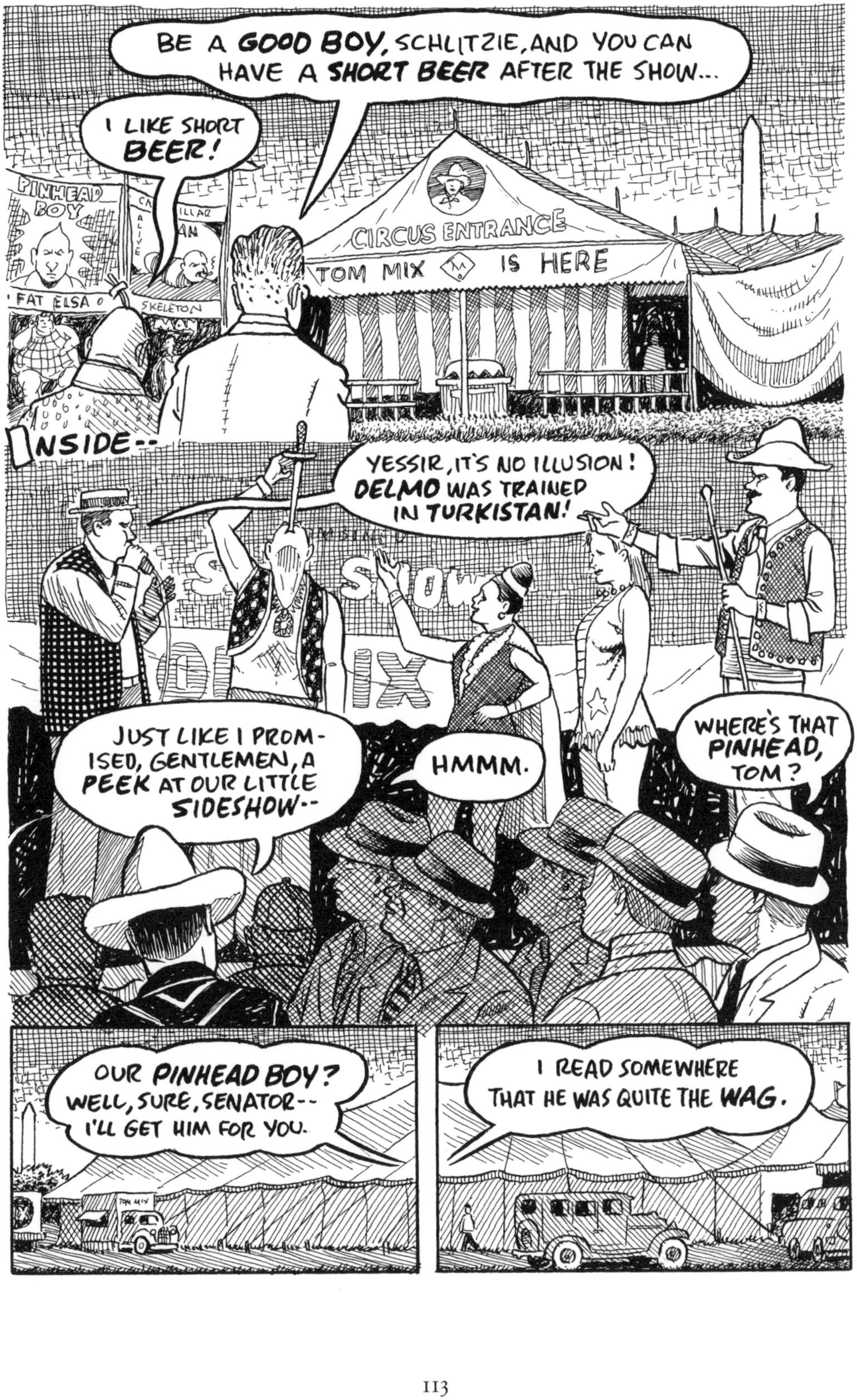
BE A GOOD BOY, SCHLITZIE, AND YOU CAN HAVE A SHORT BEER AFTER THE SHOW...
I LIKE SHORT BEER!
PINHEAD BOY
FAT ELSA
SKELETON
CIRCUS ENTRANCE
TOM MIX IS HERE
INSIDE--
YESSIR, IT'S NO ILLUSION! DELMO WAS TRAINED IN TURKISTAN!
JUST LIKE I PROMISED, GENTLEMEN, A PEEK AT OUR LITTLE SIDESHOW--
HMMM.
WHERE'S THAT PINHEAD, TOM?
OUR PINHEAD BOY? WELL, SURE, SENATOR-- I'LL GET HIM FOR YOU.
I READ SOMEWHERE THAT HE WAS QUITE THE WAG.

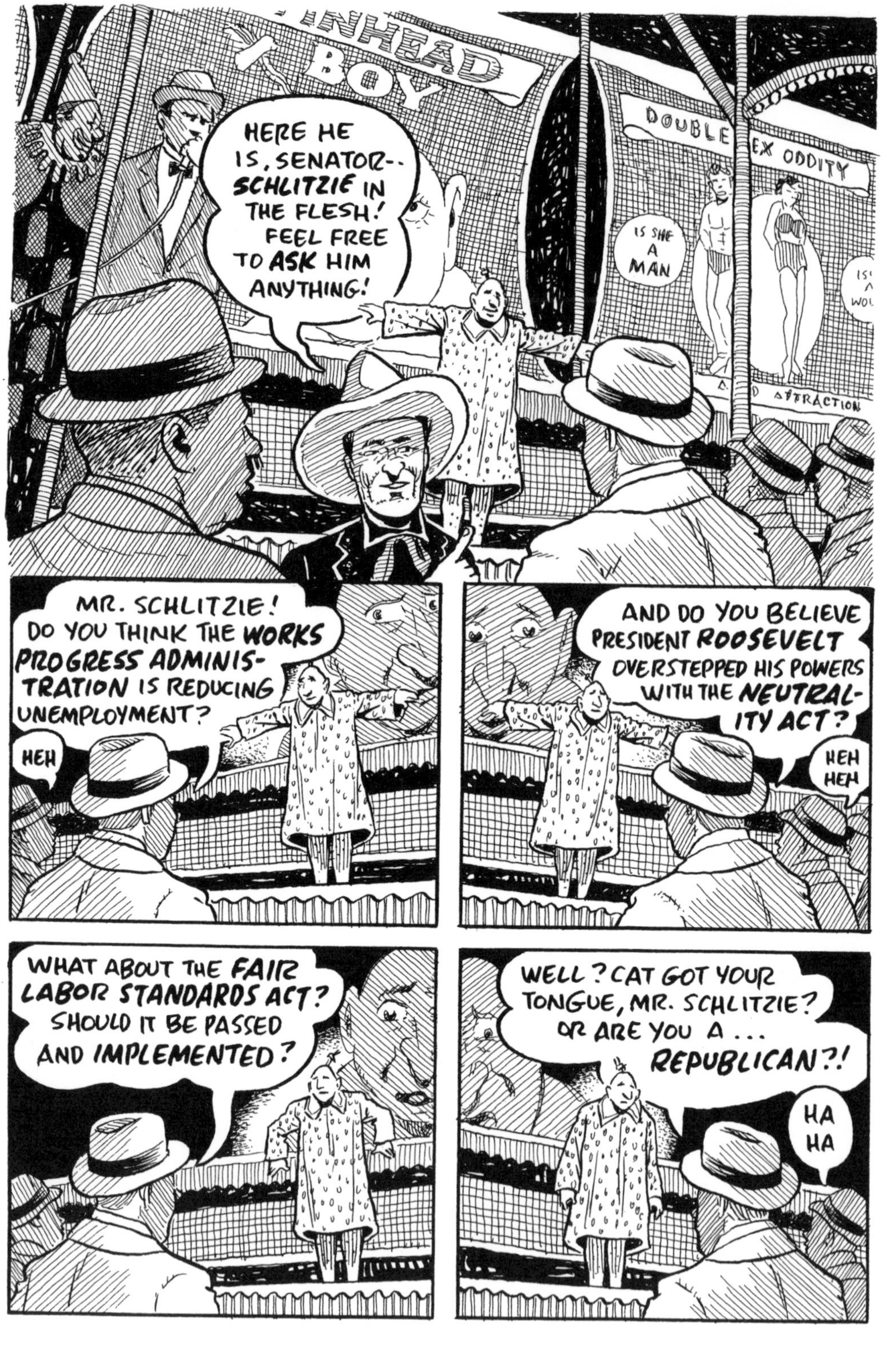
INHEAD BOY
DOUBLE EX ODDITY
HERE HE IS, SENATOR-- SCHLITZIE IN THE FLESH! FEEL FREE TO ASK HIM ANYTHING!
IS SHE A MAN
D ATTRACTION
MR. SCHLITZIE! DO YOU THINK THE WORKS PROGRESS ADMINISTRATION IS REDUCING UNEMPLOYMENT?
HEH
AND DO YOU BELIEVE PRESIDENT ROOSEVELT OVERSTEPPED HIS POWERS WITH THE NEUTRALITY ACT?
HEH HEH
WHAT ABOUT THE FAIR LABOR STANDARDS ACT? SHOULD IT BE PASSED AND IMPLEMENTED?
WELL? CAT GOT YOUR TONGUE, MR. SCHLITZIE? OR ARE YOU A ... REPUBLICAN?!
HA HA

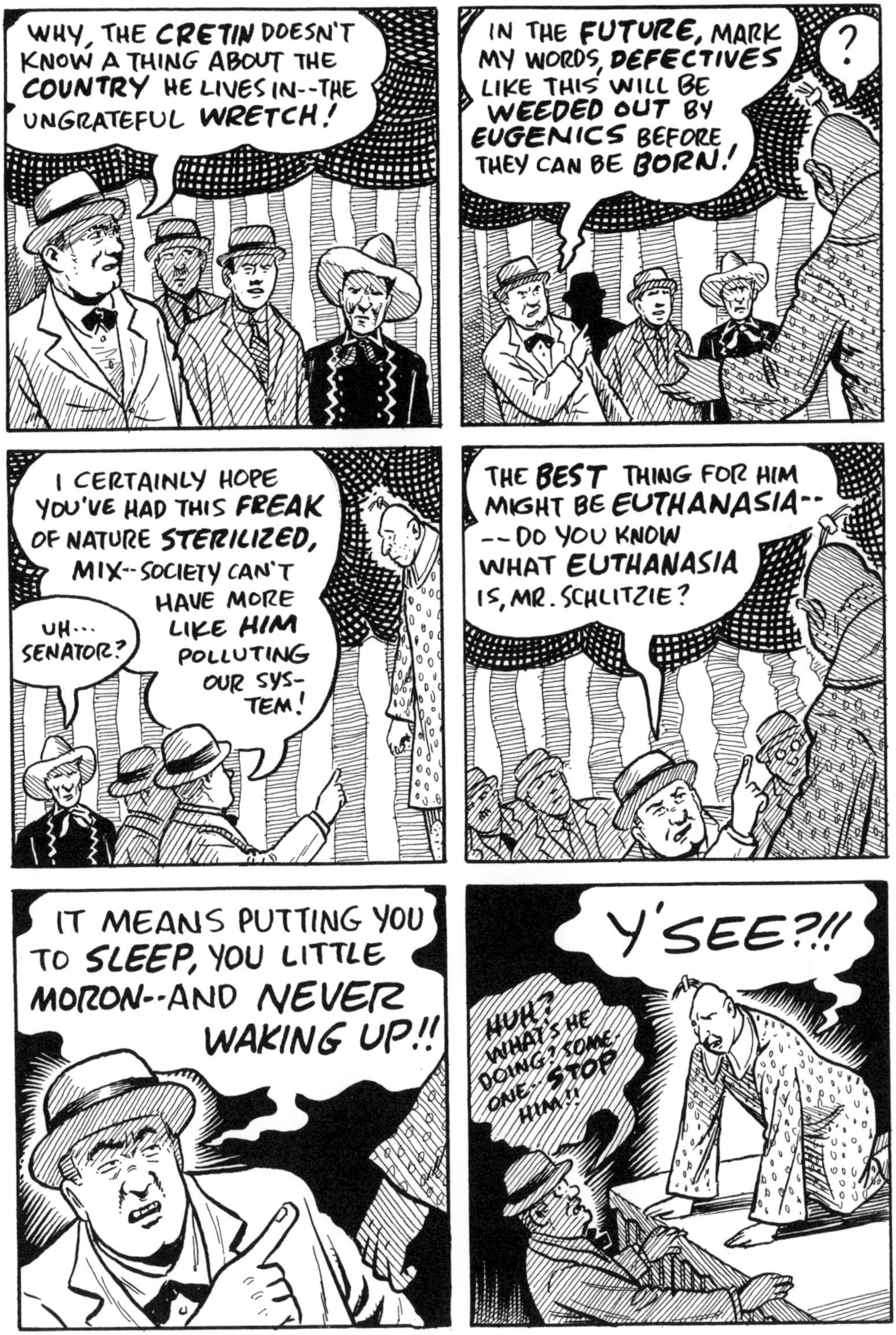
WHY, THE CRETIN DOESN'T KNOW A THING ABOUT THE COUNTRY HE LIVES IN--THE UNGRATEFUL WRETCH!
IN THE FUTURE, MARK MY WORDS, DEFECTIVES LIKE THIS WILL BE WEEDED OUT BY EUGENICS BEFORE THEY CAN BE BORN!
?
I CERTAINLY HOPE YOU'VE HAD THIS FREAK OF NATURE STERILIZED, MIX--SOCIETY CAN'T HAVE MORE LIKE HIM POLLUTING OUR SYS-TEM!
UH... SENATOR?
THE BEST THING FOR HIM MIGHT BE EUTHANASIA--
--DO YOU KNOW WHAT EUTHANASIA IS, MR. SCHLITZIE?
IT MEANS PUTTING YOU TO SLEEP, YOU LITTLE MORON--AND NEVER WAKING UP!!
Y'SEE?!!
HUH? WHAT'S HE DOING? SOME-ONE--STOP HIM!!

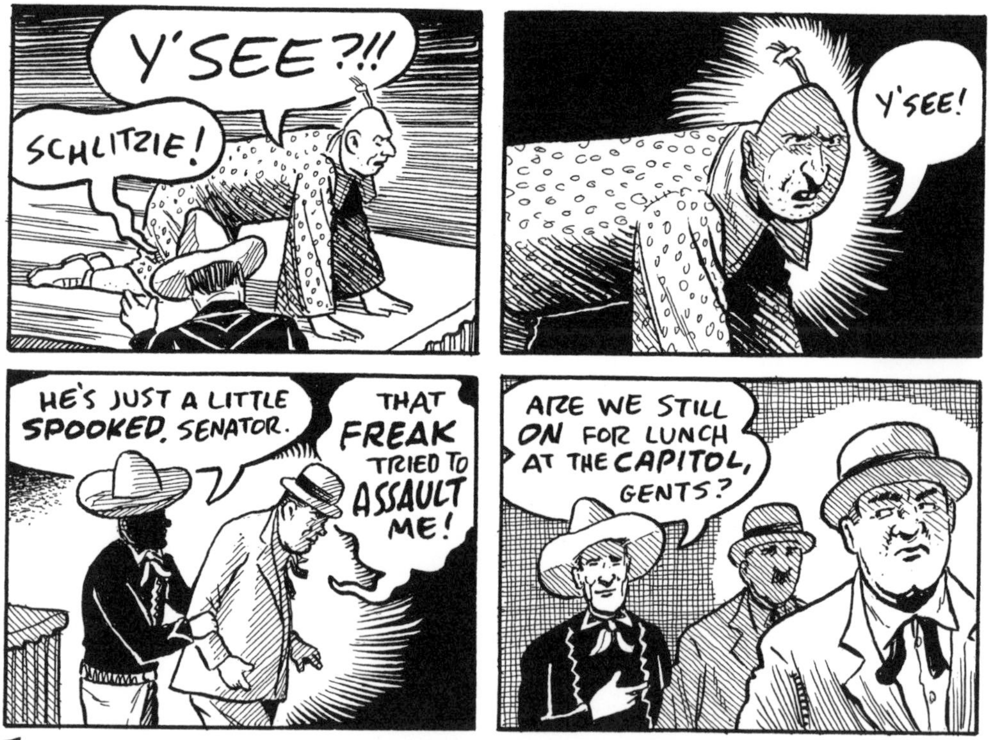
Y'SEE?!!
SCHLITZIE!
Y'SEE!
HE'S JUST A LITTLE SPOOKED, SENATOR.
THAT FREAK TRIED TO ASSAULT ME!
ARE WE STILL ON FOR LUNCH AT THE CAPITOL, GENTS?

LATER THAT YEAR, THE CIRCUS ARRIVED IN **IDAHO** FOR A TEN-DAY TOUR. BOISE, GLENNS FERRY & TWIN FALLS DREW LARGE CROWDS, ACCORDING TO THE 1937 ***CIRCUS ROUTE BOOK***, BUT AS THE ENTOURAGE REACHED **BURLEY**, DARKENING DUST CLOUDS GATHERED ON THE HORIZON.

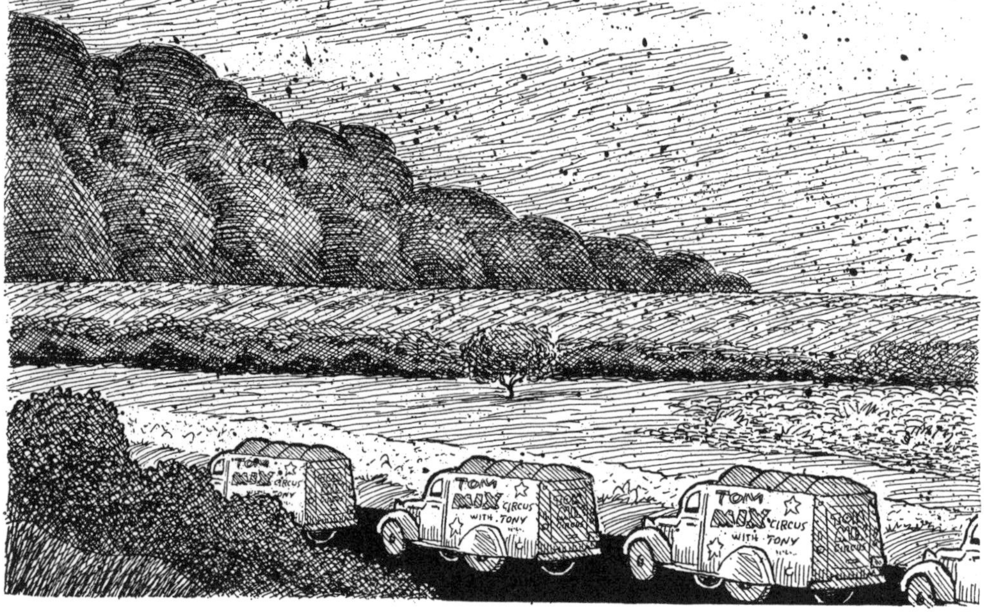
TOM MIX CIRCUS WITH TONY

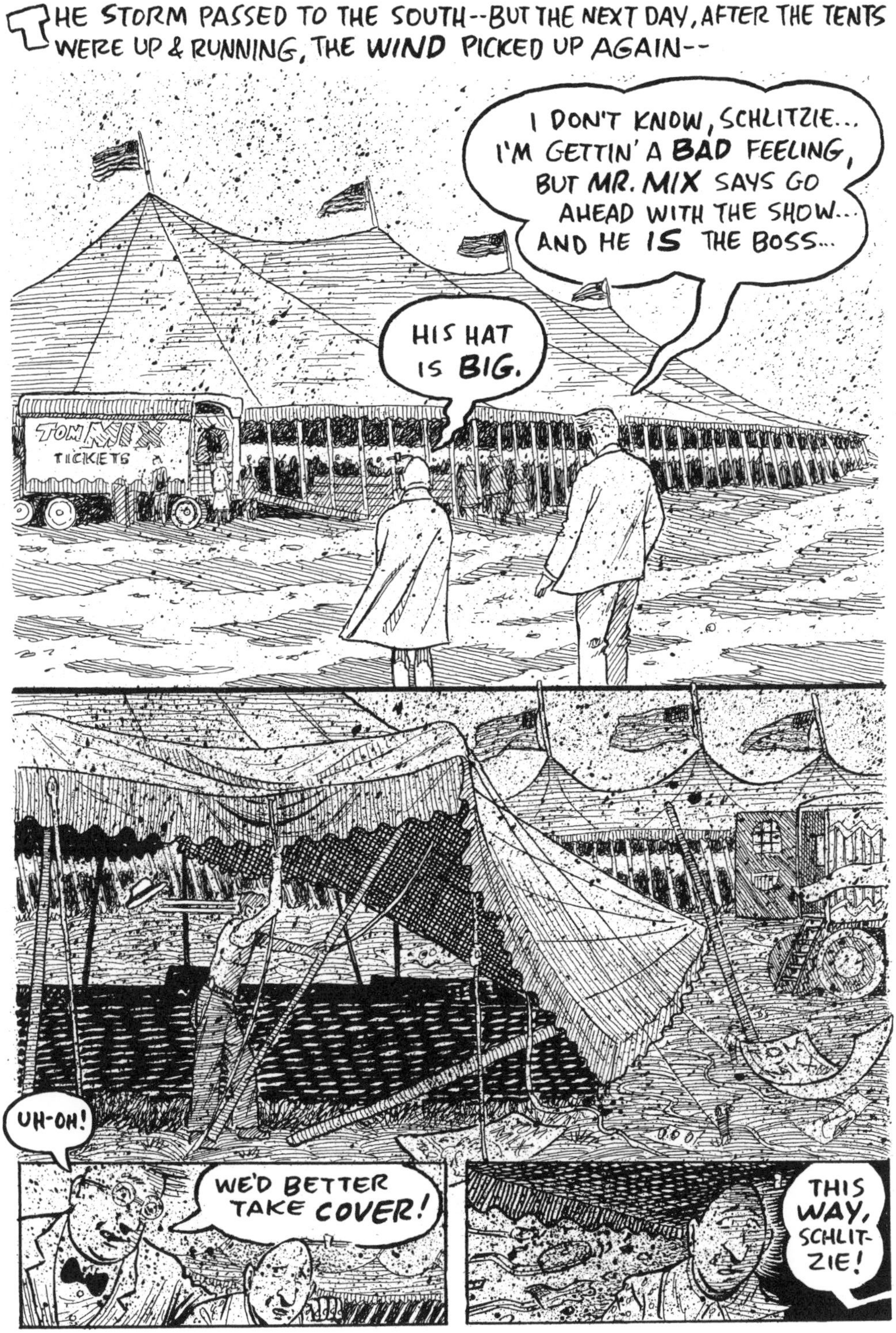
THE STORM PASSED TO THE SOUTH--BUT THE NEXT DAY, AFTER THE TENTS WERE UP & RUNNING, THE WIND PICKED UP AGAIN--
I DON'T KNOW, SCHLITZIE... I'M GETTIN' A BAD FEELING, BUT MR. MIX SAYS GO AHEAD WITH THE SHOW... AND HE IS THE BOSS...
HIS HAT IS BIG.
TOM MIX TICKETS
UH-OH!
WE'D BETTER TAKE COVER!
THIS WAY, SCHLITZIE!

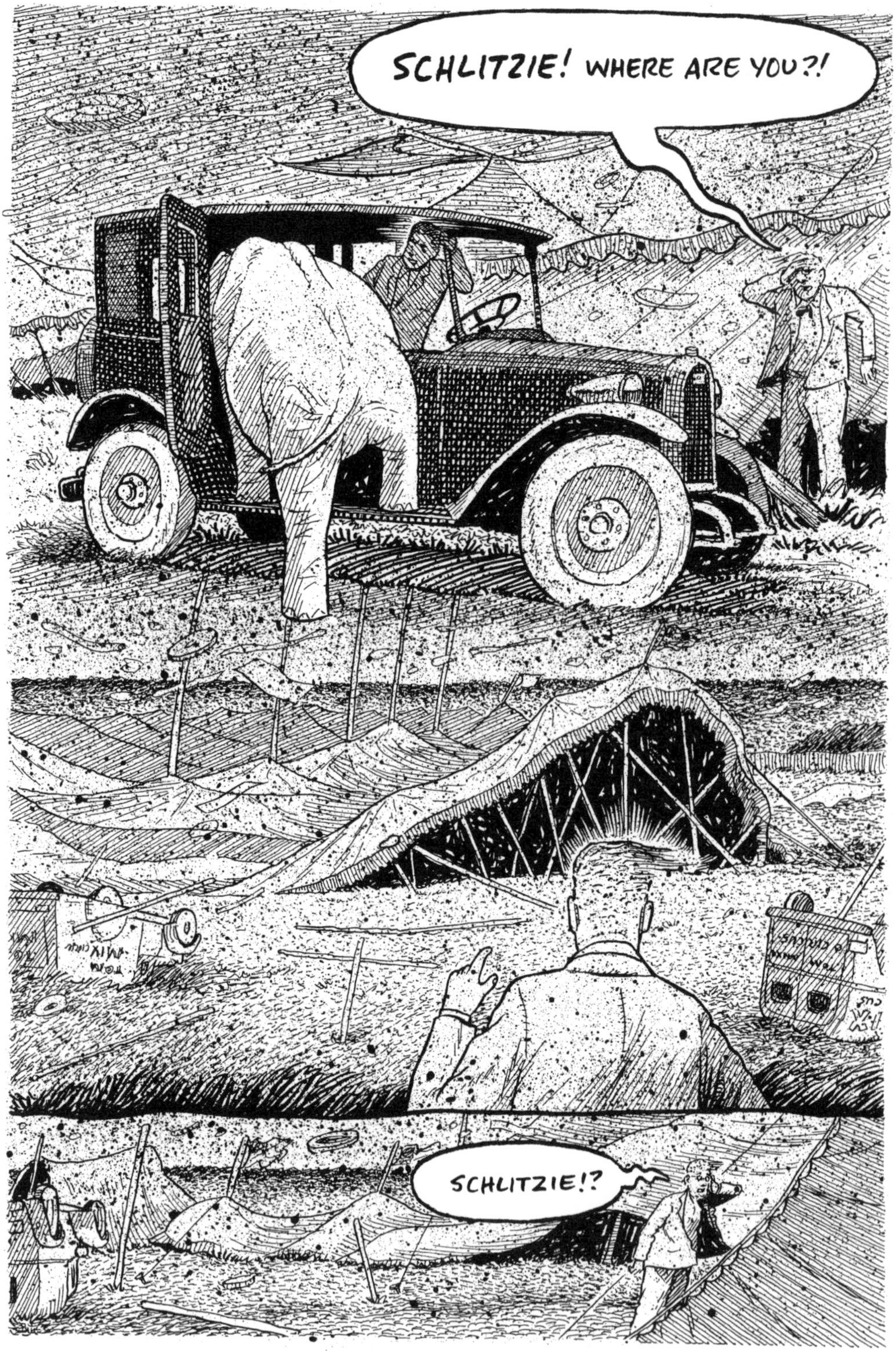
SCHLITZIE! WHERE ARE YOU?!
SCHLITZIE!?

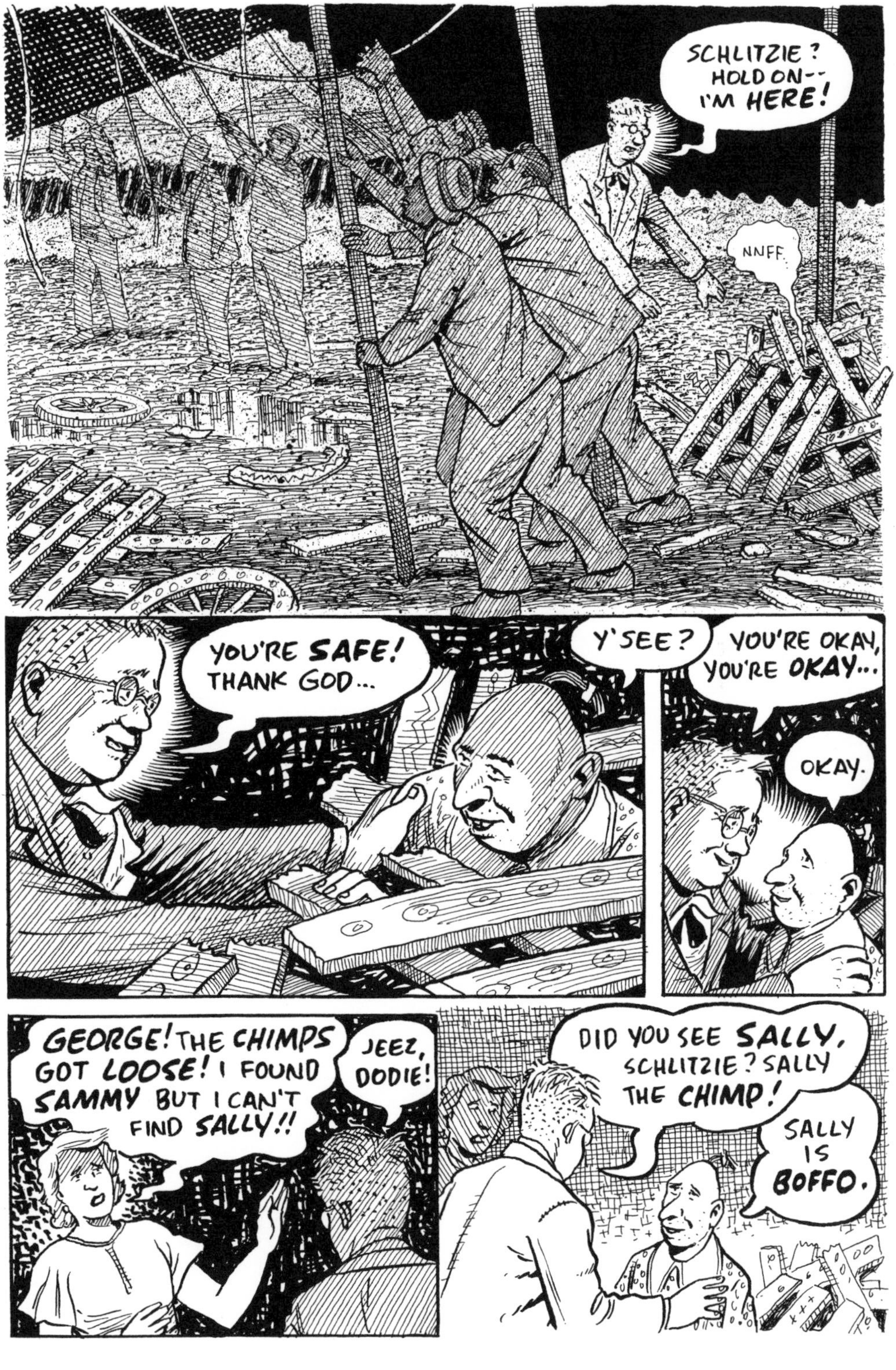
SCHLITZIE? HOLD ON-- I'M HERE!
NNFF.
YOU'RE SAFE! THANK GOD...
Y'SEE?
YOU'RE OKAY, YOU'RE OKAY...
OKAY.
GEORGE! THE CHIMPS GOT LOOSE! I FOUND SAMMY BUT I CAN'T FIND SALLY!!
JEEZ, DODIE!
DID YOU SEE SALLY, SCHLITZIE? SALLY THE CHIMP!
SALLY IS BOFFO.

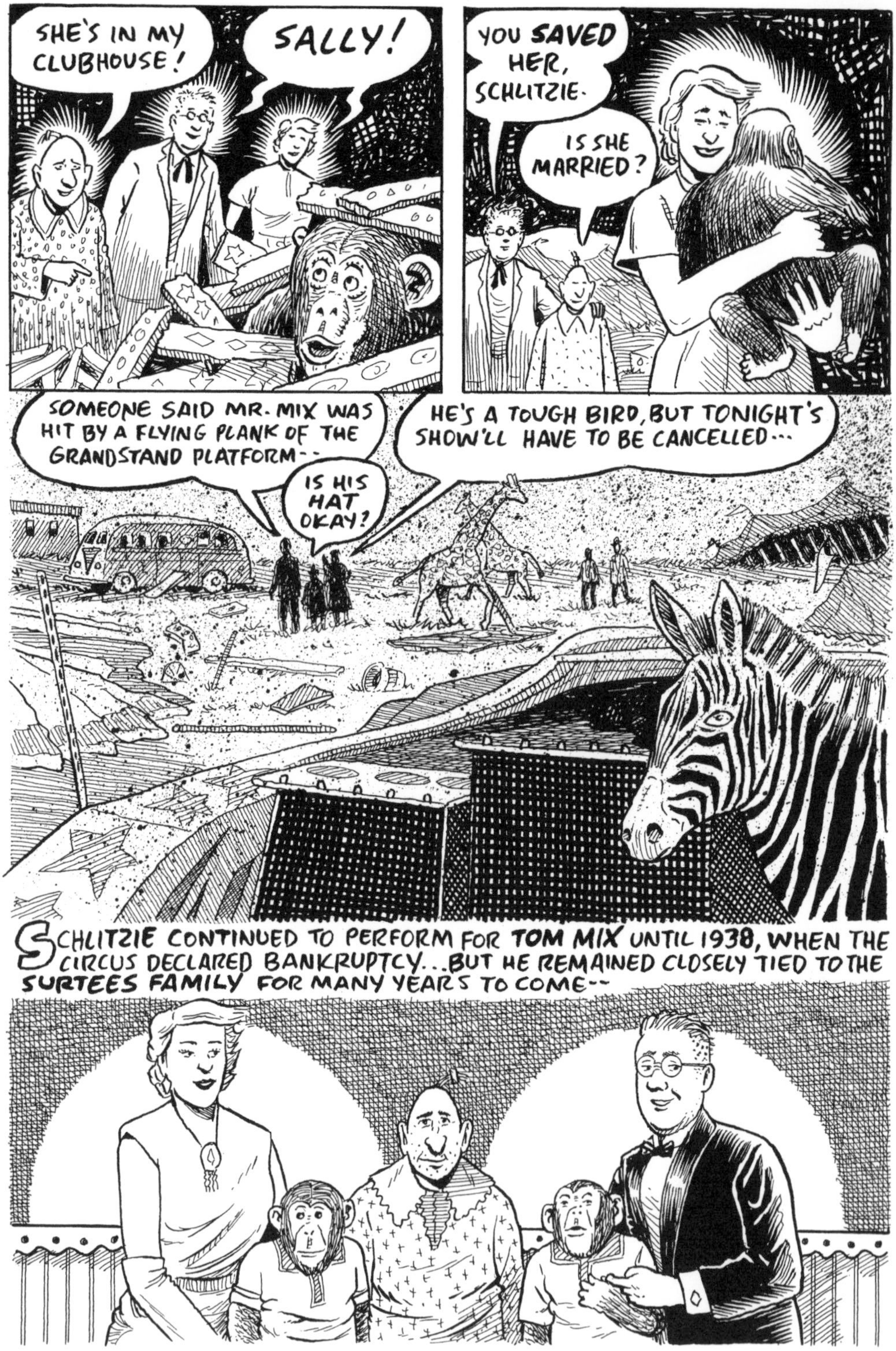
SHE'S IN MY CLUBHOUSE!
SALLY!
YOU SAVED HER, SCHLITZIE.
IS SHE MARRIED?
SOMEONE SAID MR. MIX WAS HIT BY A FLYING PLANK OF THE GRANDSTAND PLATFORM--
IS HIS HAT OKAY?
HE'S A TOUGH BIRD, BUT TONIGHT'S SHOW'LL HAVE TO BE CANCELLED...
SCHLITZIE CONTINUED TO PERFORM FOR TOM MIX UNTIL 1938, WHEN THE CIRCUS DECLARED BANKRUPTCY...BUT HE REMAINED CLOSELY TIED TO THE SURTEES FAMILY FOR MANY YEARS TO COME--

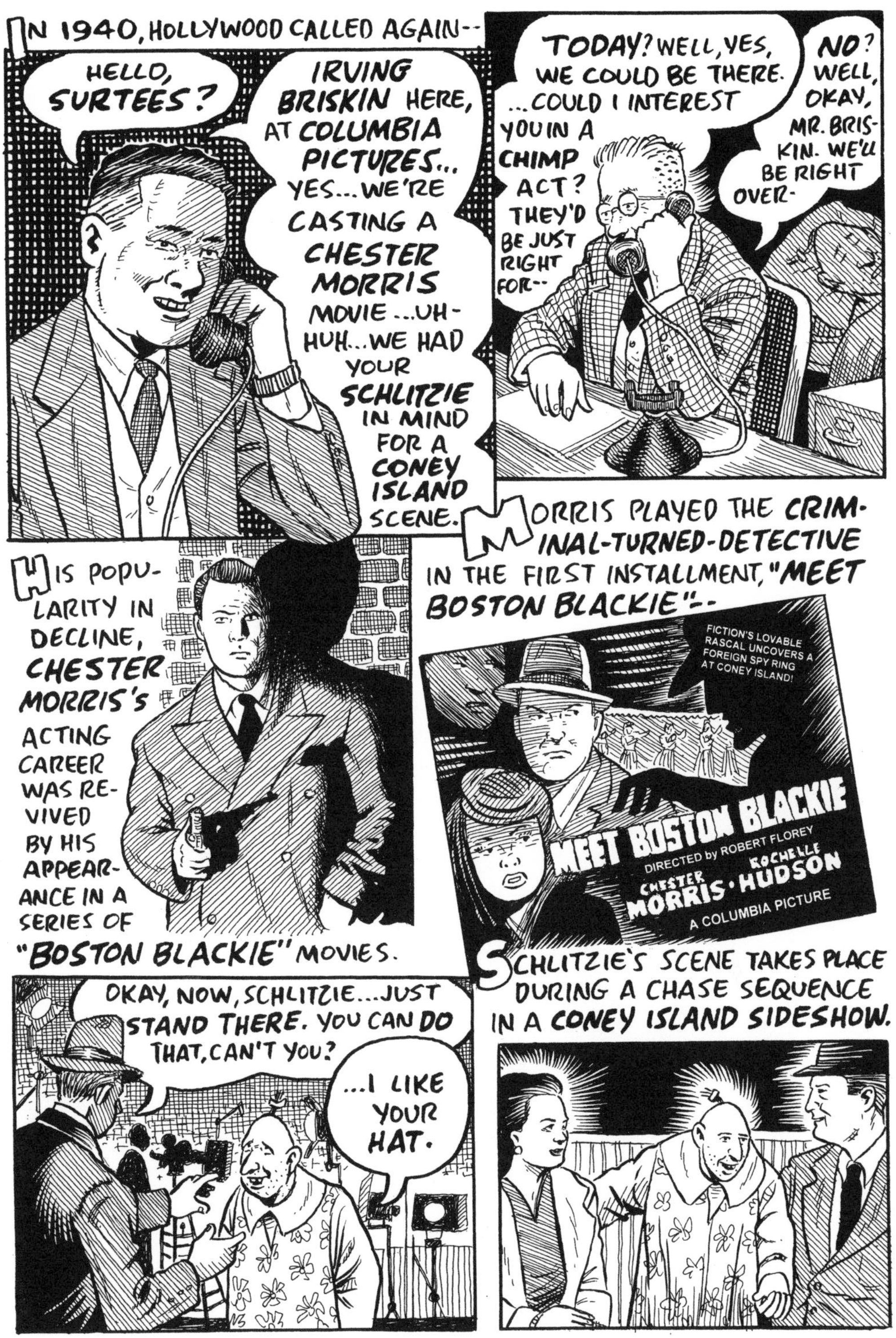
In 1940, Hollywood called again--
Hello, Surtees?
Irving Briskin here, at Columbia Pictures... yes... we're casting a Chester Morris movie... uh-huh... we had your Schlitzie in mind for a Coney Island scene.
Today? Well, yes, we could be there. ...Could I interest you in a chimp act? They'd be just right for--
No? Well, okay, Mr. Briskin. We'll be right over-
His popularity in decline, Chester Morris's acting career was revived by his appearance in a series of "Boston Blackie" movies.
Morris played the criminal-turned-detective in the first installment, "Meet Boston Blackie"--
FICTION'S LOVABLE RASCAL UNCOVERS A FOREIGN SPY RING AT CONEY ISLAND!
MEET BOSTON BLACKIE
DIRECTED by ROBERT FLOREY
CHESTER MORRIS · ROCHELLE HUDSON
A COLUMBIA PICTURE
Okay, now, Schlitzie... just stand there. You can do that, can't you?
...I like your hat.
Schlitzie's scene takes place during a chase sequence in a Coney Island sideshow.

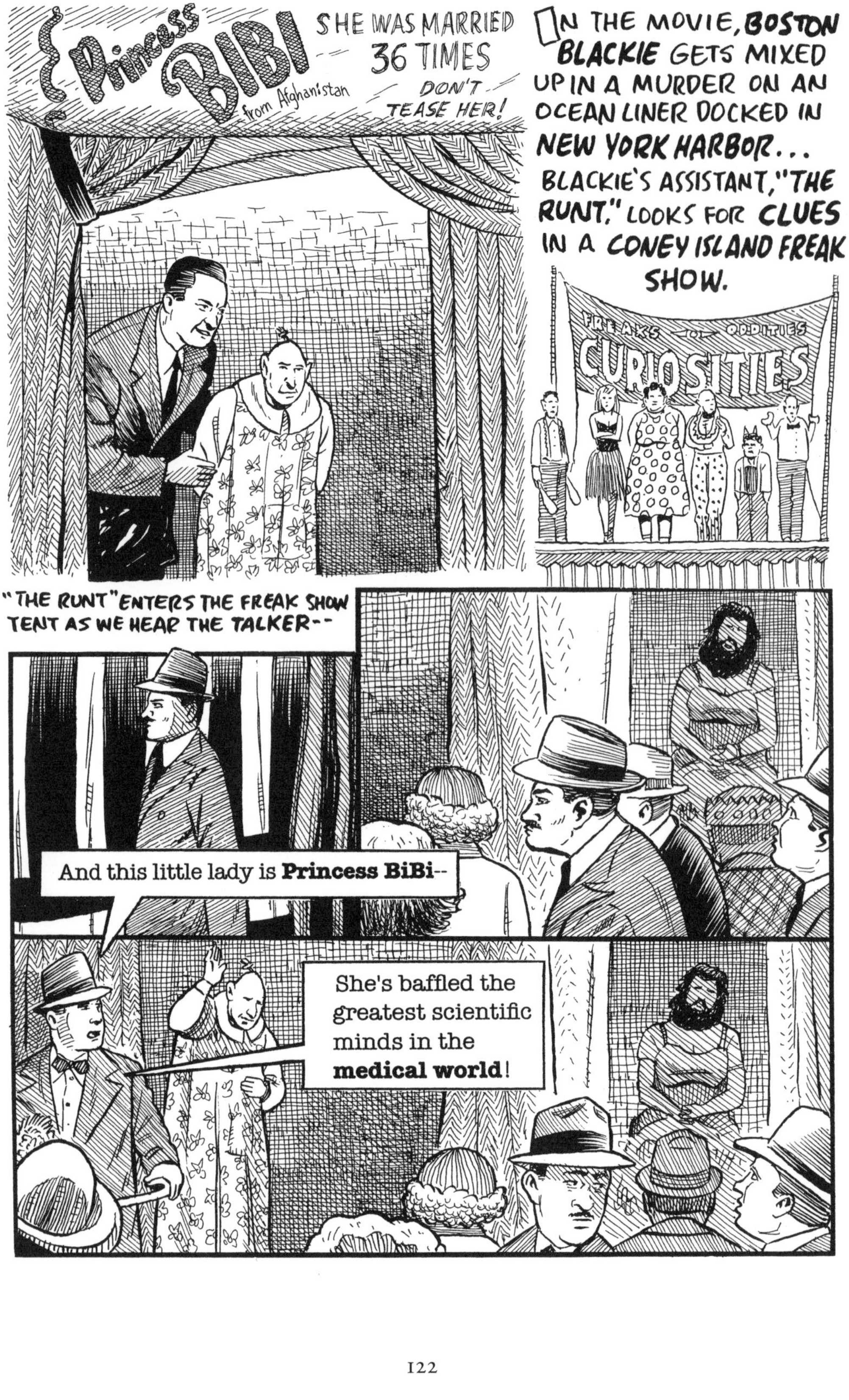

Princess BIBI from Afghanistan
SHE WAS MARRIED 36 TIMES
DON'T TEASE HER!
IN THE MOVIE, BOSTON BLACKIE GETS MIXED UP IN A MURDER ON AN OCEAN LINER DOCKED IN NEW YORK HARBOR... BLACKIE'S ASSISTANT, "THE RUNT," LOOKS FOR CLUES IN A CONEY ISLAND FREAK SHOW.
FREAKS ODDITIES
CURIOSITIES
"THE RUNT" ENTERS THE FREAK SHOW TENT AS WE HEAR THE TALKER--
And this little lady is **Princess BiBi**--
She's baffled the greatest scientific minds in the **medical world**!

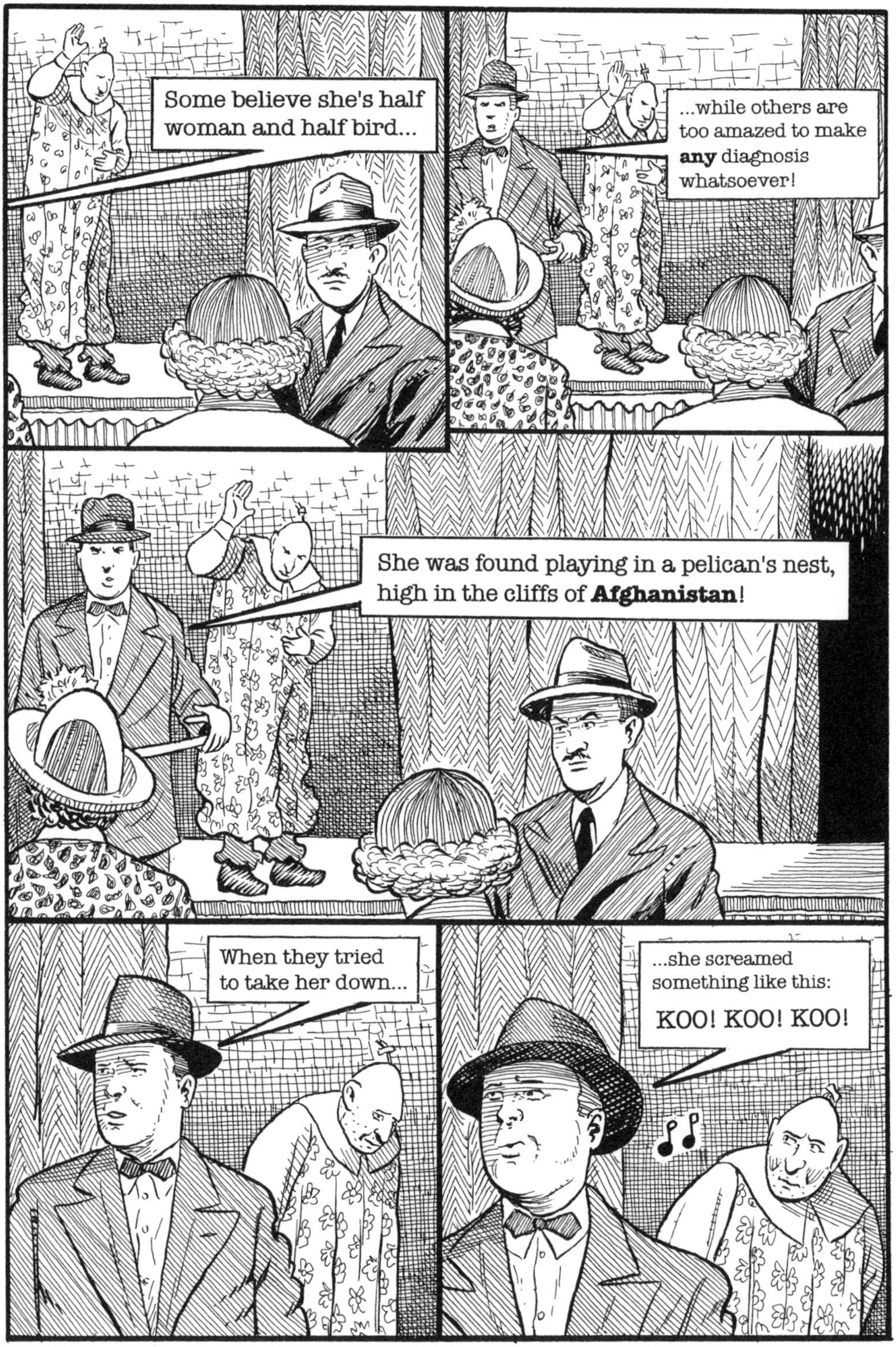
Some believe she's half woman and half bird...
...while others are too amazed to make **any** diagnosis whatsoever!
She was found playing in a pelican's nest, high in the cliffs of **Afghanistan**!
When they tried to take her down...
...she screamed something like this:
KOO! KOO! KOO!

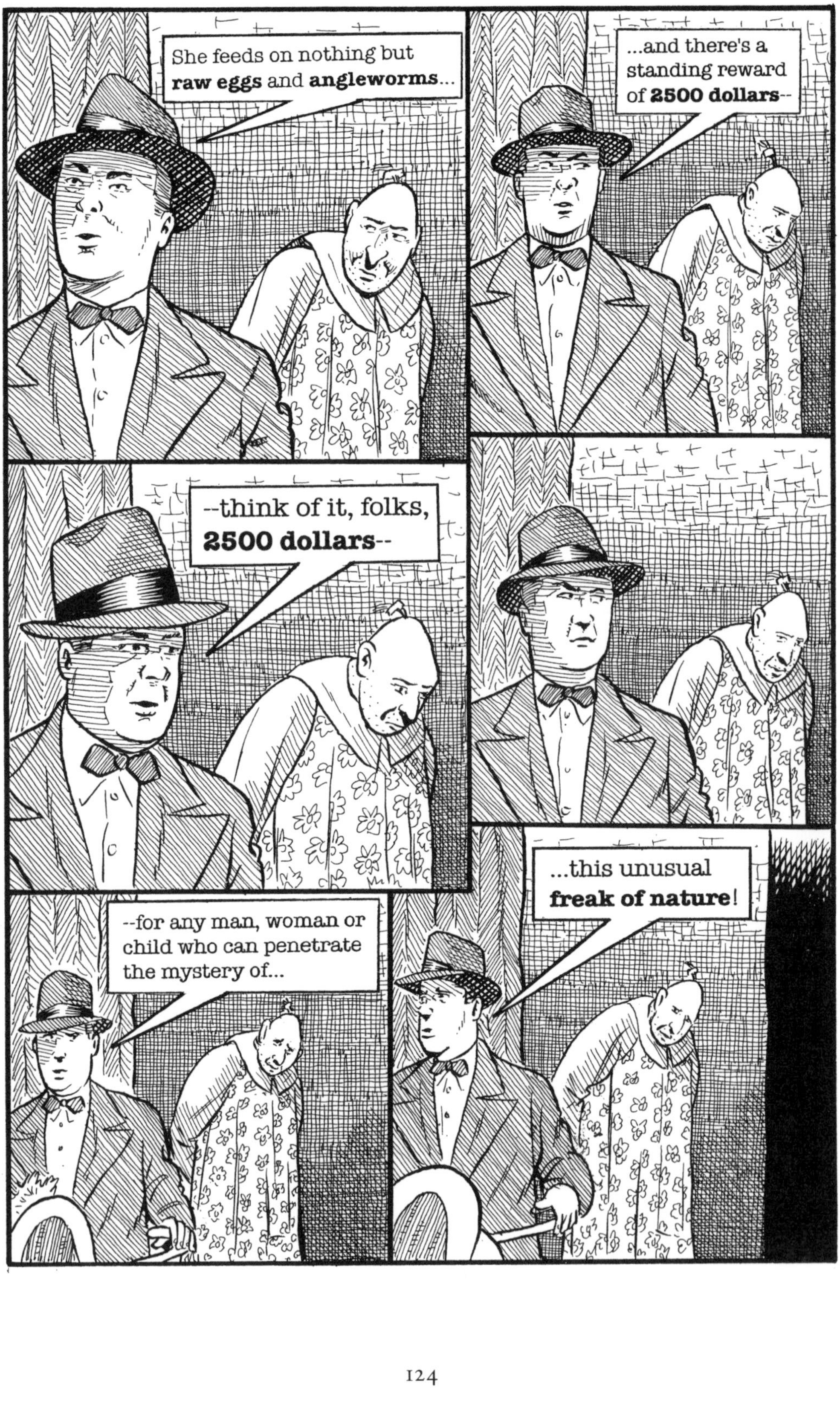
She feeds on nothing but **raw eggs** and **angleworms**...
...and there's a standing reward of **2500 dollars**--
--think of it, folks, **2500 dollars**--
--for any man, woman or child who can penetrate the mystery of...
...this unusual **freak of nature**!

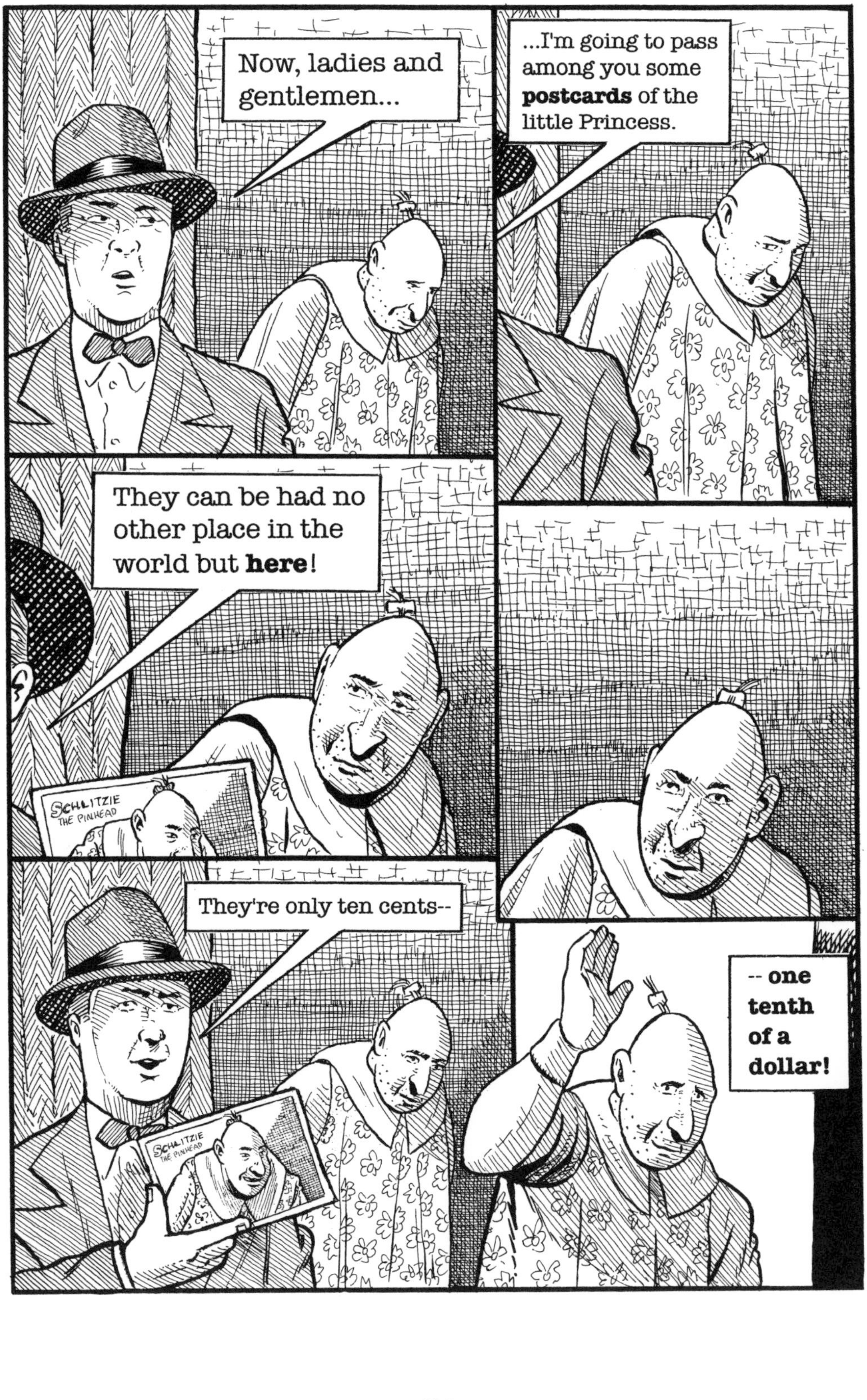
Now, ladies and gentlemen...
...I'm going to pass among you some **postcards** of the little Princess.
They can be had no other place in the world but **here**!
SCHLITZIE THE PINHEAD
They're only ten cents--
SCHLITZIE THE PINHEAD
-- one tenth of a dollar!

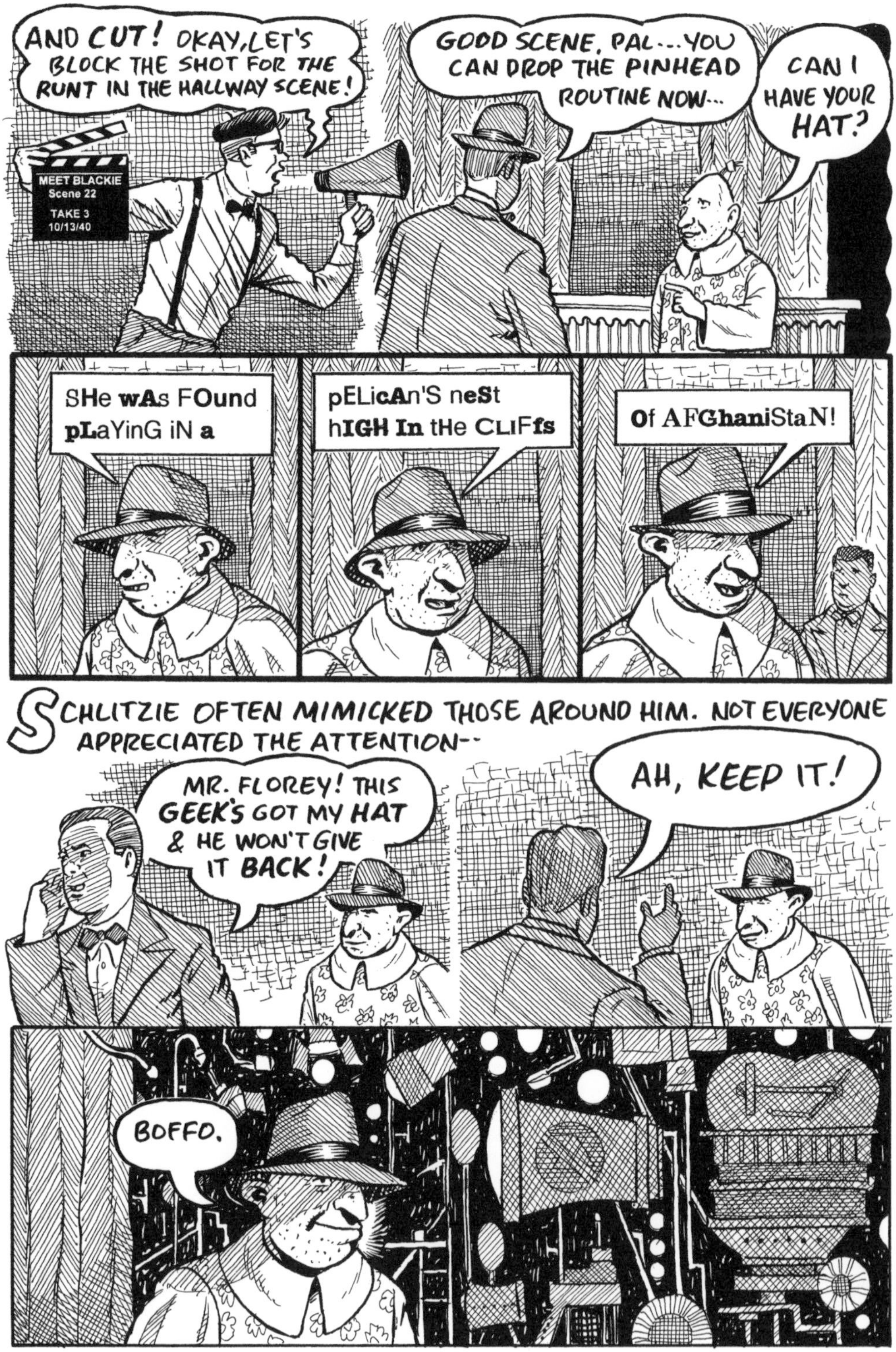
AND CUT! OKAY, LET'S BLOCK THE SHOT FOR THE RUNT IN THE HALLWAY SCENE!
MEET BLACKIE
Scene 22
TAKE 3
10/13/40
GOOD SCENE, PAL...YOU CAN DROP THE PINHEAD ROUTINE NOW...
CAN I HAVE YOUR HAT?
SHe wAs FOund pLaYinG iN a
pELicAn'S neSt hIGH In tHe CLiFfs
Of AFGhaniStaN!
SCHLITZIE OFTEN MIMICKED THOSE AROUND HIM. NOT EVERYONE APPRECIATED THE ATTENTION--
MR. FLOREY! THIS GEEK'S GOT MY HAT & HE WON'T GIVE IT BACK!
AH, KEEP IT!
BOFFO.

SIDESHOWS MAY HAVE PEAKED IN POPULAR FAVOR IN THE 1920S, BUT THEY STILL DREW LARGE CROWDS--AS WELL AS THE OCCASIONAL **RUN-IN** WITH THE LOCAL SHERIFF. STILL GOING STRONG IN 1946, SCHLITZIE TOURED THE SOUTH WITH A NEW ROSTER OF FELLOW PERFORMERS: SWORD SWALLOWER **MIMI GARNEAU,** THREE-LEGGED MAN **FRANK LENTINI,** AND **GRADY STILES,** THE "LOBSTER BOY"--

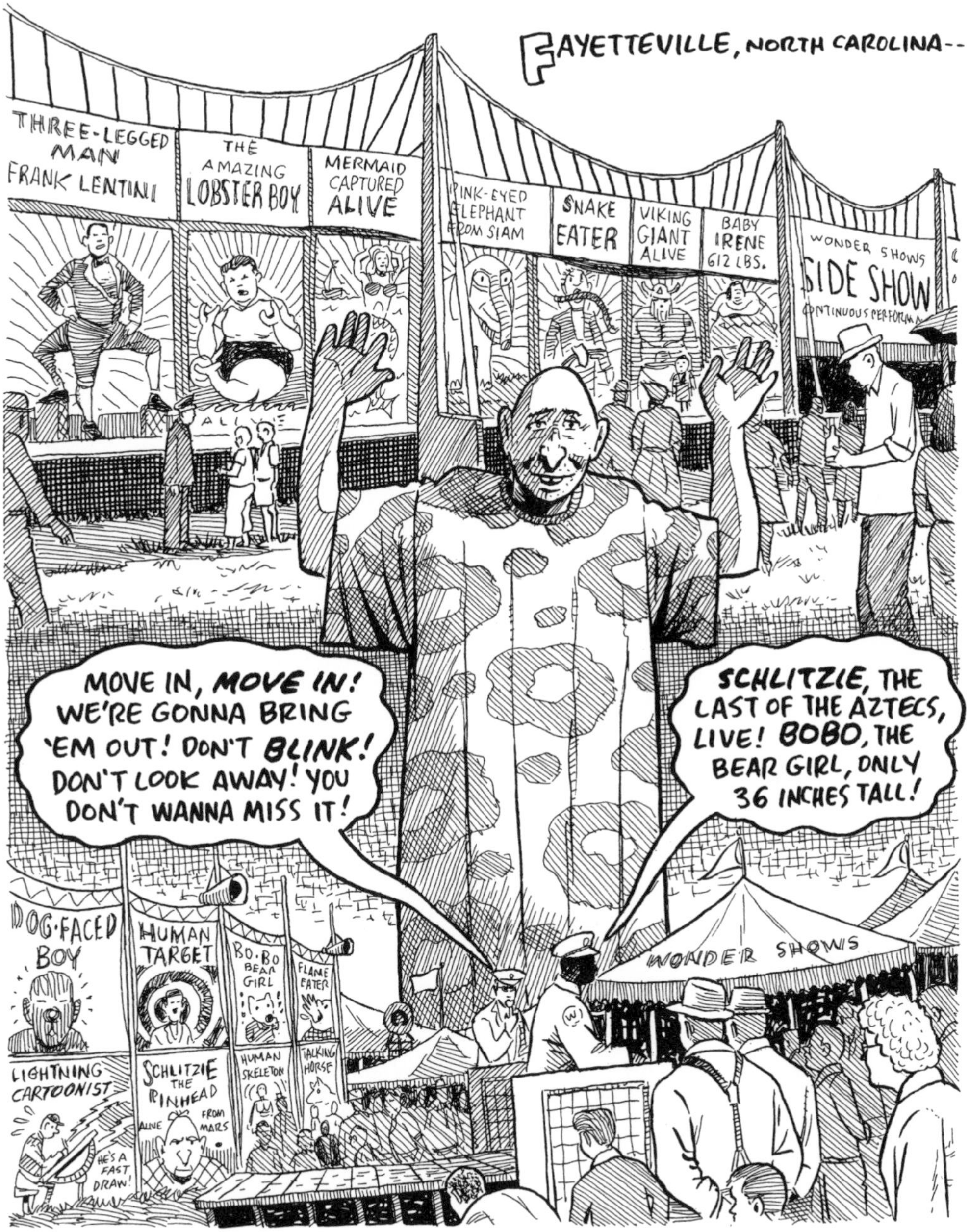
FAYETTEVILLE, NORTH CAROLINA--
THREE-LEGGED MAN FRANK LENTINI
THE AMAZING LOBSTER BOY
MERMAID CAPTURED ALIVE
PINK-EYED ELEPHANT FROM SIAM
SNAKE EATER
VIKING GIANT ALIVE
BABY IRENE 612 LBS.
WONDER SHOWS SIDE SHOW
MOVE IN, MOVE IN! WE'RE GONNA BRING 'EM OUT! DON'T BLINK! DON'T LOOK AWAY! YOU DON'T WANNA MISS IT!
SCHLITZIE, THE LAST OF THE AZTECS, LIVE! BOBO, THE BEAR GIRL, ONLY 36 INCHES TALL!
DOG-FACED BOY
HUMAN TARGET
BO-BO BEAR GIRL
FLAME EATER
LIGHTNING CARTOONIST
HE'S A FAST DRAW!
SCHLITZIE THE PINHEAD ALIVE FROM MARS
HUMAN SKELETON
TALKING HORSE
WONDER SHOWS

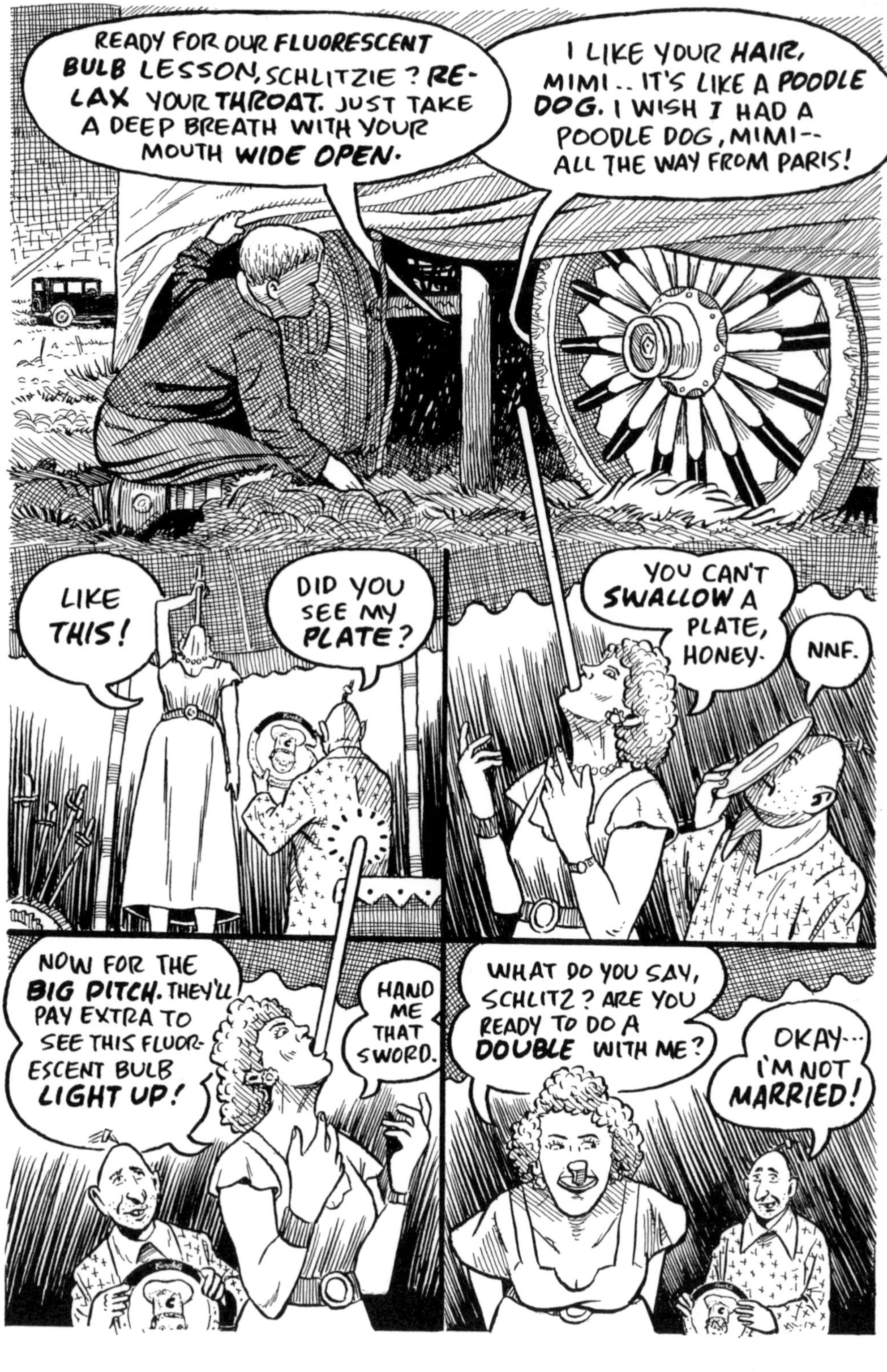
READY FOR OUR FLUORESCENT BULB LESSON, SCHLITZIE? RE-LAX YOUR THROAT. JUST TAKE A DEEP BREATH WITH YOUR MOUTH WIDE OPEN.
I LIKE YOUR HAIR, MIMI.. IT'S LIKE A POODLE DOG. I WISH I HAD A POODLE DOG, MIMI-- ALL THE WAY FROM PARIS!
LIKE THIS!
DID YOU SEE MY PLATE?
YOU CAN'T SWALLOW A PLATE, HONEY.
NNF.
NOW FOR THE BIG PITCH. THEY'LL PAY EXTRA TO SEE THIS FLUOR-ESCENT BULB LIGHT UP!
HAND ME THAT SWORD.
WHAT DO YOU SAY, SCHLITZ? ARE YOU READY TO DO A DOUBLE WITH ME?
OKAY... I'M NOT MARRIED!

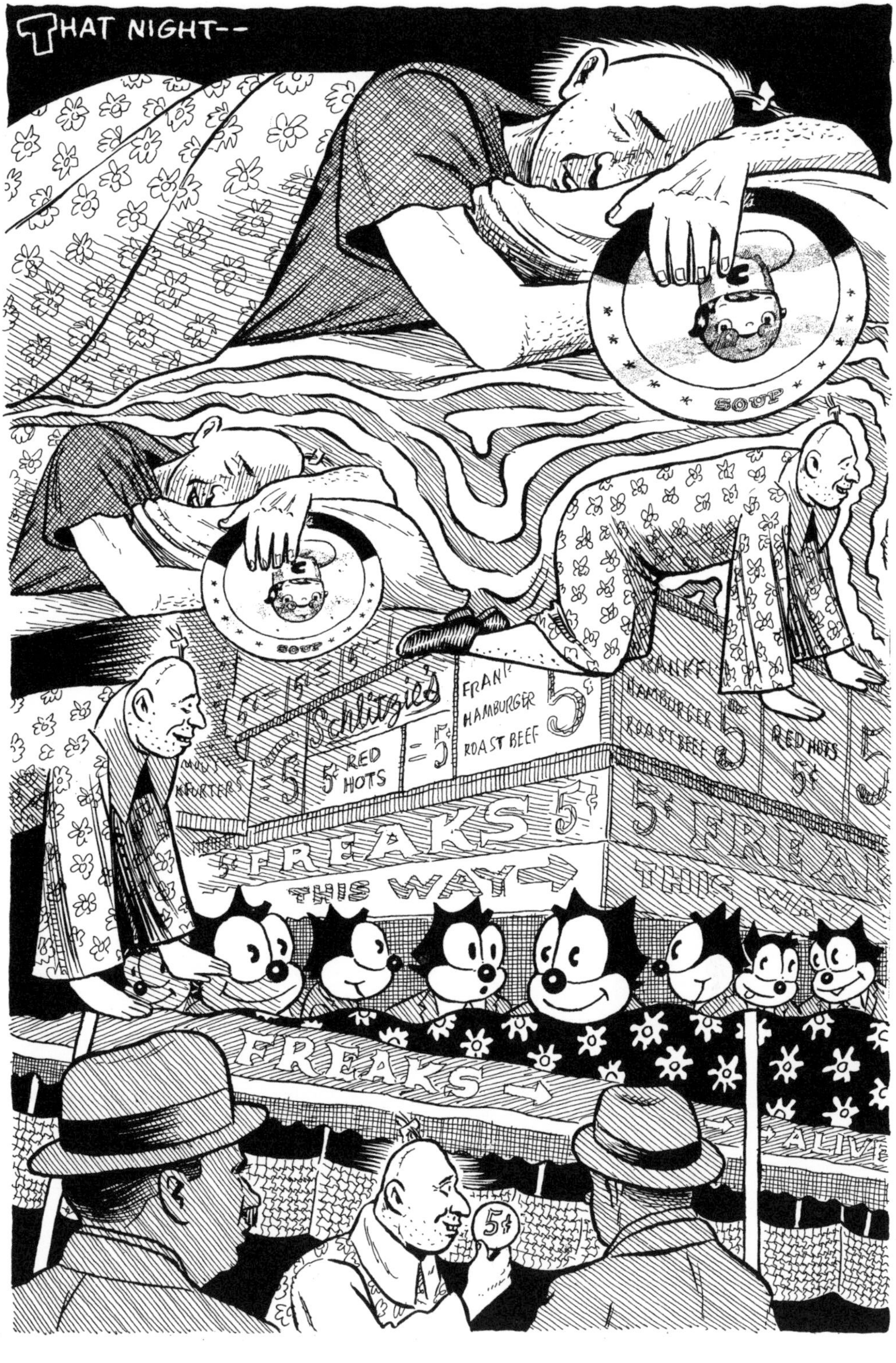
THAT NIGHT--
SOUP
SOUP
Schlitzie's
RED HOTS
FRANK
HAMBURGER
ROAST BEEF
HAMBURGER
ROAST BEEF
RED HOTS
FREAKS
FREAKS
THIS WAY
FREAKS
ALIVE
5¢

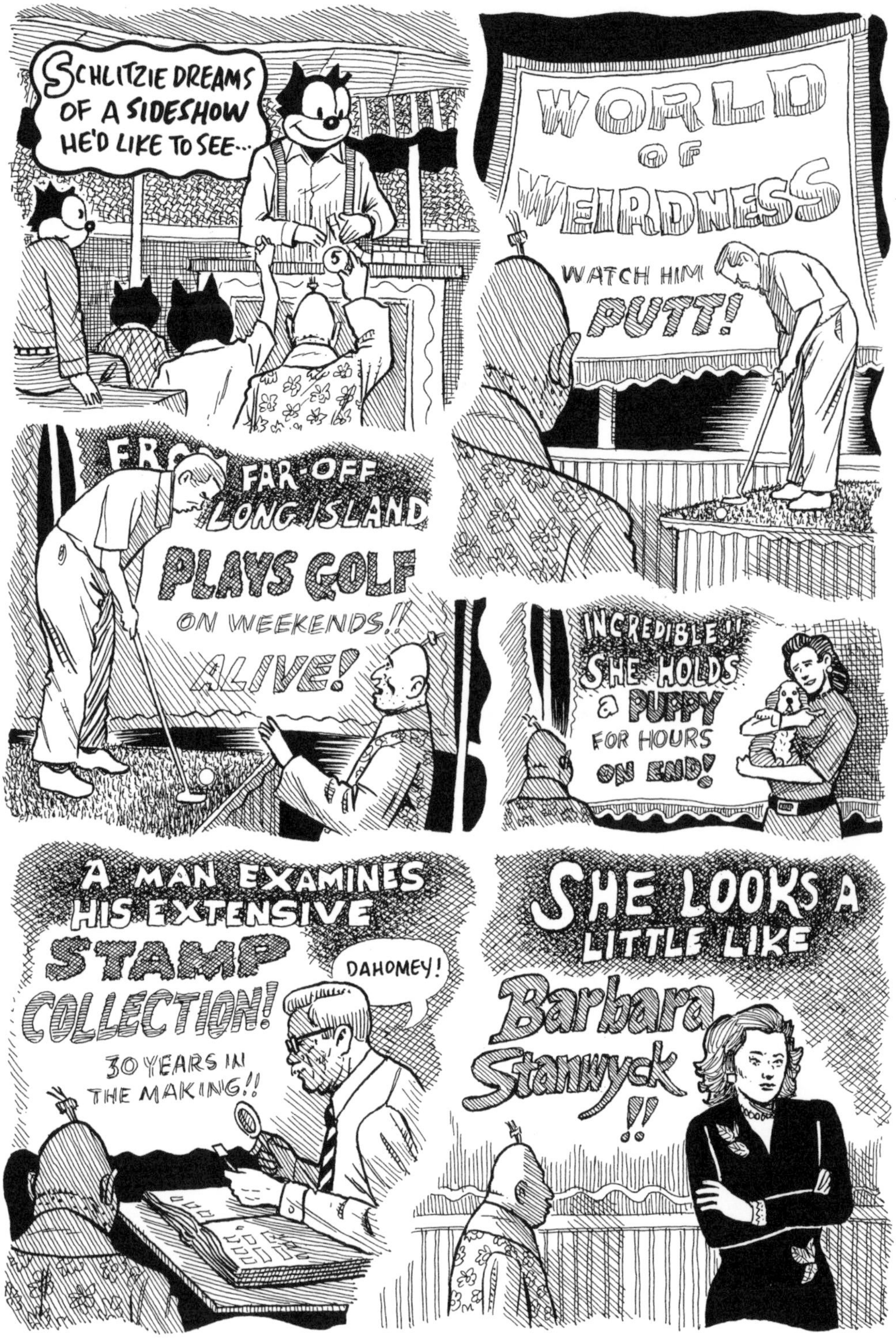
SCHLITZIE DREAMS OF A SIDESHOW HE'D LIKE TO SEE...
5
WORLD OF WEIRDNESS
WATCH HIM PUTT!
FAR-OFF LONG ISLAND
PLAYS GOLF ON WEEKENDS!!
ALIVE!
INCREDIBLE!! SHE HOLDS a PUPPY FOR HOURS ON END!
A MAN EXAMINES HIS EXTENSIVE STAMP COLLECTION!
DAHOMEY!
30 YEARS IN THE MAKING!!
SHE LOOKS A LITTLE LIKE
Barbara Stanwyck !!

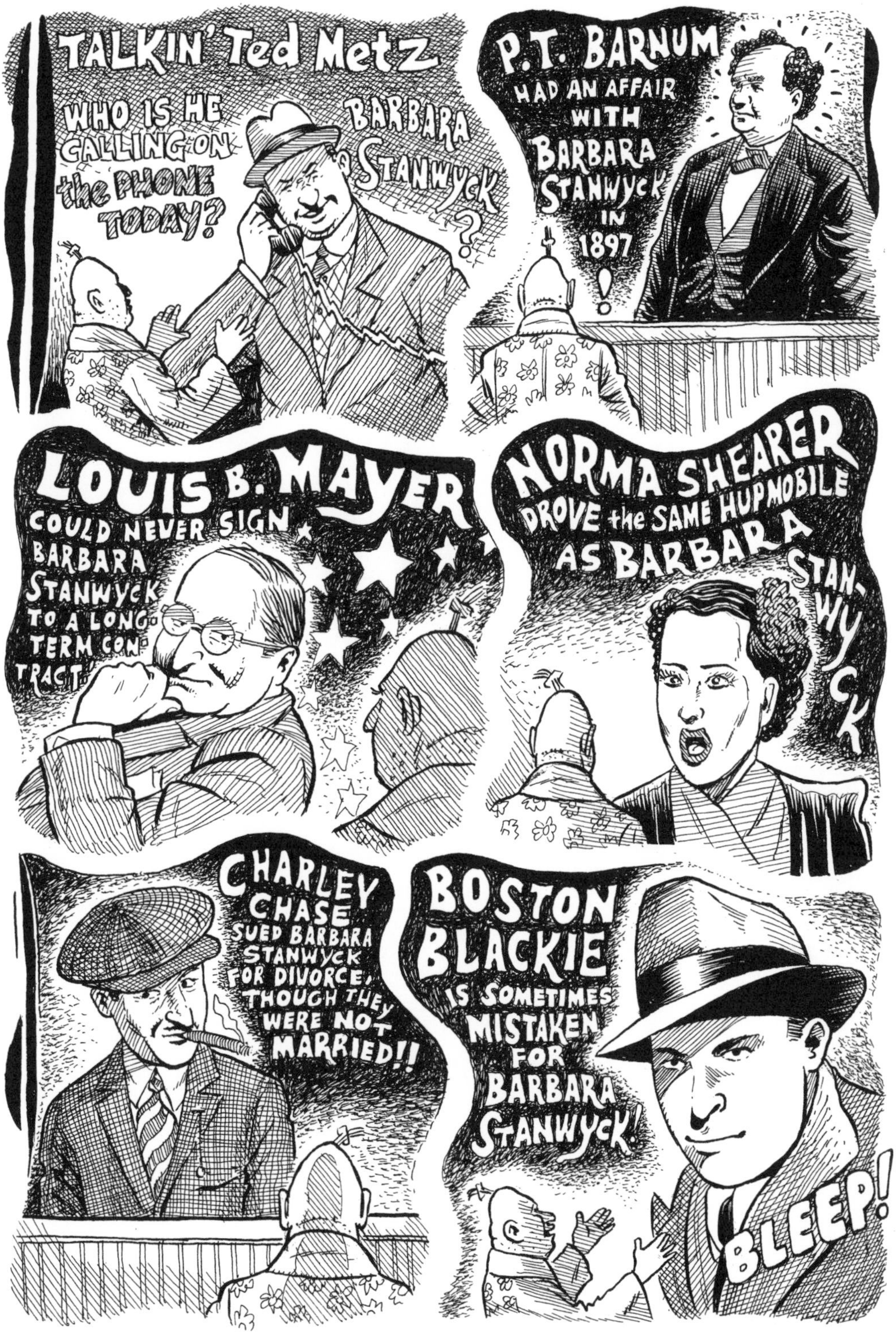
TALKIN' Ted Metz
WHO IS HE CALLING ON the PHONE TODAY?
BARBARA STANWYCK?
P.T. BARNUM HAD AN AFFAIR WITH BARBARA STANWYCK IN 1897!
LOUIS B. MAYER COULD NEVER SIGN BARBARA STANWYCK TO A LONG-TERM CON-TRACT
NORMA SHEARER DROVE the SAME HUPMOBILE AS BARBARA STAN-WYCK
CHARLEY CHASE SUED BARBARA STANWYCK FOR DIVORCE, THOUGH THEY WERE NOT MARRIED!!
BOSTON BLACKIE IS SOMETIMES MISTAKEN FOR BARBARA STANWYCK!
BLEEP!

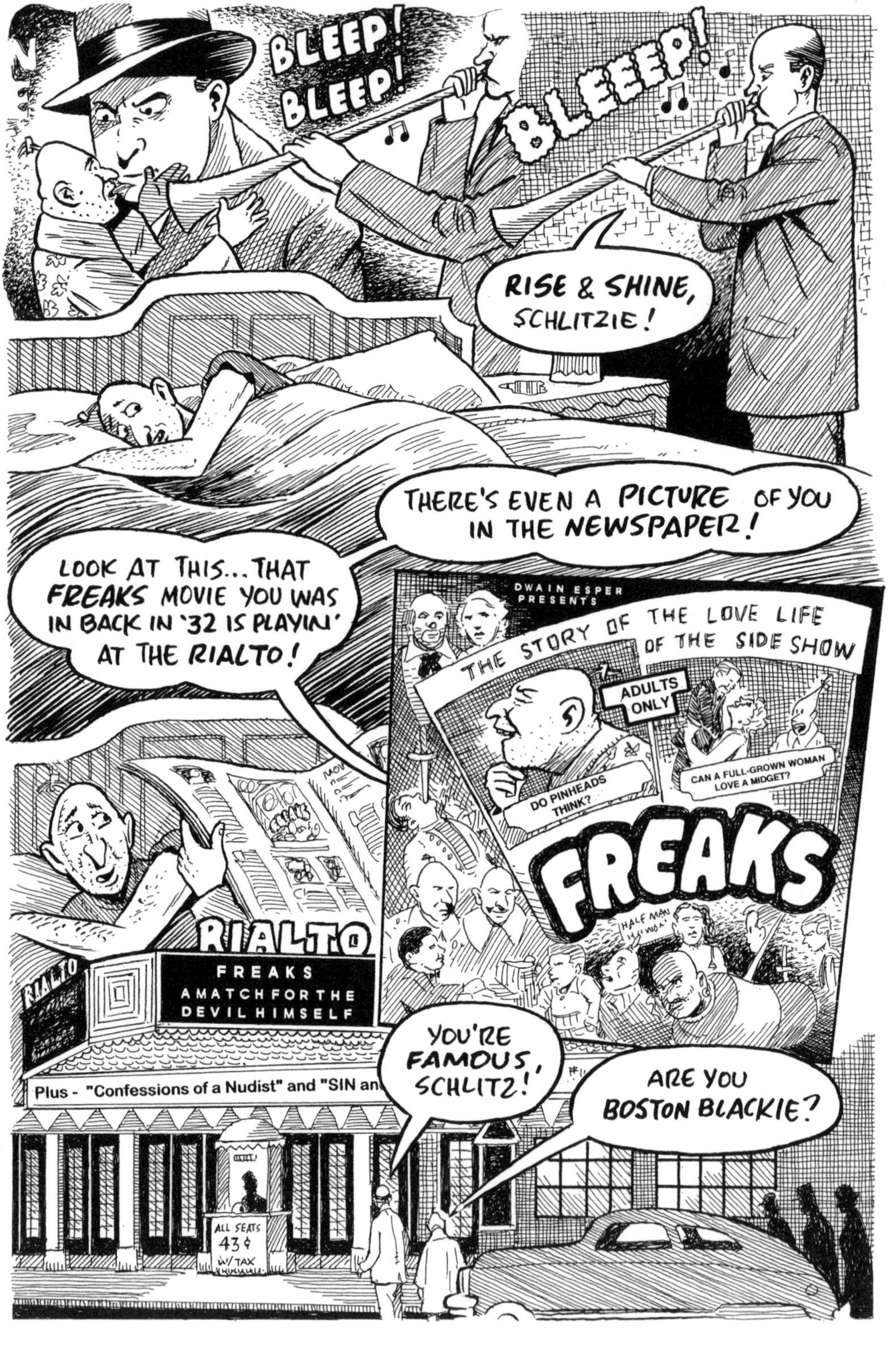
BLEEP! BLEEP!
BLEEEP!
RISE & SHINE, SCHLITZIE!
THERE'S EVEN A PICTURE OF YOU IN THE NEWSPAPER!
LOOK AT THIS... THAT FREAKS MOVIE YOU WAS IN BACK IN '32 IS PLAYIN' AT THE RIALTO!
DWAIN ESPER PRESENTS
THE STORY OF THE LOVE LIFE OF THE SIDE SHOW
ADULTS ONLY
DO PINHEADS THINK?
CAN A FULL-GROWN WOMAN LOVE A MIDGET?
FREAKS
RIALTO
FREAKS
A MATCH FOR THE DEVIL HIMSELF
Plus - "Confessions of a Nudist" and "SIN an
ALL SEATS 43¢ W/TAX
YOU'RE FAMOUS, SCHLITZ!
ARE YOU BOSTON BLACKIE?

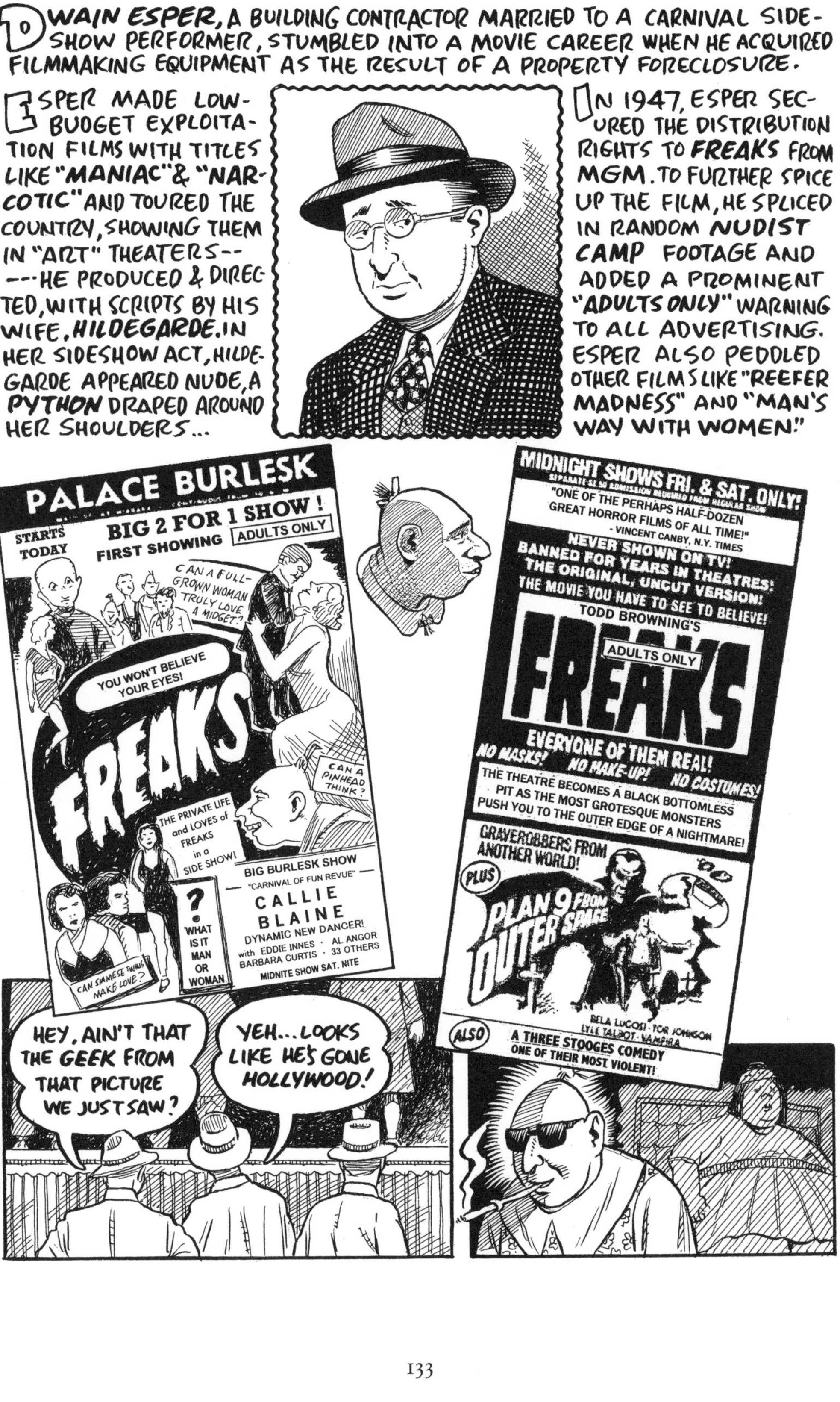
DWAIN ESPER, A BUILDING CONTRACTOR MARRIED TO A CARNIVAL SIDE-SHOW PERFORMER, STUMBLED INTO A MOVIE CAREER WHEN HE ACQUIRED FILMMAKING EQUIPMENT AS THE RESULT OF A PROPERTY FORECLOSURE.
ESPER MADE LOW-BUDGET EXPLOITATION FILMS WITH TITLES LIKE "MANIAC" & "NARCOTIC" AND TOURED THE COUNTRY, SHOWING THEM IN "ART" THEATERS---HE PRODUCED & DIRECTED, WITH SCRIPTS BY HIS WIFE, HILDEGARDE. IN HER SIDESHOW ACT, HILDEGARDE APPEARED NUDE, A PYTHON DRAPED AROUND HER SHOULDERS...
IN 1947, ESPER SECURED THE DISTRIBUTION RIGHTS TO FREAKS FROM MGM. TO FURTHER SPICE UP THE FILM, HE SPLICED IN RANDOM NUDIST CAMP FOOTAGE AND ADDED A PROMINENT "ADULTS ONLY" WARNING TO ALL ADVERTISING. ESPER ALSO PEDDLED OTHER FILMS LIKE "REEFER MADNESS" AND "MAN'S WAY WITH WOMEN."
PALACE BURLESK
STARTS TODAY
BIG 2 FOR 1 SHOW!
FIRST SHOWING
ADULTS ONLY
CAN A FULL-GROWN WOMAN TRULY LOVE A MIDGET?
YOU WON'T BELIEVE YOUR EYES!
FREAKS
CAN A PINHEAD THINK?
THE PRIVATE LIFE and LOVES of FREAKS in a SIDE SHOW!
? WHAT IS IT MAN OR WOMAN
CAN SIAMESE TWINS MAKE LOVE?
BIG BURLESK SHOW
"CARNIVAL OF FUN REVUE"
CALLIE BLAINE
DYNAMIC NEW DANCER!
with EDDIE INNES · AL ANGOR
BARBARA CURTIS · 33 OTHERS
MIDNITE SHOW SAT. NITE
MIDNIGHT SHOWS FRI. & SAT. ONLY!
"ONE OF THE PERHAPS HALF-DOZEN GREAT HORROR FILMS OF ALL TIME!"
- VINCENT CANBY, N.Y. TIMES
NEVER SHOWN ON TV!
BANNED FOR YEARS IN THEATRES!
THE ORIGINAL, UNCUT VERSION!
THE MOVIE YOU HAVE TO SEE TO BELIEVE!
TODD BROWNING'S
ADULTS ONLY
FREAKS
EVERYONE OF THEM REAL!
NO MASKS! NO MAKE-UP! NO COSTUMES!
THE THEATRE BECOMES A BLACK BOTTOMLESS PIT AS THE MOST GROTESQUE MONSTERS PUSH YOU TO THE OUTER EDGE OF A NIGHTMARE!
GRAVEROBBERS FROM ANOTHER WORLD!
PLUS
PLAN 9 FROM OUTER SPACE
ALSO
A THREE STOOGES COMEDY
ONE OF THEIR MOST VIOLENT!
HEY, AIN'T THAT THE GEEK FROM THAT PICTURE WE JUST SAW?
YEH... LOOKS LIKE HE'S GONE HOLLYWOOD!

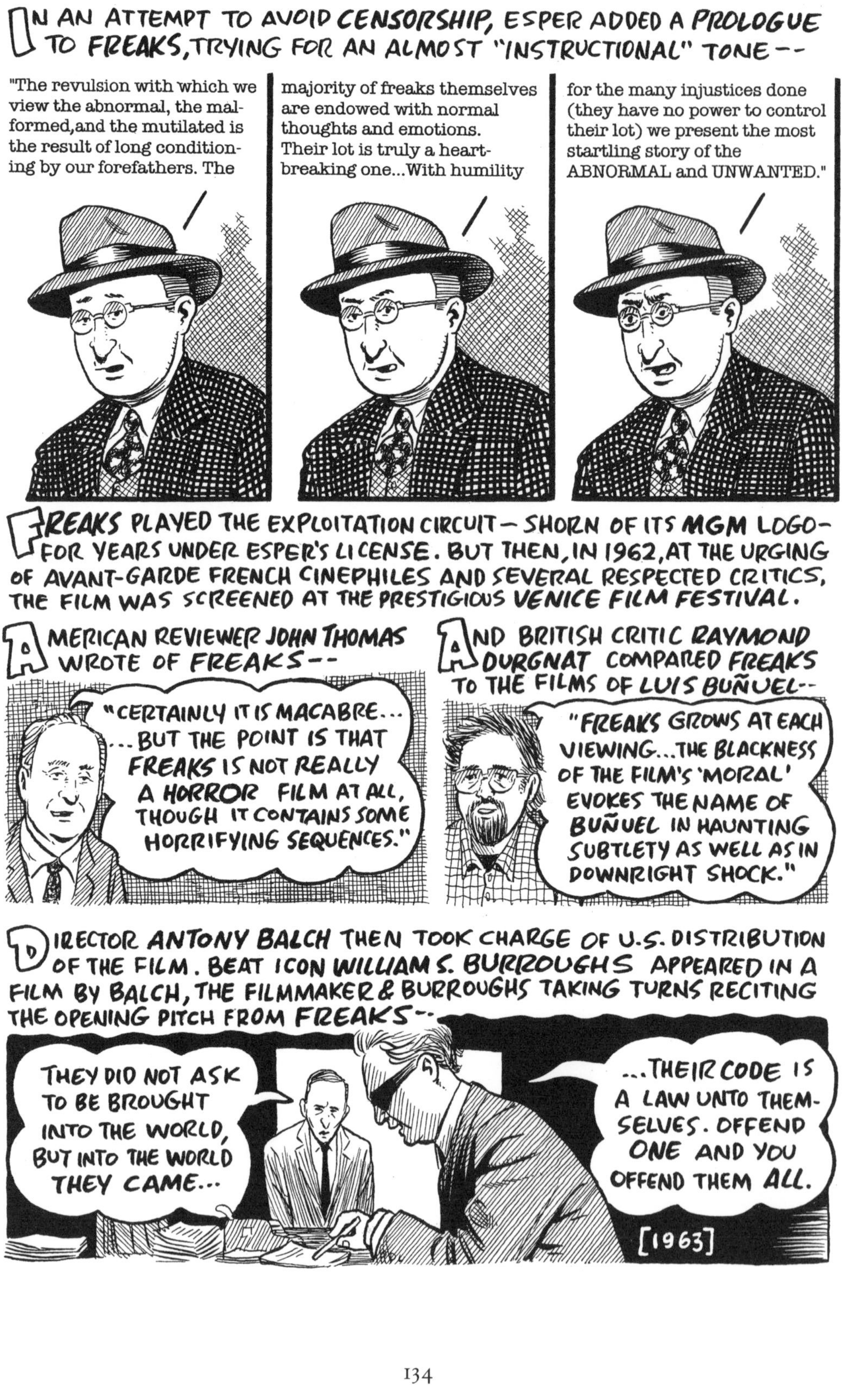
IN AN ATTEMPT TO AVOID CENSORSHIP, ESPER ADDED A PROLOGUE TO FREAKS, TRYING FOR AN ALMOST "INSTRUCTIONAL" TONE--
"The revulsion with which we view the abnormal, the malformed, and the mutilated is the result of long conditioning by our forefathers. The
majority of freaks themselves are endowed with normal thoughts and emotions. Their lot is truly a heartbreaking one...With humility
for the many injustices done (they have no power to control their lot) we present the most startling story of the ABNORMAL and UNWANTED."
FREAKS PLAYED THE EXPLOITATION CIRCUIT – SHORN OF ITS MGM LOGO – FOR YEARS UNDER ESPER'S LICENSE. BUT THEN, IN 1962, AT THE URGING OF AVANT-GARDE FRENCH CINEPHILES AND SEVERAL RESPECTED CRITICS, THE FILM WAS SCREENED AT THE PRESTIGIOUS VENICE FILM FESTIVAL.
AMERICAN REVIEWER JOHN THOMAS WROTE OF FREAKS--
"CERTAINLY IT IS MACABRE... ...BUT THE POINT IS THAT FREAKS IS NOT REALLY A HORROR FILM AT ALL, THOUGH IT CONTAINS SOME HORRIFYING SEQUENCES."
AND BRITISH CRITIC RAYMOND DURGNAT COMPARED FREAKS TO THE FILMS OF LUIS BUÑUEL--
"FREAKS GROWS AT EACH VIEWING...THE BLACKNESS OF THE FILM'S 'MORAL' EVOKES THE NAME OF BUÑUEL IN HAUNTING SUBTLETY AS WELL AS IN DOWNRIGHT SHOCK."
DIRECTOR ANTONY BALCH THEN TOOK CHARGE OF U.S. DISTRIBUTION OF THE FILM. BEAT ICON WILLIAM S. BURROUGHS APPEARED IN A FILM BY BALCH, THE FILMMAKER & BURROUGHS TAKING TURNS RECITING THE OPENING PITCH FROM FREAKS--
THEY DID NOT ASK TO BE BROUGHT INTO THE WORLD, BUT INTO THE WORLD THEY CAME...
...THEIR CODE IS A LAW UNTO THEMSELVES. OFFEND ONE AND YOU OFFEND THEM ALL.
[1963]

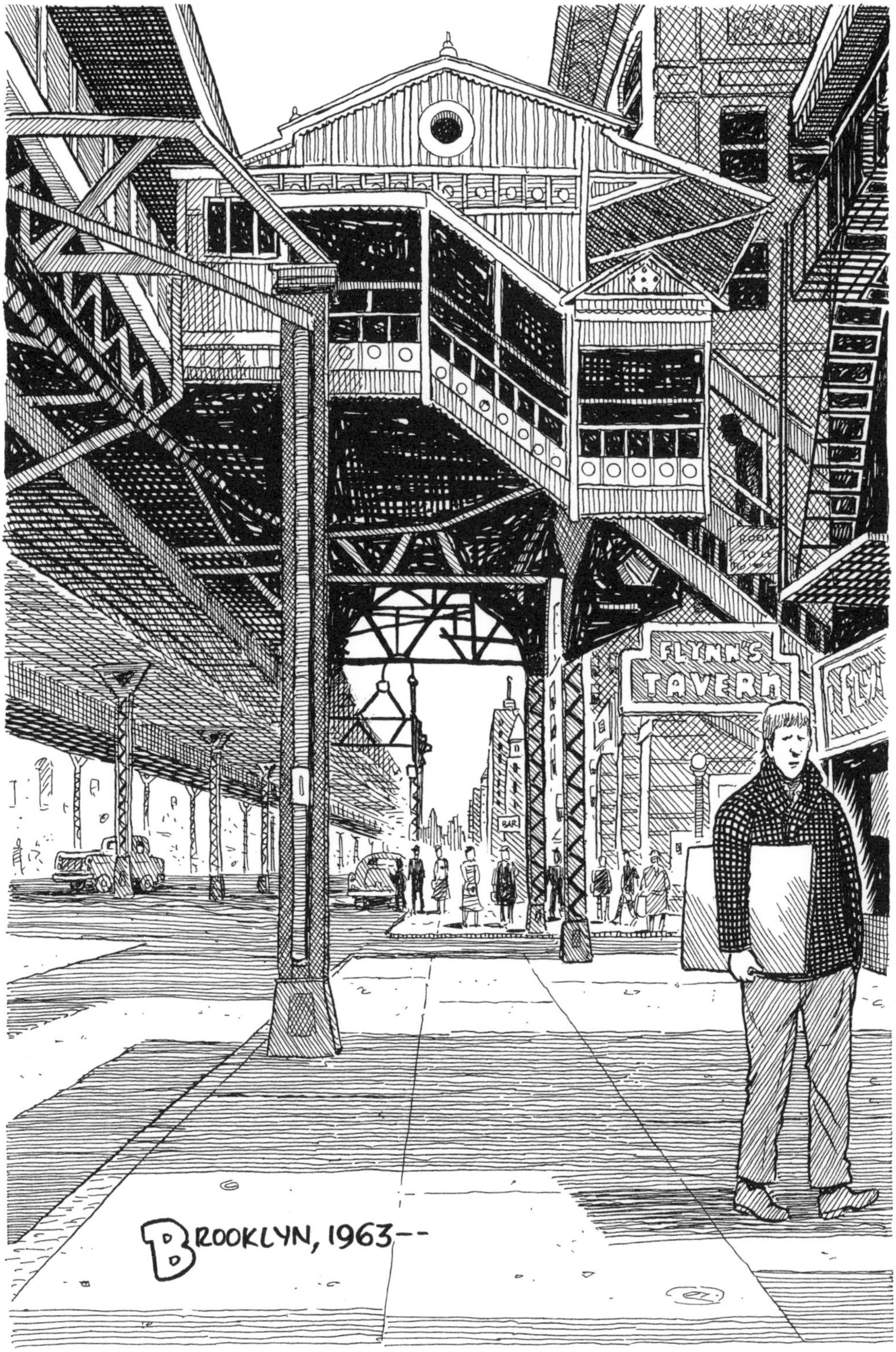
FLYNN'S TAVERN
BAR
BROOKLYN, 1963--

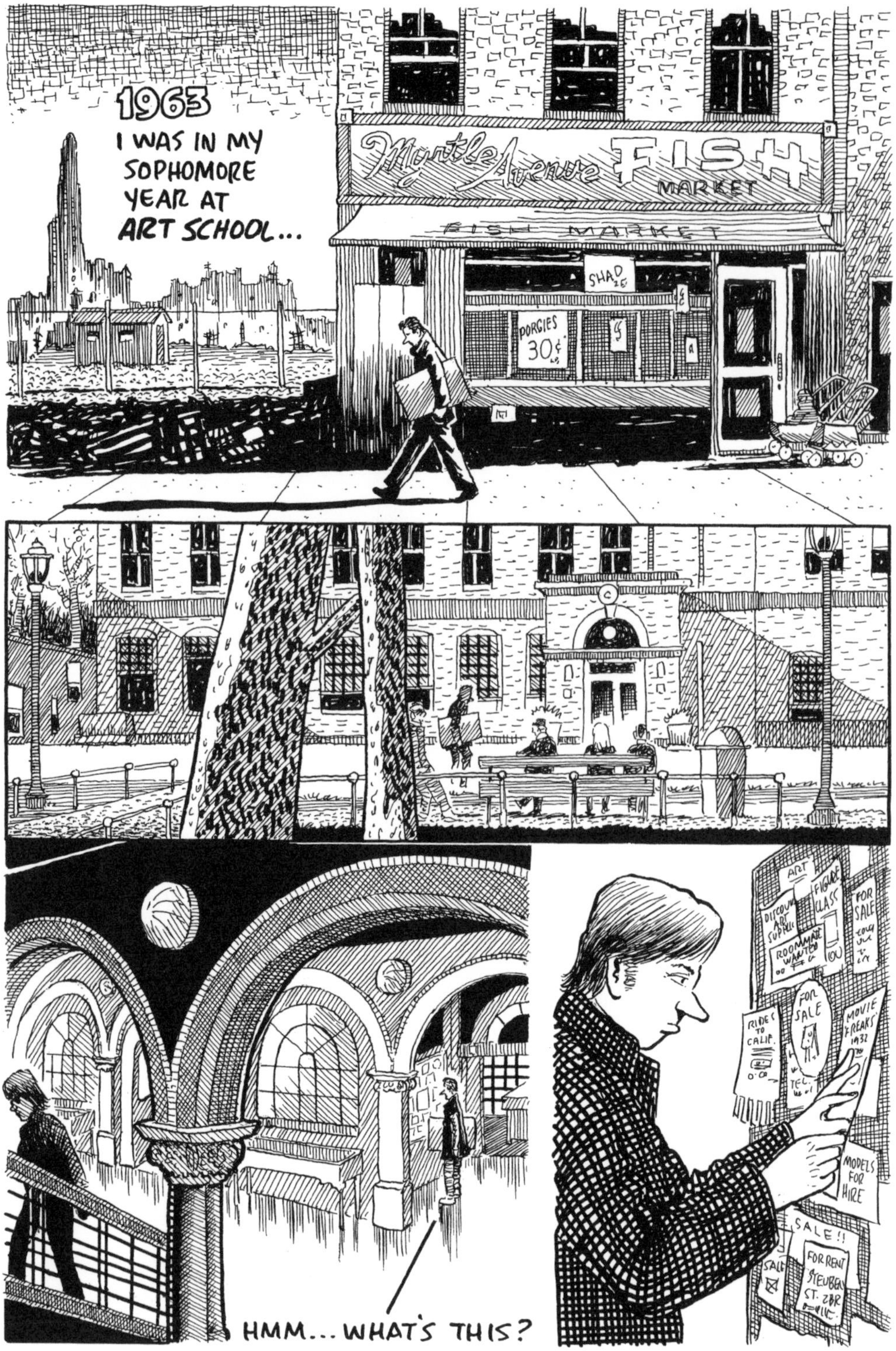
1963
I WAS IN MY SOPHOMORE YEAR AT ART SCHOOL...
Myrtle Avenue FISH MARKET
FISH MARKET
SHAD
PORGIES 30¢
HMM... WHAT'S THIS?
ART
FIGURE CLASS
FOR SALE
ROOMMATE WANTED
FOR SALE
RIDES TO CALIF.
MOVIE FREAKS' 1932
MODELS FOR HIRE
SALE!!
FOR RENT STEUBEN ST. 2BR

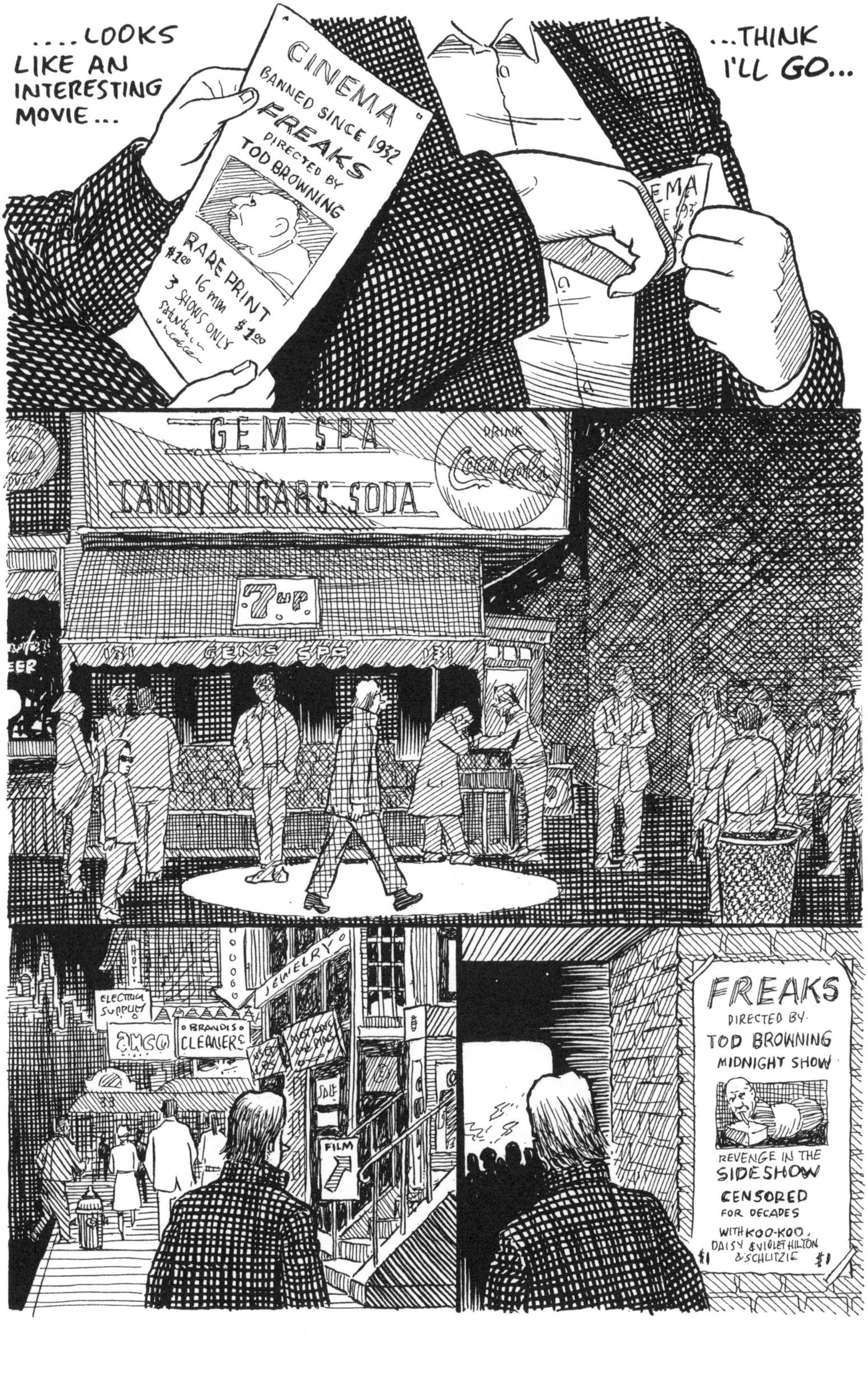
....LOOKS LIKE AN INTERESTING MOVIE...
CINEMA
BANNED SINCE 1932
FREAKS
DIRECTED BY
TOD BROWNING
RARE PRINT
16 mm
$1.00
3 SHOWS ONLY
...THINK I'LL GO...
GEM SPA
CANDY CIGARS SODA
DRINK Coca-Cola
7up
131 GEMS SPA 131
JEWELRY
ELECTRIC SUPPLY
AMCO
BRANDIS CLEANERS
FILM
FREAKS
DIRECTED BY
TOD BROWNING
MIDNIGHT SHOW
REVENGE IN THE
SIDESHOW
CENSORED
FOR DECADES
WITH KOO-KOO, DAISY & VIOLET HILTON & SCHLITZIE
$1 $1

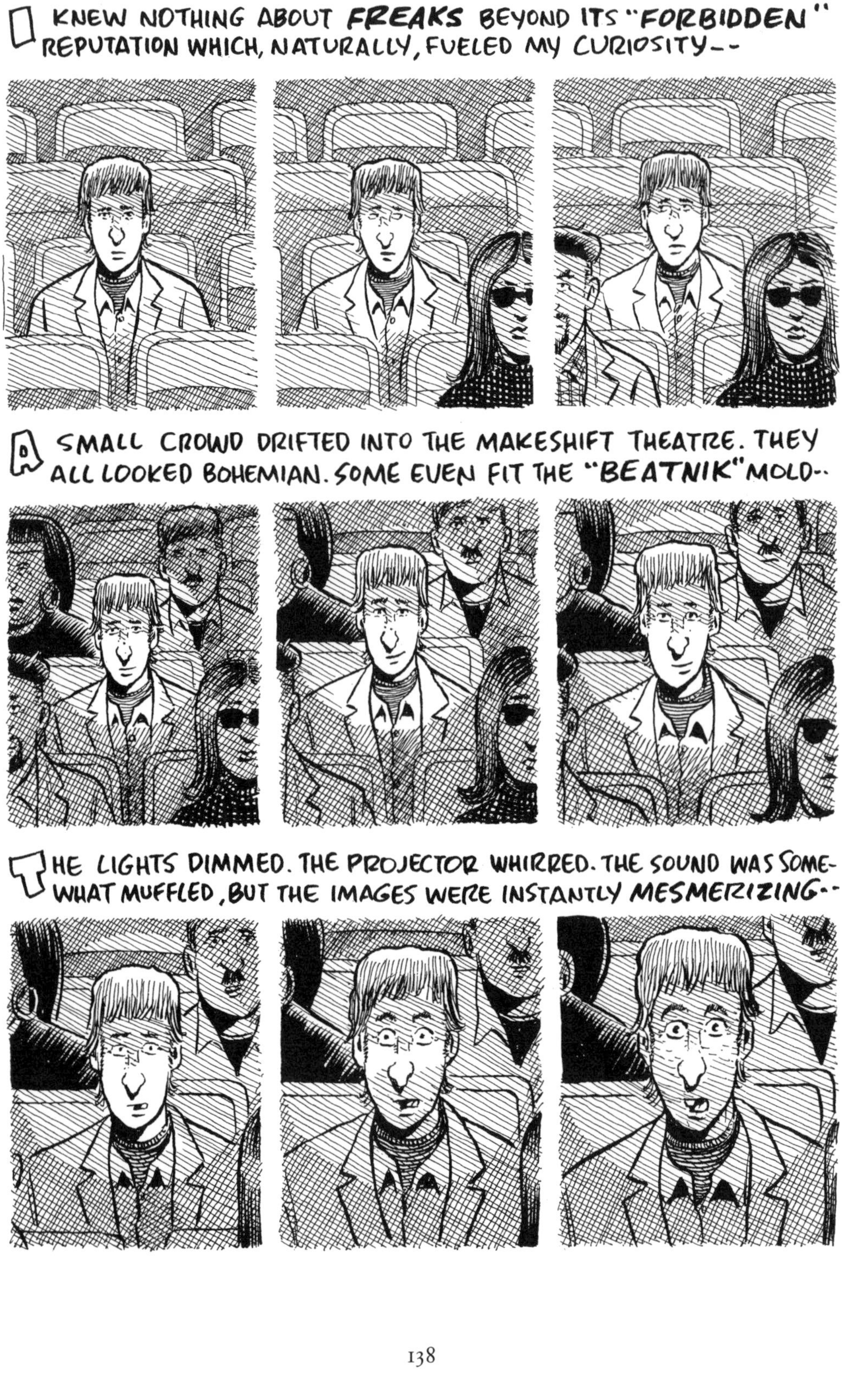
I KNEW NOTHING ABOUT FREAKS BEYOND ITS "FORBIDDEN" REPUTATION WHICH, NATURALLY, FUELED MY CURIOSITY--
A SMALL CROWD DRIFTED INTO THE MAKESHIFT THEATRE. THEY ALL LOOKED BOHEMIAN. SOME EVEN FIT THE "BEATNIK" MOLD..
THE LIGHTS DIMMED. THE PROJECTOR WHIRRED. THE SOUND WAS SOMEWHAT MUFFLED, BUT THE IMAGES WERE INSTANTLY MESMERIZING..

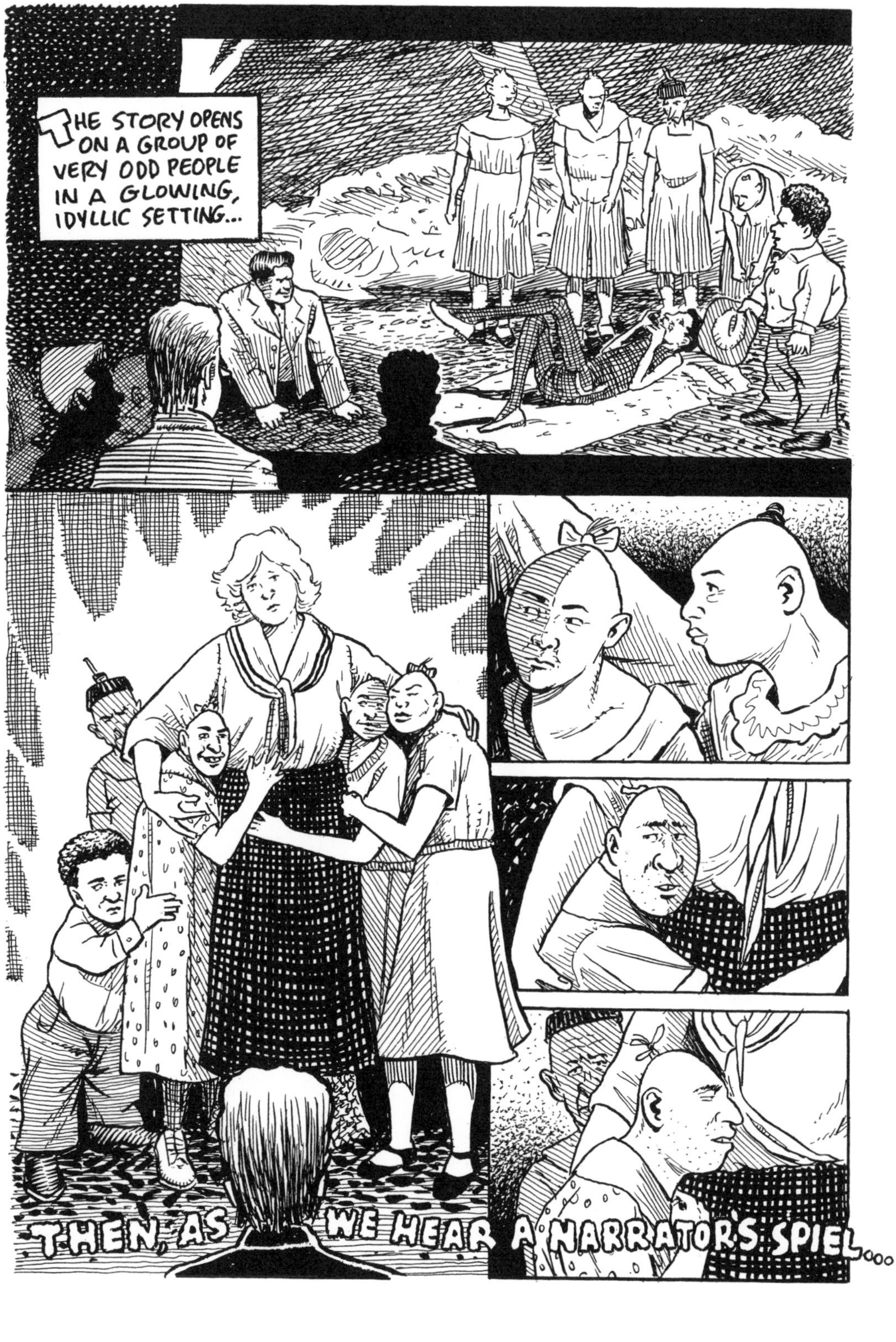
THE STORY OPENS ON A GROUP OF VERY ODD PEOPLE IN A GLOWING, IDYLLIC SETTING...
THEN, AS WE HEAR A NARRATOR'S SPIEL...

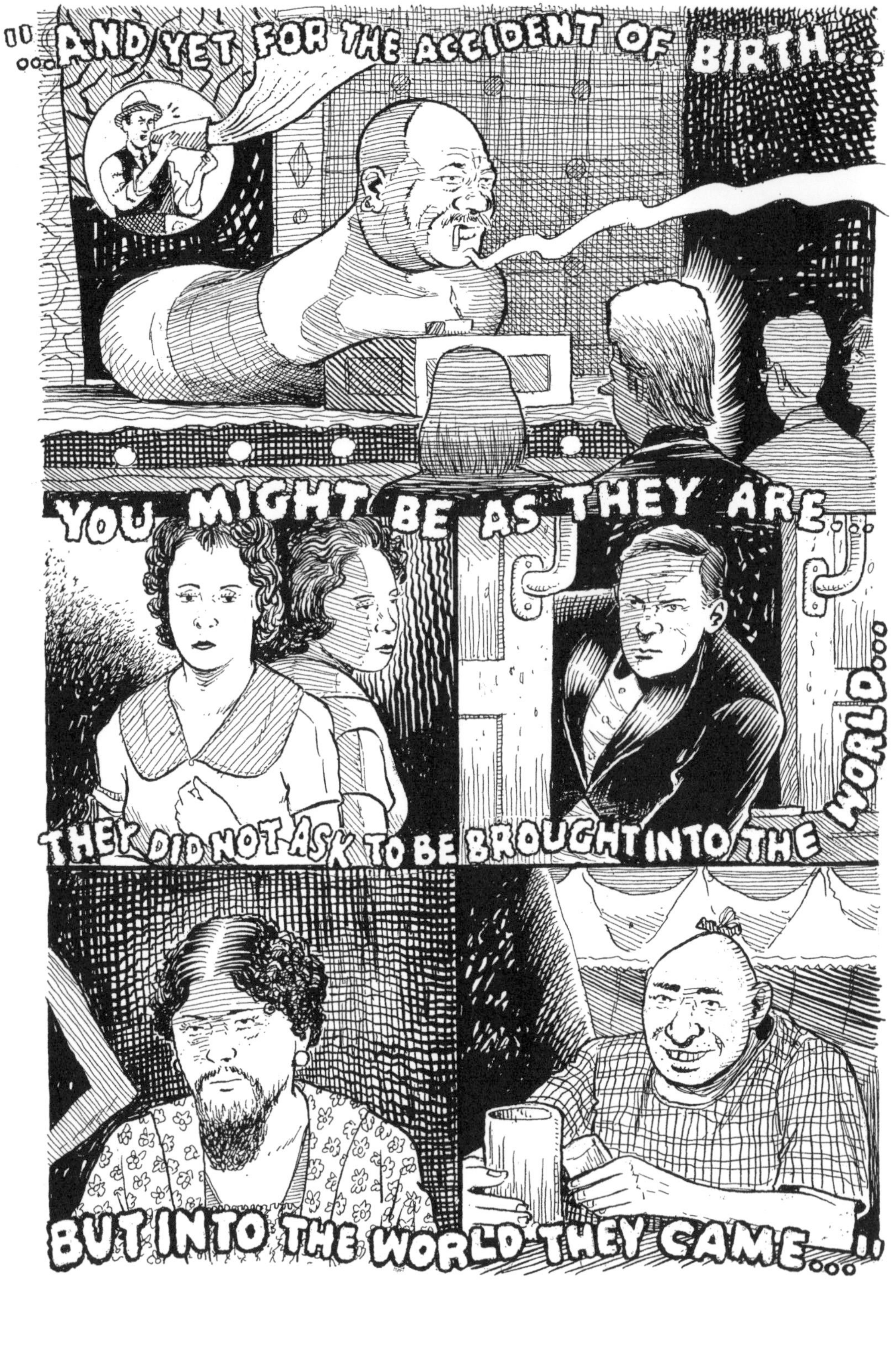
"...AND YET FOR THE ACCIDENT OF BIRTH...
YOU MIGHT BE AS THEY ARE...
THEY DID NOT ASK TO BE BROUGHT INTO THE WORLD...
BUT INTO THE WORLD THEY CAME..."

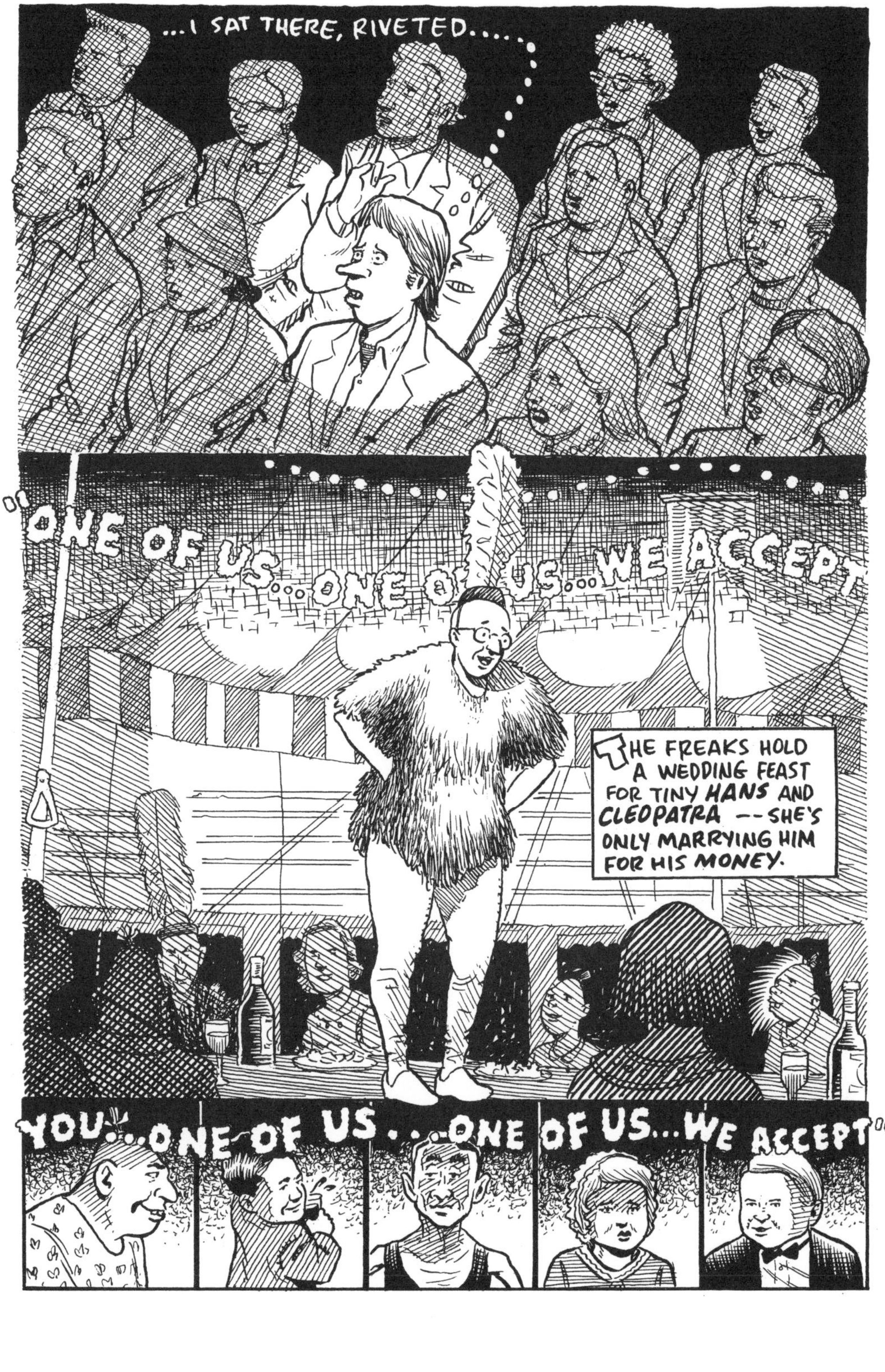
...I SAT THERE, RIVETED.....
"ONE OF US... ONE OF US... WE ACCEPT
THE FREAKS HOLD A WEDDING FEAST FOR TINY HANS AND CLEOPATRA -- SHE'S ONLY MARRYING HIM FOR HIS MONEY.
YOU... ONE OF US... ONE OF US... WE ACCEPT"

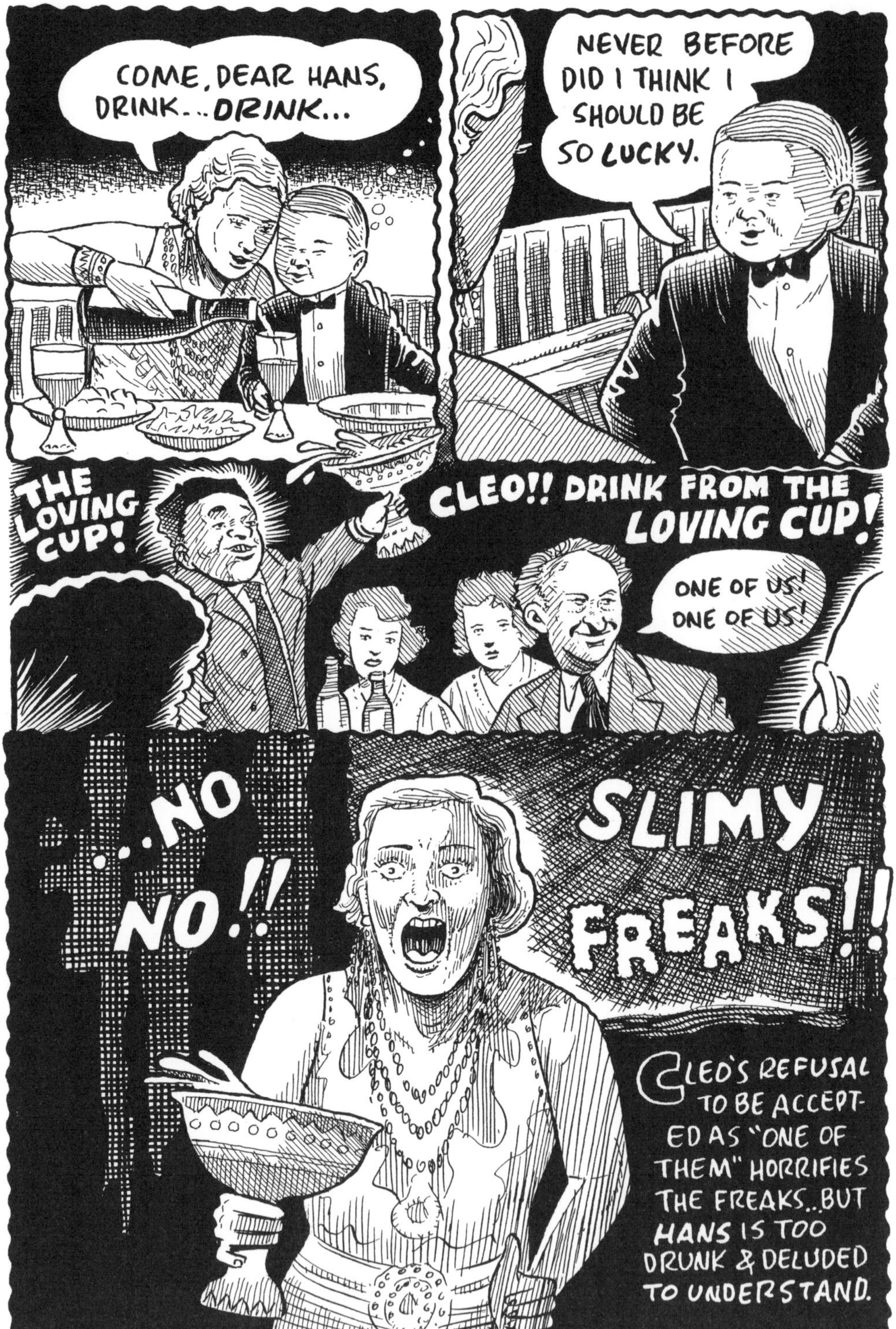
COME, DEAR HANS, DRINK...DRINK...
NEVER BEFORE DID I THINK I SHOULD BE SO LUCKY.
THE LOVING CUP!
CLEO!! DRINK FROM THE LOVING CUP!
ONE OF US! ONE OF US!
...NO NO!!
SLIMY FREAKS!!
CLEO'S REFUSAL TO BE ACCEPTED AS "ONE OF THEM" HORRIFIES THE FREAKS...BUT HANS IS TOO DRUNK & DELUDED TO UNDERSTAND.

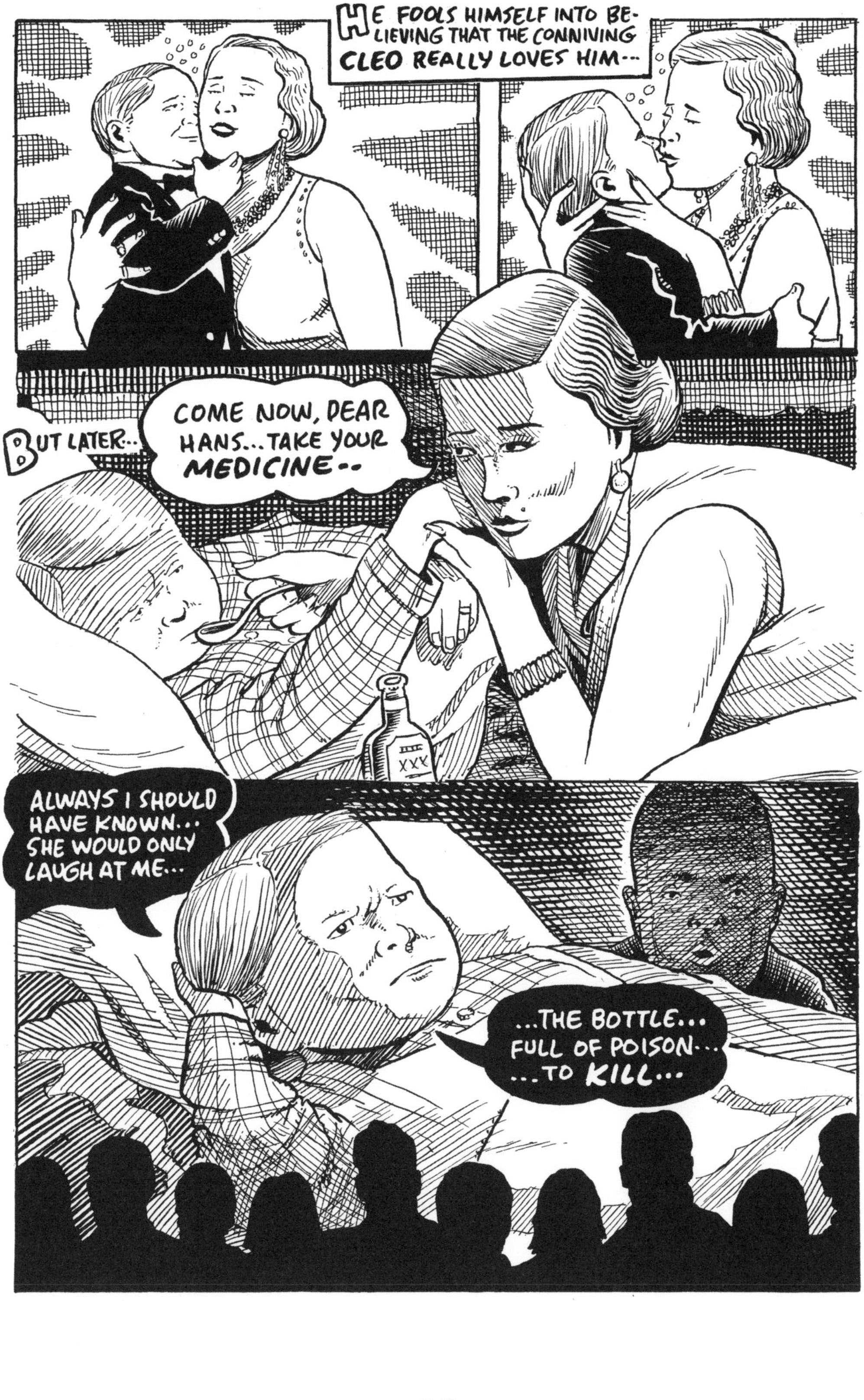
HE FOOLS HIMSELF INTO BELIEVING THAT THE CONNIVING CLEO REALLY LOVES HIM...
BUT LATER...
COME NOW, DEAR HANS... TAKE YOUR MEDICINE..
ALWAYS I SHOULD HAVE KNOWN... SHE WOULD ONLY LAUGH AT ME...
...THE BOTTLE... FULL OF POISON... ...TO KILL...

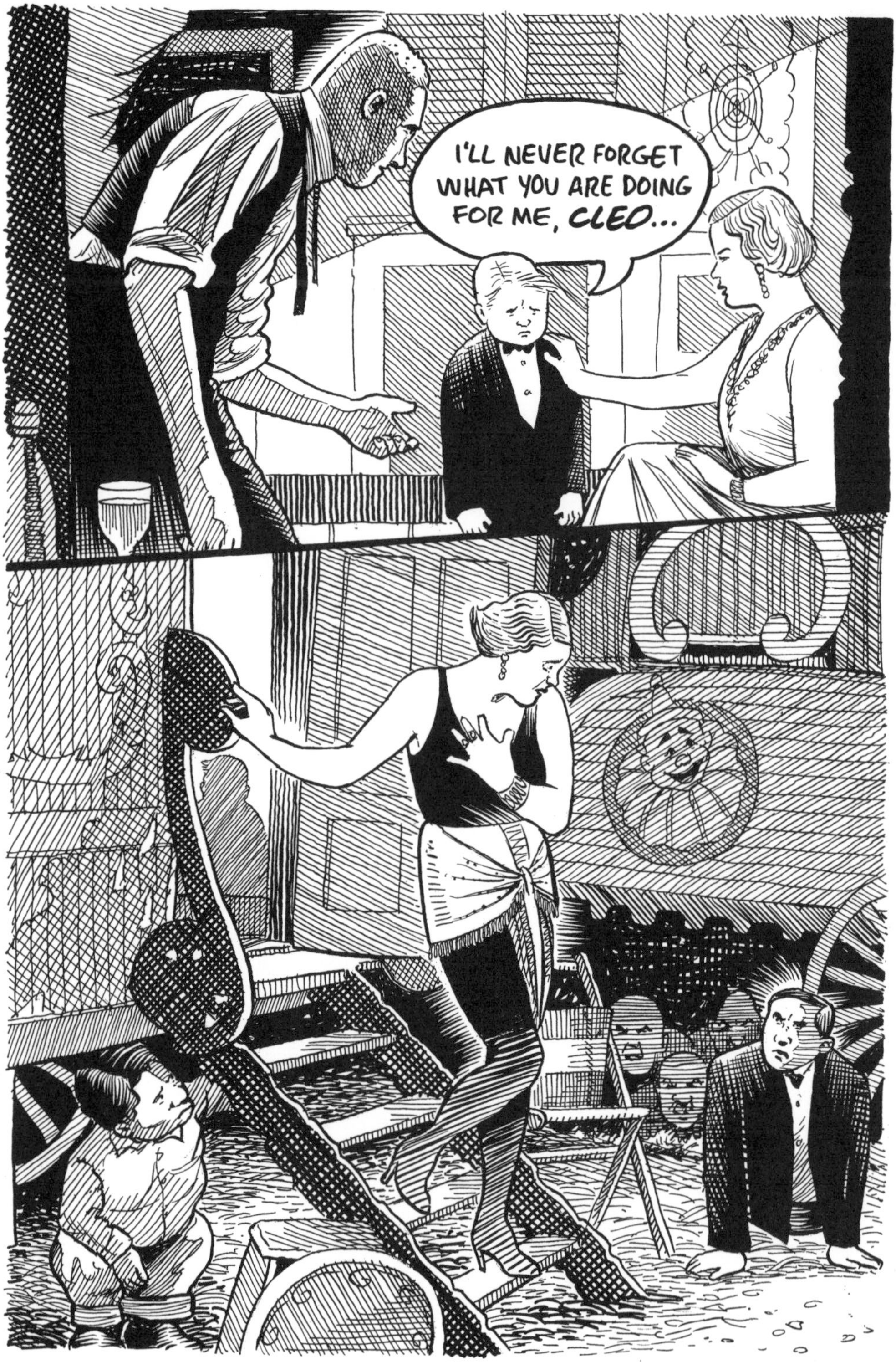
I'LL NEVER FORGET WHAT YOU ARE DOING FOR ME, CLEO...

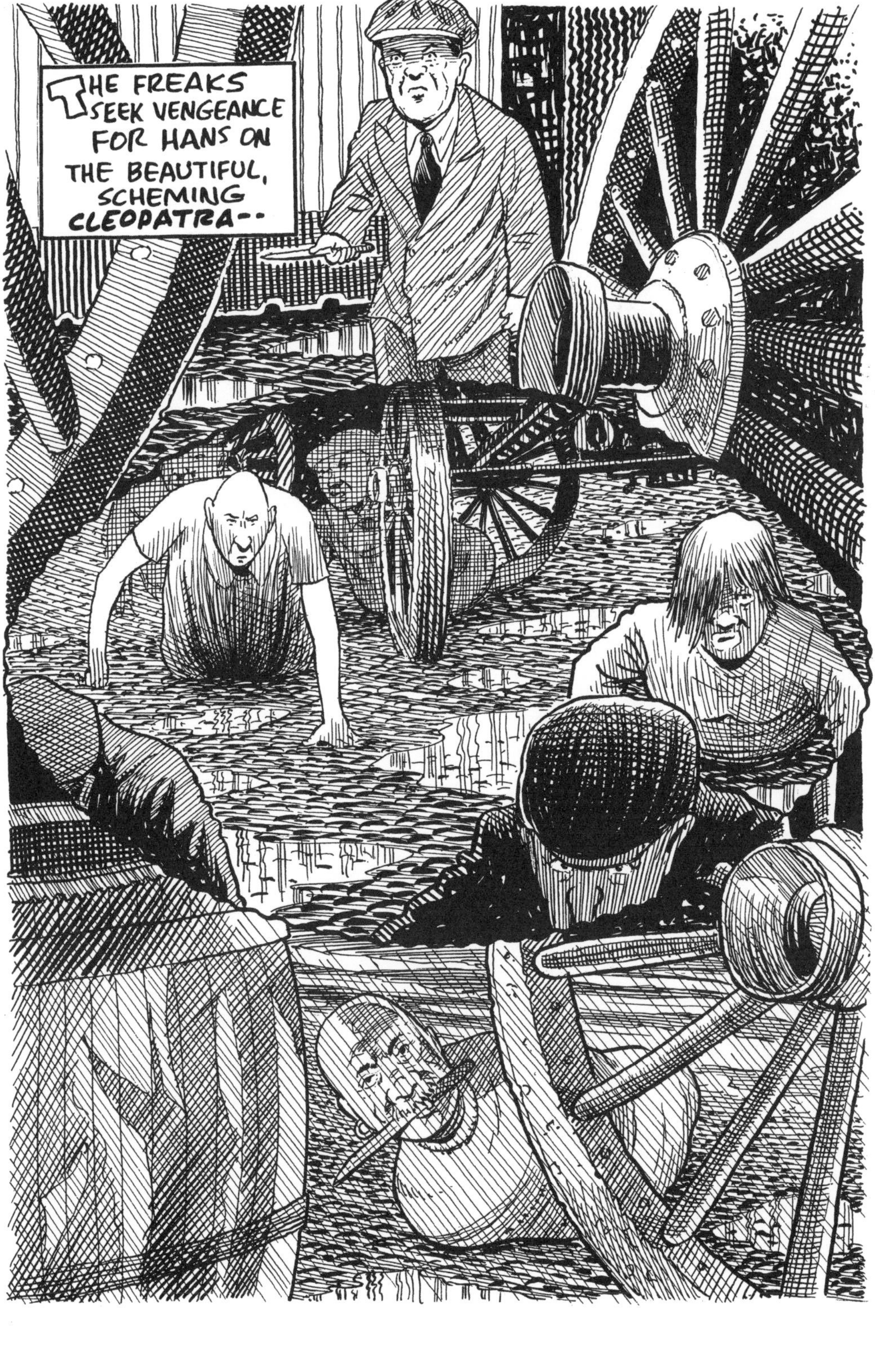
THE FREAKS SEEK VENGEANCE FOR HANS ON THE BEAUTIFUL, SCHEMING CLEOPATRA--

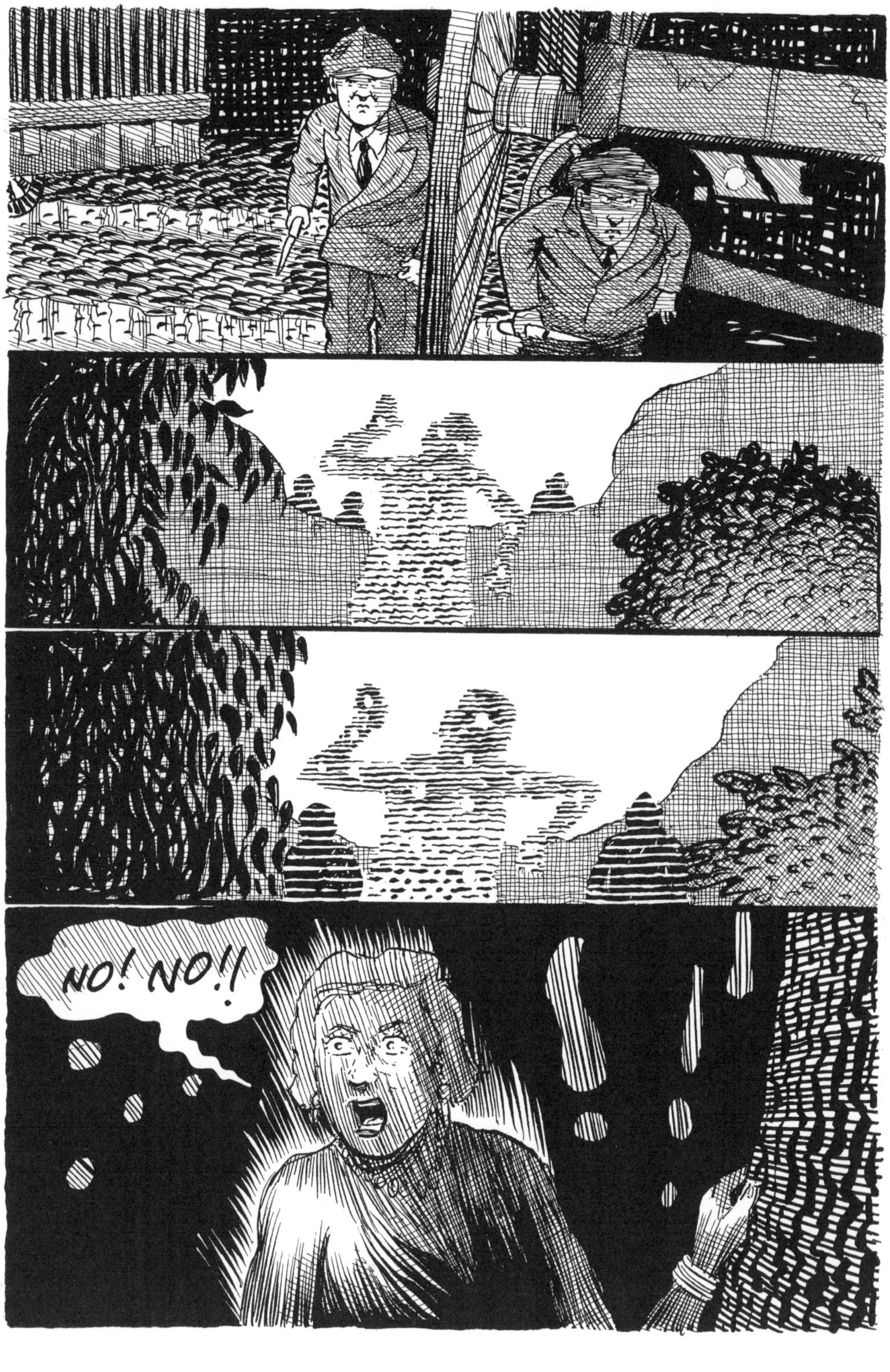
NO! NO!!

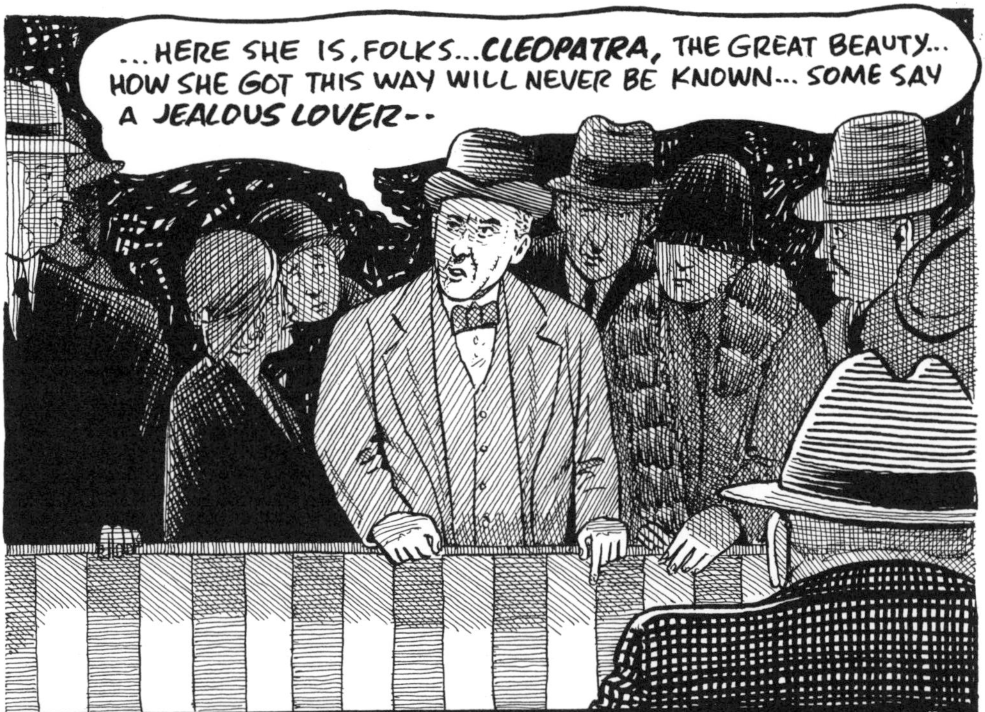
...HERE SHE IS, FOLKS...CLEOPATRA, THE GREAT BEAUTY... HOW SHE GOT THIS WAY WILL NEVER BE KNOWN... SOME SAY A JEALOUS LOVER--

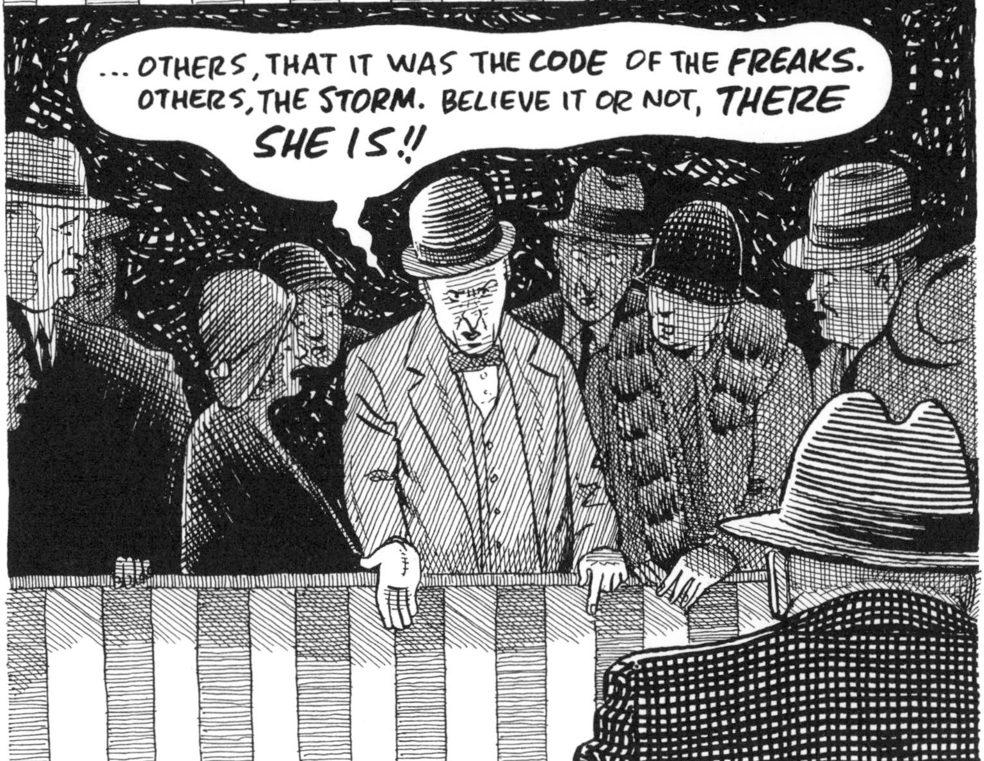
...OTHERS, THAT IT WAS THE CODE OF THE FREAKS. OTHERS, THE STORM. BELIEVE IT OR NOT, THERE SHE IS!!

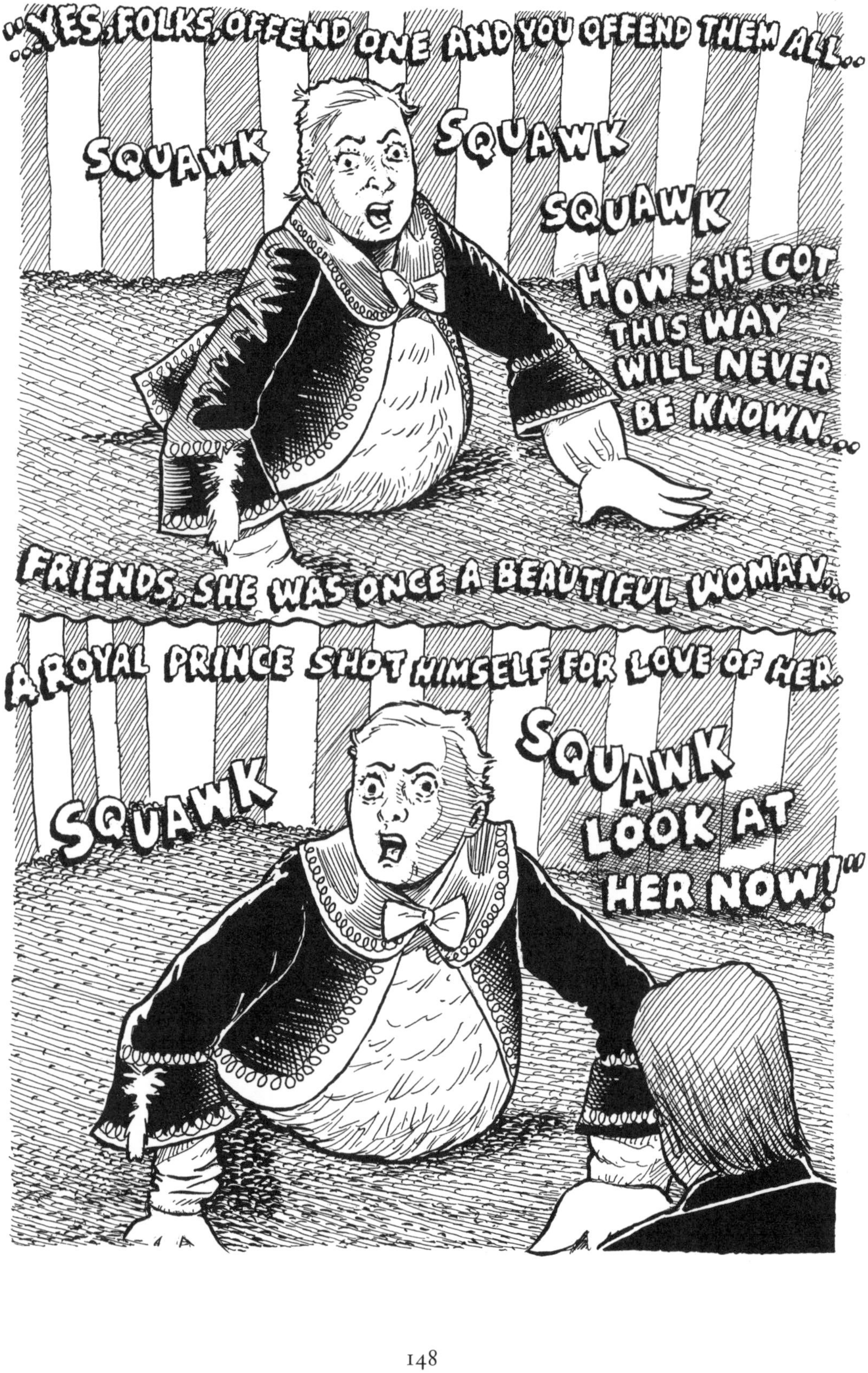
"...YES, FOLKS, OFFEND ONE AND YOU OFFEND THEM ALL...
SQUAWK
SQUAWK
SQUAWK
HOW SHE GOT THIS WAY WILL NEVER BE KNOWN...
FRIENDS, SHE WAS ONCE A BEAUTIFUL WOMAN...
A ROYAL PRINCE SHOT HIMSELF FOR LOVE OF HER.
SQUAWK
SQUAWK
LOOK AT HER NOW!"

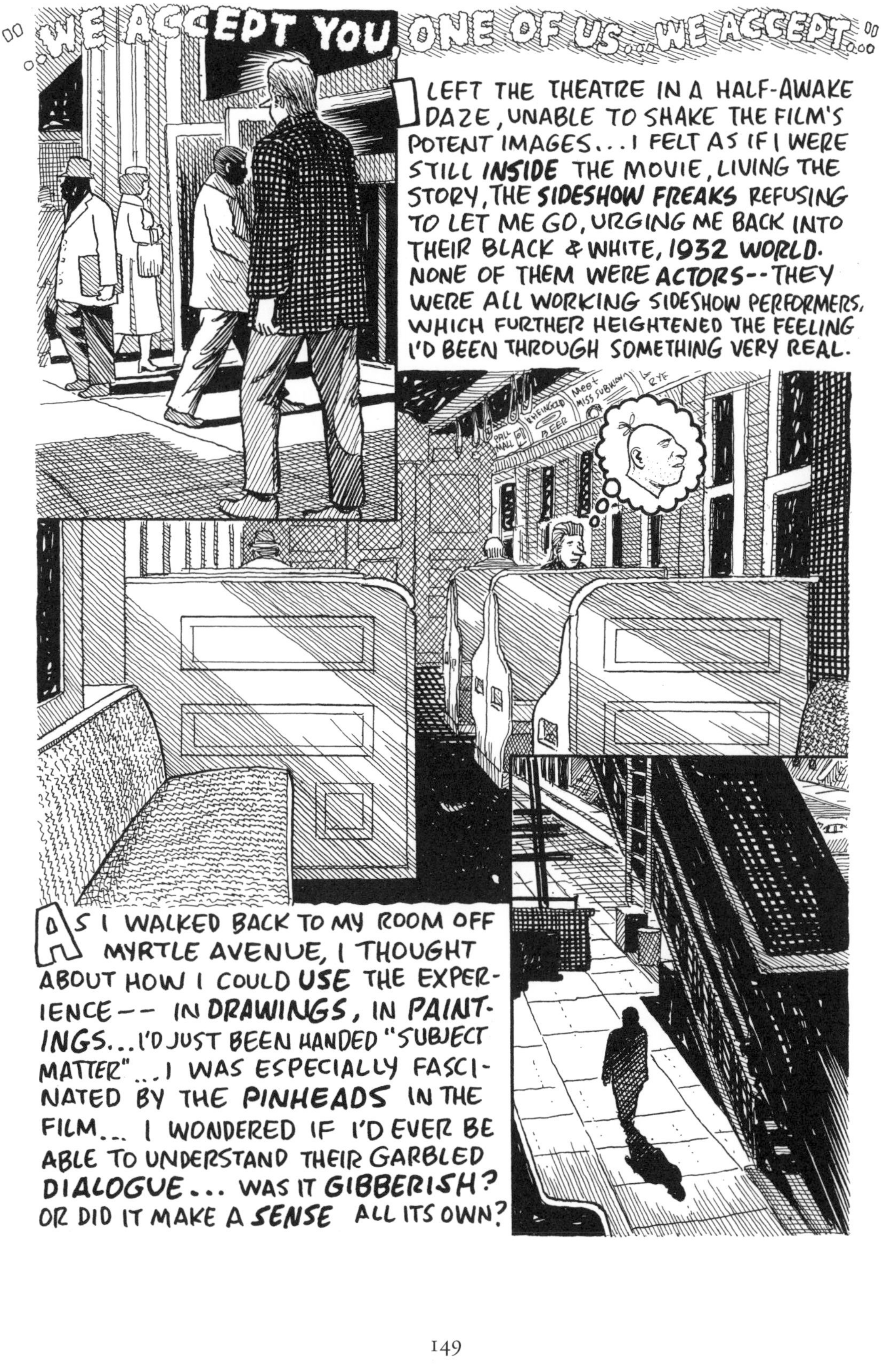

"...WE ACCEPT YOU, ONE OF US... WE ACCEPT..."
I LEFT THE THEATRE IN A HALF-AWAKE DAZE, UNABLE TO SHAKE THE FILM'S POTENT IMAGES... I FELT AS IF I WERE STILL **INSIDE** THE MOVIE, LIVING THE STORY, THE **SIDESHOW FREAKS** REFUSING TO LET ME GO, URGING ME BACK INTO THEIR BLACK & WHITE, **1932 WORLD.** NONE OF THEM WERE **ACTORS**--THEY WERE ALL WORKING SIDESHOW PERFORMERS, WHICH FURTHER HEIGHTENED THE FEELING I'D BEEN THROUGH SOMETHING VERY REAL.
PALL MALL
RHEINGOLD BEER
Meet MISS SUBWAY
RYE
AS I WALKED BACK TO MY ROOM OFF MYRTLE AVENUE, I THOUGHT ABOUT HOW I COULD **USE** THE EXPERIENCE -- IN **DRAWINGS**, IN **PAINTINGS**... I'D JUST BEEN HANDED "SUBJECT MATTER"... I WAS ESPECIALLY FASCINATED BY THE **PINHEADS** IN THE FILM... I WONDERED IF I'D EVER BE ABLE TO UNDERSTAND THEIR GARBLED **DIALOGUE**... WAS IT **GIBBERISH**? OR DID IT MAKE A ***SENSE*** ALL ITS OWN?

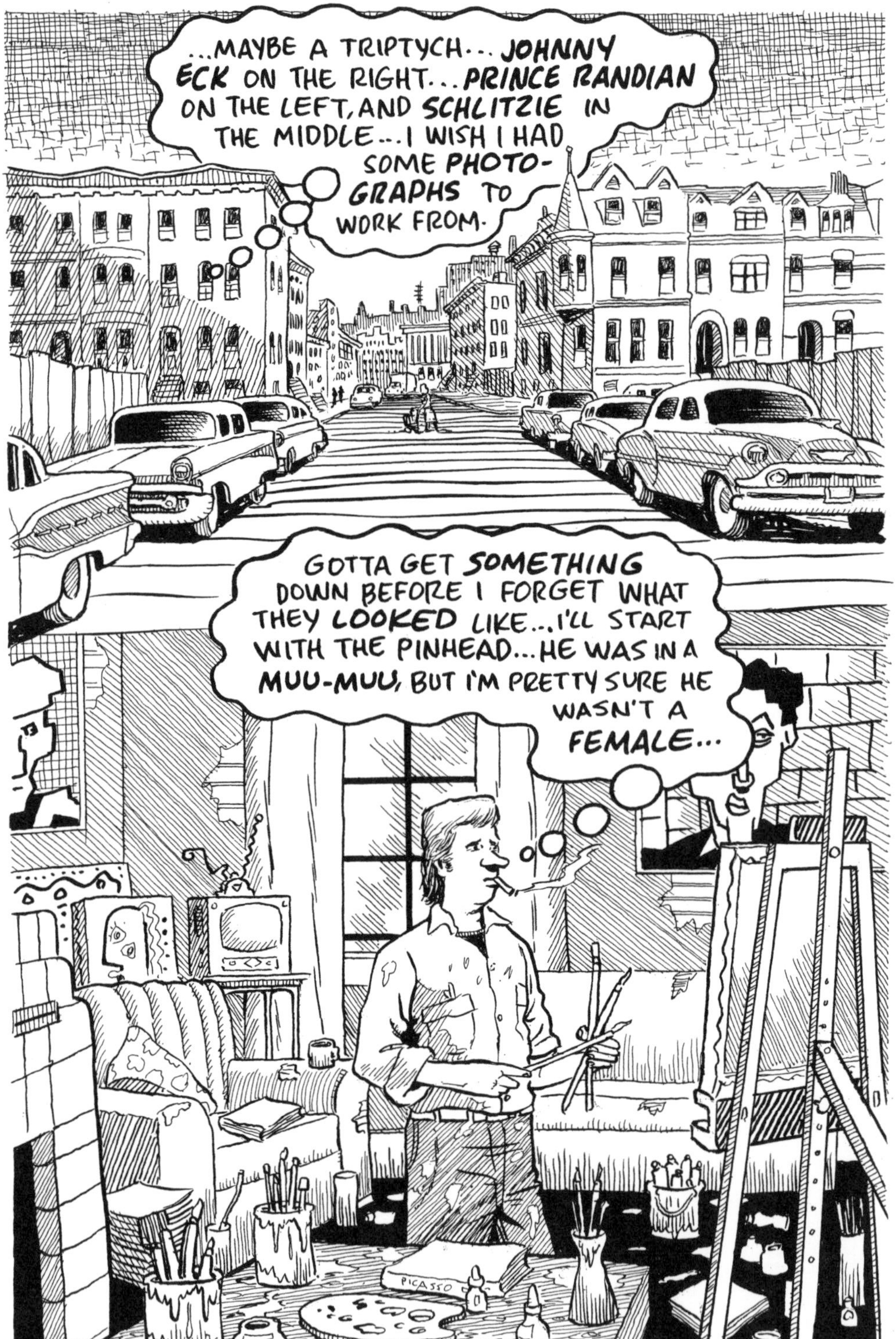
...MAYBE A TRIPTYCH... JOHNNY ECK ON THE RIGHT... PRINCE RANDIAN ON THE LEFT, AND SCHLITZIE IN THE MIDDLE... I WISH I HAD SOME PHOTOGRAPHS TO WORK FROM.
GOTTA GET SOMETHING DOWN BEFORE I FORGET WHAT THEY LOOKED LIKE... I'LL START WITH THE PINHEAD... HE WAS IN A MUU-MUU, BUT I'M PRETTY SURE HE WASN'T A FEMALE...
PICASSO

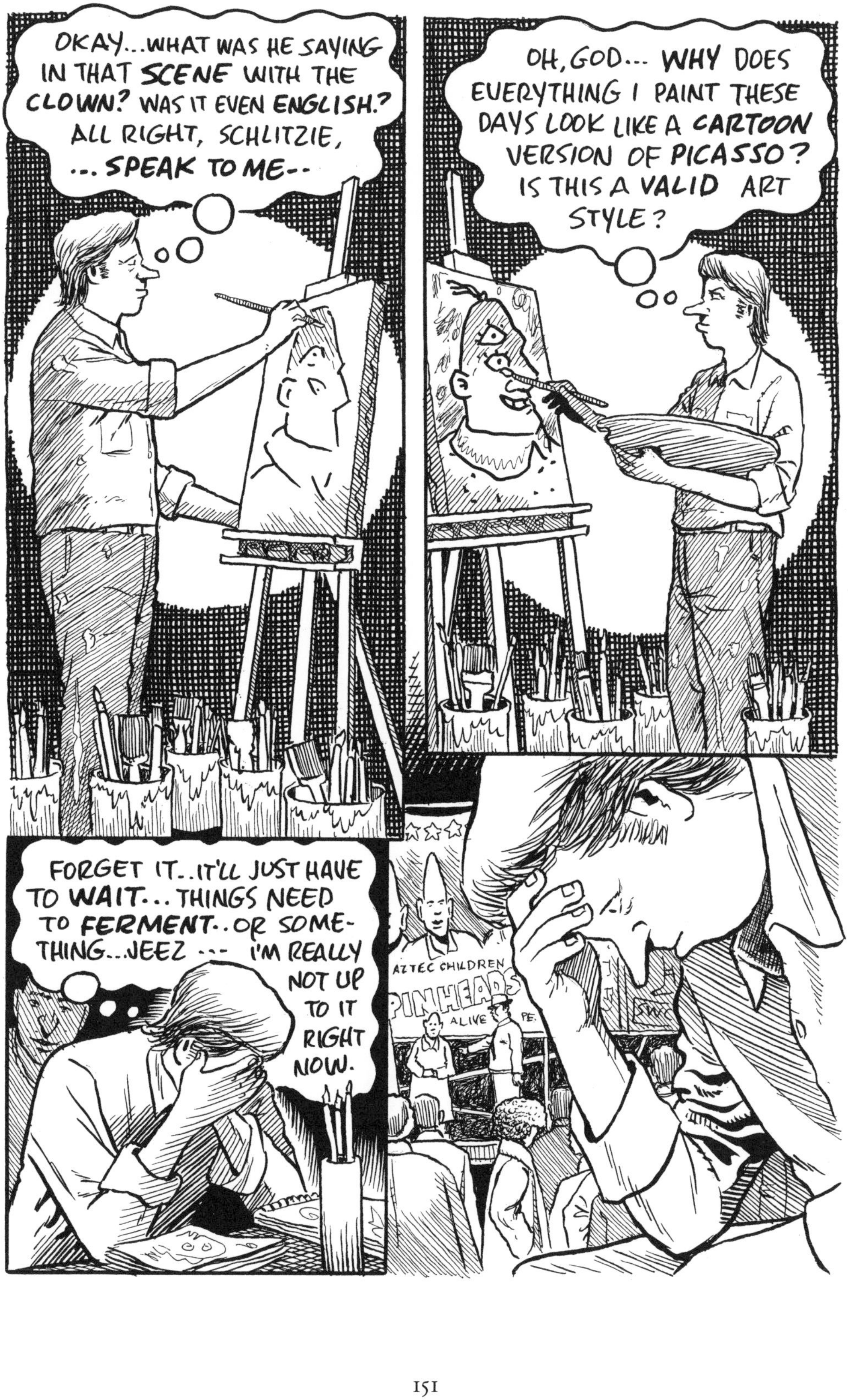
OKAY...WHAT WAS HE SAYING IN THAT SCENE WITH THE CLOWN? WAS IT EVEN ENGLISH? ALL RIGHT, SCHLITZIE, ...SPEAK TO ME--
OH, GOD... WHY DOES EVERYTHING I PAINT THESE DAYS LOOK LIKE A CARTOON VERSION OF PICASSO? IS THIS A VALID ART STYLE?
FORGET IT..IT'LL JUST HAVE TO WAIT... THINGS NEED TO FERMENT..OR SOMETHING...JEEZ --- I'M REALLY NOT UP TO IT RIGHT NOW.
AZTEC CHILDREN
PINHEADS
ALIVE

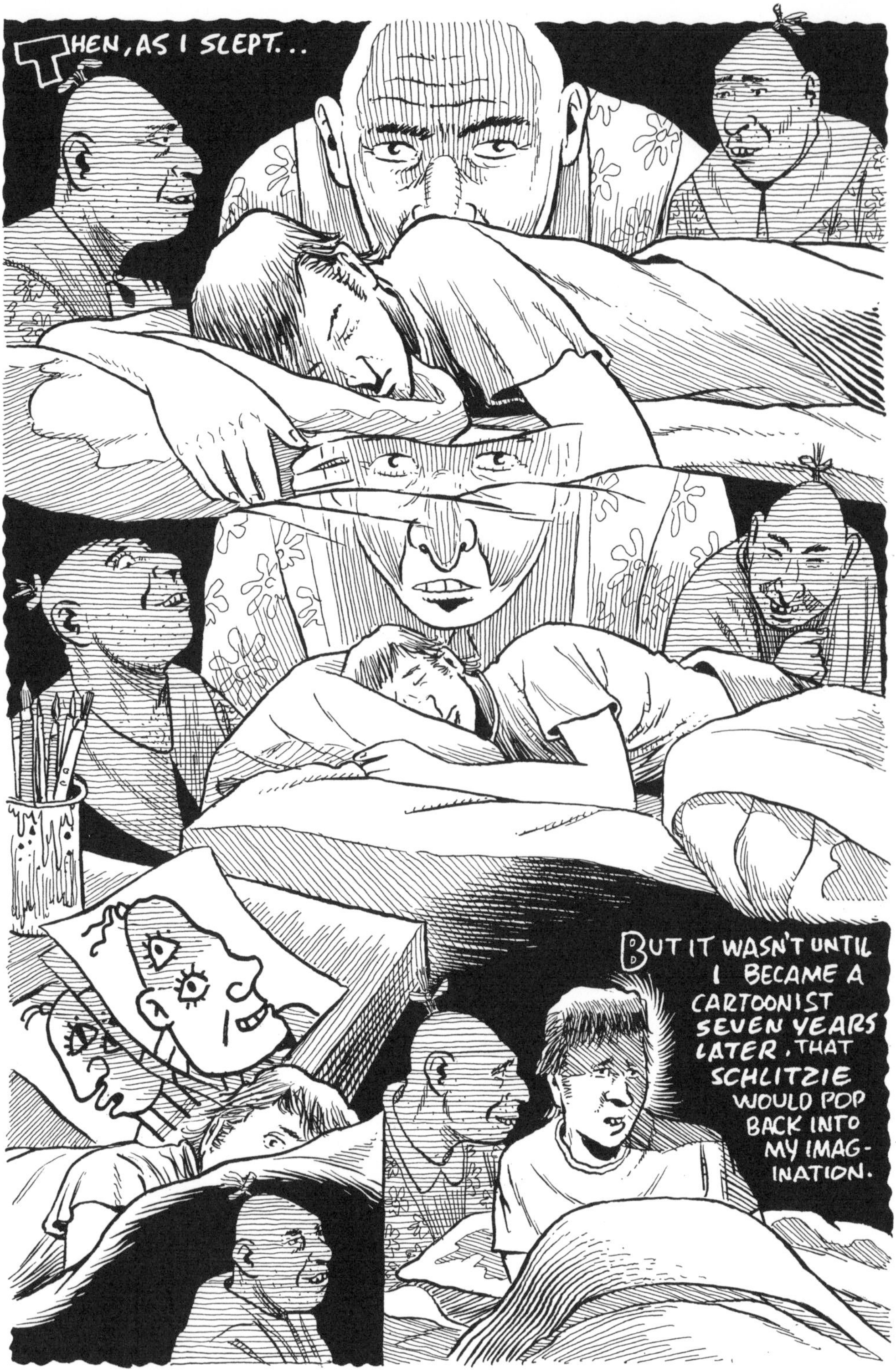
THEN, AS I SLEPT...
BUT IT WASN'T UNTIL I BECAME A CARTOONIST SEVEN YEARS LATER, THAT SCHLITZIE WOULD POP BACK INTO MY IMAGINATION.

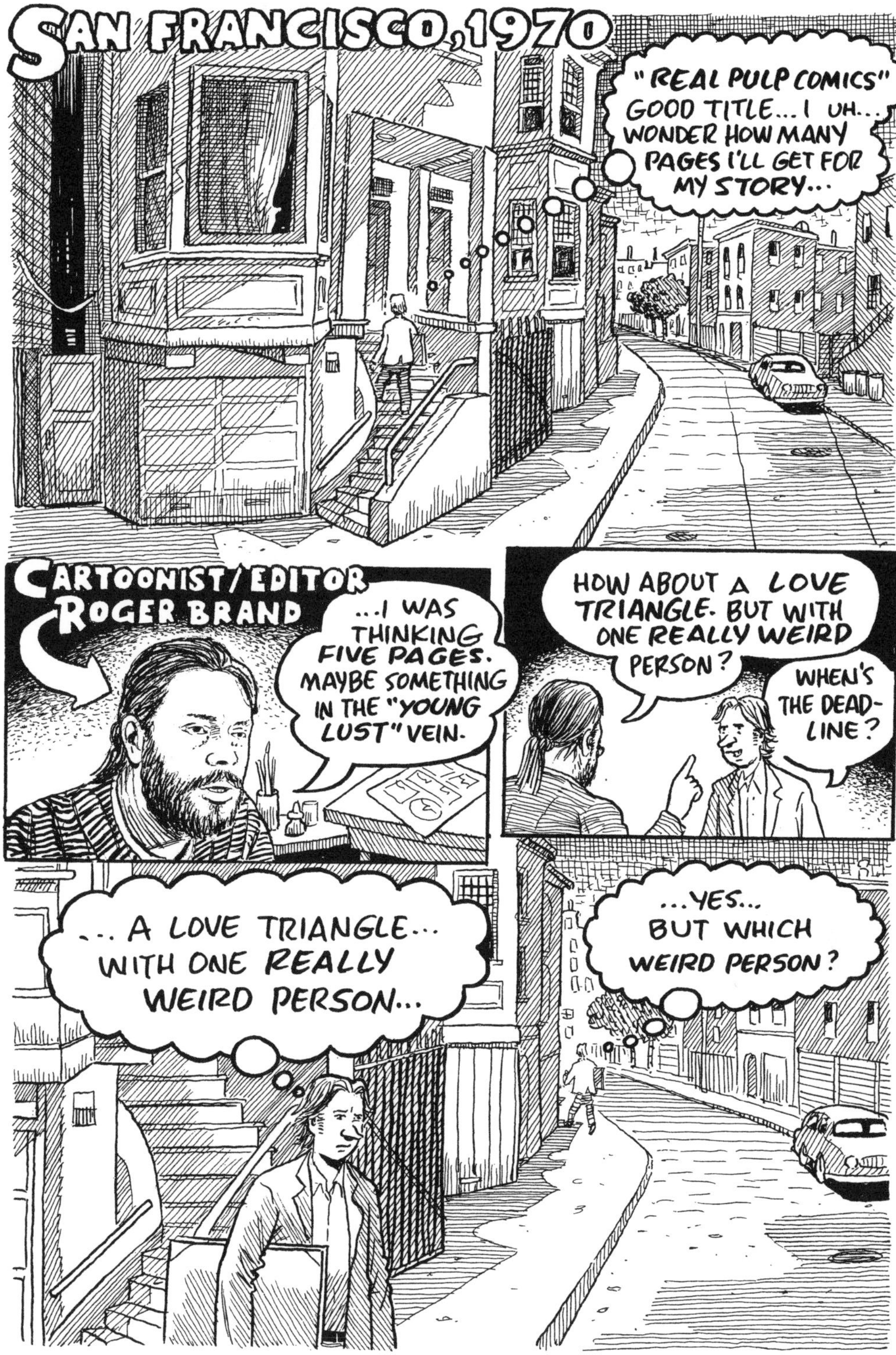
SAN FRANCISCO, 1970
"REAL PULP COMICS" GOOD TITLE... I UH... WONDER HOW MANY PAGES I'LL GET FOR MY STORY...
CARTOONIST/EDITOR ROGER BRAND
...I WAS THINKING FIVE PAGES. MAYBE SOMETHING IN THE "YOUNG LUST" VEIN.
HOW ABOUT A LOVE TRIANGLE. BUT WITH ONE REALLY WEIRD PERSON?
WHEN'S THE DEAD-LINE?
... A LOVE TRIANGLE... WITH ONE REALLY WEIRD PERSON...
...YES... BUT WHICH WEIRD PERSON?

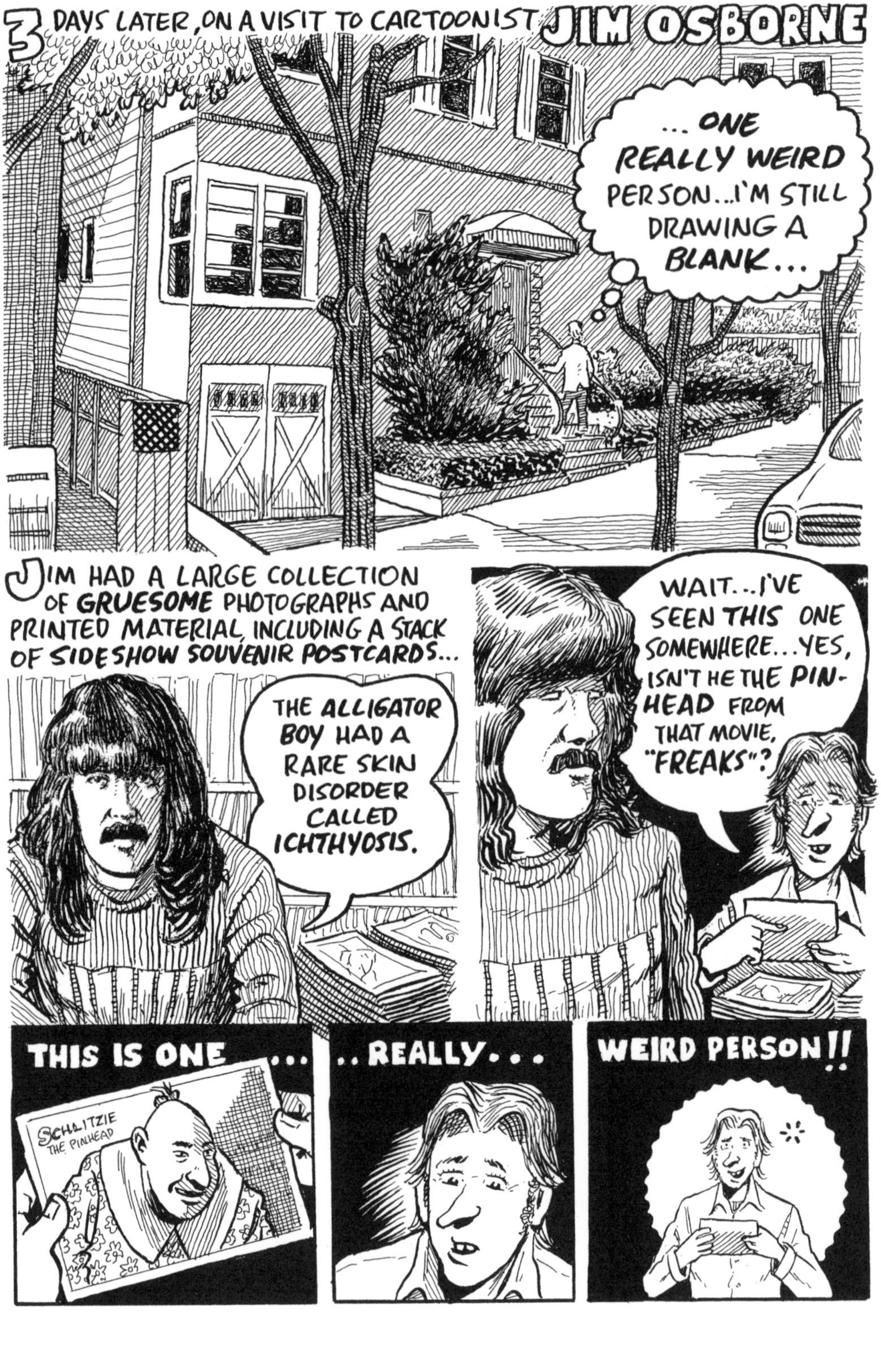
3 DAYS LATER, ON A VISIT TO CARTOONIST JIM OSBORNE
... ONE REALLY WEIRD PERSON... I'M STILL DRAWING A BLANK...
JIM HAD A LARGE COLLECTION OF GRUESOME PHOTOGRAPHS AND PRINTED MATERIAL, INCLUDING A STACK OF SIDESHOW SOUVENIR POSTCARDS...
THE ALLIGATOR BOY HAD A RARE SKIN DISORDER CALLED ICHTHYOSIS.
WAIT... I'VE SEEN THIS ONE SOMEWHERE... YES, ISN'T HE THE PIN-HEAD FROM THAT MOVIE, "FREAKS"?
THIS IS ONE ...
SCHLITZIE THE PINHEAD
.. REALLY...
WEIRD PERSON!!

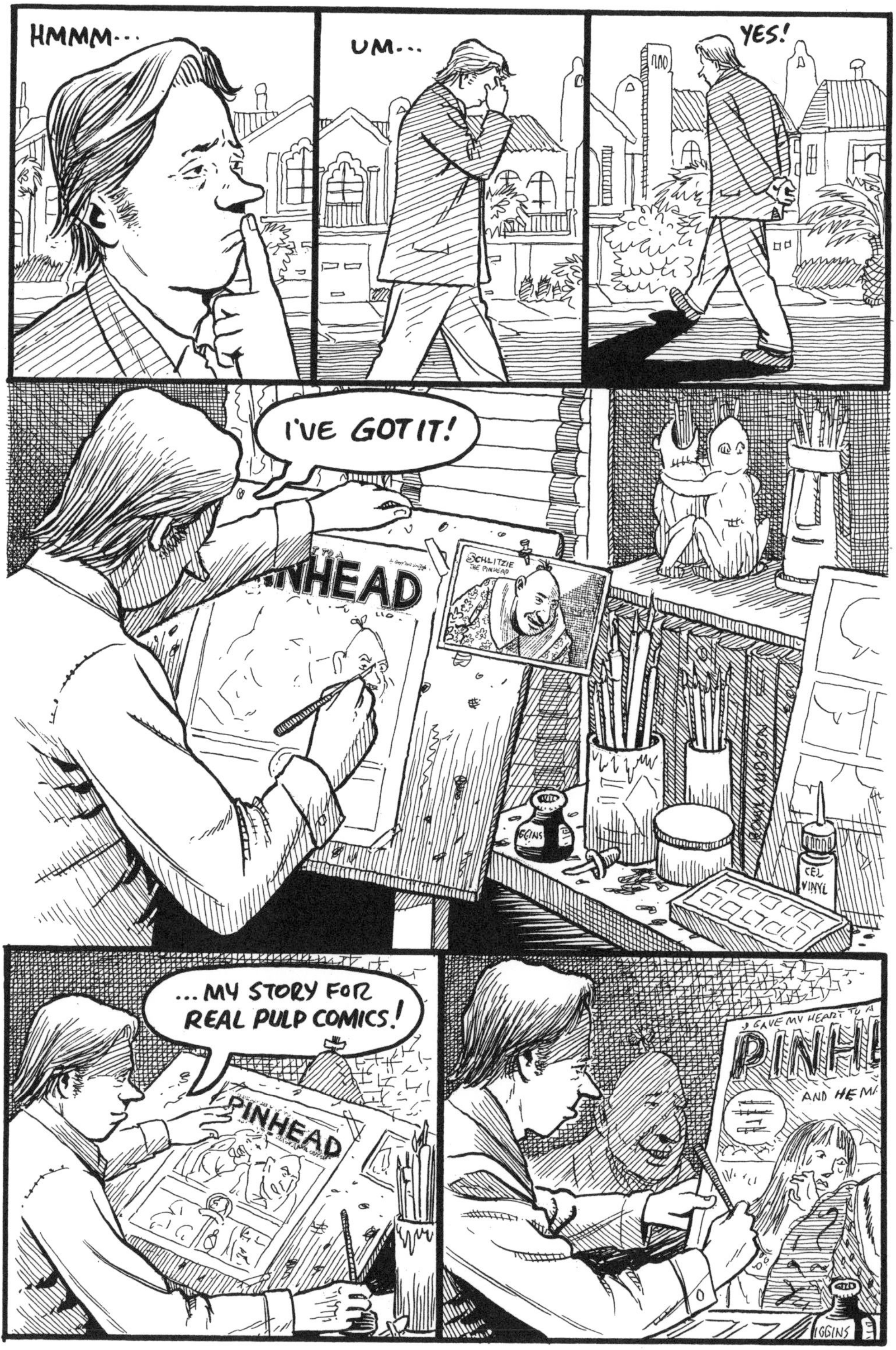
HMMM...
UM...
YES!
I'VE GOT IT!
PINHEAD
SCHLITZIE THE PINHEAD
CEL VINYL
...MY STORY FOR REAL PULP COMICS!
PINHEAD

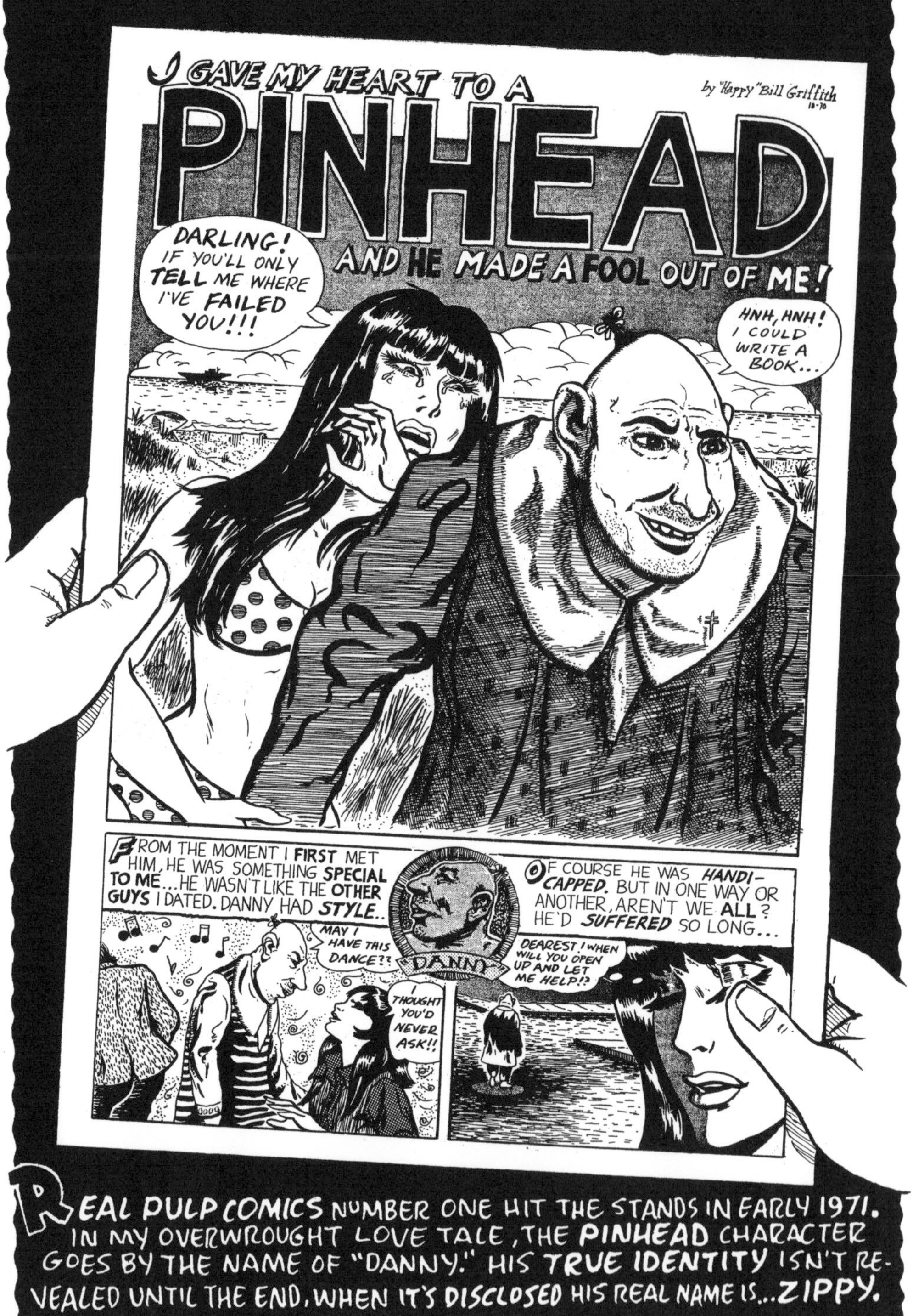
I GAVE MY HEART TO A
PINHEAD
AND HE MADE A FOOL OUT OF ME!
by "Happy" Bill Griffith 10-70
DARLING! IF YOU'LL ONLY TELL ME WHERE I'VE FAILED YOU!!!
HNH, HNH! I COULD WRITE A BOOK...
FROM THE MOMENT I FIRST MET HIM, HE WAS SOMETHING SPECIAL TO ME... HE WASN'T LIKE THE OTHER GUYS I DATED. DANNY HAD STYLE...
DANNY
OF COURSE HE WAS HANDI-CAPPED. BUT IN ONE WAY OR ANOTHER, AREN'T WE ALL? HE'D SUFFERED SO LONG...
MAY I HAVE THIS DANCE??
I THOUGHT YOU'D NEVER ASK!!
DEAREST! WHEN WILL YOU OPEN UP AND LET ME HELP!?
REAL PULP COMICS NUMBER ONE HIT THE STANDS IN EARLY 1971. IN MY OVERWROUGHT LOVE TALE, THE PINHEAD CHARACTER GOES BY THE NAME OF "DANNY." HIS TRUE IDENTITY ISN'T RE-VEALED UNTIL THE END, WHEN IT'S DISCLOSED HIS REAL NAME IS...ZIPPY.

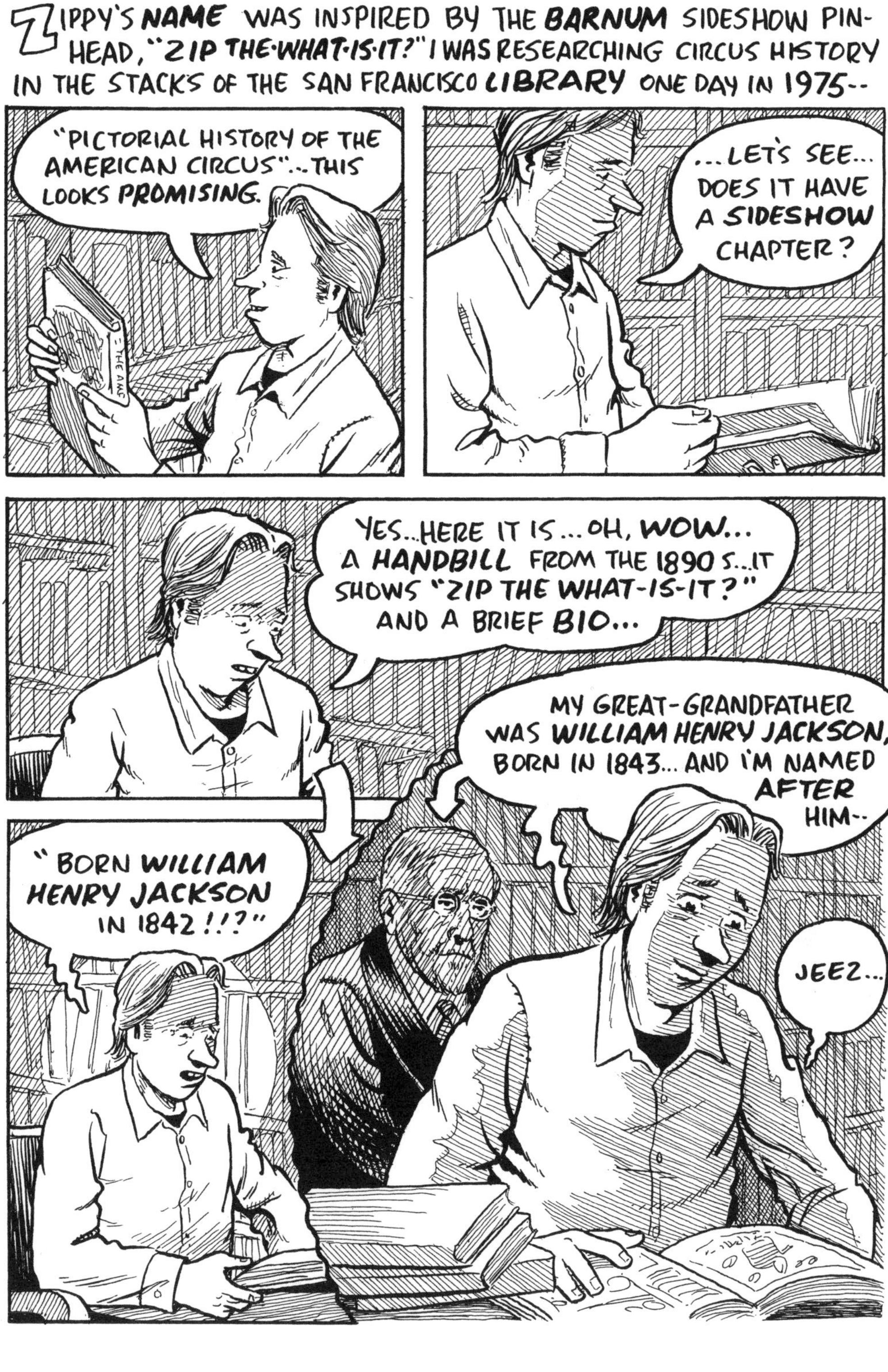
ZIPPY'S NAME WAS INSPIRED BY THE BARNUM SIDESHOW PIN-HEAD, "ZIP THE WHAT-IS-IT?" I WAS RESEARCHING CIRCUS HISTORY IN THE STACKS OF THE SAN FRANCISCO LIBRARY ONE DAY IN 1975--
"PICTORIAL HISTORY OF THE AMERICAN CIRCUS"... THIS LOOKS PROMISING.
...LET'S SEE... DOES IT HAVE A SIDESHOW CHAPTER?
YES...HERE IT IS... OH, WOW... A HANDBILL FROM THE 1890 S...IT SHOWS "ZIP THE WHAT-IS-IT?" AND A BRIEF BIO...
"BORN WILLIAM HENRY JACKSON IN 1842!!?"
MY GREAT-GRANDFATHER WAS WILLIAM HENRY JACKSON, BORN IN 1843... AND I'M NAMED AFTER HIM--
JEEZ...

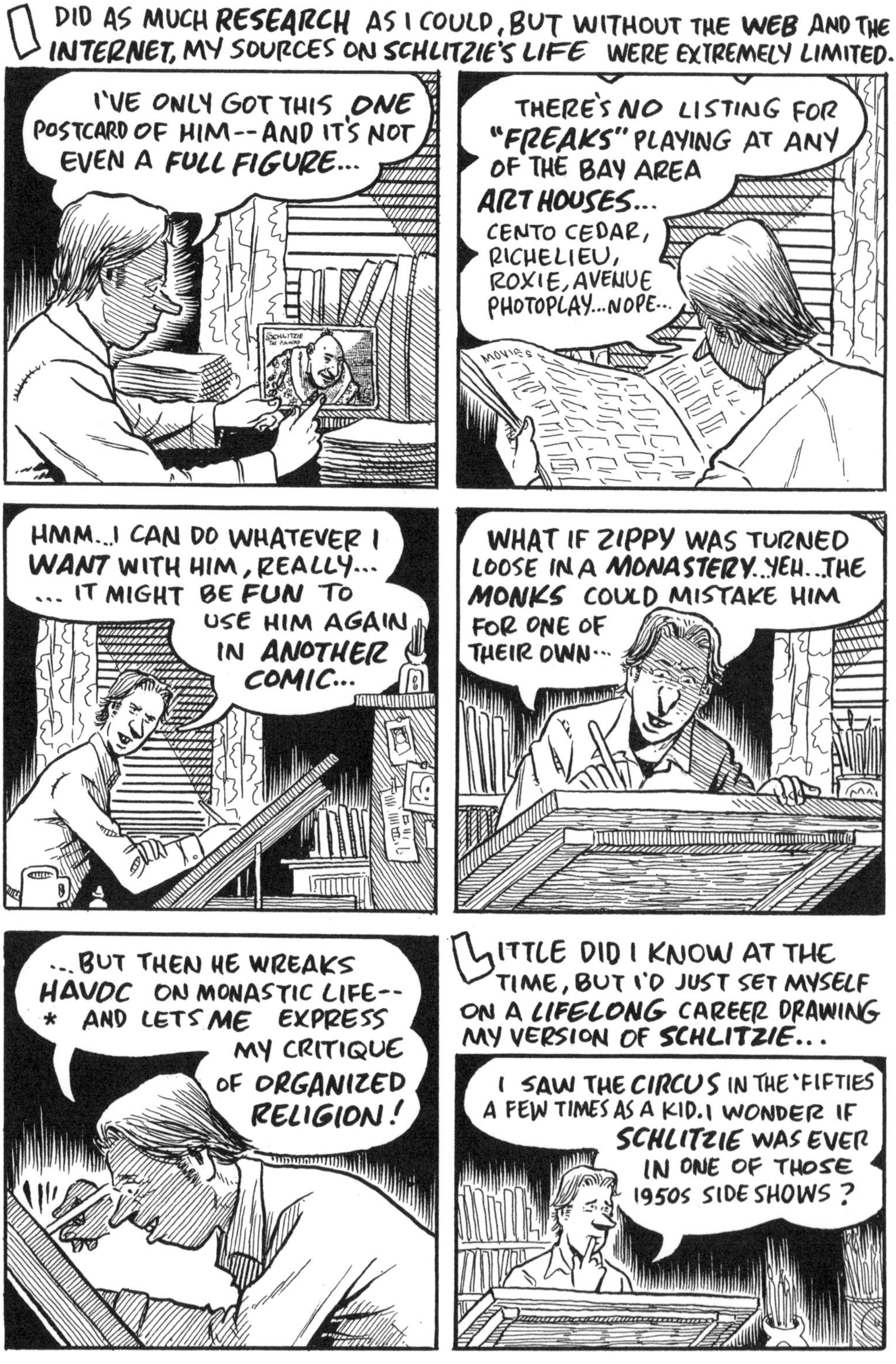
I DID AS MUCH RESEARCH AS I COULD, BUT WITHOUT THE WEB AND THE INTERNET, MY SOURCES ON SCHLITZIE'S LIFE WERE EXTREMELY LIMITED.
I'VE ONLY GOT THIS ONE POSTCARD OF HIM--AND IT'S NOT EVEN A FULL FIGURE...
SCHLITZIE
THERE'S NO LISTING FOR "FREAKS" PLAYING AT ANY OF THE BAY AREA ART HOUSES... CENTO CEDAR, RICHELIEU, ROXIE, AVENUE PHOTOPLAY...NOPE...
MOVIES
HMM...I CAN DO WHATEVER I WANT WITH HIM, REALLY... ...IT MIGHT BE FUN TO USE HIM AGAIN IN ANOTHER COMIC...
WHAT IF ZIPPY WAS TURNED LOOSE IN A MONASTERY...YEH...THE MONKS COULD MISTAKE HIM FOR ONE OF THEIR OWN...
...BUT THEN HE WREAKS HAVOC ON MONASTIC LIFE-- * AND LETS ME EXPRESS MY CRITIQUE OF ORGANIZED RELIGION!
LITTLE DID I KNOW AT THE TIME, BUT I'D JUST SET MYSELF ON A LIFELONG CAREER DRAWING MY VERSION OF SCHLITZIE...
I SAW THE CIRCUS IN THE 'FIFTIES A FEW TIMES AS A KID. I WONDER IF SCHLITZIE WAS EVER IN ONE OF THOSE 1950s SIDE SHOWS?

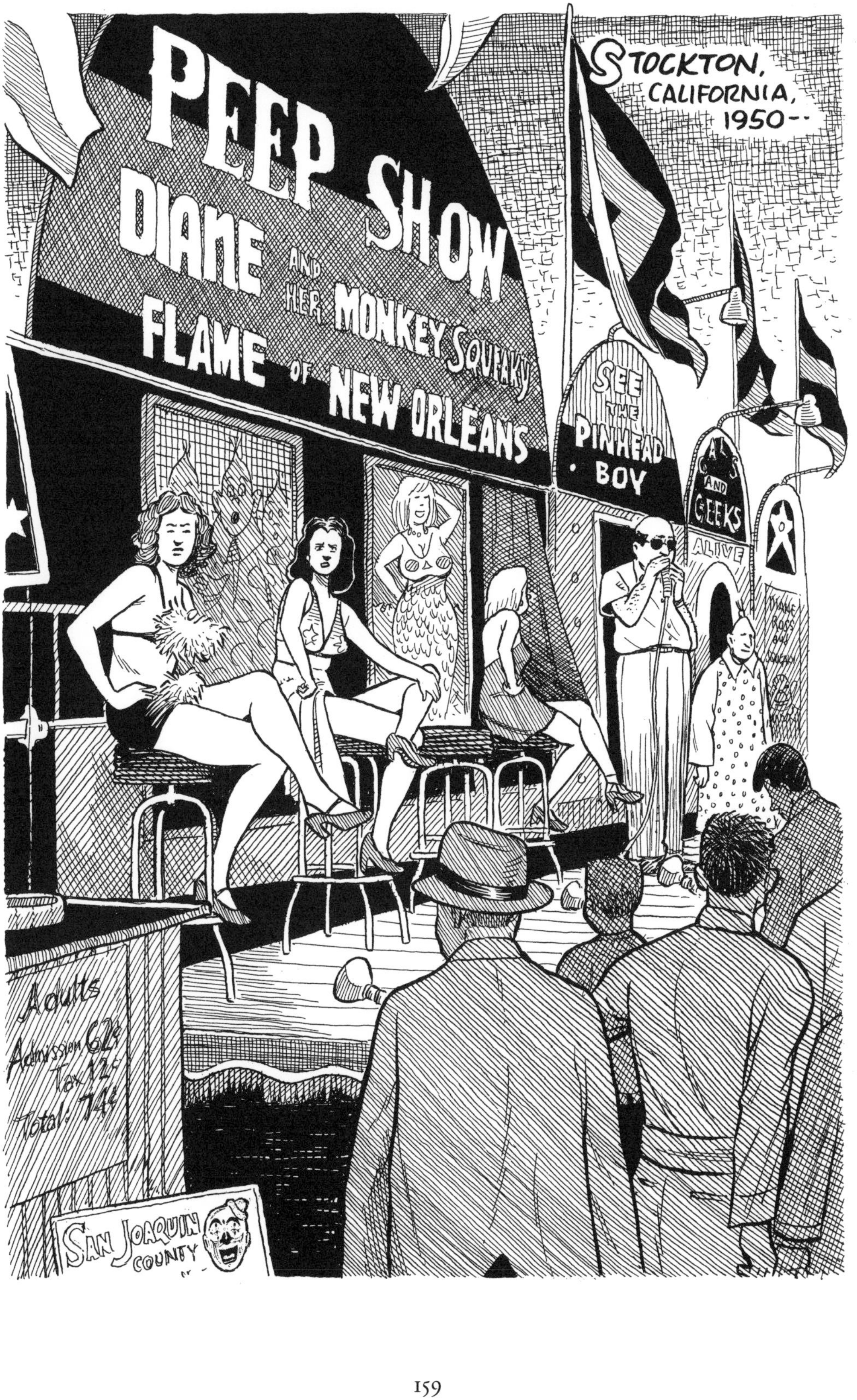
STOCKTON, CALIFORNIA, 1950--
PEEP SHOW
DIANE AND HER MONKEY SQUEAKY
FLAME OF NEW ORLEANS
SEE THE PINHEAD BOY
AND GEEKS
ALIVE
DIANE ROSS AND SQUEAKY
Adults Admission 62¢ Tax 12¢ Total: 74¢
SAN JOAQUIN COUNTY

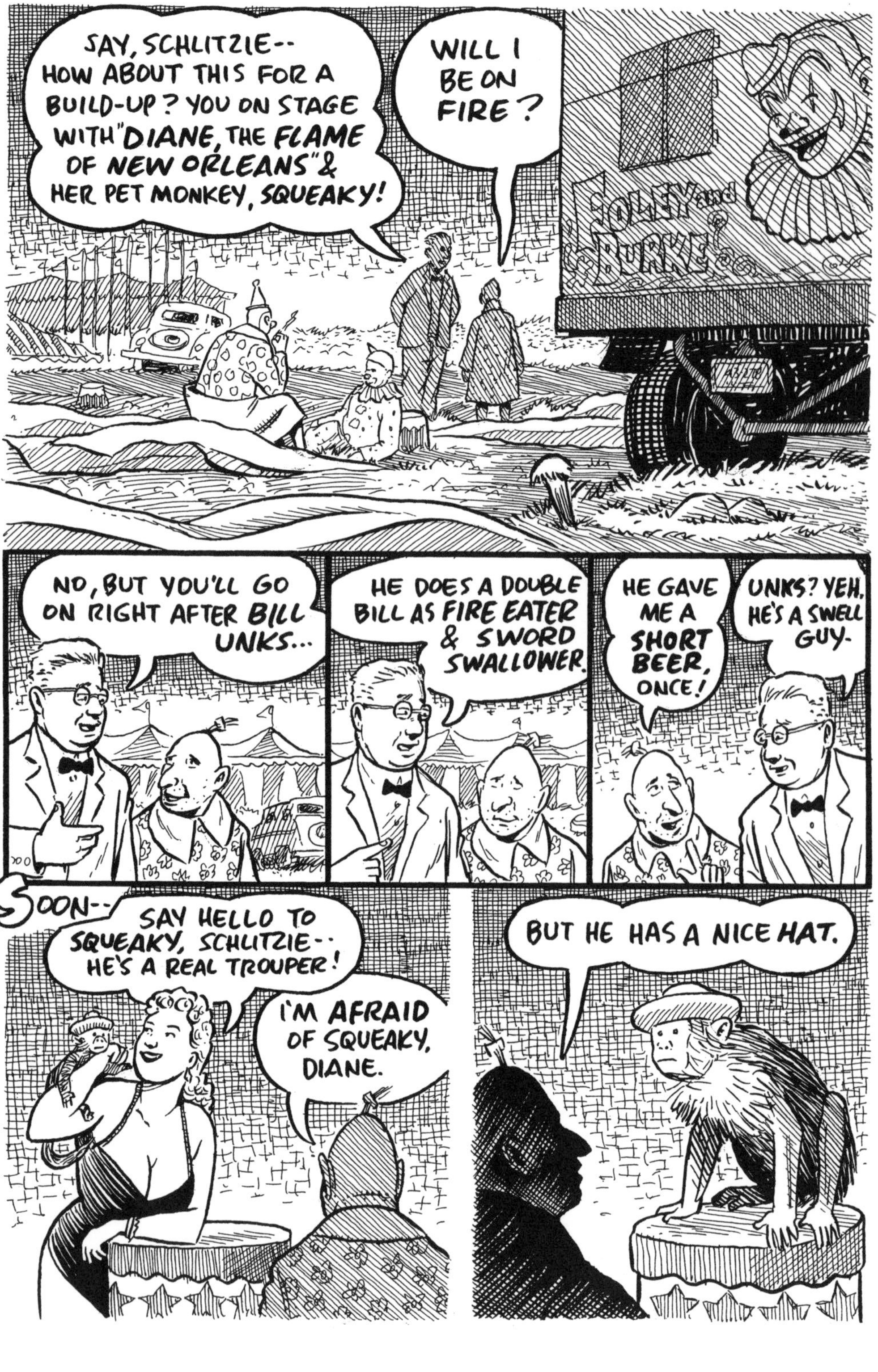
SAY, SCHLITZIE-- HOW ABOUT THIS FOR A BUILD-UP? YOU ON STAGE WITH "DIANE, THE FLAME OF NEW ORLEANS" & HER PET MONKEY, SQUEAKY!
WILL I BE ON FIRE?
NO, BUT YOU'LL GO ON RIGHT AFTER BILL UNKS...
HE DOES A DOUBLE BILL AS FIRE EATER & SWORD SWALLOWER.
HE GAVE ME A SHORT BEER, ONCE!
UNKS? YEH, HE'S A SWELL GUY-
SOON--
SAY HELLO TO SQUEAKY, SCHLITZIE-- HE'S A REAL TROUPER!
I'M AFRAID OF SQUEAKY, DIANE.
BUT HE HAS A NICE HAT.

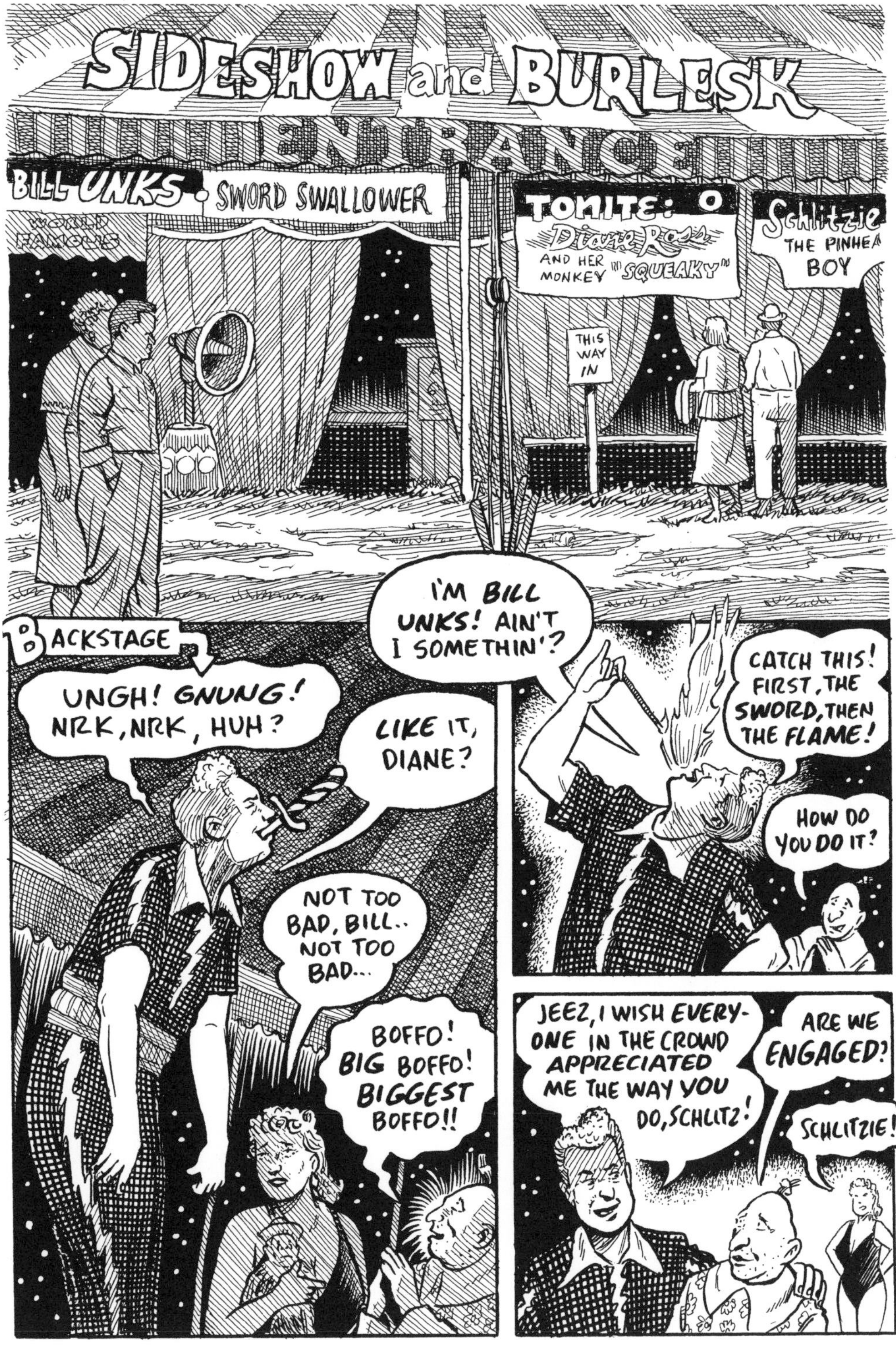

SIDESHOW and BURLESK
ENDURANCE
BILL UNKS · SWORD SWALLOWER
WORLD FAMOUS
TONITE: DIANE ROSS AND HER MONKEY "SQUEAKY"
Schlitzie THE PINHEA BOY
THIS WAY IN
BACKSTAGE
UNGH! GNUNG! NRK, NRK, HUH?
LIKE IT, DIANE?
NOT TOO BAD, BILL.. NOT TOO BAD...
BOFFO! BIG BOFFO! BIGGEST BOFFO!!
I'M BILL UNKS! AIN'T I SOMETHIN'?
CATCH THIS! FIRST, THE SWORD, THEN THE FLAME!
HOW DO YOU DO IT?
JEEZ, I WISH EVERY-ONE IN THE CROWD APPRECIATED ME THE WAY YOU DO, SCHLITZ!
ARE WE ENGAGED?
SCHLITZIE!

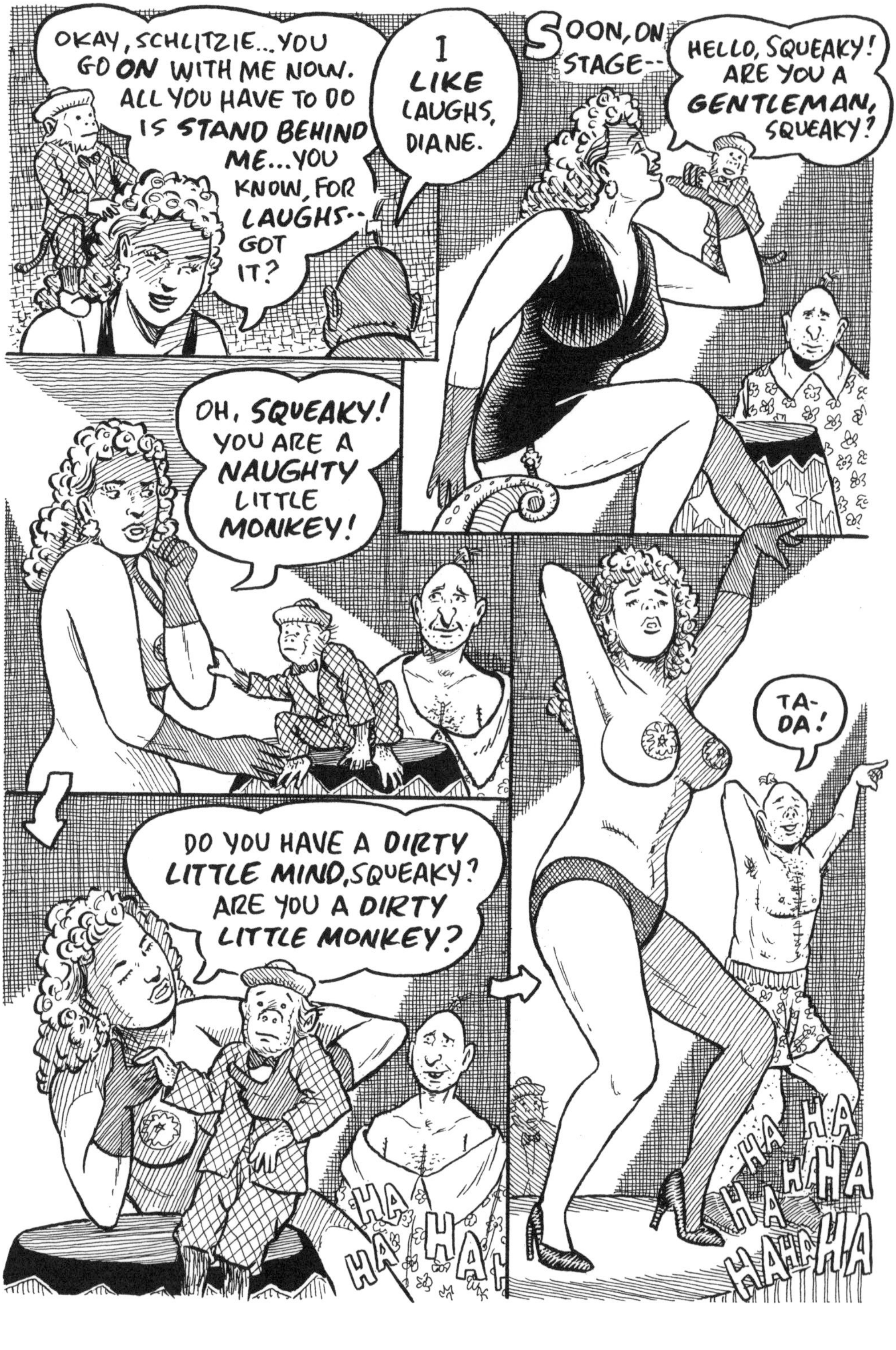
OKAY, SCHLITZIE... YOU GO ON WITH ME NOW. ALL YOU HAVE TO DO IS STAND BEHIND ME... YOU KNOW, FOR LAUGHS.. GOT IT?
I LIKE LAUGHS, DIANE.
SOON, ON STAGE--
HELLO, SQUEAKY! ARE YOU A GENTLEMAN, SQUEAKY?
OH, SQUEAKY! YOU ARE A NAUGHTY LITTLE MONKEY!
DO YOU HAVE A DIRTY LITTLE MIND, SQUEAKY? ARE YOU A DIRTY LITTLE MONKEY?
HA HA HA HA
TA-DA!
HA HA HA HA HA HA HA HA HA

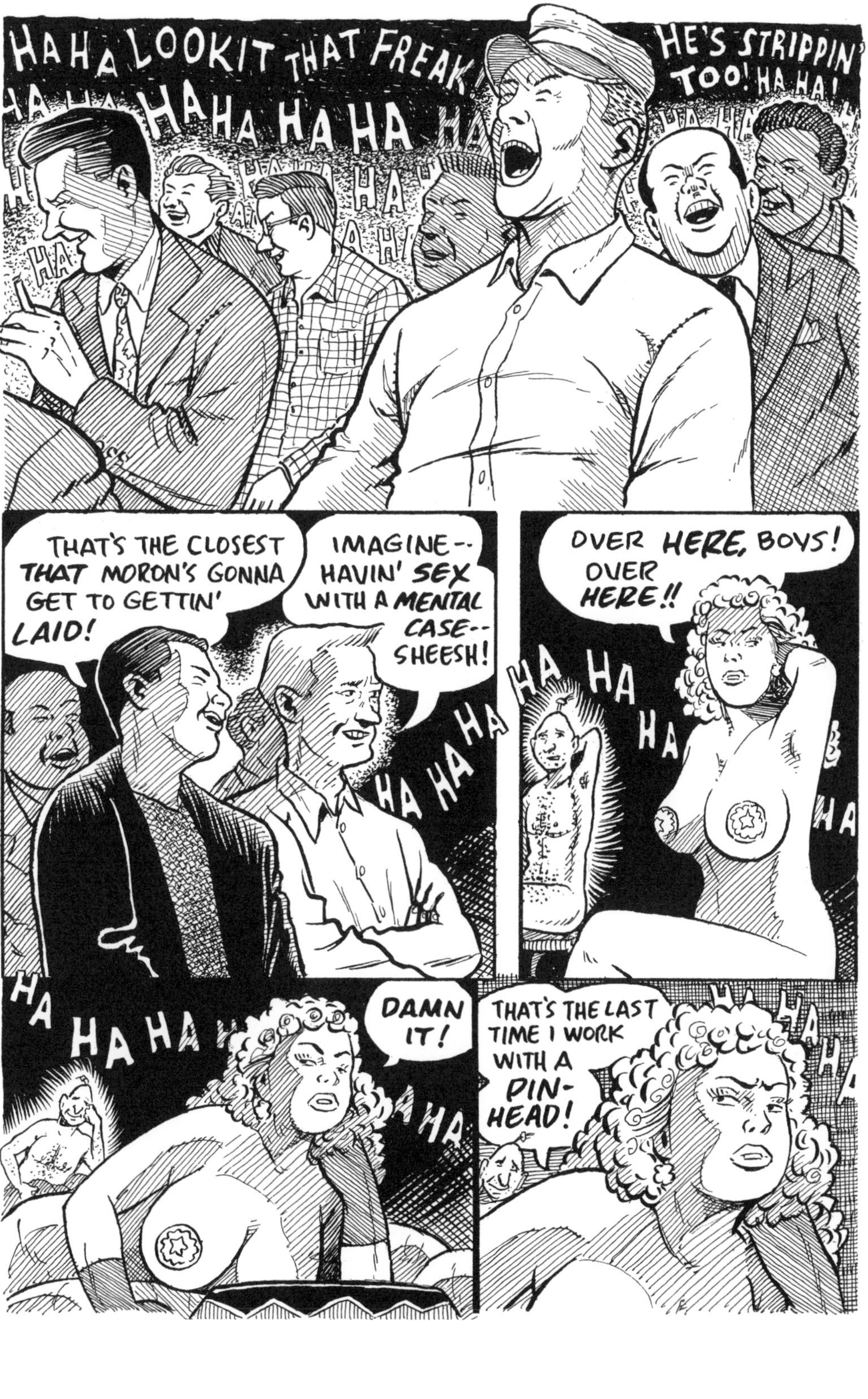
HA HA LOOKIT THAT FREAK!
HE'S STRIPPIN' TOO! HA HA!
HA HA HA HA HA HA HA
THAT'S THE CLOSEST THAT MORON'S GONNA GET TO GETTIN' LAID!
IMAGINE-- HAVIN' SEX WITH A MENTAL CASE-- SHEESH!
HA HA HA HA
OVER HERE, BOYS! OVER HERE!!
HA HA HA
HA HA HA
DAMN IT!
HA HA
THAT'S THE LAST TIME I WORK WITH A PIN-HEAD!

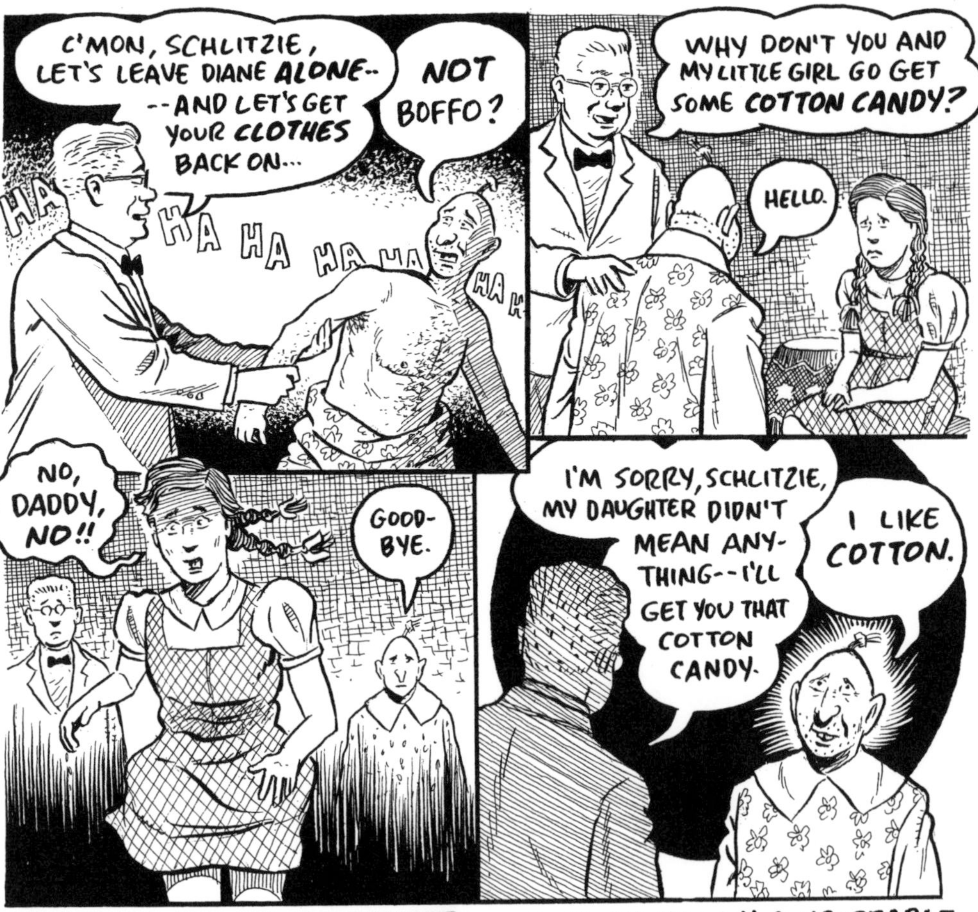
C'MON, SCHLITZIE, LET'S LEAVE DIANE ALONE-- --AND LET'S GET YOUR CLOTHES BACK ON...
NOT BOFFO?
HA HA HA HA HA HA
WHY DON'T YOU AND MY LITTLE GIRL GO GET SOME COTTON CANDY?
HELLO.
NO, DADDY, NO!!
GOOD-BYE.
I'M SORRY, SCHLITZIE, MY DAUGHTER DIDN'T MEAN ANY-THING--I'LL GET YOU THAT COTTON CANDY.
I LIKE COTTON.

GEORGE SURTEES'S DAUGHTER WAS NEVER REALLY COMFORTABLE WITH SCHLITZIE AS AN ADOPTED MEMBER OF HER FAMILY--

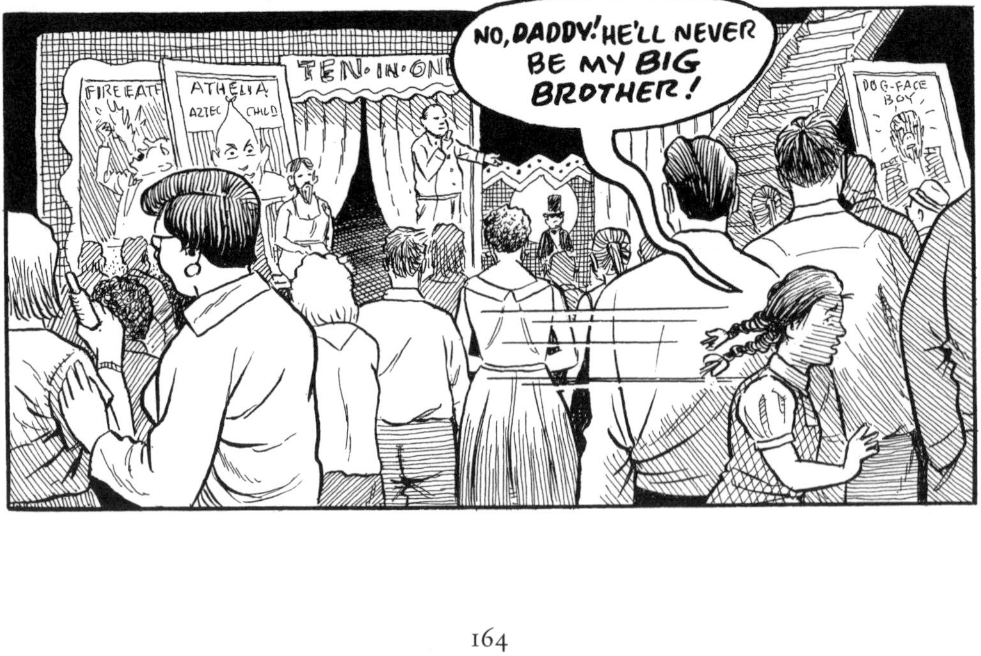
FIRE EATER
ATHELIA AZTEC CHILD
TEN-IN-ONE
DOG-FACE BOY
NO, DADDY! HE'LL NEVER BE MY BIG BROTHER!

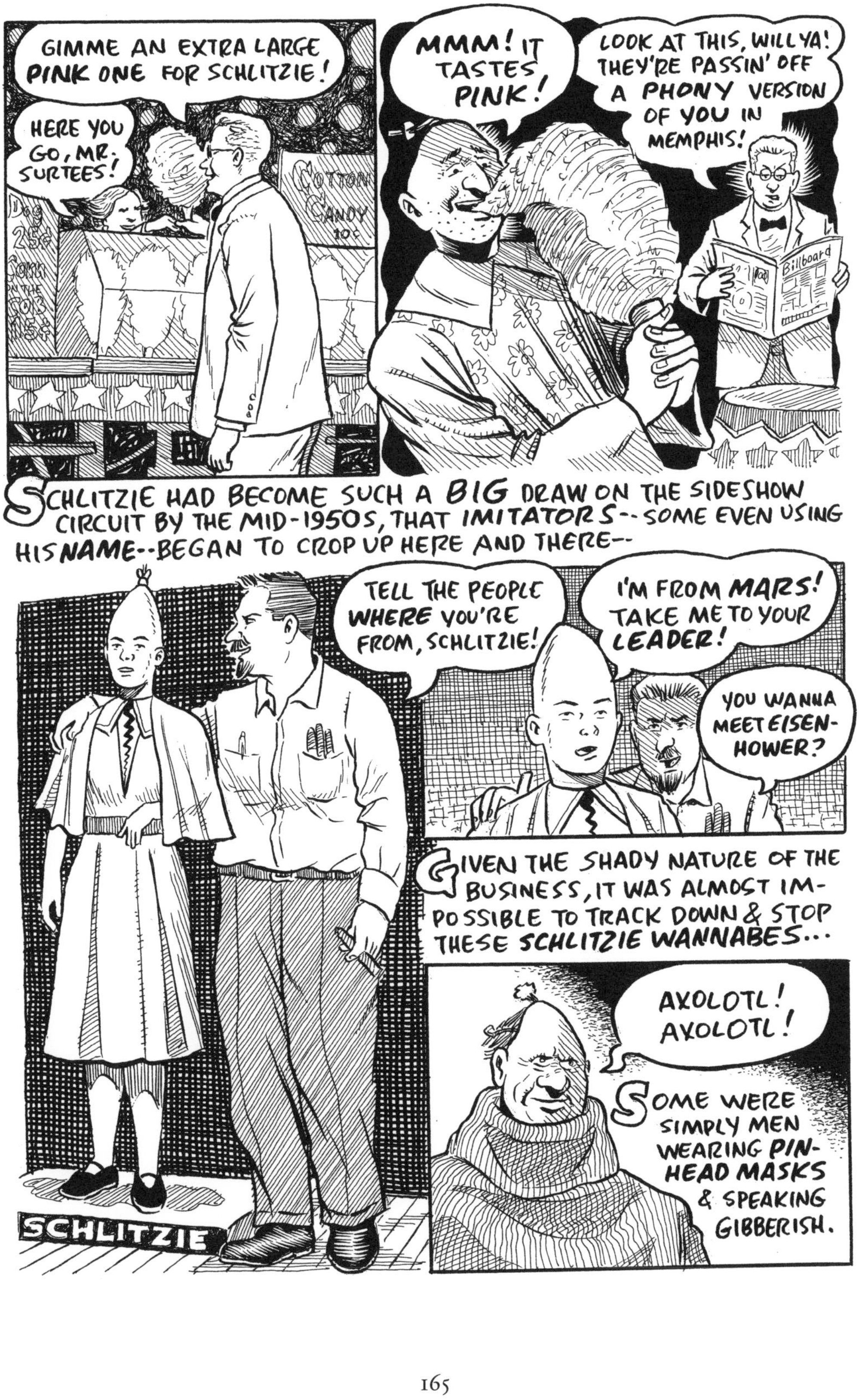
GIMME AN EXTRA LARGE PINK ONE FOR SCHLITZIE!
HERE YOU GO, MR. SURTEES!
COTTON CANDY 10¢
MMM! IT TASTES PINK!
LOOK AT THIS, WILLYA! THEY'RE PASSIN' OFF A PHONY VERSION OF YOU IN MEMPHIS!
Billboard
SCHLITZIE HAD BECOME SUCH A BIG DRAW ON THE SIDESHOW CIRCUIT BY THE MID-1950S, THAT IMITATORS--SOME EVEN USING HIS NAME--BEGAN TO CROP UP HERE AND THERE--
SCHLITZIE
TELL THE PEOPLE WHERE YOU'RE FROM, SCHLITZIE!
I'M FROM MARS! TAKE ME TO YOUR LEADER!
YOU WANNA MEET EISEN-HOWER?
GIVEN THE SHADY NATURE OF THE BUSINESS, IT WAS ALMOST IM-POSSIBLE TO TRACK DOWN & STOP THESE SCHLITZIE WANNABES...
AXOLOTL! AXOLOTL!
SOME WERE SIMPLY MEN WEARING PIN-HEAD MASKS & SPEAKING GIBBERISH.

SCHLITZIE'S PREVIOUS MANAGER, TED METZ, DIED IN 1954. THE SURTEES FAMILY PLACED AN AD IN "BILLBOARD" MAGAZINE IN HIS MEMORY EVERY YEAR FOR SOME TIME AFTERWARD--

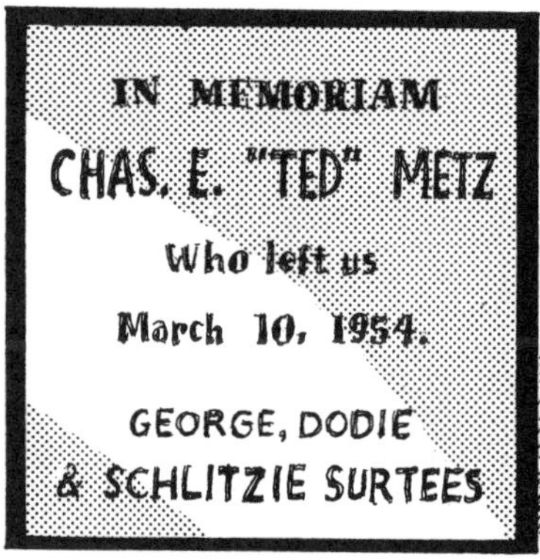
IN MEMORIAM

CHAS. E. "TED" METZ

Who left us

March 10, 1954.

GEORGE, DODIE

& SCHLITZIE SURTEES

STILL UNDER MANAGEMENT TO SURTEES, SCHLITZIE TRAVELED TO THE EAST COAST IN 1955 WITH COL. LEW ALTER'S "**I.T. SHOWS.**"

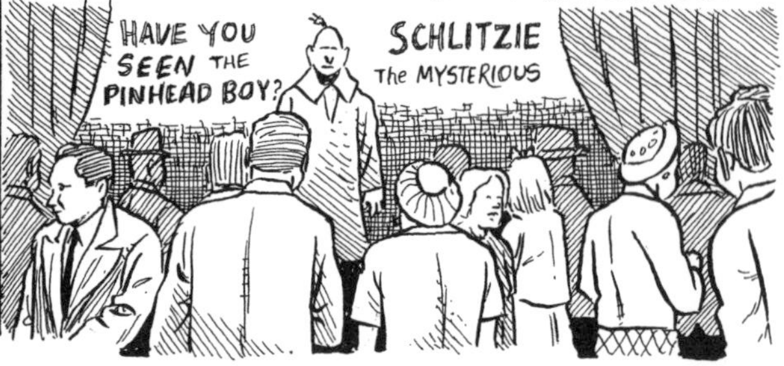
HAVE YOU SEEN THE PINHEAD BOY?
SCHLITZIE
The MYSTERIOUS

HE PLAYED TO LARGE CROWDS IN NEW ENGLAND AND AT THE **MINEOLA FAIR** IN WESTBURY, LONG ISLAND--

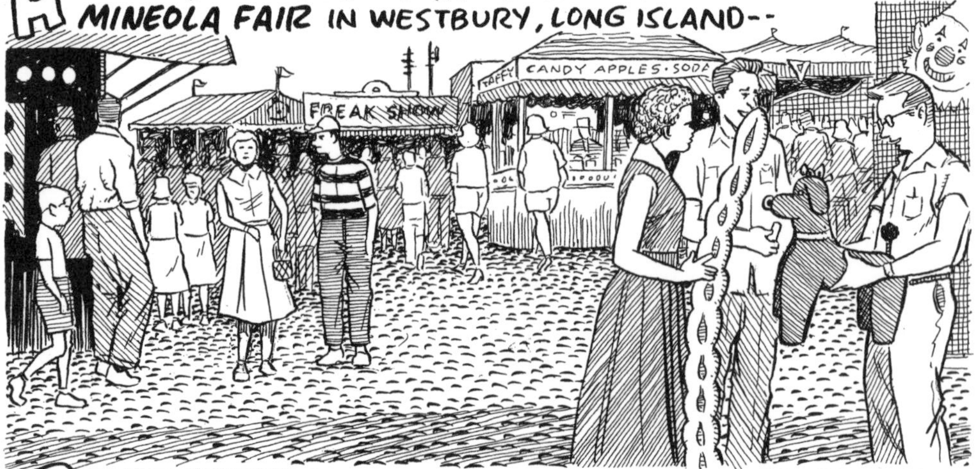
FREAK SHOW
TAFFY
CANDY APPLES · SODA

BUT THE SIDESHOW, WITH ITS USUAL CONTINGENT OF **BEARDED LADIES, LOBSTER BOYS, & PINHEADS** WAS NOT RECEIVED WITH ENTHUSIASM BY **ALL** WHO ATTENDED, ESPECIALLY THE **LAW**--

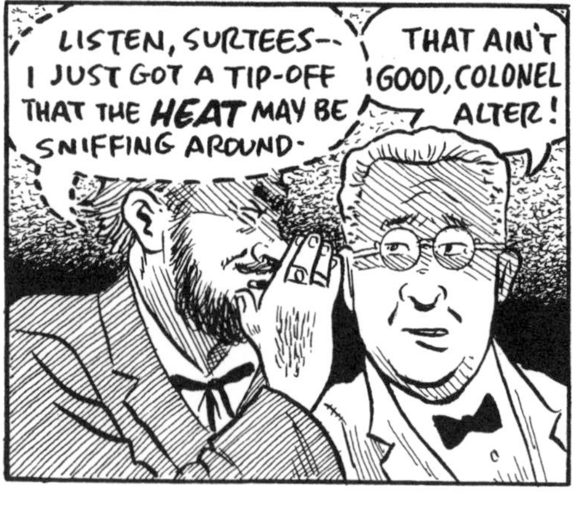
LISTEN, SURTEES-- I JUST GOT A TIP-OFF THAT THE **HEAT** MAY BE SNIFFING AROUND-
THAT AIN'T GOOD, COLONEL ALTER!

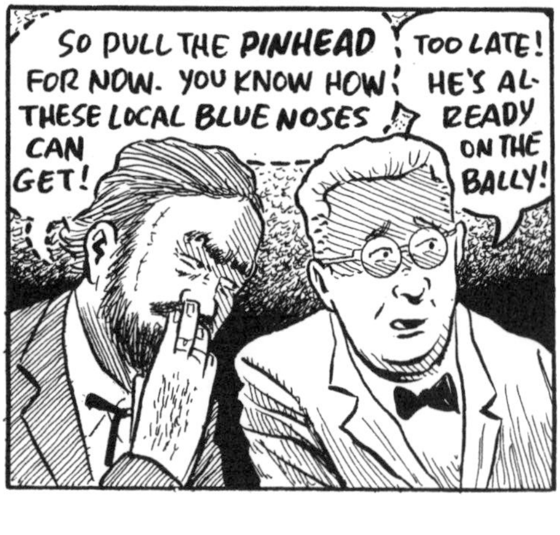
SO PULL THE **PINHEAD** FOR NOW. YOU KNOW HOW THESE LOCAL **BLUE NOSES** CAN GET!
TOO LATE! HE'S ALREADY ON THE BALLY!

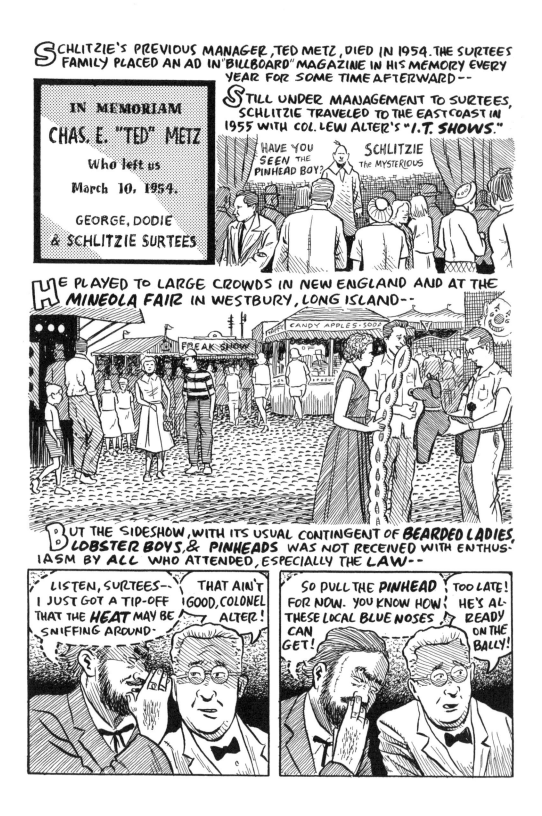

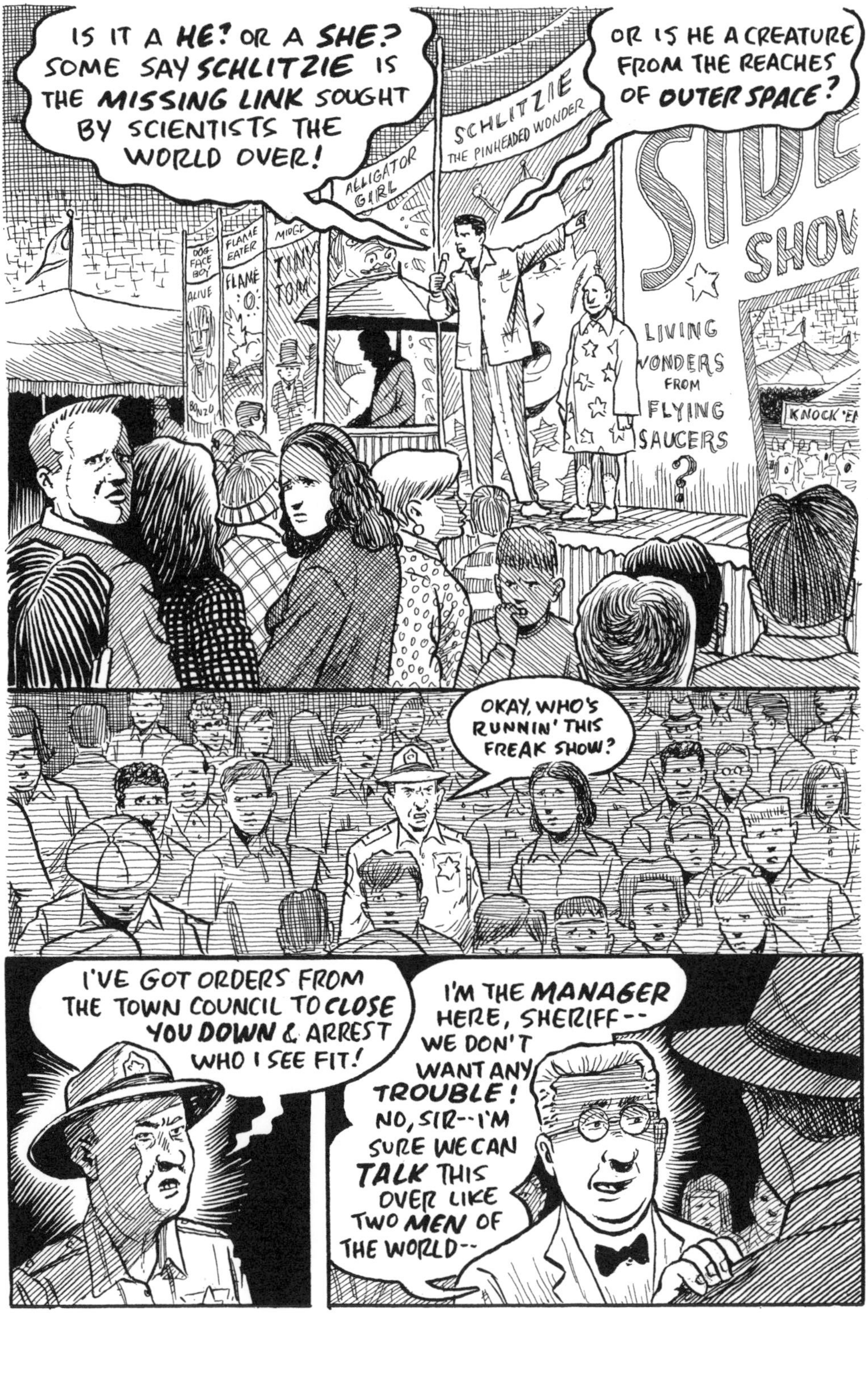
IS IT A HE? OR A SHE? SOME SAY SCHLITZIE IS THE MISSING LINK SOUGHT BY SCIENTISTS THE WORLD OVER!
OR IS HE A CREATURE FROM THE REACHES OF OUTER SPACE?
ALLIGATOR GIRL
SCHLITZIE THE PINHEADED WONDER
DOG-FACE BOY
FLAME EATER
FLAME-O
TINY TOM
LIVING WONDERS FROM FLYING SAUCERS ?
OKAY, WHO'S RUNNIN' THIS FREAK SHOW?
I'VE GOT ORDERS FROM THE TOWN COUNCIL TO CLOSE YOU DOWN & ARREST WHO I SEE FIT!
I'M THE MANAGER HERE, SHERIFF-- WE DON'T WANT ANY TROUBLE! NO, SIR--I'M SURE WE CAN TALK THIS OVER LIKE TWO MEN OF THE WORLD--

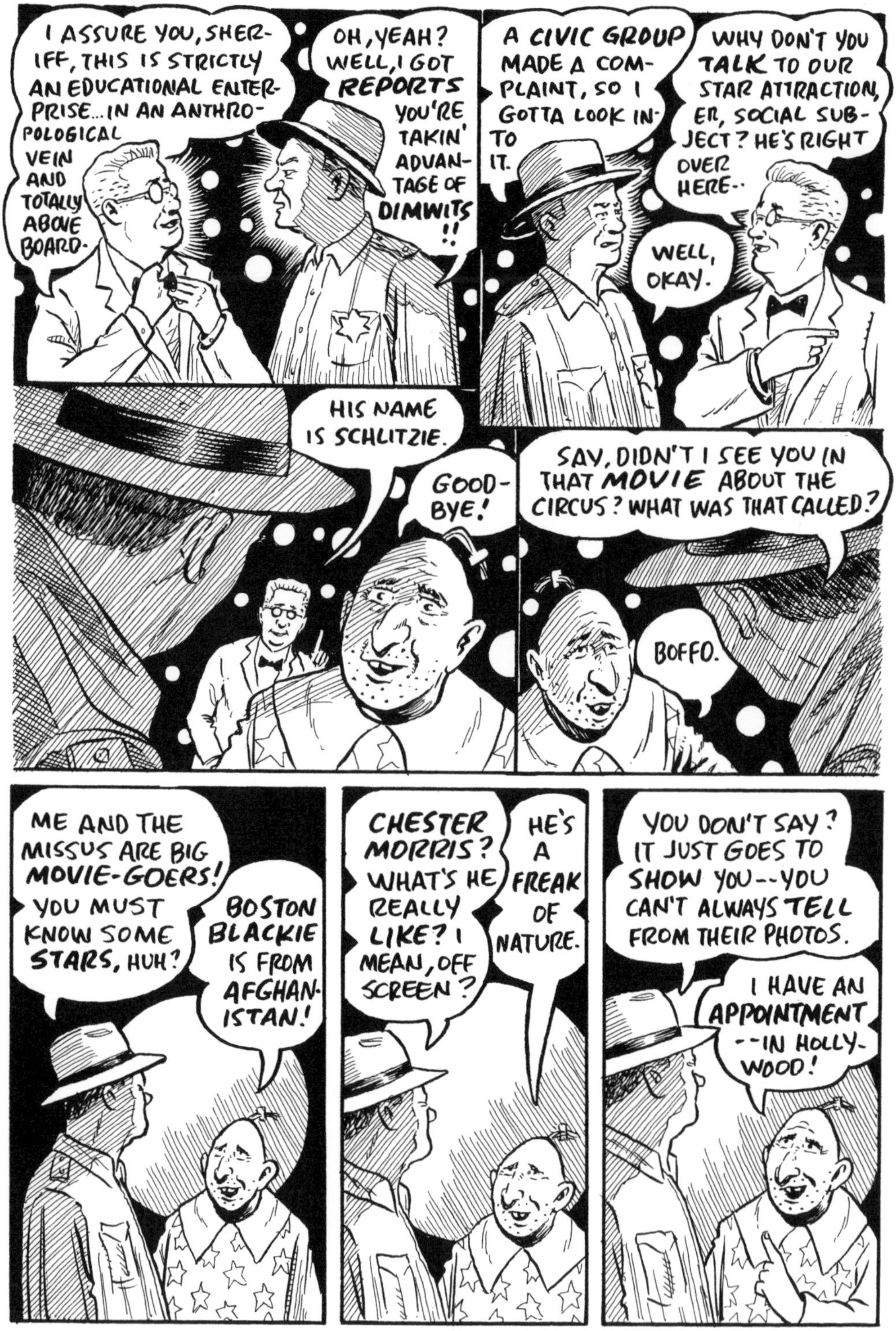
I ASSURE YOU, SHERIFF, THIS IS STRICTLY AN EDUCATIONAL ENTERPRISE... IN AN ANTHROPOLOGICAL VEIN AND TOTALLY ABOVE BOARD.
OH, YEAH? WELL, I GOT REPORTS YOU'RE TAKIN' ADVANTAGE OF DIMWITS!!
A CIVIC GROUP MADE A COMPLAINT, SO I GOTTA LOOK INTO IT.
WHY DON'T YOU TALK TO OUR STAR ATTRACTION, ER, SOCIAL SUBJECT? HE'S RIGHT OVER HERE..
WELL, OKAY.
HIS NAME IS SCHLITZIE.
GOOD-BYE!
SAY, DIDN'T I SEE YOU IN THAT MOVIE ABOUT THE CIRCUS? WHAT WAS THAT CALLED?
BOFFO.
ME AND THE MISSUS ARE BIG MOVIE-GOERS! YOU MUST KNOW SOME STARS, HUH?
BOSTON BLACKIE IS FROM AFGHANISTAN!
CHESTER MORRIS? WHAT'S HE REALLY LIKE? I MEAN, OFF SCREEN?
HE'S A FREAK OF NATURE.
YOU DON'T SAY? IT JUST GOES TO SHOW YOU--YOU CAN'T ALWAYS TELL FROM THEIR PHOTOS.
I HAVE AN APPOINTMENT--IN HOLLYWOOD!

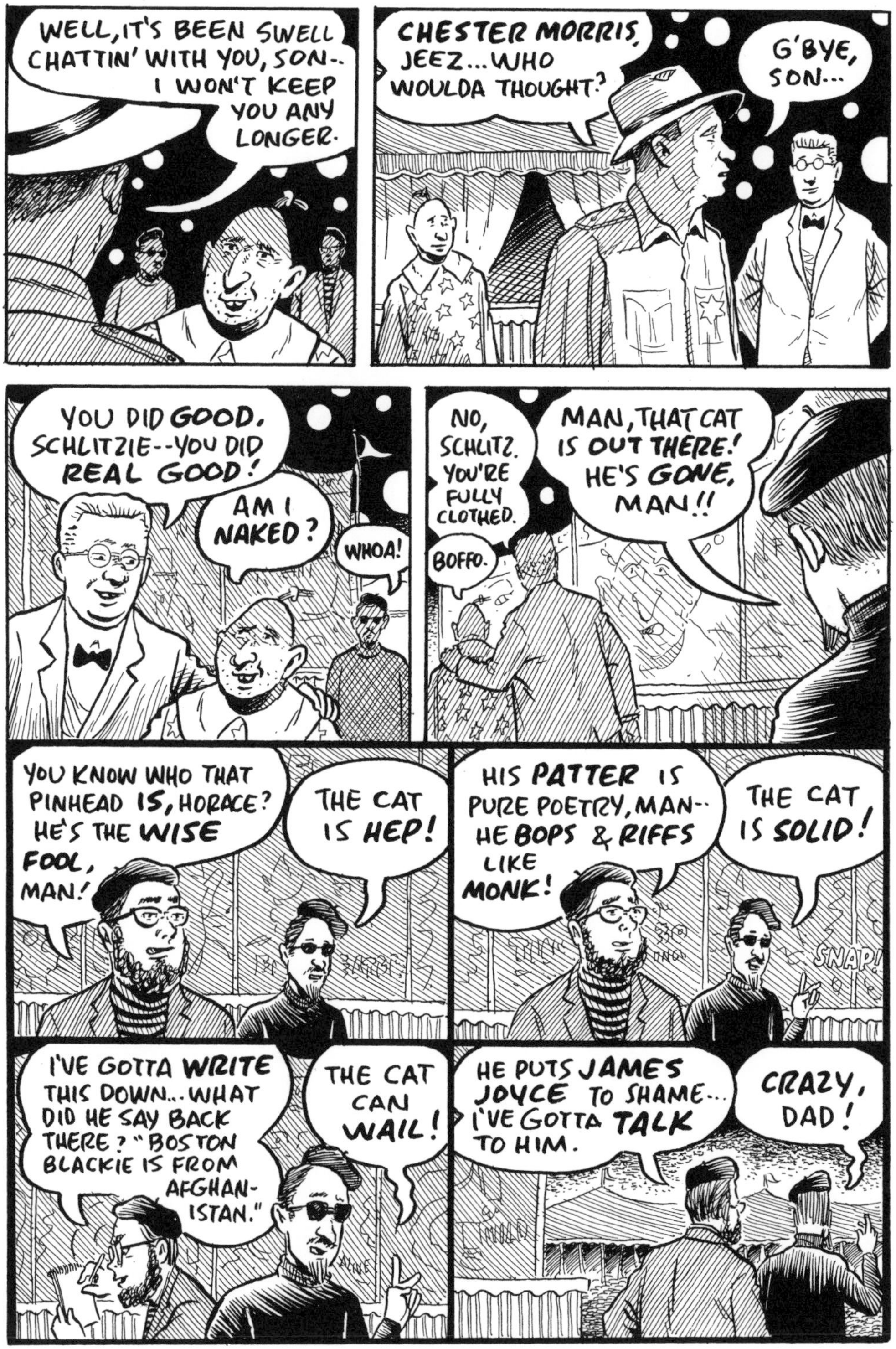
WELL, IT'S BEEN SWELL CHATTIN' WITH YOU, SON-- I WON'T KEEP YOU ANY LONGER.
CHESTER MORRIS, JEEZ... WHO WOULDA THOUGHT?
G'BYE, SON...
YOU DID GOOD, SCHLITZIE--YOU DID REAL GOOD!
AM I NAKED?
WHOA!
NO, SCHLITZ. YOU'RE FULLY CLOTHED.
BOFFO.
MAN, THAT CAT IS OUT THERE! HE'S GONE, MAN!!
YOU KNOW WHO THAT PINHEAD IS, HORACE? HE'S THE WISE FOOL, MAN!
THE CAT IS HEP!
HIS PATTER IS PURE POETRY, MAN-- HE BOPS & RIFFS LIKE MONK!
THE CAT IS SOLID!
SNAP!
I'VE GOTTA WRITE THIS DOWN... WHAT DID HE SAY BACK THERE? "BOSTON BLACKIE IS FROM AFGHAN-ISTAN."
THE CAT CAN WAIL!
HE PUTS JAMES JOYCE TO SHAME... I'VE GOTTA TALK TO HIM.
CRAZY, DAD!

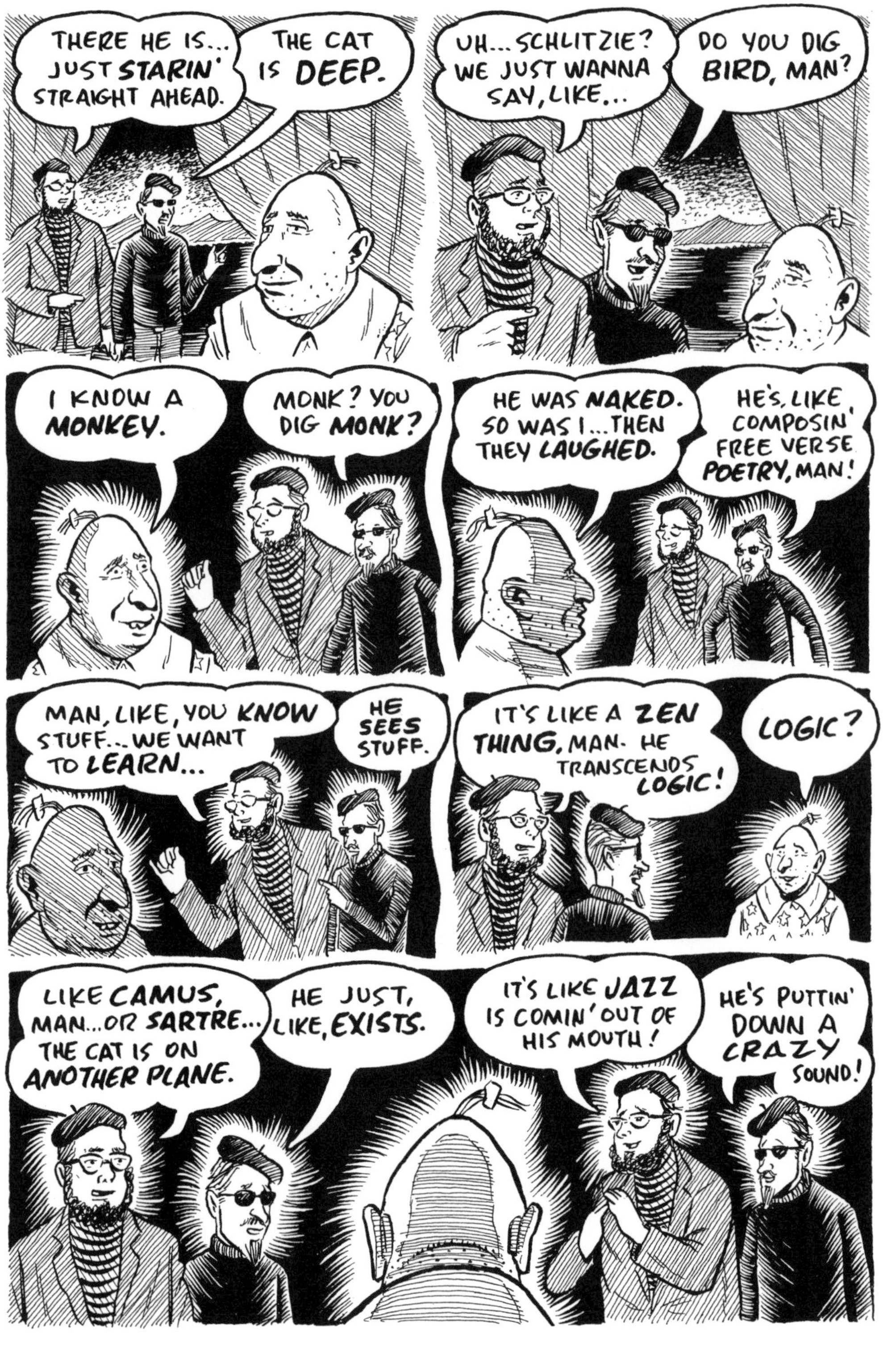
THERE HE IS... JUST STARIN' STRAIGHT AHEAD.
THE CAT IS DEEP.
UH... SCHLITZIE? WE JUST WANNA SAY, LIKE...
DO YOU DIG BIRD, MAN?
I KNOW A MONKEY.
MONK? YOU DIG MONK?
HE WAS NAKED. SO WAS I... THEN THEY LAUGHED.
HE'S, LIKE COMPOSIN' FREE VERSE POETRY, MAN!
MAN, LIKE, YOU KNOW STUFF... WE WANT TO LEARN...
HE SEES STUFF.
IT'S LIKE A ZEN THING, MAN. HE TRANSCENDS LOGIC!
LOGIC?
LIKE CAMUS, MAN... OR SARTRE... THE CAT IS ON ANOTHER PLANE.
HE JUST, LIKE, EXISTS.
IT'S LIKE JAZZ IS COMIN' OUT OF HIS MOUTH!
HE'S PUTTIN' DOWN A CRAZY SOUND!

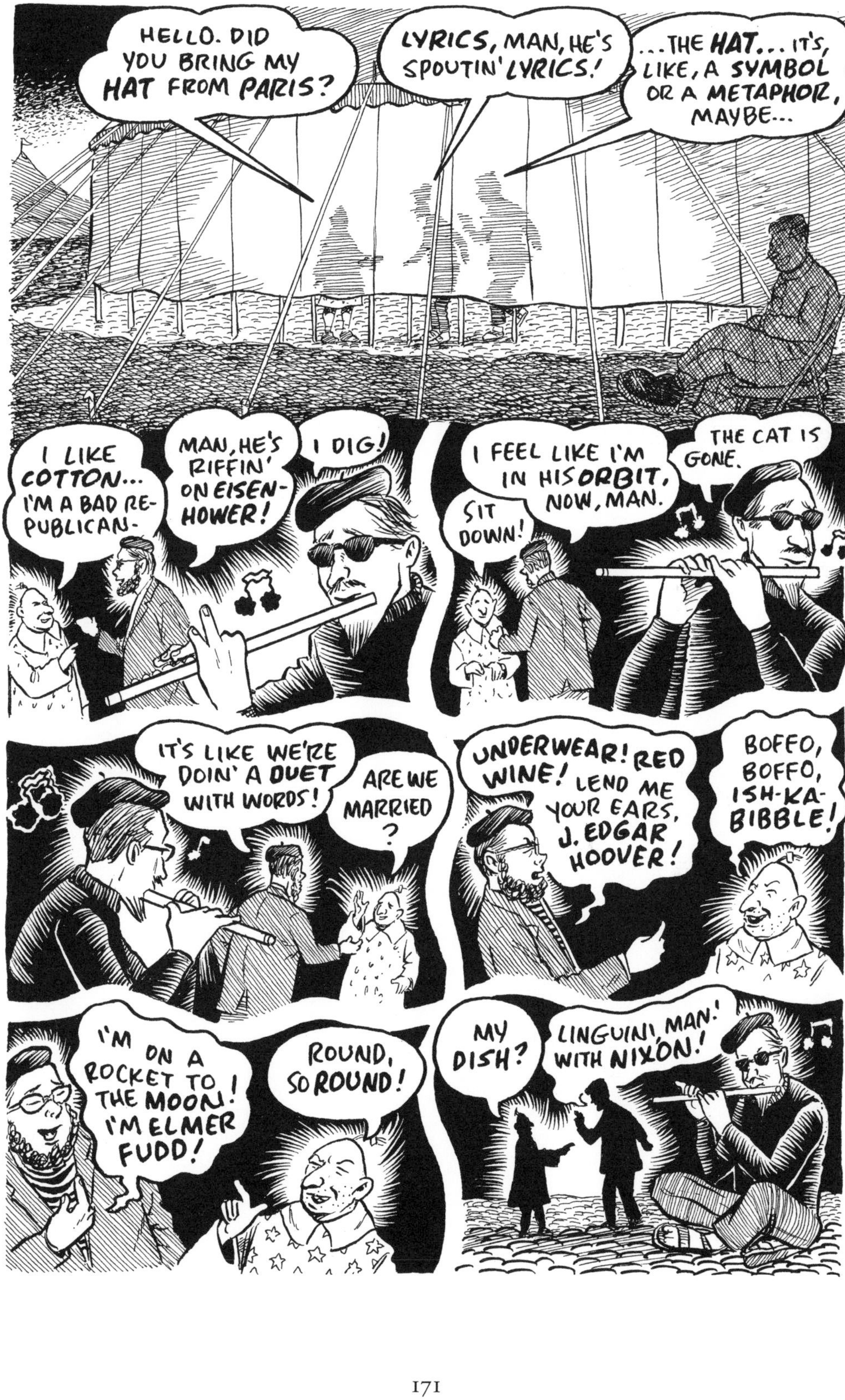
HELLO. DID YOU BRING MY HAT FROM PARIS?
LYRICS, MAN, HE'S SPOUTIN' LYRICS!
...THE HAT... IT'S, LIKE, A SYMBOL OR A METAPHOR, MAYBE...
I LIKE COTTON... I'M A BAD REPUBLICAN.
MAN, HE'S RIFFIN' ON EISENHOWER!
I DIG!
I FEEL LIKE I'M IN HIS ORBIT, NOW, MAN.
SIT DOWN!
THE CAT IS GONE.
IT'S LIKE WE'RE DOIN' A DUET WITH WORDS!
ARE WE MARRIED?
UNDERWEAR! RED WINE! LEND ME YOUR EARS, J. EDGAR HOOVER!
BOFFO, BOFFO, ISH-KA-BIBBLE!
I'M ON A ROCKET TO THE MOON! I'M ELMER FUDD!
ROUND, SO ROUND!
MY DISH?
LINGUINI, MAN! WITH NIXON!

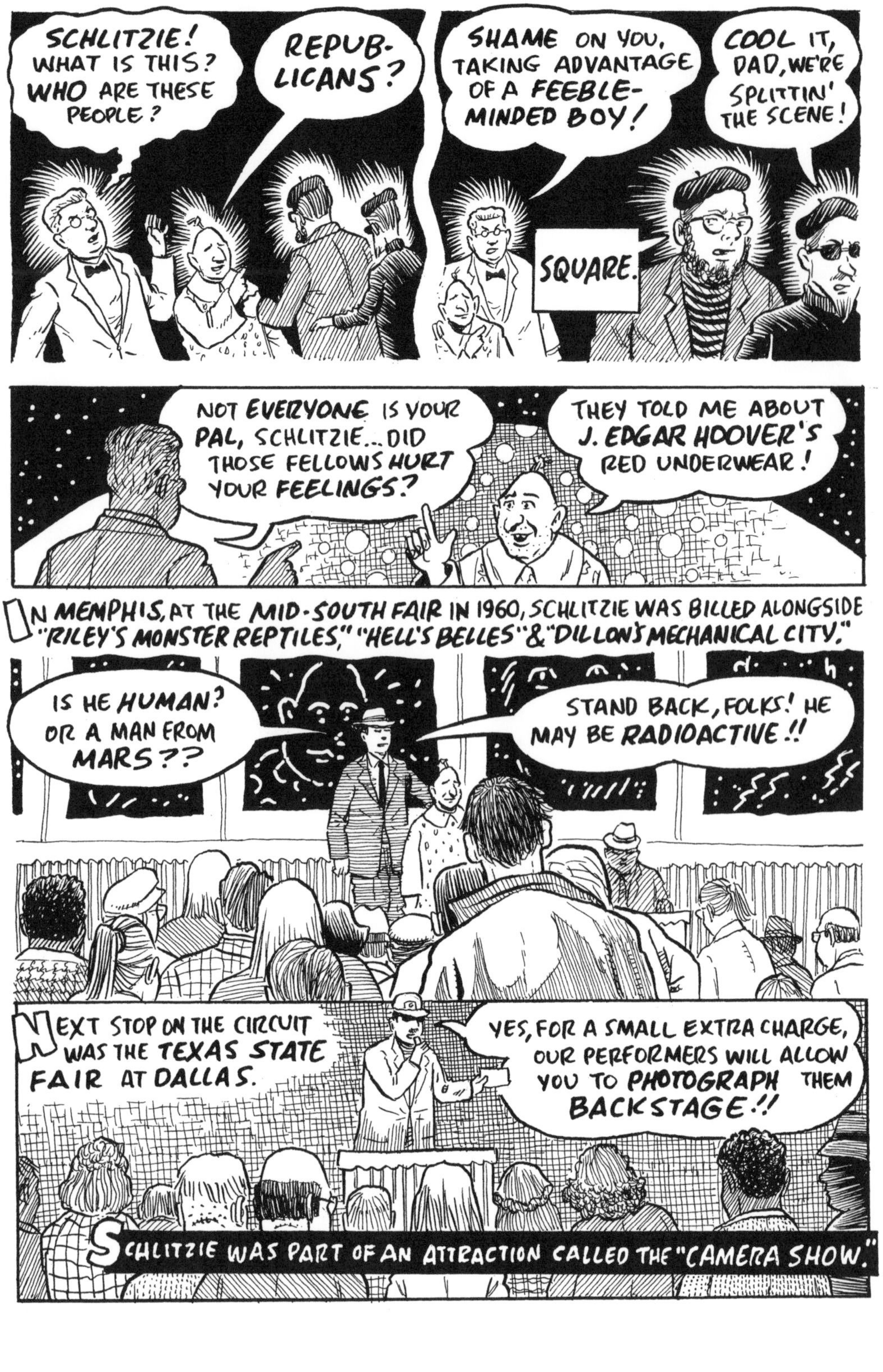
SCHLITZIE! WHAT IS THIS? WHO ARE THESE PEOPLE?
REPUBLICANS?
SHAME ON YOU, TAKING ADVANTAGE OF A FEEBLE-MINDED BOY!
COOL IT, DAD, WE'RE SPLITTIN' THE SCENE!
SQUARE.
NOT EVERYONE IS YOUR PAL, SCHLITZIE... DID THOSE FELLOWS HURT YOUR FEELINGS?
THEY TOLD ME ABOUT J. EDGAR HOOVER'S RED UNDERWEAR!
IN MEMPHIS, AT THE MID-SOUTH FAIR IN 1960, SCHLITZIE WAS BILLED ALONGSIDE "RILEY'S MONSTER REPTILES," "HELL'S BELLES" & "DILLON'S MECHANICAL CITY."
IS HE HUMAN? OR A MAN FROM MARS??
STAND BACK, FOLKS! HE MAY BE RADIOACTIVE!!
NEXT STOP ON THE CIRCUIT WAS THE TEXAS STATE FAIR AT DALLAS.
YES, FOR A SMALL EXTRA CHARGE, OUR PERFORMERS WILL ALLOW YOU TO PHOTOGRAPH THEM BACKSTAGE!!
SCHLITZIE WAS PART OF AN ATTRACTION CALLED THE "CAMERA SHOW."

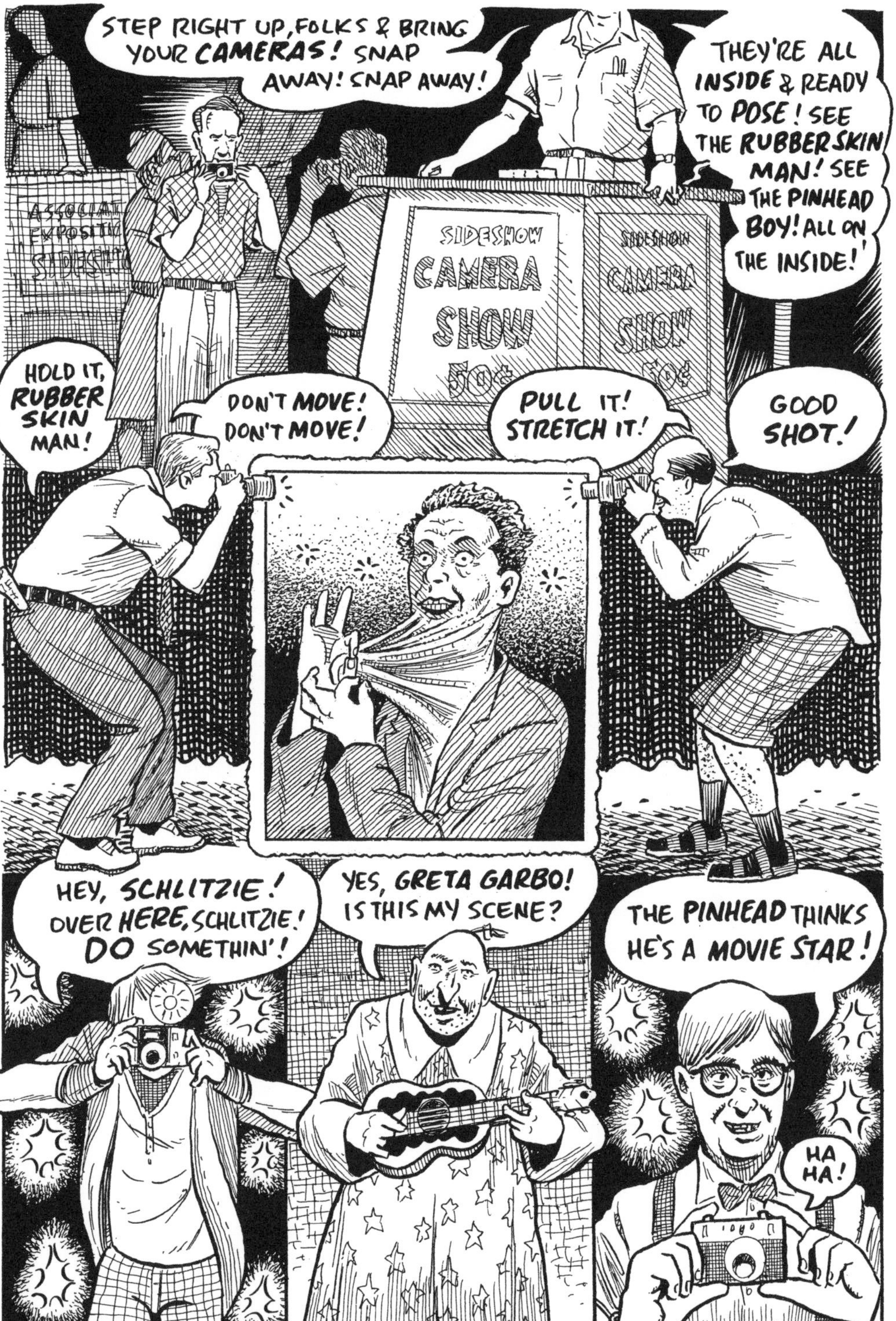

STEP RIGHT UP, FOLKS & BRING YOUR CAMERAS! SNAP AWAY! SNAP AWAY!
THEY'RE ALL INSIDE & READY TO POSE! SEE THE RUBBER SKIN MAN! SEE THE PINHEAD BOY! ALL ON THE INSIDE!
SIDESHOW CAMERA SHOW 50¢
SIDESHOW CAMERA SHOW 50¢
HOLD IT, RUBBER SKIN MAN!
DON'T MOVE! DON'T MOVE!
PULL IT! STRETCH IT!
GOOD SHOT!
HEY, SCHLITZIE! OVER HERE, SCHLITZIE! DO SOMETHIN'!
YES, GRETA GARBO! IS THIS MY SCENE?
THE PINHEAD THINKS HE'S A MOVIE STAR!
HA HA!

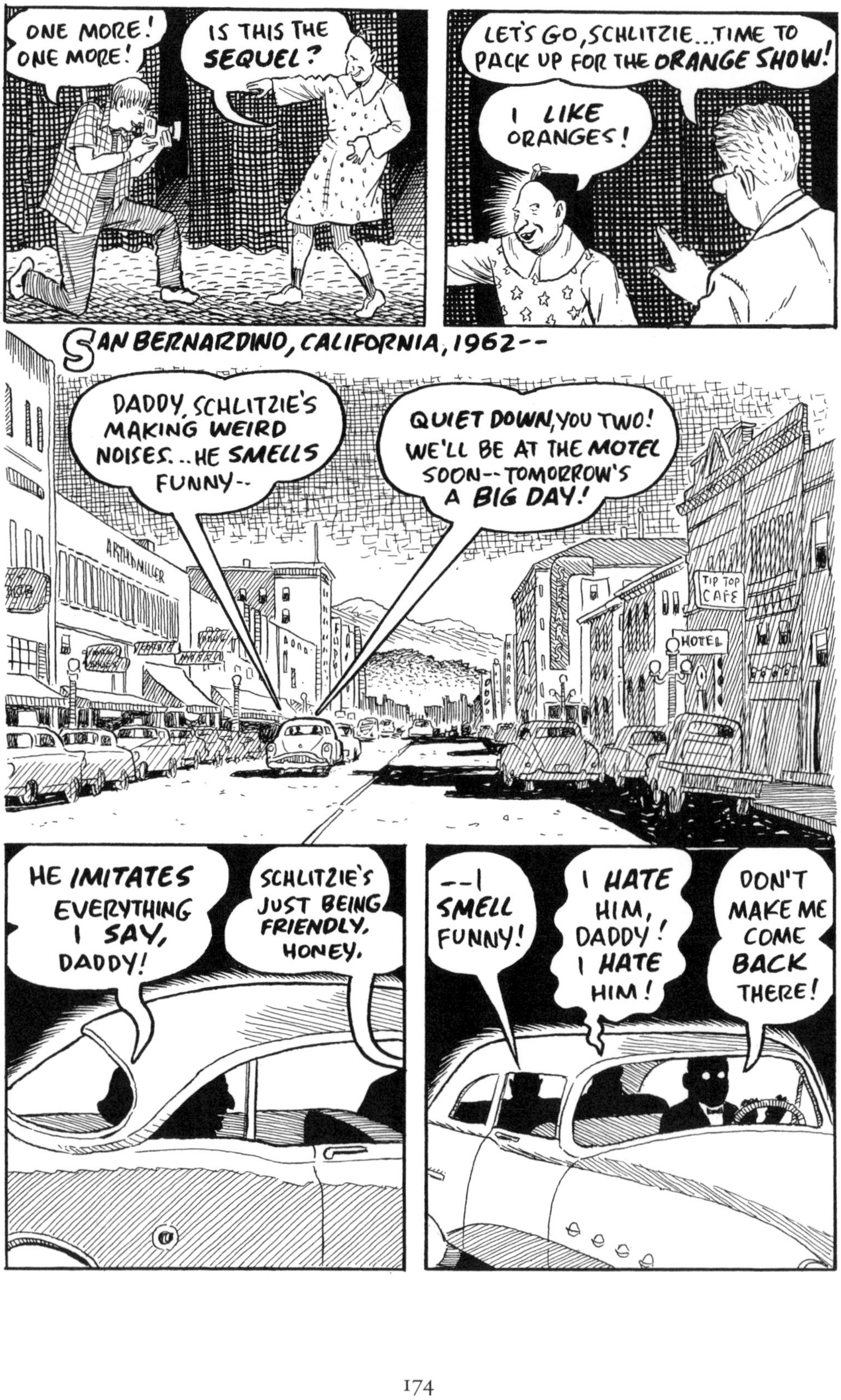
ONE MORE! ONE MORE!
IS THIS THE SEQUEL?
LET'S GO, SCHLITZIE...TIME TO PACK UP FOR THE ORANGE SHOW!
I LIKE ORANGES!
SAN BERNARDINO, CALIFORNIA, 1962--
DADDY, SCHLITZIE'S MAKING WEIRD NOISES...HE SMELLS FUNNY--
QUIET DOWN, YOU TWO! WE'LL BE AT THE MOTEL SOON--TOMORROW'S A BIG DAY!
TIP TOP CAFE
HOTEL
HARRIS
HE IMITATES EVERYTHING I SAY, DADDY!
SCHLITZIE'S JUST BEING FRIENDLY, HONEY.
--I SMELL FUNNY!
I HATE HIM, DADDY! I HATE HIM!
DON'T MAKE ME COME BACK THERE!

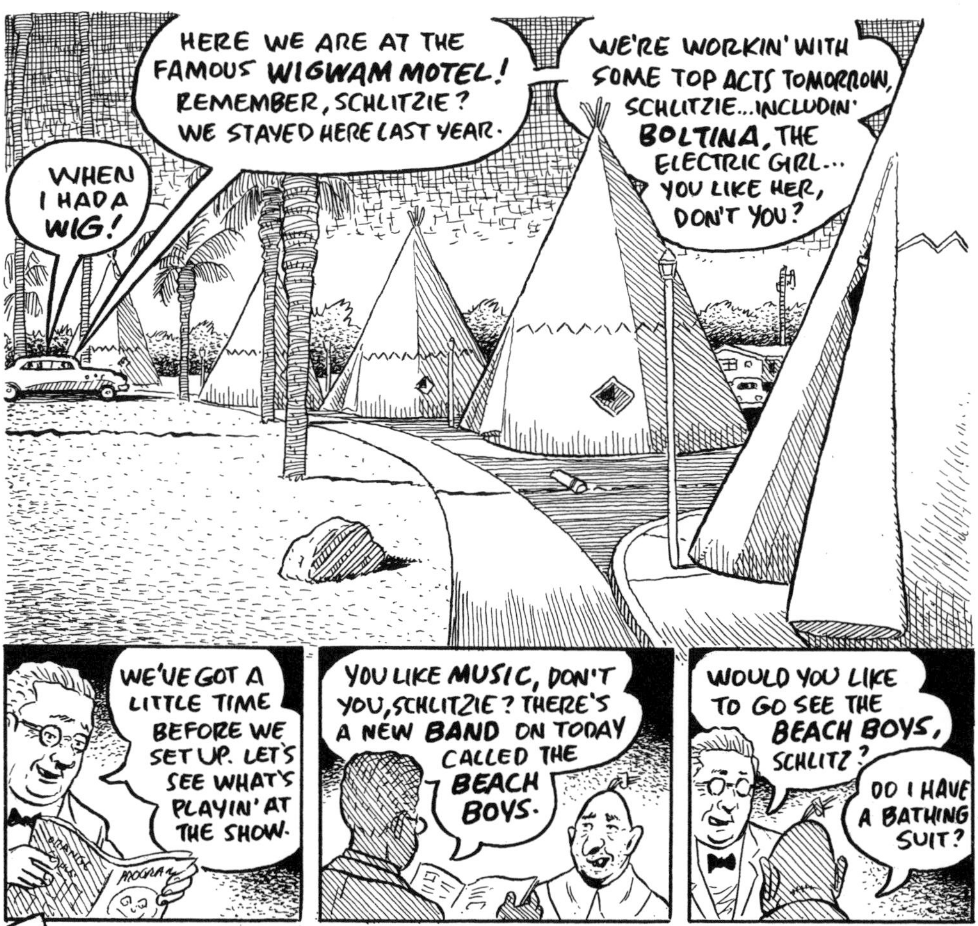
HERE WE ARE AT THE FAMOUS WIGWAM MOTEL! REMEMBER, SCHLITZIE? WE STAYED HERE LAST YEAR.
WHEN I HAD A WIG!
WE'RE WORKIN' WITH SOME TOP ACTS TOMORROW, SCHLITZIE... INCLUDIN' BOLTINA, THE ELECTRIC GIRL... YOU LIKE HER, DON'T YOU?
WE'VE GOT A LITTLE TIME BEFORE WE SET UP. LET'S SEE WHAT'S PLAYIN' AT THE SHOW.
PROGRAM
YOU LIKE MUSIC, DON'T YOU, SCHLITZIE? THERE'S A NEW BAND ON TODAY CALLED THE BEACH BOYS.
WOULD YOU LIKE TO GO SEE THE BEACH BOYS, SCHLITZ?
DO I HAVE A BATHING SUIT?

THE **NATIONAL ORANGE SHOW** WAS HELD EVERY MARCH IN SAN BERNARDINO. ORIGINALLY CREATED TO PROMOTE CITRUS GROWING, BY 1962 IT ALSO FEATURED MUSICAL ACTS AND A CARNIVAL MIDWAY. **SIDESHOWS** WERE BEGINNING TO LOSE FAVOR WITH AUDIENCES AT THIS TIME, BUT SCHLITZIE PERFORMED HERE WITH THE 3-LEGGED MAN, THE SIAMESE TWINS, AND-- THE **BEACH BOYS**...

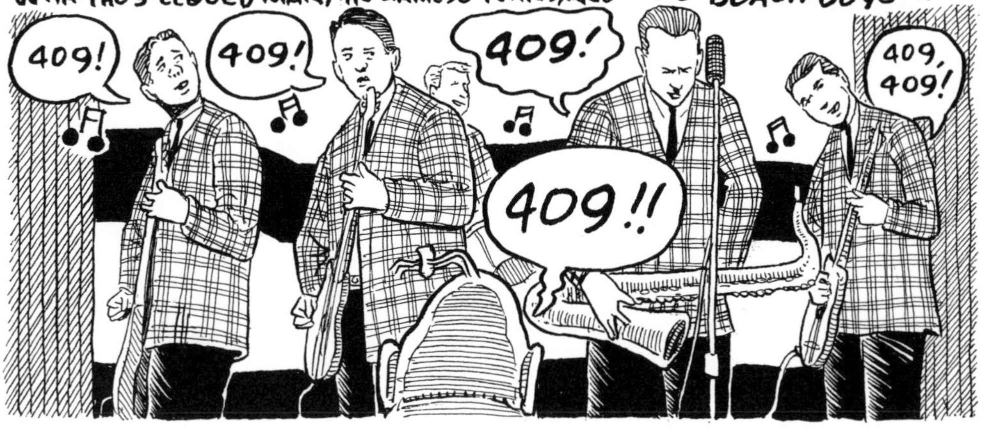
409!
409!
409!
409, 409!
409!!

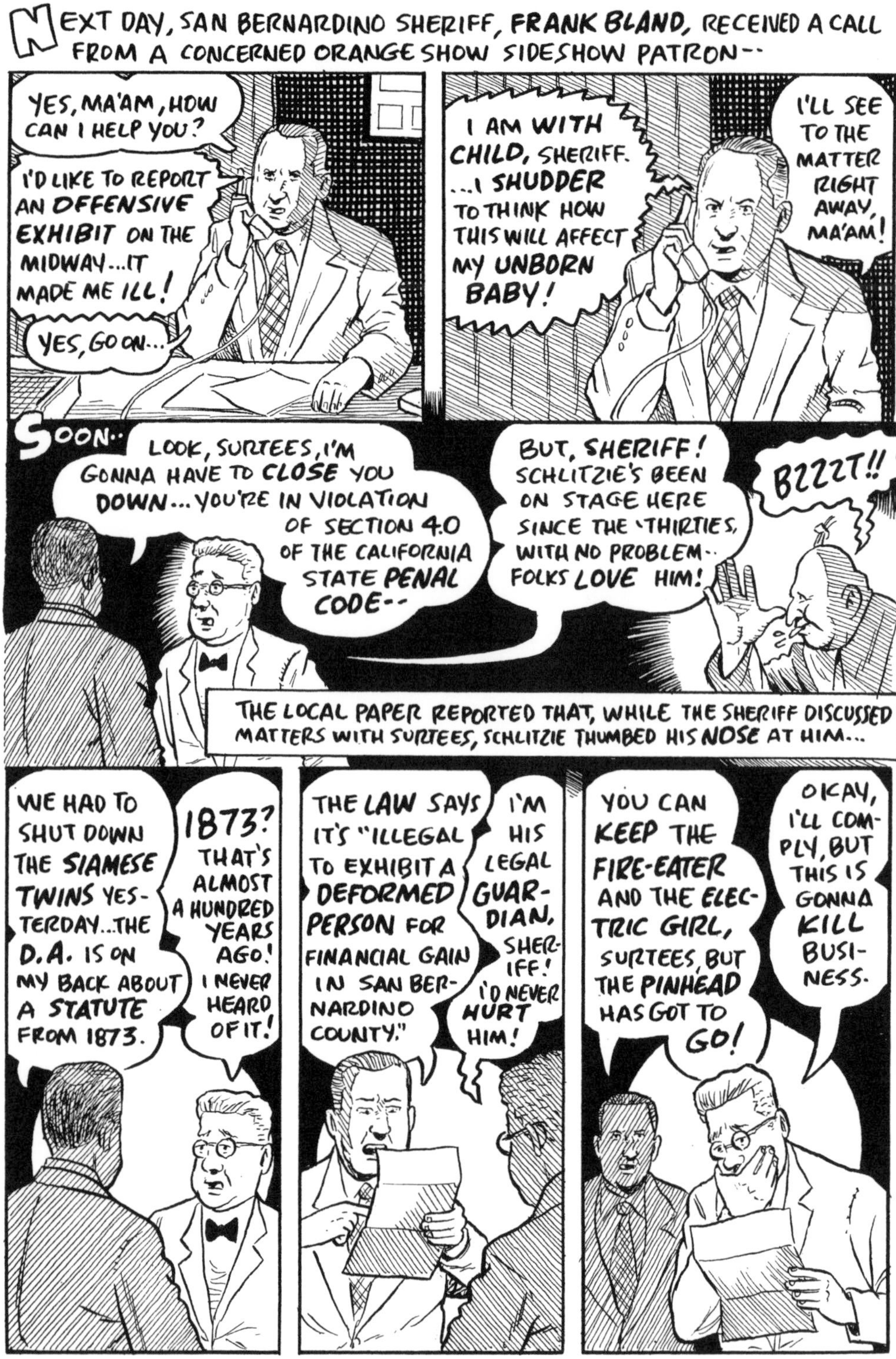
NEXT DAY, SAN BERNARDINO SHERIFF, FRANK BLAND, RECEIVED A CALL FROM A CONCERNED ORANGE SHOW SIDESHOW PATRON--
YES, MA'AM, HOW CAN I HELP YOU?
I'D LIKE TO REPORT AN OFFENSIVE EXHIBIT ON THE MIDWAY...IT MADE ME ILL!
YES, GO ON...
I AM WITH CHILD, SHERIFF. ...I SHUDDER TO THINK HOW THIS WILL AFFECT MY UNBORN BABY!
I'LL SEE TO THE MATTER RIGHT AWAY, MA'AM!
SOON..
LOOK, SURTEES, I'M GONNA HAVE TO CLOSE YOU DOWN... YOU'RE IN VIOLATION OF SECTION 4.0 OF THE CALIFORNIA STATE PENAL CODE--
BUT, SHERIFF! SCHLITZIE'S BEEN ON STAGE HERE SINCE THE 'THIRTIES, WITH NO PROBLEM.. FOLKS LOVE HIM!
BZZZT!!
THE LOCAL PAPER REPORTED THAT, WHILE THE SHERIFF DISCUSSED MATTERS WITH SURTEES, SCHLITZIE THUMBED HIS NOSE AT HIM...
WE HAD TO SHUT DOWN THE SIAMESE TWINS YESTERDAY...THE D.A. IS ON MY BACK ABOUT A STATUTE FROM 1873.
1873? THAT'S ALMOST A HUNDRED YEARS AGO! I NEVER HEARD OF IT!
THE LAW SAYS IT'S "ILLEGAL TO EXHIBIT A DEFORMED PERSON FOR FINANCIAL GAIN IN SAN BERNARDINO COUNTY."
I'M HIS LEGAL GUARDIAN, SHERIFF! I'D NEVER HURT HIM!
YOU CAN KEEP THE FIRE-EATER AND THE ELECTRIC GIRL, SURTEES, BUT THE PINHEAD HAS GOT TO GO!
OKAY, I'LL COMPLY, BUT THIS IS GONNA KILL BUSINESS.

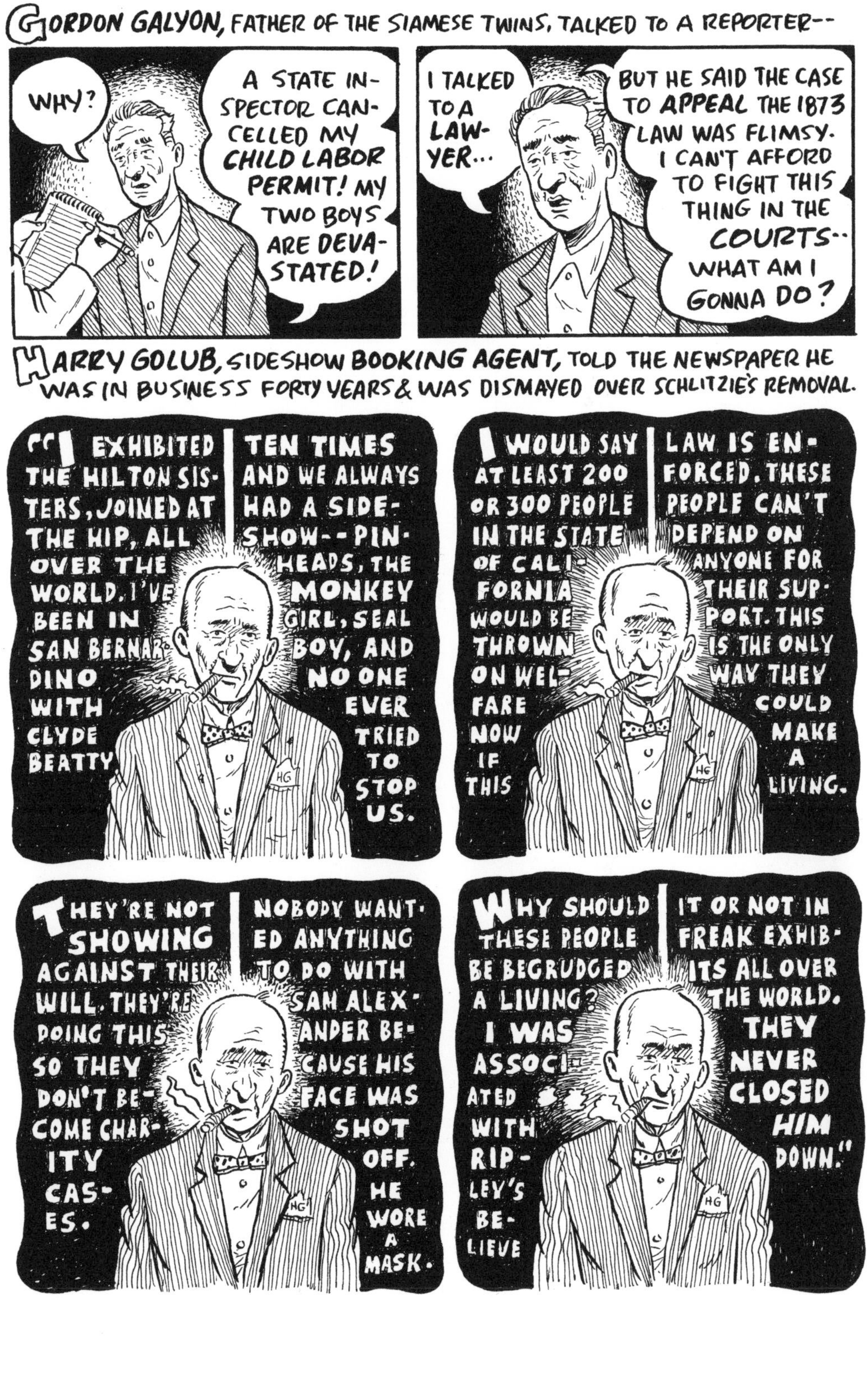
GORDON GALYON, FATHER OF THE SIAMESE TWINS, TALKED TO A REPORTER--
WHY?
A STATE INSPECTOR CANCELLED MY CHILD LABOR PERMIT! MY TWO BOYS ARE DEVASTATED!
I TALKED TO A LAWYER...
BUT HE SAID THE CASE TO APPEAL THE 1873 LAW WAS FLIMSY. I CAN'T AFFORD TO FIGHT THIS THING IN THE COURTS.. WHAT AM I GONNA DO?
HARRY GOLUB, SIDESHOW BOOKING AGENT, TOLD THE NEWSPAPER HE WAS IN BUSINESS FORTY YEARS & WAS DISMAYED OVER SCHLITZIE'S REMOVAL.
"I EXHIBITED THE HILTON SISTERS, JOINED AT THE HIP, ALL OVER THE WORLD. I'VE BEEN IN SAN BERNARDINO WITH CLYDE BEATTY TEN TIMES AND WE ALWAYS HAD A SIDESHOW--PINHEADS, THE MONKEY GIRL, SEAL BOY, AND NO ONE EVER TRIED TO STOP US.
I WOULD SAY AT LEAST 200 OR 300 PEOPLE IN THE STATE OF CALIFORNIA WOULD BE THROWN ON WELFARE NOW IF THIS LAW IS ENFORCED. THESE PEOPLE CAN'T DEPEND ON ANYONE FOR THEIR SUPPORT. THIS IS THE ONLY WAY THEY COULD MAKE A LIVING.
THEY'RE NOT SHOWING AGAINST THEIR WILL. THEY'RE DOING THIS SO THEY DON'T BECOME CHARITY CASES. NOBODY WANTED ANYTHING TO DO WITH SAM ALEXANDER BECAUSE HIS FACE WAS SHOT OFF. HE WORE A MASK.
WHY SHOULD THESE PEOPLE BE BEGRUDGED A LIVING? I WAS ASSOCIATED WITH RIPLEY'S BELIEVE IT OR NOT IN FREAK EXHIBITS ALL OVER THE WORLD. THEY NEVER CLOSED HIM DOWN."

AL FRIEDMAN, OWNER OF THE ROYAL WEST CARNIVAL SHOWS, GAVE THE REPORTER HIS THOUGHTS ON SCHLITZIE'S CLOSING--

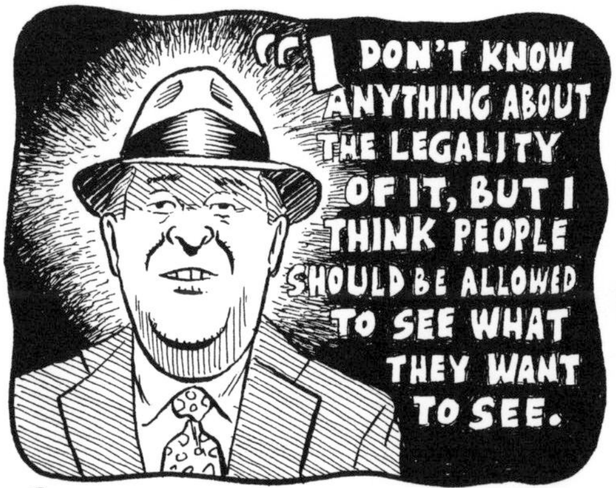
"I DON'T KNOW ANYTHING ABOUT THE LEGALITY OF IT, BUT I THINK PEOPLE SHOULD BE ALLOWED TO SEE WHAT THEY WANT TO SEE.

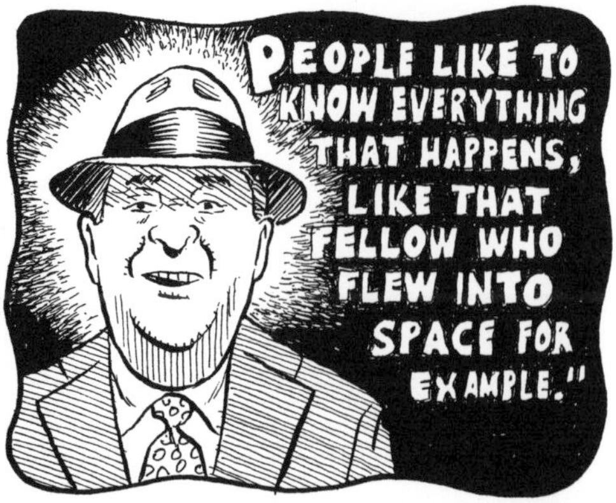
PEOPLE LIKE TO KNOW EVERYTHING THAT HAPPENS, LIKE THAT FELLOW WHO FLEW INTO SPACE FOR EXAMPLE."

FINALLY, TED LEVITT, CARNIVAL BUSINESS AGENT, CHIMED IN-

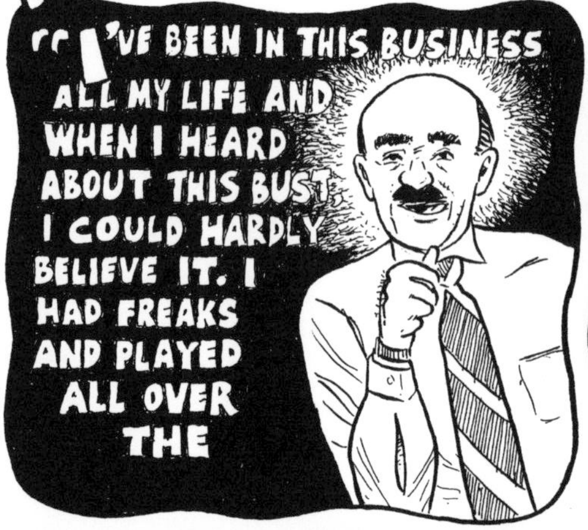
"I'VE BEEN IN THIS BUSINESS ALL MY LIFE AND WHEN I HEARD ABOUT THIS BUST, I COULD HARDLY BELIEVE IT. I HAD FREAKS AND PLAYED ALL OVER THE

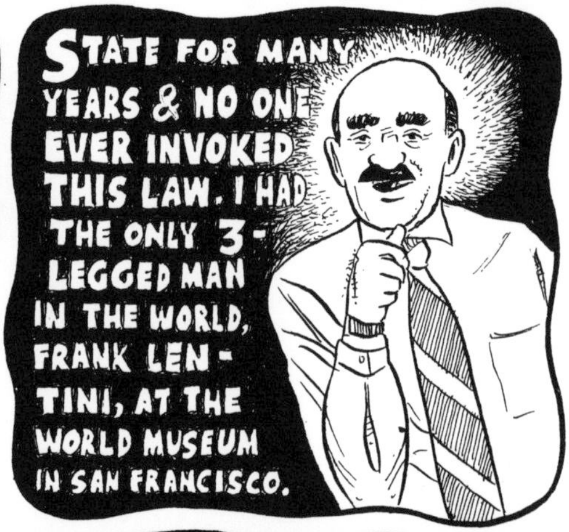
STATE FOR MANY YEARS & NO ONE EVER INVOKED THIS LAW. I HAD THE ONLY 3-LEGGED MAN IN THE WORLD, FRANK LENTINI, AT THE WORLD MUSEUM IN SAN FRANCISCO.

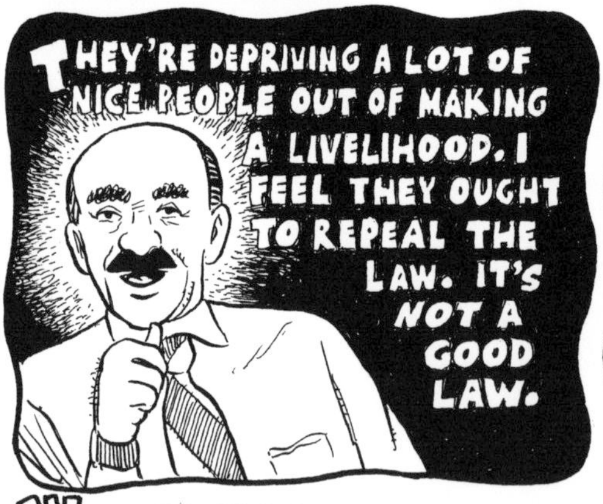
THEY'RE DEPRIVING A LOT OF NICE PEOPLE OUT OF MAKING A LIVELIHOOD. I FEEL THEY OUGHT TO REPEAL THE LAW. IT'S NOT A GOOD LAW.

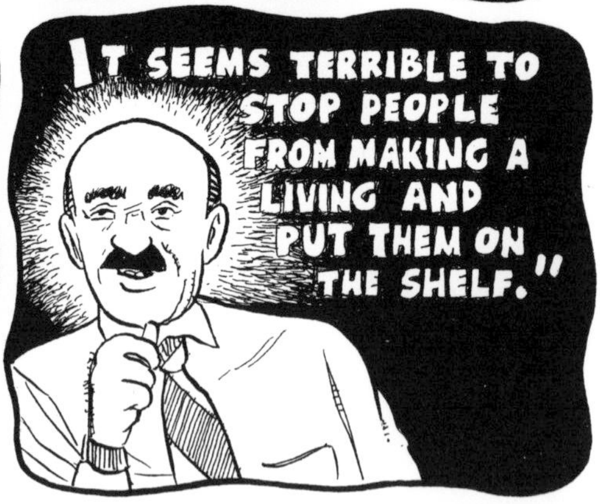
IT SEEMS TERRIBLE TO STOP PEOPLE FROM MAKING A LIVING AND PUT THEM ON THE SHELF."

WHAT THESE MEN WERE TALKING ABOUT, HOWEVER OBLIQUELY, WAS THE FACT THAT THIS MOMENT, IN 1962, HERALDED THE BEGINNING OF THE END OF THE AMERICAN SIDESHOW AS A FORM OF POPULAR ENTERTAINMENT.

UPON HIS RETURN TO LOS ANGELES, SCHLITZIE WAS LOANED OUT TO SIDESHOW MANAGER, **SAM ALEXANDER**. ALEXANDER WAS A FREAK HIMSELF, BILLED AS "**THE MAN WITH TWO FACES**" --

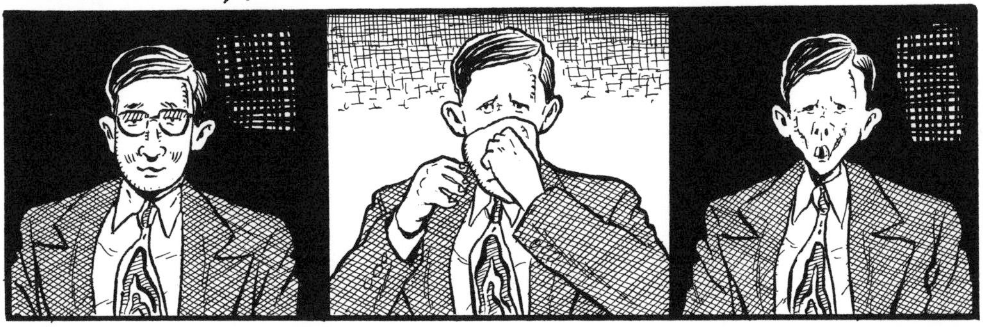

HIS DISFIGUREMENT WAS THE RESULT OF AN ACCIDENTAL **EXPLOSION**, CAUSING HIM TO WEAR A **PLASTIC MASK** IN PUBLIC. HE WOULD TELL HIS STORY ON STAGE, THEN TURN AROUND & REVEAL HIS MANGLED FEATURES TO THE CROWD. HE BROUGHT SCHLITZIE TO **HAWAII** IN 1962 WITH THE **E.K. FERNANDEZ CIRCUS**.

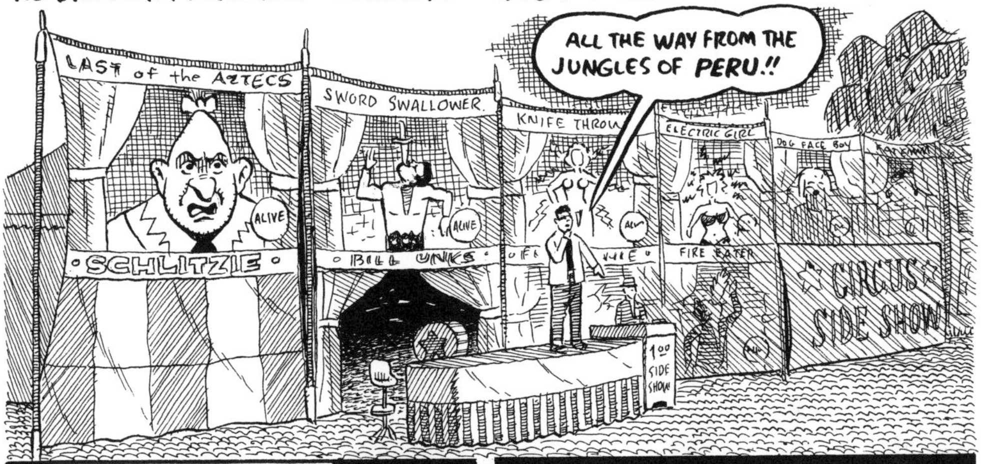

ALL THE WAY FROM THE JUNGLES OF PERU!!
LAST of the AZTECS
SCHLITZIE
ALIVE
SWORD SWALLOWER
BILL UNKS
ALIVE
KNIFE THROW
ELECTRIC GIRL
FIRE EATER
DOG FACE BOY
CIRCUS SIDE SHOW
1.00 SIDE SHOW

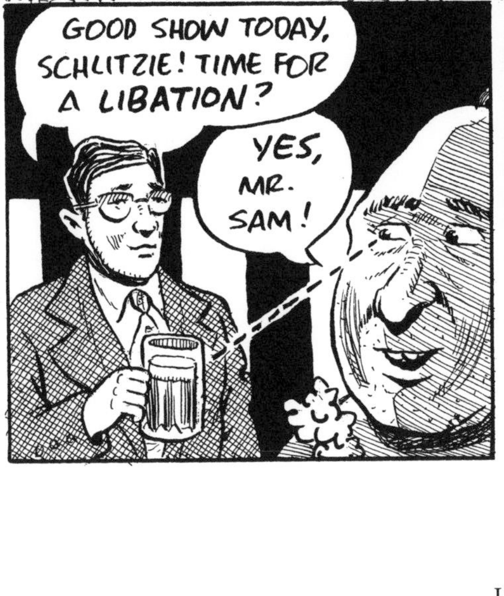

GOOD SHOW TODAY, SCHLITZIE! TIME FOR A LIBATION?
YES, MR. SAM!

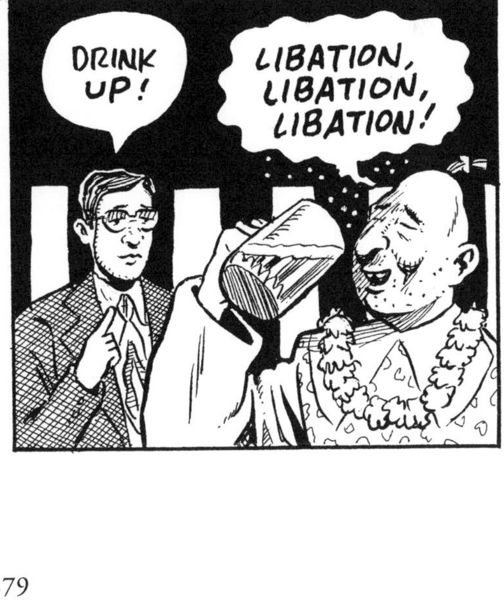

DRINK UP!
LIBATION, LIBATION, LIBATION!

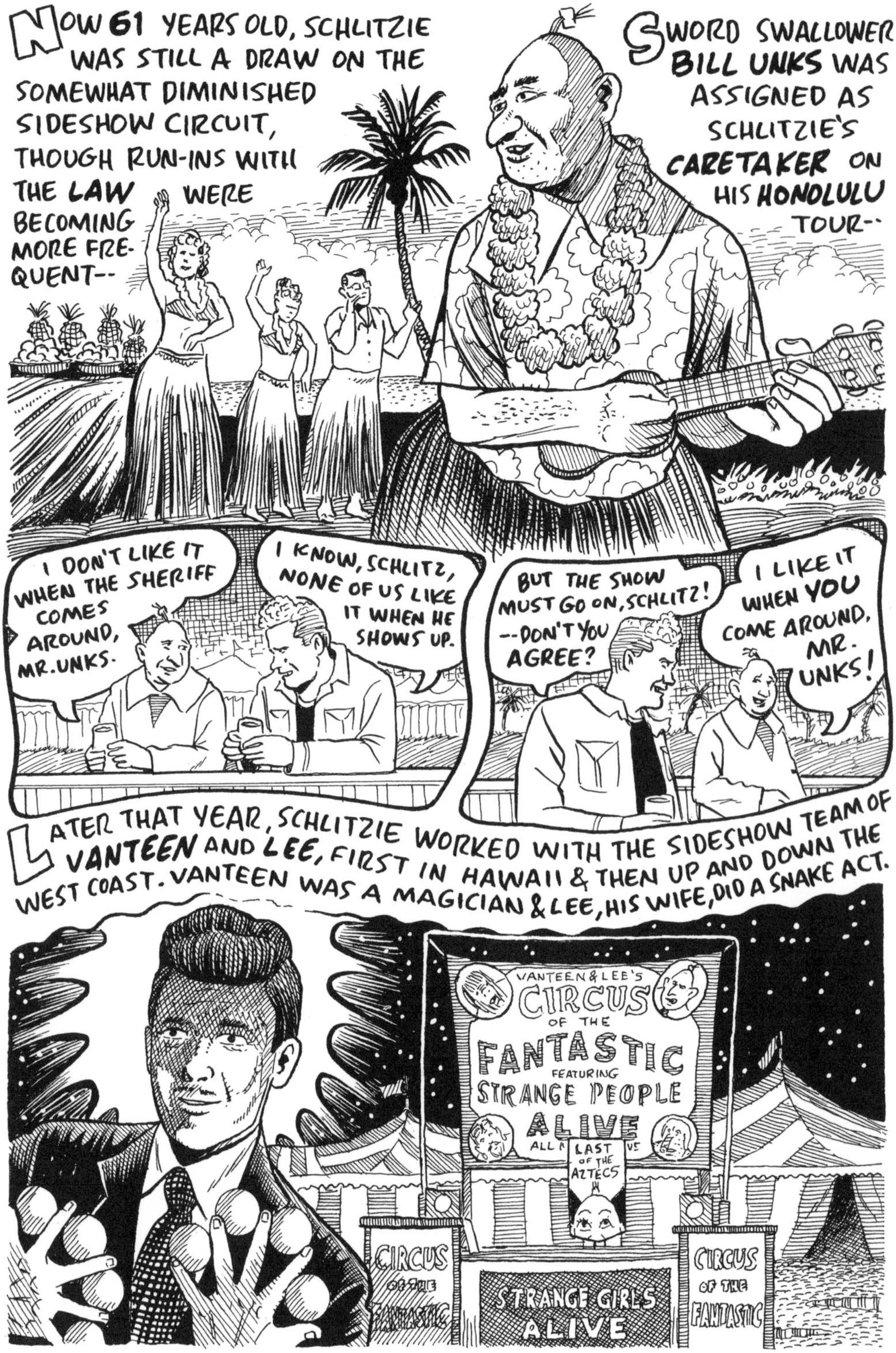
NOW 61 YEARS OLD, SCHLITZIE WAS STILL A DRAW ON THE SOMEWHAT DIMINISHED SIDESHOW CIRCUIT, THOUGH RUN-INS WITH THE LAW WERE BECOMING MORE FRE-QUENT--
SWORD SWALLOWER BILL UNKS WAS ASSIGNED AS SCHLITZIE'S CARETAKER ON HIS HONOLULU TOUR--
I DON'T LIKE IT WHEN THE SHERIFF COMES AROUND, MR. UNKS.
I KNOW, SCHLITZ, NONE OF US LIKE IT WHEN HE SHOWS UP.
BUT THE SHOW MUST GO ON, SCHLITZ! --DON'T YOU AGREE?
I LIKE IT WHEN YOU COME AROUND, MR. UNKS!
LATER THAT YEAR, SCHLITZIE WORKED WITH THE SIDESHOW TEAM OF VANTEEN AND LEE, FIRST IN HAWAII & THEN UP AND DOWN THE WEST COAST. VANTEEN WAS A MAGICIAN & LEE, HIS WIFE, DID A SNAKE ACT.
VANTEEN & LEE'S CIRCUS OF THE FANTASTIC FEATURING STRANGE PEOPLE ALIVE
LAST OF THE AZTECS
CIRCUS OF THE FANTASTIC
STRANGE GIRLS ALIVE
CIRCUS OF THE FANTASTIC

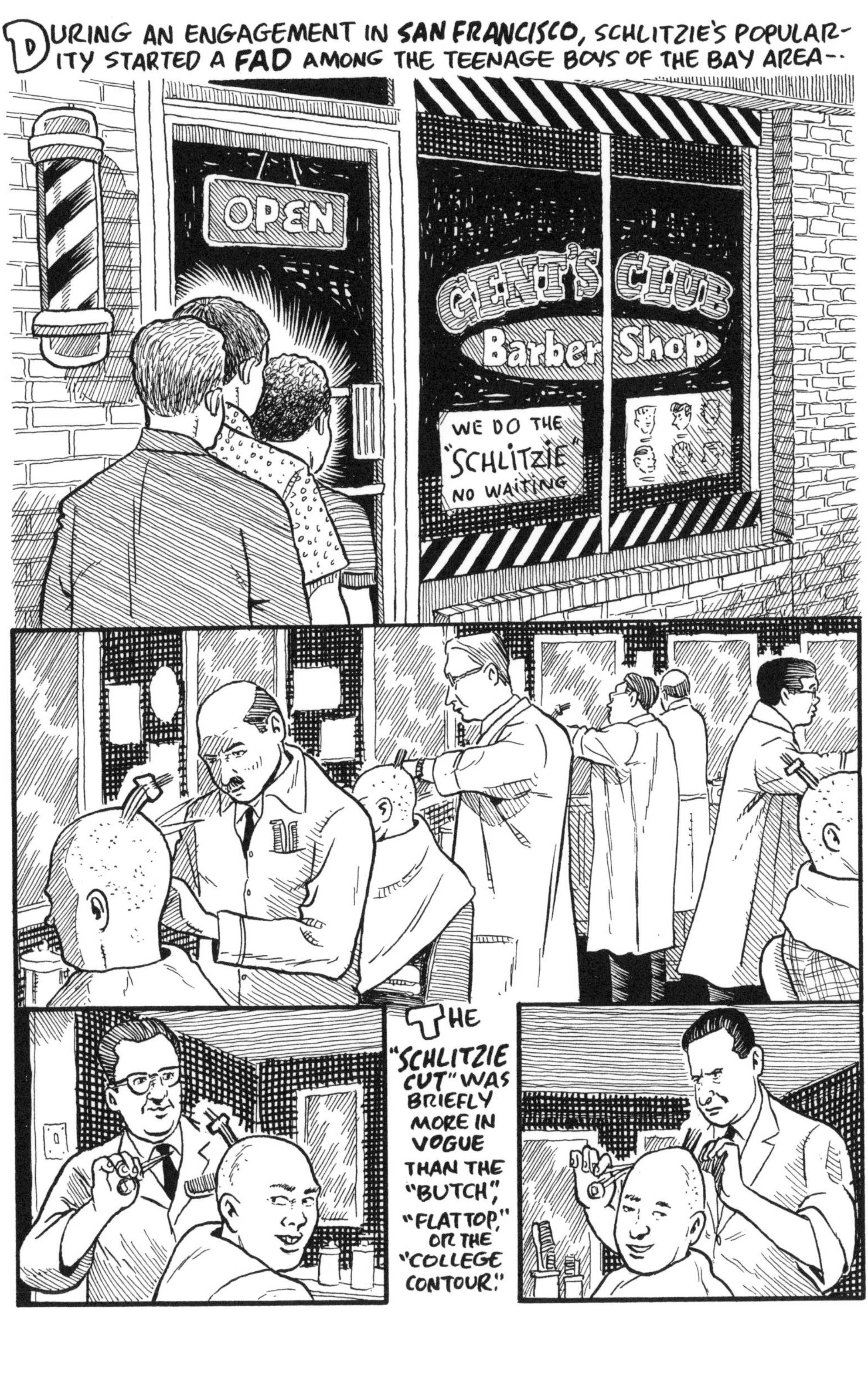
DURING AN ENGAGEMENT IN SAN FRANCISCO, SCHLITZIE'S POPULARITY STARTED A FAD AMONG THE TEENAGE BOYS OF THE BAY AREA--
OPEN
GENT'S CLUB
Barber Shop
WE DO THE "SCHLITZIE" NO WAITING
THE "SCHLITZIE CUT" WAS BRIEFLY MORE IN VOGUE THAN THE "BUTCH", "FLATTOP," OR THE "COLLEGE CONTOUR."

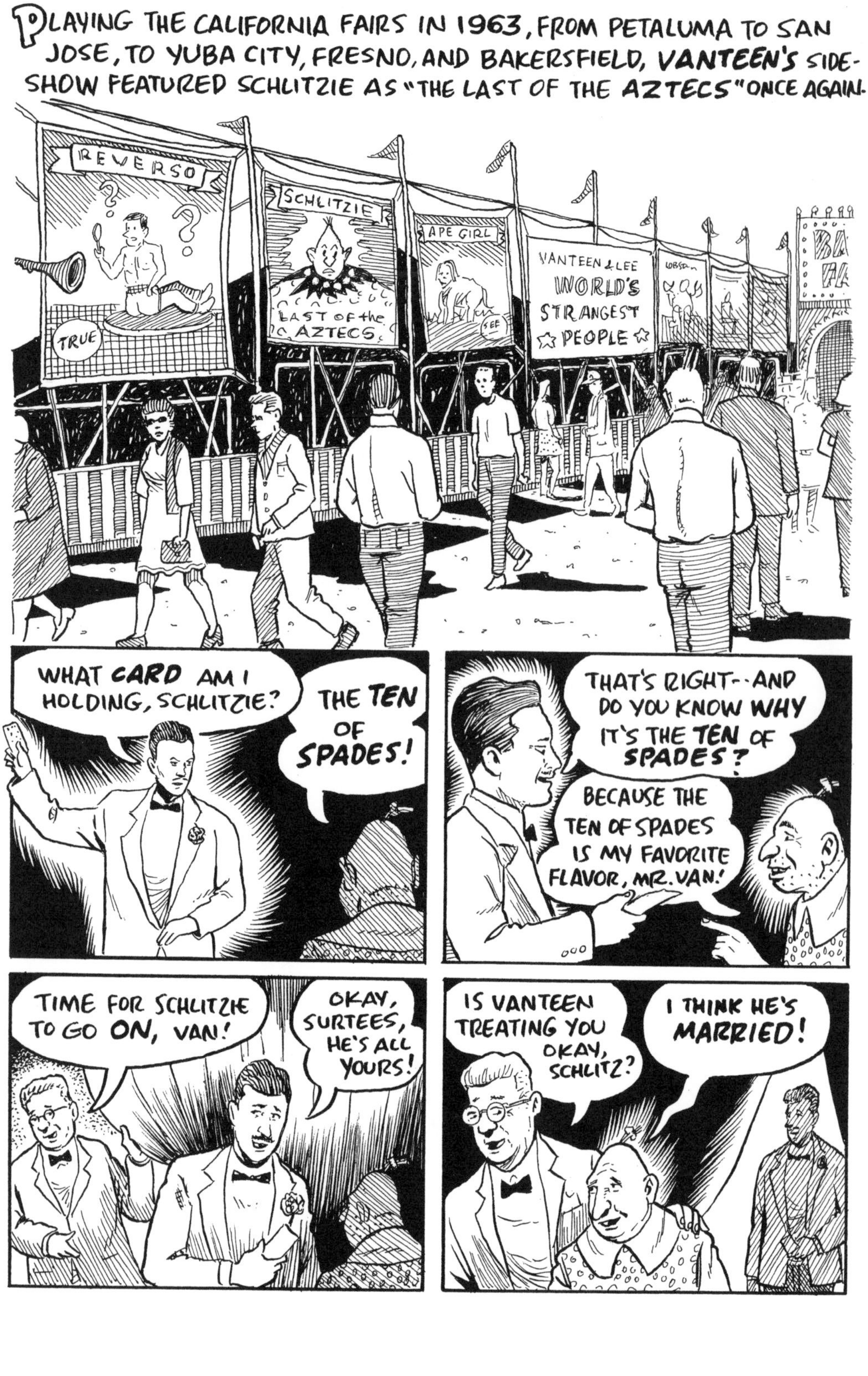
PLAYING THE CALIFORNIA FAIRS IN 1963, FROM PETALUMA TO SAN JOSE, TO YUBA CITY, FRESNO, AND BAKERSFIELD, VANTEEN'S SIDESHOW FEATURED SCHLITZIE AS "THE LAST OF THE AZTECS" ONCE AGAIN.
REWERSO
TRUE
SCHLITZIE
LAST OF the AZTECS
APE GIRL
SEE
VANTEEN & LEE WORLD'S STRANGEST PEOPLE
WHAT CARD AM I HOLDING, SCHLITZIE?
THE TEN OF SPADES!
THAT'S RIGHT--AND DO YOU KNOW WHY IT'S THE TEN OF SPADES?
BECAUSE THE TEN OF SPADES IS MY FAVORITE FLAVOR, MR. VAN!
TIME FOR SCHLITZIE TO GO ON, VAN!
OKAY, SURTEES, HE'S ALL YOURS!
IS VANTEEN TREATING YOU OKAY, SCHLITZ?
I THINK HE'S MARRIED!

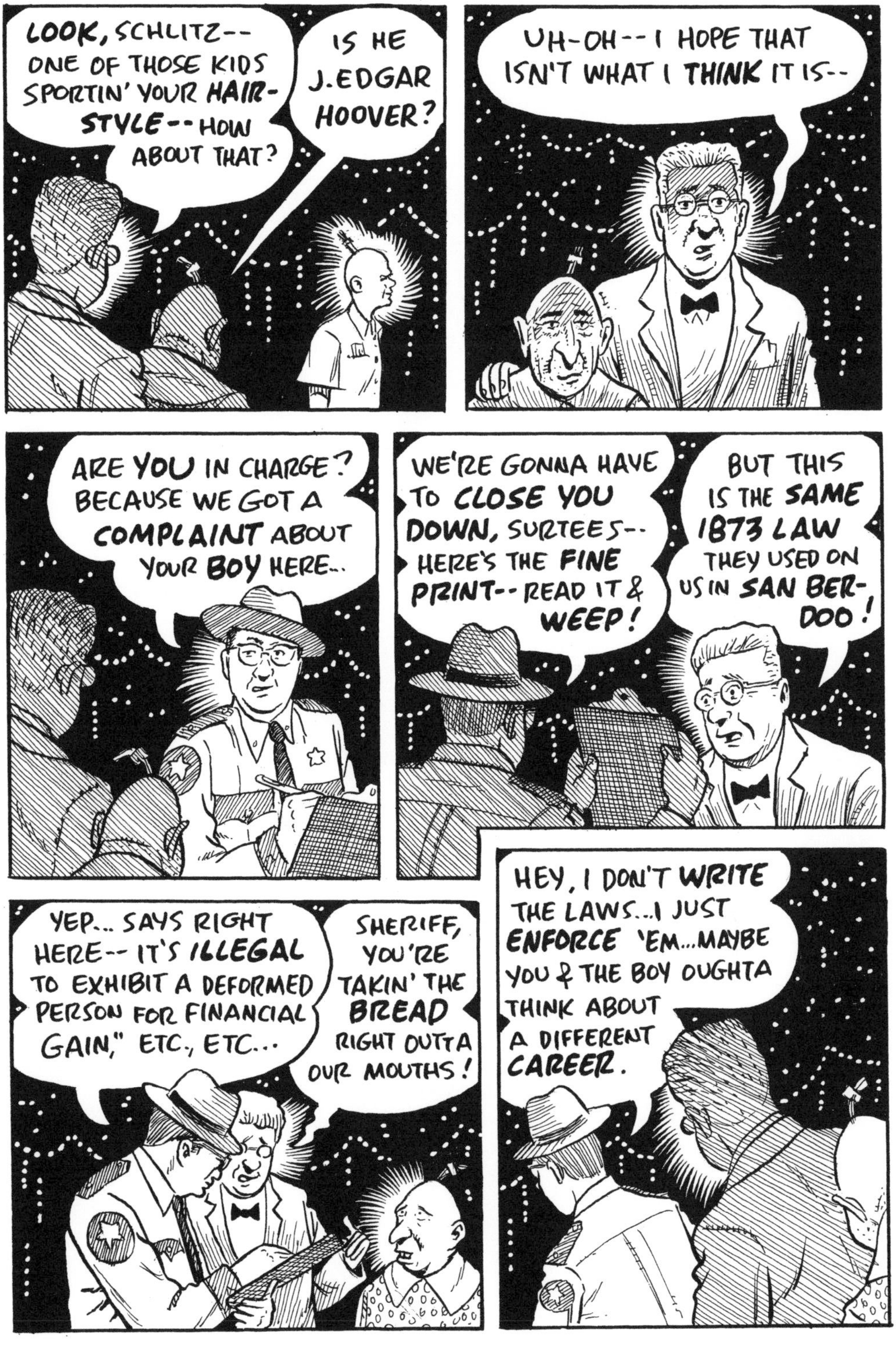
LOOK, SCHLITZ-- ONE OF THOSE KIDS SPORTIN' YOUR HAIR-STYLE--HOW ABOUT THAT?
IS HE J. EDGAR HOOVER?
UH-OH--I HOPE THAT ISN'T WHAT I THINK IT IS--
ARE YOU IN CHARGE? BECAUSE WE GOT A COMPLAINT ABOUT YOUR BOY HERE..
WE'RE GONNA HAVE TO CLOSE YOU DOWN, SURTEES-- HERE'S THE FINE PRINT--READ IT & WEEP!
BUT THIS IS THE SAME 1873 LAW THEY USED ON US IN SAN BER-DOO!
YEP... SAYS RIGHT HERE-- IT'S ILLEGAL TO EXHIBIT A DEFORMED PERSON FOR FINANCIAL GAIN," ETC., ETC...
SHERIFF, YOU'RE TAKIN' THE BREAD RIGHT OUTTA OUR MOUTHS!
HEY, I DON'T WRITE THE LAWS...I JUST ENFORCE 'EM...MAYBE YOU & THE BOY OUGHTA THINK ABOUT A DIFFERENT CAREER.

LEGAL PROBLEMS WERE NOT THE ONLY PUSHBACKS FACING THE SIDESHOW IN 1963-- IN BAKERSFIELD, HOME TO MANY MEXICAN-AMERICANS, THE HISPANIC COMMUNITY MADE THEIR UNHAPPINESS ABOUT SCHLITZIE'S "LAST OF THE AZTECS ORIGINS" KNOWN TO MANAGEMENT--

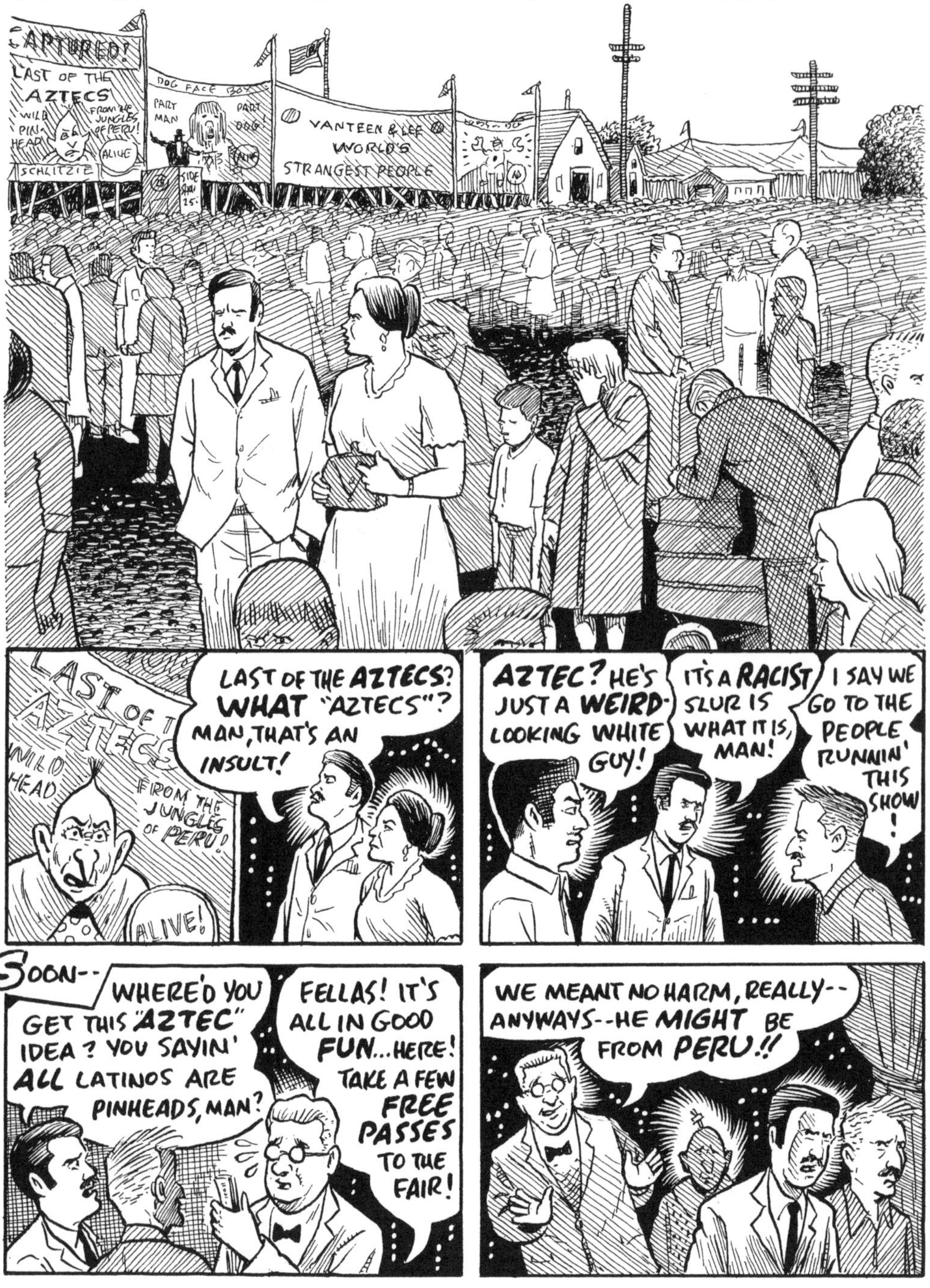

CAPTURED!
LAST OF THE AZTECS
WILD PIN-HEAD
FROM THE JUNGLES OF PERU
ALIVE
SCHLITZIE
DOG FACE BOY
PART MAN
PART DOG!
VANTEEN & LEE WORLD'S STRANGEST PEOPLE
SIDE SHOW 25¢
LAST OF THE AZTECS? WHAT "AZTECS"? MAN, THAT'S AN INSULT!
AZTEC? HE'S JUST A WEIRD-LOOKING WHITE GUY!
IT'S A RACIST SLUR IS WHAT IT IS, MAN!
I SAY WE GO TO THE PEOPLE RUNNIN' THIS SHOW!
SOON--
WHERE'D YOU GET THIS "AZTEC" IDEA? YOU SAYIN' ALL LATINOS ARE PINHEADS, MAN?
FELLAS! IT'S ALL IN GOOD FUN... HERE! TAKE A FEW FREE PASSES TO THE FAIR!
WE MEANT NO HARM, REALLY-- ANYWAYS--HE MIGHT BE FROM PERU!!

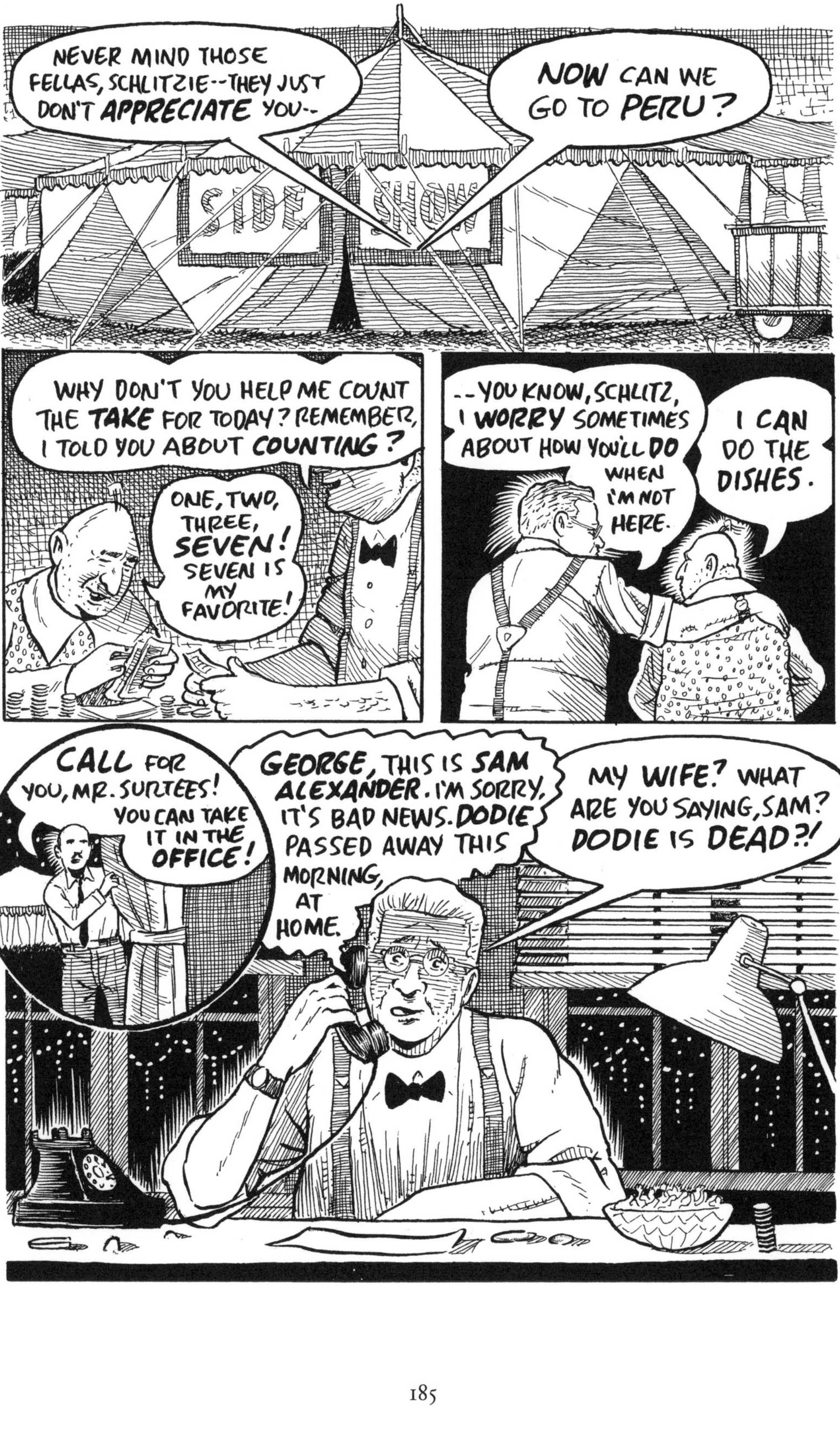
NEVER MIND THOSE FELLAS, SCHLITZIE--THEY JUST DON'T APPRECIATE YOU--
NOW CAN WE GO TO PERU?
WHY DON'T YOU HELP ME COUNT THE TAKE FOR TODAY? REMEMBER, I TOLD YOU ABOUT COUNTING?
ONE, TWO, THREE, SEVEN! SEVEN IS MY FAVORITE!
--YOU KNOW, SCHLITZ, I WORRY SOMETIMES ABOUT HOW YOU'LL DO WHEN I'M NOT HERE.
I CAN DO THE DISHES.
CALL FOR YOU, MR. SURTEES! YOU CAN TAKE IT IN THE OFFICE!
GEORGE, THIS IS SAM ALEXANDER. I'M SORRY, IT'S BAD NEWS. DODIE PASSED AWAY THIS MORNING, AT HOME.
MY WIFE? WHAT ARE YOU SAYING, SAM? DODIE IS DEAD?!

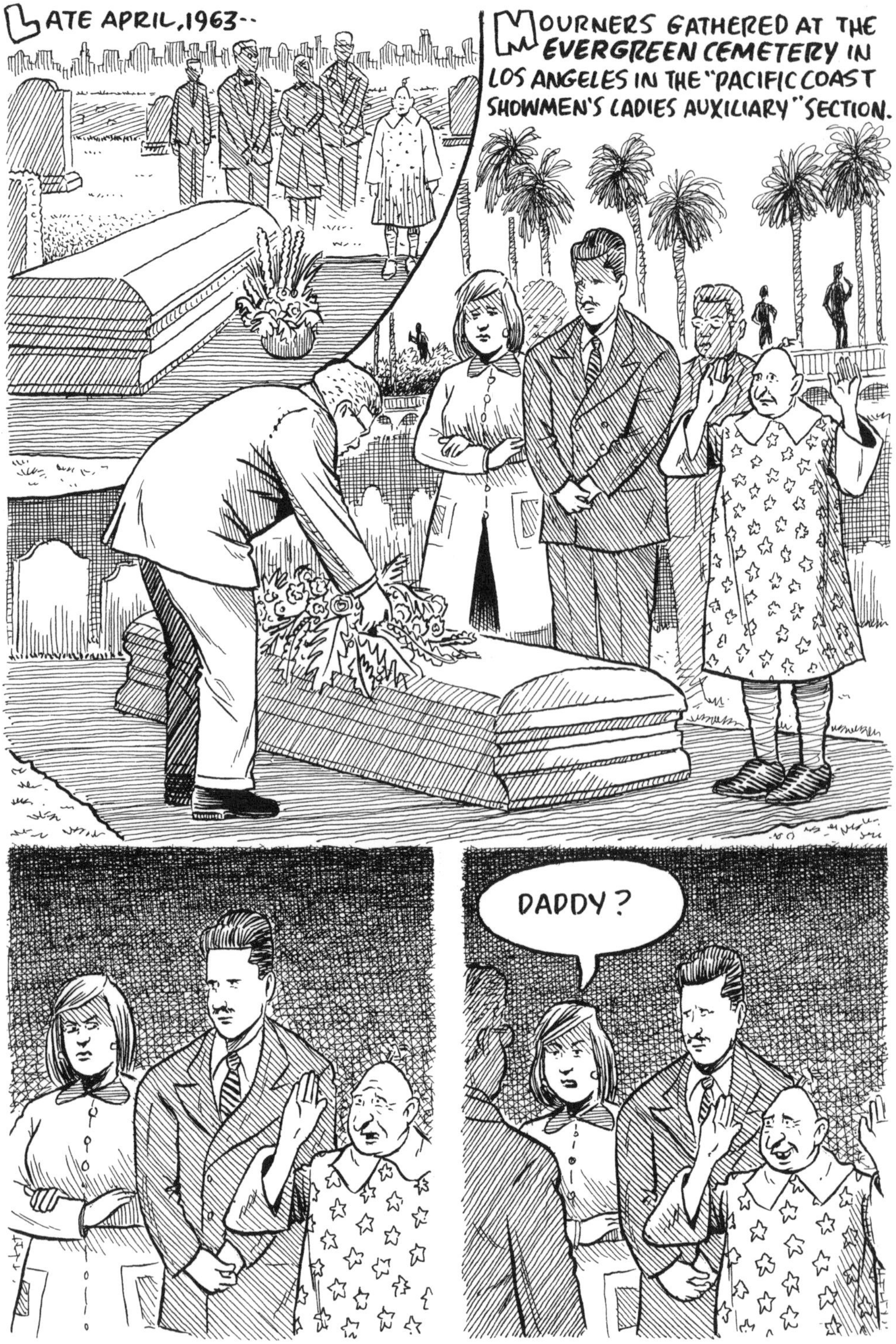
LATE APRIL, 1963--
MOURNERS GATHERED AT THE EVERGREEN CEMETERY IN LOS ANGELES IN THE "PACIFIC COAST SHOWMEN'S LADIES AUXILIARY" SECTION.
DADDY?

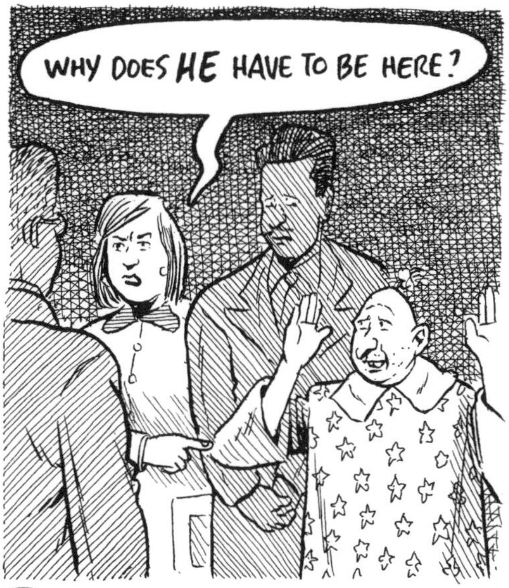
WHY DOES HE HAVE TO BE HERE?

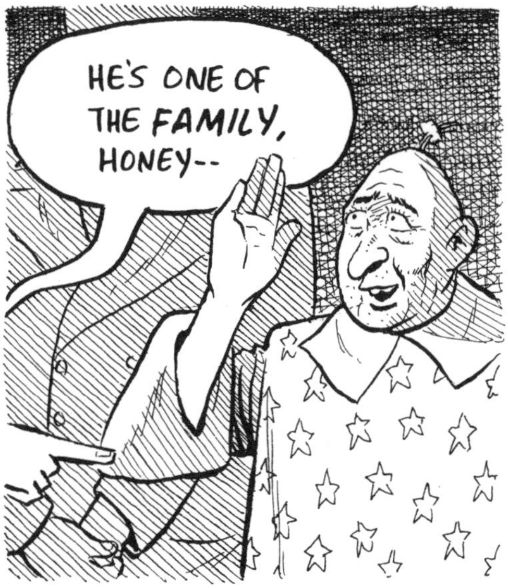
HE'S ONE OF THE FAMILY, HONEY--

BACK ON THE CIRCUIT, SCHLITZIE PLAYED CIRCUSES, CARNIVALS, AND PEEP SHOWS UP & DOWN THE WEST COAST DURING 1963 AND INTO 1964 --

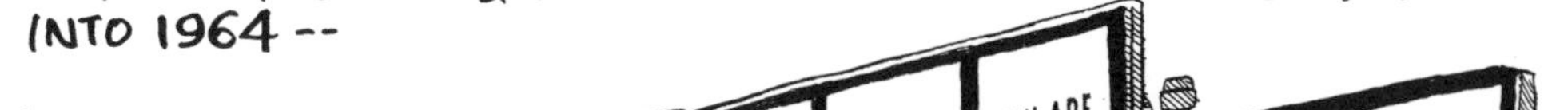
EVER SINCE EVE
WE DARE TO TELL THE 'TRUTH' ...
MEN ARE ATTRACTED WOMEN ARE FASCINATED ...
"ADULTS ONLY.
SEE
CHILDREN NOT ADMITTED
ADULT ONLY
WHAT EVERY YOUNG WOMAN SHOULD KNOW ...
FATHERS DARE YOU TELL YOUR SONS ?
? WHAT IS WOMAN WHO IS WOMAN ?
NATURE REVEALED
IT'S 'REAL' IT'S 'HUMAN'
'EVER SINCE' EVE YOU HAVE ASKED WHY

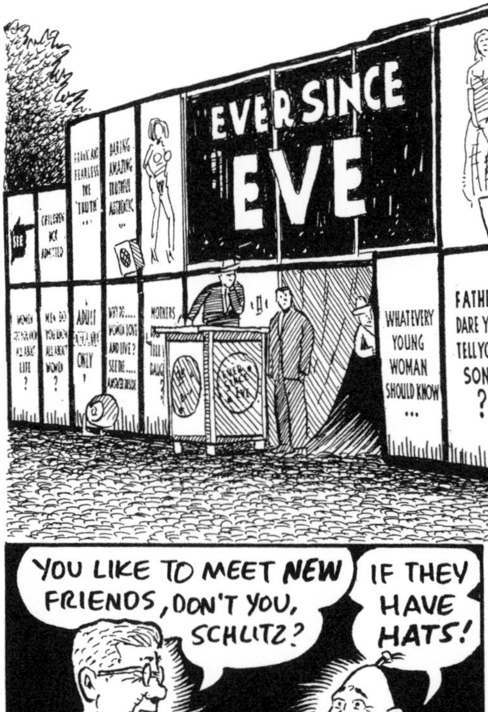
YOU LIKE TO MEET NEW FRIENDS, DON'T YOU, SCHLITZ?
IF THEY HAVE HATS!

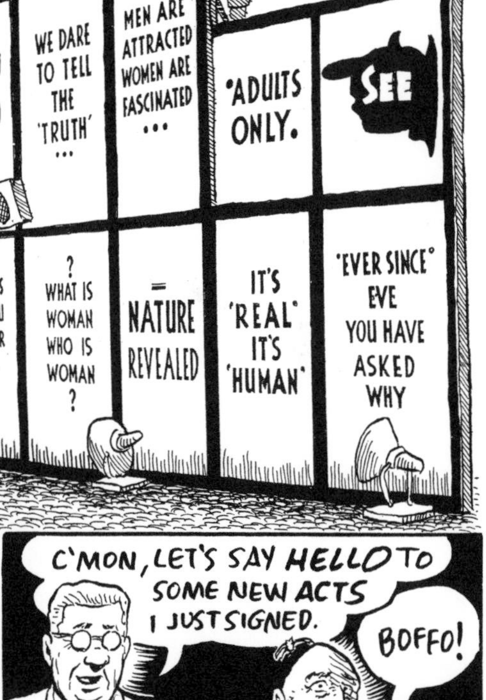
C'MON, LET'S SAY HELLO TO SOME NEW ACTS I JUST SIGNED.
BOFFO!

BY 1964, SIDESHOW ACTS BEGAN TO REFLECT THE GROWING UNEASE WITH THE DISPLAY OF PEOPLE WITH HANDICAPS OR UNUSUAL ANATOMIES. ***SNAKE CHARMERS & KNIFE THROWERS*** TOOK THE PLACE OF THE ***BEARDED LADY*** OR THE ***HUMAN TORSO***-- BUT NOT ***ALWAYS***.

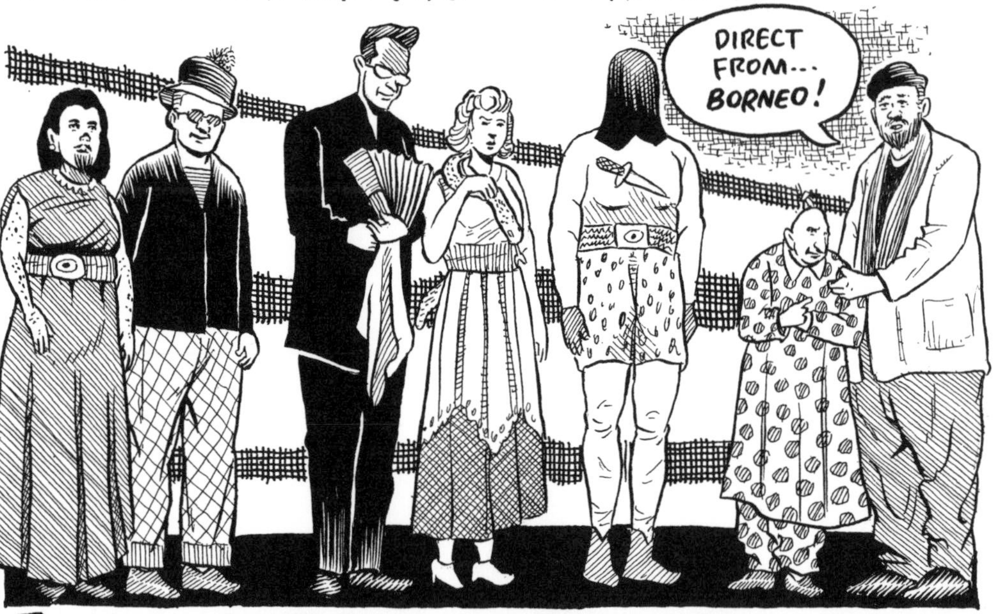
DIRECT FROM... BORNEO!

TO AVOID LEGAL PROBLEMS, SOME SHOWS ELIMINATED HUMAN ATTRACTIONS ALTOGETHER & SIMPLY PUT **FREAK PHOTOS** ON EXHIBIT, INCLUDING ONES OF **SCHLITZIE**... SURTEES LOOKED ASKANCE AT THIS PRACTICE.

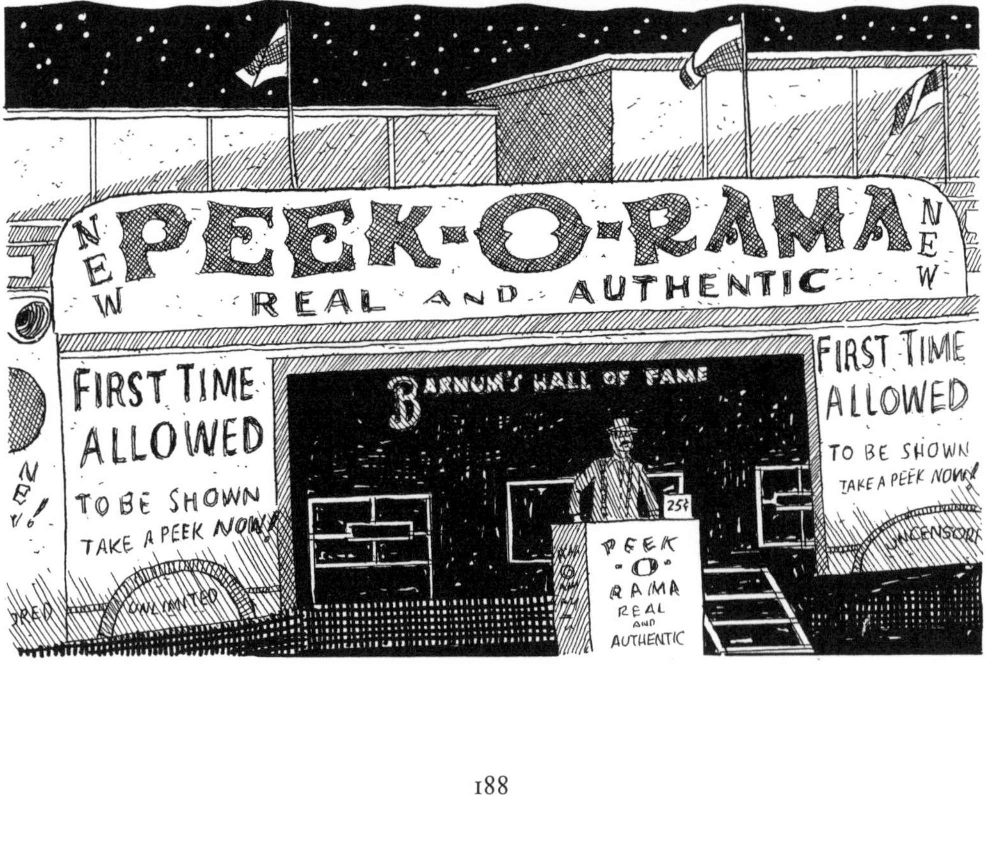
NEW PEEK-O-RAMA NEW
REAL AND AUTHENTIC
FIRST TIME ALLOWED TO BE SHOWN TAKE A PEEK NOW!
BARNUM'S HALL OF FAME
FIRST TIME ALLOWED TO BE SHOWN TAKE A PEEK NOW!
25¢
PEEK -O- RAMA REAL AND AUTHENTIC
UNLIMITED

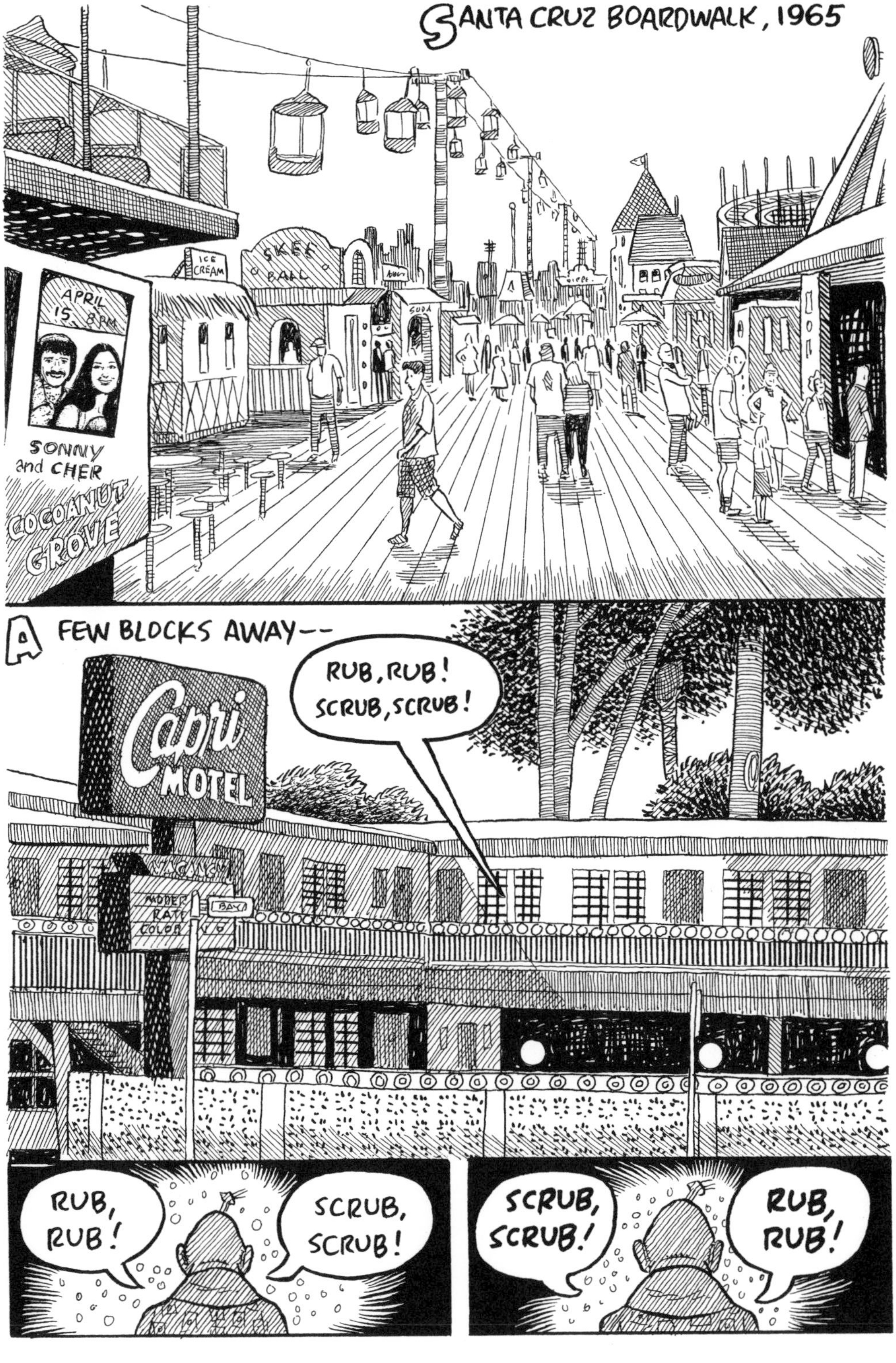
SANTA CRUZ BOARDWALK, 1965
APRIL 15 8PM
SONNY and CHER
COCOANUT GROVE
ICE CREAM
SKEE BALL
A FEW BLOCKS AWAY--
Capri MOTEL
RUB, RUB! SCRUB, SCRUB!
RUB, RUB!
SCRUB, SCRUB!
SCRUB, SCRUB!
RUB, RUB!

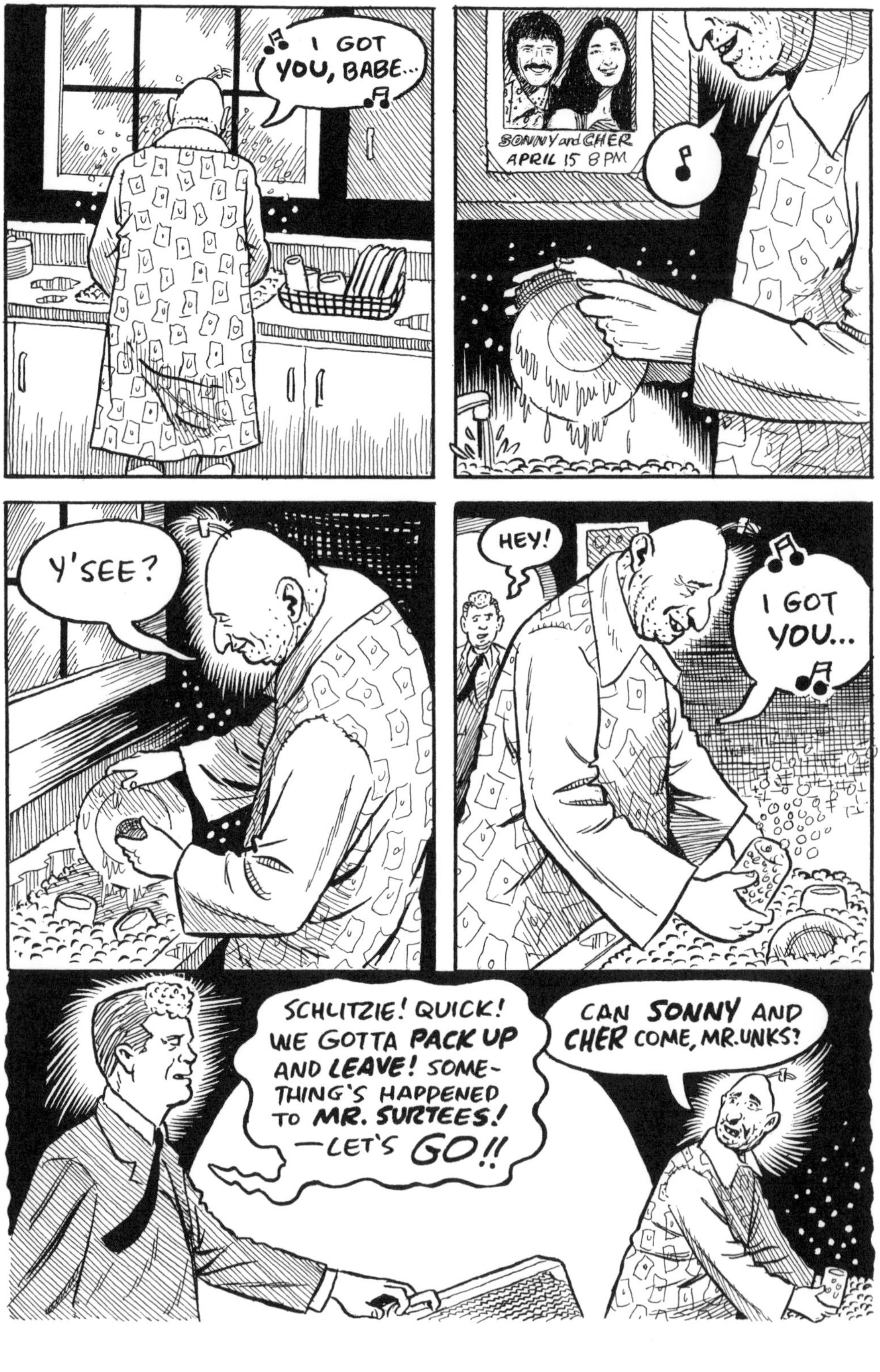
I GOT YOU, BABE...
SONNY and CHER
APRIL 15 8 PM
Y'SEE?
HEY!
I GOT YOU...
SCHLITZIE! QUICK! WE GOTTA PACK UP AND LEAVE! SOMETHING'S HAPPENED TO MR. SURTEES! —LET'S GO!!
CAN SONNY AND CHER COME, MR. UNKS?

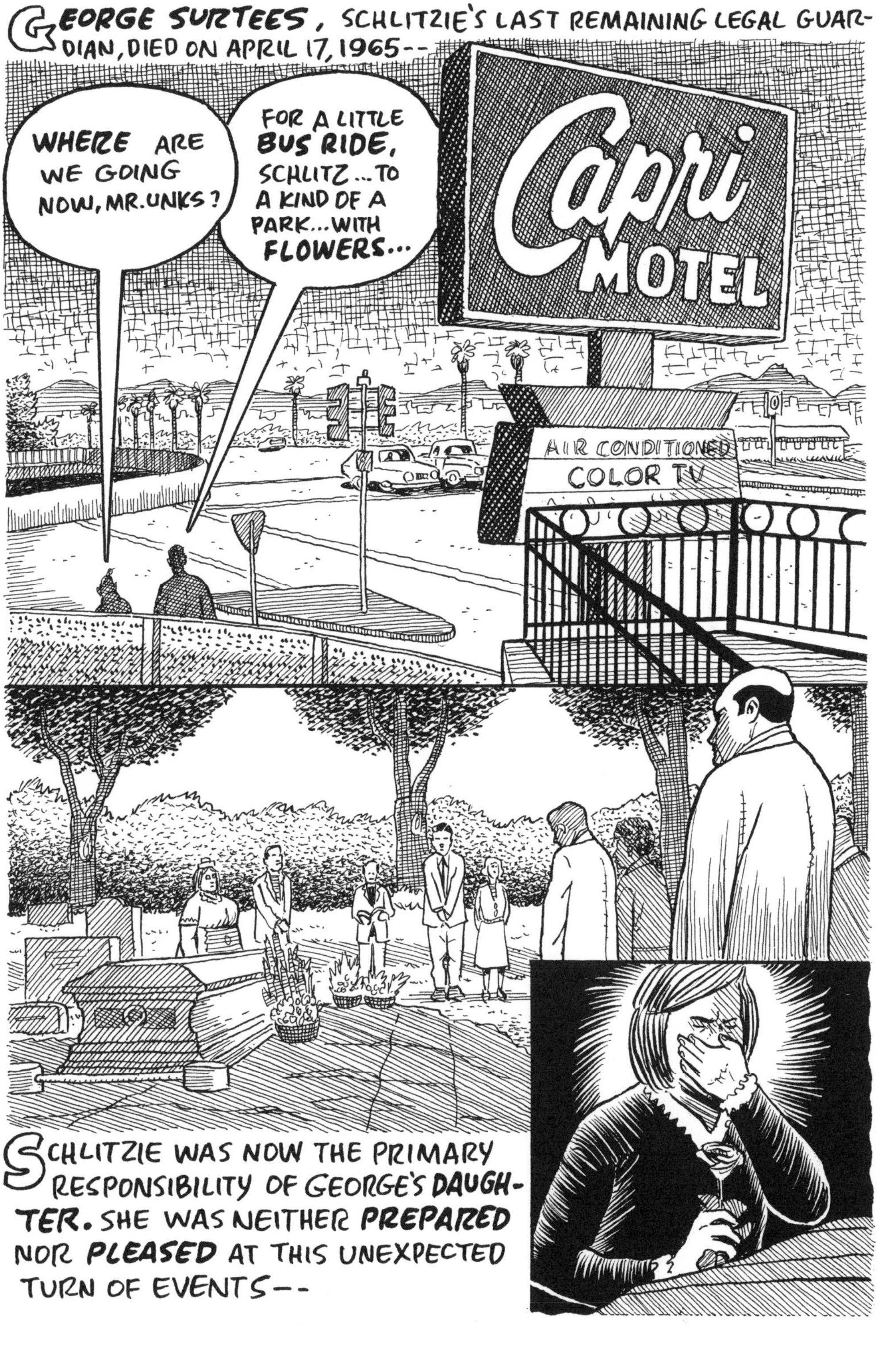
GEORGE SURTEES, SCHLITZIE'S LAST REMAINING LEGAL GUARDIAN, DIED ON APRIL 17, 1965--
WHERE ARE WE GOING NOW, MR. UNKS?
FOR A LITTLE BUS RIDE, SCHLITZ... TO A KIND OF A PARK... WITH FLOWERS...
Capri MOTEL
AIR CONDITIONED
COLOR TV
SCHLITZIE WAS NOW THE PRIMARY RESPONSIBILITY OF GEORGE'S DAUGHTER. SHE WAS NEITHER PREPARED NOR PLEASED AT THIS UNEXPECTED TURN OF EVENTS--

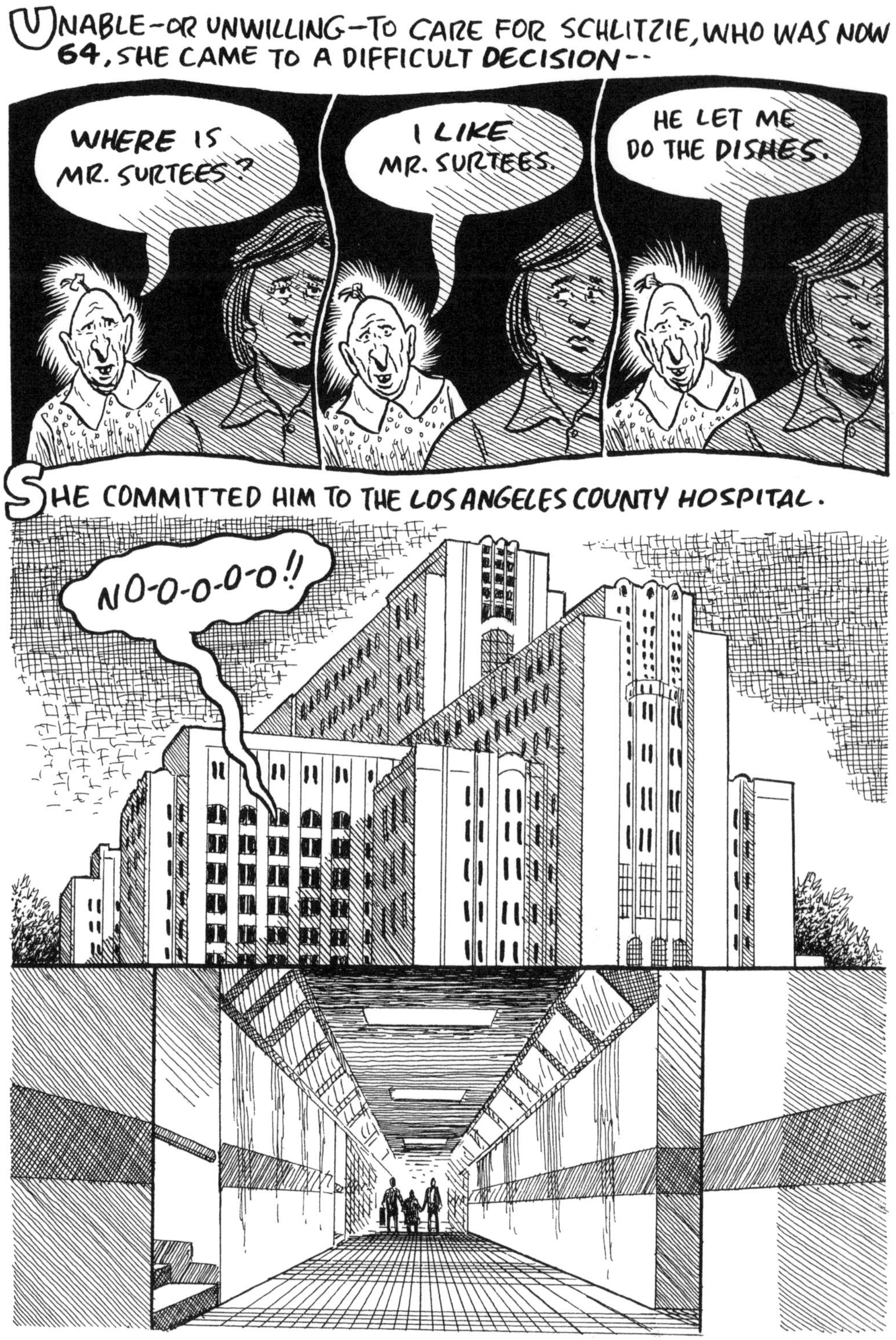
UNABLE—OR UNWILLING—TO CARE FOR SCHLITZIE, WHO WAS NOW 64, SHE CAME TO A DIFFICULT DECISION--
WHERE IS MR. SURTEES?
I LIKE MR. SURTEES.
HE LET ME DO THE DISHES.
SHE COMMITTED HIM TO THE LOS ANGELES COUNTY HOSPITAL.
NO-O-O-O-O-O!!

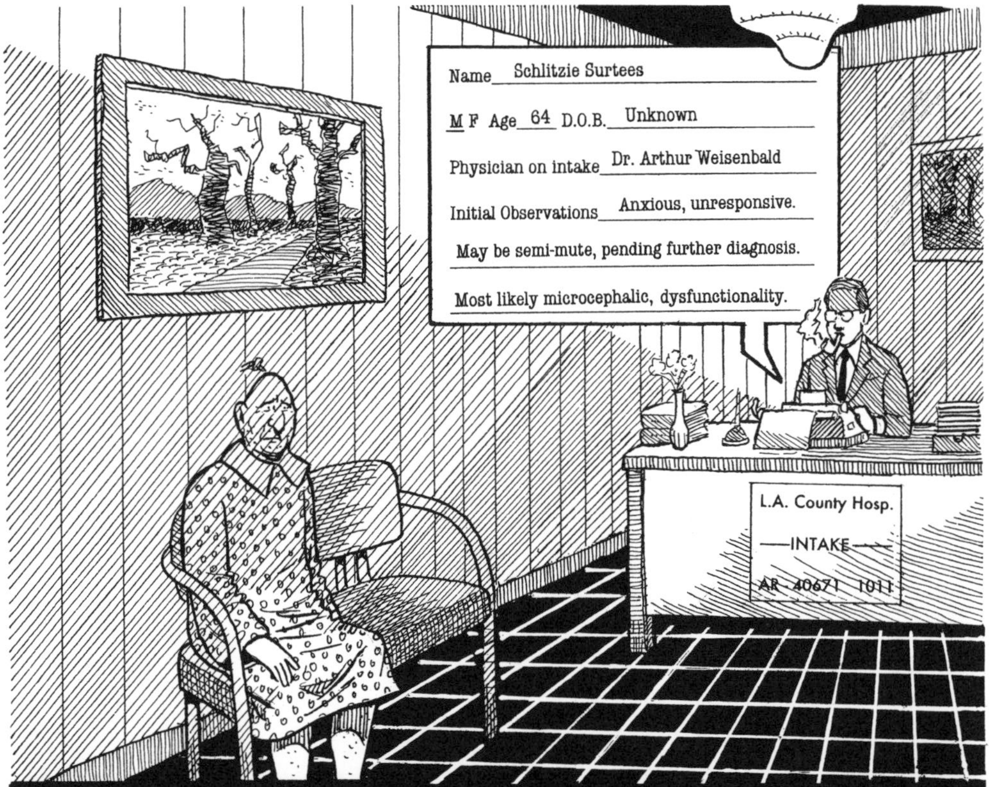
Name Schlitzie Surtees
M F Age 64 D.O.B. Unknown
Physician on intake Dr. Arthur Weisenbald
Initial Observations Anxious, unresponsive.
May be semi-mute, pending further diagnosis.
Most likely microcephalic, dysfunctionality.
L.A. County Hosp.
—INTAKE—
AR-40671 1011

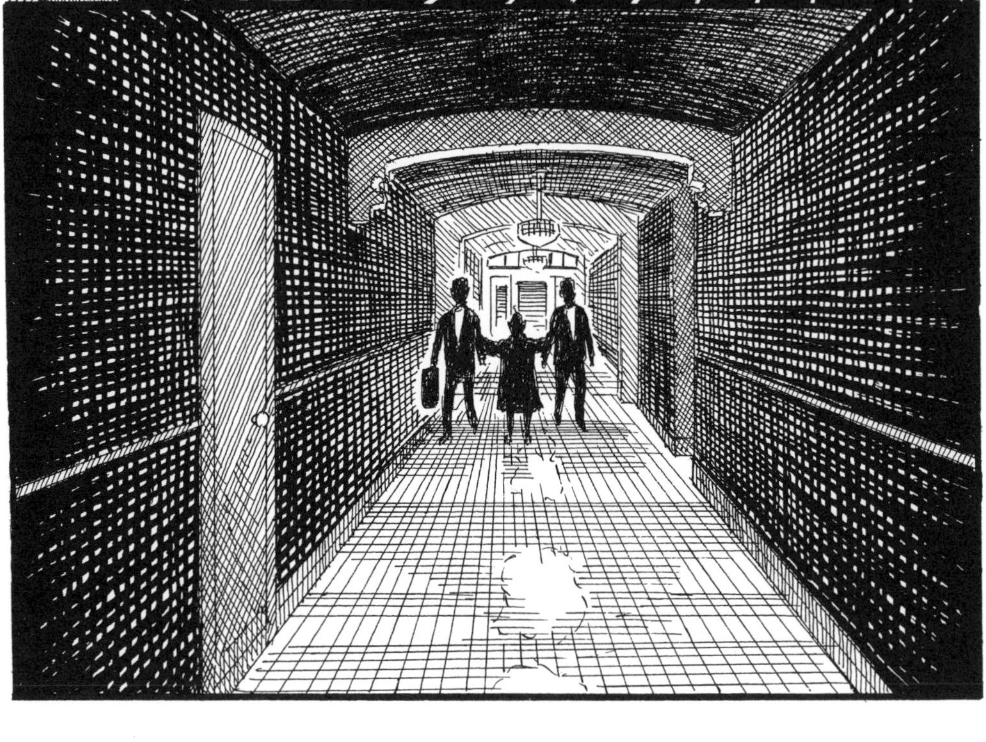

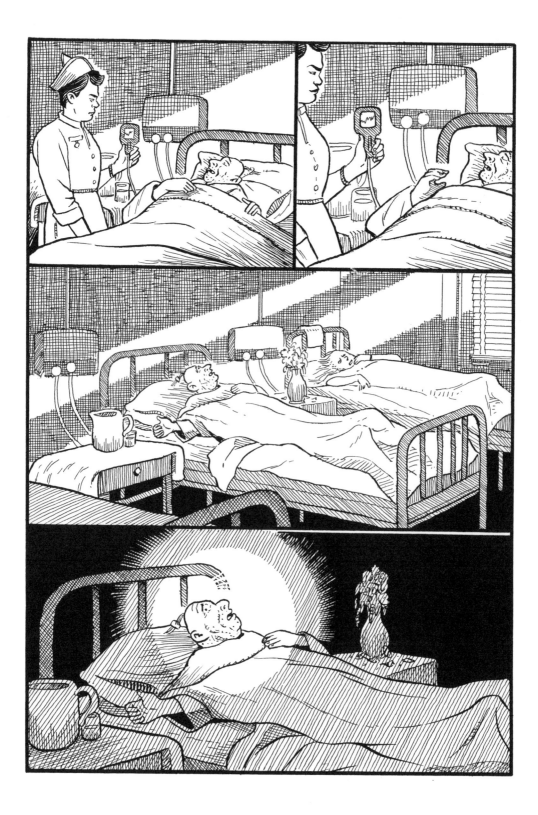

194

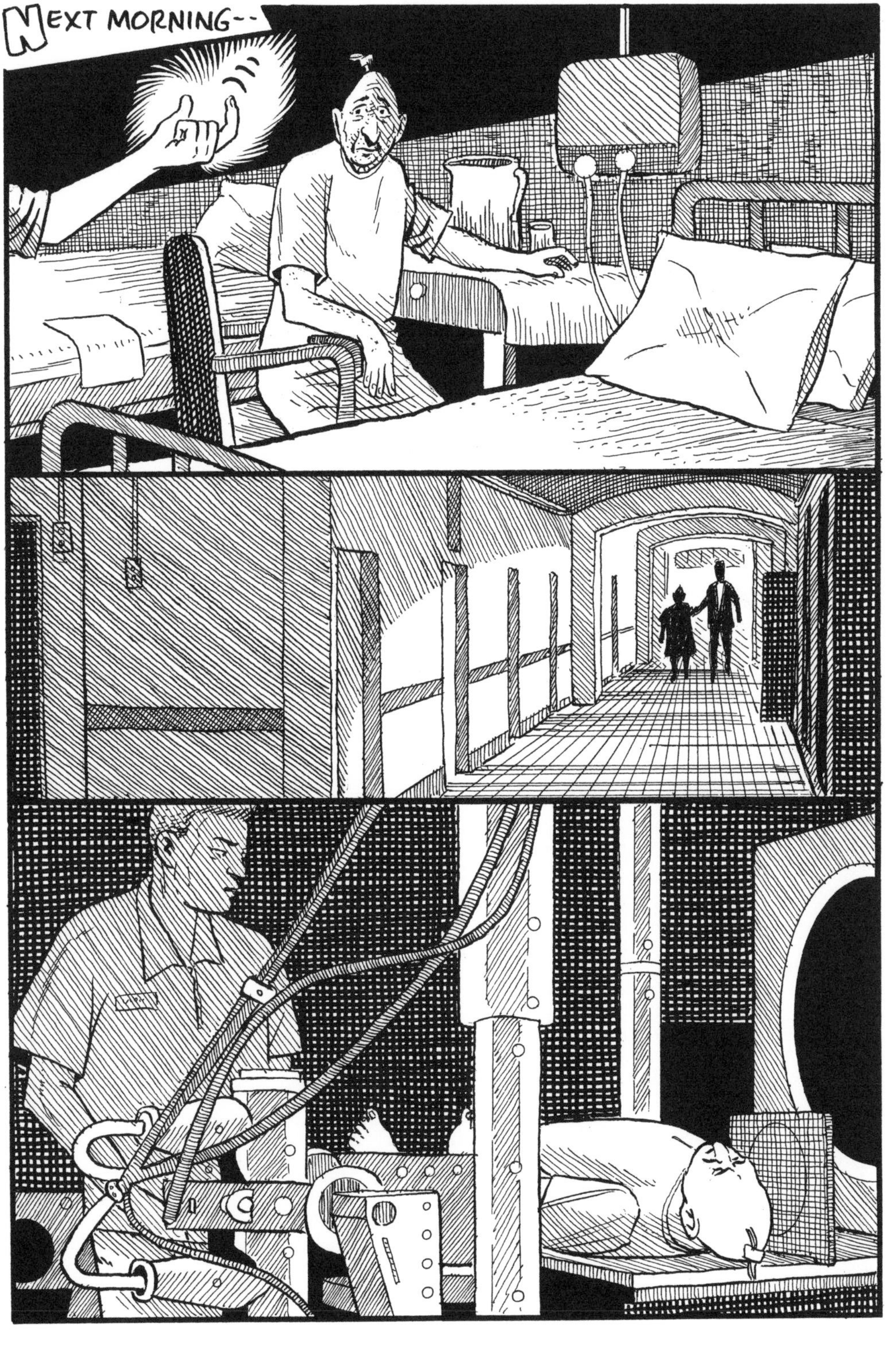
NEXT MORNING--

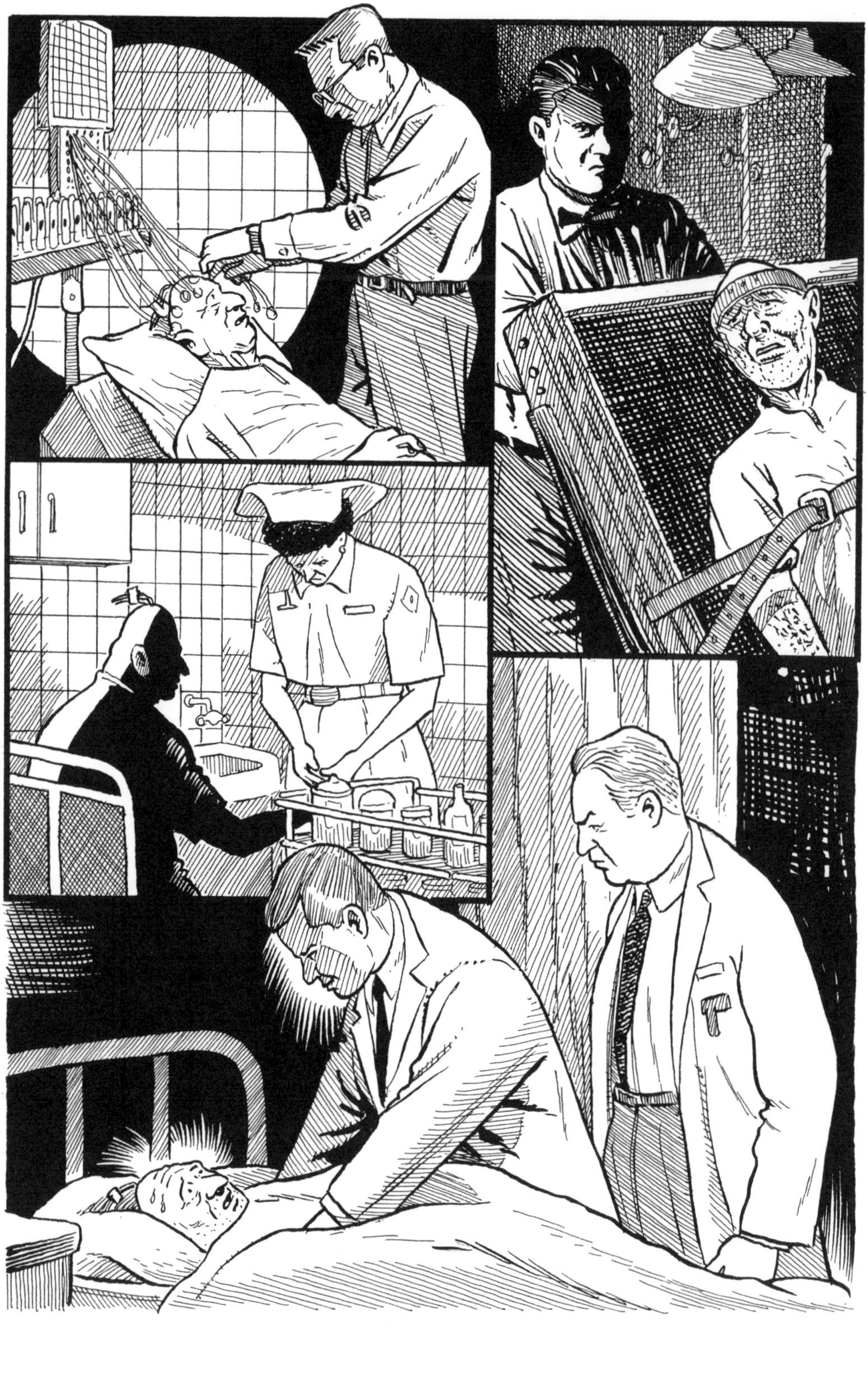

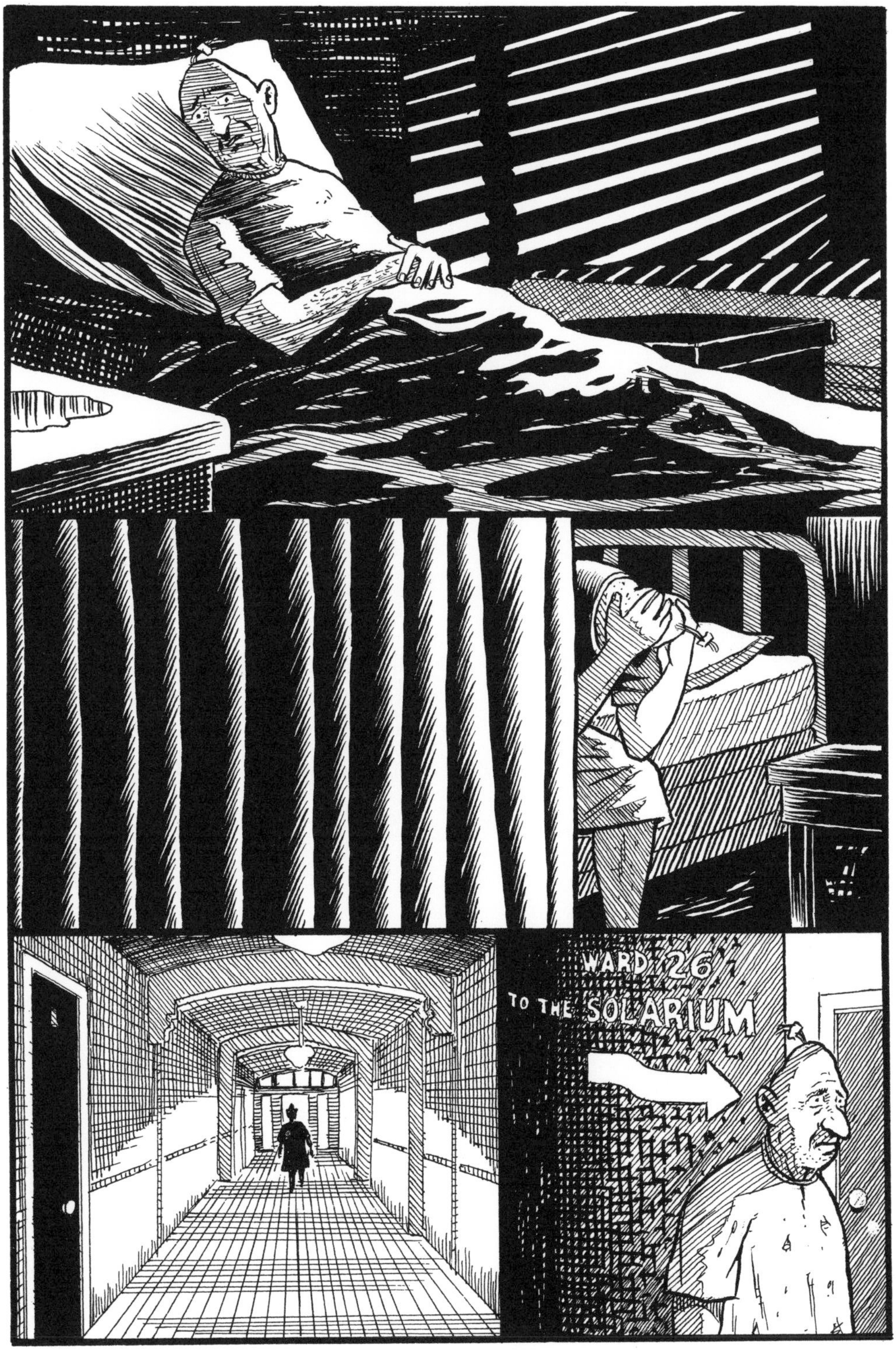
WARD 26
TO THE SOLARIUM

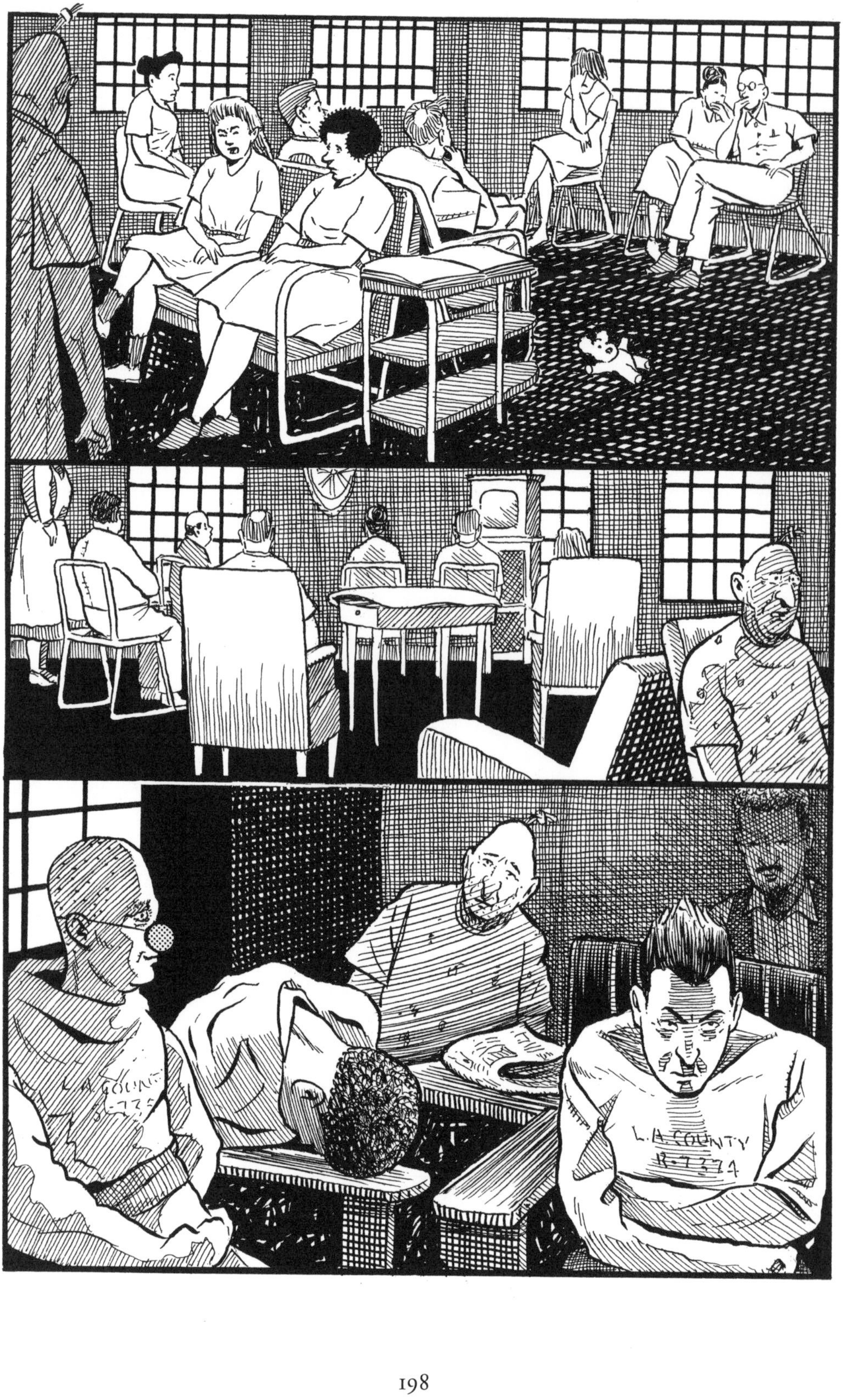
L.A. COUNTY
R-7374

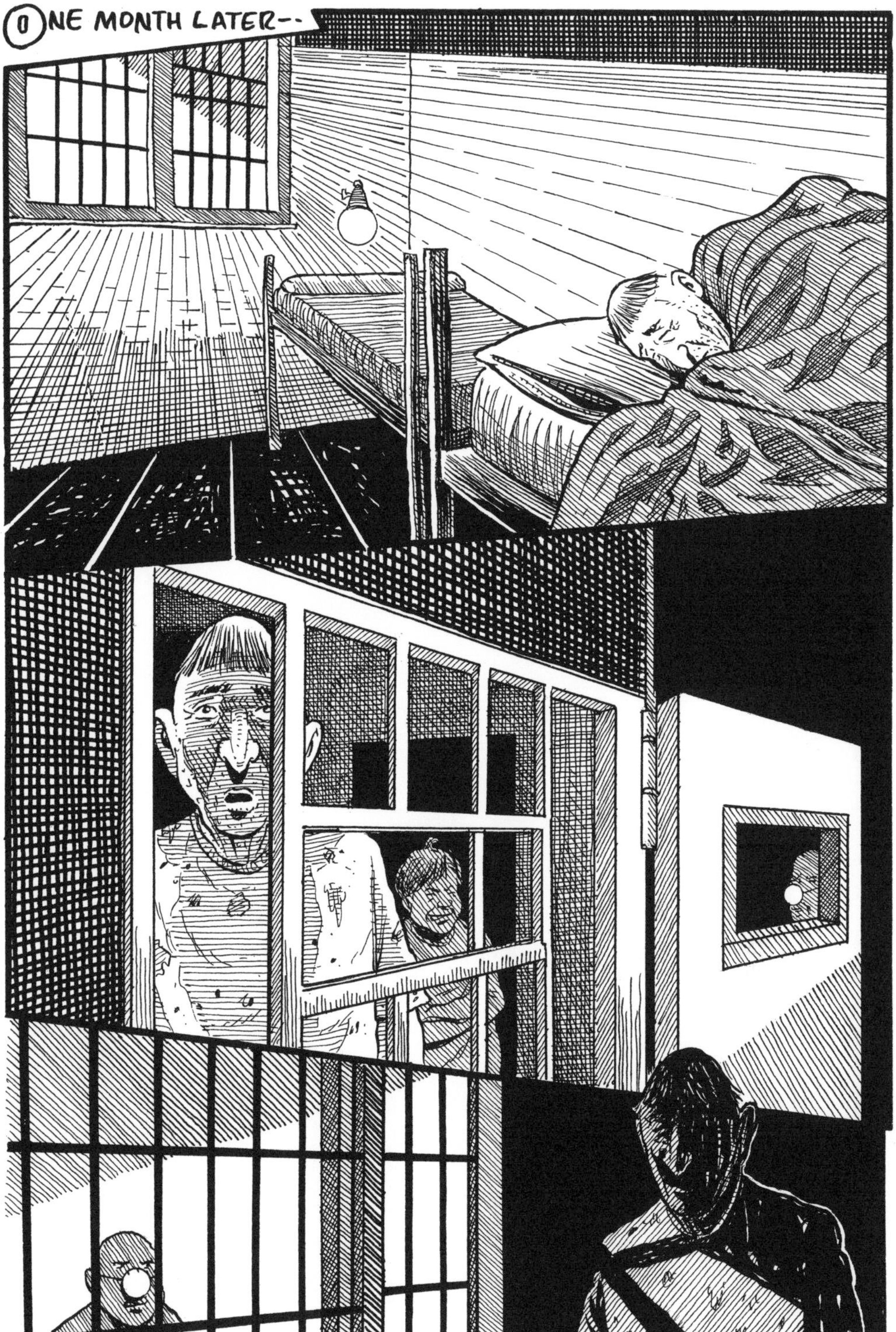
ONE MONTH LATER--

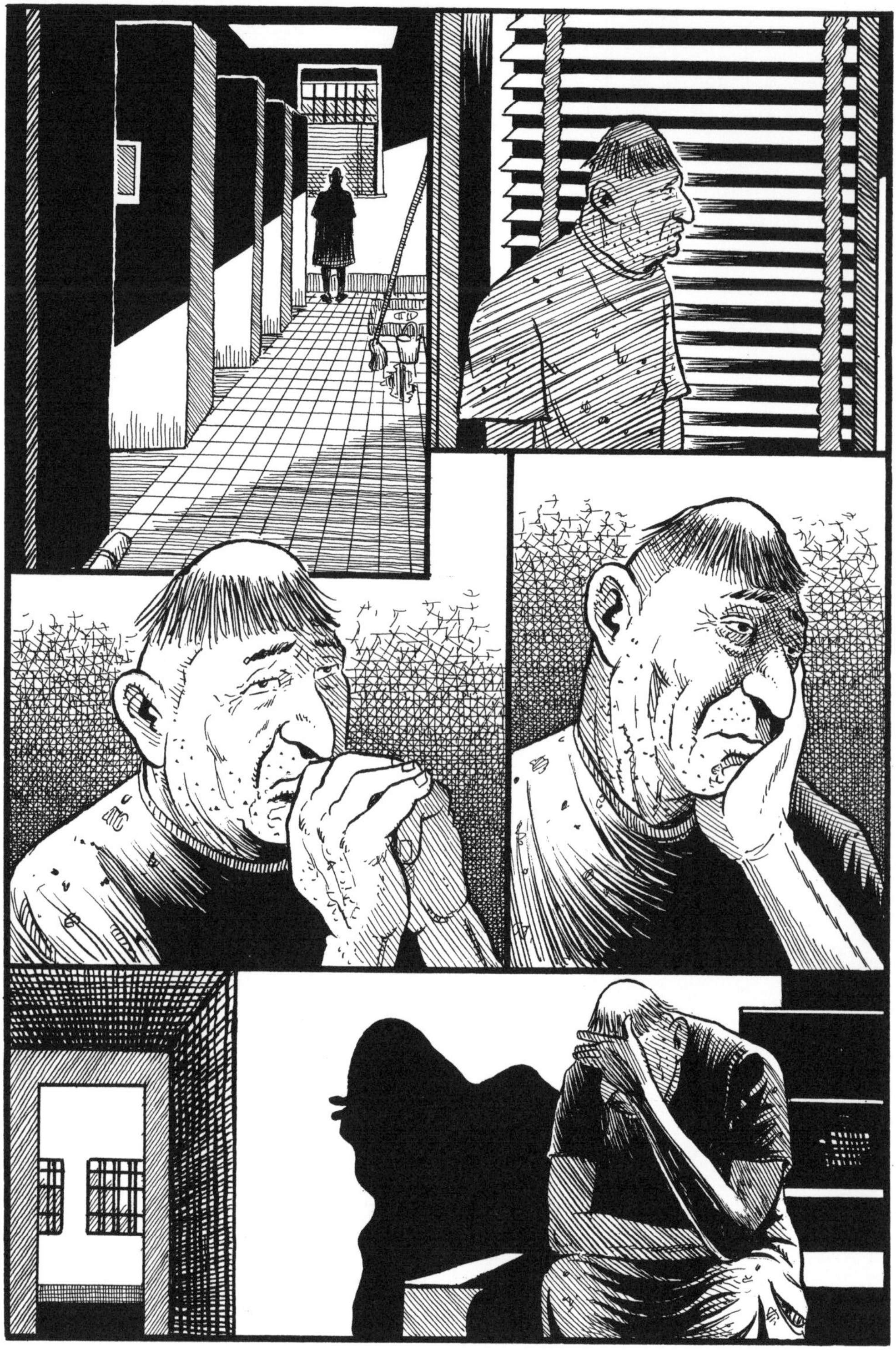

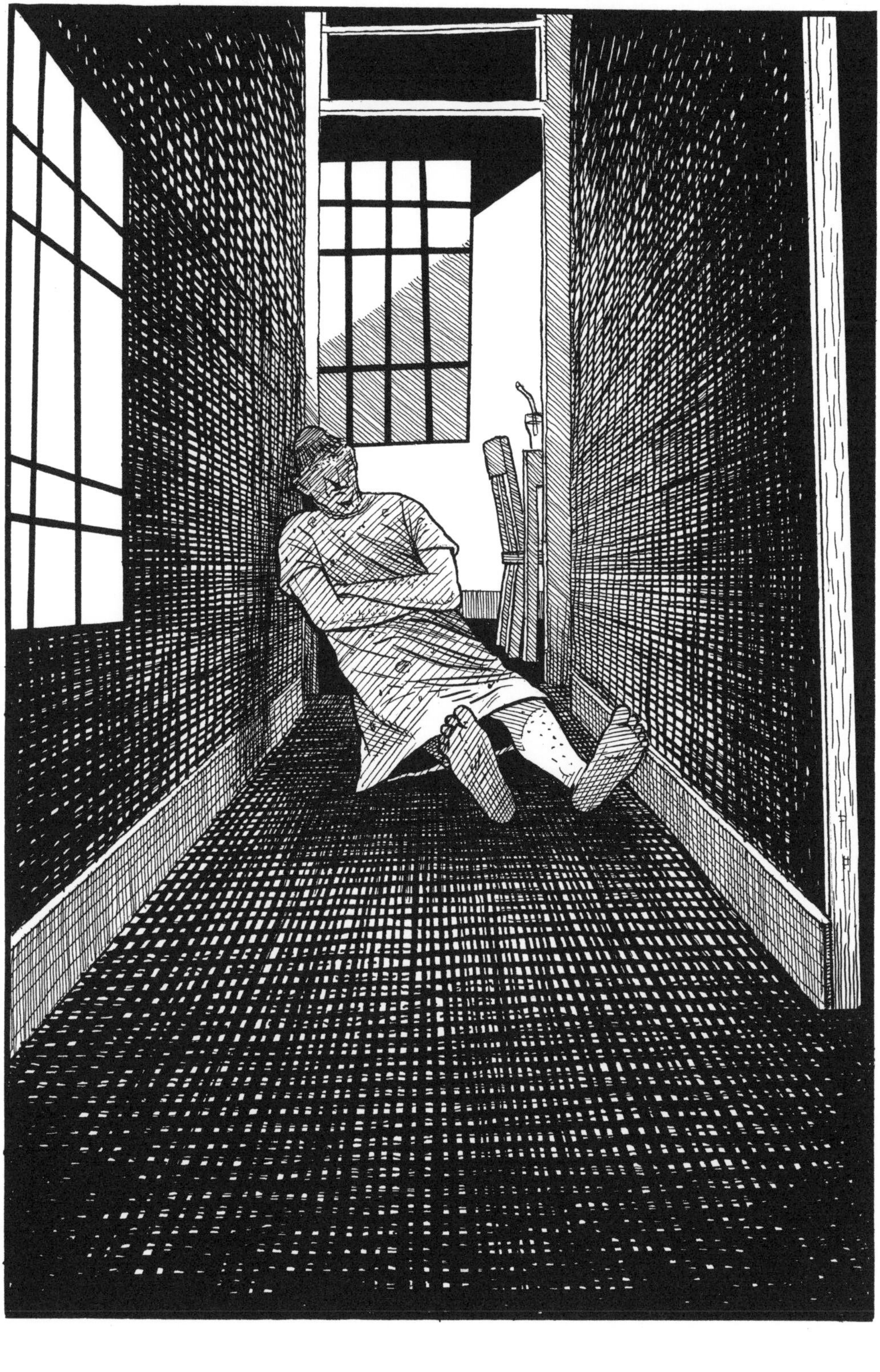

THE HOSPITAL ENTRANCE, SEVEN MONTHS LATER--

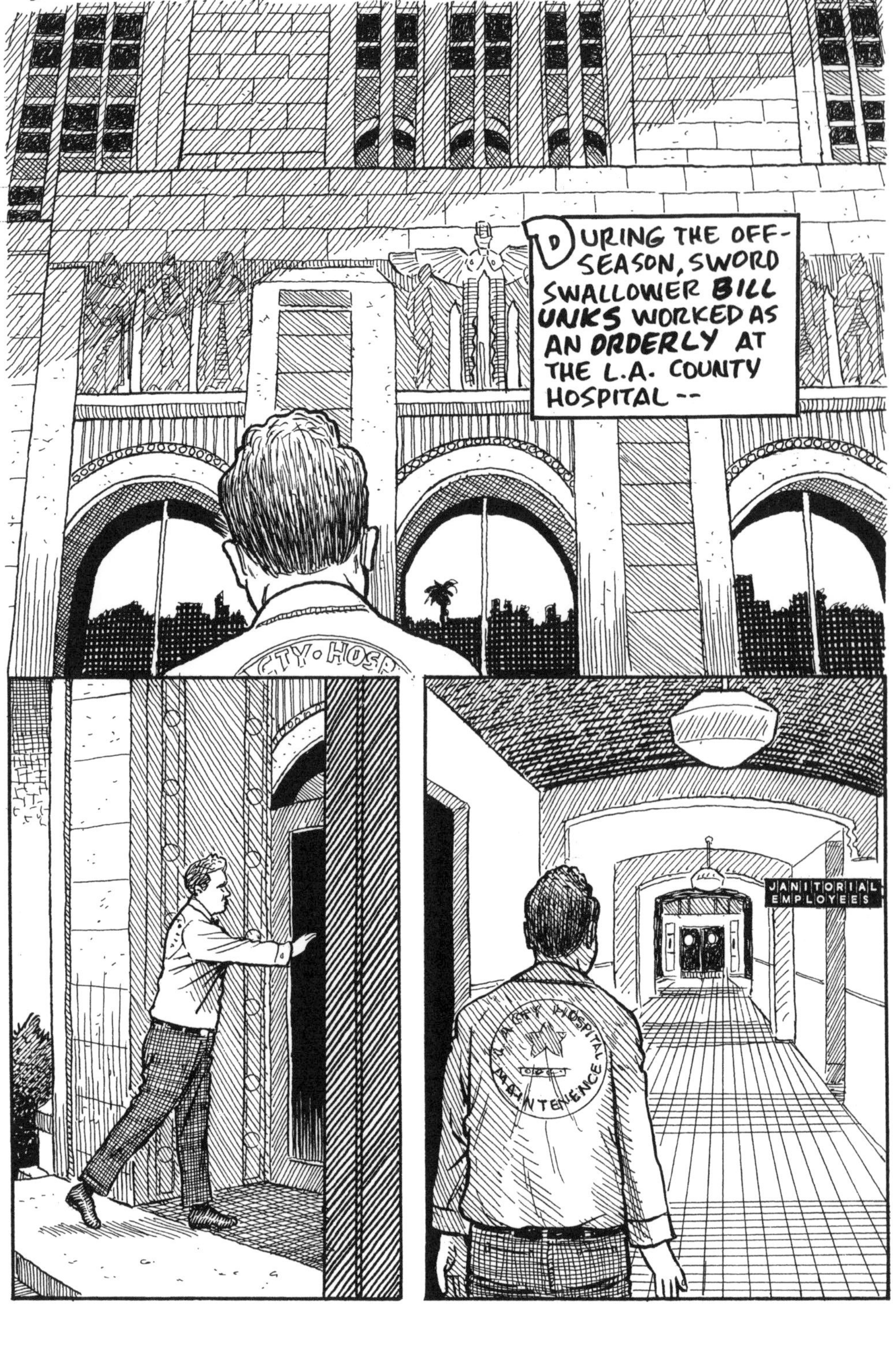
DURING THE OFF-SEASON, SWORD SWALLOWER **BILL UNKS** WORKED AS AN **ORDERLY** AT THE L.A. COUNTY HOSPITAL--
JANITORIAL EMPLOYEES
MAINTENENCE

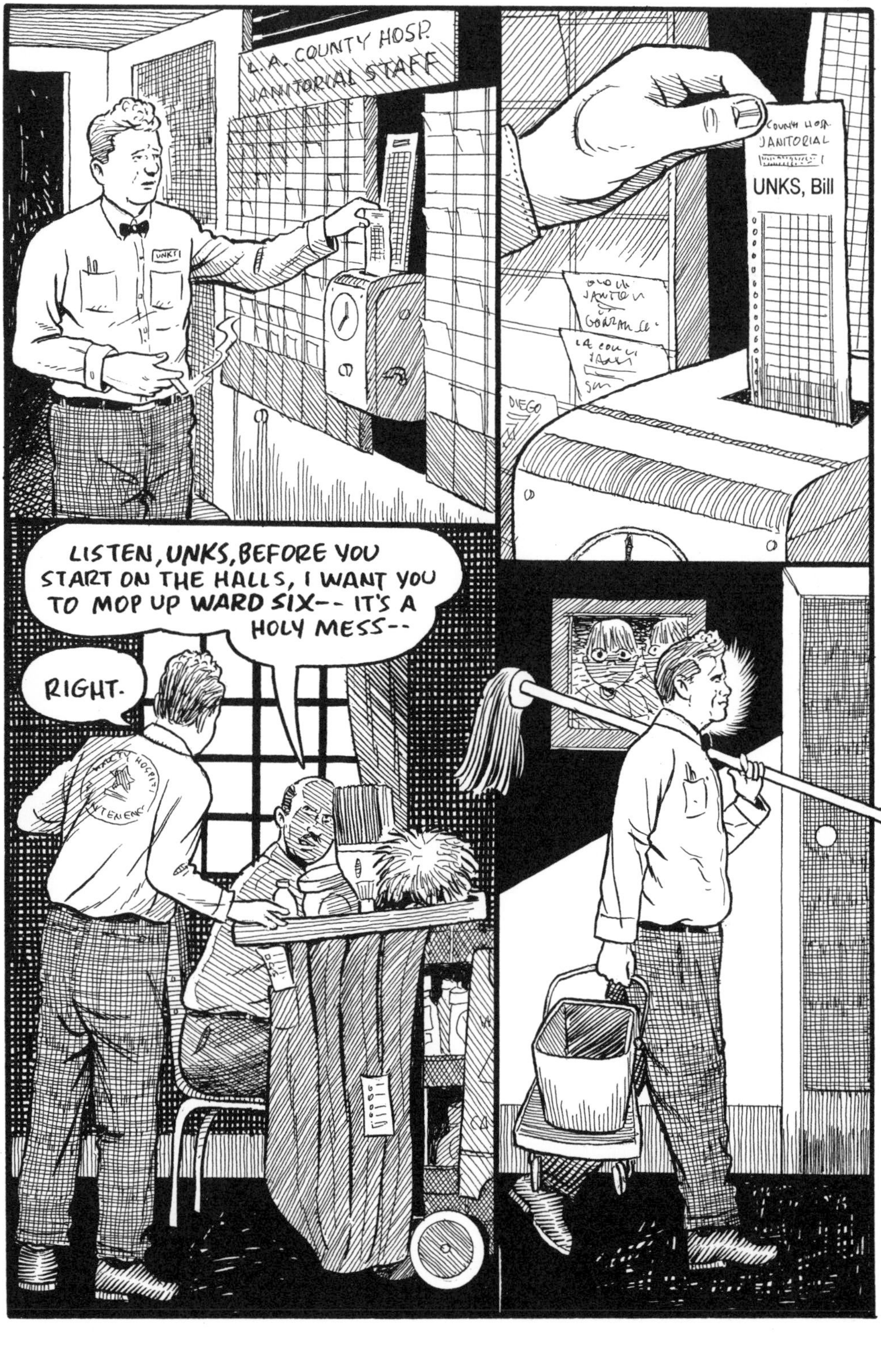
L. A. COUNTY HOSP.
JANITORIAL STAFF
COUNTY HOSP.
JANITORIAL
UNKS, Bill
DIEGO
LISTEN, UNKS, BEFORE YOU START ON THE HALLS, I WANT YOU TO MOP UP WARD SIX-- IT'S A HOLY MESS--
RIGHT.

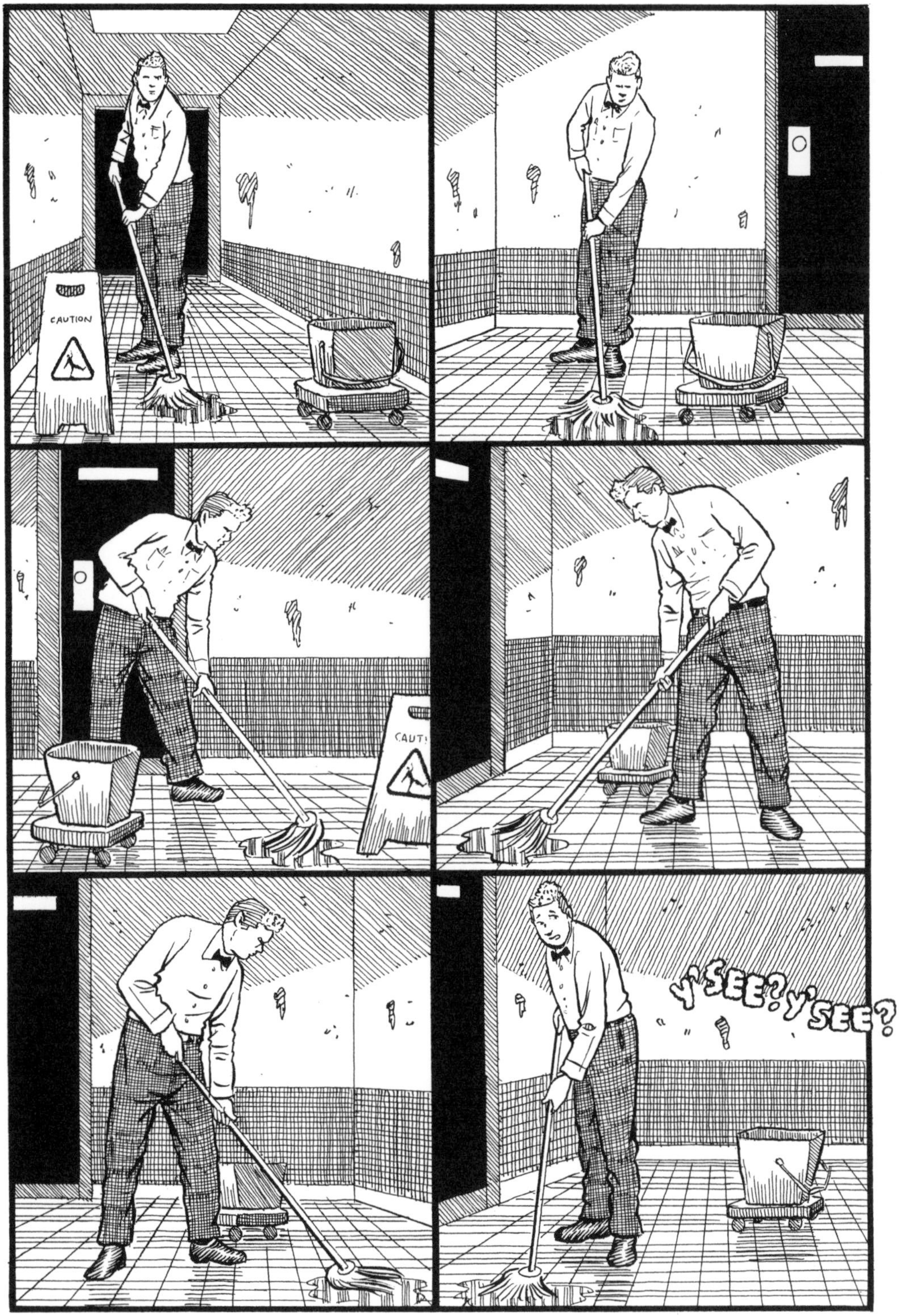
CAUTION
CAUTI
Y'SEE? Y'SEE?

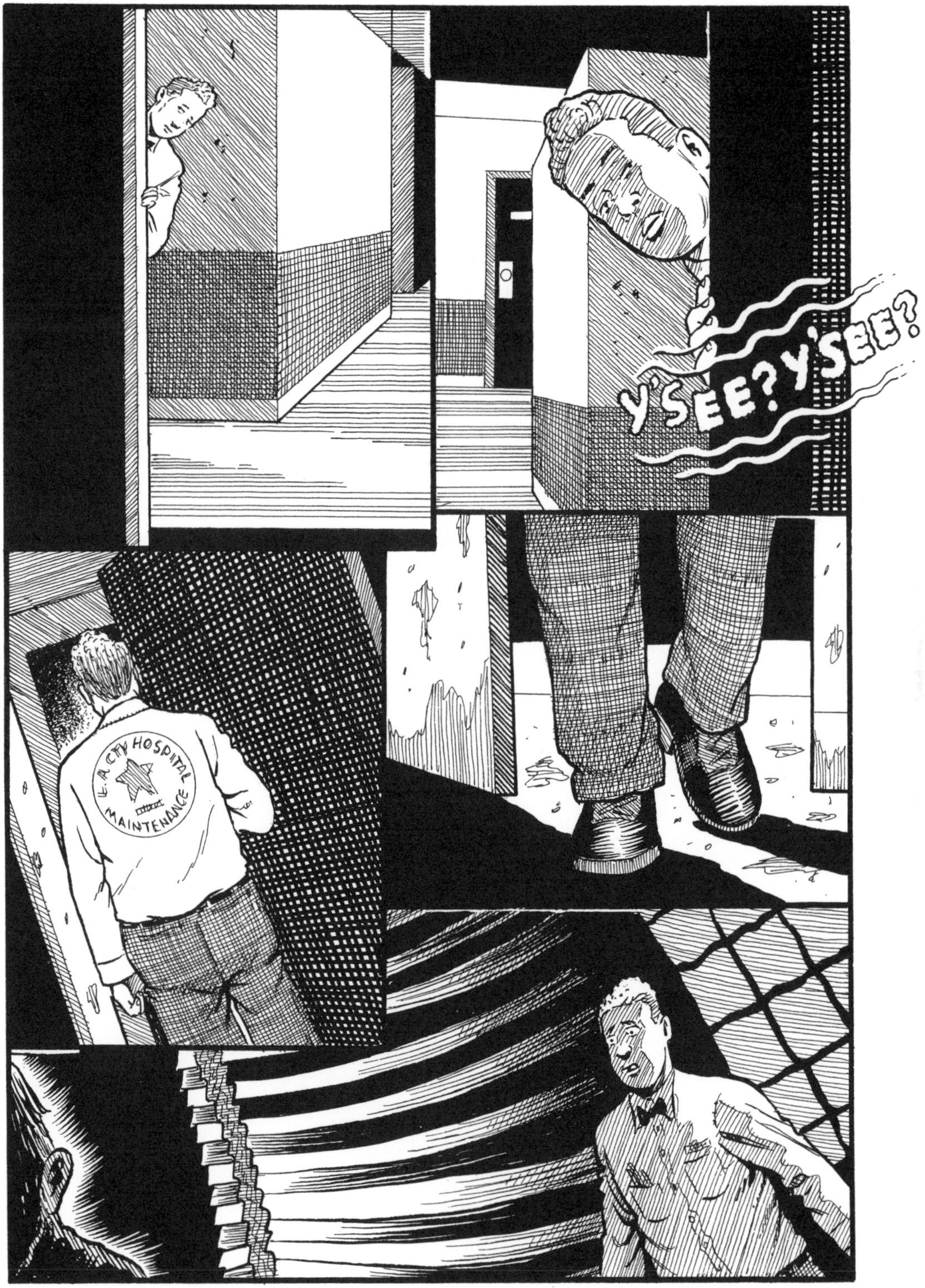
Y'SEE? Y'SEE?
L.A. CITY HOSPITAL
MAINTENANCE

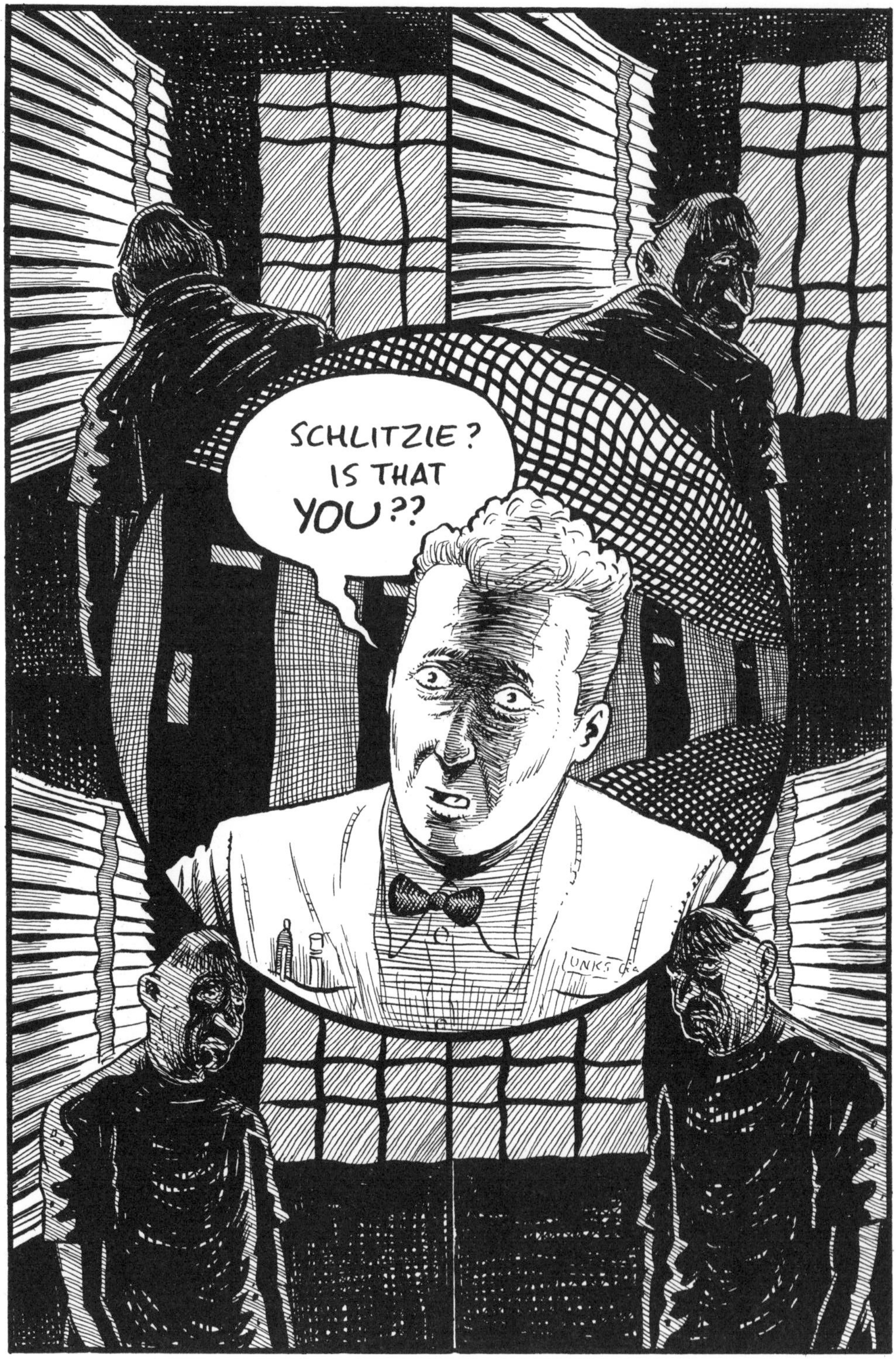
SCHLITZIE? IS THAT YOU??

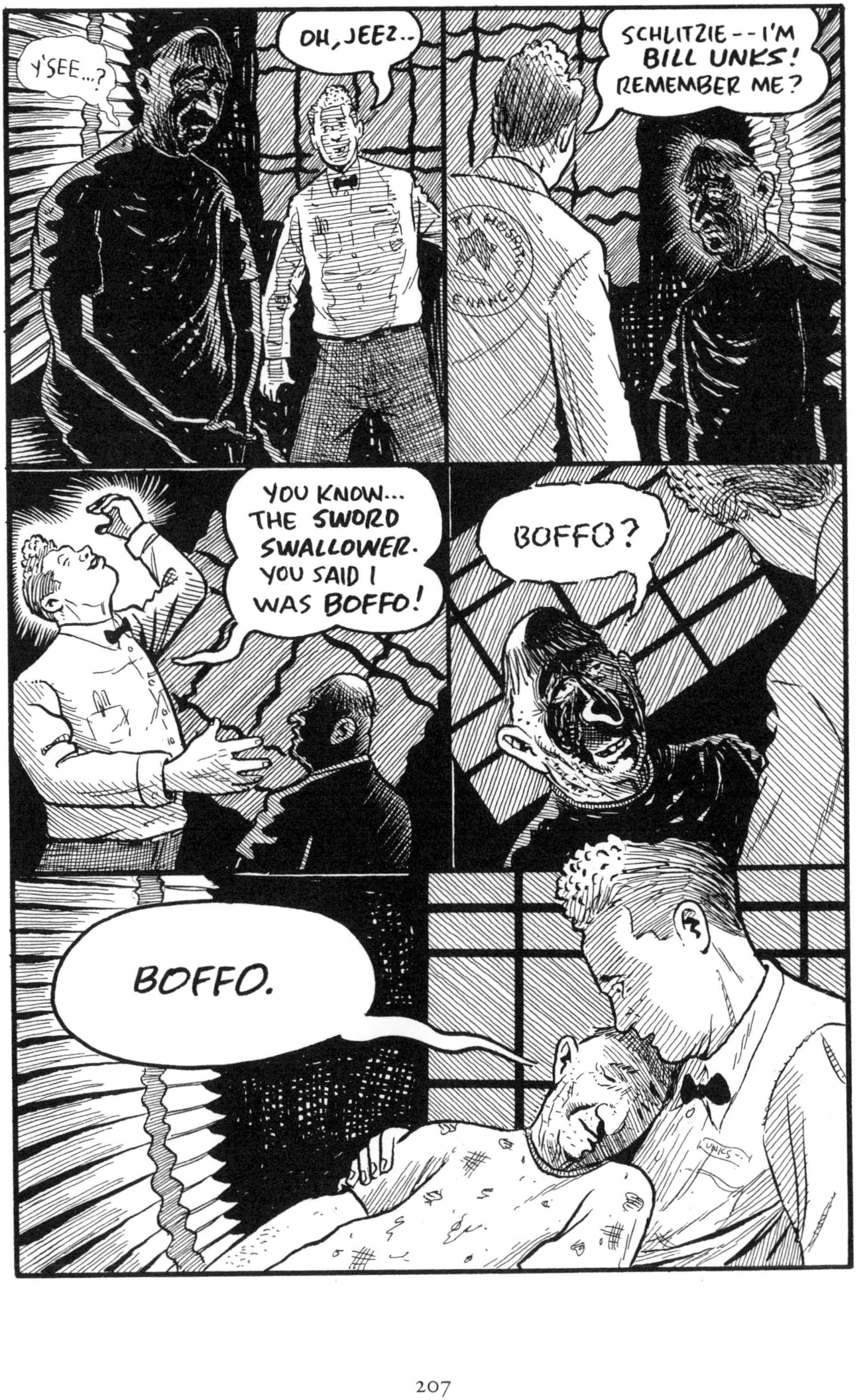
Y'SEE...?
OH, JEEZ..
SCHLITZIE--I'M BILL UNKS! REMEMBER ME?
YOU KNOW... THE SWORD SWALLOWER. YOU SAID I WAS BOFFO!
BOFFO?
BOFFO.

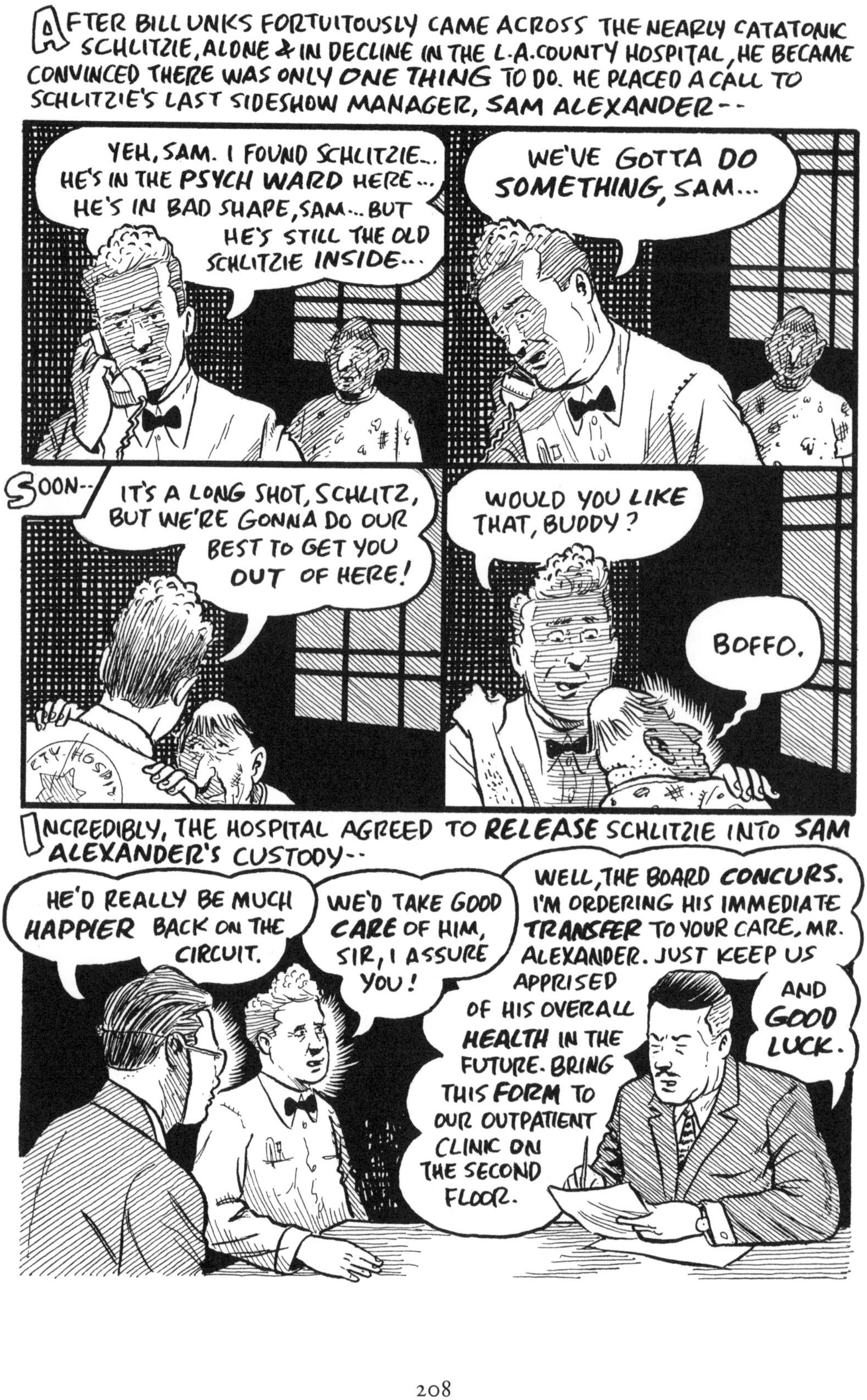
AFTER BILL UNKS FORTUITOUSLY CAME ACROSS THE NEARLY CATATONIC SCHLITZIE, ALONE & IN DECLINE IN THE L.A. COUNTY HOSPITAL, HE BECAME CONVINCED THERE WAS ONLY ONE THING TO DO. HE PLACED A CALL TO SCHLITZIE'S LAST SIDESHOW MANAGER, SAM ALEXANDER--
YEH, SAM. I FOUND SCHLITZIE... HE'S IN THE PSYCH WARD HERE... HE'S IN BAD SHAPE, SAM... BUT HE'S STILL THE OLD SCHLITZIE INSIDE...
WE'VE GOTTA DO SOMETHING, SAM...
SOON--
IT'S A LONG SHOT, SCHLITZ, BUT WE'RE GONNA DO OUR BEST TO GET YOU OUT OF HERE!
CTY. HOSPIT
WOULD YOU LIKE THAT, BUDDY?
BOFFO.
INCREDIBLY, THE HOSPITAL AGREED TO RELEASE SCHLITZIE INTO SAM ALEXANDER'S CUSTODY--
HE'D REALLY BE MUCH HAPPIER BACK ON THE CIRCUIT.
WE'D TAKE GOOD CARE OF HIM, SIR, I ASSURE YOU!
WELL, THE BOARD CONCURS. I'M ORDERING HIS IMMEDIATE TRANSFER TO YOUR CARE, MR. ALEXANDER. JUST KEEP US APPRISED OF HIS OVERALL HEALTH IN THE FUTURE. BRING THIS FORM TO OUR OUTPATIENT CLINIC ON THE SECOND FLOOR.
AND GOOD LUCK.

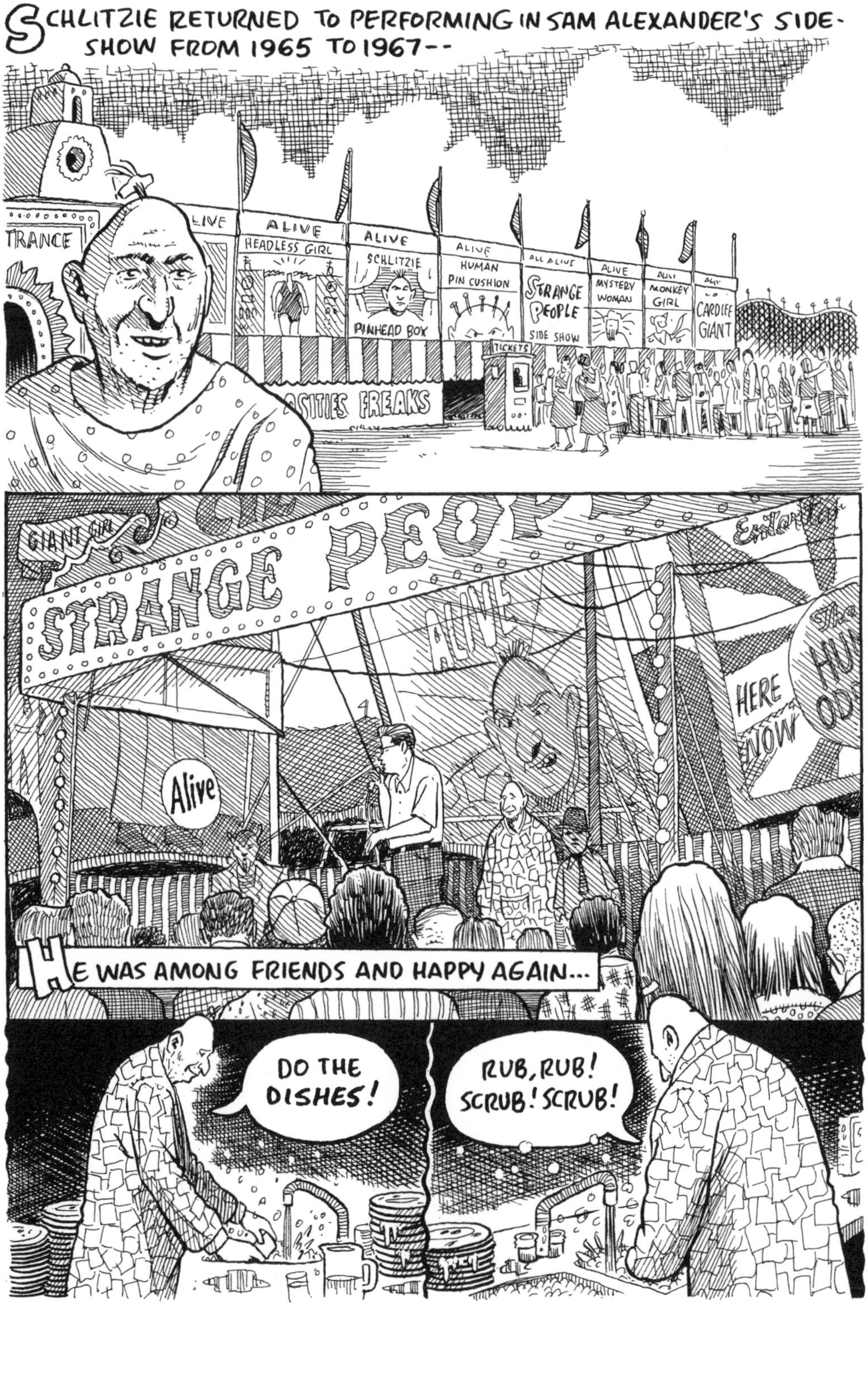
SCHLITZIE RETURNED TO PERFORMING IN SAM ALEXANDER'S SIDE-SHOW FROM 1965 TO 1967--
TRANCE
ALIVE
ALIVE
HEADLESS GIRL
ALIVE
SCHLITZIE
PINHEAD BOX
ALIVE
HUMAN
PIN CUSHION
ALL ALIVE
STRANGE PEOPLE
SIDE SHOW
ALIVE
MYSTERY WOMAN
ALIVE
MONKEY GIRL
ALIVE
CARDIFF GIANT
TICKETS
FREAKS
GIANT GIRL
STRANGE PEOP
ALIVE
Alive
HERE NOW
HE WAS AMONG FRIENDS AND HAPPY AGAIN...
DO THE DISHES!
RUB, RUB! SCRUB! SCRUB!

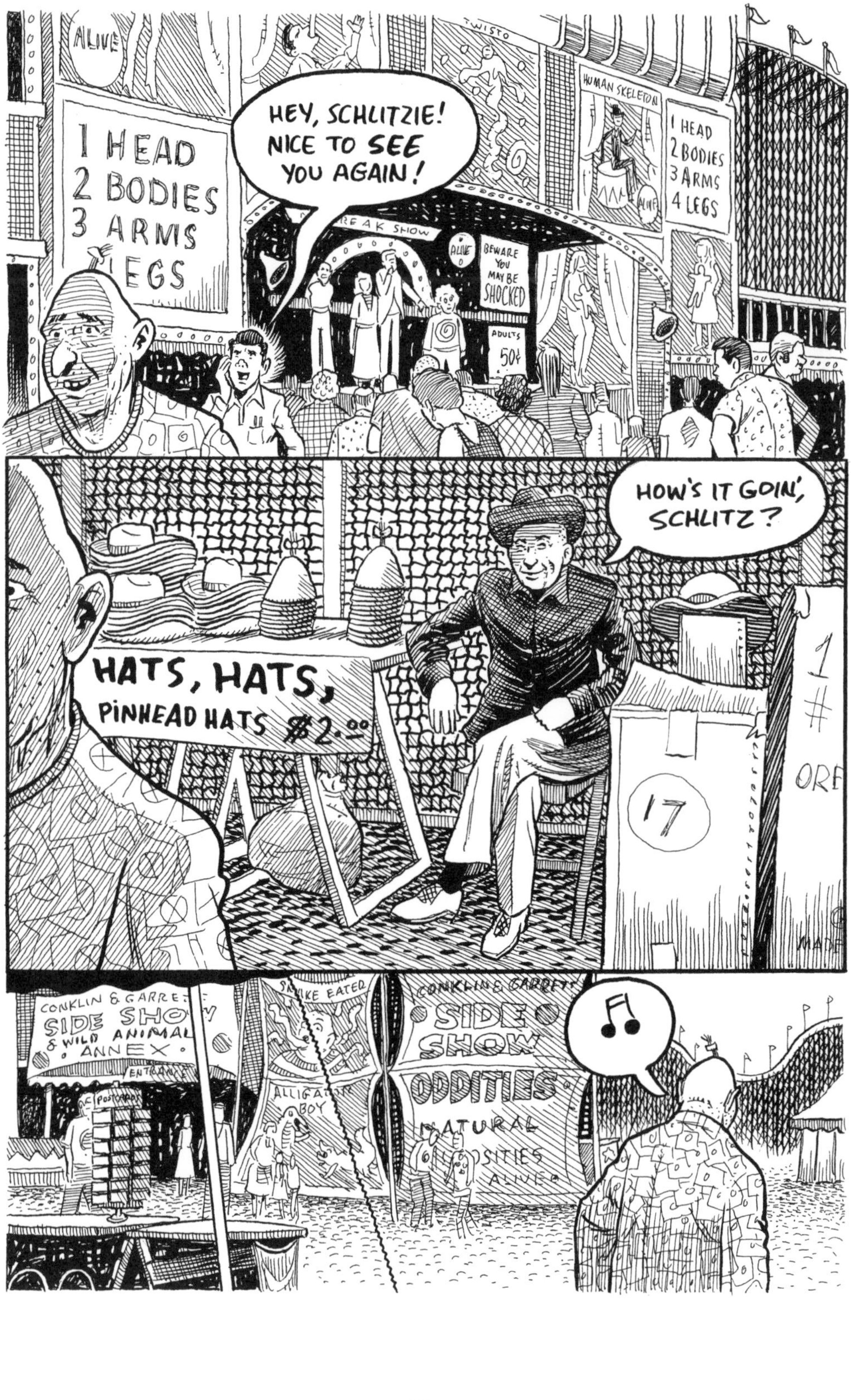
ALIVE
1 HEAD
2 BODIES
3 ARMS
HUMAN SKELETON
1 HEAD
2 BODIES
3 ARMS
4 LEGS
HEY, SCHLITZIE! NICE TO SEE YOU AGAIN!
BEWARE YOU MAY BE SHOCKED
ADULTS 50¢
HOW'S IT GOIN', SCHLITZ?
HATS, HATS, PINHEAD HATS $2.00
17
SIDE SHOW
ODDITIES

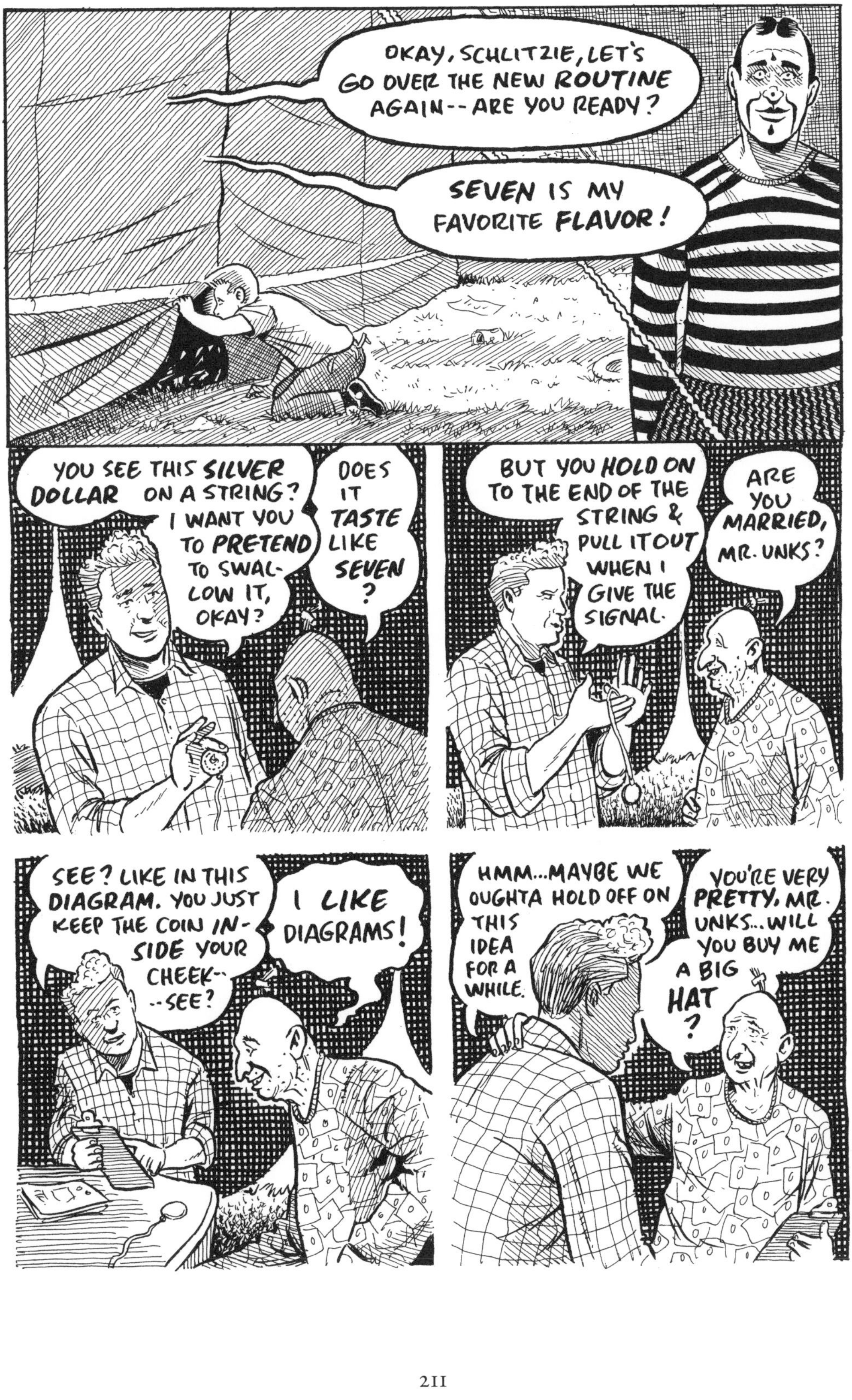
OKAY, SCHLITZIE, LET'S GO OVER THE NEW ROUTINE AGAIN-- ARE YOU READY?
SEVEN IS MY FAVORITE FLAVOR!
YOU SEE THIS SILVER DOLLAR ON A STRING? I WANT YOU TO PRETEND TO SWALLOW IT, OKAY?
DOES IT TASTE LIKE SEVEN?
BUT YOU HOLD ON TO THE END OF THE STRING & PULL IT OUT WHEN I GIVE THE SIGNAL.
ARE YOU MARRIED, MR. UNKS?
SEE? LIKE IN THIS DIAGRAM. YOU JUST KEEP THE COIN INSIDE YOUR CHEEK-- --SEE?
I LIKE DIAGRAMS!
HMM...MAYBE WE OUGHTA HOLD OFF ON THIS IDEA FOR A WHILE.
YOU'RE VERY PRETTY, MR. UNKS...WILL YOU BUY ME A BIG HAT?

THE SAM ALEXANDER SIDESHOW TRAVELED THROUGHOUT CANADA, INCLUDING A STOP AT BELMONT PARK IN MONTREAL, WHERE SCHLITZIE WAS BILLED AS "THE MONKEY GIRL"--

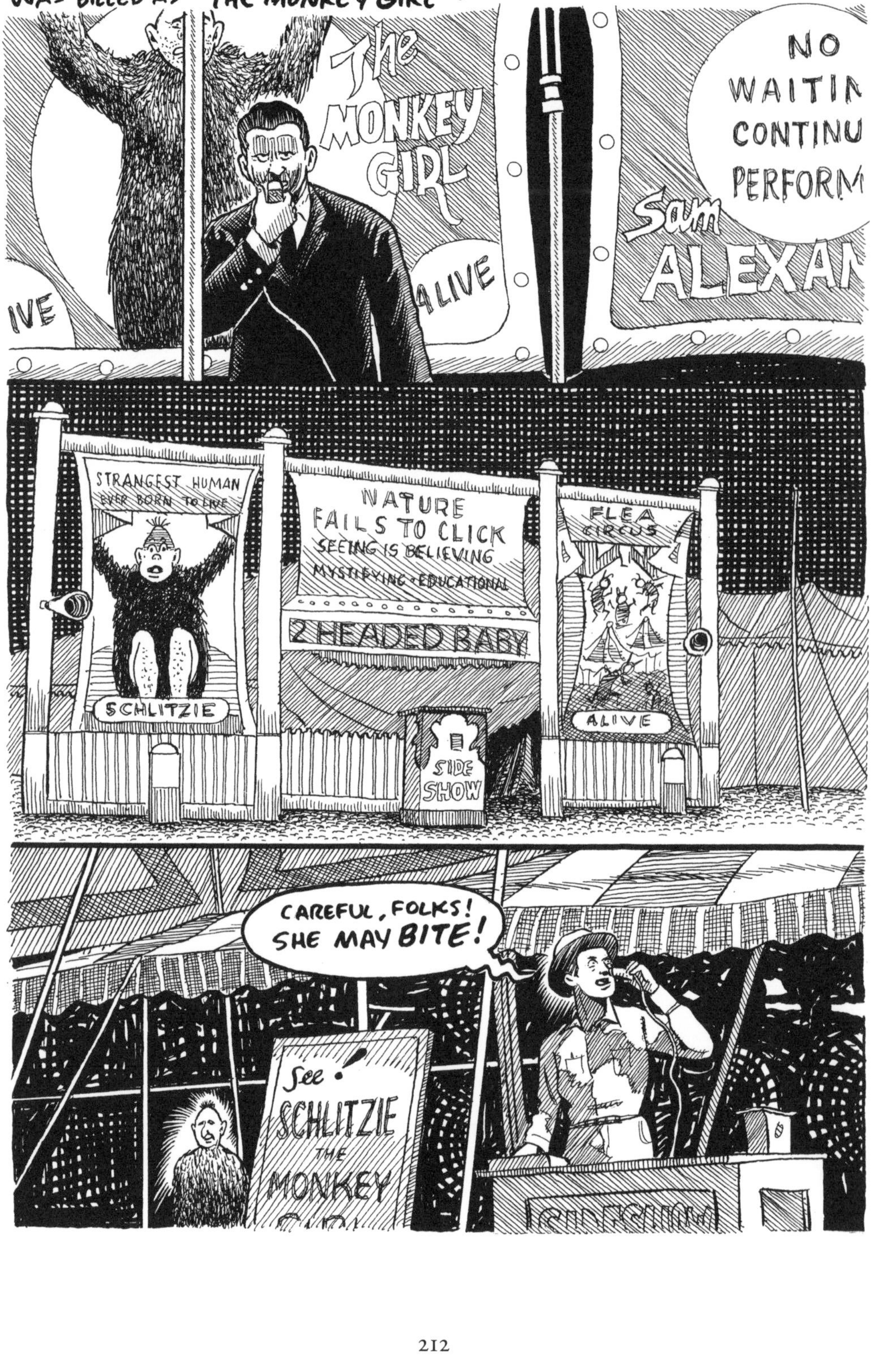

The MONKEY GIRL
ALIVE
IVE
NO WAITIN CONTINU PERFORM
Sam ALEXAN
STRANGEST HUMAN EVER BORN TO LIVE
SCHLITZIE
NATURE FAILS TO CLICK
SEEING IS BELIEVING
MYSTIFYING - EDUCATIONAL
2 HEADED BABY
FLEA CIRCUS
ALIVE
SIDE SHOW
CAREFUL, FOLKS! SHE MAY BITE!
See! SCHLITZIE THE MONKEY

THE SHOW ROLLED INTO **TORONTO** THAT SUMMER AND SET UP AT THE **CANADIAN NATIONAL EXHIBITION** OUTSIDE THE CITY--

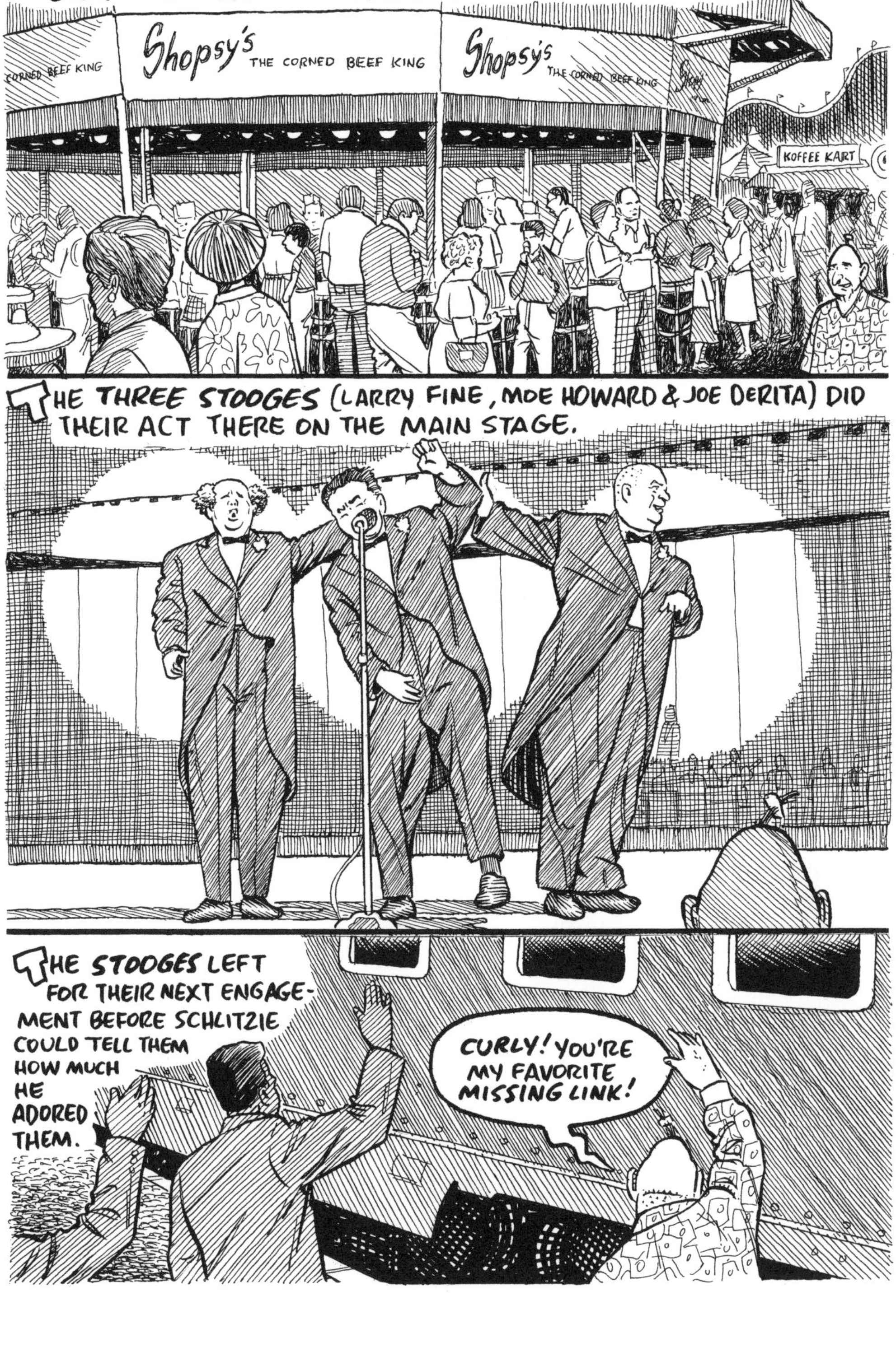
CORNED BEEF KING
Shopsy's THE CORNED BEEF KING
Shopsy's THE CORNED BEEF KING
KOFFEE KART
THE THREE STOOGES (LARRY FINE, MOE HOWARD & JOE DERITA) DID THEIR ACT THERE ON THE MAIN STAGE.
THE STOOGES LEFT FOR THEIR NEXT ENGAGEMENT BEFORE SCHLITZIE COULD TELL THEM HOW MUCH HE ADORED THEM.
CURLY! YOU'RE MY FAVORITE MISSING LINK!

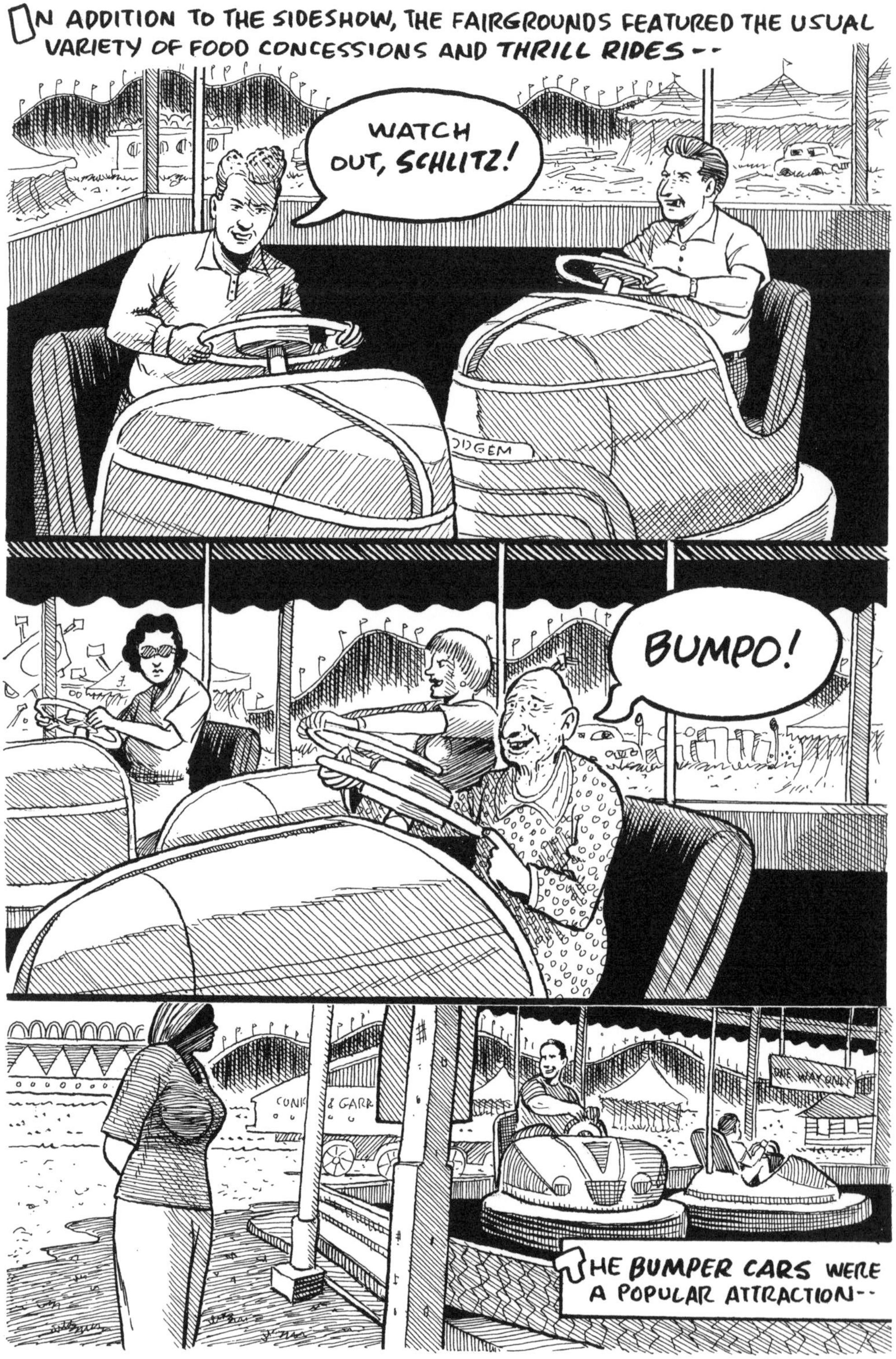
IN ADDITION TO THE SIDESHOW, THE FAIRGROUNDS FEATURED THE USUAL VARIETY OF FOOD CONCESSIONS AND THRILL RIDES--
WATCH OUT, SCHLITZ!
BUMPO!
THE BUMPER CARS WERE A POPULAR ATTRACTION--

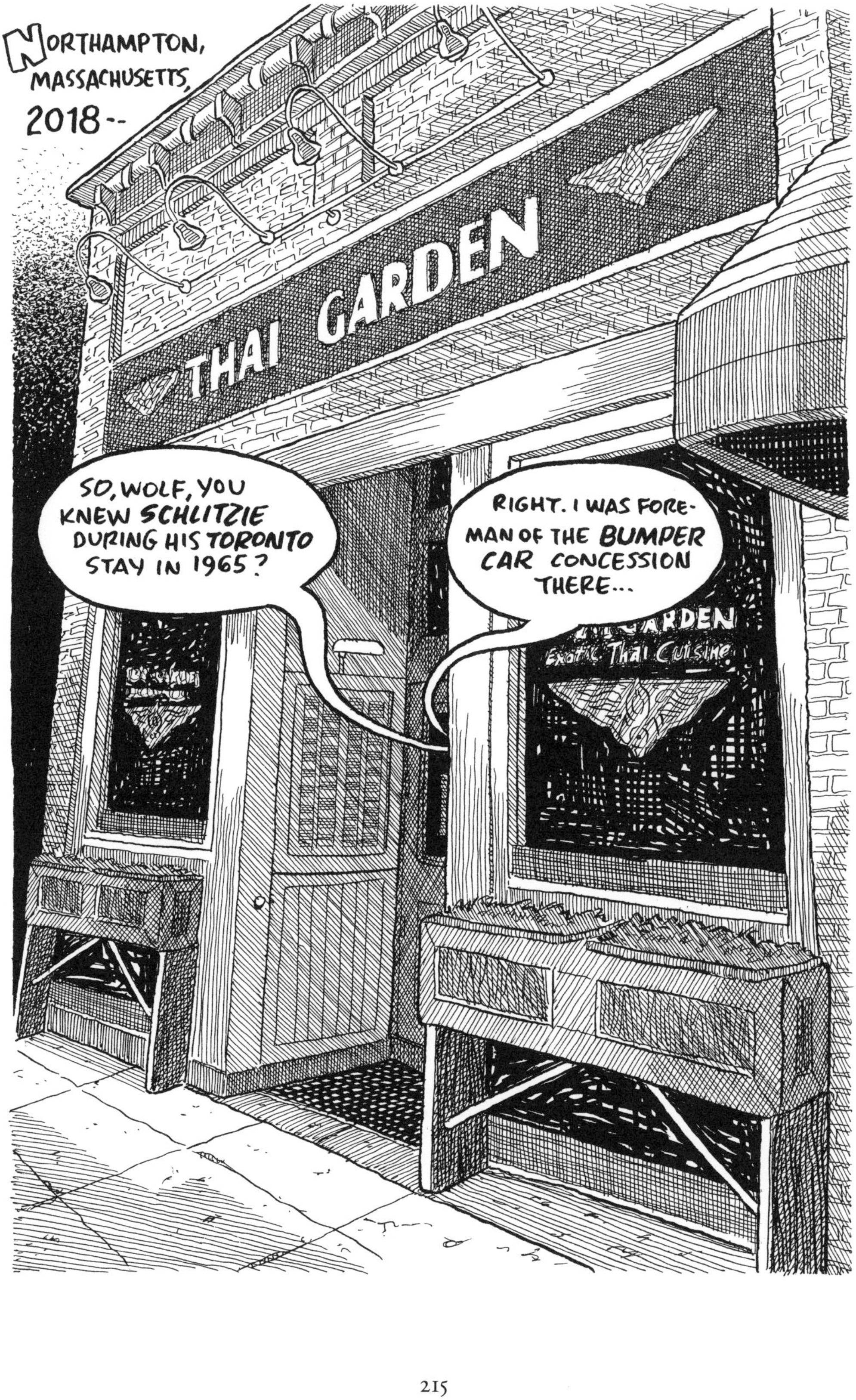
NORTHAMPTON, MASSACHUSETTS, 2018--
THAI GARDEN
SO, WOLF, YOU KNEW SCHLITZIE DURING HIS TORONTO STAY IN 1965?
RIGHT. I WAS FOREMAN OF THE BUMPER CAR CONCESSION THERE...
GARDEN
Exotic Thai Cuisine

THE CLARENDON HOTEL IN LONDON, ONTARIO, WAS HOME THAT SUMMER TO WOLF KRAKOWSKI, SCHLITZIE & HIS CARETAKER, AS WELL AS A FEW OTHER SIDESHOW PERFORMERS, INCLUDING "THE HUMAN PINCUSHION" & A KNIFE-THROWING COUPLE. WOLF ALSO REMEMBERS "A SHELL-SHOCKED PERMANENT RESIDENT" AND A "WAN, SMALL-TOWN HOOKER" WHO CRUISED THE DANK HALLWAYS.

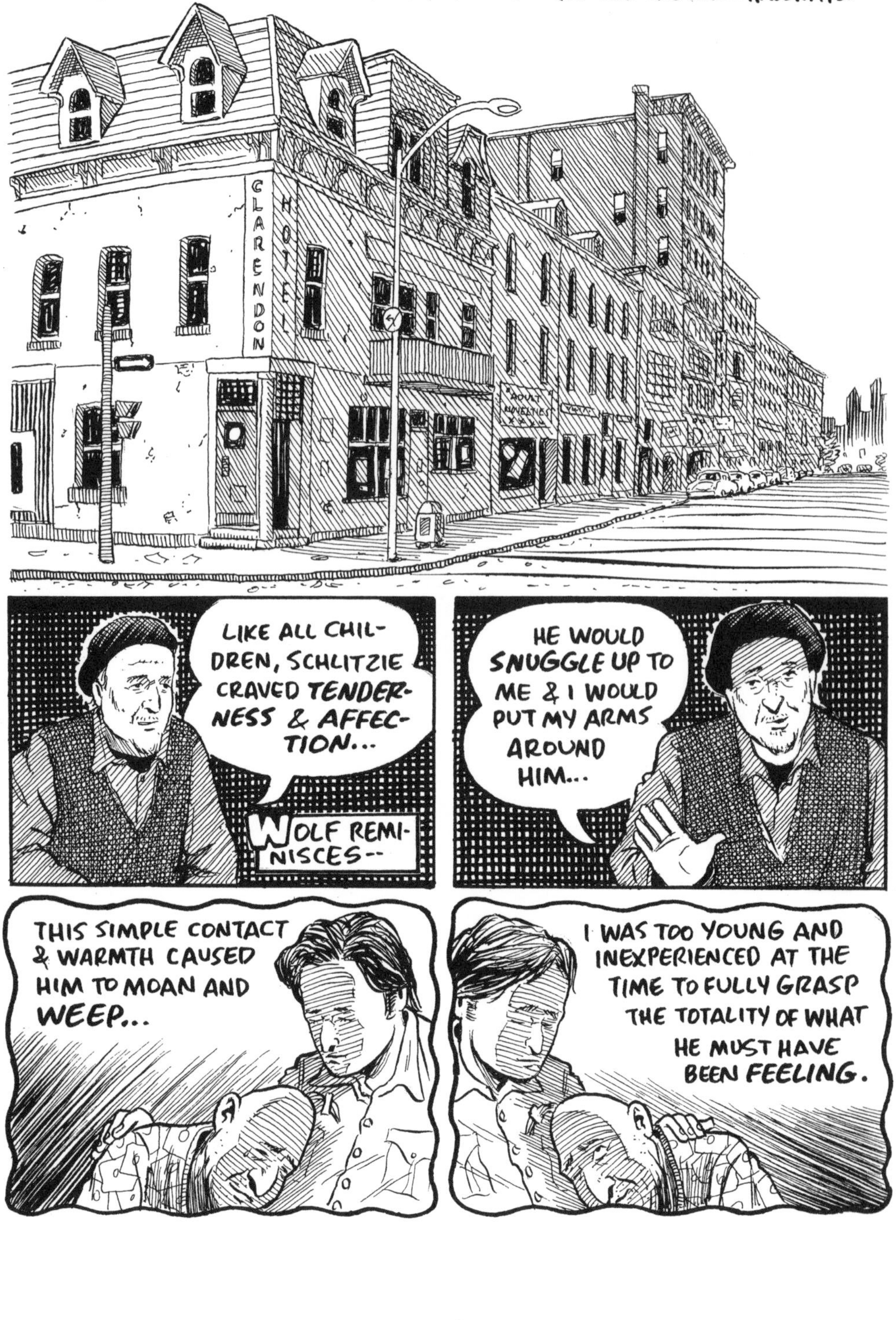
CLARENDON
HOTEL
LIKE ALL CHILDREN, SCHLITZIE CRAVED TENDERNESS & AFFECTION...
WOLF REMINISCES--
HE WOULD SNUGGLE UP TO ME & I WOULD PUT MY ARMS AROUND HIM...
THIS SIMPLE CONTACT & WARMTH CAUSED HIM TO MOAN AND WEEP...
I WAS TOO YOUNG AND INEXPERIENCED AT THE TIME TO FULLY GRASP THE TOTALITY OF WHAT HE MUST HAVE BEEN FEELING.

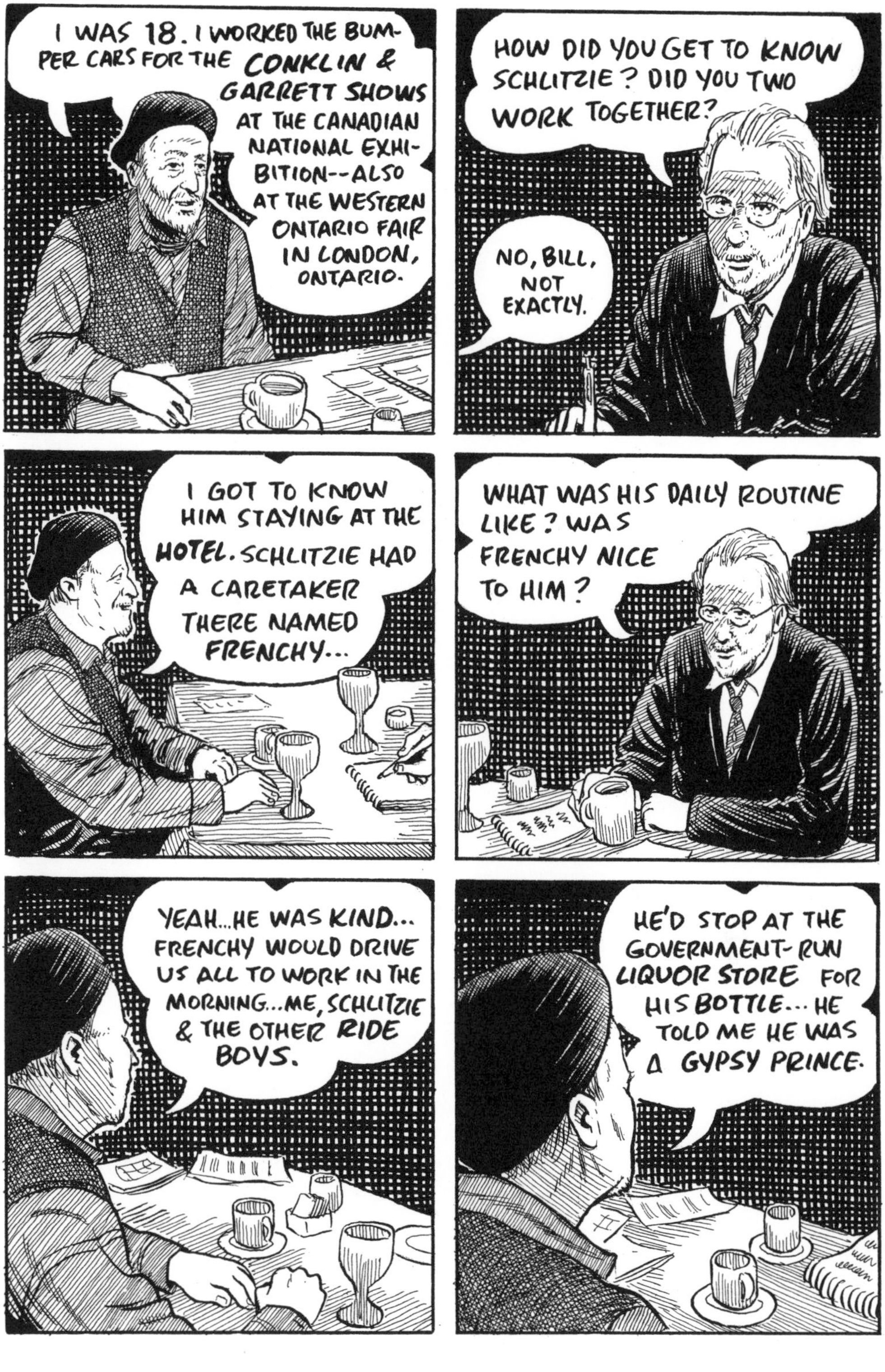
I WAS 18. I WORKED THE BUMPER CARS FOR THE CONKLIN & GARRETT SHOWS AT THE CANADIAN NATIONAL EXHIBITION--ALSO AT THE WESTERN ONTARIO FAIR IN LONDON, ONTARIO.
HOW DID YOU GET TO KNOW SCHLITZIE? DID YOU TWO WORK TOGETHER?
NO, BILL, NOT EXACTLY.
I GOT TO KNOW HIM STAYING AT THE HOTEL. SCHLITZIE HAD A CARETAKER THERE NAMED FRENCHY...
WHAT WAS HIS DAILY ROUTINE LIKE? WAS FRENCHY NICE TO HIM?
YEAH...HE WAS KIND... FRENCHY WOULD DRIVE US ALL TO WORK IN THE MORNING...ME, SCHLITZIE & THE OTHER RIDE BOYS.
HE'D STOP AT THE GOVERNMENT-RUN LIQUOR STORE FOR HIS BOTTLE... HE TOLD ME HE WAS A GYPSY PRINCE.

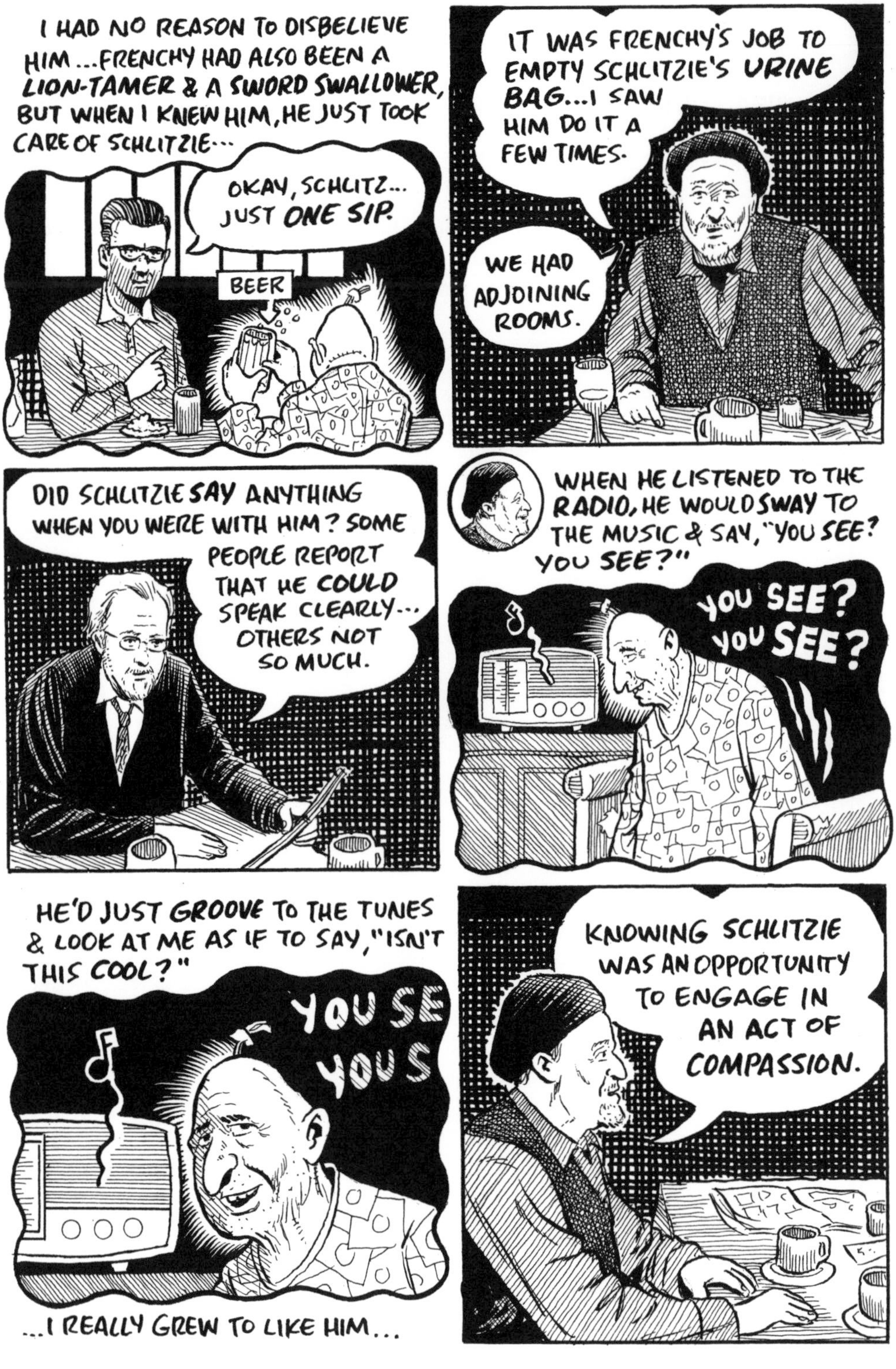
I HAD NO REASON TO DISBELIEVE HIM...FRENCHY HAD ALSO BEEN A LION-TAMER & A SWORD SWALLOWER, BUT WHEN I KNEW HIM, HE JUST TOOK CARE OF SCHLITZIE...
OKAY, SCHLITZ... JUST ONE SIP.
BEER
IT WAS FRENCHY'S JOB TO EMPTY SCHLITZIE'S URINE BAG...I SAW HIM DO IT A FEW TIMES.
WE HAD ADJOINING ROOMS.
DID SCHLITZIE SAY ANYTHING WHEN YOU WERE WITH HIM? SOME PEOPLE REPORT THAT HE COULD SPEAK CLEARLY... OTHERS NOT SO MUCH.
WHEN HE LISTENED TO THE RADIO, HE WOULD SWAY TO THE MUSIC & SAY, "YOU SEE? YOU SEE?"
YOU SEE? YOU SEE?
HE'D JUST GROOVE TO THE TUNES & LOOK AT ME AS IF TO SAY, "ISN'T THIS COOL?"
YOU SE
YOU S
...I REALLY GREW TO LIKE HIM...
KNOWING SCHLITZIE WAS AN OPPORTUNITY TO ENGAGE IN AN ACT OF COMPASSION.

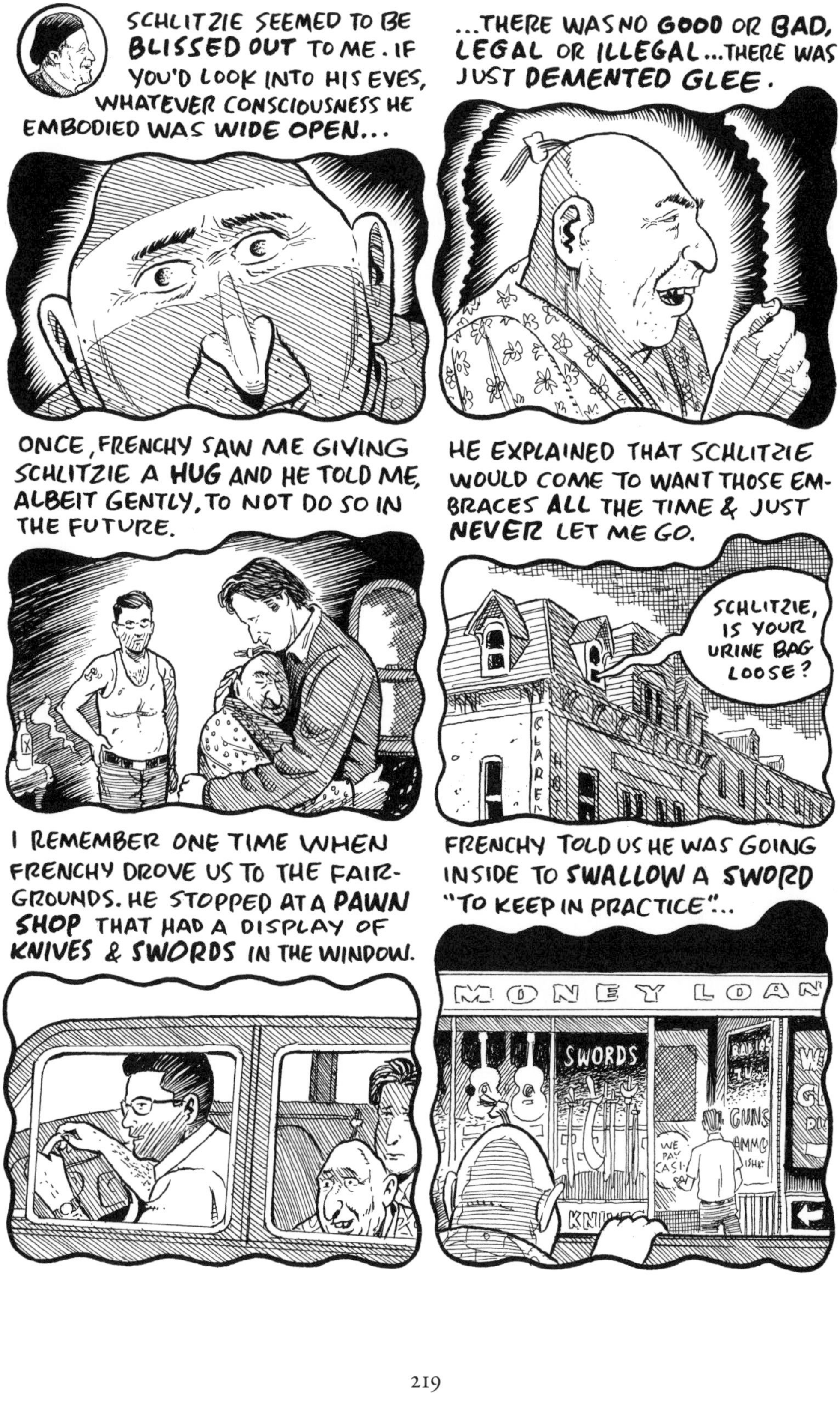
SCHLITZIE SEEMED TO BE BLISSED OUT TO ME. IF YOU'D LOOK INTO HIS EYES, WHATEVER CONSCIOUSNESS HE EMBODIED WAS WIDE OPEN...
...THERE WAS NO GOOD OR BAD, LEGAL OR ILLEGAL...THERE WAS JUST DEMENTED GLEE.
ONCE, FRENCHY SAW ME GIVING SCHLITZIE A HUG AND HE TOLD ME, ALBEIT GENTLY, TO NOT DO SO IN THE FUTURE.
HE EXPLAINED THAT SCHLITZIE WOULD COME TO WANT THOSE EMBRACES ALL THE TIME & JUST NEVER LET ME GO.
SCHLITZIE, IS YOUR URINE BAG LOOSE?
I REMEMBER ONE TIME WHEN FRENCHY DROVE US TO THE FAIRGROUNDS. HE STOPPED AT A PAWN SHOP THAT HAD A DISPLAY OF KNIVES & SWORDS IN THE WINDOW.
FRENCHY TOLD US HE WAS GOING INSIDE TO SWALLOW A SWORD "TO KEEP IN PRACTICE"...
MONEY LOAN
SWORDS
GUNS

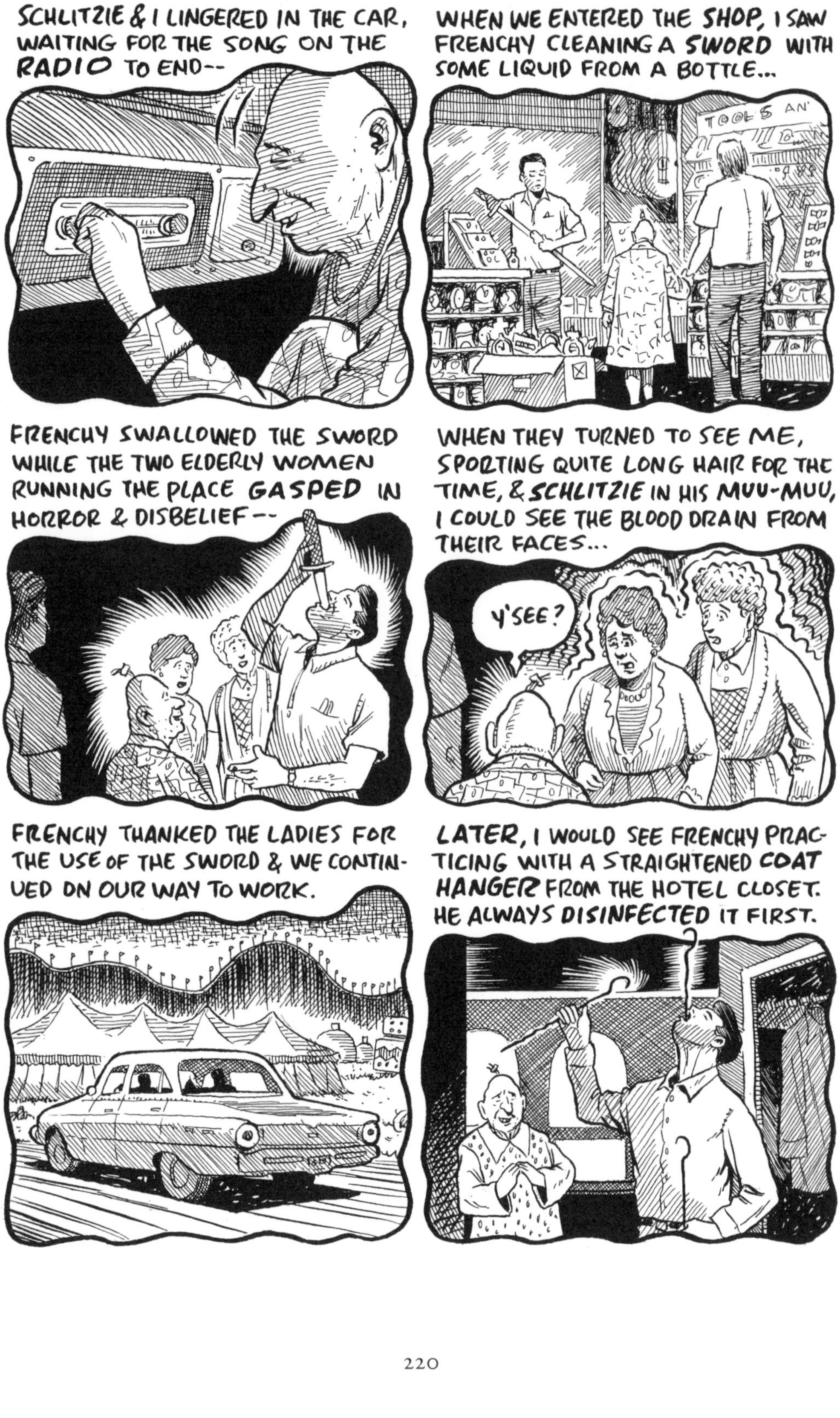
SCHLITZIE & I LINGERED IN THE CAR, WAITING FOR THE SONG ON THE RADIO TO END--
WHEN WE ENTERED THE SHOP, I SAW FRENCHY CLEANING A SWORD WITH SOME LIQUID FROM A BOTTLE...
TOOLS AN'
FRENCHY SWALLOWED THE SWORD WHILE THE TWO ELDERLY WOMEN RUNNING THE PLACE GASPED IN HORROR & DISBELIEF--
WHEN THEY TURNED TO SEE ME, SPORTING QUITE LONG HAIR FOR THE TIME, & SCHLITZIE IN HIS MUU-MUU, I COULD SEE THE BLOOD DRAIN FROM THEIR FACES...
Y'SEE?
FRENCHY THANKED THE LADIES FOR THE USE OF THE SWORD & WE CONTINUED ON OUR WAY TO WORK.
LATER, I WOULD SEE FRENCHY PRACTICING WITH A STRAIGHTENED COAT HANGER FROM THE HOTEL CLOSET. HE ALWAYS DISINFECTED IT FIRST.

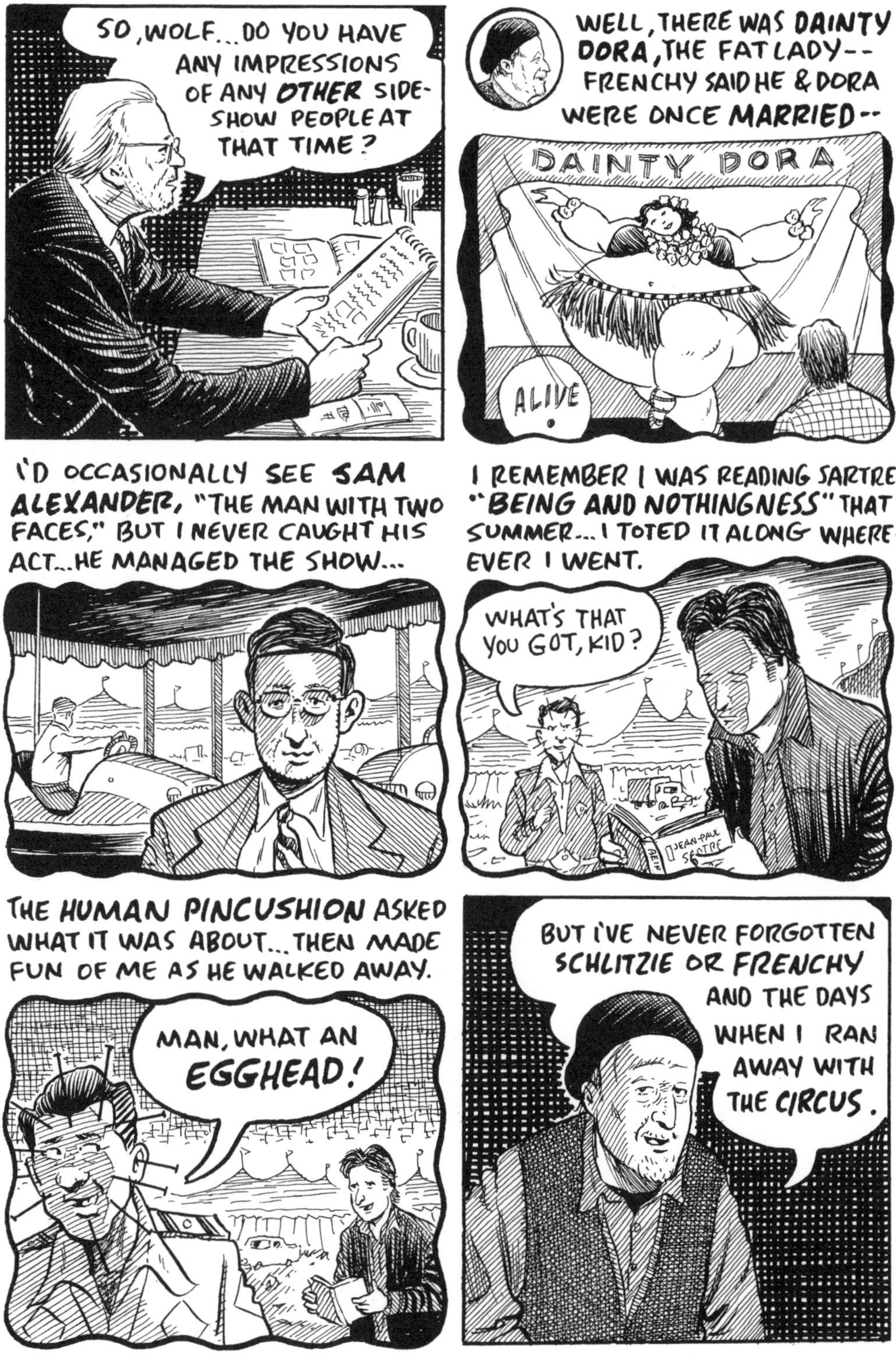
SO, WOLF... DO YOU HAVE ANY IMPRESSIONS OF ANY OTHER SIDE-SHOW PEOPLE AT THAT TIME?
WELL, THERE WAS DAINTY DORA, THE FAT LADY-- FRENCHY SAID HE & DORA WERE ONCE MARRIED--
DAINTY DORA
ALIVE
I'D OCCASIONALLY SEE SAM ALEXANDER, "THE MAN WITH TWO FACES," BUT I NEVER CAUGHT HIS ACT... HE MANAGED THE SHOW...
I REMEMBER I WAS READING SARTRE'S "BEING AND NOTHINGNESS" THAT SUMMER... I TOTED IT ALONG WHERE-EVER I WENT.
WHAT'S THAT YOU GOT, KID?
JEAN-PAUL SARTRE
THE HUMAN PINCUSHION ASKED WHAT IT WAS ABOUT... THEN MADE FUN OF ME AS HE WALKED AWAY.
MAN, WHAT AN EGGHEAD!
BUT I'VE NEVER FORGOTTEN SCHLITZIE OR FRENCHY AND THE DAYS WHEN I RAN AWAY WITH THE CIRCUS.

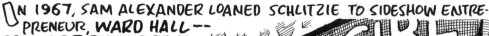

IN 1967, SAM ALEXANDER LOANED SCHLITZIE TO SIDESHOW ENTREPRENEUR, **WARD HALL** --

AT VENUES LIKE THE *BLOOMSBURG FAIR* IN BLOOMSBURG, PENNSYLVANIA, SCHLITZIE SAT IN A BIG *EASY CHAIR* ON STAGE BECAUSE, ACCORDING TO HALL, "HE WAS GETTING OLD AND HAD A HARD TIME GETTING ON AND OFF STAGE LIKE THE OTHER ACTS."

HALF MONKEY, HALF HUMAN, WITH A BRAIN **THE SIZE OF A GOLF BALL!**

SCHLITZIE'S PARENTS WERE WEALTHY *SOCIETY PEOPLE* WHO KEPT SCHLITZIE & HIS SISTER, ATHELIA, IN AN APARTMENT IN THEIR MANSION IN SANTA FE, NEW MEXICO!

EVER THE *SHOWMAN,* HALL OFTEN REGALED AUDIENCES WITH ONE OF THE MANY EXTREMELY UNLIKELY SCHLITZIE *"ORIGIN"* STORIES.

HALL'S CIRCUS & SIDESHOW CAREER GOT ITS START IN 1946 WHEN HE WAS FIFTEEN... BY THE MID-1950S, HE HAD HIS OWN SIDESHOW. EARLIER IN HIS LONG CAREER, HE HAD A KNIFE-THROWING ACT WITH **HARRY LEONARD** AND A VENTRILOQUIST ACT WITH HIS DUMMY, "**PERKY PERKINS.**"

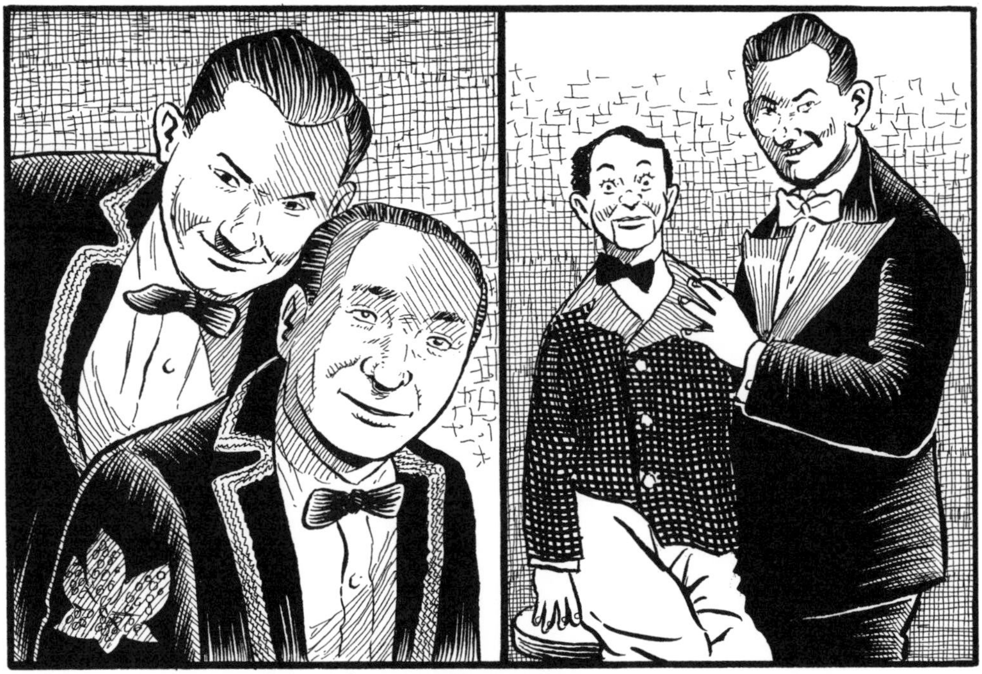

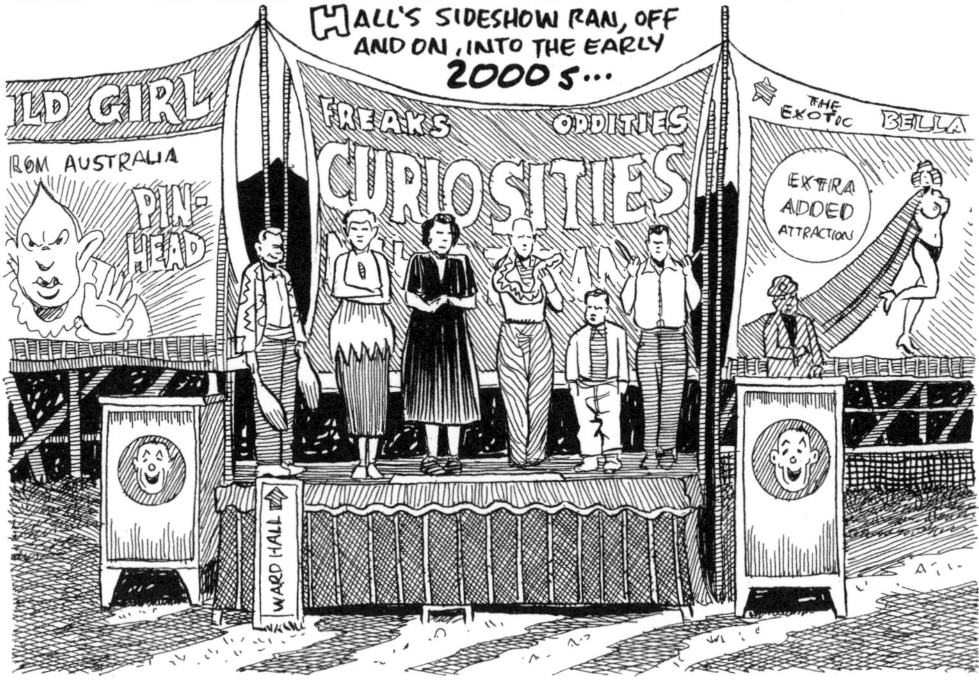
HALL'S SIDESHOW RAN, OFF AND ON, INTO THE EARLY 2000S...
LD GIRL
ROM AUSTRALIA
PIN-HEAD
FREAKS
ODDITIES
CURIOSITIES
THE EXOTIC BELLA
EXTRA ADDED ATTRACTION
WARD HALL

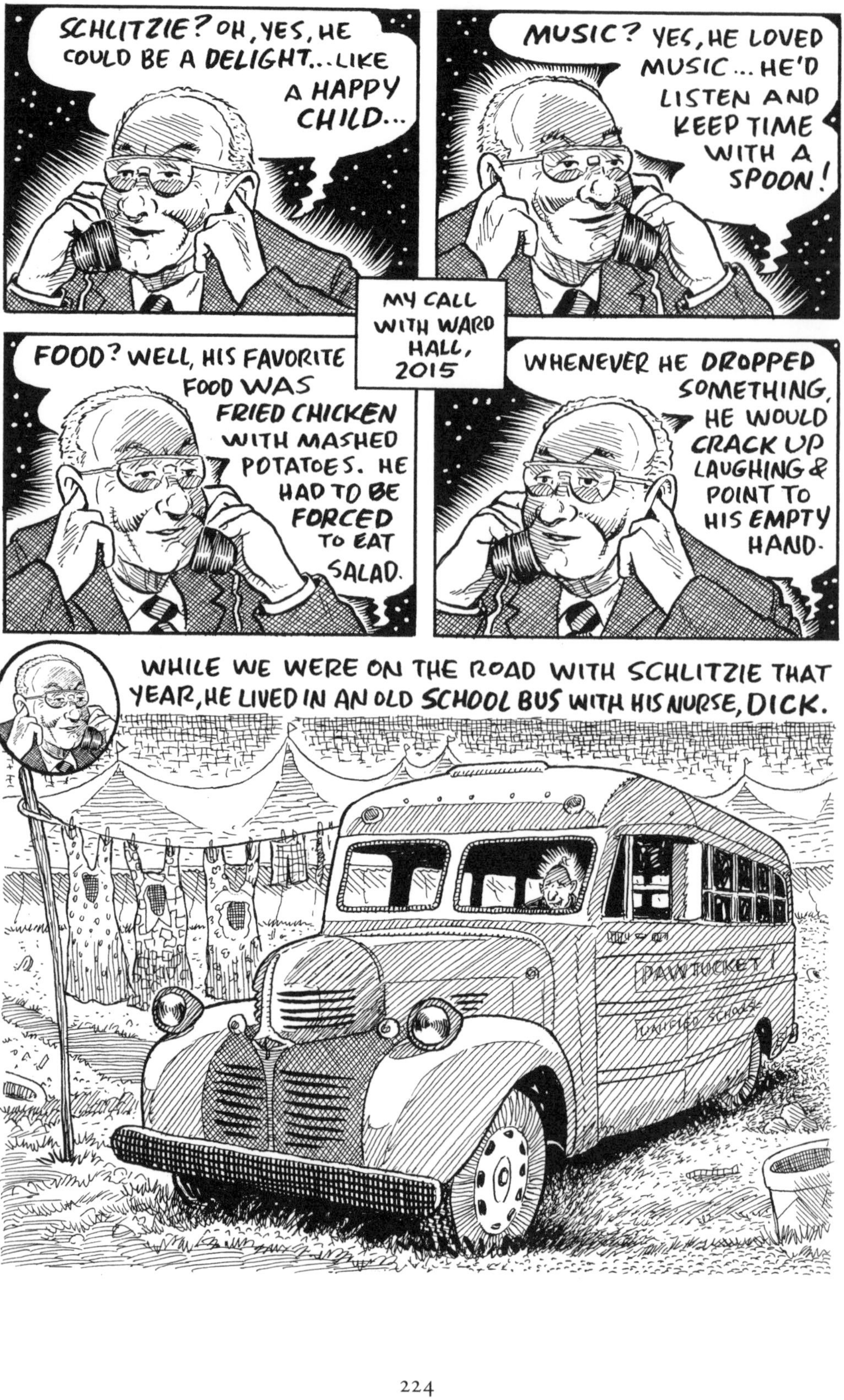
SCHLITZIE? OH, YES, HE COULD BE A DELIGHT... LIKE A HAPPY CHILD...
MUSIC? YES, HE LOVED MUSIC... HE'D LISTEN AND KEEP TIME WITH A SPOON!
MY CALL WITH WARD HALL, 2015
FOOD? WELL, HIS FAVORITE FOOD WAS FRIED CHICKEN WITH MASHED POTATOES. HE HAD TO BE FORCED TO EAT SALAD.
WHENEVER HE DROPPED SOMETHING, HE WOULD CRACK UP LAUGHING & POINT TO HIS EMPTY HAND.
WHILE WE WERE ON THE ROAD WITH SCHLITZIE THAT YEAR, HE LIVED IN AN OLD SCHOOL BUS WITH HIS NURSE, DICK.
PAWTUCKET

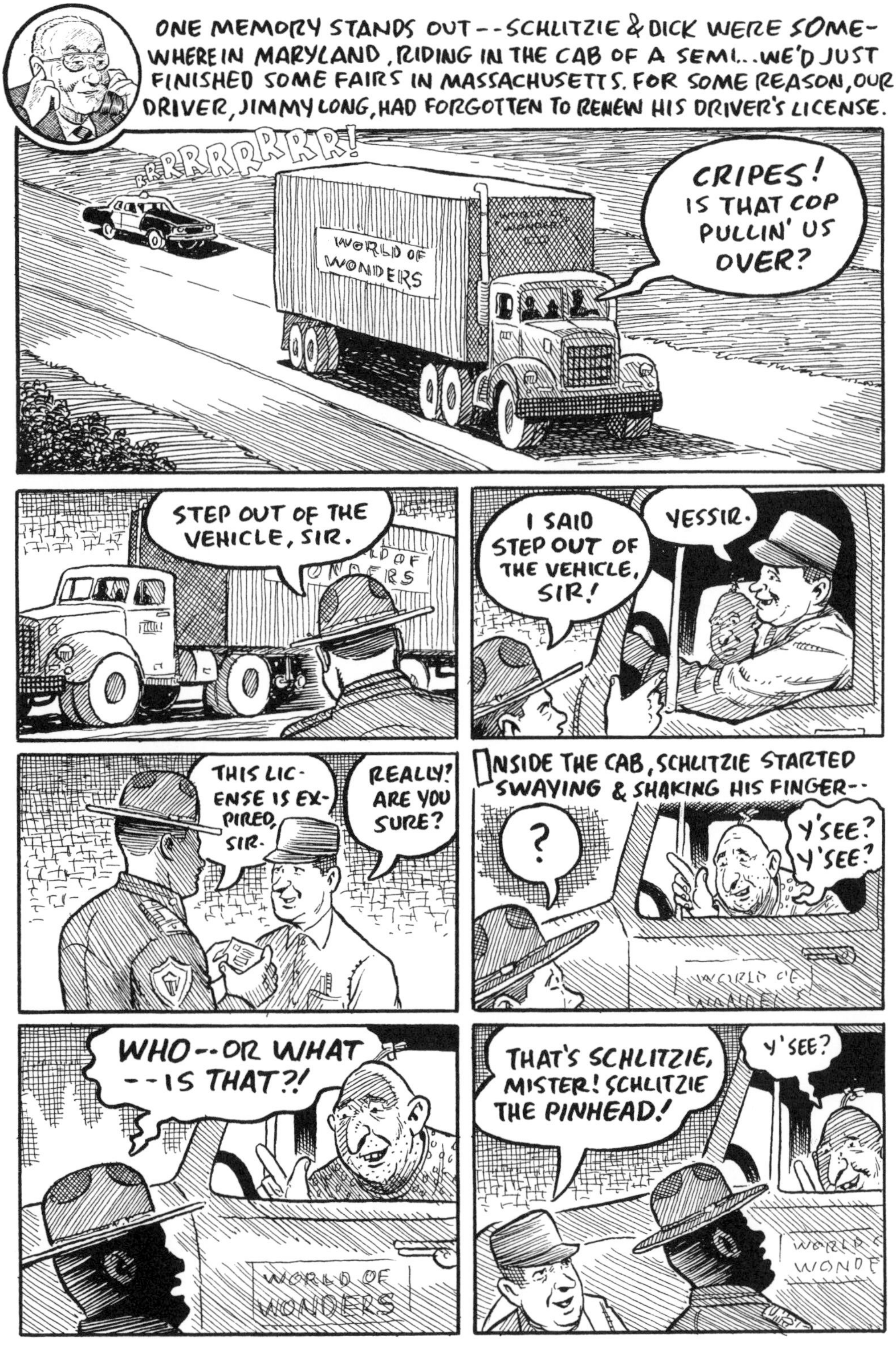
ONE MEMORY STANDS OUT--SCHLITZIE & DICK WERE SOMEWHERE IN MARYLAND, RIDING IN THE CAB OF A SEMI...WE'D JUST FINISHED SOME FAIRS IN MASSACHUSETTS. FOR SOME REASON, OUR DRIVER, JIMMY LONG, HAD FORGOTTEN TO RENEW HIS DRIVER'S LICENSE.
RRRRRRRRR!
WORLD OF WONDERS
CRIPES! IS THAT COP PULLIN' US OVER?
STEP OUT OF THE VEHICLE, SIR.
I SAID STEP OUT OF THE VEHICLE, SIR!
YESSIR.
THIS LICENSE IS EXPIRED, SIR.
REALLY? ARE YOU SURE?
INSIDE THE CAB, SCHLITZIE STARTED SWAYING & SHAKING HIS FINGER--
?
Y'SEE? Y'SEE?
WHO--OR WHAT--IS THAT?!
WORLD OF WONDERS
THAT'S SCHLITZIE, MISTER! SCHLITZIE THE PINHEAD!
Y'SEE?

THAT'S WHEN THE OFFICER TURNED TO JIMMY AND SAID:

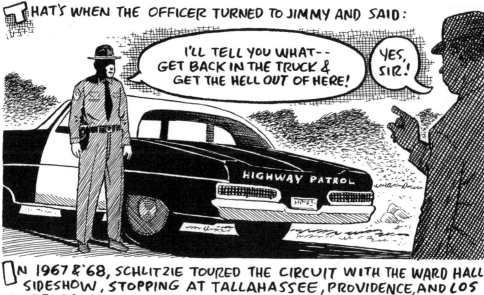

I'LL TELL YOU WHAT-- GET BACK IN THE TRUCK & GET THE HELL OUT OF HERE!

YES, SIR!

HIGHWAY PATROL

IN 1967 & '68, SCHLITZIE TOURED THE CIRCUIT WITH THE WARD HALL SIDESHOW, STOPPING AT TALLAHASSEE, PROVIDENCE, AND LOS ANGELES, WHERE THEY JOINED THE DOBRITCH INTERNATIONAL CIRCUS, ONE OF SCHLITZIE'S LAST KNOWN APPEARANCES--

YOU'LL SEE SCHLITZIE, THE MONKEY GIRL, THE STRANGEST LIVING HUMAN BEING IN THE ENTIRE WORLD! SHE HAS A HEAD THE SIZE OF A COCONUT, WHICH COMES TO A POINT LIKE AN ICE CREAM CONE!

SHE HAS NO MORE BRAINS THAN A MONKEY! SHE'S ON STAGE NOW, AMONG THE STRANGE & UNUSUAL, THE STRANGEST OF ALL IS SCHLITZIE, THE MONKEY GIRL!!

SCHLITZIE the MONKEY GIRL

HUMAN PINC

SCHLITZIE RETURNED TO **SAM ALEXANDER** IN 1969, AS HIS CAREER BEGAN TO **WIND DOWN.**

YOU FEEL UP TO A SHOW TONIGHT, SCHLITZ?

UP?

ARE YOU TIRED?

I LIKE CHICKEN!

WHY DON'T YOU JUST GO OVER TO THE COOK-HOUSE & GET YOUR DINNER?

DISHES!

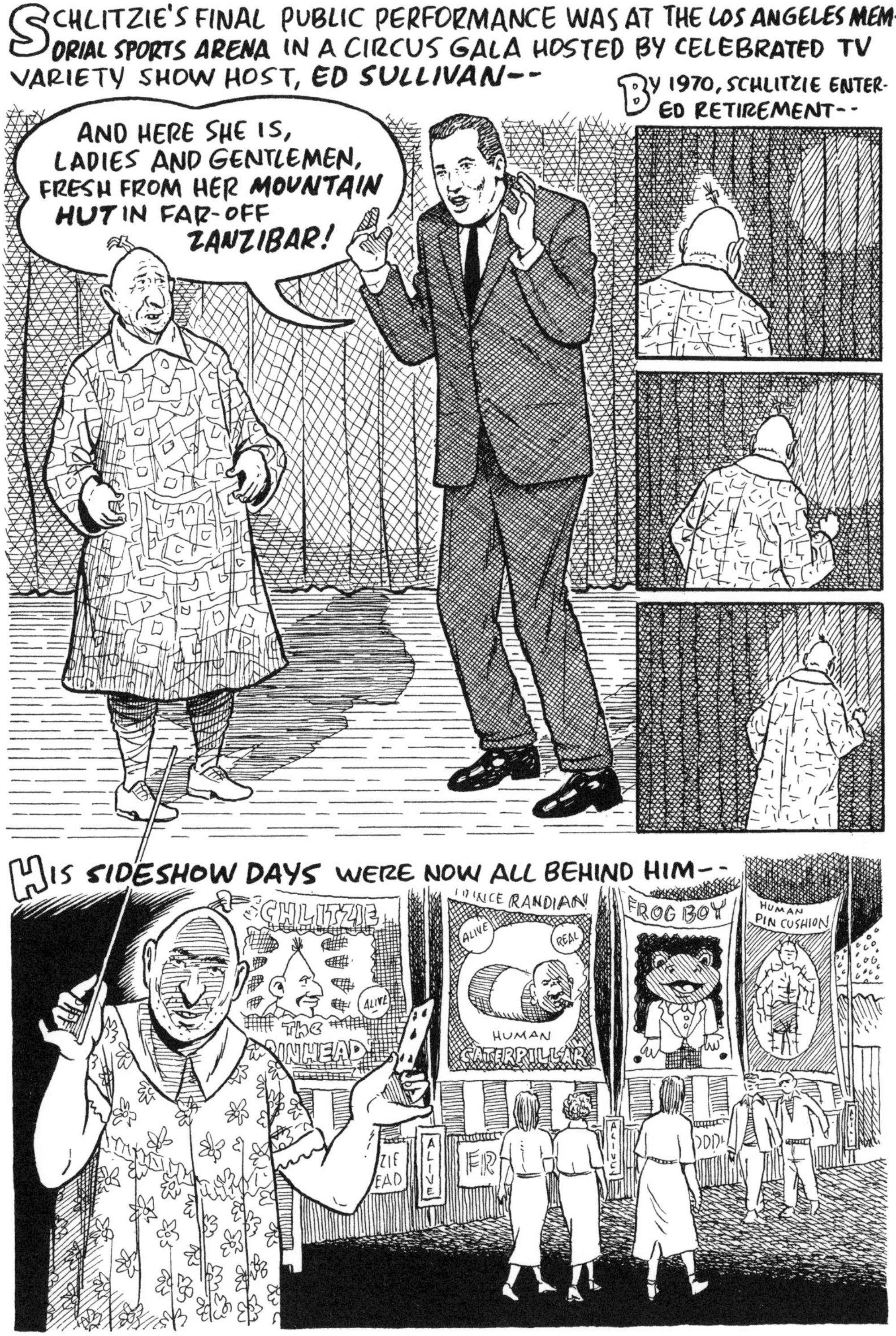
SCHLITZIE'S FINAL PUBLIC PERFORMANCE WAS AT THE LOS ANGELES MEMORIAL SPORTS ARENA IN A CIRCUS GALA HOSTED BY CELEBRATED TV VARIETY SHOW HOST, ED SULLIVAN--
AND HERE SHE IS, LADIES AND GENTLEMEN, FRESH FROM HER MOUNTAIN HUT IN FAR-OFF ZANZIBAR!
BY 1970, SCHLITZIE ENTERED RETIREMENT--
HIS SIDESHOW DAYS WERE NOW ALL BEHIND HIM--
ALIVE
the
ALIVE
REAL
HUMAN
CATERPILLAR
FROG BOY
HUMAN PIN CUSHION
ALIVE
ALIVE

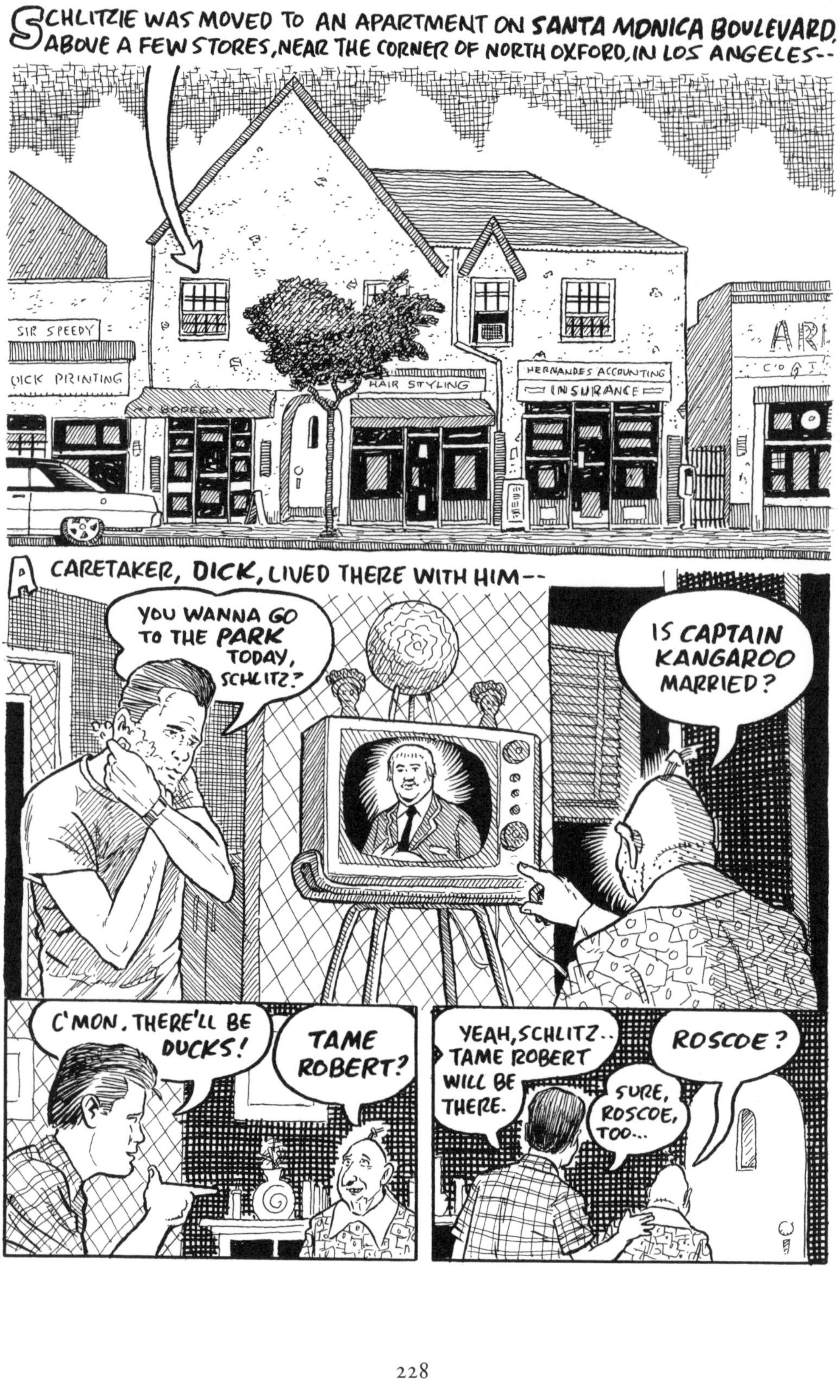
SCHLITZIE WAS MOVED TO AN APARTMENT ON SANTA MONICA BOULEVARD, ABOVE A FEW STORES, NEAR THE CORNER OF NORTH OXFORD, IN LOS ANGELES--
SIR SPEEDY
ICK PRINTING
BODEGA
HAIR STYLING
HERNANDES ACCOUNTING
INSURANCE
A CARETAKER, DICK, LIVED THERE WITH HIM--
YOU WANNA GO TO THE PARK TODAY, SCHLITZ?
IS CAPTAIN KANGAROO MARRIED?
C'MON. THERE'LL BE DUCKS!
TAME ROBERT?
YEAH, SCHLITZ.. TAME ROBERT WILL BE THERE.
ROSCOE?
SURE, ROSCOE, TOO...

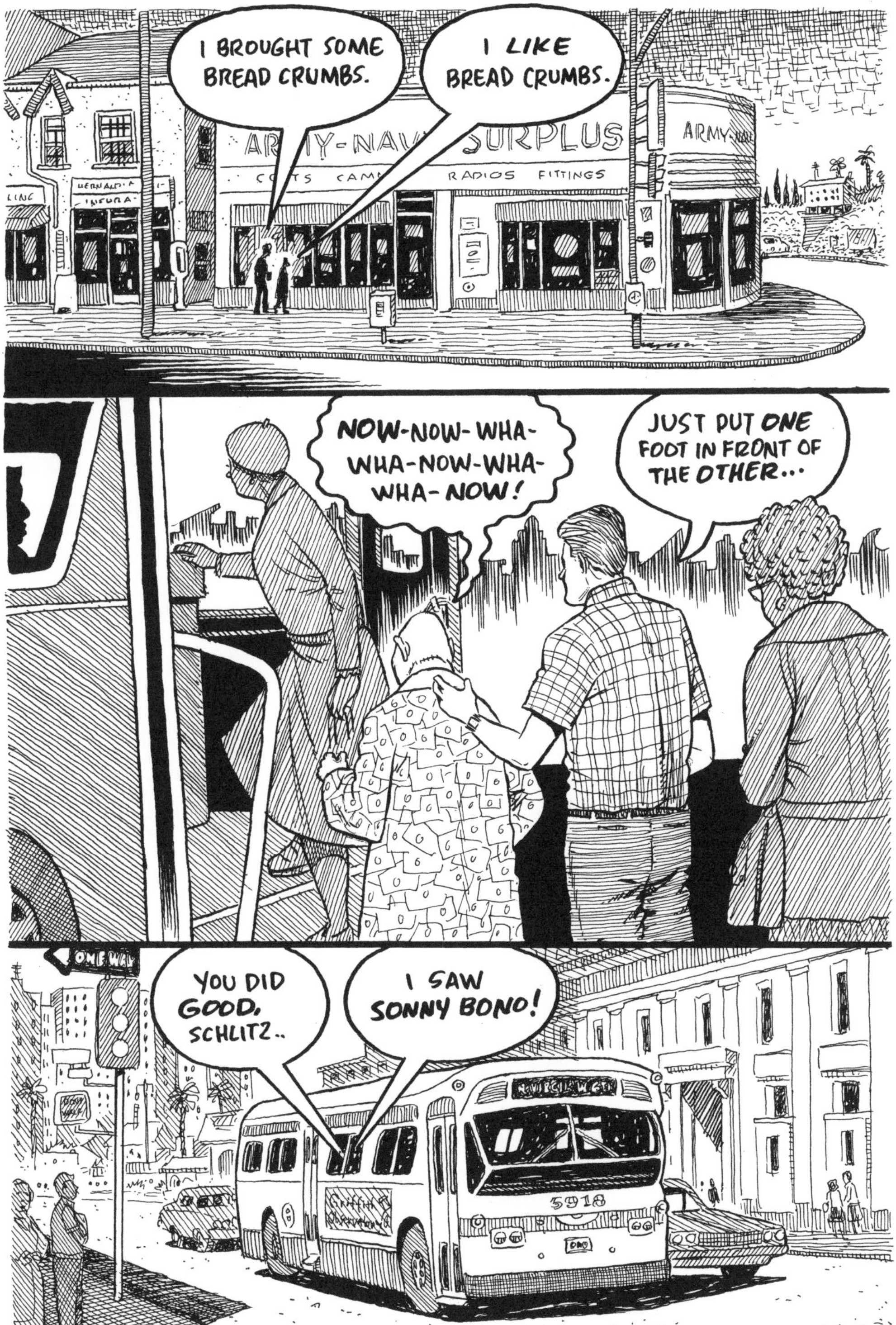
I BROUGHT SOME BREAD CRUMBS.
I LIKE BREAD CRUMBS.
ARMY-NAVY SURPLUS
RADIOS FITTINGS
NOW-NOW-WHA-WHA-NOW-WHA-WHA-NOW!
JUST PUT ONE FOOT IN FRONT OF THE OTHER...
YOU DID GOOD, SCHLITZ..
I SAW SONNY BONO!
5918

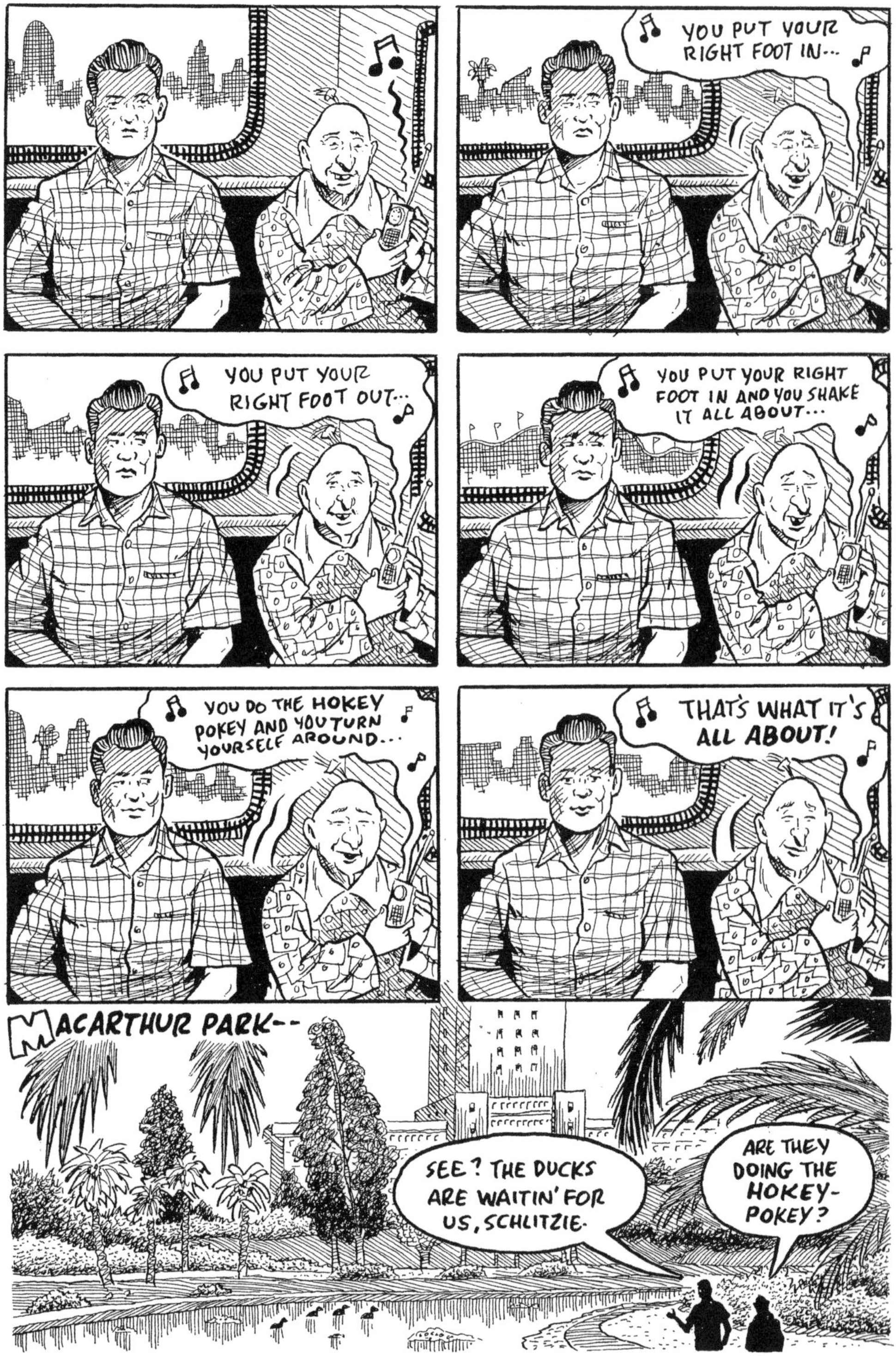
YOU PUT YOUR RIGHT FOOT IN...
YOU PUT YOUR RIGHT FOOT OUT...
YOU PUT YOUR RIGHT FOOT IN AND YOU SHAKE IT ALL ABOUT...
YOU DO THE HOKEY POKEY AND YOU TURN YOURSELF AROUND...
THAT'S WHAT IT'S ALL ABOUT!
MACARTHUR PARK--
SEE? THE DUCKS ARE WAITIN' FOR US, SCHLITZIE.
ARE THEY DOING THE HOKEY-POKEY?

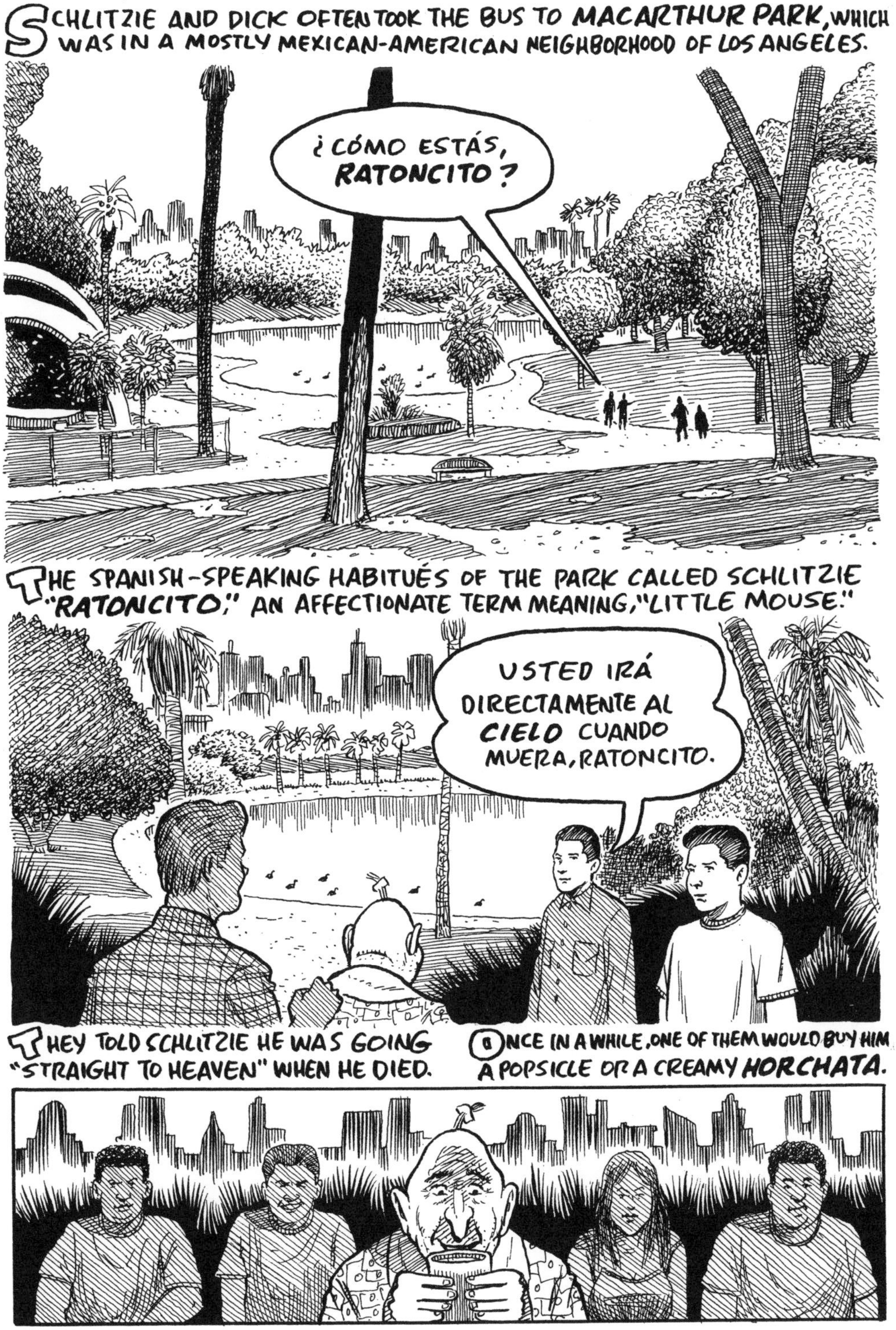
SCHLITZIE AND DICK OFTEN TOOK THE BUS TO MACARTHUR PARK, WHICH WAS IN A MOSTLY MEXICAN-AMERICAN NEIGHBORHOOD OF LOS ANGELES.
¿CÓMO ESTÁS, RATONCITO?
THE SPANISH-SPEAKING HABITUÉS OF THE PARK CALLED SCHLITZIE "RATONCITO," AN AFFECTIONATE TERM MEANING, "LITTLE MOUSE."
USTED IRÁ DIRECTAMENTE AL CIELO CUANDO MUERA, RATONCITO.
THEY TOLD SCHLITZIE HE WAS GOING "STRAIGHT TO HEAVEN" WHEN HE DIED.
ONCE IN A WHILE, ONE OF THEM WOULD BUY HIM A POPSICLE OR A CREAMY HORCHATA.

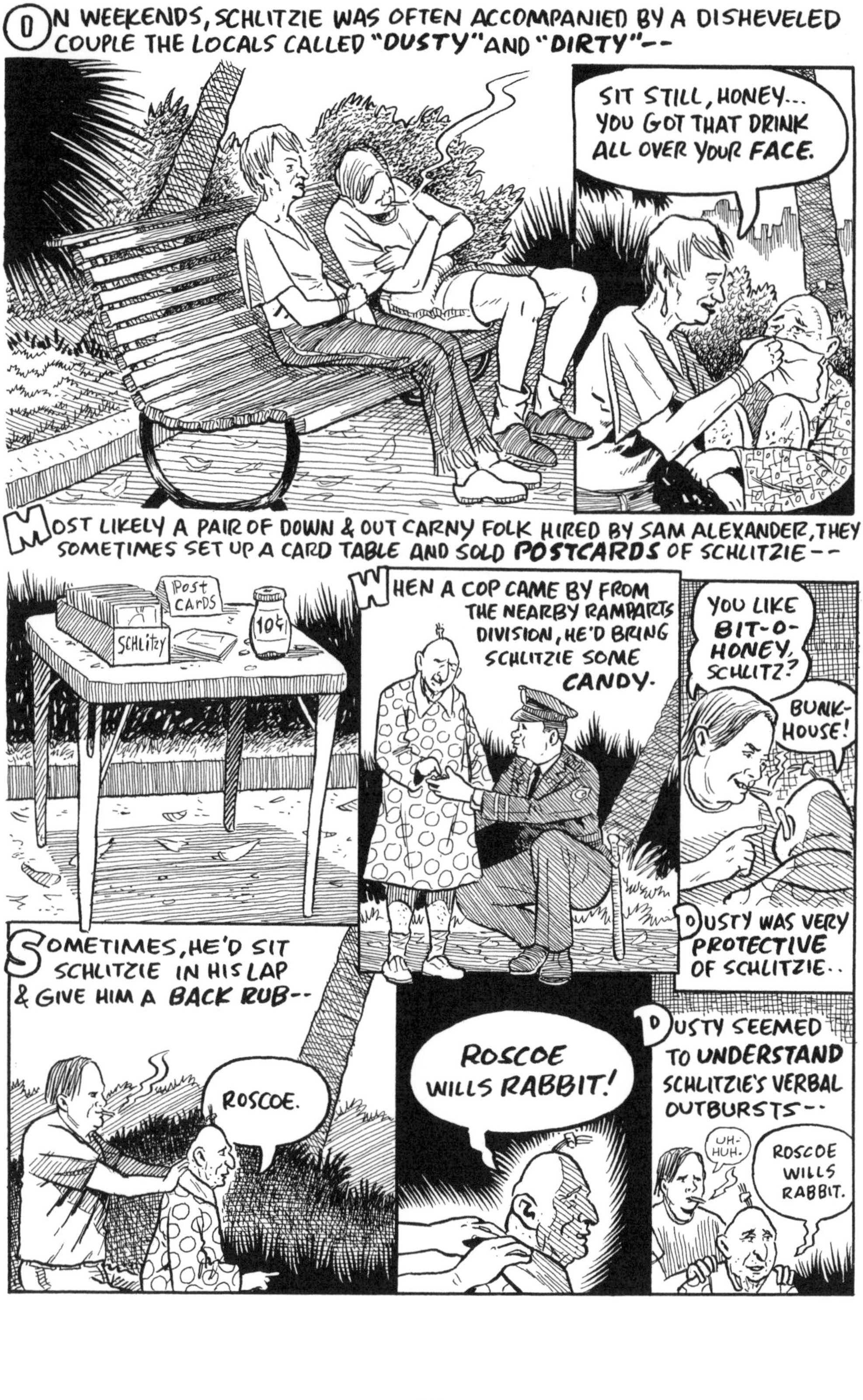
ON WEEKENDS, SCHLITZIE WAS OFTEN ACCOMPANIED BY A DISHEVELED COUPLE THE LOCALS CALLED "DUSTY" AND "DIRTY"--
SIT STILL, HONEY... YOU GOT THAT DRINK ALL OVER YOUR FACE.
MOST LIKELY A PAIR OF DOWN & OUT CARNY FOLK HIRED BY SAM ALEXANDER, THEY SOMETIMES SET UP A CARD TABLE AND SOLD POSTCARDS OF SCHLITZIE--
POST CARDS
SCHLITZY
10¢
WHEN A COP CAME BY FROM THE NEARBY RAMPARTS DIVISION, HE'D BRING SCHLITZIE SOME CANDY.
YOU LIKE BIT-O-HONEY, SCHLITZ?
BUNK-HOUSE!
DUSTY WAS VERY PROTECTIVE OF SCHLITZIE..
SOMETIMES, HE'D SIT SCHLITZIE IN HIS LAP & GIVE HIM A BACK RUB--
ROSCOE.
ROSCOE WILLS RABBIT!
DUSTY SEEMED TO UNDERSTAND SCHLITZIE'S VERBAL OUTBURSTS--
UH-HUH.
ROSCOE WILLS RABBIT.

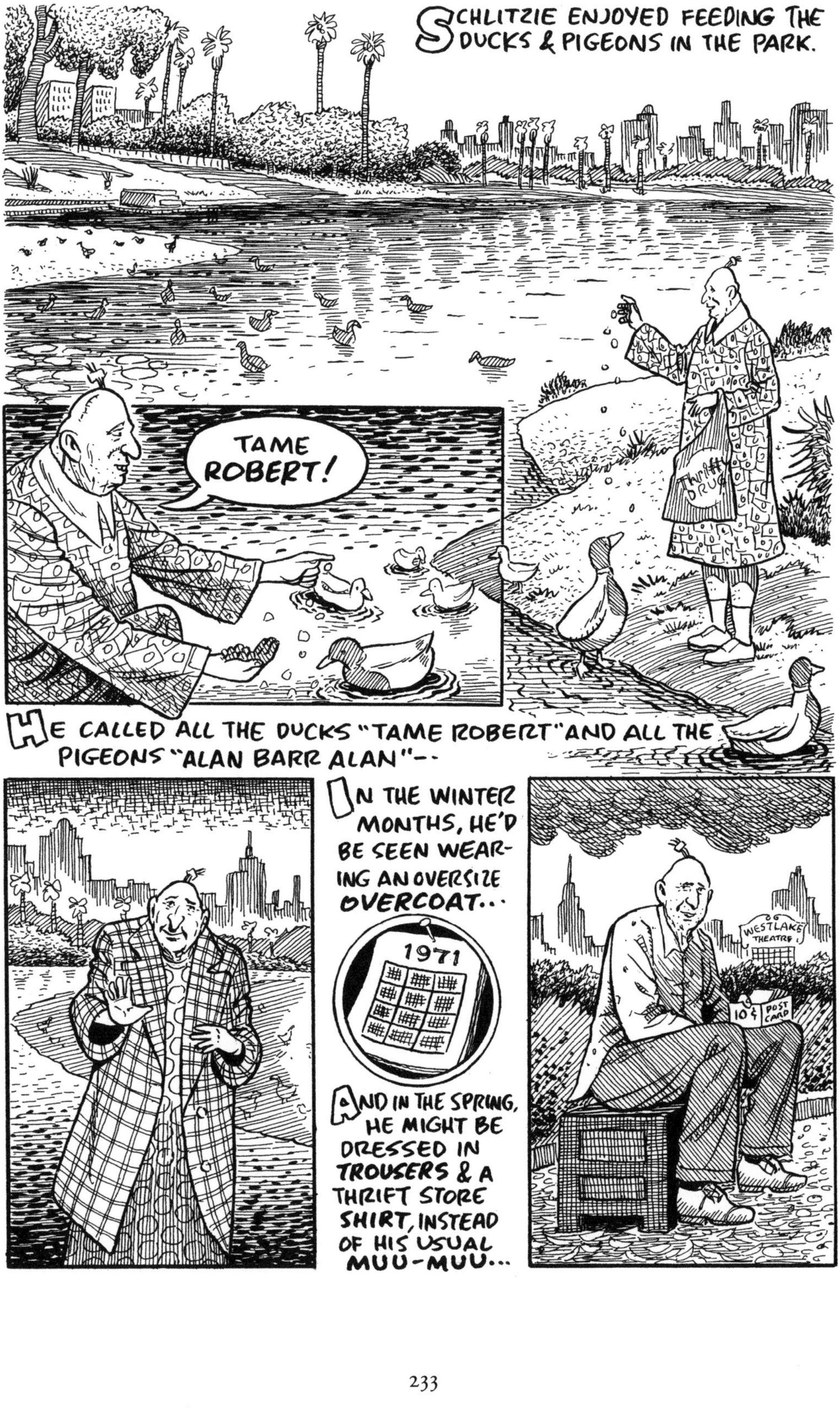

SCHLITZIE ENJOYED FEEDING THE DUCKS & PIGEONS IN THE PARK.
TAME ROBERT!
THRIFTY DRUG
HE CALLED ALL THE DUCKS "TAME ROBERT" AND ALL THE PIGEONS "ALAN BARR ALAN"--
IN THE WINTER MONTHS, HE'D BE SEEN WEARING AN OVERSIZE OVERCOAT...
1971
AND IN THE SPRING, HE MIGHT BE DRESSED IN TROUSERS & A THRIFT STORE SHIRT, INSTEAD OF HIS USUAL MUU-MUU...
WESTLAKE THEATRE
10¢
POST CARD

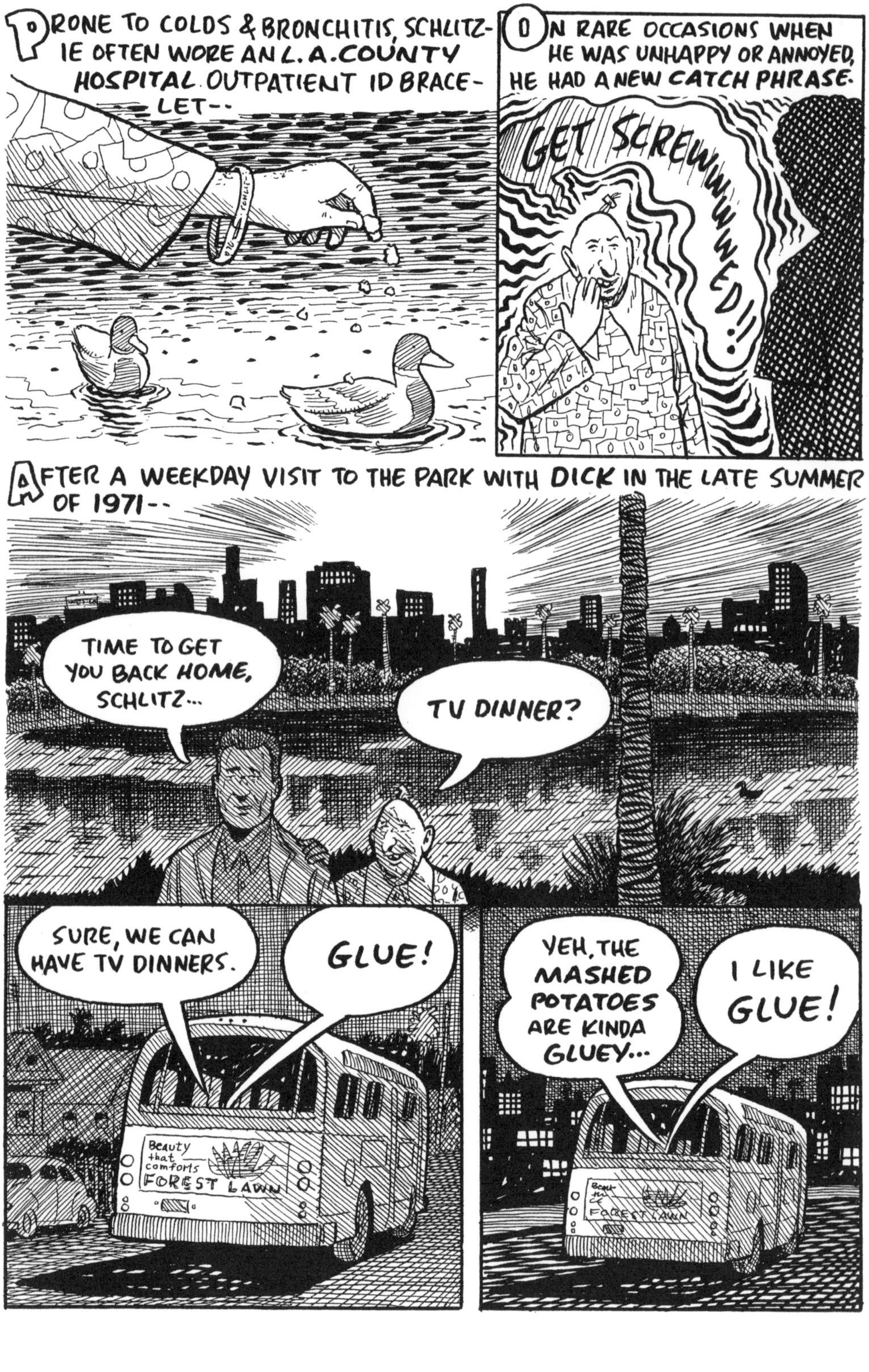
PRONE TO COLDS & BRONCHITIS, SCHLITZIE OFTEN WORE AN L.A. COUNTY HOSPITAL OUTPATIENT ID BRACELET--
ON RARE OCCASIONS WHEN HE WAS UNHAPPY OR ANNOYED, HE HAD A NEW CATCH PHRASE.
GET SCREWWWWWED!!
AFTER A WEEKDAY VISIT TO THE PARK WITH DICK IN THE LATE SUMMER OF 1971--
TIME TO GET YOU BACK HOME, SCHLITZ...
TV DINNER?
SURE, WE CAN HAVE TV DINNERS.
GLUE!
Beauty that comforts FOREST LAWN
YEH, THE MASHED POTATOES ARE KINDA GLUEY...
I LIKE GLUE!
FOREST LAWN

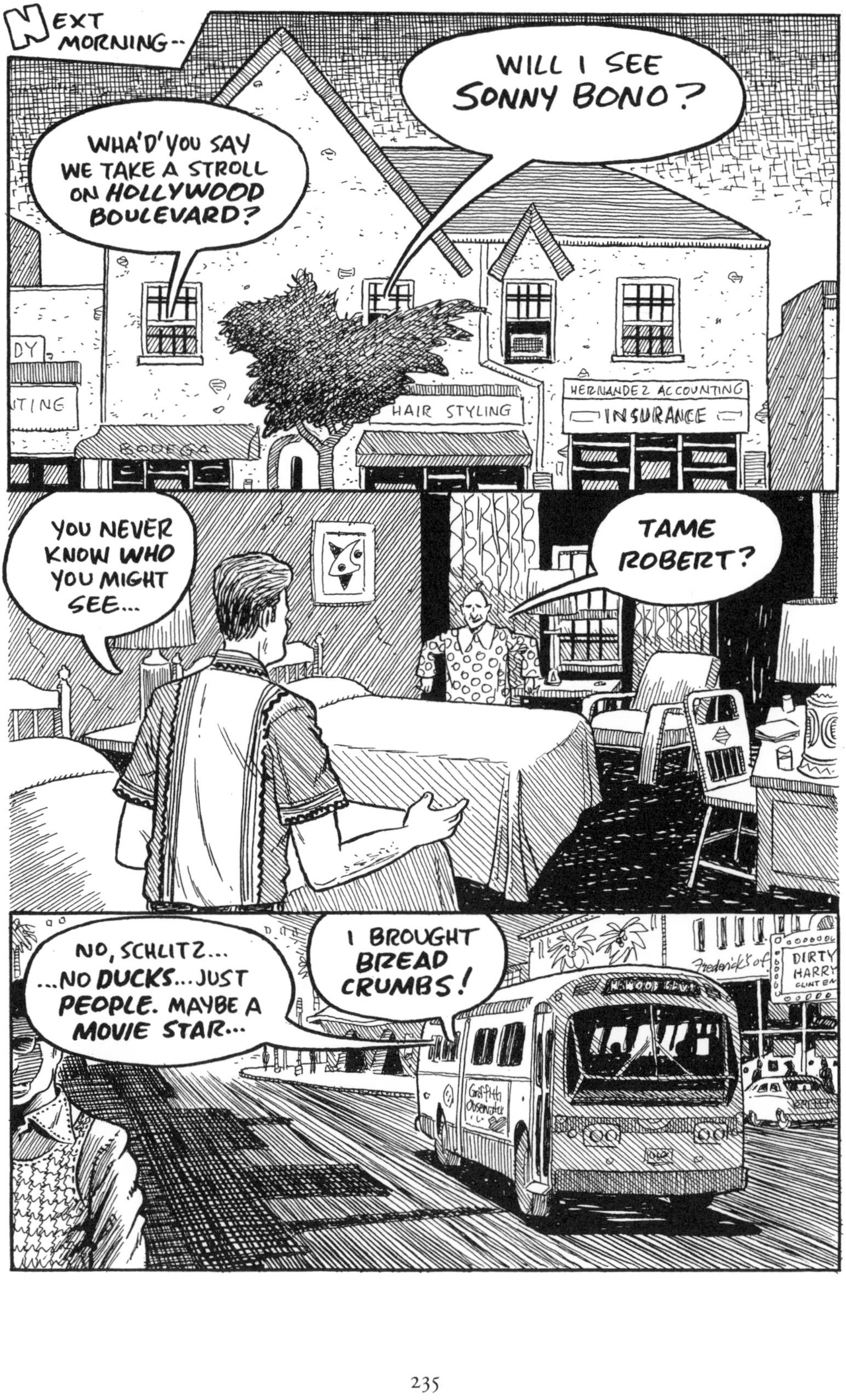
NEXT MORNING...
WHA'D'YOU SAY WE TAKE A STROLL ON HOLLYWOOD BOULEVARD?
WILL I SEE SONNY BONO?
HAIR STYLING
HERNANDEZ ACCOUNTING
INSURANCE
BODEGA
YOU NEVER KNOW WHO YOU MIGHT SEE...
TAME ROBERT?
NO, SCHLITZ... ...NO DUCKS... JUST PEOPLE. MAYBE A MOVIE STAR...
I BROUGHT BREAD CRUMBS!
Frederick's of
DIRTY HARRY

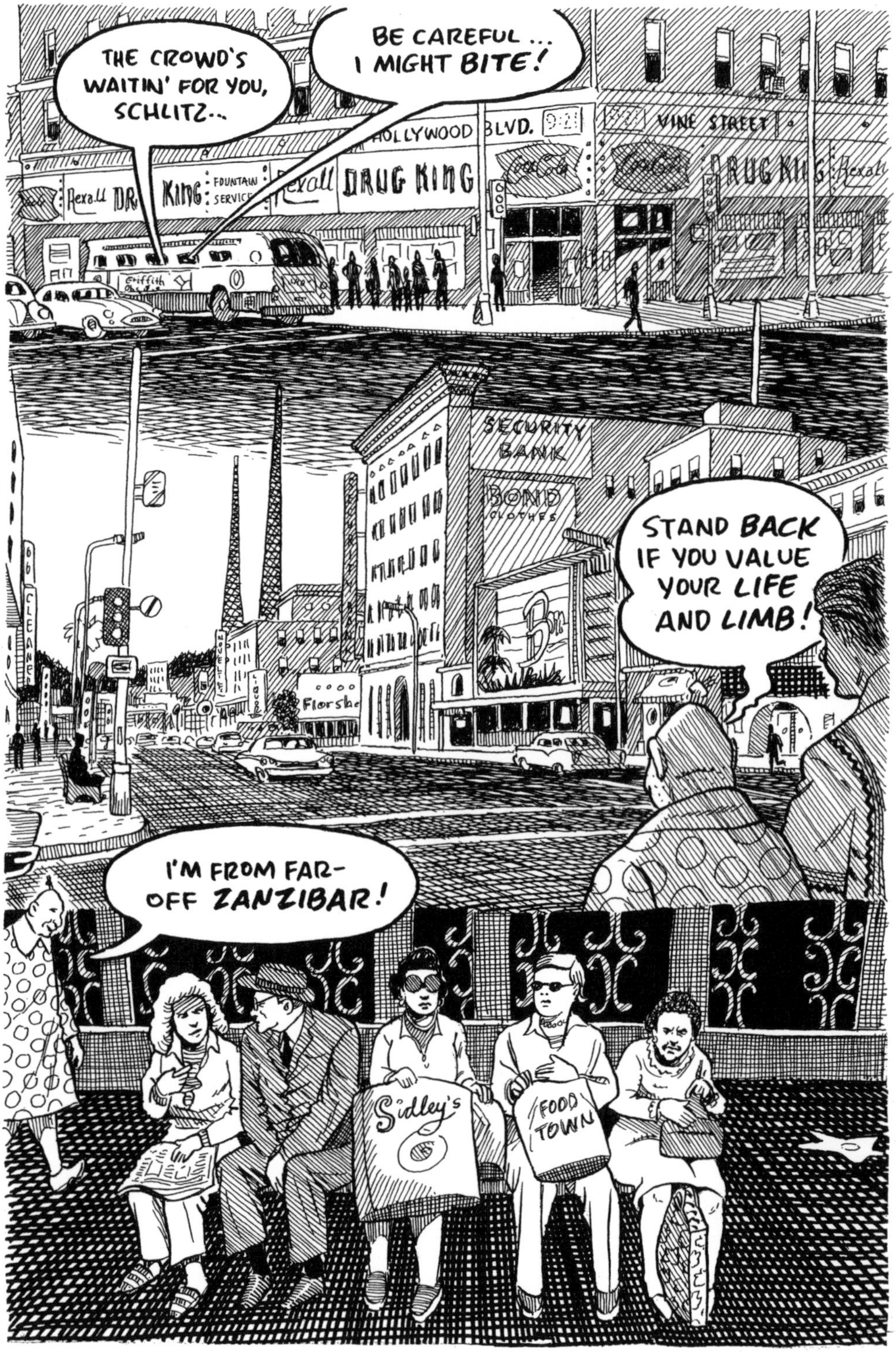
THE CROWD'S WAITIN' FOR YOU, SCHLITZ...
BE CAREFUL ... I MIGHT BITE!
HOLLYWOOD BLVD.
VINE STREET
Rexall
DRUG KING
FOUNTAIN SERVICE
SECURITY BANK
BOND CLOTHES
STAND BACK IF YOU VALUE YOUR LIFE AND LIMB!
I'M FROM FAR-OFF ZANZIBAR!
Sidley's
FOOD TOWN

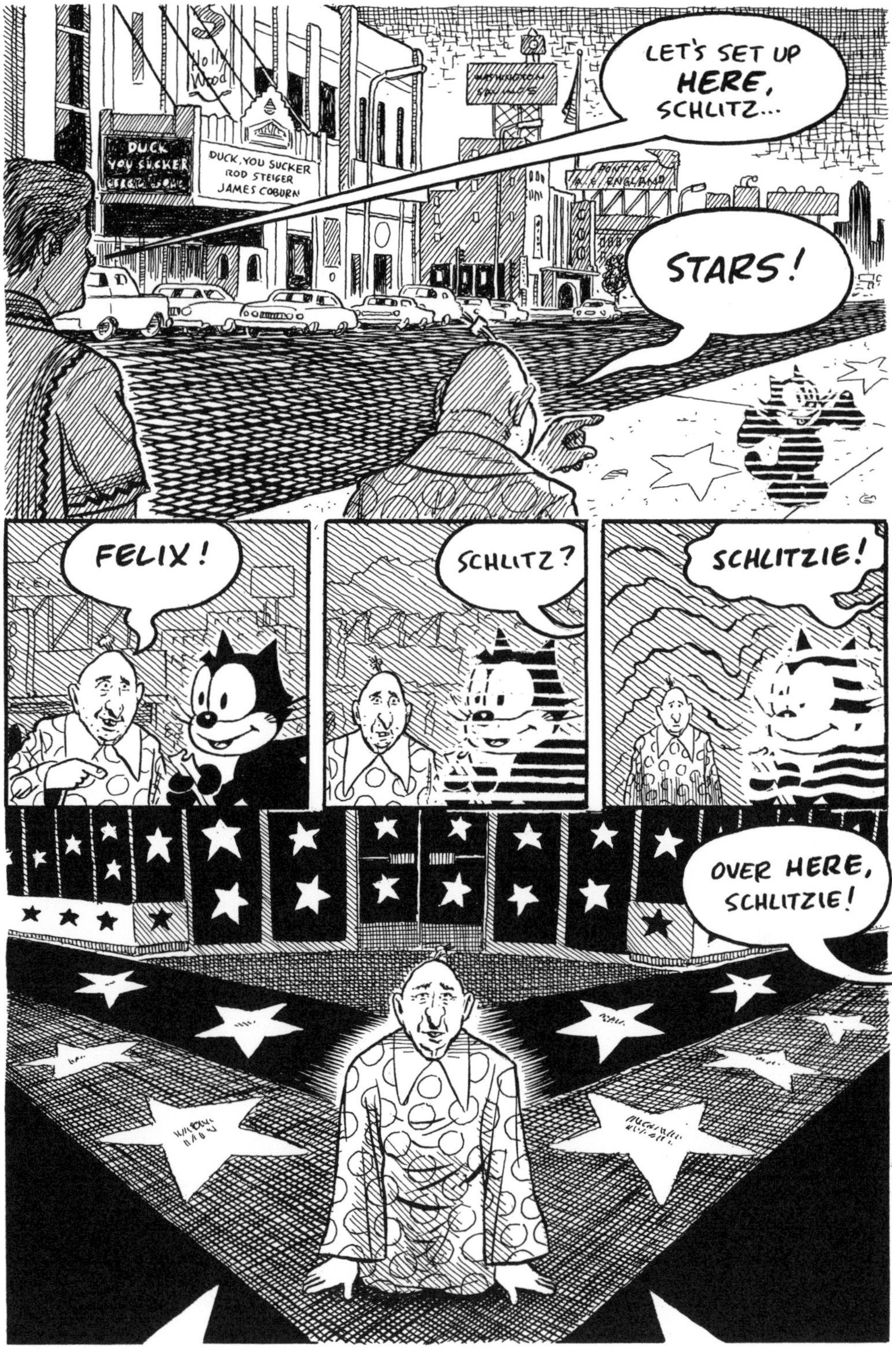
DUCK YOU SUCKER
DUCK, YOU SUCKER
ROD STEIGER
JAMES COBURN
LET'S SET UP HERE, SCHLITZ...
STARS!
FELIX!
SCHLITZ?
SCHLITZIE!
OVER HERE, SCHLITZIE!

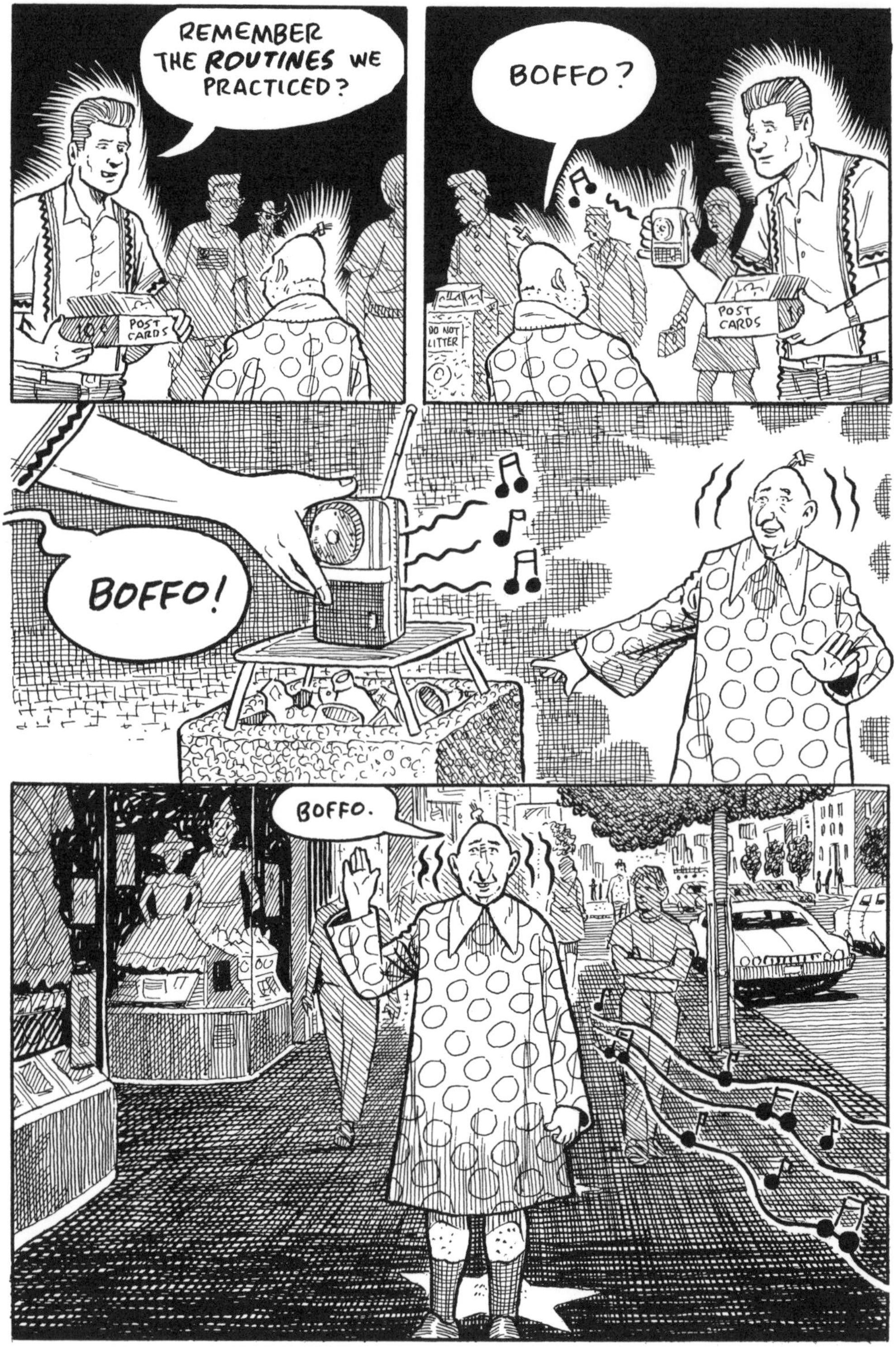
REMEMBER THE ROUTINES WE PRACTICED?
10¢
POST CARDS
BOFFO?
DO NOT LITTER
POST CARDS
BOFFO!
BOFFO.

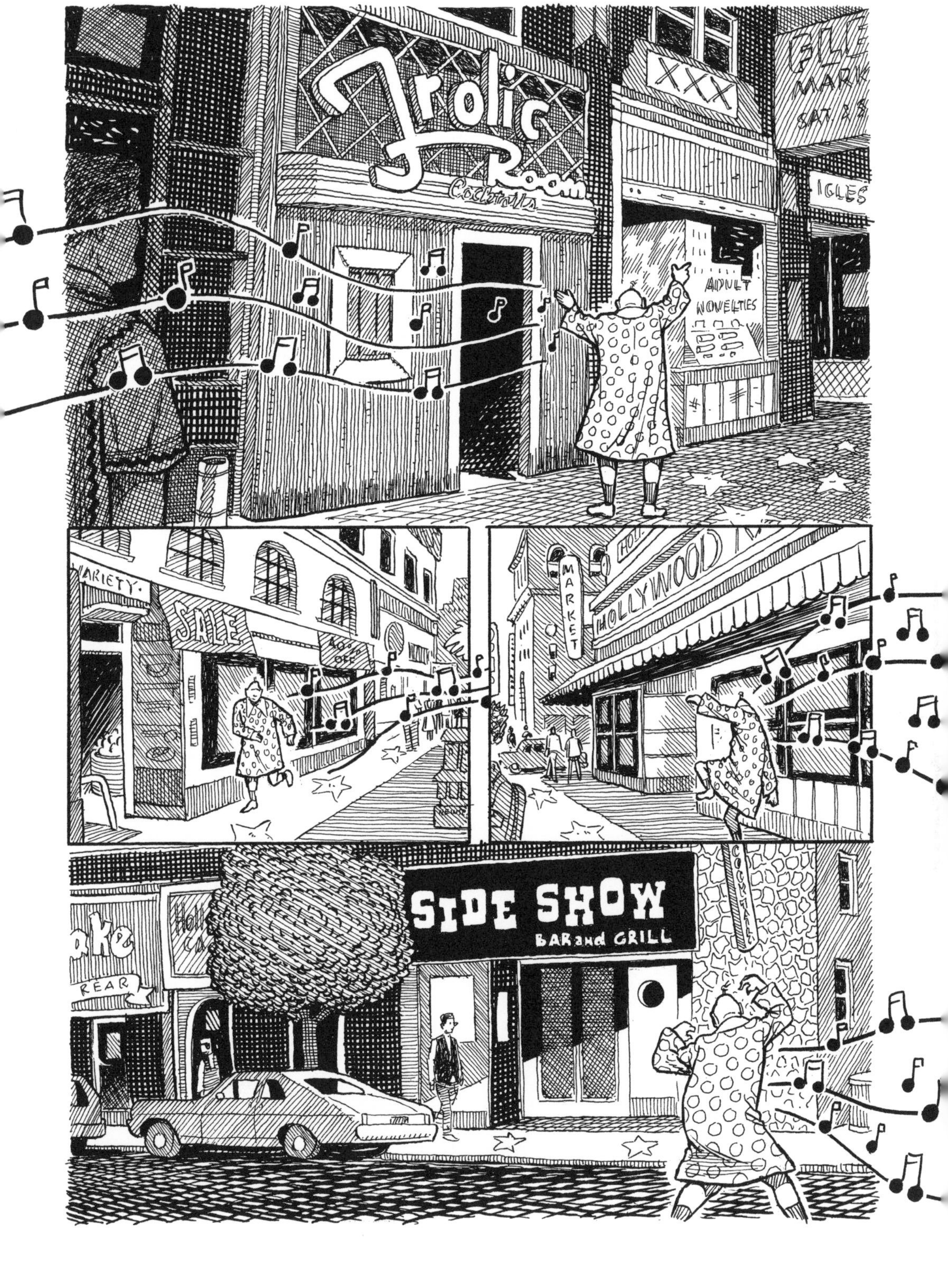
Frolic Room
Cocktails
XXX
ADULT NOVELTIES
SALE
VARIETY
MARKET
HOLLYWOOD
SIDE SHOW
BAR and GRILL
COCKTAILS
REAR

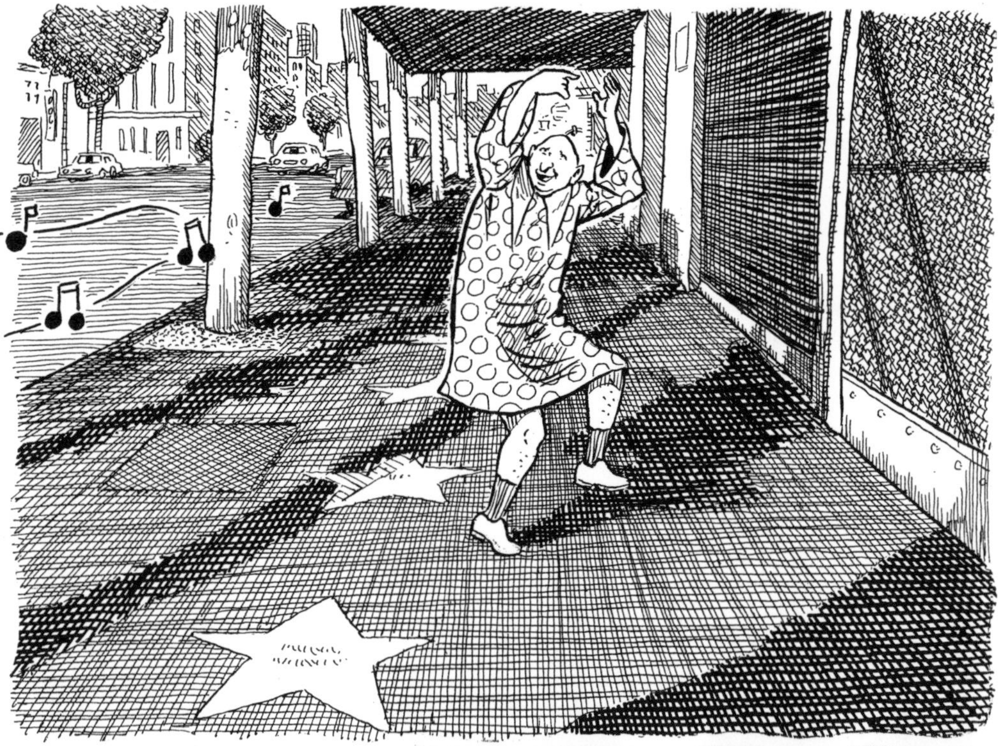

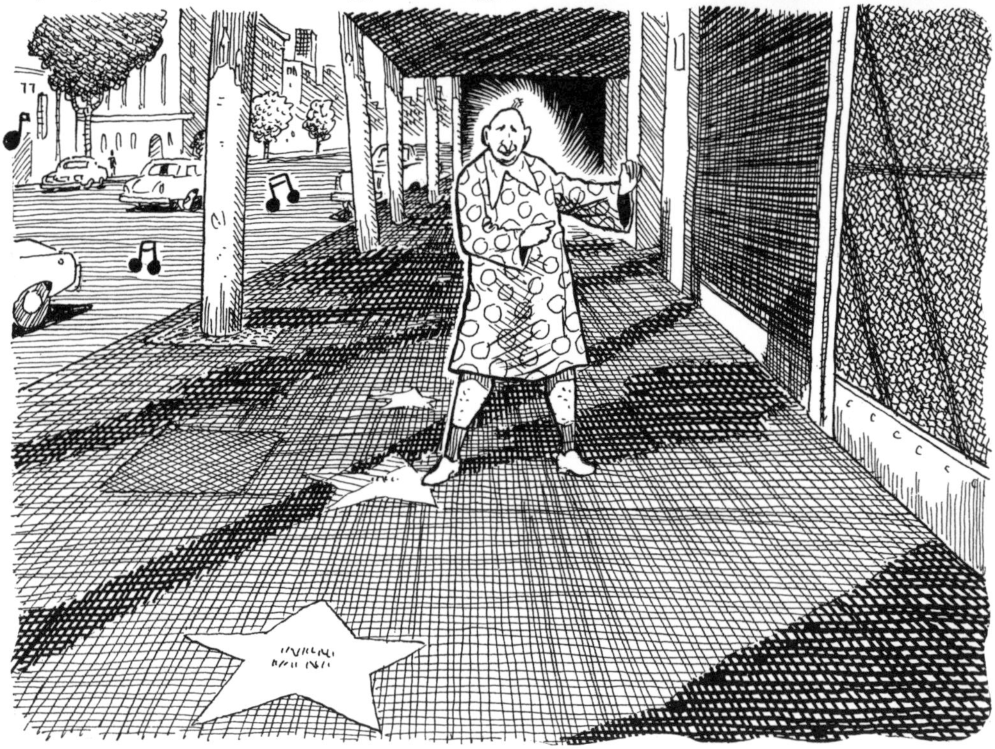

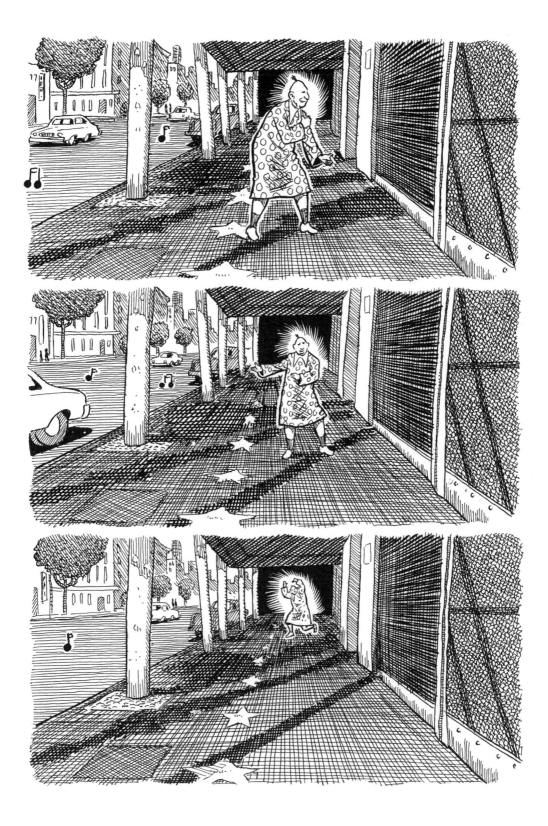

241

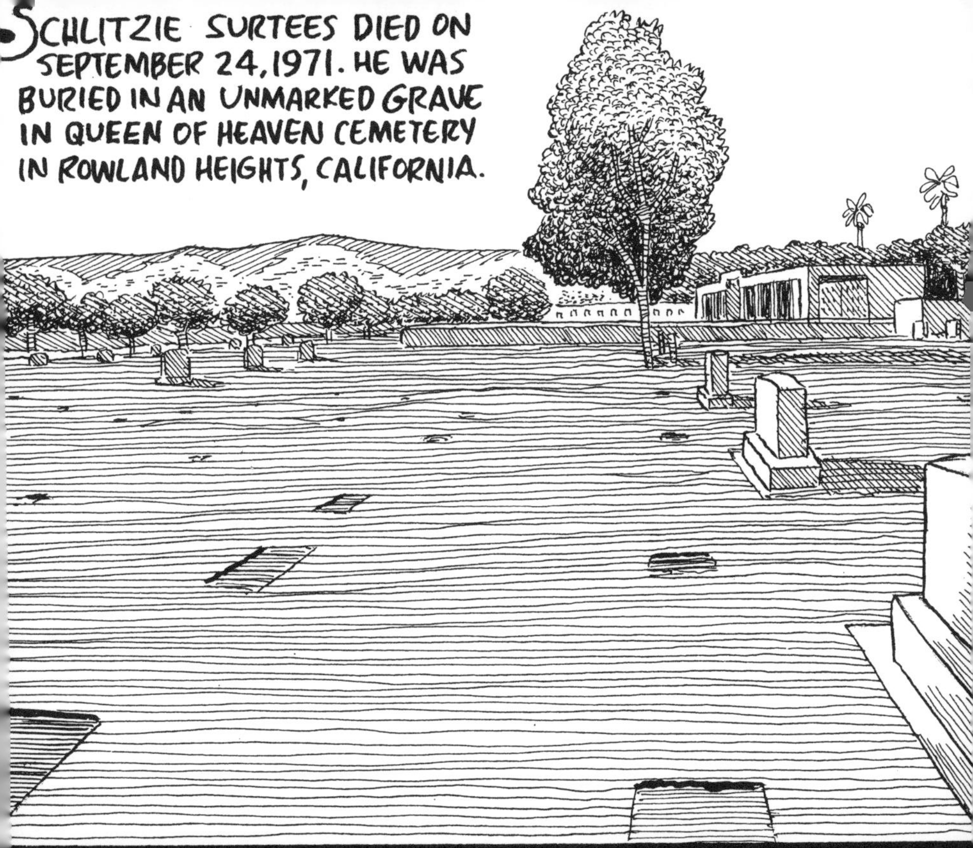
SCHLITZIE SURTEES DIED ON SEPTEMBER 24, 1971. HE WAS BURIED IN AN UNMARKED GRAVE IN QUEEN OF HEAVEN CEMETERY IN ROWLAND HEIGHTS, CALIFORNIA.

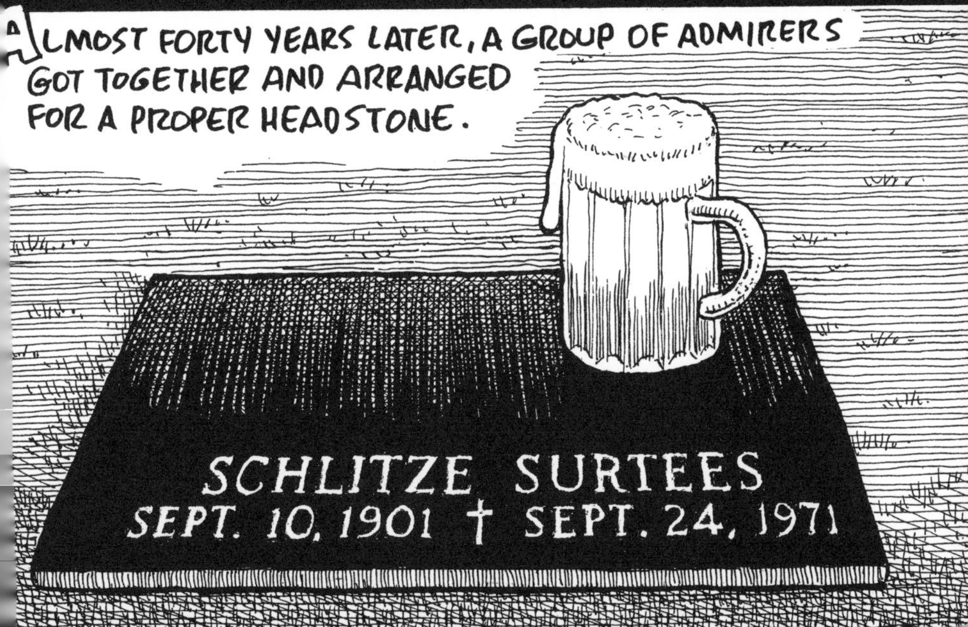
ALMOST FORTY YEARS LATER, A GROUP OF ADMIRERS GOT TOGETHER AND ARRANGED FOR A PROPER HEADSTONE.
SCHLITZE SURTEES
SEPT. 10, 1901 † SEPT. 24, 1971

SOURCES

Barth, Mark and Alan Siegel. *Step Right This Way: The Photographs of Edward J. Kelty.* New York: Barnes & Noble Books, 2002.

Bogdan, Robert. *Freak Show: Presenting Human Oddities for Amusement and Profit.* Chicago: University of Chicago Press, 1988.

Drimmer, Frederick. *Very Special People: The Struggles, Loves, and Triumphs of Human Oddities.* New York: Amjon Publishers, 1973.

Durant, John and Alice Durant. *Pictorial History of the American Circus.* New York: A. S. Barnes and Company, 1957.

Erlich, Andrew. *The Long Shadows: The Story of Jake Erlich.* Scottsdale, AZ: Multicultural Publications, 2012.

Hartzman Marc. *American Sideshow: An Encyclopedia of History's Most Wondrous and Curiously Strange Performers.* New York: Jeremy Tarcher/Penguin Books, 2005.

Hawkins, Joan. *Cutting Edge: Art-Horror and the Horrific Avant-Garde.* University of Minnesota Press, 2000.

Macy, Beth. *Truevine: Two Brothers, a Kidnapping, and a Mother's Quest: A True Story of the Jim Crow South.* New York: Little, Brown and Company, 2016.

Nickell, Joe. *Secrets of the Sideshows.* Lexington, KY: University Press of Kentucky, 2008.

O'Brien, Tim. *Ward Hall: King of the Sideshow!* Nashville: Casa Flamingo Literary Arts, 2014.

Skal, David J. and Elias Savada. *Dark Carnival: The Secret World of Tod Browning.* New York: Anchor Books/ Doubleday, 1995.

Sloan, Mark. *Wild, Weird and Wonderful: The American Circus 1901–1927, as Seen by F. W. Glasier.* New York: Quantuck Lane Press, 2002.

Stencell, A. W. *Seeing is Believing: America's Sideshows.* Toronto: ECW Press, 2002.

WEBSITES

Altered Dimensions. "Schlitzie the Pinhead—Tragic Story of a Famous Sideshow 'Freak' Performer." December 26, 2012. altereddimensions.net/2012/ schlitzie-the-pinhead.

FindADeath by Scott Michaels. "Shlitze." findadeath.com/directory/s/Shlitze/index. html.

"Memories of Schlitzie in His Last Years at MacArthur Park in Los Angeles" by Jaime D'Arcy Garcia. Although no longer available online, this essay was of great help in depicting Schlitzie in the years just before his death in 1971.

Sideshow World (Preserving the Past . . . Promoting the Future). Professor Lee Kolozsy. "Great Bally Talkers." sideshowworld.com/13-TGOD/L-K/37-Talkers/tgodgbt.html.

Sideshow World (Preserving the Past . . . Promoting the Future). John R. Robinson, Rick West, Shawnee Robinson, Patt Kelley, Lori Ballard, Mephisto the Fire Eater, and James Zajickk. Schlitzie and historical sideshow information, including memories of Ward Hall: sideshowworld.com.

Westland Network. "Coney Island—Rides & Shows List." Jeffrey Stanton. Revised June 3, 1998. westland.net/coneyisland/articles/ridelist.htm.

Wikipedia. "Schlitzie." en.wikipedia.org/wiki/Schlitzie.

Wikipedia. "Zip the Pinhead." en.wikipedia.org/wiki/Zip_the_Pinhead.

FREAKS

Freaks Picture Gallery. Olga Baclanova: The Ultimate Cinemantrap. "The *Freaks* Show: Exhibit 5." olgabaclanova.com/picture_gallery/movies/freaks_show_gallery.htm.

Freaks Script Synopsis. Olga Baclanova: The Ultimate Cinemantrap."The *Freaks* Show: Exhibit 1." olgabaclanova.com/freaks_script_synopsis.htm.

IMDb (Internet Movie Database). "*Freaks* (1932) Trivia." imdb.com/title/tt0022913/trivia.

TCM Movie Database, Turner Classic Movies. "*Freaks* (1932) Articles." tcm.com/tcmdb/title/163/Freaks/articles.html.

Wikipedia. "*Freaks*." en.wikipedia.org/wiki/Freaks.

YouTube. Search *Freaks* for Schlitzie's big scene.

NOTES

Page 25, panel 5: Translation: "I hope you like it here."

Page 66, last panel: Sideshow manager Ward Hall told me that Schllitzie would often say "Is he married?" when referring to men he liked or those who were kind to him.

Page 70: Personal note: My Uncle, Bill Jackson, was a barker (the sideshow term is "outside talker") at Playland at this time. It's likely he was out front on the bally stage there, drawing in the crowds to see Schlitzie.

Page 74: This scene takes place entirely in Schlitzie's imagination.

Page 153, panel 2: *Young Lust*: a series of underground comics published from 1970 to 1993, parodying the genre of romance comics of the 1960s and 1970s, co-edited by the author.

Page 158, panel 5: "Zippy the Zany Zealot," *Short Order Comix* no. 1, 1973.

Page 176, panel 3: *San Bernadino Daily Sun*, March 23, 1962.

Page 243: On September 24, 1971, at age seventy, Schlitzie died from bronchial pneumonia at Fountain View Convalescent Home in Los Angeles. His death certificate lists his official name as "Shlitze Surtees" and his birth date as September 10, 1901. Under "Last Occupation," it says "Side Show Freak."

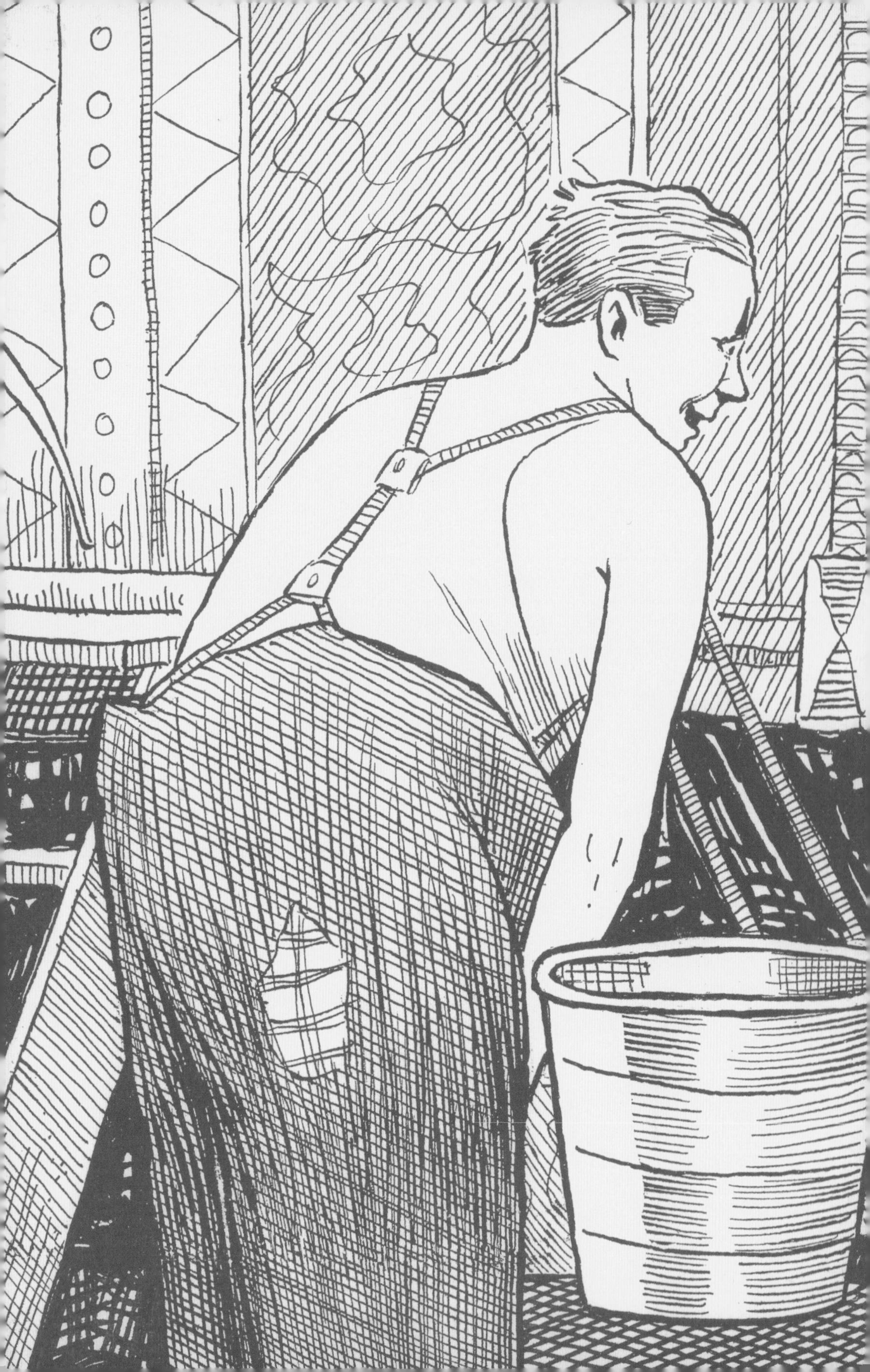

RIGHT AS RAIN

right

as

rain

LINDSEY STODDARD

HARPER
An Imprint of HarperCollinsPublishers

Right as Rain

www.harpercollinschildrens.com

Library of Congress Cataloging-in-Publication Data

Names: Stoddard, Lindsey, author.
Title: Right as Rain / Lindsey Stoddard.
Description: First edition. | New York, NY : Harper, an imprint of HarperCollinsPublishers, [2019] | Summary: "Eleven-year-old Rain must adjust to a new normal after her brother dies and her family moves to New York City"-- Provided by publisher.
Identifiers: LCCN 2018034251 | ISBN 978-0-06-265294-2 (hardback)
Subjects: | CYAC: Grief--Fiction. | Moving, Household--Fiction. | Running--Fiction. | Family life--New York (State)--New York--Fiction. | Friendship--Fiction. | New York (N.Y.)--Fiction. | BISAC: JUVENILE FICTION / Family / General (see also headings under Social Issues). | JUVENILE FICTION / Social Issues / Emotions & Feelings. | JUVENILE FICTION / Social Issues / Friendship.
Classification: LCC PZ7.1.S7525 Ri 2019 | DDC [Fic]--dc23 LC record available at https://lccn.loc.gov/2018034251

Typography by Sarah Nichole Kaufman
19 20 21 22 23 CG/LSCH 10 9 8 7 6 5 4 3 2 1
❖
First Edition

For Tyler,
My big brother and first-ever teammate.

CHAPTER 1

Dirt

The earliest thing I can remember is dirt jammed beneath my fingernails.

My mom studies the brain, so I know about childhood amnesia. It means we can't remember anything before the age of three or four. That's a fact because when I close my eyes and play memory games—Mom gives me a word and I try to connect it to moments I remember as far back as I can go—the earliest I can ever come up with is the dirt. Everything before that, before I was three, is just a big who-knows.

The dirt jammed under my fingernails when I was three felt good, though. Like it was supposed to be there and I wasn't my whole full self without it.

My mom says that memories stick best when we tell

them into stories with feelings and smells and colors. Maybe that's why I remember the dirt so well, because it felt so good, and because my family has been telling that story my whole life, so I know all the details even if I didn't recall them on my own.

Here's how it goes:

I'd wait until my mom and dad weren't looking. Then my little fingers would get to work on the line of buttons or long zipper that started at the back of my neck, whatever dress my mom stuck me in that day. She thought a dress made out of denim or corduroy was a compromise, but a dress is a dress, and I wouldn't be caught dead in one. I only ever wanted my brother's hand-me-downs, knee-ripped overalls and flannel shirts.

Once I got free of the zipper or buttons or stretched the fabric off over my head, I'd make a break for it and run my three-year-old, bare-naked butt to my dad's garden in the backyard and I'd bury it. I'd bury my dress as deep as I could, in with the downward-growing carrots and among the potatoes bigger than my little-kid fists.

Then I felt free. I felt just right with the dress deep in the earth, my baby skin open to the summer sun, and the Vermont soil packed under my nails.

It would only last a few minutes before my mom would find me in the yard and ask, "Rain, where is your dress?" I'd shrug and say that's a big who-knows, and that maybe it ran off to be with a little girl who would love it more than I did.

Until one day when I made my naked break to the garden with a patchwork dress bunched up in my right fist, and stopped dead in my tracks. There were dresses everywhere. Every dress I had ever buried and more. Pink lace, yellow cotton, long denim with buttons, corduroy with big front pockets, white tulle, and navy striped ruffles hanging from the tomato plants and strewn across the thick-growing kale.

Then I felt my mom's hand on my head. "Remember, Rain, when you bury things deep, they grow up twice as tall."

I remember the screen door slam and my dad walking out to the garden. He draped his arm around my mom's shoulders. "Look what sprouted up," he said, and they both tried to hide little laughs behind their hands.

The screen door slammed again and Guthrie rushed out to the yard and snapped a picture that lives in one of our family albums—his naked baby sister wide-eyed and jaw-dropped among the colorful gowns budding up. He laughed too and patted my head, but the idea of a dress garden made me cry big tears, so they bit their tongues and helped me harvest all the frill and lace in the dirty wicker basket that usually carried leaves of red lettuce and sun-warmed tomatoes.

That day, with my nails still full of dirt, I swore to myself that I'd never bury anything that deep again.

But that was before I was ten years old, when my parents laughed and talked to each other in normal tones. When we were a family of four.

Before that night.

CHAPTER 2

That Night

"Promise you won't tell," he said.

"Promise." I stuck out my hand and we locked our pinkies in a pact.

CHAPTER 3

Moving

"That's it?" I ask. "It's technically not even a truck. It's a van." That's a fact, because vans have those sliding doors on the sides and so does the vehicle parked in our driveway.

"Yes, Rain." My mom's pulling clear tape across a box marked *Towels*. "That's it, for the hundredth time."

I've actually only asked three times, but each time I can't believe it. We're moving 288 miles to New York City, and everything we're taking with us can fit through the sliding doors of that van.

"That's what selling the house furnished means. We leave the furniture."

I want to tell her that I might have agreed to moving, but I never agreed to leaving all my stuff. Especially my bed. I like my bed because it has two inches of foam on top that remembers the shape of my body no matter what position I sleep in.

And then there's my last memory of him, kneeling down and shaking me awake, whispering.

Hey, sleepyhead.

Locking pinkies.

Maybe it won't be so bad to leave the bed behind.

My mom presses the tape down over the edge of the box and rips it off the roll with her teeth. "This way we'll start fresh," she says. "We'll just get what we need when we get there." She tries to smooth the wrinkles out of the tape, but there's one right down the middle that sticks up and won't go away.

Instead of telling her that maybe I want my dresser or my desk or something from Guthrie's room, I try to think of what Dr. Cyn says about fresh starts.

Then my mom pops up from the box. "I have to go grab the . . ." But I can't hear what she's going to grab because she's already hustling up the stairs to their bedroom. She's always hustling off somewhere. Up the stairs, out to work, over to the grocery store. All the way to New York City.

I want to yell at her. Yell that she can get a new bed, a new apartment, and a new brain research job at Columbia Presbyterian Hospital in New York City, but that I don't want new friends, new teachers, and a new track coach when we're so close to the end of the school year. Especially this year.

But every time I really want to yell, I remember that when she sat me down forty-five days ago and asked about moving before the year was out, I nodded and said OK. I said OK because they need someone at the hospital by June first for a team-building week before a big conference, and people who study the brain know that building a team is important. I said OK because even though I've never met Dr. Cyn, I've been following her blog on families and grief for 278 days, and she says fresh starts can help a grieving family cope.

And I said OK because I remember what I did, and how nobody knows, and how if I hadn't done it, everything would be normal and no one would want to hustle off anywhere or stayed locked in a bedroom all day.

So instead of shouting at the back of my mom's head as she hustles up the stairs, I crack my knuckles and count the boxes stacked by the front door. *Towels. Books. Clothes—Maggie. Clothes—Henry. Clothes—Rain. Kitchen. School supplies—Rain. Garden.* There are thirteen in all, which feels unlucky.

I'm surprised to see the *Garden* box. Dad wants to leave his gardening stuff here, and Mom thinks he's just being difficult. I know because I heard them arguing about it when they first sold the house and were starting to pack. I was supposed to be shoveling the front walk. I'd already packed my big winter jacket, not thinking we'd get another storm because it was April. So instead of shoveling I was crouched in the back of my closet looking for an extra sweatshirt in my *Donations* box. Their bedroom is right on the other side of my closet wall, and I could hear every word.

Of course you're bringing it, Henry. You're not staying in the bedroom all day when we get there. You're acting like your life is over.

You're acting like yours isn't.

Don't.

Everything stays in this house. Isn't that your plan? So I'll leave it here, with all the other important stuff you're so ready to leave behind.

Henry—

Nothing to grow in New York City anyway.

Then the door slammed and I could hear my mom's feet hustling off somewhere. My dad didn't even call, *Maggie!* like he used to. Instead, I heard him slump on the bed and click off the light, even though it was only four o'clock in the afternoon.

I wanted to go crawl in with him, pull the comforter over our heads, and close my eyes tight against the slivers of late-afternoon light sneaking in through the blinds, and just let our hearts hurt. But the front walk needed to be shoveled, so I pulled on an old sweatshirt that would belong to some other kid by next month, and opened the door to the cold outside.

When I was shoveling the walk that afternoon I counted each pile of snow I dug out and tossed over my shoulder. My brain kept telling me if I could just get to thirty, then everything would go back to normal. I breathed in with each thrust, and out with each toss. The snow was wet and heavy because it was spring and too warm for the fluffy, pretty stuff. It felt good. It burned in my back and my shoulders, and I just kept counting. *Sixteen, seventeen, eighteen* . . .

After thirty, I dropped the shovel, fell back into the big pile I'd made, and looked up at the darkening sky. I knew nothing had actually changed, because shoveling thirty shovels never brought anyone back from the dead. And that's a fact.

Dad will come downstairs eventually, probably with his hair sticking up, and probably right before it's time to carry the boxes outside and get in the van and drive away. He'll see the box with *Garden* written in Mom's handwriting and they'll start up that stupid fight about whether it should stay or go.

Mom's feet are hustling back down the stairs. "OK,

I got them," she says, clutching a stack of three family photo albums. We used to keep them on the coffee table in the TV room and I'd look through them when the commercials were boring.

But after that night, they disappeared up behind the closed door of my parents' bedroom.

"I think they'll fit in here," she says, peeling the tape back off the *Towels* box and burying the albums down into the yellow terry cloth. My naked-butt-dress-garden photo is in the one on top. Then she pulls the tape back down across the box, but it doesn't stick as well and she still can't smooth out that wrinkle.

I wonder where she'll put the albums when we get to our new apartment.

"I'll start loading," I say, and grab the *Garden* box. I push my feet into my Converse and head down the front walk to the moving van. The box isn't heavy. Seedlings mostly, I bet, and from the sound of it, a couple of clinking trowels, and maybe a few pots. But there's no way to move the whole shed, the whole garden, the whole back-yard where Dad taught Guthrie and me to measure, and till, and plant, and water.

I slide open the van door and put the box inside with mom's handwriting, *Garden*, hidden against the back of the driver's seat so Dad won't see.

Mom is walking down the path with two boxes labeled

Books stacked in her arms. "Keep that door open," she calls. "And go tell your dad we're packing the truck."

"Van," I say. "It's only a van." And before I yell something that I don't deserve to yell, I turn fast and crack my knuckles back up the path.

Their bedroom door is closed like it has been for the last 350 days. I knock as quietly as I can and put my ear to the door. "Dad?" I whisper.

I hear the comforter crinkle and my dad clear his throat. "Coming."

I back up on my tiptoes even though I know he's awake and I can't possibly ruin anything else by walking normally, or even stomping my feet hard on our wood floors like I really want to, but walking silently seems safer, just in case.

Guthrie's door has been closed for the last 350 days too. Or at least my mom thinks so. I've snuck in there exactly six times since that night just to lie on his floor in my sleeping bag, like I used to every Christmas Eve for as long as I can remember. When I was little we stayed up and made plans to catch Santa, even though now I know he hadn't believed in Santa for a long time, and was just playing along for me.

Each of those six times since that night, I've woken early, rolled up my sleeping bag, scuffed up his shag rug to hide the memory of my body, and snuck out before my mom could find me there. Even though I hate that she shut up his bedroom, I don't want to upset her any more by opening a door that she wants closed.

Now that I'm walking by his room, it feels like I should go in one last time before we leave forever. I know everything will be the same on the other side, but seven times seems lucky. So I turn his doorknob quietly and push it open.

It's exactly the same. His quilt is pulled back, and both pillows are still on the floor, where Mom threw them that night when she found them bunched under his sheets pretending to be his sleeping body. His English 12 textbook is open to page 194, and his coffee mug is still half-full and on his desk, like he's just in the bathroom and will be back any minute to slurp a sip and finish reading "A Sound of Thunder" by Ray Bradbury.

It's weird that Mom hasn't come in to make his bed and throw his textbook in the donation box, or return it to the school, or rinse his coffee mug and put it back in our fully furnished kitchen for the next teenage son who lives here to make his coffee black and walk upstairs to his room to read his English homework. She cleaned every other inch of the house, but she closed this door that night, and just hustles past it on her way to somewhere else.

"Rain! Henry! Are you coming?" Mom's voice breaks the silence of Guthrie's room.

"Coming!" I call. And without even thinking I reach into the guitar case that's lying open on the floor and grab one of Guthrie's guitar picks. I press the triangle of plastic between my fingers and imagine his fingers there. Then I stuff it in my jeans pocket.

I pull his door closed just as Dad opens their bedroom door and steps out. "Hey," he says. His voice sounds like it hasn't been used in days. His hair is sticking up on one side, his beard is grayer and scruffier and longer than I've ever seen it, and his flannel shirt is off by a button.

"Hey," I whisper back.

Then I'm the one hustling off and down the stairs.

CHAPTER 4

Goodbye

The morning is crisp, and the muddy ground is still solid from a colder-than-usual night. My Converse high-tops land hard every time I stride, but this is still the shortest way to Izzy's house, and when my mom said ten minutes, she sounded serious, like she was going to stand in the driveway by the moving van and count until I reemerged from the woods. Even though she's never the one to count. That's Dad's thing, and mine, ever since he taught me how to measure the tomato plants three feet apart, and how to plant the seeds $1/8$ inch below the surface and cover them lightly with soil so they have the chance to break through when they start sprouting.

My dad's always been in charge of our family garden,

and 350 days ago he used to work on a team that renovates houses too, measuring new spaces for windows and doors, and the distance between each stair leading to the basement. For those things you have to be exact. I like being exact.

My best time to Izzy's house is three minutes, seventeen seconds. Guthrie and his friends cleared this path two summers ago so they could mountain bike through the woods, and it cut the time between our house and Izzy's by a whole two minutes.

Even with the cool conditions, no warm-up, and my trail running shoes in the bottom of a box, I think I'm beating my best time, which is good because I like to win. My legs stretch long, and each foot strikes the ground just enough to spring me forward.

The early morning air fills my lungs easily. Roots and leaves and pinecones stick up through the traces of mud, so I keep my eyes one step ahead. *Anticipate.* I can hear Coach Scottie's voice in my head, like I always do when I run—*Eyes up the hill. Hut hut hut!*—until I veer off the path, past the tree house my dad designed for us in second grade. He measured, and cut the wood, and hammered around the trunk of a sturdy oak tree, and we still sleep in it on hot summer nights. Seven long strides past the tree house and I'm in Izzy's yard.

Three minutes, twelve seconds. It feels good to break

something, even if it's just my own record.

Izzy will be leaving for the bus stop in three minutes, which is about how much time I have to say goodbye, if I run my fastest time back to our house too.

I knock three times hard on her door. "Iz!"

"Rain!" The door swings open fast, and before I can even say anything we're hugging so hard and my eyes are burning, and after such a short run why my legs are buckling and giving out is a big who-knows. And then we're in a big heap on her front step.

"I can't believe you're really—"

"I don't want to—"

"How will I get through the rest of sixth grade without you?"

"I won't have anyone."

And then I cry. It's the first time I've cried since the memorial that spilled out of the high school auditorium where Guthrie used to play his guitar at talent shows, across the parking lot, and into the baseball fields behind the school. Here I have all those people, a whole crowd of people, who want to read poems and sing songs and tell funny stories about how my brother was the best. And maybe it feels pretty terrible to have all of his old teachers look at me with big sad eyes in the hallway and ask me if I'm OK all the time, but starting tomorrow I'll have no one. Not any sad-eyed teachers, not Coach Scottie, not Izzy, not our backyard garden, and not Guthrie's bedroom floor.

I hug her tighter. "I have to go. My mom said ten—"

"Screw what your mom said," she snaps. "This is her fault. She *really* needs a new job right now? At the end of the school year? In a whole different state?"

"Yeah." I sniff. "Screw her," which are definitely words I'm not supposed to say, but I don't really mean it, because not even Izzy knows what I know. She doesn't know that I said OK to moving, and that none of this is my mom's fault.

"I have to go."

We stand up from the front step and she grabs her book bag. "I'll miss you so much." Tears are still wet on her cheeks.

"I'll write," I say. "Real letters, with paper and envelopes and stamps and everything." My mom says that we develop empathy when we turn off our devices, have actual conversations, read books made of paper, and write long letters to people we miss, thinking of them the whole way through. Sometimes I write Izzy letters and send them in the mail even though I can run to her house in three minutes, seventeen seconds.

"I'll keep an eye on the mailbox," she says.

I hug her one more time, then I take off through her backyard, past the tree house, and onto the path. I breathe deep the smell of pine and wonder what would happen if I just keep running, curve with the path down toward the Morrisons' house and on as far as my brother and his friends cleared, until the mud warms and sloshes up my Converse. I wonder what would happen if I just keep running instead of popping out in our yard, and through the sliding door of the moving van.

I can feel the corner of his guitar pick against my thigh each time I lift my leg. It feels good knowing I have something of his. It's sticking and chafing just enough to remind me over and over that I have it. It's there.

I slow down when I get to our yard.

Their voices reach me before I can see them.

"We don't have to get there exactly at three."

"Henry. We get the keys at three o'clock. They didn't say 'around three' or 'whenever you get here.' They said three o'clock."

"If we leave in thirty minutes and drive sixty-five miles per hour with one ten-minute stop, we'll get there at three o'clock."

I smile big because that's exactly what I was thinking.

"Aren't we just getting the keys from the superintendent anyway? Doesn't he live in the building? I'm sure it's fine," he says.

"The furniture is supposed to arrive between five and six. I'd like to be settled before then."

"We don't have anything to settle."

She shakes her head and points at his shirt. "Fix your buttons."

"Seriously?"

Then Mom looks up and sees me. "Good. There she is. Let's go!" She's waving me over, and Dad isn't fixing his buttons.

The back of the van is packed tight with our thirteen boxes.

And for a split second I think if there isn't a seat for me, I'll just live with Izzy and her family. I'll tend our garden, go to my regular school, and run in the Vermont state championships in sixteen days while Coach Scottie and all the sad-eyed teachers cheer me on. Even though I'm only eleven, and only a sixth grader, I know I have a shot at winning. I'm faster than any of the eighth graders at my school, and Coach Scottie says I've been training smart.

But then I remember Dr. Cyn and how maybe this move is our best shot at a good, fresh start. And maybe it'll make Dad open his door and make Mom stop hustling off and stay in one place, one place where she doesn't have to walk by Guthrie's room every day, even if I want to.

"Where do I sit?" I ask.

Mom slides into the driver's seat and pats the spot next to her.

"In the middle?" I ask.

Mom yanks on the belt. "Three seats up front in this truck."

"Van," I say. Then I scooch into the middle and scrunch my knees up toward my chest. Dad slips into the passenger seat, closes the door, and settles back against the headrest.

"Ready?" Mom says as she shifts the van into gear.

Screw you! I want to yell. But instead I try to make myself smaller, pulling my shoulders in and sinking down, smushed between my parents. I give my knuckles a good crack, and look up at our house. I try not to think of the time Guthrie and I dropped bubble-wrapped and marshmallow-padded eggs out his bedroom window for his physics project. I try not to think about burying my dresses in the backyard.

I try not to think of that night.

We back out of the driveway and start off down our street, and I'm watching our house grow smaller and smaller in the rearview mirror until we turn, and it's gone.

"Goodbye," I whisper.

CHAPTER 5

That Night

"I've got it all planned," he said. "I just need your help. One favor."

My heart beat with the quickened pulse of being wanted, being needed by my big brother.

"OK," I agreed.

CHAPTER 6

288 Miles

For the first forty-seven minutes, no one says anything. We just listen to the radio and look straight ahead down the interstate.

When the music starts crackling with static, I adjust the knob left and right, but the only things I can get are Christian rock and talk radio. I leave it on talk radio because then at least someone will be talking.

The host is interviewing hikers who completed the entire Appalachian Trail from Georgia all the way to Maine. They're talking about what they carried in their packs.

My harmonica, one says. *It was a huge lifesaver, especially on rainy nights, when I was stuck in my tent.*

Anything you wish you'd left behind?

The hiker laughs. *My book. I figured I'd be doing all this reading and finish it by the time I got out of Georgia.*

Not the case? the interviewer asks.

Not a page. The hiker laughs again. *I left it in the first town we crossed.*

Another hiker butts in. *See, that's funny, because reading was my lifesaver. Books are heavy, but I ripped out the pages as I read, and recycled them when I crossed through towns.*

I like imagining the pages of a story scattered between Georgia and Maine.

I guess you just bring what you think you'll need out there, the first hiker says. *And that's different for everybody.*

Dad humphs and glances across me at Mom.

I try to change the channel, but all I can find is static.

"What, Henry?"

I keep turning the dial, but nothing is coming through clearly.

"I can't imagine having to go that far with so little," Dad says.

"Sounds pretty liberating to me," Mom retorts. "Being on the move with only what you need."

My shoulders are trapped tight between theirs, and it feels like the space in the front of the van is getting smaller.

Dad humphs again. "Put it back on that interview, Rain."

I turn the dial back toward the talk radio station, but I'm hoping that it's been taken over by static, or that they've moved on to some boring subject that Mom and Dad can't argue about. Though something tells me they'd find a way.

A voice breaks through the static.

"There," Dad says.

The hiker says the trail is about 2,190 miles long. It crosses fourteen states, and about one in four people who set out to hike the whole trail actually make it. Everyone else quits.

One in four.

That's the same odds as marriages that survive the death of a child. And that's a fact, because I've been researching.

After reading pages and pages of Dr. Cyn's blog, I basically know that most marriages don't make it. She writes about the stages of grief, and support systems, and emotional stress, and how the death of a child goes against nature.

And even though she wrote a post seventy-four days ago that finding a fresh start could help a couple come back together, she admits that a lot of why a marriage suffers or survives through it all is still a big who-knows.

And if I want my parents to be that one out of four, I know I have a big job to do. And that's a fact, because they argue over garden equipment and some stranger on the radio's hiking pack.

The thing is, you don't really know exactly what you'll need or what works for you until you're out there on the trail. It's a lot of trial and error and getting what you need along the way.

Now Mom says, "Huh, this *is* interesting."

Another hiker, a new voice, speaks up and adds, *It's not about the* what, *it's about the* who. *It's with* who *you choose to walk this trail.*

Dad crosses his arms over his chest and leans back against the headrest. Mom has both hands high on the steering wheel and looks far down the interstate.

We've only gone sixty-eight miles, and I'm already feeling like the air in the van is disappearing fast. And I want to yell. Yell at them both to just stop. Stop arguing over stupid stuff. Stop humphing and edging closer to the middle because they're taking up my space. Just stop because I already miss Izzy and right now I'm supposed to be stretched out and reading in Ms. Carol's room, but instead I returned my book to the school library yesterday when I was only forty-six pages in, and hugged Ms. Carol goodbye forever.

Instead of yelling like I really want to and taking

back all my space in the front of the van, I just crack my knuckles and stare down the interstate and my brain tells me that maybe if I can keep the station from going staticky the whole way to New York City, everything will go back to the way it was, and my parents will be one out of four.

CHAPTER 7

The Heights

"We're here, Rain! This is Washington Heights!"

Mom is nudging me awake. The radio is off, probably because it faded into static and no one bothered to fix it, and for some reason that makes me so mad at both of them for not even trying. Or maybe I'm mad at myself for falling asleep.

I'm craning my neck to see out the windows. Buildings stretch up and up four, five, six stories. A red, white, and blue flag flaps from a second-story window of a gray brick building. It's not the stars and stripes that I'm used to seeing. Instead, white lines divide the flag into four big rectangles of color.

I look at it again and memorize the blocks of colors and the little design in the middle and tell my brain to remember to look it up later.

In the next window over, an older woman leans out and calls to a man on the street. He's wearing tall boots and watering the sidewalk outside his store with a hose, and why anyone needs to water pavement is a big who-knows. The water is washing over the curb and down into the gutter. He looks up and waves to the woman overhead.

"My hospital and your school are on the same street just ten blocks north or so," Mom says, gesturing behind us. "And our apartment isn't far. We can walk together in the mornings! Can't you feel the energy here already?"

My dad lets out a little snort. And I know what he's thinking—*Where's the grass?*—because it's what I'm thinking too.

"I guess," I answer.

"You guess? Oh, come on. Look around!" She's trying to get me excited, but if I show any enthusiasm, then my dad will keep sighing and resting his bed head against the closed window and it'll look like I'm taking my mom's side in this whole new-job-move thing. Which I'm not. But I'm not *not* either.

My mom only started looking for new brain research opportunities and planning this big hustling-off after that night. And if I hadn't done what I did, I don't know what we'd be doing. But it wouldn't be this.

We stop at a red light. The average red light lasts 120 seconds, and that's a fact, because I've counted many times before.

Before the light turns green again, ten people cross the street in front of our van. And that's just at this light! When I look down the avenue I can see three more red lights and people crossing in front of those stopped cars too. Plus, all the people walking along the sidewalks, on both sides, in both directions, and there are people sitting on benches in the median that divides the four lanes of traffic. And all the people in the cars that are bumper-to-bumper from here all the way down Broadway, probably all the way through Times Square, where the big lights flash all night, and down to whatever's past that.

In our neighborhood back home, there are four houses around a cul-de-sac and fourteen residents. That means that over 70 percent of our neighborhood's population back home just crossed in front of our van in 120 seconds at this one red light in Washington Heights.

"Come on, Henry," Mom says, and points to a restaurant on the corner. "Look, barbecue! You love barbecue."

Dad nods and looks out the window like maybe he's trying, but he doesn't say anything.

Then I remember that our neighborhood's population isn't fourteen anymore. It's thirteen. And it will be ten until the next family moves in tomorrow.

And all of a sudden, three people in this little van is too crammed. I'm feeling hot and it's hard to breathe and I want to get out now. I reach over my dad and roll down his window.

"Looking for fresh air?" he asks. "Good luck."

"Your dad can make any opportunity negative," Mom says. "Don't mind him."

"And your mom insists that all things be made positive and shiny and fine."

Then we stop at another red light.

I unbutton my flannel shirt to the tank top underneath, and six people cross in front of our van.

One woman wears too many layers for a sunny day and pushes a cart overflowing with big, clear garbage bags full of cans and bottles. The cart has a wobbly wheel and the glass clinks as she pushes. Two young guys with book bags rush around either side of her and disappear down below the pavement where it says *Subway*. Another woman, whose head is wrapped with a blue-and-gold scarf, pulls the hand of a little dark-haired boy and says something that makes him hurry up.

There are just so many people. And so much stuff.

There's a deli right next door to another deli and three barbershops on the same side of the street, and all the chairs are full. Barbers wear colorful smocks and carefully drag electric razors behind the ears of their customers. Fruits and vegetables are piled on displays outside of tiny corner stores, and one woman sells doughnuts shaped like sticks from a plastic shopping cart. Another ladles something hot out of a big orange cooler into Styrofoam cups and passes it to outstretched hands clutching dollar bills. A man peels oranges in perfect circles and sells them on sticks next to whole pineapples. Another spreads out used CDs and books on a red sheet across the sidewalk and calls to all the people passing by to take a look. Music blasts from a parked car, and five men sit on milk crates in short sleeves, talking in loud tones and shuffling their feet to the beat.

All the signs taped to the store windows are handwritten in Spanish. *Se necesita lavaplatos . . . Tenemos cincuenta colores . . . Especial de jueves: sancocho.* After two years of taking Spanish in school, this is the first place I've actually seen Spanish outside of my textbook or the back half of the manual that came with our new TV that we left in Vermont. And after two years of Spanish, I still don't understand all the window signs. One needs wash plates? And I know that *sancocho* is Thursday's special, but I don't know what *sancocho* is.

We cross over 158th Street, and 157th, and I like that the streets are numbers. It makes things feel organized and exact, and at least I won't have to memorize a complicated map with streets like Oak and Elm and Main, like the ones we have at home.

When we cross 155th Street, Mom says, "Now we're in Hamilton Heights—at least that's what the real-estate agent called it."

Hamilton Heights looks just like Washington Heights, with buildings that go up and up and up. I count two more barbershops and one salon with chairs tipped all the way backward, and the employees with long dark ponytails and pink aprons are doing something to the women's eyebrows with what looks like sewing thread. I tell my brain to remember to look that up too.

Next door, people sit shoulder to shoulder at picnic tables outside a bar that has *Grand Opening* drawn in bubbly handwriting with colorful markers right on the window and a big wooden sign above the door that says *Hamilton's Bar and Grill*. They eat French fries out of fancy cone-shaped holders, lean in to hear each other talk, and order foamy beers off a long list etched on a chalkboard.

It's sixty-seven degrees here, which is twenty-four degrees warmer than it was when we left Vermont this morning, and everyone is shedding layers and pulling sunglasses down from the tops of their heads. Fast-food wrappers and supersize cups litter the curbs, and daisies, carnations, and irises wrapped in plastic bloom from buckets on either side of the automatic sliding doors of a supermarket.

"There it is," Mom says. "152nd Street."

All the streets are one way, so we drive down 151st and back up 152nd, and we have to double-park the van because cars are squeezed all the way down both sides of the street with just inches between them. You wouldn't even plant seeds in a vegetable garden that close. That's why there were seven years and one month between Guthrie and me. Dad says you have to give things space to grow.

"We're supposed to buzz the super when we get here." Mom unbuckles her seat belt. "Doesn't that sound so *urban*? So cool? Let's go *buzz the super!*"

"I'll stay with the van," Dad says.

"Suit yourself." Mom swings open her door and a car honks and swerves and screeches past us. She gasps and yanks the door back.

"Whew!" she says. "This city will keep you on your toes." She's trying to make her voice sound steady and bright and fine, but I can tell it scared her.

The screeching tires.

My heart is beating fast, and that terrible feeling of remembering is rising up from my gut.

She opens her door again, slower this time, and I scoot across the seat and out onto 152nd Street. It feels good to be out of that van, reaching toward my Converse high-tops and stretching out my hamstrings.

"Come on." Mom nudges me. She already has a box in her arms.

There are three steps that go up to the front door of the building, and on the sidewalk out front, four men sit around a folding table, slapping dominoes. A crowd gathers around them, two deep, watching and exclaiming in Spanish.

"*Perdón*," Mom says as she walks past, and a rush of heat flushes up my face in embarrassment because they actually speak Spanish and I just know stupid phrases like *Tengo hambre* and *Quisiera un vaso de agua, por favor* and my mom knows even less, and both of our accents sound like twigs getting caught up in a weed whacker.

When they say *Hola* and *Bienvenido* back, it sounds like they're singing.

Mom hustles up the stairs past a girl who's sitting on the top step, tying a pair of Nike Flyknit Racers. Her hair is buzzed short all over her head, like maybe she goes to the barbers we drove by on Broadway, and even though she's skinny, she has muscles that pop out around her shoulders, and her calves are so strong I can see the muscles bulge from the front of her leg as she pulls her laces tight. She looks fast.

"I'll let you do the honors," Mom says, dropping the box to the side of the door. "Buzz the super! I'll grab more boxes."

The girl looks up from her laces and kind of smirks, and I feel embarrassed all over again because I'm pretty sure we sound really stupid, even in English.

"You're moving into thirty-one?" she asks.

"Yeah," I say. "My name's R—"

"Great," she mumbles. Then she tugs a double knot in her sneaker and I see that same red, white, and blue flag printed on the back of her T-shirt. *Dominican Republic*, it reads.

The way she says *Great* doesn't sound like she really thinks it's great. Not at all. And that's a fact, because as soon as she says it my chest aches hard and I start missing Izzy and my house and Coach Scottie. And Guthrie.

I press the black button that says *Superintendent*, and I can hear it ring. In a minute, the door makes a loud buzzing sound, and it takes me six seconds to realize that no one is coming to greet us and open the door, that a buzzer isn't a doorbell and you're supposed to push open the door when you hear that buzzing sound.

But before I can figure out what to do, the buzzing sound stops and Mom reaches around me and presses *Superintendent* again. I hear the ringing and then the buzzing, and this time I quickly push the door open.

The girl shakes her head and hops down the steps and strides long and even down the street, and all the dominoes men yell after her, "*¡Corre como el viento!*" And even though I don't know what they're saying, it must be something about how she's flying, because she is.

CHAPTER 8

Apartment Thirty-One

Our super's name is Héctor, and when he introduces himself to us, he pronounces the *H*, but when he crosses the street to help us unload the van, the dominoes men call out to him, *¡Héctor!* dropping the *H* and hammering the *éc* like a tomato plant stake driving against rocky soil.

He nods in their direction and calls them *¡hermanos!* and says something about *el sol*.

Dad gets out of the van and shakes Héctor's hand. "I'm Henry Andrews. Nice to meet you," he says. His buttons are still off by one, so the left side of his shirt hangs one inch lower than the right side, and I wonder if Mom is going to say something again.

"I'm Héctor," he says. "Welcome." He cups his hand

against the van's back window and peers in. "This is all you have?"

Dad shoots a look at Mom. "Hard to believe, isn't it?"

"We're traveling light and starting fresh," Mom cuts in. She shoots a look back at Dad and tugs at her own shirt and mouths, *button*. Dad pretends he doesn't see and slides open the van door. "We ordered new furniture. It should arrive in a couple of hours," she says.

"I'll get you some cards for a locksmith," Héctor says. "You'll need a new dead bolt too." Then he stacks *Clothes—Rain* and *Clothes—Maggie* in his arms. I slide *Garden* out before Dad sees it, pressing Mom's handwriting against my body and crossing the street, up the three steps, and through the doors that are propped open by thick newspapers folded and jammed in the hinges.

Héctor goes out for another armful, and Mom drops the *Towels* box on the lobby floor with the others. I keep *Garden* tight against my chest and look at the long row of silver mailboxes next to the elevator.

I find number thirty-one, which I don't like because prime numbers feel so exclusive, and cold, and closed, like there's no room.

Mom puts her hands on my shoulders. "Our first city mailbox, Rain!"

I nod and try not to think about Twelve Cloverfield Lane in Vermont.

"I know you miss Izzy." She squeezes my shoulder a little bit and then hugs me from behind. "And I know this timing is pretty rotten. But it'll be a great adventure for all of us."

"It's not just Izzy," I say, looking right at #31 etched with Sharpie on the front of our mailbox. Some other family's name—*Muñoz*—is written on the white tag, and I wonder if their mail is still inside.

"I know," she says, and squeezes my shoulder harder like she's really sorry.

My throat starts to burn, and I don't want to cry in front of any new neighbors who live in nice, divisible numbers like thirty-two or forty-four and who might come in through the buzzing front doors any second, so I shake out of her hug and say, "Let's bring these upstairs."

We slide all thirteen boxes into the elevator, and Héctor, my mom, and my dad squeeze in and press three. I take the stairs and race the elevator up. I can hear it chug through the floors, and I'm listening to coach Scottie's *hut hut hut!* in my head. Guthrie's guitar pick shifts in my pocket and rubs against my thigh as I pump my arms and fly over the steps two at a time. I win.

When the elevator opens on the third floor, I'm breathing hard, but I reach in to pull out the *Garden* box. Héctor unlocks the apartment door, helps us slide the boxes in, and hands the keys to my mom.

"Small key is for the mailbox," he says. "Call me if you need anything."

"*Gracias*," Mom says, and the hot flushes my cheeks again because his English is way better than her Spanish.

"No problem." He smiles and closes the door behind him.

Now I know why people say they live in a shoe box in New York City. Our apartment is not much bigger than the box for a new pair of my size-seven Adidas Ultraboosts. That's not exactly true, but if you lined the boxes up edge to edge, you'd only need sixteen to reach from one end of the living room to the other, and that's a fact because I count my steps as I look around the empty rooms.

There's no place to hide *Garden*. There isn't even a closet in the smaller bedroom, which I assume is mine, so I just keep carrying the box because I don't want Dad to see it and have our first moments in apartment thirty-one be the same old argument about whether or not the *Garden* box should have come the 288 miles. Even though it's mostly full of seeds and trowels, it's awkward and starting to feel heavy.

How anyone hides a secret in a New York City apartment is a big who-knows.

"What the— They painted right over all the finishes." Dad inspects a window, then walks into the bigger bedroom. "Right over the damn closet doors." He marches back out.

Mom pulls open a hall closet door and breaks the seal of white paint. "Feels like a fresh start to me," she says.

"It's not a fresh start, it's a sloppy job."

Mom shakes her head and grabs my elbow. "Put that down, Rain. Let's look around." I slide *Garden* against the wall, and I know it's only a matter of time before Dad sees it. But at least it's out of my arms.

We don't even have to move our feet to see the whole apartment. There's a kitchen that opens up over a new, shiny marble counter to a living room with three big windows that look out across an alley to the back of another tall, brick building. There are two bedrooms and one bathroom, which is one bedroom and one bathroom less than our house in Vermont.

Dad is opening all the living room windows. He sticks his head out of the last one and looks left and right. "Where is that coming from?"

"What?" Mom asks.

"You don't hear that?"

"Obviously not, Henry, if I asked *What?*"

I step between them. "Music," I say. The lyrics are

in Spanish, and it's impossible to tell where it's coming from because the beat is bouncing around the alley, back and forth between our building and the one across.

"Three thirty on a Thursday afternoon and there's a party?"

"I doubt it's a party," Mom says.

"So it's just always like this, then? No special occasion?"

"Henry."

"Maggie."

Before their voices can climb up and up into a six-story fight, I ask if I can put my stuff in my room. Mom says of course and that she'll give me a hand. She picks up *Clothes—Rain*, and I take *School supplies—Rain* to the smaller bedroom. The room is a perfect square with one window looking out toward the music-bouncing alley, and a silver radiator that sticks out from the wall.

"We can make a closet for you in no time," Mom says, inspecting the walls. "Maybe buy you one of those armoires, or make something urban and cool with a shower curtain rod here in the corner."

I rip the tape off the box holding my school supplies.

"Bed could go here." She points next to the window. "Maybe a desk over here, so you can do your homework. And maybe—"

"That's it, Mom," I say. "Just a bed and desk. Nothing

else will fit." And that's a fact because even if I get a twin bed, which is smaller than the bed I left behind, it will cover almost half the width of the room. Already this apartment is starting to feel like the front of the moving van.

She pats my shoulder. "It's going to be so cozy."

I nod and try not to let her see the tears filling my eyes, but she's already hustling off to the kitchen and starting to peel the tape off more boxes.

Out my bedroom window, rust-colored fire escape ladders zigzag up the building across the alley and they remind me of the ladder we lean up to the tree house in the woods behind Izzy's backyard. I grab my notebook and a pen from my *School supplies* box, sit on the floor against the far wall, and start writing.

Dear Izzy,

I tell her how tall the buildings are and how different an apartment is than a house, and about the ladders that rise up and up at perfect forty-five-degree angles right in front of the rectangular windows, and how I already miss our tree house sleepovers. Even though I'm only writing about rusty old ladders on the side of a big building where hundreds of people live, writing to Izzy makes me feel better, and I almost forget about the 288 miles.

I start to sketch a picture of a building in the corner of the page. I swipe little lines for the rungs of the fire escape ladder, and it's hard to believe all these people live on top of each other, and beneath, and side by side, stacked up and up and up.

Through a window on the third floor, in a room right across the alley from my bedroom, I can see a woman standing at the sink, washing dishes. In the next window over, a man paces the room and talks on his cell phone, and I wonder if they are in the same apartment, or maybe they live in side-by-side apartments and don't even know that the other exists. You would think washing dishes six feet from someone else and not even being aware of him is impossible, but from this angle I can see how two people might live side by side and never know each other.

Mom's voice calls from the kitchen. "The music's kind of festive! It's like they knew we were moving in."

"Yeah, what a welcome," Dad says. He slams closed a window.

I press the pen harder and make the fire escape outside my bedroom window darker, the angles sharper.

"I like it open," Mom says. "Let the neighborhood in!"

He pulls down another window.

And before he closes the third one, there's a knock at the door.

"I'll get it," I say, and put down my pen. I wonder if it's someone with home-baked cookies for us like we delivered to the Morrisons when they first moved to Cloverfield Lane.

It's only nine steps from my bedroom to the front door, but it seems longer walking between Mom and Dad.

When I click the lock and pull open the door, the front-stoop Nike Flyknit Racers girl is standing there. She's still wearing her running shorts, and now a navy blue sweatshirt that's zipped up halfway, the hood pulled over her head.

"My dad said to give these to you." She holds out two business cards and doesn't even come close to eye contact. I know that eye contact comes from the cerebellum, which is the most ancient part of the brain, because my mom told me. She says it probably traces back to hunting, and our ability to hone in on a target. So maybe it's good that Nike Flyknit girl isn't looking right at me.

I take the cards she's holding out. They're for hardware stores on Broadway. "OK," I say.

Then she looks up and right past me, like I'm in the way, and she studies our small, empty apartment.

My mom comes up behind me and puts her hands on my shoulders. "You must be Héctor's daughter," she says, and reaches out.

The girl shakes my mom's hand.

"I'm Maggie, and this is Rain. And that's Henry."

Mom points, and Dad waves from the living room, where he's crouched down, inspecting the brand-new but uneven floorboards.

The girl is still peering past us. Then she mutters, "It looks different." She says it with a clenched jaw and no smile, and she still hasn't looked up to meet our eyes.

Then my mom starts in about how our furniture arrives today, and as soon as we have some places to sit, she'd love to have her back up for lunch someday, and how she and I are probably about the same age and we're both runners, so maybe we could go for a jog together sometime.

For the first time since she knocked on our door, the girl looks at me. Right at me. And I can't help but think of a spear cutting through the air at its prey.

"You're a runner?" she stabs.

"Yeah," I answer.

"You race?" She narrows her eyes.

I nod.

"Great," she says. But this time she doesn't say it like she doesn't mean it. She says it with a growing smirk, like it's going to be so great when she smokes past me and leaves me in the dust.

We'll see about that.

Then Mom says, "I don't think I caught your name."

"Frankie."

"Well, Frankie," she says. "Tell your dad thanks for the locksmith recommendations."

I hold up the cards and kind of fan them in my fingers, and try to smile at her.

She nods and turns, and in a flash she's jumping over all six stairs, absorbing the shock with slightly bent knees at each landing, all the way down to her basement super's apartment.

It takes two hours and thirty-seven minutes from the time Frankie hands me the business cards for a locksmith to come install a new dead bolt on our front door, two men to deliver two bed frames and mattresses, and three other men to squeeze a couch and then a recliner chair into the elevator, and to remove the legs from a desk to fit it through my bedroom door and reattach them on the other side.

Once all the furniture is in, I count that we'll need four shims to stick under two legs of the couch and two legs of my desk, and that's a fact, because Dad taught me about uneven flooring in older buildings.

My new bed doesn't have any inches of foam on top and, it doesn't remember my body when I roll from one side to the other. And even though it's brand-new and 288 miles from my old one, I still wake up at exactly 10:43, I still hear him whisper, and my heart still speeds up to 110 beats per minute, which is really fast for a runner at rest.

I need a favor.

And before I can roll back over and try to find a spot that remembers me, my dad's voice breaks through the music tinging in the alley.

"Jesus, Maggie! I thought I told you—"

He found the *Garden* box.

"Henry, you can't just sit around and—"

"Actually, I can. I can do whatever I need. Just like you are. Except my needs aren't affecting the whole family."

"You think that staying in the bedroom all day isn't affecting Rain?"

"No. I think moving to a new state is."

"Henry—"

"Where do you expect me to use a trowel anyway?" He drops it back in the box and it lands with a clunk. "This city is paved solid from river to dirty river."

I reach for my jeans on the floor and find Guthrie's pick in the pocket. I hold it in my fingers and imagine his fingers holding it too, and strumming it against the strings of his guitar. Then I slide it into my pillowcase until morning, and wonder if anyone is looking in our windows like I'm peering in across the alley. There's a light on in the kitchen across the way and the woman I saw earlier is sipping from a mug at the small table, and one window over the glow of a TV screen strobes across the man's face.

Whether they belong together or are total strangers is still a big who-knows.

The *Garden* box thuds on the floor, and I can hear my mom mutter, "Impossible."

This isn't feeling like such a fresh start at all.

CHAPTER 9

That Night

"When will you be—"

But he held a finger to his lips.

"I'm not going to tell you when," he whispered. "Because I know you, and you'll start counting. No counting, Rain. No worrying."

I nodded OK, but I was 98 percent certain that I couldn't keep that promise, because counting is what I do when I want to erase my brain, and I didn't want to think of all the scary things that could happen when you break a rule like curfew.

CHAPTER 10

Like a Girl

"Wakey, wakey!" Mom's pulling on my toes. "I'm walking you to school."

"School?" I'm wide awake now and sitting up fast. "Today? It's Friday. I'll just wait until Monday." I pull my comforter back over my head.

"Rain—"

"Can't I just wait until next school year? It's already June."

"No, Rain. We talked about this." She pulls the comforter back down. "Your principal's expecting you today. Plus I have to stop by the hospital for . . ." But she's hustling off somewhere, so I don't hear the end.

"Mom!"

"Let's get some of those doughnut sticks we saw

yesterday for breakfast!"

I want to yell that there's no reason I need to start school today. All my stuff is in boxes and I don't even know what supplies I need, and I just don't want to. I've had enough new.

I give my knuckles a good crack and push the comforter off.

My clothes box is full of jeans, T-shirts, flannel shirts, sweatshirts, running warm-ups, tank tops, and sneakers, but what kids here even wear to school is a big who-knows. I pull on a pair of jeans and my *Run Like a Girl* shirt. This is what I would wear if I were waking up in Vermont and getting ready to go meet Izzy at the bus stop, but for some reason it feels all wrong now.

I slip Guthrie's guitar pick back in my pocket, and dig for my book bag in my school supplies box. It's full of notebooks from my old school, but I didn't think to ask for new ones, for my own fresh start.

I pull out a box of envelopes and book of stamps and tear Izzy's letter out of my notebook carefully along the perforated edge. I fold it into three even parts and seal it in the envelope. Then I realize I don't know how to mail it. At home, I'd put it in the mailbox at the end of our driveway and raise the little red flag so the mailman knew I had a letter to take. But our metal locked box downstairs with *#31* etched on it doesn't have a little red flag to raise. It doesn't even have the right name on it.

Mom's in the kitchen slurping coffee. "Ready?" She takes a last sip, leaves the mug in the sink, and picks up her bag.

"How do I mail this?" I hold up Izzy's letter.

She smiles. "I'll show you on the way." Then she puts her arm around my shoulders and steers us toward the door. "Oh, my little Raindrop. I love you so." She's been saying that for as long as I can remember, all the way back to the dirt, and it makes me feel like maybe today can be OK, and maybe even New York City can be OK.

But when I'm tying up my Converse, I see that their bedroom door is closed, and if Dr. Cyn is right and a fresh start can help, I wonder how long it'll take for him to open up and come out. I try to send my dad a little secret message like I do sometimes. *Get up, Dad. Come out.* But the door stays shut because sending someone secret messages has never put their heart back together again. And that's a fact.

The doughnut sticks that the woman sells from her cart are called *churros*, and I will never be able to roll my *r*s enough to order one in Spanish. But they are delicious and I wish I had gotten two because I eat mine before we get to 157th Street. And the way you mail something in New York City is to find one of those blue post office boxes on the street, pull down the handle, and just drop it in.

Before we get started walking again, Mom takes me by the shoulders. "This is a new place, Rain. You have to be aware of your surroundings at all times. Things can happen anywhere, but here there are more people, more cars, more trucks, more streets, more lights."

I nod.

"Follow the signals at each crosswalk. Don't walk against lights. Ever. And remember the streets just count up and down, from 152nd Street to 168th Street, so you can't get lost. Just look at the numbers."

I nod. And even though it doesn't feel anything like walking down Cloverfield Lane and taking a right on Elm, walking up Broadway past all the numbered streets isn't as scary as I thought.

It's already warm outside and the sun hasn't even gotten high enough to sneak over the tall buildings and shine down over us on Broadway. Store owners are unlocking big gates that roll up like our garage doors at home, and carrying big boxes down into dark basements through clanging metal doors that open up from the sidewalk. Then all of a sudden I realize that not only are people filling the sidewalks and living six stories up and up, but below my feet in deli basements and restaurant kitchens, there are people moving about and working, and whooshing by on rumbling subway trains.

The Spanish whooshes fast by me too. In four blocks I don't recognize any of the words or phrases from my two years of Spanish class. It flies too fast, and before I can grab a word or sound, it's gone and bouncing back and forth between passersby on the street.

"There are so many people here," I say to my mom.

"I know," she says, with a mouthful of *churro*, and it makes me jealous that she hasn't finished hers yet. "I told you. Isn't it wild?"

Four people hustle down the stairs to a bakery, and a line winds around the corner from a Starbucks just one block up, and there are at least ten tiny stores with ripped awnings between.

A tall, skinny boy with a backward Yankees cap holds the hand of a small boy with a Teenage Mutant Ninja Turtles book bag that hangs down to his knees, and a woman kisses the forehead of a little girl in a school uniform and watches her hop up the stairs of a bus labeled M4 and wave from her window seat.

"Guthrie would love this." I say his name before I can pull it back, and it drops hard on the sidewalk between us. Mom hasn't said his name since that night. She hasn't opened his door. She hasn't even cried. She's hustled around and planned his memorial, and applied for new jobs, and shown our house to new families, and packed up boxes. But she hasn't said his name. Not once.

And that's a fact because I've been listening.

"Sorry," I mutter.

Mom puts her arm around me and says, "You never have to be sorry, Rain." She points to another woman selling *churros* from a cart on the corner. "Round two?"

We approach the woman and I hold up one finger and point to the *churros*, and as the woman is handing me a sugar-and-cinnamon-coated doughnut stick in a sheet of wax paper, Mom says, "He would. He would love it here."

I take a bite and nod my head.

"Can you imagine?" she asks. "He'd have chowed ten *churros* by now and stopped in every store along the way to say what's up." She's smiling, but her eyes aren't happy. It looks like she's squinting against something too bright to look at, but we're still walking in the shadows of the big buildings that stretch up and up and up. "He'd know everyone in the neighborhood already."

"That's a fact," I say.

It feels OK to talk about Guthrie. Even though the remembering rises up heavy from my gut, it feels like it's supposed to be there. Like when Mom washes my cuts and scrapes with warm salt water. It stings worse than you can imagine, but it also feels right and good.

The school is three stories high and takes up half the block. *Middle School 423* is stamped in the concrete over the doorway, and the first people we see when we walk in are wearing security uniforms and have tiny, static-hissing walkie-talkie radios pinned to their collars.

We sign in and an agent points up the stairs. "Second floor, to the left."

The hallways are empty because it's only eight fifteen, but a few teachers are walking quickly in and out of classrooms carrying stacks of copy paper and rolled-up charts under their arms. My stomach does flip-flops, and I tug on my mom's hand. "Can't I just come to the hospital with you today?"

She stops outside the principal's office and looks right at me. "You're going to be great, Rain. First days are hard, but you just have to jump in and start swimming."

"And if I sink?"

"No chance." Then she knocks on the office door and it swings open, and before I can even tell my brain to remember to look up the Mirabal Sisters because there's a poster of them on the office wall, the principal gives me a paper describing the school uniform she says I'll need to have by Monday and a copy of my schedule, and points down the hallway toward Ms. Merrill's homeroom class.

The bell's ringing, and I hug my mom.

"Are you sure you want to walk home yourself? I can

come get you," she says, and I blink back all the tears I want to cry.

"I'll be fine."

"Remember. Just count down the streets to 152nd. And if you feel uncomfortable—"

"Stop in a store. I know, Mom."

"See you at home, little Raindrop." She kisses my forehead like that woman kissed the little school-uniformed girl as she hopped up the steps of a big city bus on her own. If a second grader can travel alone, so can I.

Then more kids than I've ever seen in one place at one time, except when we went to Disney World when I was in third grade, swarm up the stairs and through the doors into the hallway. They are all wearing white button-down shirts and navy blue pants or skirts, and Spanish words roll off their tongues and slide among all the bodies in the crowded hall. The beads braided into one girl's hair clink and clank as she tells a fast story to another girl, and I don't understand one word, but now they're laughing and I wish I were laughing with them. Boys tip basketballs over the heads of their friends and off the walls. They laugh and shove each other and open their lockers and squeeze their basketballs inside.

And as if I could feel any more wrong—wrong clothes, wrong language, wrong hair, wrong skin, and like this whole New York City move was the worst idea my mom ever had and I ever agreed to—I slink through the bodies toward Ms. Merrill's classroom, and who's sitting there but Nike Flyknit Racers Frankie.

"Figures," she mumbles and shakes her head.

Ms. Merrill smiles and shakes my hand and points to an empty desk in the third row. At my old school, we sat at tables of four and had exactly sixteen kids in our class.

I slide into the empty seat and start counting the blue-painted bricks of the classroom wall. Two, four, six, eight. And I remember how the hiker on the radio said he had to take it one day at a time, one step at a time. So that's what I'll do. I'll get through today. But Flyknit Frankie is peering out of the corner of her eye at my desk, and I wish at least that I were wearing navy blue and white so I could try to blend in, but as more students come in through the classroom door and stop their Spanish short when they see my face in the third row, I have this feeling that I won't be blending in here.

Ms. Merrill doesn't make me stand up and say three things about myself or anything like that, which makes me like her immediately. She comes to my desk when everyone is unzipping their book bags and taking their seats and sneaking quick glances in my direction, and she asks if I want to introduce myself to everyone or if I'd rather just meet a couple of people first, which is good, because I count thirty-three kids in this class already, and I'm not even sure everyone's here yet. Standing up in my *Run Like a Girl* shirt and regular old jeans with my straight blond hair pulled back in a messy, unbrushed blob and talking about how I'm from Vermont, which feels about nine thousand miles away from here even though it's only 288, sounds terrible.

"This is Amelia," Ms. Merrill says. The girl at the desk next to me is small and skinny. She wears her dark hair in two curly pigtails, and has bright aqua-framed glasses and matching rubber bands around her braces. She says hi, but it takes her a while to get the *H* started because she's stuttering. At first I think she's as nervous as I am, and maybe she's new too, but then I realize her stutter is bigger than nerves. It's permanent.

"Hi," I answer.

Ms. Merrill says that Amelia can help me understand my schedule and where all the classrooms are. "She's very responsible. You're in good hands."

Amelia smiles and nods her head. I can tell she's shy and doesn't want to talk much and didn't volunteer for this, but her smile is real, and that makes me feel 16 percent better.

Then Ms. Merrill slides a folder onto my desk with *Homeroom* written on the front. Inside are a bunch of papers about current events, and a canned food drive, and community service.

Students need to complete twenty-five hours of community service before June eighteenth to be promoted to the seventh grade.

There's a grid to fill out with what service you did and for how many hours, and a spot for signatures that prove that you actually helped someone.

Just as I'm thinking I definitely won't have to do any community service hours because I just got here and it's already June first, and eighteen days is definitely not enough time to think of what to do, Ms. Merrill says, "And make sure Amelia explains those community service hours to you. You're getting a little bit of a late start, so you can just do ten."

I nod my head, but I'm already thinking that's not proportional. That if they had 180 days to do twenty-five hours, I should only have to do two and a half hours. Ms. Merrill is definitely not a math teacher.

I'll have to do thirty-three minutes a day of community service, and that's if I start today, which I can't because after school I have to go buy navy blue pants and white shirts and notebooks that don't have my old schoolwork in them.

I want to yell at Ms. Merrill that this isn't fair, and she can't even do simple math, and that I don't even know anything about my community yet, and it's almost the end of the year, so can't I just skip it? But I just give my knuckles a good crack and try not to think of what Izzy is doing right now, and if some other kid has checked out the book I didn't get to finish from the library yet.

Ms. Merrill starts playing a song and projects the lyrics on the SMART board screen. Everyone quiets down and follows along. A couple of kids start singing out the chorus in loud voices, and Ms. Merrill is smiling and encouraging them. I'm running my finger over the name that's sketched on my desk in purple marker. *Reggie*. And I wonder if Reggie got in trouble for writing on a desk and if Ms. Merrill ever tried to clean it.

I can feel Frankie staring, and when I peek over at her, it's not me she's staring at, it's my finger tracing over and over the name *Reggie*. And this time her jaw's not clenched. Her face is soft, and her eyes look sad like maybe she has some remembering that rises up and up too.

Then the song ends, and everyone is dragging their desks into groups of three. Amelia's trying to tell me which way my desk turns, but her stutter takes too long, so she just gestures me over until I'm turned next to her, and face-to-face with Frankie.

"Discussion groups," Amelia whispers. The *d* gets

stuck in her mouth over and over, and two boys in the group behind us mutter something in Spanish and snicker into their navy blue sweatshirt sleeves. It makes me mad because Amelia's being nice and those boys deserve to trip on their faces. I want to whip around and tell them that too, but I already stick out like a cucumber plant trying to survive in a potato patch, so I just watch as Ms. Merrill puts some discussion questions up on the SMART board.

Frankie's sitting back in her chair with her arms folded across her chest, and Amelia's staring at her hands.

The silence is awkward for a full minute, which feels like at least three minutes, before Ms. Merrill notices that we aren't discussing the song lyrics, or anything else.

She bends down next to our desks. "Have you both met Rain?" she asks. "Rain, you know Amelia. And this is Frankie."

Frankie nods, but she doesn't look up.

"Maybe you two could help Rain go over the schedule before we go to first period?" Ms. Merrill smiles, then she moves on to another discussion group.

I pull out the copy of our schedule from my folder and lay it over the purple-markered "Reggie" on my desk. We have all the same classes I had in Vermont, except

I don't see art or music. "When do we have art?" I ask.

"W-w," Amelia starts, and the longer she stutters on that *W*, the more terrible I feel that I asked a question in the first place.

"We had it first quarter," Frankie finishes for her.

"You mean it's just over?"

"Yup," Frankie says.

"Sucks," Amelia spurts out all in one syllable, and even if *sucks* is one of the words I'm not supposed to say, it makes me feel better that she said it. I'm glad that sometimes she can just shoot out an idea while she's having it.

"It doesn't suck," Frankie argues. "Because now we get gym instead. What *really* sucks is that we don't get gym the whole year."

I look back down at the schedule, and I focus on the little boxes under Friday. Next is science, then math, then lunch. English isn't until the end of the day. Gym is last period.

But what I'm really thinking is that none of this actually sucks. Having art or not having it, or how much gym you get. What *actually* sucks is that Guthrie's gone and I don't know anyone, and I miss Izzy and the two inches of foam on my bed, and no matter how many secret little messages I send, I can't get my dad out of his room, and that being in apartment number thirty-one makes me feel like an overwatered plant whose soil has no more air pockets and whose roots can't breathe because they're drowning.

So whining about gym seems kind of small.

Frankie starts mumbling, "Gym should be every—"

"Just shut up," I say, but it's too late to pull it back. That was supposed to stay in my brain not fly out in Frankie's face, and *shut up* is another thing I'm not supposed to say, and she hates me enough already, and why is a big who-knows.

When I look up, she's glaring at me.

"I didn't mean—"

But the bell is ringing and Frankie is already yanking the zipper closed on her book bag and pushing past everyone toward the door. A girl from another discussion group is shaking her head like why the heck did I say that, and Amelia starts asking me something, but it's turning over and over in her mouth like a lawn mower that won't start, so she jots on the side of my schedule. *Are you OK?*

I nod yes, but my eyes are filling up, so I bend down and pretend to be busy with my book bag. When I sit back up, Amelia is gone, but on my schedule she added, *Are you sure? We can talk, even though I suck at it.*

And I'm thinking maybe having that stutter does actually suck.

• • •

The only class I really like is English. Mrs. Baldwin has quotes hanging all over her room, which gives me something to look at while they all discuss poems they read earlier in the week. It's weird to think that while they were sitting in this classroom reading poetry, I was sitting 288 miles away in Vermont reading the first forty-six pages of *The One and Only Ivan* in Ms. Carol's room during independent reading. Which makes me wonder where the library is in this school because I want to finish my book.

I scribble on a page of my old English notebook: *Where's the school library?* Then I hand it to Amelia. She hands it back. All it has is a frowny face, and Amelia's gesturing behind us to Mrs. Baldwin's classroom library in the corner, which has bins and bins of books all labeled with her own genre signs. *Sports, Romance, Friendship, Family Drama, Mrs. Baldwin's Weekly Favorites* . . . There are forty-two bins, which is a lot, but it's not a whole room like the library in my old school, where there were shelves and shelves and a whole system for finding all the books you could ever wish to find, and a librarian, Ms. Trish, who could get a book for you overnight like magic if you couldn't find it on one of the shelves.

No art. No school library. No librarian.

Mrs. Baldwin asks to see me after class for a minute,

which makes me nervous for two reasons. First, in every book you ever read, if the teacher wants to see you, it's bad news. Two, if I talk to Mrs. Baldwin even for forty-five seconds the whole class will leave without me and I'll have no one to follow through the halls to last period, and I have no idea where the gym is. But I nod my head and put my notebook back in my book bag and hurry up to the front of the room.

"I just wanted to show you our classroom library, in case you want to check out a book. You're always welcome."

I smile and hope she's like Ms. Trish and knows exactly where to find any book I ask for.

"Do you have *The One and Only Ivan?*"

Mrs. Baldwin grins and puts her hand on my shoulder. "Oh, we are going to get along great." We walk to the corner classroom library, and she pulls *Ivan* out from *Mrs. Baldwin's Weekly Favorites.* "This one is in here every week."

She teaches me how to fill out the card from the back of the book. It's not like the system from my old library with a bar code that scans and puts your name in the computer and prints out a receipt that tells you when the book is due. It's just an index card, and it's written in the same handwriting as all the genres on the bins and all the quotes on the walls.

The last person to sign out this book was Reggie, on April 22, and I'm not sure if Reggie is in our class and I just haven't figured out who it is yet, or in another class and I'm just the lucky one who gets to share all the Reggie-graffitied desks.

I sign my name and write June first on the card, and Mrs. Baldwin slides it into a pocket chart that hangs on the wall. "You're number thirty-four," she says. "Monday I'll catch you up on some of the poetry we've been reading, but for this weekend, just enjoy *Ivan*." She pats my shoulder and I smile. And for one second I don't feel like the only kid who doesn't understand Spanish and who isn't wearing navy blue and white, and who gets lost in the hallways, and doesn't have a locker or any hours of community service. I'm not feeling so much like I don't belong.

And when I zip *Ivan* into my book bag and leave the classroom, Amelia is waiting for me outside the door. She holds up a scrap of paper that reads, *Gym. This way.* We walk side by side down the hall and up the stairs to the second floor. And just when I'm feeling like everything might be going OK, we swing open the big doors to the gym and the whole class turns to look at us.

The gym teacher is younger than Mrs. Baldwin and looks like he played football in high school. He wears tear-away warm-up pants and a tight Under Armour

T-shirt, and keeps his chest puffed out like some tough guy. A whistle hangs around his neck.

"New kid?" he shouts, and it echoes across the gym. "You're late!"

Amelia and I hustle over, and as I'm sitting down with the rest of the kids on the gym floor, he sees my shirt and says, "Run like a girl, huh?" He raises his eyebrows and nods his head in a way that makes me not want to sit because I don't want him looking down on me any more than he already is.

The boys who snickered at Amelia's stutter in homeroom snicker again now, and I swear I see Mr. Meathead sharing a secret nod with them. But then I accidentally share a look with Frankie, who's sitting in the front row too and turned around like everyone else to read my shirt. It's the first time I've caught her looking at me that she doesn't seem like she wants to squash me.

She rolls her eyes. But not at me. At Mr. Meathead. And even if I can't get my messages to my dad, I think Frankie gets my secret little message right now—*Let's show this stupid teacher how girls run*—because she's nodding her head and there's a little smirk growing on her face. And I don't even care that *stupid* is another one of the words I'm not supposed to use.

I want to raise my hand and tell him what a stereotype he is. Actually, I want to just shout it out. That all gym teachers in books are just like him, but I just give my knuckles a good crack and wait.

He goes on about how middle school gym is serious and important and it sets the stage for our athletic lives and how we need to start stepping it up and end the year with a bang.

"This isn't about playing anymore," he says. "Today we run." He explains that we're going to do a quick stamina test. A few kids groan and call out that he's never made them run before and can't they just shoot hoops? Then everyone starts chiming in and saying it isn't fair and they don't want to get sweaty. Everyone except the boys in the front row. And Frankie and me.

"The sidewalk that circles around the school is exactly a quarter mile," he says. "You will run that twice. No stopping." He blows his whistle through the complaints and starts walking toward the gym doors, and we're all following him down the stairs and outside into the afternoon sun.

I'm not wearing navy blue gym sweatpants and sneakers like everyone else is. Frankie's got on her Nike Flyknit Racers and navy blue warm-ups. She starts unbuttoning her white school shirt to the T-shirt she has on underneath.

"New kid," Mr. Meathead grunts, looking at my jeans and Converse high-tops. "You can sit out today."

"No thanks." I push up my sleeves and go join Frankie at the starting line.

The front row boys are stripping down to their T-shirts too and pushing up to the front, where Mr. Meathead has his hand raised and his whistle between his lips. Frankie's bending down for a real track start, even though we don't have starting blocks, and I know how to do that too, so I crouch into my position and feel the rough sidewalk beneath my fingertips. A couple of boys join us in starts, but they're positioned all wrong, and it'll take them longer to get up and out. I'm not about to say anything because they think they look all cool doing it, and I intend on beating them.

I can feel the edge of Guthrie's guitar pick against my thigh. Then the whistle screams through the air and we're off.

Frankie pulls out first and moves toward the inside of the sidewalk. I'm right on her heels, but my muscles are tight and cold and my feet fall hard on the concrete in my Converse. I match Frankie's pace and stay right with her. We're already rounding the front of the building, and I can hear footsteps turning over fast behind me, someone with a short, quick stride, and it's making me turn up the heat. I use my arms to dig like Coach Scottie taught me and I'm starting to feel my rhythm, like I'm flying over tree roots and slippery rocks on the way to Izzy's house. We round the first lap and dash past Mr. Meathead.

"Pace yourselves, girls!" he calls. I can see Frankie shake her head and I'm shaking mine too. Going out of the gate too hard is a rookie mistake. And we're no rookies.

We round the front of the building for our second lap, and the footsteps are pulling up fast behind me. I'm picturing one of those front-row bad-start boys who shared a secret nod with Mr. Meathead gaining on me, and I want to look so I can see who I'm racing, but I know it's bad technique and could cost me my lead, so I exhale hard and turn my stride over faster and faster. The steps stay right on my tail and no matter how hard I push I can't pull away from them, and I can't pull up next to Frankie.

We round the back of the building. Just a straight-away to the finish line and Mr. Meathead.

I stretch long and gain half a stride on Frankie, but she crosses first and pumps her fists toward the sky. "Yeah!" she exhales, and slows to a stop.

I finish just behind her but ahead of the footsteps that chased me the whole way. I'm bent over my knees when I feel a pat on my back. "G-g-good race." I look up and see Amelia, little wispy, tiny, stuttering Amelia.

"That was you?" I pant.

She smiles, her big mouth full of braces.

"Th-th-th-third place," she says. "But I'd still r-rather have art."

I give her a high five and check out her sneakers—Brooks Adrenalines in a bright aqua that matches her braces and glasses.

Frankie saunters over and puts up a hand for a high five, and Amelia and I both go for it at the same time, so our hands all kind of meet. And even if the high five feels kind of off and goofy at first, and makes us all giggle a little, even Frankie, I can't help but think about how a triangle is the strongest geometric shape.

Everyone has crossed the line now, and the bell is ringing for us to return to our homerooms.

We three walk past Mr. Meathead, who's talking to a group of kids about some knee injury he had when he was playing football in high school and that's why he couldn't do the run with us.

We kind of slow down as we pass him and I wait until he looks up.

"That's how you run like a girl," I tell him.

CHAPTER 11

Hamilton Heights Café

At first I wish I could rewind seven hours and tell my mom I do want her to pick me up from school, even if it makes me look like a little second grader, or makes me stick out even more, because 152nd Street feels farther away than sixteen blocks. There are three other schools letting out at the same time on this one street, so the sidewalks are crowded with kids chasing each other, pulling on each other's book bags and laughing, shouting quick phrases in Spanish, lining up to buy shaved ice in tiny little cups from carts with green-and-white-striped umbrellas, and bumping into people who are trying to pass through.

I should have told her to meet me around the corner at Starbucks and to not even talk to me in case kids from my school were watching, and we'd just walk home side by side. I wish I had thought of that before.

But once I get to Broadway, I start subtracting the numbers from 168 to 167 to 166, and each block I feel better. I even recognize some of the people who were opening their shops on the walk to school this morning, and I smile at them and they smile back.

The *churros* women, both of them, are now selling *tamales*, and I buy three. One for me, one for Mom, and one for Dad. And I tell my brain to remember to look up whether or not you eat the corn husk that's wrapped around the meat and cheese.

The man who was watering the sidewalk is now stacking hairy coconuts outside his market, and he gives me a nod and an *hola* and I nod back.

And just like that, walking home with my *tamales*, and my own set of apartment keys, and nodding to all the people I saw this morning, and my legs a little shaky from running so hard, I'm starting to feel a little more cool and urban, like my mom said.

Before I can feel cool and urban for two whole minutes, I see somebody lying down right on the sidewalk, curled up in the corner of a vacant storefront. They're covered by a tattered green sleeping bag with dirty brown stuffing that bursts from the seam, and one bare, cracked foot sticks out from the bottom. The sleeping bag is pulled over their head and face, and I can't even tell whether this person is just sleeping or isn't alive. I stand there, staring at the bare foot, waiting for a twitch, and twenty-nine people pass by before I take a deep breath and walk off just like them.

On the next block, two kids race on scooters and a dog squats and poops right there on the curb.

The same guys are out in front of our building playing dominoes, and they smile and say *hola* and wave like I've been living here three years instead of one day. I smile back and hop up the three steps and unlock the two doors into our building. I race up to the third floor because I can't wait to tell them about how I showed Mr. Meathead, but I can hear my mom's voice before I reach our apartment door.

"Not once all day?" She's not exactly yelling, but I can tell she's not patting his shoulder and trying to understand either.

"We don't all have team-building events to attend," he responds.

I stick the key in the new dead bolt on our door and hear Mom say, "Shh, she's home. Just act happy, if that's not too much to ask."

"Act?" he whispers. "You want me to act?"

I push open the door.

"Rain!" Mom says. "You're home!"

Dad is wearing the flannel shirt he was wearing yesterday in the moving van, and it's still off a button, and I wonder if he ever even changed or if he slept like that. If so, he's been in that shirt, buttoned all wrong, for at least thirty-two hours. And that makes me feel terrible because before, Dad only wore shabby flannel shirts when he was gardening. And now he's wearing a shabby flannel and he doesn't even have a garden anymore.

"How was your first day? How was the walk home? Tell us everything," Mom says.

"It was OK." Except now it feels bad to talk about how I think I made a friend, maybe even two, so I just add, "I like my English teacher."

"That's good!" Mom says.

"And I need navy blue pants and white shirts for Monday."

She claps her hands once and grabs her keys from the counter. "Well, let's go!" But just then there's a knock at the door and it's a guy in a denim shirt.

"Cable," he mumbles.

Dad disappears into the bedroom and closes the door.

"Come in." Mom gestures toward the living room, and the cable guy starts unpacking a small box and playing with our new TV.

"And the landline here," Mom says, pointing to a

spot on the wall by the kitchen.

I roll my eyes because I'm the only kid in middle school who doesn't have a cell phone. Mom says there's enough research now to show how "all this technology" affects the brain and I have to wait until I'm thirteen.

She knocks on the bedroom door and calls to my dad that the cable guy is here and to come out because she has to leave with me to go shopping, but Dad's not responding.

"It's OK, Mom."

The cable guy is asking her a question and she's half talking to him, a quarter talking to me, and a quarter calling to my dad.

"I saw a couple of shops on Broadway with clothes in the windows," I tell her. I can just check them out. Really I'm thinking there's no way I'm going in any of those shops on Broadway by myself, but I'm definitely not staying in here for one more minute either, and maybe I'll just sit on the front stoop and read *Ivan* for a while.

The cable guy is drilling into the wrong spot for the landline phone, and Mom tells him to hold on.

"Are you sure? If you can't find anything, we'll go together this weekend. Promise." She hands me fifty dollars and tells me to put it in my wallet in the bottom of my book bag and not to take it out unless I'm buying something.

I nod.

"Sorry," she says, and puts her hands on my shoulders. "Be back in an hour. No later." She looks at her watch and I look at mine.

I nod.

Frankie's sitting on the stoop when I get outside.

"Hey!" I say, and she looks up.

"Hey yourself." Then she looks back down, like we didn't just smoke our whole class in the half mile, like we didn't just show Mr. Meathead to watch what he says about girls, and like we never made that triangle high five with Amelia.

And now I'm feeling stupid because even though she doesn't seem like the shopping type, neither am I, and for one second I thought maybe she'd come with me, and I wouldn't have to go in those shops alone. I thought maybe she could help me pick out navy blue pants and a white button-down shirt so I wouldn't stick out so much in school, and if they didn't speak English in the store she could translate for me because even though I know blue is *azul*, I don't know what navy blue is.

But she doesn't even look at me again.

"Guess I'll see you Monday," I say.

She crosses her arms over her knees and puts her head down. "Guess so."

And now I'm feeling even more stupid because I can't even sit on the front stoop and read and I don't have any place to go.

It isn't until I round the corner onto Broadway that I realize I'm still carrying the *tamales*. I never looked up how to eat them, and they're probably cold anyway, so I toss the bag in a trash can on the corner.

Broadway is crowded with people and sounds. A group of boys is playing three on three on the sidewalk outside a barbershop, faking left and right, weaving between people passing by, jumping over the heads of their opponents, and letting the basketball roll off their fingers through the bottom rung of a fire escape ladder. Friends cheer and chant for each basket from the hoods of parked cars and seats made of coolers and big, black speakers that vibrate with the same Spanish music that bounces around the alley and in through our apartment windows.

A delivery truck double-parks, and three men jump out and slide crates of food down a metal ramp to the street, load the boxes high onto handcarts, and wheel them to the grocery store. Cabs and buses honk, and drivers gesture out their windows and swerve into the next lane.

A woman on the corner sings a church song from deep in her chest and hands out pamphlets as people walk past.

I try to count all the people on the street, but they're moving too fast from block to block, and I have to start over three times before I give up.

I pass one of the stores with clothes hanging in the window. There are two racks outside the door on the sidewalk jammed with pants and shirts in no order with a sign that says *descuento*, and a cardboard box of white socks that come in packages of eight. Inside looks small and dark, and I wonder if it even has dressing rooms. I hear two men in the store speaking in Spanish that's too fast to catch and I try to remember the lesson from our textbook about buying items. *¿Cuánto cuesta esta camiseta?* But everything sounds wrong in my head, and they'd probably respond too quickly for me to understand the answer anyway.

I pretend to look through the clothing on the racks for thirty seconds, then I keep walking before anyone can come out and ask me if I need any help. I can't go home yet, and walk past hot-and-cold Frankie sulking on the stoop, and back up to apartment thirty-one, where there are too many closed doors, so I just keep going along Broadway.

I pass by the bar where people sit outside on long picnic tables, clinking glasses of beer, and next door there's a sandwich board sign open on the sidewalk that says *Hamilton Heights Café* with an arrow pointing down five stairs into a basement. I peek into the café and see people sitting around small tables with steaming mugs. Some stare at laptops, some read and write notes in the margins of their books, some are sitting back with their legs crossed and chatting.

This is the kind of place where I could read *Ivan*, so I hurry down the stairs and order a big hot chocolate with extra whipped cream from a barista with long hair and a backward baseball hat who says, "Enjoy!" I take out my book and read at a little square table for the whole forty-eight minutes that I have left to be away from the apartment before I'm late.

In my book, the main character, a silverback gorilla named Ivan, is describing his domain in the zoo-themed mall, and I think I know how he feels. He's the only one of his kind there, and he's lonely, and has that same missing that rises up.

It isn't until I look up from page seventy-nine that I realize that this café is different from my building, and different from my school, and different from the street. I hear mostly English, and my skin matches lots of other skin here. And why is a big who-knows because I don't match fourteen out of fifteen of the people who walk by outside. And I don't match any of the thirty-three kids in my class.

Frankie is gone from the stoop when I get there. Our cable is hooked up and working, and mounted on the wall outside the kitchen is a landline telephone. And it's not even cordless. Ten boxes are empty, broken down, and leaning by the door, which means there's one more, besides my two, that is packed up and tucked away somewhere, and I'm 98 percent certain it's the *Garden* box.

And the bedroom door is still closed.

"Rain!" Mom says the second she hears me click open our dead bolt. She stands up from the wires she's trying to reroute around the bookshelf. "I'm so sorry. We ended up with a different cable package, and I had to—"

"It's OK."

"Did you find anything?" Mom asks.

"Just hot chocolate."

She gives me a big hug. "Oh, my little Raindrop. I love you so," she says and kind of rocks me back and forth once. Then she holds me out at arm's length and starts listing all the best shopping spots in the city, and which subways go there, and how she's already called and knows where every pair of navy blue pants from here to Fifty-Ninth Street is.

Tears sting behind my eyes because I wish she would rock me back and forth one or two more times and repeat, *Oh, my little Raindrop*, over and over again. I wish she'd just cry so that I could cry too and it wouldn't feel like we're a retaining wall holding back soil that just wants to crumble out and is so tired of being packed in tight.

But I know she can't. She has to hold me out by the shoulders and she has to keep everything packed inside like she has since that night.

"I need ten hours of community service by June eighteenth," I tell her because it's the only thing I can think to say.

She points at me and smiles. "I'm on it," she says.

CHAPTER 12

That Night

I made my footsteps as quiet as possible, staying up on the balls of my feet as I passed their bedroom. From the bathroom I could see right down the stairs to the front door, where Guthrie had his hand on the knob.

Then we locked eyes, held up our hands, and counted out together silently on our fingers.

One, two, three.

CHAPTER 13

A Man Named Nestor

"Wakey, wakey!" Mom's pulling on my toes. "We're going to church!" And never in my eleven years, four months, and one day have I ever heard my mom say that. And that's a fact.

In Vermont, what Sundays were for depended on the season. In the winter, Sundays were for skiing. "Closer to God up here anyway," Dad would say as we'd ride the quad chairlift, side by side by side by side, high up into the mountain. In the spring, Sundays were for tilling, and weeding, and planting. Summer was for barbecues and swimming, and eating vegetables right off the branch. Fall was for harvesting, and canning, and prepping the garden for a long winter. But never once was a Sunday for church.

It's our first Sunday in New York City and all of a sudden I'm getting up, putting on a new pair of navy blue pants, and buttoning up one of my new white shirts that Mom and I bought yesterday in a neighborhood five subway stops away, but felt like a whole different city. They're the nicest clothes I have now, and Mom says I can't wear jeans and a T-shirt to church. This feels way different, way worse, than dirt under my fingernails, and it's June, so Sundays should be for dirt.

"We're not going for the service," Mom says. "We're going to help cook a meal for the homeless. Community service, remember?" Then she's hustling off to the kitchen to silence a whistling kettle and I'm thinking about the cracked, bare foot I saw sticking out from the green sleeping bag on Broadway and wondering if that person is still there.

My parents' bedroom door is closed when I slide into my shoes and I try a secret little message to my dad again. I try telling him that I don't really want to go to a church either, but I wish he'd come with us anyway.

"Let's go," Mom says, and we open the door and click the dead bolt locked.

It's only three blocks from our apartment, but the whole walk I'm tugging at my shirt and wishing I were wearing overalls and working compost into the soil.

The church has a bell tower that stretches up taller than all the buildings around it. It has high arched windows, and heavy front doors, and old gray stones that look like they belong in a history book.

The music inside soars. It breaks through the heavy doors, pushes against the thick stone walls, and tumbles down the wide front stairs. The sound of hundreds of voices breaking apart and coming together makes my heart beat fast. And I'm thinking that Guthrie would love this.

A few people walking by stop on the street and listen too. Some make imaginary crosses by tapping their forehead, then each shoulder, mumbling a quiet prayer, and closing their eyes.

"Beautiful," Mom whispers. And we just stand and stare toward the doors, as if we can see the music in the air. And I can tell the voices sing right to my mom's heart too, because she breathes in so deep I can hear it, and she closes her eyes. But before she really lets the voices sink in too deep, she pulls on my hand. "We're supposed to meet in the kitchen in the basement." Then we hustle off around the side of the church, down a set of stairs, and knock on a little red door.

A small woman with gray-streaked hair pulled back in a short braid opens the door, and my mom starts in about how she had called to volunteer.

"*Bienvenido, bienvenido. Gracias,*" the woman says and waves us in.

She doesn't speak much English, but we find out her name is Claudia and she pronounces it like the clouds in the sky and I think it's just as beautiful as the singing that's tumbling down the front steps of the church.

Claudia speaks in short English sentences, and my mom responds with a couple of words in Spanish.

"Sandwich. Bread." Claudia points toward a counter and opens a drawer with knives. Then she points to the refrigerator and takes out sandwich meat and cheese.

"*Está bien,*" Mom replies. "*¿Aquí?*"

"Yes, yes, *sí.*"

Before too long we're making turkey and cheese sandwiches and chopping cucumbers for a salad. Another woman shows up at the little door and hugs Claudia and speaks one-hundred-miles-per-hour Spanish that I can't catch a word of. Then another arrives with a tray of food that she slides into the oven. There are six of us by the end, and Claudia introduces us to them all. They come here every Sunday. I can tell because of how fast they talk and tight they hug. Today is just our first time, but everyone is as warm as this kitchen, with bread baking and rice simmering and a basket of cookies covered with a red-checked cloth keeping the chocolate chips melty.

Then Claudia asks me to come here and shows me

how to stir the soup in a big pot on the stove. I move the wooden spoon in big, slow, clockwise circles and watch the chicken and vegetables follow around and around. Then I switch to counterclockwise and the chicken and vegetables scatter and resist and sink and bob, and it takes a few circles for them to follow their new direction.

It makes me think of Dad, and I wonder if he's just sinking and scattering and soon he'll catch on and come out and change his shirt and kiss my forehead like he used to, even if I'm too old for that now.

It's hard when someone switches your direction on you fast. And that's a fact.

Before the remembering can rise up too fast, there's a quiet knock on the door and it creaks open, and this time it's not someone here to help. It's someone who needs help.

He's tall and his shoulders are wide. His face is a map of old lines that's been folded over and over along the same creases and his hair is tight and gray and curls all over his head, thinning at the top. His clothes are dirty and loose, and he walks favoring his left foot.

He smiles at Claudia and she takes his arm. "*¿Como está*, Nestor?"

"Can't complain," he says, and his voice is as deep and rumbling as the subway trains that pass under our feet on Broadway. I don't know if Claudia understands his English, but she smiles and nods and pats his arm, leads him to a table and pours him a cup of water.

For one minute I think this might be the person I saw on the street, and I'm relieved that he was just sleeping. But when he sits down I notice his shoes, worn and ripped, plastic bags shoved into holes and taped over, socks loose and brown and sinking below his ankles. The person beneath the green sleeping bag didn't have shoes.

Now more people are coming through the church basement door. Another older man walks in with a black hat and three layers of T-shirts poking out from the neck of his baggy sweater, then a woman younger than my mom who's holding the hand of a little girl who's holding the hand of a teddy bear. The little girl is wearing pajamas with feet and a too-big black jacket.

"*Hola*, Natasha," Claudia says, bending down and tucking the girl's hair behind her ears. The girl smiles and wags her bear, and Claudia gestures toward the tables.

I'm stirring the soup and pouring two ladles full in each bowl like Claudia showed me and I'm feeling uncomfortable in my new white shirt. Mom is spreading mayonnaise on sandwich bread. She gives me a half smile across the kitchen, and I know what it means. This is hard. It's hard to see people who need. But it's good we're helping, and not just to get hours for some piece of paper so I can go on to seventh grade.

Claudia grabs two bowls of soup and gestures for me to do the same, and I follow her out to the tables, where there are now eighteen people waiting for water and sandwiches and soup. They chat with each other or stare off somewhere else; some fold their arms on the table and bury their faces in their sleeves.

I place a bowl in front of Nestor. He looks up. "You're new."

I nod.

"I'm old," he says, and smiles. And it makes me laugh a little, but I stop fast because I don't want to be laughing at him.

"No, no, laugh out loud, new kid," he says, and he lets out a big, rumbling laugh, so I laugh again with him and he gets going pretty good but manages to chuckle out, "Old as dirt, I am."

He puts out his hand. "Nestor."

I shake it because it's polite, but his nails are dirty and it's not because he's been digging potatoes. "Rain," I say.

I return to the kitchen and when Nestor's not looking I wash my hands with lots of soap and it makes me feel terrible. Then I serve the rest of the soup bowls and fill water cups and I watch Nestor as he slurps his soup and takes small bites of his sandwich until it's all gone.

When everyone leaves, Claudia puts a brown bag of leftovers in each hand. They say *thank you* and *adiós* and *gracias* and *see you next week*. Mom and I stay to scrub the pots and take out the garbage, and it feels wrong to pull out my community service log and have Claudia sign it, but I have to pass to the seventh grade, so I do.

"*Muchas gracias*," she says and when she smiles she has three little wrinkles that reach out from her eyes, lines that my mom calls crow's-feet. They're the mark of a kind life, she tells me on the way home. And I hope that I get crow's-feet when I get old, old like Claudia. Old like Nestor.

CHAPTER 14

A Deal with Frankie

I get to Mrs. Baldwin's English class before everyone else and enter on my own because Amelia gets pulled for speech therapy at lunch on Mondays, so we can't walk in together.

I take out my folder. It feels better to have two hours of community service signed on my log, clothes that match everyone else's, and new notebooks that aren't filled with all my classwork from my old school, but I still feel like the only silverback gorilla in a domain that doesn't quite fit right.

Kids arrive two by two or in groups of three, jumping up to slam the top of the door frame like basketball stars, and laughing about something that I missed.

Finally Amelia comes in, and it already makes me feel a little better.

She smiles big and waves when she sees me and sits down at her desk on my right.

Frankie comes in next and slumps into her desk on my left and she's still not looking in my direction. Amelia raises her eyebrows like *What's wrong with her?* and I shrug.

Mrs. Baldwin is calling for attention. Kids are still talking, most in Spanish, and even though I'm really trying, they're talking too fast for me to pick out all the words I recognize and then make those into a sentence that makes sense, like the word jumble puzzles Dad used to pull out of the newspaper and help me unscramble until the letters turned into meaning.

I stick my hands in my desk even though I know I haven't put anything in there, and I feel a piece of paper. It's crinkled in a ball, so I open it up and flatten it out against my desk. Little jotted notes in two different handwritings fill the page, two different-colored pens, back and forth. I can't really follow the conversation, even though it's mostly in English, because it twists down the margin and crams into the corners and has arrows pointing to the back.

Before I can figure out where the notes start, Frankie

grabs it out of my hand and crumples it back up into a ball.

"None of your business," she says, and before I can say sorry, there's a knock on the classroom door. It's a tall, dark-skinned man, my dad's age, with a thick accent that doesn't sound like our super's or any of the people's at the church kitchen. He's wearing a navy zip-up track jacket and mesh running cap, the kind you can dunk in the stream and put back on your head and your whole body cools down and feels like it can go one more mile. And I'm wondering where runners dunk their caps here in New York City.

"A minute with these three, please," he says to Mrs. Baldwin. And he's pointing his long finger at Frankie, then at Amelia. Then at me.

I look behind me and jab my thumb to my chest. "Me?"

"You."

Frankie grumbles. "Coach . . ."

But he gives her a look that makes her stop. She sighs and takes her time walking to the door. Amelia and I follow.

"I'm Coach Okeke," he says. "And I hear you can run."

I nod my head yes, because that's a fact.

"Frankie's already on my team, and even though she's only in the sixth grade, she has a definite shot at

winning the 100m at the middle school city championships in a couple of weeks."

Frankie smiles and puts her hands on her hips.

"And she *did* have a real shot at winning the 4x100m
relay," he adds.

Frankie's smile disappears.

"But one of her teammates moved, one pulled a muscle in practice last week, and one can't get out of a family
reunion." Coach Okeke pauses, and I can tell he wants
to roll his eyes about that last one, but instead he says,
"So right now, it's just Frankie, and she can't run it by
herself. If we want to send a relay to the city championships meet, we have to fill those spots."

"Coach, we have—"

He cuts her off and points a long finger right down at
her. "You want to win?"

Frankie looks right back at him. "You know I do,"
she answers.

"Then from what I've heard you are going to want
these two on your team." He nudges his head in our
direction.

Frankie looks down at her Flyknit Racers. She still
has the note from my desk in her right hand, and she's
crushing it into a smaller ball in her fist.

"Practice starts at three." He says it like we've
already agreed and had our parents sign papers and

paid for a uniform and everything. Like he won't take no for an answer.

Every muscle in my running legs wants to join the track team and run every day and win the relay and write to Coach Scottie so she could be proud, but I know that even if I help at the church both Sundays until the community service hours are due I will still only have six hours, so I have to get busy after school too, which doesn't include training for the city championships, and I just want to yell that it's all so unfair.

I crack my knuckles hard, but before I can tell Coach Okeke that I wish I could, Amelia is shaking her head no and saying thanks anyway, but the words get stuck in her mouth, so she reaches for the classroom door and disappears inside.

"I can't either," I tell him. "I just moved here and I have all this community service to catch up on. I'll never be able to finish it."

Now both Frankie and Coach Okeke are looking at me like they wish I'd change my answer to yes because I really can run. I wish I could say yes too, because Frankie's the kind of girl you want on your team. And that's a fact.

"Sorry." I open the door and walk back to my desk.

Frankie stays in the hallway with Coach Okeke for another few minutes, and just as she gets back to her desk, Mrs. Baldwin is calling for us to open our note-books and draw a big heart right in the middle of the page.

I'm not the best at drawing, and I want to get the heart perfectly symmetrical, but I can't, so I keep erasing and starting again. We're supposed to be filling our heart with things and people that are important to us, but I can't even get the dumb heart to look right.

"Can we write important places too?" a boy behind me asks.

"What a bright idea," Mrs. Baldwin responds. Then she adds something to her own heart, which is drawn up on the SMART board.

A boy in the front row punches the boy next to him in the shoulder and snickers, "I bet I know someone you're writing in your heart." The whole row erupts and even Amelia giggles. The boy punches his friend back in the shoulder and says, "I bet I know someone who *isn't* putting *you* in her heart."

This makes Frankie crack up too and everyone says, "Ohhhhh," and even Mrs. Baldwin seems like she's in on the joke because I can tell she's trying not to laugh and then she says, "OK, OK, very funny. But I don't want you *all* writing about love and heartbreak. I'm not sure I can handle that much sappy poetry."

This makes the class laugh harder and go, "Ohhhhh!"

again like Mrs. Baldwin is the coolest for being in on all the crush drama. And now I really feel like a one-and-only.

Mrs. Baldwin gets the class to calm down and start jotting in their notebooks again, and Frankie reaches over and kind of taps my arm, which makes a blip in the bottom of my heart just when I was about to get it perfect.

"We could make a deal," she says.

I write *Mom and Dad* right in the middle of my heart so I have something there in case Mrs. Baldwin starts circling around and checking our progress. Then I look up at Frankie.

"I'll tell you a place you can get your community service hours fast, if you join the track team." She taps her pencil on her desk. "I want to win," she says.

Then she's telling me about a place called Ms. Dacie's and how kids go there after school to get help with homework, or attend events, play games, or just to talk.

"How is that community service?" I ask.

"Dacie always says, 'You are serving this community just by being here.' Plus, she rounds up. I already have thirty hours," Frankie says, "and I haven't missed a track practice yet."

The whole time she's telling me, she's staring at my desk. At the eraser shavings I made into little ski mountains evenly spaced along the pencil groove, and at the corner of my folder that I creased into a perfect equilateral triangle, and at the *Guthrie* that I wrote at the very bottom of my heart because that's where I keep him. But I wrote it in small letters because it also hurts.

"Practice is at three," she says. "Then I'll show you Ms. Dacie's."

I look at Amelia, and she's still shaking her head no.

It's enough getting through school, she writes on her notebook page and passes it to me, and the way she's looking at me I know that she doesn't mean schoolwork is too hard for her: she means being around people and trying to talk all day is enough. She doesn't need a whole other group of people to feel embarrassed around after school.

The bell's ringing and Mrs. Baldwin's telling us to add to our hearts tonight because we're going to use them to write poetry tomorrow.

Someone calls out, *"Oooh, las rosas son rojas,"* and I actually understand all the words, so I laugh with the rest of the class and Mrs. Baldwin, and for three seconds it feels good.

Then I remember what Mrs. Baldwin said. That we're going to be writing poetry. I want to tell her that I don't write poetry, but I could write her an OK essay with organized paragraphs and a thesis statement if she wants, but before I can say anything she squats down by my desk.

"How's Ivan?" she asks.

"Sad," I tell her.

"And how are you?"

I don't even know how to respond because no one's asked me that for a long time and I don't actually know. I'm sad like Ivan, and scared, and every once in a while I feel pretty good, which makes me feel guilty and terrible.

"OK," I answer.

"I'm looking forward to reading your poetry," she says. I almost tell her I won't be writing any poetry because it's too loosey-goosey and I'll never get it right, but I crack my knuckles instead and she stands up from my desk.

Before I pack my bag and throw it over my shoulder, I peek at Frankie's desk. Her heart isn't symmetrical either, and she wrote *Ms. Dacie* right there in the middle. Then I see *Reggie* down at the bottom and it's in small writing too. She closes her notebook fast and stuffs it in her bag.

"Do we have a deal?" she asks.

And I'm thinking how much I miss my team back home, and how good it feels to run, and then I think about my dad's shirt buttons, and that maybe if I join track he'll come out and change into shorts and a clean T-shirt and stand next to Mom and cheer for me like he used to. And if we win the city championships, we'll have something to celebrate all together.

And then maybe this fresh start will begin working, and they could be that one out of four.

"Deal," I say.

CHAPTER 15

Secret Team Handshake

Fourteen of us girls are standing in the park behind the school, and even though I'm the only one without an MS 423 running tank top, this already feels more like my domain. Everyone is bouncing and stretching and looks like they're ready to spring into motion and cut through the air. I know that feeling. Frankie is hopping up and down too, warming her hamstrings, and reaching down to touch her Racers.

I'm calculating how many hours of community service I need to get each week if I keep up at the church kitchen on Sundays, and wishing that Amelia were here too. Then I'm replaying my dad's voice in my head when I called home to get permission to stay for track practice today. I had to call three times right in a row before he answered, and he had morning groggy pre-shower voice even though it was 2:49 in the afternoon. I wonder if he's been outside today.

Coach Okeke introduces me to the group and everyone smiles and says hi and some shout out their names. "I'm Cristina!" and "I'm Ariel." I hear Daniela and Ashley and Roxanna, and then all the other voices blend together. I smile and wave.

They're all hopping and stretching and wanting to know where we're running today.

"Follow me!" Coach Okeke says, and takes off through the park.

"*¡Vámanos!*" yells one of the girls, and we all take off after Coach.

We circle around a swimming pool with six lanes and a diving board that isn't open yet for the season, and down a steep set of stairs. We're running along a path behind the school and then across basketball courts where a group of boys are changing their sneakers on the sidelines and getting ready to play, then down a sidewalk with big buildings stretching up and up, and weaving around people walking their dogs.

Frankie is out front, right on Coach Okeke's heels, and I'm just behind her, but we're running in a big pack of fourteen girls and I can hear all the footsteps on the pavement around us and I like the way that sounds. Like rain.

Coach Scottie's voice is in my head. *Eyes up. Hut hut hut!* I lift my eyes and look forward—down the sidewalk and toward the car-jammed bridge that leads over the river.

"That's Yankee Stadium!" Coach Okeke shouts back to me, and points across the river. Tall white pillars reach up and up and tower over kids playing in the parks below.

And just like that, even though Guthrie's guitar pick rubs against my left thigh each stride, I'm not thinking about how many hours I need for anything, or that I'm not wearing the right running clothes because I didn't know I'd be joining the track team today. I'm not thinking about any closed doors, or the pained faces of people who need, or anything about that night. It's just one step, then the next, and the air that I'm cutting through, and the burn in my legs. It's just my inhale and exhale and my arms pumping and my feet turning over and over. It's just forward and forward and never back.

Then I hear footsteps pull up next to mine and a girl with dark skin and dark curly hair pulled into two tight buns on the top of her head says, "I'm Ana."

"Rain," I say, with my next inhale.

She's built like Amelia, short and slight, and takes

quick strides that turn over fast.

And before we've run five more blocks I learn that she's in sixth grade too, but in a different homeroom, and that she just started racing this year.

"You're fast," I breathe.

Out of the corner of my eye I can tell she's smiling. "You too."

Coach Okeke ends practice back in the park and holds his cap under the stream of a water fountain before we cool down and stretch. I tell my brain that I can forget about looking that up.

After, when Frankie and I are heading toward the school to grab our bags and go see Ms. Dacie, he calls out, "Teach her the secret team handshake!"

We look back and I see Ana waving bye. I wave back. And that feels good.

"Don't forget!" Coach Okeke yells. "She needs to know it!"

Frankie nods, and we keep on walking.

Ms. Dacie's is between school and home, which is perfect because I can't waste any minutes getting to community service if I'm going to finish my hours, figure out how to write poetry, and win the state championships.

On the way there, Frankie doesn't teach me any handshake, and we don't really talk about anything, but when we pass the vacant storefront I notice the body is gone, but the green sleeping bag and a dented plastic water bottle without its cap are still there, pushed into the corner of the sidewalk. And now I'm wondering if that person actually lives there and will just return back when they're tired to take a swig of water and sleep.

Ms. Dacie's is on a street of three-story buildings that look more like houses, with swooping front steps that lead to heavy wooden doors. There's even a strip of space between Ms. Dacie's and the place next to hers. It's full of overgrown and tangled green, but a garden used to be there. And that's a fact because I can see the raised wooden beds beneath the snarls of weeds.

There's a faded sign—*Ms. Dacie's*—that hangs on the unkempt garden's gate.

We hop up the steps and Frankie rings the doorbell. Above the bell is a peephole and a sticker—an equilateral triangle with one stripe for each color of the rainbow, ROY G BIV, in order. Beneath the triangle it says *Safe Space*. There's another sticker that has a cross like the one on top of the bell tower at the church, next to a six-pointed star made from two triangles, next to a waning crescent moon with a five-pointed star cradled in its nook, and a couple of other symbols I don't recognize. Beneath all the symbols it says *Welcome*.

A boy answers the door. He looks a little older than

we are, and he doesn't make eye contact, but not in the same way Frankie didn't make eye contact when she first showed up at our apartment door. He seems quiet and shy.

"Hey, Frankie," he says, looking down at the welcome mat, and I wonder if he recognizes her by her Flyknit Racers.

"Hey, Casey. This is Rain."

I put my hand out to shake his, and Frankie pulls my arm back gently. "Casey doesn't like shaking hands," she says, and I kind of push the toe of my Adidas Ultraboosts forward into his vision instead.

"Welcome," he says and opens the door wide. "Frankie's here!" he hollers. "She brought a friend!" When he says *friend*, I look at Frankie and Frankie looks at me.

"She just needs community service," she tells him, but she doesn't say I'm *not* her friend.

We follow Casey down a skinny hallway, past a bulletin board stuck with old-fashioned Polaroid photographs of smiling kids, and dozens of fliers for events like Saturday tutoring sessions and an evening music class. The hallway leads into a big open room with couches and tables and chairs and two old desktop computers and shelves stacked high with books and games and school supplies. Three kids are playing cards at one table, slapping their hands down hard and laughing, and two others are doing homework on the couch.

Someone else is stretched out and propped up on her elbows on the floor with a sketch pad and is drawing some kind of superhero comic strip. And I actually do a double take, because when she looks up, I realize it's Ana from the track team. She must be even faster than I thought because she beat us here and we left school before she did.

"Hi!" she says when she sees us.

"You really *are* fast," I tell her.

She smiles. "I ran."

Her comic strip is black and white, except for the superhero's cape, which she's shading in with a bright red colored pencil. The cape is the same design as the flag I saw hanging in the apartment window when we first drove into Washington Heights, the flag I saw on Frankie's shirt.

Her drawing is good. Really good. It looks like it could be in the graphic novels bin of Mrs. Baldwin's classroom library.

I hear pans clang from the kitchen, and Frankie nudges me in that direction. There are two kids at the counter rolling cookie dough into balls and placing them on a foil-covered baking sheet. Flour dusts the kitchen floor and puffs big white polka dots on the kids' aprons. Open bags of sugar and measuring spoons and a cutting board of chopped walnuts clutter the counter, and it smells amazing.

"Dacie," Frankie says. A tall, curvy, pillowy woman with gray curly hair pulled back in a big purple clip turns around from the oven.

She smiles at Frankie and gives her a big hug, which surprises me because Frankie doesn't seem like the kind of person who would want someone hugging her, but her skinny body disappears easily into Ms. Dacie's embrace.

Then she holds out a big wooden mixing spoon. "Dough?" she offers. "Chocolate chip today."

Frankie takes a glob in her fingers. "My favorite."

Then Ms. Dacie spots me and she peers over the frames of her round, purple glasses. "And who do we have here?"

"This is Rain."

"Rain," she says, and the way she says it *sounds* like rain, like the kind of rain that comes when the sun is still shining, unexpected and calm and falling off easy, leaving everyone looking up in wonder.

"Welcome, Rain," she says. Then she's pulling me into a hug too, even though I just met her four seconds ago. Then I'm pressing a pinch of cookie dough to the roof of my mouth, and Dacie is telling me how a kitchen is no kitchen at all unless it smells like cookies baking.

She introduces me to everyone there. Alia and

Edwin are in the kitchen and Matthew, Jer, and Trevor are playing cards. Yasmin and Cris are doing homework, and Ana is still sketching her comic. Even though I don't recognize anyone else but Ana from my school, and my skin doesn't match any skin here either, I'm not sticking out, because Edwin's hair is blue and spiky, and Cris has short shaved hair like Frankie, but with a tiny Mohawk and zigzags shaved above her ears. Jer has black makeup on his eyes and Alia wears a silver-and-red scarf over her head, even in the hot kitchen with the oven running. Casey is organizing the books on the shelves from largest to smallest and I secretly want to hug him because that's how I would organize it too. But something tells me that Casey doesn't like hugs much, not even from Ms. Dacie.

Everyone looks up and smiles and says hi and asks about where I'm from and what my name means. And it doesn't even feel bad to tell them I'm from 288 miles away in Vermont and my dad is this hippie gardener guy so he named me Rain, and my brother Guthrie, which means wind, and he used to sing this silly song to us that went, *Oh, the wind and rain* . . .

Saying Guthrie's name doesn't even feel so bad, maybe because there's more furniture and people and things in this little place than in ours on 152nd Street, so it settles into the soft spaces instead of dropping hard on the brand-new wood floors of apartment number thirty-one.

"Make yourself at home," Dacie says. So I pull up a chair at one of the computers in the living room to look up all the things I've told my brain to remember, like who the Mirabal Sisters are, and how to eat a *tamal*.

Then I check to see if Dr. Cyn has added anything to her blog about marriage and grief because even though I want Mom's big fresh start in New York City to be working, I don't think it is yet.

I'm reading that finding ways to remember him is important. Looking at photographs and sharing happy memories might help, or finding a way to honor him. But even reading about remembering makes that feeling rise on up and I log off.

"Rain? Want to help me with these dishes?" Dacie is calling from the kitchen.

She hands me yellow plastic gloves and shows me how to plug up the sink with soapy hot water. There's a big mixing bowl and a small one, measuring cups and spoons, and glasses still frothy from milk.

Dacie hands Frankie a broom and dustpan, and I turn the water hotter. It feels good, burning even through the yellow gloves. I scrub hard at the big mixing bowl with the rough side of the sponge, and then I scrub the glasses. Steam rises up from the sink and settles on my face as I bend over and scour hard, trying to get rid of every last speck on a cutting board that has years of discolored slices across the plastic surface.

"That's OK, now, Child," Dacie says. Her hand is light on my back. "You can't expect it to go back to good as new." She takes the cutting board from my hands and starts drying it with a green dish towel. "But this'll do."

I nod, then wash the measuring cups and pass them to Dacie, who dries and puts things back where they belong. Then I drain the sink and watch the suds circle down and settle on the bottom of the sink with a layer of bubbles.

Before we leave, Dacie signs our community service logs, and even though I only really helped out for sixteen minutes of washing dishes and wiping up, she signs for the whole hour we were there.

"Thank you for coming," Dacie says. "And please come back." Her smile sends out those crow's-feet from the corners of her eyes, and I know what that means.

I say goodbye to Ana, who is still bent over her drawing. She looks up and waves. "See you tomorrow."

And that feels good. That no matter how the day goes tomorrow, whether I have to write a poem, or if I get in on a big class laugh, or if Mr. Meathead says something else that gets right under my skin, at least I have track practice to look forward to, running with

Frankie and Ana and all the other girls through Washington Heights.

When we're walking down the long hall, I glance at some of the old Polaroid pictures thumbtacked to the bulletin board. There's one of Alia and Jer holding a big platter of orange-frosted cookies and underneath it says, *Halloween Party.* Then there's one of Frankie with her arm around another girl. They're wearing track uniforms and both are laughing so hard the picture is kind of blurred. I don't recognize the girl in the picture from the team today.

Underneath the photo it says, *Frankie and Reggie, first track meet.*

I remember the purple marker *Reggie* across my homeroom desk, and the note that Frankie snatched fast from me today in English class, and the name at the bottom of her heart.

"She's my best friend," Frankie says. "She used to be in our class. Before you got here." And the way she says it tells me that she doesn't want to say anymore. She pushes open the heavy wooden door and opens the latch on the gate to the street.

The whole walk home I'm wondering if my parents' bedroom door will be open when I get there, and where Reggie went, and if that's her real name, and if Izzy got my letter yet. I have three chocolate chip cookies still warm from the oven wrapped in a paper towel in my book bag and I wonder if we have milk in our brand-new refrigerator.

The dominoes men tip their caps and say *hola* and hi as Frankie and I bounce up the three steps to our building.

"Dacie's is cool. I think I'll go back," I say before I start up the steps to the third floor.

Frankie doesn't say anything. She's unlocking the mailbox farthest to the right but before she pulls out the mail she calls, "Hey." I turn back and she walks up to me with her right fist clenched tight and I'm thinking she's going to punch my lights out for taking Reggie's seat in Ms. Merrill's homeroom class, but instead she bops her fist up and down three times in the air in front of me.

"Secret team handshake," she says.

She bounces her fist again and I match it with mine and then we're clutching palms and raising our arms up and waggling our fingers on the way back down and ending with a fist bump, a full-body spin around, and a head nod.

"Not bad," she says, then grabs her mail from the mailbox. "See you tomorrow."

CHAPTER 16

Anniversary

Their bedroom door is closed, but I'm feeling really good
from track practice, and meeting Ana, and Ms. Dacie's,
and the secret team handshake, and I want to creak it
open and tell my dad all about everything, but I'm afraid
if I do I'll see his off-by-a-button flannel and then I'll
have to feel that remembering rising up and ruining all
the good feeling I have.

Mom's unloading groceries into the refrigerator and
telling me about this great new market that just opened
up by the hospital and how they have organic produce
and we just might have to use our new oven tonight.

"There's something about a brand-new, fully renovated kitchen that feels clean and fresh," she says.
"Look! The manuals are still in all the appliances." She

pulls an instruction booklet from the top shelf of the refrigerator before she slides in a half gallon of milk.

Then she looks up. "Well," she says, "tell me about track! And community service!" She's putting red-leaf kale into the crisper. That's Dad's favorite to grow. *Easy, and plentiful, and downright delicious,* he always used to say, popping a still-sandy leaf in his mouth straight from the garden row.

We used to have this rule that for exciting news you had to wait for the whole family so that no one got to know first, and the teller would only have to share the story once so they could make it really good and not leave out any of the details. It already feels a little bad that I have exciting news to share at all and now if I wait for my whole family I'd be waiting forever.

What I really want is to tell Guthrie. He would love Ms. Dacie's.

I look at the closed bedroom door again and I take a big breath and walk over quietly on the balls of my feet. I knock lightly and Mom closes the refrigerator and stands up. I knock again, louder.

"Dad?"

There's rustling, and Dad clears his voice. "Yeah?"

"Can I come in?"

More rustling. "Yeah, yeah, of course."

I open the door slowly. He's propping himself up on

two pillows, like it's only a really bad cold and congestion he has, and if he just keeps upright and drinks lots of fluids, it'll clear up in a few days. There are three books and a newspaper scattered across the bed, and I wonder if he's done the word scramble yet or if he saved it for me. An empty plate and glass sit on the nightstand and he reaches over them to click on the bedside lamp.

"Hey there," he says. "I was just feeling a little tired, so I . . ." but I don't want him to explain because I already know what he's feeling tired of. Tired of how heavy his heart is and tired from carrying it around all day. And tired of watching Mom use her heavy heart as momentum, throwing its weight ahead and letting it drag her forward and forward, not looking back for him because she can't.

"Track was great," I blurt. "I'm only running one event at the city championship meet, the 4x100m relay, because I'm technically a last-minute alternate, but we're going to win," I say. "And we have a secret handshake."

He scooches over and I sit next to him on the edge of the bed. He's wearing a different shirt and his hair looks like it's been washed, but it's still sticking up all wild.

"Well, that is the best news I've heard in a long time," he says.

The same music starts up in the alley and the notes

ping back and forth off the buildings. Dad rolls his eyes and does a funny little dance. Then Mom comes in and sits next to me on the bed and Dad sits up taller and crosses his legs like a little kid in school ready for story time.

I tell them all about Mr. Meathead and how Frankie, Amelia, and I smoked our whole class, running like girls. Then I'm describing Coach Okeke and Ana and Ms. Dacie and all the kids there and how nice they are.

"And you wouldn't believe how overgrown her garden is. You can barely see the raised beds beneath all the weeds. Oh! And I brought back some cookies." I unzip my bag and pull out the paper towel that Dacie handed me on my way out the door. They are still warm and gooey and falling apart just the way I like them.

Mom hustles off to the kitchen, but comes right back with three glasses of milk, and Dad has a smudge of melty chocolate on his lip that makes Mom and me giggle.

"What?" he says, and even though he knows what, he pretends he doesn't and smears even more chocolate on his mouth the next bite. Then for a minute, he's my Dad from 354 days ago, making a goofy face and pushing his chocolaty lips out toward me. "What? I can't kiss my own daughter on the forehead?"

I scream and giggle and swipe at him with a pillow.

Chocolate smears across the brand-new white pillowcase. "Oh!" he says. "Why didn't you tell me I had chocolate on my face? I'm so embarrassed!"

We all laugh and finish the cookies and chug the milk and I show them the secret track team handshake.

"You have to stand up for the last part."

I pull the covers off Dad and grab his hand. He stands up and I'm surprised when I see his jeans. It must feel weird and uncomfortable to have on regular daytime clothes in bed, and I'm wondering if he really tried today. Really tried to get up and take a shower and go outside and turn on his computer and check to see if there are any companies who need a contractor to help with renovations. But then he just couldn't. Not yet.

"You start with a fist, like this." I show them all the moves of the secret handshake and how you spin your whole body around at the end.

"Here, try it with Mom. I'll judge."

They stand there face-to-face for eleven seconds without saying anything, and for all those seconds I wonder if this is the longest they've looked right at each other since that night, and if they're thinking about the track team or Dacie or the new refrigerator or what we'll have for dinner.

Or if they're always thinking about Guthrie.

Then Mom raises her fist and starts bopping it three

times. Dad joins in and then they're spinning and their fist bump is a little off, but they remember all the parts.

For five seconds, I think maybe all they needed was a team handshake. And now maybe they can start talking in quieter tones and not getting so frustrated and maybe we can all go to a museum or a restaurant or a big Broadway play, and they could be that one out of four.

But that's when I pull out the paperwork from Coach Okeke. It falls open to the team's calendar and right there on June fifteenth in big block letters with lots of exclamation points is *city championships!!!!*

We all see it at the same time and no one is laughing anymore, or doing any team handshake. Dad sits back down on the bed and Mom hustles off to the kitchen with the milk glasses and I can hear her drop them in the sink. The running water makes her seem two miles away, even though she's just six steps from us.

The city championships meet was supposed to give my parents something to do, together, like they used to, something to watch, and cheer. And it's on the worst day. The day we all wish we could just skip over and never see again ever. I wish the whole June fifteenth square of every calendar would just erase and everyone would go to bed on June fourteenth and wake up on June sixteenth so that we wouldn't have to figure out how to stop that terrible feeling from rising up harder than it usually does.

Even Dr. Cyn says that this day will be the toughest.

"Sorry," I whisper. "I don't have to—"

Dad reaches out and rests his hand on mine. Then he folds the calendar over so we don't have to look at that day. "Don't be sorry," he says. "Don't ever be sorry. It's not your fault."

I shove the papers back in my book bag and I try to smile at him before I leave, but I just want to crawl in with him and hide my face in the chocolate-smeared pillow and forget about blinking back the tears that burn behind my eyes.

I hear him say, "You're going to win that race, Rain." But I can't look back at him, propped up on his pillows with his outside clothes creased and wrinkled and given up on and twisted beneath the covers. Because he doesn't know. It is my fault.

CHAPTER 17

That Night

I tried to wait four whole minutes between each time I pressed the light on my digital watch beneath the comforter to check the time. I counted out perfect seconds in my head, one-one-thousand, two-one-thousand, three-one-thousand, and tried not to peek.

12:34 . . . 12:38 . . . 1:02 . . . 1:06 . . . 1:10 . . .

Until the phone rang at 2:41. It rang four long rings. Four-one-thousand, five-one-thousand. I kept counting, thinking that if I could just keep count, keep track of the minutes, that everything would be OK.

But counting out perfectly even seconds never kept anyone safe. And that's a fact.

CHAPTER 18

One and Only

Now that I know who she is, I'm seeing little signs of Reggie everywhere. A poster board project about the water cycle in our science classroom has her name on it, and even though Mrs. Baldwin tried to cover her name with a white sticker label on my used classroom binder, you can still see *Reggie* peeking through. I wrote Rain on the new label in black marker, tracing Reggie's *R*, but I couldn't make my name stretch as long as hers to cover it all up. She still has a locker in the sixth-grade hallway with her name spelled out in blue star stickers across the metal. I wonder why she left before the end of the year, and I wonder if her mom got some new fancy job and they had to leave all their furniture behind too.

I don't know how to tell Frankie that I can't be on

the track team and that I definitely can't run in the city championships on June fifteenth, so I do what Amelia does when she thinks she can't get something out. I jot it on a piece of notebook paper—*I can't be on track anymore. Sorry.*—and pass it to my right. Frankie grabs it quick when Mrs. Baldwin is looking the other way.

She writes something and passes it back. *Too bad. You're running.*

No, I'm not. I hand it back.

This time, she just crosses out what I wrote and leaves the note there on her desk like she doesn't even have time for this.

And even though it feels good that Frankie's starting to be nice to me again, introducing me to Dacie and helping me with community service, and not glaring at me, I know she wants me to race so she has a shot at winning the relay. And I know that when I quit, Frankie will go back to glaring at me.

They'll probably have to change the secret handshake too. Which sucks. And I don't even care if I'm not supposed to use the word *sucks*, because it's been feeling pretty good to have fourteen other hands that I can bop and bump, and do a complete turn around, wiggle, and nod with.

Amelia is tugging on my sleeve and raising her eyebrows like *What?*

I whisper, "I'm quitting track."

"Alr-r-ready?"

Someone behind us giggles and Mrs. Baldwin looks over. Then she tells us to get in our groups of three to share the hearts we created yesterday.

Frankie and Amelia slide their desks toward me and we're back in a triangle, with our notebooks out.

"You're not quitting," Frankie states, like it's up to her.

"Yes, I am," I say back, matching her tone, because it's actually my decision and not hers, and she doesn't know anything about why I can't run.

Amelia raises her eyebrows again. She wants to know why.

"The city championships. I just—can't run that day."

Her eyebrows are still up, and now Frankie's are too.

"It's just a bad day for me," I say. "A really, really bad day."

"Th-th-that's wh-why you should run," Amelia starts, but then she writes the rest in her notebook and passes it to me. *You told me running empties your brain. Sounds like a good activity for a bad day.*

I don't respond.

"Sorry," I say to Frankie.

"Whatever," she says.

And just like that Frankie's back to hating me.

Mrs. Baldwin kneels down by our group and asks us a couple of questions about what's on our notebook hearts. I tell her about Vermont and Izzy and all the things that are high up in my heart, but I cover the small letters at the bottom with the palms of my hands.

When she stands back up, Mrs. Baldwin announces that "Poetry is born of feelings," and she tells us that we can write things on our hearts that are important to us, but also things that make us feel other emotions, like anger, or sadness, or missing.

That feeling rises on up and even though I don't want to ever see that day again, my hand starts writing in tiny letters down by Guthrie's name, *June fifteenth*. Amelia presses her lips together and lowers her eyes like she understands now how hard that day must be.

Mrs. Baldwin starts showing us how to take one thing from our notebook hearts and turn it into a poem.

Most everyone in the class is excited about poetry because poetry means no rules. No sentences, no periods, lines can be short or long, or anything you want. But I like rules; they make me feel safe and contained and that's why no one should sneak out or break curfew, and that's why I don't write poetry. And that's a fact.

Amelia slides her notebook to me again. *I still think you should run.*

"You're not running," I say. "Just because you have a stutter and don't want to have to talk more . . ." I snap it a little too quick and a little too loud, but once it's out I can't quiet it down and or pull it back, and Amelia looks down at her hands and when she does I see what's written at the bottom of her heart, in tiny little handwriting. *Stutter.*

She picks up her stuff and asks Mrs. Baldwin if she can work in the classroom library by pointing to her notebook and pointing to the corner where the couch and all of Mrs. Baldwin's bins of books are. Mrs. Baldwin nods and Amelia sits down with her back to the rest of the class.

Frankie's shaking her head and still not looking at me either and I'm feeling more alone than the one and only Ivan, because even he has Bob the dog and Stella the elephant, at least for a little while.

Then Mrs. Baldwin stops by our group again and Frankie's telling her about how she's writing a poem about track. Mrs. Baldwin nods her head and touches her shoulder like she knows that's important and a perfect thing to write a poem about. Frankie's poem is already stretching toward the bottom of her notebook. She's biting her tongue and flipping the page and writing more.

How anyone can just write a poem like that is a big who-knows.

I'm looking over at Amelia, who has her head bent over her notebook too, and I wonder what she's writing, and I know that I should go say sorry, because I am, but Mrs. Baldwin is still at our group and now she's looking at me.

"I don't really write poetry," I tell her.

She sits down in Amelia's empty chair and points at my notebook heart. "Have you chosen a topic?"

I point at *Izzy* because I don't want her eyes drifting to the bottom of my heart and seeing what I've written in little letters there.

"Great," Mrs. Baldwin says. "Finding a topic is the first step." But the bell's ringing and it's time to go. "Well, give it a shot tonight. Write about Izzy. See what happens."

I nod my head, but what I'm really thinking is, *I can write about Izzy all I want, but it's not going to come out as a poem.*

It's time for gym but Mrs. Baldwin asks if she can see me quick after class. Frankie's first out the door because gym's her favorite period and she's not missing one minute. Everyone else is packing up their book bags and starting loud conversations that will roll out with them into the hallway. Amelia finishes writing in her notebook and is the last one to leave.

I catch up to her before she reaches the door, and I don't know why it's so hard to say I'm sorry, but it gets caught up in my throat, and so I jot it down on the corner of her notebook tucked under her arm.

She reads it and gives me a sort of half smile like she understands, but her heart probably still hurts.

OK, she jots on the corner of my notebook, and then she leaves.

I pack up my book bag and zip it shut and turn around to see what Mrs. Baldwin wants to talk to me about.

"Just checking in to see how Ivan is," she says.

"He's awful." I take out the book and show her where my bookmark sticks out from the pages.

"Have you gotten to the part where . . ."

I nod because I know exactly what horrible, horrible part she's talking about. The part about Stella the elephant, and how that makes Ivan even more alone.

Now Ruby, the new baby elephant, is the one and only of her kind too. Thinking about it again makes me wish I'd had a better apology for Amelia, and I almost run to catch up with her, but I can tell Mrs. Baldwin is waiting for me to tell her more.

"Ivan just made this impossible promise to take care of Ruby and make sure she doesn't grow up in that domain like Stella did. But I don't know how he's going to get her out. He's just a gorilla."

"He's an awfully loyal gorilla," Mrs. Baldwin says.

I nod.

Then Mrs. Baldwin gestures toward the library. "Why don't you grab a book of poetry too? Maybe reading a few poems will help you write some of your own."

I nod and search her *Poetic Novels* bin, because if I have to read poetry, I at least want it to be a story too.

I pull out *The Crossover* by Kwame Alexander, because it has a cool cover with a basketball player on the front. I'm about to write my name on the index card in the back when I see that the last person to read this book too was Reggie and I'm wondering if we have the exact same taste in books, and if she plays basketball and if our school even has a basketball team.

She checked out the book on May seventeenth in curvy handwriting.

Reggie Muñoz.

And then my brain makes one hundred clicks. Our mailbox. *Muñoz.* Frankie's face on the stoop when she first found out I was moving into apartment thirty-one. Her face when she peered past me and into our living room, and how she said, *It looks different.* The picture of them in their track uniforms, laughing. Thirty-four kids in our class minus one is thirty-three, and plus one back is thirty-four.

I canceled out Reggie Muñoz.

I moved into her apartment. I'm sitting at her empty desk. I took her spot on the relay team. I wrote my name right over hers on a brand-new white label.

And I feel worse than I did ten minutes ago when I quit on Frankie and lashed out at Amelia, and I want to run 288 miles home, or 355 days backward and say no or yell to wake my parents or block the door and shake my head and push him back and tell him to follow the rules so there would be no that night. Then there would be no new brain research job and instead of moving into apartment number thirty-one I could sink back into my two inches of foam and sleep a whole night through and Frankie could keep Reggie as her best friend and teammate.

I slide *The Crossover* into my book bag and thank Mrs. Baldwin. Then I walk toward the gym. But this time Amelia isn't waiting for me outside the classroom door. I'm on my own.

CHAPTER 19

Something I Could Do

When I get to gym, the class is running sprints, squatting down to touch the lines of the basketball court, pivoting and running back, then back again. The last person to finish each sprint sits out on the bleachers.

Right now five boys, Frankie, and Amelia are left on the line.

Mr. Meathead is blowing his whistle for the next one to start, and Frankie's in the lead. They touch the half-court line and sprint back to the end of the court.

One of the boys is eliminated. He slams his fist on the bleacher and sits down with the rest of the class.

"Jump in if you want," Meathead says to me. "Show them how it's done." He gives me a smile, which makes me feel like maybe I don't need to call him Mr. Meathead anymore and Mr. Rayder, his real name, would be fine, at least for now.

"It's OK," I say. "I have fresh legs. It's not fair."

"Suit yourself," he says.

But before he can blow the whistle for the next sprint, Frankie calls out, "Run!" She's not even out of breath. "We can take it. Come on!"

And my legs really feel like running, so I drop my book bag and join them on the line. The whistle blares and we're off. I reach for the half-court line with my fingers, pivot, and shoot back toward the end line under the basketball hoop. Frankie finishes first. Another boy is eliminated. In the next sprint I'm gaining on Frankie and Amelia's gaining on me, and another boy is eliminated, until it's just us three again, taking our mark and waiting for Mr. Rayder's whistle.

We shoot off the line and stay neck and neck and neck as we bend to touch the half-court line, change directions fast, then charge back toward the end. We're still in a perfect line, and it's by our noses that we'll win or lose the sprint, but even though I want to look left and right and see us all lined up, I can hear Coach Scottie's voice saying to keep my eyes ahead, focus forward, so I do, and we all cross the line together. Frankie's out of breath now, and so is Amelia. Her cheeks are pink and we're all sweating.

"Tie! Line back up," Mr. Rayder says. "All three of you."

At first we all groan for the extra sprint, but then we take off, side by side by side, when he blows the whistle.

"Tie! Line up again."

This happens three more times and we're panting and huffing and chugging water from the fountain in between, and on our fourth sprint something happens. We make this little agreement, but not out loud, and not even with a look, it's something that just happens in each of us, that we decide we're crossing together every time. I can't really explain it, it's just this pact we make silently, inside, like a little secret message, and I know that we're going to be neck and neck and neck, side by side by side, the whole class cheering us on, the whistle blowing over and over, until the bell rings.

And that's exactly what happens.

The bell rings and we cross the line, together, for the last time. The whole class cheers from the bleachers and we're bending over our knees, gulping for air, and Mr. Rayder announces us class champs and we raise our fists in the air and then do one of our triangle high fives.

As soon as our hands touch I remember how running erases my brain, and that's a fact because now that my feet are still I'm remembering that Frankie's mad at me for quitting track, and that even though I apologized, I hate that I snapped at Amelia, and that I'm living in Reggie Muñoz's apartment, probably even her bedroom, and sitting at her desk in class, and now she's at the bottom of Frankie's notebook heart.

And I'm wondering if it's possible that our little secret inside message to stick together in the sprints erased how mad they were.

On our way back to homeroom we walk side by side by side even though we're not racing anymore, and even though we're not talking, not even one word.

Before we open the door to homeroom I blurt out, "I know that I'm living in Reggie's old apartment."

Frankie nods, but her face is hard and unmoving like compacted soil that will take lots of work to break up and soften.

"I'm sorry," I say, and even though it's a word I'm not supposed to use, I add, "That must really suck."

Frankie nods again, but her face doesn't soften.

"I wish there were something I could do—"

"Run," she says, staring down at her Nikes.

"I can't—"

"You said you wished there were something you could do." Then she pushes open the door of our homeroom class. "You could run. We could win the relay. That's something." The door slams behind her, and through the little square window I can see her slump down at her desk.

Amelia and I follow her in and my heart starts beating ten beats faster per minute, and why is a big who-knows because I ran hard in gym but had lots of time to recover my pulse.

Then before I can figure out why my heart is pounding, I say, "I will if she will," and point at Amelia.

She drops her jaw and points to her chest. "I t-t-told you—"

"You told me that it's hard enough getting through the school day. Well, it'll be hard for me to get through June fifteenth. But if you do it, I will. We'll do it together." I take a deep breath to try to steady my heart. "Like friends."

Now her face looks as hard and unmoving as Frankie's.

"You're fast," I tell her. "And you won't have to talk that much. Just run."

She sits down quickly in her chair and reaches into her book bag. She pulls out a notebook, scribbles something hard onto a page. and turns it around.

Fine.

I look at Frankie. "Fine," I say. "We're in." And then her face crumbles into a smile, and so does Amelia's.

"F-friends," she says.

CHAPTER 20

Closed Doors

Amelia only has to say five words at her first practice today, and she says them to Coach Okeke.

"Here to r-run. Not t-talk."

He smiles big and teaches her the secret team handshake, which she practices with Ana and at least five of the girls on the team, and no one makes her say anything else either, because doing a team handshake says enough.

We do a different loop for practice, running through the park and down the steep stairs, but this time across a footbridge over a river into the Bronx.

Ana runs next to Amelia the whole way and says, "I can't believe this is your first practice ever! You're good."

At first I want to cut in and tell her that Amelia's not here to talk, but before I can, she responds, "I j-just n-needed a little p-push." Then she looks over at me and smiles, and I get such a happy feeling I could hop hurdles over all the fire hydrants.

After practice we walk side by side by side by side down Broadway, weaving around groups of kids speaking Spanish and moms pushing strollers and doctors and nurses in their scrubs carrying Starbucks cups back toward the hospital where my mom is researching the brain right now.

Frankie and Ana turn toward Dacie's house and Amelia stops and puts out her fingers—one, five, three because she lives on 153rd Street. Frankie waves her to come on and that we're all going to Ms. Dacie's house and she should come too. Amelia raises her eyebrows like, *Who is Dacie?* And even though she sighs like she just wants to go home now, she pulls out her phone and sends a message with the fastest thumbs I have ever seen. We all follow Frankie down the street and climb the stairs to the big wooden door with all the stickers that show everyone's welcome.

Casey answers the door and keeps his eyes down toward the welcome mat like last time. He yells, "Frankie, Ana, and Rain are here! They brought a friend!" And why that makes me feel so good is a big who-knows, but it's like I belong already.

When we introduce Amelia, Dacie looks over her

purple glasses and right through Amelia's aqua frames and says, "Those glasses are the coolest. I'm going to have to get myself a pair."

Amelia smiles and nods.

"Welcome, Amelia. Let me show you around." Dacie takes Amelia by the arm and hurries her into the kitchen, and the next time I peek in, I notice that Ms. Dacie has an old landline hanging from her kitchen wall too, and that Amelia is kneeling on the counter and pulling down a bag of Hershey's Kisses from the top shelf.

Yasmin and Edwin pour out flour and sugar, and Ms. Dacie is glopping a big spoonful of peanut butter into a measuring cup.

Frankie sits with Ana, who is pulling all of Dacie's art supplies out of a big plastic bin and spreading out the panels of her superhero comic across the floor. She has one more panel than she did yesterday. The superhero, whose hair is pulled up into the same two tight buns as Ana's, is holding the hand of a tiny girl with matching hair, and they're soaring through a dark sky.

Trevor is working with a tutor who's wearing a City College sweatshirt and counting out blocks to balance an algebraic equation, but he stops before he comes to a solution and tells Ana that her art is really good.

"Thanks," she says, and continues to shade the dark night sky.

I start helping Casey organize the DVDs that are stacked beneath the TV. "Who even watches these anymore?" I ask, and it makes him laugh.

"She has records too," he tells me, and points to five milk crates and a record player.

Her voice rings out from the kitchen, "I can hear you! You sure know how to make a lady feel old!" And that makes us both laugh even more.

"And you have a landline!" I call back. "I thought my mom was the only dinosaur alive who insisted on having a landline." And everyone laughs, and that makes me feel even more like I belong right there.

Then Ms. Dacie comes out of the kitchen with a dish towel over her shoulder. "Funny, funny," she says. "You all laugh now, but I bet my memory's sharper than all of yours! How many phone numbers do *you* have memorized?" She can hardly keep from laughing herself, and all of us are giggling when Jer says he doesn't even know his mom's number by heart.

"See?" she says. Then she taps the side of her head with her flour-dusted finger.

It makes me think of Mom and that even though she's probably right that my brain is better off without a cell phone, I still kind of want one so I can message fast back and forth with Amelia.

"And," she adds, "music sounds better on one of these."

She shows us how the records slide out of their sleeves and how to load them onto the player and how they spin around and around. I don't tell her that I already know all that because Guthrie listened to records too, and he used to say the same thing about music sounding better on vinyl.

Casey could watch the spinning all day, and I could too, because I want to count how many rotations make a song and I want to know how all those little grooves remember the melodies and harmonies and all the words to every song.

I remember pulling the records from Guthrie's shelf, sliding them out from their covers, running my fingers along the grooves, and pushing them back in exactly where they belonged. That remembering rises up and up.

Then Casey puts on a Michael Jackson record and that gets Cris to tapping her foot and then Jer, and before the fifteenth rotation they're both up and trying to moonwalk across Ms. Dacie's wood floors. "Who can listen to Michael Jackson and *not* dance?" Jer exclaims.

Frankie and I snort and shake our heads, because there is no way I'm dancing, and that's a fact. But for some reason it feels good that they are.

In the kitchen Amelia is showing Yasmin and Edwin how to make the peanut butter cookie dough into balls and roll them in sugar. "Th-these are my f-favorite."

Then they're pulling a batch out of the oven and pressing Hershey's Kisses into the warm dough. "L-let them sit for a m-minute," Amelia tells them. "They get all m-m-melty." And I don't know if it's because there aren't any pens or paper in Ms. Dacie's kitchen, or if everything just feels easier here, but Amelia doesn't seem to care how much she talks or how long she stutters on her syllables. And neither does anyone else.

I take out my poetry notebook because even if it's not going to be a poem, I have to have something on my page about Izzy for English class tomorrow so Mrs. Baldwin can see I at least tried and it didn't work. Then maybe she'll let me write an essay.

Ms. Dacie sees me tapping the eraser of my pencil against my temple at one hundred twenty beats per minute, and sits down next to me.

"I don't really write poetry," I tell her.

She pulls a purple pen out of her curly gray hair and says, "Sure you do." Then draws six long dashes across my page.

"Just six words," she says. "Start there. See what happens." Then she walks off to check on the kids in the kitchen.

I stare at the six purple dashes, and my brain is immediately calculating words about Izzy.

— — — — — —

I try a few out in my brain first to see how they sound. Then I jot them in a list on my page.

Izzy is my best friend ever.

I miss Izzy. She misses me.

Then Ms. Dacie is back and asking me all about Izzy. What does she look like? What kinds of things did you do together? When did you meet? What do you miss most? What's your favorite memory? And I'm telling her all about the tree house and our sleepovers and how she's always been there for me, since kindergarten, and how I didn't cry once about moving until I hugged her goodbye.

"Now try another six words," she says. "Describe a memory. Don't worry if it's a complete sentence or not."

Tree fort sleepover. Please no squirrels!

Goodbye to her was hardest ever.

~~There for me after that night.~~

~~Even she doesn't know my secret.~~

I scribble out the last ones, even though they're the only ones that kind of sound like poems to me because poems are always mysterious and hard to understand and make people say *oooo* or *ahhh* after reading the last line.

Dacie points to the scribbled-out ones. "I wouldn't throw those out just yet," but she doesn't ask me about that night or my secret or anything, which is good, because I wouldn't have told her anyway.

Then she tells me about a couple of different kinds

of poems that she thinks I might like. A haiku, where I have to count the exact syllables per line, which sounds more like my kind of poem, and a way to rhyme that has rules and a pattern that I could follow. I'm excellent at rules and patterns.

"And if those don't feel right, you can always give yourself a number. Try writing that many words, or that many syllables, or that many lines. Make up the rules," she says. "Then follow them."

I nod and say thanks and all of a sudden poetry isn't feeling quite so impossible.

An hour passes fast and Ms. Dacie signs our community service sheets and hands Ana a plastic bag with foil-covered plates that she takes from her refrigerator. "I made your mom's favorite last night, and have just too many leftovers to tackle by myself," she says. "Pass them on for me?" Ana takes the bag and thanks her and they both nod like they're sharing a secret little message too.

Ms. Dacie walks us out. There are fliers on the bulletin board about an art camp here this summer, and a study group for the SATs. When I see Frankie and Reggie's track meet picture I try not to feel bad, but I can't help it.

Ms. Dacie sees me looking and puts her hand on Frankie's shoulder. "We miss our Reggie, don't we?" she says. "Change is hard."

And that's a fact.

We're all standing on the stoop looking over the tangled garden when Dacie breathes out big and says, "I'm afraid I have some hard news about change too." She pushes her purple glasses up on her nose. "I received news that the funding for Ms. Dacie's House is ending," she tells us. "And I'm not sure how long I can keep this old door open on my own."

"What?" Frankie snaps. "How can—who took it?"

"Change is hard," she says again, and pats Frankie's shoulder.

"That sucks," Amelia spits out in one whole piece.

Ms. Dacie chuckles and says, "When you're right, you're right. This sucks." It feels weird hearing a grown-up say *sucks*, but that's the best word to describe it.

She tells us we can talk more about it tomorrow and hands us each one of Amelia's peanut butter Hershey's Kiss cookies. "Maybe this can help sweeten your walk."

When Dacie closes the door, a big lump rises up in my throat and I can't help but think about Dad's closed bedroom door and how all the people that make me feel good and OK are closing big, heavy doors right in my face.

CHAPTER 21

Wash Cycle

There's yelling on the other side of our apartment door, and it's climbing up and up. Before I can make out any of the words, or stick my key in our dead bolt lock to let myself in, I turn right around and hop down the stairs two at a time, and head back out the front doors.

Even though I know my parents will worry, like really worry, when I'm not home on time, because when a kid is missing it's serious business, and they of all people know that, I head back to Broadway, down the five stairs, and into the café with the good hot chocolate.

I order a hot chocolate with extra whipped cream from the same backward-baseball-cap barista. He slides the hot chocolate across the counter to me in a big blue mug, and then punches a hole in a little card and hands it to me. The card says *Frequent Flier.*

"I've seen you here before," he says. "Your tenth one's on us."

I slip the card into my book bag. "Thanks," I say. And it makes me feel 6 percent better, knowing that I'm a regular somewhere. Like I might have someplace that won't close its door on me.

I'm worrying that my parents will be worrying when they realize I'm late, but I also want them to stop yelling at each other, and maybe giving them something to figure out together, like where I am, will make them have to think like a team.

I sit in the same seat I sat in before, and I even recognize two of the people from when I was here last time. One is looking through a big stack of papers and reading the same sentences over and over again to himself. I think he's an actor and practicing his lines. He makes small gestures to the open air, and the steam from his coffee swirls from his mug. The other is a woman who leans forward over a textbook, writing notes in the margin and highlighting big blocks of text.

Everyone else is busy typing on laptops, reading, and sipping hot drinks.

I take out my notebook and I pick the number twelve, because I used to live at Twelve Cloverfield Lane, and twelve is a good, even number. Then I make twelve dashes across my page just like Ms. Dacie did.

———————————————

I calculate a few lines about Izzy in my head and list them in my notebook.

This one time we laughed so hard milk came out our noses.
~~I haven't laughed that hard, or much at all, since that night.~~

Then I try doing the rhyming pattern that Dacie taught me. She said that I could use ABAB or AABB to help me keep lines organized. A rhymes with A, and B rhymes with B. It sounds hard, but it's more like a math problem, so I think I could probably do it.

A: I wonder what Izzy is doing now.
B: Maybe she's in the tree house thinking about me.
A: While I'm here in the café wondering how
B: Poetry is supposed to be.

I kind of even like that one a little. I try another and another and before I look up to see that some people have left and some new ones have come to take their seats, I've written all these lines about Izzy and other things, and I don't know if any of it is poetry, but it feels OK and not all loosey-goosey, even if most of it is crossed out.

> A: When you feel all jumbled, go for a run.
> A: It's more than just exercise and fun.
> B: It empties your brain,
> B: At least if you're Rain.

> A: ~~Everything was different before,~~
> A: ~~Now my dad's stuck behind his door.~~
> B: ~~Nobody knows the whole truth of that night,~~
> B: ~~I just wish my parents would stop their fight.~~

I even try one of those haikus, counting out five syllables in the first line, then seven, then five, like Dacie taught me.

> Best place to sleep is
> a tall tree fort with your friend.
> Hard can be OK.

When I look up next from my notebook and out the window of the café, I watch all the legs passing by on the sidewalk and I immediately recognize two shoes—ripped, dirty sneakers, plastic bags shoved into holes and taped over, the same loose socks sinking down to the floppy tongues. And I don't know why I stand up and leave my notebook and pencil and book bag and hot chocolate and everything and rush out the door and up the five steps, but I do, and then I'm calling, "Nestor!"

He turns slowly and squints his eyes at me, then smiles and waves. "New Rain," he replies. He's a little hunched over, hobbling back toward me, still favoring his left foot, and all of a sudden I kind of panic and I don't know why I called out to him in the first place.

If there were any homeless people in my town in Vermont, I didn't ever see them, but here, you do. You see them sitting or sleeping on benches, beneath old sleeping bags on the street, collecting bottles from garbage cans, pushing carts, and huddled at bus stops, and in the subway stations. Some talk to themselves or preach to a pretend audience on the street, big long sermons that I only catch a few words of because I hustle past fast.

As he gets closer to me I feel scared. Not scared of Nestor, because I talked to him before, and he was nice and funny at the church, but scared that he doesn't have a home, and what that could do to you, and scared that I can't do anything about it, or think of anything to say once he gets within talking distance.

"This your stomping ground now?" He points down the stairs to the café.

"They have good hot chocolate," I say.

Then I don't even know why I do it, but I ask him if he wants one. "It's on me," I offer, which makes me feel kind of bad because he's an adult and I'm just a kid.

He looks down the stairs and into the window. "I haven't been down here in a dog's age," he replies. Then he nods his head and follows me down the steps, hanging tight to the railing.

I'm wondering if by a dog's age he means seven years, which is one year in human years, or if he means the average age of a dog, which varies depending on the breed, but is probably around ten to thirteen years. Either way, that's a really long time, and I wonder where he's been instead.

The bells on the door chime when we walk in and everyone glances up from their laptops and books and looks at Nestor following behind me through all the tables and up to the counter. I can tell they're trying not to stare, but they're not very good at it, because I see them raise their eyebrows and peer over their screens. They didn't stare when it was just me.

They're staring because Nestor doesn't fit here. He doesn't smell like coffee and pages, he smells like weather and rot, and it's hard to ignore it when you're in a small space like the café.

I order him a hot chocolate with extra whipped cream and the barista pushes the buttons on his screen, steams the milk, and takes my money, and punches my frequent flier card.

Then we sit at my table and I'm wishing I hadn't asked him down here because I can't think of one single thing to say and I don't even really know him and I'm sure my parents will be worried soon, and would be really mad if they ever found out I was talking to a stranger, especially a stranger like Nestor.

The people at the two tables closest to us have moved away and even though I think they're overreacting, or should at least fake it and stay put so they don't make him feel bad, I kind of wish I could move away too. But before I can wish that too long, Nestor says, "A poet, are you?" and taps my notebook with his finger.

I cover my page with my arm. "Not really. I have to write something for school."

"Looks like you've got a good start there." His voice rumbles just like I remember from the church kitchen, and I wish I could ask him anything without it being rude, like what happened or what didn't happen to make him like he is, and where he sleeps at night and if he gets cold.

The barista comes over to clear mugs from the table next to us and asks if I'm OK and if I know this man. "Do your parents know you're here?"

The answer to all of those questions is actually no, but I just nod my head, and the barista tells me that he'll be right here behind the counter if I need anything.

"I can take this hot chocolate to go," Nestor says. I want to say OK, but then I look outside, and even though it's bright out and people are walking by in short sleeves, I know that when the sun goes down it'll get cooler, and that makes me feel bad because even if it's not Twelve Cloverfield Lane, I have a home, and even if it doesn't have two inches of foam, I have a bed too.

"It's OK," I respond. But I keep my eye on the barista and I can see he's keeping his eye on me and that makes me feel bad but better too.

"Bet you wouldn't believe I used to work here," Nestor says.

And that's a fact.

I take a sip of my hot chocolate, which is now cold chocolate, and shake my head no way.

"Back then it was a Laundromat." He points to the far wall. "The washing machines were lined up there. And the dryers here."

I try to imagine the café back then, but it's hard because I've never even been in a Laundromat before. We had our own washer and dryer in our house in Vermont, and there were brand-new machines with the instruction manuals still in them behind the hall closet door in apartment thirty-one when we got there.

He takes a noisy slurp from his mug, and a little

chocolate sticks on the gray stubble of his unshaven lip.

"I guess you couldn't really call it *working*," he says.

I raise my eyebrows because I want to know the story, but I don't want to pressure him to share more because it obviously ends with him not working here, and wearing dirty socks and fall-apart shoes.

"I had a deal with the Almonte family, who owned the business." He takes another slurp and wipes his mouth with his sleeve.

"The neighborhood had just started changing. People were moving in with money to spend, so the Almontes started a delivery service for $1.25 per pound of laundry. I delivered the clean, pressed, folded clothes to the newly renovated apartment buildings, and the Almontes let me toss my own clothing into the smaller loads for free."

Then he starts to chuckle a little. "I still love thinking about what those rich people would think if they knew their clothes were swishing around with mine."

I laugh too because he's laughing and because it's pretty funny to imagine, but the wooden café chair is starting to feel uncomfortable, and I shift my weight a little because I'm not sure if I'm rich and I wonder if we're one of those families moving in, because apartment thirty-one is newly renovated.

"It kept me clean and dry," Nestor continues. "And sometimes I'd even get a delivery tip to tuck in my pocket. Not a bad deal."

"So what happened?" I ask.

"Too much change. The people moving in wanted to start their own businesses, and things got too expensive for a lot of the people already here. The Almontes lost their shop. And I lost my deal."

He wraps his hands around the warm mug, and I look around the café. I wonder if all these people lived here when this was the Laundromat, and if their clothes swirled around with Nestor's, and if it makes them feel weird knowing that they're drinking chai lattes and eating almond croissants where the Almontes' washing machines used to be. Or maybe they just moved here, and didn't know that this was ever anything but a café. Maybe they're new like me.

I look quickly at my watch and realize I'm now officially twenty-three minutes late, and I wonder what my parents are doing.

Now I wish I had never just hustled off, even if they were fighting, because now *I'm* worrying. Worrying that they're worrying. And worrying that maybe Reggie Muñoz had to move like the Almontes had to move, and that maybe Dacie will have to move too.

And I like cafés, but the only things that should be in Ms. Dacie's House are Ms. Dacie and her art supplies, and cookie ingredients, and college tutors, and bookshelves, and Polaroid photos, and event fliers, and records, even if they're old and sometimes skip, and the stickers on the door, and all the mismatched kids that go there every day.

"Change is hard," I say, because that's what Dacie said, and it feels right to tell Nestor that now. "I'm sorry."

He looks up from his hot chocolate. "Let me give this poetry a try. I was pretty good with words way back when."

Even though I don't want him to see my poems, I slide my notebook over. He reaches for my pencil and taps it against the tight gray curls on the side of his head, then he scratches something quick on the page, closes the cover, and passes my notebook back.

"I still got it," he says and snaps his dry fingers.

That makes me laugh, and he gets to laughing too. A few people look up from their laptops to see what could be so funny. And that gets us both laughing even more, I think because we both might be imagining their clothes getting sudsy with his in the same washing machine.

I look at my watch and tell him I have to be getting home, and the second I say *home* I feel terrible and sorry all over again. He tips his head back for his last sip, we put our mugs in the dirty dish bin, and he follows me out. Everyone watches us walk by, and I want to yell that he was here first and to quit staring, but instead I give my knuckles a good crack and walk up the five stairs to Broadway.

"Thanks for the hot chocolate."

"Anytime," I say, even though I kind of doubt we'll ever have hot chocolate together again.

Then I watch him walk down the sidewalk, favoring his left foot, and I wish I could do more.

I open my notebook to his page and head toward 152nd Street, reading as I walk, swerving around the outdoor seating of the bar next door, the shelves of fruit stretching from the market, teenagers flying by on short bikes, their knees pumping high to their chests, and through the different beats and rhythms blasting from car windows.

He wrote a haiku with all the syllables counted out perfectly across the three lines.

Change is hard. Don't be
Sorry. Be something great while
You are still so young.

I'm thirty-two minutes late, so I start to run, and even though I'm running, it's hard to empty my brain because it's turning around and around like a wash cycle, wondering what great thing I could possibly be.

CHAPTER 22

A Little Space

Even though I'm already thirty-seven minutes late, I stop in the lobby to get the mail because maybe if I do something helpful they'll forget about most of those minutes. But as I walk up to the third floor I'm mainly worrying that they won't have even noticed I'm not there yet.

As soon as I reach the second floor I can hear their voices, still loud and rising, back and forth.

When I get to the door, I slide my key into the dead bolt, and before I can even turn it, the door flies open and my dad is scooping me up in his arms like I'm five years old and not eleven.

"Oh, thank God," he's whispering, and because I'm eleven and not five, and in the seventy-first percentile in height for my age, I'm kind of falling out of his arms and we're collapsing in a heap on the apartment floor.

Then Mom sinks to her knees and wraps her arms around us both and says, "Oh, my little Raindrop, I love you so."

And why I start crying is a big who-knows. Maybe it's because I'm so relieved that they stopped fighting long enough to notice I was late, or maybe it's because this feels like the exact position we were in that night, except instead of brand-new wood floors it was rough pavement beneath my knees.

Guthrie's guitar pick is digging into my leg, but we're all tangled up and I can't really move, and I don't even try to adjust because I should feel it, pushing against me, reminding me of what I did.

Dad is crying too. I can tell because his shoulders are shaking up and down like they do whenever he laughs or cries. But I know he's not laughing now. He's holding me close and rocking me back and forth and his shoulders are bouncing and bouncing and I can feel his tears sticking to my face and mixing with mine.

Mom starts to say, "Oh, my little Raindrop . . ." again, but before she can finish, she sniffs and her voice catches and then she starts crying too. "You were thirty-seven minutes late," she blubbers, and I can't believe it because my mom never counts things out the way I do.

"A long and terrible thirty-seven minutes."

Dad's shoulders are still bouncing, and he's still hold-ing me so tight that I couldn't go anywhere if I wanted to, which I don't.

Then Mom wipes the tears from her face fast and sighs big like this is the end of her crying and now she wants some answers.

"You scared us," she says. "Where on earth were you? And why didn't you pick up a phone to call us?"

I want to tell her I shouldn't have to ask some store owner for their phone, I should have my own, but she's pulling away from our heap and turning my chin toward her so I can't look away.

"We called the school, we called the track coach, we called Ms. Dacie, and Frankie, and you were nowhere. Nowhere, Rain."

And I'm mad that she won't just stay in our pile on the floor a minute longer and let us cry and send little silent secret messages to each other about how much we miss everything and how sorry we are and how we'll all try a little harder.

"Rain—"

"Maybe I should have a cell phone," I say.

Then Dad cuts in, "She's safe, Maggie. Just give it a minute, would you?"

"Are you kidding? Do you remember how scared we—"

"Of course I do. I just think we could—"

But before my mom can cut him off again and answer back, I blurt out, "I was having hot chocolate in the café with a homeless guy."

That shuts them both up really fast, which is perfect because I wanted to yell *shut up*, but that's something I'm not supposed to say. They're both just looking at me, like I got their attention and I can go ahead and explain now, but instead I stand up, and I walk the nine steps to my bedroom.

Mom's not the only one who can hustle off.

And Dad's not the only one who can close a door.

They give me six minutes by myself before they knock quietly on my door, and all I do for the whole six minutes is lie on my bed and count the bricks on the building across the alley from window to window until I lose count and start over. It doesn't empty my brain like running does, but it gets close. It pushes June fifteenth, and Dacie, and Reggie, and Nestor, and the Almontes, and all the hard changes, and Mom and Dad's rising voices to the back of my brain because all I can really focus on is seventy-one, seventy-two, seventy-three . . .

"Rain?" Dad taps lightly on my door.

"Open the door, please," Mom says.

"We just want to listen, Rain," Dad whispers. "Promise."

But I just keep counting the bricks, squinting my eyes to make sure I don't skip any.

"Rain . . ."

Their voices make me lose count, and that makes me mad because all the thoughts I don't want to think come rushing back in and before I can crack my knuckles and start again, I yell, "Leave me alone!"

And at that exact second I start feeling bad because even though they're the ones yelling and hustling off and hiding, I'm the one who did anything wrong.

There's another soft knock on my door, and I'm secretly relieved that they aren't giving up and leaving me alone like I told them to.

"I'm going to go pick up some dinner," Dad says. "When I get back, we'll all eat together." Then he taps three quiet taps on my door like he's saying *all right then*, or *goodbye for now*. "We can eat in there if you want," he adds. "But we're eating together."

"OK," I agree, because if my dad is going to put on shoes and go outside the apartment, and talk to people, order food, and carry it back, I can open my door too.

I hear the click of the dead bolt lock and picture Dad walking down Broadway and reading all the menus in the restaurant windows. He doesn't know any more

Spanish than *hola*, so I bet he comes back with burgers from the bar next to the café, the one with picnic tables outside, and the chalkboard menu, and the French fries that come in big fancy cones. That's another place where my skin matches most other skin. But now I'm wondering what it was before, and if a family like the Almontes owned it, and if someone like Nestor worked there, and where they all are now.

Then Mom's voice says, "Maybe we can talk about you getting a cell phone. For safety calls only, so we know where you are."

I don't say anything.

"But until then, if you are going to be late, even five seconds late, you have to ask to use the phone where you are to call us."

I think about how embarrassing that would be, to ask the backward-baseball-cap barista if I can use the phone to call my mom.

"I'm just going to sit right here against your door until Dad gets back. OK, Rain? In case you want to talk." Her knees crack like loud, snapping twigs the way they always do when she bends them, and even though her knees are fine and she's athletic like I am, Guthrie used to cover his ears every time Mom bent down, and he'd call her Old Crotchety and laugh.

I get up from my bed and sit down on the floor too,

leaning my back against my door, and I can feel her weight against me, and it feels good, being back-to-back with Mom. We sit there quiet, just breathing, for a whole minute before I say, "Old Crotchety."

And that gets Mom to laughing. Her chuckles rise up and up until I hear her trying to catch her breath. "I haven't thought about that since . . ." But she's hooting and snorting so hard she can't finish and I can hear her stand up and sit back down again, making her knees crack. "Old Crotchety," she repeats, and laughs. "Old Crotchety . . ."

I feel her sit down against the door, so we're back-to-back again. And then something changes and I'm 70 percent certain her laughs are turning to cries. Then I'm 100 percent certain because I hear her sniffing and heaving.

I turn around and put my hand on the door and press hard and hope she can feel it. I lay my cheek by my hand too and whisper through the wood, "It's OK, Mom." And maybe it's because there's a door between us, but she doesn't try to stop. She cries so hard it vibrates the door against my cheek and I pat three little pats and tell her it's OK because even if it's not, I can't think of anything else to say. She cries for two minutes and forty-five seconds, and the whole time I press my cheek into the door and pat my hand where I think her back is.

Then she stops, clears her throat, and stands up. And I hear the faucet running and plates clanking.

Then I hear the dead bolt unlock. Dad's home with dinner.

"What'd you get?" Mom chimes, as if she didn't just cry for two minutes and forty-five seconds.

"*Tamales*," he answers. "I don't even really know what they are, but they looked good, and the woman selling them was really nice."

That makes me open the door fast and blurt, "They're a traditional food from Mexico. You don't eat the corn husk." And that's a fact, because I looked it up at Ms. Dacie's.

"There's my Rain," Dad says, putting the brown paper bag down on the kitchen counter.

Mom is laying three place mats on the counter. It's the first time since that night that we'll actually sit down for a real dinner, all together. At home in Vermont, we never ate at the table again. But maybe here it's a little different, because Guthrie never had a spot at this counter like he did in our old house, a spot that would just be empty if we laid out place mats and had dinner, a spot that would only make us think of how much we miss him.

Mom pours water into three glasses and puts out three plates and forks. Dad rips the brown paper bag down the side and shows us the steaming meat and cheese *tamales*, all perfectly wrapped and tied in corn husks.

We sit down and I put one on my plate and show them how to untie the husk and unwrap it. "You can eat it with your fingers or with a fork," I say, but I know we're fork people. Even when we order Chinese food. Mom always starts with chopsticks but gets frustrated with the little grains of rice, so she gives up and caves for silverware.

"They're delicious!" Mom says.

And that's a fact.

I'm happy that Dad didn't get burgers from the chalkboard menu bar, even if it looks like a fun place to be and the food always smells so good when I walk by, because I think the *tamal* lady is nice too, and if people start buying burgers and fancy cone fries instead of *tamales*, I wonder where she'll have to push her cart.

"So," Dad starts. "Hot chocolate with a homeless guy?"

And the way he says it makes me laugh. He snickers too, until Mom says, "It's not funny!"

But even she knows it kind of is, and lets out a little laugh.

"But really, Rain. What happened?"

I tell them about hearing them fighting and how I

just couldn't put the key in the lock and open the door so I left. I tell them how Ms. Dacie helped me with poetry so I ordered a hot chocolate and started writing at the café and that I don't even know exactly how it all happened, but I recognized Nestor from the church kitchen, and all of a sudden we were drinking hot chocolate together and talking about how the café used to be a Laundromat.

"Rain—"

"I know," I say. "I probably shouldn't make a habit of having hot chocolate with strangers. But Nestor didn't feel so strange."

Dad scrapes the last bits of meat out of a husk with a fork. "You are always thinking of others," he says. "I love that about you." He starts unwrapping another *tamal* from the bag. "But we just love you so damn much, Rain . . ."

I'm pretty sure *damn* is something I'm not supposed to say, but when Dad uses the word it makes me pay attention and really believe him. And I'm 88 percent certain he can't finish that thought because the words are caught in his throat.

"Just so damn much . . ." he repeats. "And if anything ever . . . If . . ."

Mom reaches over and taps his hand like they're a relay team and it's her turn to take over. "Your dad and

I just want to keep you safe. And we would never forgive ourselves if you ran off and got hurt because we were fighting."

And that's a fact that I understand.

"That's why . . ." Mom says. She clears her throat and takes a deep breath. "That's why your dad and I are going to try giving each other a little space."

I'm wondering how much more space they really need with Mom at her job all day and Dad in the bedroom, doing whatever he's doing. And then my brain makes one hundred clicks and I realize they aren't just talking about a little elbow room, they mean they don't want to live together anymore, that they're giving up, that they aren't one out of four, and I try to take a deep breath and finish my *tamal*, but I have a feeling I'll never like *tamales* again, which sucks. And it's all my fault.

"Rain—"

"We think this is best for everyone—"

"It's not best for me!" I snap. Then I do something I've never done before. I slam my brand-new dinner plate against the brand-new marble countertop that I'm 99 percent certain weren't here when Reggie Muñoz lived in this apartment. I slam it so hard it cracks right down the middle into two pieces in my hands. The juice from the meat escapes and runs onto the counter and falls

~ 171 ~

in big splats on the brand-new wood floor. I push back my stool and do something else I've never done before. I slam my door. And if I had anything hanging on my walls, it would have fallen to the floor and shattered too. That's how hard I slam it.

I flop on my bed and try to block out their whispers from the kitchen. So I start counting the bricks on the building across the alley again. Sixteen, seventeen, eighteen . . . until a light turns on in one of the windows and I lose count. It's the woman I saw before. She's reaching for something in a high kitchen cabinet. In the next window over, the same man is sitting on the couch again, watching TV. I still don't know if they are in separate apartments, living side by side, or if they live together but are just in two different rooms. Maybe they're giving each other space. Or maybe she's just reaching for a bag of chips and pretty soon she'll join him in front of the TV and they'll watch movies all night, like we used to.

I want to stay up so I can know the ending, but my eyes are feeling heavy, and when I lie back I crinkle the mail I brought upstairs for my parents. I pull it out from under me and push it to the floor, except I can't help but see that one of the envelopes is addressed to Mr. Muñoz, as if I don't already feel like a big pile of dry, cracked, untillable dirt.

I fall asleep pinching Guthrie's guitar pick so hard

between my fingers it's leaving a big red crease, and thinking that in books the parents always get back together, and it's never the kid's fault if they don't.

But I can't forget what Dr. Cyn says, and one out of four is not great odds.

And I can't forget that night, and how it *is* my fault. And how Guthrie would be here if I hadn't done what I'd done.

CHAPTER 23

That Night

The pavement was rough, and little pebbles stuck hard in my knees, but I didn't dare move, because if I did, if I shifted my weight and moved from this heap of arms and legs and tight-holding hugs and fast-beating hearts between my parents, I'd have to see it again—the flares sparking on the blacktop, the tape keeping us back, away from him, the silent, rotating lights of the ambulance.

Maybe we could stay in a heap like this, holding close for the rest of our lives.

CHAPTER 24

Plans

Nobody says wakey wakey to me this morning and tugs at my toes, because I'm up early. My brain wakes me up wondering if last night was a dream, if I really had hot chocolate with Nestor, and if Mom and Dad really said what they said. I wake up in my regular clothes at 4:43 in the morning, on top of my bed, and Guthrie's guitar pick is stuck to my right palm.

I finish *The One and Only Ivan* before the sun comes up. Then I change into my running clothes. Even though running by myself without Coach Okeke and the fourteen girls on the track team on my heels feels scary, and like I wouldn't even know where to go, I still need to move, to erase my brain. So I decide I'll run repeats up the steep hill from Riverside Drive back to our building stoop. It's 100 percent impossible to get lost half a block from your own apartment.

I creak open my bedroom door and for one minute I think my dad is back looking for work because he's not behind the bedroom door. He's sitting on a stool in the kitchen, his laptop is open on the counter, and he's jotting things on a notepad. And I wonder if he's been there all night.

"Hi, there." He says it so softly it's almost like he just breathes the words out.

When I circle around him and peek over his shoulder I see that he's not back looking for work at all. He's looking up apartments in New Jersey.

"A whole different state?" I ask. "You need that much space?"

"We're just looking at what we can afford. Trying to make plans." He closes the screen. "I know this is hard, Rain. It's hard for all of us. I'm sorry."

Then Mom hustles into the kitchen. Her hair is wet from the shower.

"You're up early! Good morning!" I'm not sure if she's talking to Dad, or to me, or to Dad and me, or if people who are getting separated, but aren't actually separated yet, even say anything to each other anymore, or if they just pretend the other person isn't there, like practice for when they really won't be.

"I'm going for a run," I say.

Mom and Dad look at each other like they're deciding which one of them is going to stop me.

"Just repeats up the hill from Riverside. I'll be in sight of the building the whole time."

"By yourself? Rain, maybe I'll come watch you from the—"

"Maybe you should see if Frankie can go with you?"

They look at each other again and Mom nods. I can't believe they actually agree for once. I don't think they can believe it either. For five seconds I think maybe they'll remember how great everything was when they used to agree with each other more and how much they should be together and how stupid they are for thinking they need space.

But then Dad lifts his laptop screen back up and Mom hustles into the bedroom to change.

"Fine," I say. "I'll see if Frankie's up." Then I take my keys and tie them into my shoelace, and let the door slam behind me. I can hear them both say, "Rain, wait," as I leave, but I'm too fast, hopping down three steps at a time until I'm at Frankie's apartment.

I knock quietly and she's the one who answers the door.

"I need to run," I say.

She nods like she doesn't even need to know more.

"Me too." Then she disappears for one minute and when she's back, she's in her running clothes and tying her apartment key into her shoes the way I do. Héctor is outside watering the sidewalk and Frankie calls to him that we're going for a run. He waves and we're off.

And before I can tell Frankie that I was just thinking of doing some repeats up the hill to erase my brain, she's leading me down 152nd Street and through a big cemetery, under a bridge, and onto a path that winds its way up the Hudson River. It's different down here, away from traffic, from honking cabs, and double-parked delivery trucks, away from shuffling feet, and shouts, and blasting music, and people running after buses that are closing their doors and letting out big puffs of exhaust.

We're running side by side past baseball fields, playgrounds, volleyball nets, and picnic tables, and all I'm thinking about is *forward forward forward*.

We pick up the pace and get to a straightaway past eight tennis courts that leads to a little gravel path and up to a red lighthouse perched right on the water. Frankie points to the lighthouse, and I know what she means. *Race you to the end.*

And we do.

My feet land on the ground just long enough to spring me forward again, and I feel like I'm flying. Frankie is a stride ahead of me and I'm pushing to keep up and all I'm thinking about is the next stride, then the next and the next until we slap our hands against the gate that surrounds the red lighthouse. Frankie first, then me one second behind.

We do the secret handshake and bend over our knees to catch our breath.

"I needed that," I gasp.

"Me too."

After a sip at the water fountain, we start to jog back easy, cooling down, and I'm wondering why Frankie needed to run, and if it has to do with Reggie. I wonder a hundred things about Reggie, actually. And before I can keep my mouth shut because no one wants to talk while running, I'm asking her questions, and I can't believe she's answering. Maybe it's because we're side by side and don't have to look at each other, so it doesn't feel so weird, but Frankie starts in.

"She was the only one in our class who was like me," she says.

And even though I don't really know exactly what she means, I understand how it feels to be a one-and-only. Like Ivan. And I'm sad that Frankie's friend is all the way in Florida now.

"Reggie just gets me. And I get her."

Then she's telling me all about the day in fifth grade they gave each other their nicknames. "Regina and

Franchesca became Reggie and Frankie," she says. "Felt as free as running."

I want to tell her that is a perfect twelve-word poem and she should write it down. I'm also thinking that I can't believe her real name is Franchesca and I can't imagine calling her anything but Frankie, because Frankie just fits.

"We buzzed off our hair together too. And she introduced me to Dacie and all the kids there. At least I have them now." Then she exhales hard and I can see her shake her head out of my peripheral vision. "Well, maybe."

We're running long, slow strides as we reach the stairs that will bring us back up from the park to Riverside Drive.

"At the beginning, kids would sometimes joke about us in class, our names and the way we dressed more like boys, but we had each other and we both liked being who we were. That didn't always fit with the other girls at school. But we fit together, so it didn't matter."

She picks up the pace as we run the stairs up from the park, and through puffing breaths she says, "Everyone at school's used to me now, and no one really says anything, but Reggie was there from the beginning."

She's sharing so much with me, I almost tell her about my parents. Almost, but I don't, because them deciding to take space is just the last part of a longer story that I don't want to remember, and definitely don't want to tell. A story that's buried down deep. A story that started that night.

But as we wind along Riverside Drive toward home, I think of them making plans. Plans for my dad to move to New Jersey, plans to separate and make me travel back and forth between them on weekends, plans for who will pay for what, and how much time they'll give it before they split for good. And I want to run faster so my brain empties out and all I can think about is *forward*, but with every step I'm thinking about what Dr. Cyn says, how the anniversary could be the hardest day, and how they need to find something to celebrate together, and how they should try participating in something they used to enjoy as a couple, and then maybe they could be that one out of four. That one out of four who makes it.

And I'm thinking how Ivan made plans. Plans to save the baby elephant Ruby from the zoo-themed mall so she could grow up in a better domain with other elephants like her. And how even though he's just a silverback gorilla, his plans worked.

And before we turn the corner from Riverside Drive back to 152nd Street, I'm making my own plans. Plans to push my parents back together.

I'm going to win that relay race at the city championships.

CHAPTER 25

Operation Save Ms. Dacie's

The next day in English class, Mrs. Baldwin announces
that we have a small poetry collection due on Thursday
June fourteenth, which is exactly seven days from now
and exactly one day before the city championships and
the worst day ever.

Kids shout questions in the air before she can say
anything else.

"How many poems?"

"How long do they have to be?"

"Are you serious? Isn't it basically summer already?"

I want to ask if poems can be twelve words long and
if they rhyme do we get extra credit?

She doesn't answer any of the questions. Instead she
says, "On that Thursday, we will have a poetry slam

celebration in class. You'll choose your best poem and read it aloud to your classmates. I'll bring cookies!"

Everyone's calling out. Some are protesting, "There's no way I'm reading any poem out loud!" and some are asking if they can bring chips and soda.

She starts passing out an assignment sheet with all the directions on it, and announces over all the calling-out voices, "Read this over, and then if anyone has any *real* questions, come talk to me. I don't want to take away any more of your work time, so—ready, set, write!"

For the first seven minutes, kids are still complaining and telling each other they're not getting up in front of anyone and reading anything, and how every time they've presented so far this year they got to do it in partners, and how come they have to write poetry anyway because it's too personal.

One kid, Anthony, stands up from the back row and says, "Roses are red, violets are blue, this is my poem, how did I do?" Everyone laughs and claps and Anthony takes a bow and asks Mrs. Baldwin, "Does that count? I presented my poem."

But Mrs. Baldwin doesn't respond to any of it. She just opens her own notebook and starts writing, and I'm wondering if she's doing that to get everyone to quiet down, or if she's really working on a poem too.

Either way, it works, and little by little kids quiet

down and move their desks to sit in pairs and start sharing what they're writing about.

A boy in front of me, named José, says he's been trying to write a poem about his dad but he definitely doesn't want to read it out loud. He slides his notebook to his friend and his friend takes his time reading it.

When he looks up, he tells José, "You have to read this one. It's really good."

José says, "Nah," but then his friend is sliding his own notebook over and saying, "If you read that one, I'll read this one."

And then I keep hearing little pacts like that around the classroom and seeing kids lean over each other's notebooks, reading and asking questions, and I hear erasers scratching and big exhales as kids clear the dust from their lines and revise until everything sounds just right. Some kids stand up and move into the far corners of the room and practice reading aloud to an audience of three friends.

Mrs. Baldwin is visiting groups now and pointing to notebook pages and asking students how they chose this word or that word.

Before I can even open my notebook to the poems I have so far, Amelia walks over to the corner library again and starts pushing her pen fast across the page, and I'm thinking if anyone has the right to complain, it's her.

Every once in a while, she stops writing and puts her head between her hands and looks down at her shoes.

I look over at Frankie to see if she's noticing Amelia too, and maybe we should go sit with her, but Frankie has her desk turned toward Michael's desk and is listening to him read his poem. Mrs. Baldwin is kneeling by their desks and listening too.

Michael's poem is about basketball, and when he finishes they give him high fives and Mrs. Baldwin says, "I love the way you describe how it feels to be on that court. It makes me wonder how it sounds to be out there. What are some things you hear during a basketball game like that?"

He starts listing things like squeaking sneakers and panting players.

I see Frankie jot something in her notebook too, like that gave her an idea for her own poem.

Then Mrs. Baldwin is off to the next group and Frankie is reading a poem to Michael about running, which is what I'm going to write about too, and all of a sudden I realize I haven't even taken out my notebook and there aren't any other desks to turn toward and share.

I'm about to get up and go sit by Amelia, even if she wants to be alone, and tell her that it's going to be OK and maybe she can pick a really short poem, like one that's only six words, but the bell rings for next period, and this time instead of asking me to stay and chat after class, Mrs. Baldwin is asking Amelia if she'll stay back for a minute before gym.

I hear someone behind me mumble something about how if she gets out of this it's not fair, and I mean to bite my tongue and crack my knuckles and pack up my book bag, but I whip around in my chair instead and kind of whisper-yell right back to him, "No, what's not fair is that she lives with her stutter every day and no one tries to understand what that might feel like."

That shuts him up.

And when I look back down, there's a little note scribbled on ripped paper on my desk. *Thanks.*

I smile at Amelia, zip up my book bag, and stop to wait for her outside the door so we can walk up to gym together. When Frankie comes out, she stops too and waits, even though gym is her favorite class and she never wants to waste even one minute.

I tell her that it's OK, I can wait, and she says, "No competition up there without you guys anyway." And that gets us laughing until Amelia comes out.

"What'd Mrs. Baldwin say?" I ask.

"Th-that I d-don't have to do it out loud."

"Good," Frankie says. "That's fair."

And that's a fact.

Then she scribbles on her notebook, *She said a friend can read it for me.*

I pat her on the back and say, "I'll read it," and she gives me a little smile, but she doesn't look as happy as I thought she might, and I'm 91 percent certain it's because she wishes she could read it on her own.

"L-let's r-run," she says. So we hustle off down the hall and up to gym.

That day at practice Coach Okeke calls over Frankie, Amelia, Ana, and me.

"You four," he says, looking at each one of us. "This is your relay team. It's official. The first-ever all-sixth-grade relay team I've ever sent to city championships."

That makes us smile. Ana giggles.

"Rain leads off. Then Amelia, and Ana, and Frankie is your anchor." Before he calls everyone else around to start practice, he looks back at us and says, "You're going to show those eighth graders."

Frankie puts her hand up and we all high-five together, and I'm thinking that even though in geometry a square isn't as strong as a triangle, it feels good to have another side to our structure.

For the whole hour, we four practice handoffs. Coach Okeke gives us a baton and I practice running in and placing it in Amelia's outstretched hand. It's my responsibility to get it into her palm safe because she'll be running forward and trusting that by reaching back she'll feel the baton and can take off. We practice passing from me to Amelia to Ana to Frankie and before the end of practice we've got it down and Coach Okeke gives us all the secret team handshake before we go.

We're heading down Broadway toward Ms. Dacie's and we're all so excited we're still running and couldn't stop if we wanted to. We're crossing the streets against the walk lights, which my mom told me never to do, and kind of scares me a little, but it also feels good to rush out in the breaks of traffic and skip over the curb and weave between the people walking on the street.

"The first-ever all-sixth-grade team!" Ana exclaims.

"If we win, we'll make history!" Frankie raises her fist to the sky.

"Let's w-w-win."

I'm thinking that we *have* to win, and *have* to make history, because that's my plan to push my parents back together. They're going to be there watching me race on the worst day ever, but when we win the relay, Mom and Dad will cheer and celebrate and then like they do in books, they'll jump up and hug, even though they don't exactly mean to, but then they'll look at each other and laugh and smile and remember how good it feels to laugh and smile, and then they'll want to bring the whole team out for ice cream, and maybe they'll even remember the secret team handshake and decide they need one of their own. Then maybe Dad will stop looking at apartments in New Jersey. And the space that they think they need will shrink.

When we knock on Dacie's door, Casey answers and calls, "Frankie, Rain, Ana, and Amelia are here!"

We pass the bulletin board with Frankie and Reggie's picture and drop our book bags in the living room. But something doesn't feel right. It doesn't smell like cookies, and no one has turned on the record player.

Edwin twists one of his blue spikes of hair between his fingers and nods toward the other side of the room. A tall man wearing a black suit is carrying a briefcase and taking notes on a little pad with a short pencil that he puts behind his ear in between jots. The pencil sticks right in there and doesn't move because his hair has something in it that makes it look shiny and hard and fake.

Dacie gives us a half smile. "I'll be with you in one minute."

She brings the man into the kitchen. He looks around and takes more notes.

"This is bull," Trevor mumbles. He's pulling a textbook out of his book bag. "That guy wants to buy Dacie's place.

Where else am I supposed to get free math tutoring?"

"I'm supposed to be coming to art camp here this summer," Ana says.

"Ms. Dacie is like my mom." Jer bows his head.

Cris sighs and Yasmin says, "This sucks."

And that's a fact.

The man follows Ms. Dacie down the hall and outside to the yard with all the tangled garden beds. I'm hoping the overgrown weeds change his mind about wanting Dacie's place, because he doesn't look like the kind of guy who could spend a day getting dirt under his nails to make those gardens healthy again.

Then I start wondering what he wants this house for anyway. And if he's thinking about changing it into a café or a new bar with chalkboard menus and what will happen to Ms. Dacie.

I bet Mr. Slick Suit won't even try to revive the gardens. And I bet whatever he turns this place into won't have anything that tastes half as good as a homemade cookie from Dacie's kitchen.

And even though I already have one big plan to focus on, and even though I can't think of the first step, I say, "We have to make a plan." And that makes everyone pull really close into a circle right there on the living room floor and nod and say *yes* and *I'm in* and Alia starts erasing Ms. Dacie's whiteboard easel, where she wrote out the recipe for oatmeal raisin cookies, and writes, *Operation Save Ms. Dacie's.*

Then we all just kind of look at each other. I look at Jer, then Matthew, then Frankie. I look at Cris and Ana, and we all look at Alia because she's the one standing up with the whiteboard marker ready to jot down our plan.

"We n-need m-m-money," Amelia says, finally.

That makes everyone laugh, not because she stuttered, but because it was so obvious and none of us really had any.

"I have ten dollars," Matthew says, holding up two wrinkled fives.

That makes us laugh even more, and even though we all know it's ridiculous we're emptying our pockets and among the eleven of us here, we have $52.55.

"We'll never have enough," Jer says.

"We don't even know how much we need," Cris responds. "Maybe we should ask Ms. Dacie."

We all agree that we shouldn't tell Ms. Dacie anything until we have a solid plan because she wouldn't want us worrying and feeling responsible.

Then Trevor says, "We could have a bake sale. Do those things ever work?"

"We just had one at my school," Cris says. "It was to raise money for the cheerleaders' uniforms." She shrugs her shoulders. "But it worked. They all have matching skirts and sneakers now."

Jer says he bought a brownie every day for a week from that bake sale and they weren't half as good as cookies from Ms. Dacie's.

Everyone's starting to get excited until Matthew says, "A cheerleading uniform is way cheaper than Ms. Dacie's rent. We'd have to sell like a gazillion cookies."

"Or charge fifty dollars a cookie," Alia says, and everyone shakes their heads because we're running out of ideas.

"It'll never work."

Then we hear the front door open and Ms. Dacie saying she'll grab a couple of glasses of water and they can tour the grounds. The slick suit man says OK, and through the window I can see him on the front stoop staring out over the tangled gardens.

Ms. Dacie's footsteps shuffle down the hall and Alia quickly erases *Operation Save Ms. Dacie's* from the whiteboard and we all go back to normal, pretending to work on superhero comics and math homework, but really all of our brains are trying to make one hundred clicks to come up with a better plan.

CHAPTER 26

Best Hot Chocolate Ever

On our way out from Ms. Dacie's Frankie says, "I've got the perfect place for us to go. We can keep talking about the plan." Then she takes off down Ms. Dacie's front steps, past the slick suit man, who's measuring the side yard, and around the corner faster than I can say, "Wait!"

I have seventy-two minutes until I'm late, and I want to keep brainstorming a plan for Ms. Dacie, so Amelia, Ana, and I take off too and catch up to Frankie on Broadway and we try to jog side by side by side but the sidewalk is busy with deliverymen on bikes, weaving in and out of people strolling and chatting, and hustling to the subway, and others who are dragging plastic chairs into the sun and gathering on the corners to enjoy the weather.

Frankie stops outside a place called La Cocina. "This is it," she says and pushes open the door. There are six stools at a counter, all taken, and three little tables with mismatched chairs. The music playing is in Spanish and so are all the words on the menu hanging on the wall.

Frankie sees me looking and says if I think some new café in the neighborhood has good hot chocolates, I haven't tried anything yet.

A woman behind the counter calls out, "*Hola*," and something else that's too quick for me to understand, but must be *seat yourself wherever*, because Frankie, Amelia, and Ana start walking to one of the tables. I follow them and we all sit down. Everyone at the counter turns around and nods and smiles to us, and one man says, "*Hola*," to Frankie and, "*¿Como está tu padre?*" and Frankie replies in Spanish, and he tips his hat, and no one is typing on laptops.

My chair wobbles, and there's yellow foam stuffing sticking out of a rip in the fabric, but it's comfortable and I lean back and sink in just the right amount.

"*Cuatro*," Frankie says to the woman behind the counter and holds up four fingers, and she doesn't even have to say *cuatro* what because the woman just knows and nods and in three minutes there are big steaming mugs of hot chocolate in front of us.

And Frankie is right. This is the best hot chocolate

I've ever had, and that's a fact, because I know my hot chocolate. It tastes like there are at least two extra ingredients that I've never tasted in hot chocolate before that are melted up in the mug with the milk and cocoa. It makes it a tiny bit spicy, but then the milk washes it away and it's perfect.

My face must tell Frankie exactly what I'm thinking, because she says, "I told you so."

For some reason, this place and the hot chocolate make me feel even more determined to save Dacie's, and before our mugs are half-empty we're trying to come up with better ideas than a bake sale.

"I wish Reggie were here," Frankie says. "She's the best at coming up with ideas and organizing this kind of stuff."

"I wish she were here too," I tell her. "I'm sorry."

She takes another sip. "It's not your fault."

But I still feel like a rotten, wrinkled tomato, long fallen from the branch.

And I want to tell her how it is my fault. That it's my fault that my mom needed to hustle all the way away to New York City, and how if my family weren't here, maybe Reggie's still would be. And how it's not working anyway, that we hustled off to New York City for a fresh start, and after eight days my parents already need more space.

Maybe it's because I'm looking down into my hot chocolate and not directly up at them, but I just start talking about my parents and how they want to separate, and how if anything can save them it'll be winning the relay.

"How can the relay save them?" Ana asks.

I take a breath and remember. "They used to come to all my track meets together and get excited, and cheer, and be happy. They need to do something that makes them happy like that again. So if we win . . ."

They all nod like they understand, and Amelia runs her finger around the rim of her mug and a smudge of hot chocolate lodges under her nail like dirt.

Our mugs are empty, and the waitress takes them away and fills them up without even asking if we want more.

"We'll w-w-win," Amelia says and reaches out and covers my hand on the table with hers.

Then Ana reaches out and covers Amelia's so our hands are stacked up like three pancakes. "We'll make history," she says.

Then Frankie stacks her hand on top and says, "We'll win the relay. And we'll save Dacie's. We have to."

And just then, with our hands all stacked up like that, I stare at the smudge of chocolate beneath Amelia's fingernail and my brain makes one hundred clicks and I'm 91 percent certain I've got a plan to save my parents *and* Ms. Dacie's.

So with our hands still pressed together I say, "I've got it! I've got a plan." And I tell them all about what my brain is thinking and how not only will it save Ms. Dacie's house, it could help my parents too, and with winning the relay and this, Ms. Dacie and my parents can defeat the odds. And no one moves their hand, not an inch, the whole time I'm telling them. And they're nodding and saying *yes* and *this might actually work!*

Then we start chanting, "One, two, three, four!" and throw our hands up and laugh, and how is a big who-knows because we didn't plan this cheer out ahead of time, so it must be that we're really good at sending little secret messages. Like a team.

Frankie looks at the clock above the counter. "I have to get home."

Amelia and Ana say, "Me too."

I look at my watch. I have thirty-three minutes until I'm late, and even though at first I didn't feel as comfortable here in La Cocina as I do in the café, I like it here more now, even if my skin doesn't match and the Spanish is too fast for me to pick up. Maybe it has something to do with the free refill and the easy smiles.

It means I'll have to walk home alone, but I say, "I think I'll stay for a bit," anyway. Walking home alone doesn't feel so scary anymore, because I know at least twenty-four other people will be on every block the whole way home, and some I might even recognize and nod to, and that's not so alone at all.

"You s-sure?"

"Yeah, I might try to work on Mrs. Baldwin's poems," I say.

They nod OK and take their last sips, push in their chairs, then we all do the team handshake before they leave. The six people at the stools sipping coffee chant along with each of our fist bumps, cheering us on—¡eh eh eh eh!—and I get up from my seat to do the last part, the full-body spin and head nod. At the end, everyone breaks into cheers and laughter, even the waitress, and calls us *las chicas rítmicas* and I'm 98 percent certain that means that we girls have a good rhythm together.

"We got this," Frankie says.

And for some reason that makes my throat feel tight and my eyes get blurry and stingy. They each leave a couple of dollars on the table and everyone at the counter goes back to their coffee and chitchatting. The doors chime when Frankie, Amelia, and Ana walk out and I reach into my book bag for my notebook and turn to the pages where I've been working on poems. The last one is in Nestor's handwriting.

Change *is* hard. Don't be
Sorry. Be something great while
You are still so young.

And now I'm thinking that instead of wasting time writing poems, I should be starting to plan the details for Operation Save Ms. Dacie's. I've got one hundred ideas in my brain, and I've got to write them down so I can start making them real. Then I'm thinking maybe I can write them into poems.

What makes a poem is still a big who-knows, but I think it's kind of in the way it sounds, so I'll only know if I've written one if I try. If it sings a little like music when I say it out loud, or makes a big punch sound, then it might be a poem.

I draw out twelve dashes across my notebook page.

Sorry Mr. Slick Suit. Ms. Dacie's is ours. We're not for sale.

That one feels a little like a punch, and that makes me feel good, so I try another.

That garden will be growing in no time. It just needs love.

If everyone lends a hand we can pull out all the weeds.

When the weeds are all gone something new can grow up tall.

I read them out loud, and even though I'm not the only one at La Cocina I don't feel embarrassed at all, and they sound kind of like songs, and it still feels good, so I keep going. This time I try to do the rhyming ones like Ms. Dacie taught me.

A: We'll need the whole neighborhood,
B: Even Dad.
A: And we'll make change for good.
B: Mr. Slick Suit will be mad.

A: We'll sell cookies and we'll rent plots
B: Everyone'll own a piece of Dacie's place
A: It'll take work, lots
B: Sorry, Slick Suit. Close your briefcase.

The waitress raps her knuckles on the table next to my empty mug and raises her eyebrows, wondering if I want another refill. I shake my head no thanks, and she smiles and takes away my mug. I have to be home in eleven minutes.

I leave her a 50 percent tip because even though she

heard everything I told Frankie, Amelia, and Ana about my parents, and that's a fact because she refilled our mugs with hot chocolate without us even asking so we had something to do with our hands while we sat there, she didn't say anything, and she didn't give me sad eyes.

On the walk home I pass the café and for the first time notice a faded *Almonte's Laundry* painted on the brick above the new wooden *Hamilton Heights Café* sign. I pass the bar next door where everyone sits outside with fancy French fry cones, and then the lady selling *tamales* from her cart on the corner. The next block down, a man stands on a short stepladder and hammers boards over a restaurant window that used to advertise *especiales del día*. I've been here eight whole days and I haven't been in there yet, and now it's too late. I wonder what will open behind those doors, and where the man on the stepladder will go.

And I can't believe it took me eight days to have the actual best hot chocolate in the neighborhood, and I hope La Cocina stays here forever.

I check our mailbox in the lobby, and there's just one thing in there—a long white envelope with Izzy's bubbly handwriting on the front. Seeing her name in the top left corner and knowing that just seventy-two hours ago this envelope was in Vermont, and in her hands, makes my throat feel tight and my eyes burn.

I'm early by two minutes, but my parents are still standing right there by the door when I get home.

"I'm not late."

They both act like they just happened to be by the door doing something else, not waiting around for me, or listening for my footsteps, or the sound of the key in the front door. My dad starts looking through the pockets of his rain jacket that hangs from our front hooks, like he lost something important, but it's so obvious he's not really searching for anything.

"What are you looking for?" Mom asks, trying to hide her grin.

"My—uh—the—" Then they both just crack up.

Mom stops pretending to dust the windowsill with her shirtsleeve and covers her face.

"OK, OK, the truth comes out. We've had our ears pressed against the door for five minutes."

"And peeking through the peephole," Dad adds.

The image of them doing that gets me laughing too. "I'm not even late!" I say through my laughs. "I'm two whole minutes early."

"I know," Dad says. "We just— We're not used to not driving you everywhere and picking you up. This is a big change for us."

"Change is hard," I tell them.

Dad nods his head. "We just—"

"Love you so much," Mom finishes.

"Maybe even enough for a cell phone," Dad says.

I'm expecting Mom to sigh and say, *Henry! We're supposed to be on the same page about this!* but instead she just nods her head and says, "I think so."

Dad kisses me on the forehead, then the oven timer goes off and Mom hustles into the kitchen to take out roasting sweet potatoes and beets, and Dad walks back into the bedroom.

"Dinner in fifteen minutes," Mom calls. But right now I just want to be alone and read Izzy's letter and try not to get too excited that for ninety seconds it seemed like they were on the same team again.

I close the door and drop my bag and carefully open the sealed envelope because I don't want to rip through any part of Izzy's writing. I unfold her letter and start at *Dear Rain* and don't stop, not even at the periods, until I get to *Your Best Friend, Izzy.*

It makes me sad that everything she wrote on all the lines in between—like how they're having a field day, and how she has a solo in the final chorus concert, and how the whole class is making Ms. Carol a T-shirt—has already happened now, between the time she wrote them down with her pink pen to the time it arrived in my apartment-number-thirty-one mailbox.

That makes me feel even more than 288 miles away.

I start a letter back to her right away because I want her to know about Frankie and how she used to hate me but now we're teammates, and how she, Amelia, Ana, and I are the first-ever all-sixth-grade relay team to go to the state championships, and about Nestor, and how I actually *can* write poetry, and how I finished *The One and Only Ivan*, and all about Ms. Dacie and how she might lose funding for her house, but not if I can do something about it. And I want to write it quick because I don't want anything to change before I drop the letter in the big blue box on the corner and it arrives in her green plastic mailbox that sticks out from her front yard at the end of her driveway.

I sign it *Love, Rain*, fold it into three equal parts, and seal it in an envelope.

It feels a little weird that I didn't tell her about my parents, because I told my relay team already, and I used to tell Izzy everything, but if my plan works, then maybe they'll be back together and forget their whole plan to separate before this letter even gets to Vermont.

Mom knocks on the door with two garden bowls— sweet potatoes, beets, and spinach all mixed up with brown rice cooked with butter that you can still taste. "I thought we'd have a girls' dinner in here," she says.

I say OK, even though Dad invented the garden bowl, and none of the vegetables in this bowl are from our garden, and I know the only reason we're having a girls' dinner in here is to get me used to a table for two.

I was just getting used to three.

We sit on the edge of my bed, and Mom spreads a towel across my comforter for a tablecloth. We take a bite of our garden bowls at the same time and even though we don't say it out loud, we're both thinking the same thing—it doesn't taste quite as good here. And that's a fact, because we don't say, *Now* that's *good!* like we did every time we took our first bites in Vermont. And Dad isn't here to say *Like a garden in a bowl!* Vegetables just taste better when you planted them from a seed and watered them every day and watched them grow up from the soil toward the sky.

But the garden bowl makes me think of my plan for Ms. Dacie's house and how I know it can work.

Mom asks me about school and track, and I ask her if Izzy can visit this summer.

"Of course!" she says, and I'm already thinking about how I'll open the letter and add *PS: My mom says you can visit this summer! Ask your mom!*

I can't finish my bowl, probably because I'm full of hot chocolate. Mom says it's OK and takes our dishes to the kitchen. "Ice cream?" she calls.

"That's OK," I call back, and I'm 75 percent certain it's the first time I've ever turned down ice cream.

She pokes her head back into my room. "You feeling all right?" she jokes. "I found a store that sells Ben & Jerry's. I have cookie dough."

And I'm 100 percent certain it's the first time I've ever turned down Ben & Jerry's. "Just full," I say. "I'm going to read."

"OK, then," she says.

In the kitchen window across the alley, I can see the woman wiping down her counter. I can't see the man anywhere, so I still don't know if they're living in the same apartment or are just side-by-side neighbors. I watch her for a few minutes hoping she walks into the room with the TV, the one where I've seen the man sitting, but she doesn't. She turns out the light and disappears down the hall. So it's still a big who-knows.

I change into my pajamas and clip my book light to the pages of *The Crossover* by Kwame Alexander from Mrs. Baldwin's library. I read beneath my comforter more poems than I've read before in my whole life combined. All of his poems sing and all of them punch and every one of them follows a rhythm that's as clear as the music bouncing around the alley outside my window.

My eyes get droopy, and all the lights in our apartment are turned off except the little glow from my book light. I push the button on my digital watch. 10:12. Then I turn off my book light, let my eyes get used to the dark, slide the comforter off my body, and walk up on the balls of my feet, quietly, out of my room so I can go find what I'm looking for.

Their bedroom door is closed. I wonder if they say good night to each other or not, or if they draw an invisible line lengthwise down the bed like Guthrie and I used to when we had to share hotel beds on vacation.

I check the closet outside the bathroom first and can't see any boxes in there, just toilet paper and towels. Then I stand in front of the hall closet, which is right outside their bedroom, and for one second I think about flushing the toilet before I try opening the door so it drowns out the click and creak, but I don't. I just open it slowly and stop when it starts to squeak. It's stuffed with winter jackets that hang to the floor and boots and shoes all toppled over one another. Gym bags and hiking packs and water bottles and tennis racquets. We had a closet like this in Vermont. Mom called it our catch-all closet. Dad called it a mess.

Then I see it in the far back corner, behind all the long winter jackets and under two sleeping bags. The *Garden* box.

The tape stretched across the top is unbroken. I lift the box over the boots and shoes, pull it through the long-hanging coats, and carry it as quietly as I can back to my room.

I close the door, peel the tape from the top, and count what's in there.

Four trowels.

Six small pots.

Eight wooden stakes that still have Vermont soil caked on the pointed ends.

Four pairs of gardening gloves.

Ten seed packets: two tomato, two carrot, two peas, two green bell pepper, one summer squash, and one red-leaf kale.

I'm 100 percent certain it's too late in the season to plant tomatoes and summer squash, and I tell my brain to remember to look up the rest.

I take my pen from my book bag and make a list of what we'll need for sure on a Post-it note:

More seeds that can be planted in June
Soil
More gardening gloves

I know we'll need at least eight other things that I can't think of right now, and I try to tuck myself back into bed and go to sleep, but my brain can't stop thinking about getting dirt beneath my nails.

CHAPTER 27

Our All

The next day at Ms. Dacie's house we get everyone around in a circle, even Ms. Dacie, and map out our plan. Frankie explains how we're going to keep Trevor's idea of a bake sale, but add to it.

"Everything will be two dollars each and we'll have two bakers rotating in the kitchen so we always have oven-warmed cookies and no one will be able to resist."

Ana says we can make lemonade too, and everyone's already nodding their heads and saying, "Yeah," and they haven't even heard the best part yet.

Then I explain the garden. How right now it's just a tangled mess and not worth anything, but with a little love and care it could be something that produces vegetables and flowers and looks beautiful and everyone will want to visit.

Trevor asks how that will make money, and that's when I reveal the biggest part of my plan. "We'll rent little plots of the garden to people in the neighborhood who want to grow their own vegetables and flowers and take care of it."

Everyone's nodding their heads again and saying, "Yes! Good idea!"

"They'll pay every month for their plots, and Ms. Dacie can use the money to help pay the rent since she won't have the funding."

Cris and Edwin high-five, and Yasmin stands right up and starts a little happy dance. Everyone else is still nodding their heads.

"W-we st-still have to m-measure to s-see how many p-plots we can make," Amelia says.

"I can help with that!" Trevor says.

When I look, I notice Ms. Dacie isn't nodding her head. She's smiling, though, and looking over the top of her purple glasses at Frankie, then Amelia and Ana, then me, then at everyone around the circle. "You all are too sweet," she says. "And it means the world to me that you want to help, but it might be more money than a bake sale and a garden can make up."

A few kids groan, and my heart starts beating one

hundred beats per minute because I haven't thought about the plan not working.

"We at least have to try!" Frankie blurts. "We can't just do nothing."

"Yeah!" Casey says.

"You c-c-can't stop us from t-trying," Amelia adds.

Dacie smiles and I think there might be tears caught up in the corners of her eyes.

"OK," she says. "Let's give it our all. But if we don't raise enough, promise me we won't be disappointed. We'll be proud that we tried, and we'll donate what we *do* make to the library. Deal?"

"Deal!"

"I'll make the fliers and signs!" Ana says and starts pulling out the art supplies.

"We'll make a grocery list for all the ingredients we need for cookies!" Yasmin and Cris grab hands and hustle off to the kitchen.

Casey says he'll start cleaning up for the guests so the house looks good and organized.

Trevor says he'll make a big donation jar out of the old jumbo pretzel jug from last weekend's movie night. "Maybe some people will just want to make a donation. Every little bit counts!"

Everyone says they'll hang fliers at their schools and tell their parents to tell their friends too.

"I'll put it online!" Edwin jumps up and turns on one of Ms. Dacie's old desktops.

Matthew starts going through Dacie's records because every fun event has to have music, and Alia says we should call a newspaper. "Maybe they'll write a story and that'll make more people want to come!"

And while everyone is thinking of ideas and jumping up and organizing, I watch Ms. Dacie, and now I'm 100 percent certain that those were tears caught in the corners of her eyes, because they're not caught anymore, they're running free down her face. Like we already saved her house.

Then she clears her throat and says, "Just one more thing. I haven't touched those garden beds in years. We're going to need someone who really knows what they're doing. An expert."

That's when I pipe up. "I've got that covered."

And I don't care how my dad buttons his shirt, or what direction his hair sticks in, he's opening that bedroom door, and he's going through that *Garden* box, and walking up the street to Ms. Dacie's, and getting his hands dirty.

Frankie nods her head at me because she knows the other part of my plan: to get them here, to get them gardening, side by side, like they used to, to push them back together before it's too late.

Before we leave, Ana's drawn a huge sign on poster board with colorful blooming gardens and a table of the most realistic and delicious-looking cookies.

Ms. Dacie's House Fund-raiser and Community Event

Saturday June 16 ALL DAY

All Welcome

Jer helps Ana tie it tight to the gate out front so that everyone walking by sees it and with all of us gathering around and buzzing with energy and Ms. Dacie touching us all on the shoulder to say *Thanks*, with those crow's-feet wrinkles spreading out from her eyes, it makes it feel official and real.

In exactly eight days we will give it our all.

CHAPTER 28

Garden Box

Later that night, under my covers, I try to think of how I can convince my dad to help, to leave the apartment, assess Ms. Dacie's garden beds, find a planting store, stock up on supplies, and get his hands dirty in the soil again.

I think of three different ways that I could ask him, but none of them sounds right. I don't think he'll say no, but I think he might not say yes. He'll say that he'll think about it, or maybe, or that it sounds like a lot of work, an impossible job, and before he can say a yes or no, it'll be too late and Slick Suit will sign a big check and Ms. Dacie's will be gone.

Then I decide I'll let him say the first words instead. I push back the covers and climb out of bed and tiptoe with the *Garden* box in both hands. I set it down carefully outside their doorway and make sure it's in the exact center so he can't shuffle around it on the way to the bathroom or sidestep it to get his coffee from the kitchen. It'll be right there, tape pulled back and top opened, twelve inches from his feet, dead center, when he opens the door in the morning.

I tiptoe back to my room and pull the comforter over me, and even though I don't think it'll make too much of a difference, I fall asleep with all my fingers crossed.

I wake up to my dad's voice. "What in the— Maggie, I thought I said—"

I jump out of bed and open my door fast before dad pulls the tape back across the *Garden* box and gives it a little kick out of his way. It slides across the floor toward the kitchen.

Mom comes out of the room, tying her bathrobe around her waist. "I didn't put it there."

They both look up at me and I realize I didn't think about this part, what I would say if he kicked the box instead of opening it wider to see what he could do with what's inside.

"Rain?"

I don't even give myself one second to take a big breath, I just start in about Ms. Dacie's gardens and how they're a tangled mess and we need an expert because otherwise Ms. Dacie's will have to close and all these kids who are so nice to me won't have a place to bake cookies or do their homework or go to summer art camp.

"Whoa, whoa," Mom says. "Breathe." She gestures toward a kitchen stool and I sit down.

I take a big breath that lasts three seconds going in and three seconds coming out, and I start over.

"Ms. Dacie is losing her funding. She can't afford to run her place on her own." I tell them about Operation Save Ms. Dacie's and our plan for a big fund-raiser event. How we'll bake cookies, and make lemonade, and rent out the garden plots for people in the neighborhood to grow their own vegetables and flowers.

"You should see her house, Dad," I say. I tell him about the math tutors, and the bookshelves, and her records, and baking cookies, and the art supplies, and how she even helped me write poetry when no one else could.

"I'm sure it's a great place." He puts his hand on my shoulder. "And you are very sweet to come up with a plan, but this might be a bigger job than a fund-raiser."

He takes one step away toward the hall closet, where the *Garden* box used to hide behind the long-hanging coats and among the boots, and I'm not 100 percent certain where my voice rises from so fast, but I think the same place where the missing reaches up and up, and I forget about giving my knuckles a good crack and let my voice out loud.

"Stop!"

And he does. Right in his tracks.

"You can't just walk off!"

And he doesn't. He just stands there frozen, waiting.

"And don't even think about putting that *Garden* box away, because if you're not going to use it, I am." I take a big breath again. "I'm at least going to try."

"Rain—"

"You're in or you're out," I tell him. And I wish I hadn't said it that way, because I'm 88 percent certain he's out and maybe he just needs a little more time to think about how it just might work, and even if it doesn't, he'll get to have dirt under his nails and make something grow.

He doesn't say anything for three seconds and I don't want to wait one second longer, so I take the *Garden* box back to my room and close the door.

I count fifty-two bricks on the building across the alley before my heart starts beating its normal beats, and when my blood is moving calm like that through my body again I decide I'm not giving up on Dad so quickly, and I know the exact place that will make him want to help. I just have to get him there.

CHAPTER 29

Church

On Sunday I'm up early and I'm the one pulling on my parents' toes and saying, "Wakey, wakey!"

I don't even know if my dad's ever been to church before, but I have to get him to go today because Frankie and Amelia and Ana will be there and they're going to help me convince him to help us with Dacie's garden for the fund-raiser.

Plus, if Mom and Dad come with me to the church for community service today, it'll be like a warm-up for Ms. Dacie's house. Even if it's just washing dishes or making a salad, they can remember what it was like to do something next to each other.

I open their door a crack and peek in. And I think I'm right about them making an invisible line down the middle of the bed because they are two separate humps of comforter with space between like two rows of different crops in a vegetable garden.

The door creaks a little as I open it wider, and Dad sits up so fast it scares me. "What happened? Rain? Is everything OK?"

Then Mom shoots up fast too. "What's wrong?"

And it makes my throat get all scratchy and that burning rise up behind my eyes because I'm 98 percent certain that if a little door creak makes them shoot straight out of sleep, then they probably don't ever fall down into that deep sleep that feels so good and takes you one million miles away and that Mom always says is so important to make your brain a more efficient learner. I'm scared of deep sleep after that night too.

"Just me," I say. "Everything's fine."

They both release huge sighs, and even though it's because they were scared first thing in the morning, and I'm the one who scared them, I'm glad they at least did it together.

"Will you come with me to help at the church?" I ask.

"I thought you were getting all your hours at Ms. Dacie's," Mom says.

"I am," I say. "But I still want to go. It's important."

She looks at me and smiles, and I think she's sending me a secret message that says she's proud of me.

"I'm in," she says.

"Dad?"

"Oh—I think I should probably . . ."

What I want to do is scream that he has nothing else he should probably do but get out of bed and get dressed and go help some people who don't have food or homes even if it means he won't be taking space from Mom today.

But instead I crack my knuckles and say, "You're going," and turn around fast before he can say anything else.

Before I get the six steps back to my bedroom he calls, "OK. I'm coming," and I pump my fist like we already won the city championships and saved Ms. Dacie's house.

It's raining when we leave for the church, and the rain here isn't like the rain in Vermont. It smells different, like hot street instead of heavy grass, and it collects in big puddles at the curbs that we hop over at each intersection.

The weather muffles the voices that sing from the church doors, like the songs are caught up in each raindrop and washing down the street. I recognize the music from last week. This time, my dad stops, right there in the rain, and listens.

"Wow," he whispers. "It's really something."

The rain drips from the hood of his raincoat, and I imagine little songs traveling in streams down his face and splashing open on the sidewalk.

And it really is something. And that's a fact, because I've heard church music three times before in Vermont, and the singing never sounded like this. Like great joy bursting out from darkness, like happiness that rises up and up above the tops of the tallest buildings all mixed up with sadness that sinks down below the deepest subways.

I can tell the music is singing right to my dad's heart, because I'm 92 percent certain that tears are mixing up with the raindrops on his face and I'm 100 percent certain I know what's trapped up in his tears and splashing open on the sidewalk and washing down the street. The songs that Guthrie used to play on his guitar, and the stories of him we haven't told for 360 days.

I'm about to reach up and grab his hand sticking out from his raincoat and send him a little secret message that my heart hurts too and sometimes music makes it hurt worse, when Mom says, "We should get inside. Come on." Then she's hustling off, and Dad and I follow her sneaker squish marks up the sidewalk, around the corner of the church, and down the steps to the kitchen.

Ms. Claudia is there and she offers us a towel and hangs our rain jackets to dry. Two other women are already there washing lettuce for a salad, and Ms. Claudia assigns my mom and dad to sandwiches. Dad will smear the bread with mayonnaise and Mom will load it with turkey and cheese.

I'm opening big bags of oranges and putting them into a basket, but really I'm watching Mom and Dad out of the corner of my eye. They're not saying anything, just smearing mayonnaise and layering cheese slices, but I think they make a pretty good team, because the sandwiches are stacking up high on the platter fast.

Frankie shows up, then Amelia and Ana. I can tell from their drippy jackets that it's still raining outside. Claudia greets them and they all talk in Spanish and hang their raincoats next to ours. Then Claudia says the four of us can start putting out the boxes of plastic forks and spoons and cups and napkins. We also need to fill the big coolers with water and unfold all the chairs and fit them around the tables. We put our hands up for a quadruple high five and get to work, and I know we're a good team because we finish all our tasks before the door opens and the first hungry person walks in.

I recognize some people from last time. The little girl, Natasha, with her teddy bear and her mom, is wearing a black trash bag today, cut with holes and turned into a poncho. Rain drips from the bottom of the plastic onto a pair of adult sneakers tied tight over her footed pajamas. The shoes are worn through on the sides, and too big, and make her feet look like they've walked too many miles for her little years.

Claudia helps her out of the poncho, and Ana bends down and speaks to her in Spanish. Natasha smiles and shows her the teddy bear and Ana kisses its nose and they run off together, giggling, to one of the tables.

"Does Ana know her?" I ask Frankie.

She shrugs. "Kind of seems like it."

I deliver the basket of oranges to the table where the coolers are so people can help themselves and Ana calls to me, "Toss one!"

I raise my eyebrows and point to the oranges.

She nods her head and puts up her hands. "I'm open!"

I underhand toss her an orange, and in thirty seconds she and Natasha are bowling the orange into plastic cups and watching them crash to the floor. Natasha cracks up hard each time, and when I turn back toward the kitchen I can see that her mom's eyes are red, and not just because she's tired.

My mom walks Natasha's mom to the table, and my dad takes over stirring the pot of soup on the stove and ladling it into paper bowls.

The door opens again and it's Nestor. He's shivering hard from the rain, so Claudia helps him out of his top layer, an oversize sweatshirt with a split zipper, and the same second that Claudia peels it from his shoulders and hangs it by the hood on the hooks in the back, I can smell the rot coming from the layers of clothes still pressed to his skin. It makes me wonder where he sleeps and when was the last time he took a shower, and a sadness rolls deep through me.

"New Rain," he says. "You came back."

I smile and say hi, and before he can shake the drops from his gray beard I say, "I found a way better hot chocolate."

Frankie comes up next and says, "It's the best in the neighborhood."

"That's a fact," I say.

Nestor chuckles. "I bet I know just where you're talking about too. La Cocina," he says. "Emilio and Rosalie's place. Been there forever."

Frankie nods, and my parents come over to meet Nestor. "We're Rain's parents," they say, and even though both of them raised me to put out my hand for a shake when I'm meeting someone new, neither one of them do, and I can't help but think it's because Nestor's hands are cracked and caked and smeared with filth and grime right down to the fingerprints, and unlike us after a potato harvest day, he doesn't have a garden hose to rinse the dirt right off.

Claudia runs the water in the kitchen sink and

invites everyone to wash up before lunch is served. Ana bounces Natasha over piggyback, and Nestor gets last in line and when it's his turn he washes his hands over and over, squirting a second and third glob of soap into his palms and scrubbing hard between each finger.

There are twelve people here this week, sitting and eating, resting their heads, or chatting with each other in short, tired sentences, and looking out the one small basement window and hoping the rain stops bouncing against the sidewalk outside.

"*That's* really something too," my dad says, watching them from the kitchen. And this time I know that he's talking about how many people live hard like this. Moms and kids and old guys who should be living easy. It really is something. And it takes your breath away and makes your heart ache, just like the music from the church does. And that's a fact.

Because in this little basement, on this one corner there are twelve people that need. And it makes me wonder who else in this neighborhood needs and who doesn't know about this kitchen, and how many more people there are, stretching down and down toward Times Square where all the big lights flash and beyond. And what these twelve do when it's not Sunday. And if Natasha goes to school yet, or if she will, and if she'll have enough clothes and shoes that fit, and if other kids will be nice to her.

"Really something," my dad says again, and shakes his head.

Frankie brings an empty plate of sandwiches into the kitchen and Dad helps her reload with more.

"You know, Mr. Andrews," she says, "Ms. Dacie is in need of some help too."

Dad looks up at her and then at me and kind of gives me a half smile. "So I heard."

"She's losing her funding and someone wants to buy her house and turn it into something else that won't help kids at all."

There are seven full seconds of silence as they stack sandwiches together.

"Ms. Dacie's always been there for me when things were hard. I want to be there for her now," Frankie says. Then she stops stacking and looks up at my dad. "We could use your help too, Mr. Andrews."

Before he can say anything, Amelia's there too and she's trying her best to tell him all about the tangled gardens and how no one else knows how to weed and plant and make anything grow.

Ana piggybacks Natasha over, and I slip away with the platter of sandwiches. I walk around the tables and offer seconds to everyone. Nestor takes two and pats the seat next to him, so I sit.

"How's that poetry going?"

"It's OK," I tell him.

"What are you writing about?"

"Mostly about how much I miss my friend Izzy."

"Ah, because you're New Rain." Nestor sighs. "Tell me, where were you before you were new?"

I start telling him all about Vermont and Izzy's tree house and Ms. Carol's classroom and the library and the garden in our backyard behind the house.

"It hurts," he tells me. And it isn't a question, so I just let the words settle on the table between us. "I know a thing or two about loss."

I let those words settle too and wonder about all the things he must have lost, including his deal with the Almontes at the Laundromat when it turned into the café.

"A thing or two about loss, indeed," he repeats.

"Me too," I say.

Nestor lets my words settle in with his. He nods and his forehead crinkles up into a hundred wrinkles and he presses his lips together tight like he knows I'm talking about something more than just a tree house, a loss deep below the surface, past where carrots grow or trains rumble.

"It hurts," he says again.

And that's a fact.

I'm looking at my dad with Frankie and Amelia and Ana. Amelia is nodding her head, and I can hear Ana saying how Ms. Dacie has always been there for her and her mom, through the worst times. "I don't know where I'd be without her."

I remember the bag of leftovers Ms. Dacie passed to Ana on the way out one day, and I wonder if it was more than just a nice gesture. I wonder if she'd passed brown bags of leftover food to Ana before. I wonder if Ana and her mom need like some of the people here need.

Now my mom is there, next to my dad, and she's jotting something down on a Post-it and I can hear my dad say, "End of season, so we'll have to . . ." and I know he's in.

Frankie gives me a little thumbs-up.

Before I can give my brain two seconds to remember that Nestor has nothing to donate, I'm turning back to him and saying he should come next Saturday to Ms. Dacie's place. We're having a big fund-raiser and we're renting garden plots and selling cookies and lemonade and we want to help Ms. Dacie save her house. The second I say it, I turn red and hot and wish I could take it all back. But before I can, Nestor smiles.

"I'll be there."

Frankie, Amelia, and Ana walk with us on the way home. It's still raining, and we all pull up our hoods and walk two by two, weaving around people who duck under umbrellas along the sidewalk. I'm keeping pace with Ana, our heads down, faces out of the rain.

"Did you know that girl?" I ask. "Natasha?"

We keep slosh-sloshing through the puddles and shaking drops from our hoods.

"No," she says.

"It seemed like—"

"I just know what it feels like," she says. The rain is falling hard and muffling her voice. "Being a kid like her."

"Oh." It barely comes out as a whisper, and the wind carries it off fast.

A car honks and swerves around a garbage truck, and a woman struggles with an umbrella that turns inside out in the wind.

"So I guess, in a way, I kind of knew her."

Frankie turns around and says, "Race ya!" and in one second we all four take off, leaving my parents behind, and sprint side by side by side by side up the hill to Ana's street, then Amelia's, then Frankie and I tear around the corner onto 152nd Street. And with each step I try to erase all the loss. Nestor and the Almontes, Ms. Dacie, and Ana, and with each stride I try to pull myself away from that night.

CHAPTER 30

That Night

For one second I thought that if maybe I just opened my eyes I would see him sitting on the back of an ambulance with a blanket wrapped around his shoulders. The medics would tell us that he was lucky and if it had been one second sooner, or one inch to the left, he wouldn't have survived. They'd tell us that he was OK and could go home with us, and I'd curl up in my sleeping bag on his bedroom floor every night that week.

But just opening your eyes never got a heart started beating again, and that's a fact. Not everything happens like it does in books.

CHAPTER 31

Brave

All I've done for the past two days, besides practice relay starts and handoffs, is make posters for the fund-raiser, hang fliers in store windows and slide them under apartment doors, fill a grocery cart with baking ingredients and lemons for all-day cookie baking and fresh-squeezed lemonade making, and measure the raised garden plots and divide them into equal parts that people can rent.

Since Sunday at the church, Dad has been visiting Ms. Dacie's and taking the subway to a garden nursery on the Upper West Side and buying more seed packets and plants and extra gardening tools. The *Garden* box is wide open and in Ms. Dacie's hallway, and Dad has already started weeding and working the soil. And yesterday when I got there after practice his fingernails were jammed with dirt and when he walked me home, we stopped at La Cocina for two hot chocolates to go.

Even though things are starting to feel pretty good and ready for the fund-raiser, I haven't written one more word of poetry this week because even in English class yesterday I was busy drafting a thank-you letter that we could give to people if they donate on Saturday. Every time Mrs. Baldwin walked by my desk, I flipped back to my page of poems and tapped my eraser on my temple like I was thinking of the next perfect word, and it worked for the whole period.

But now the poetry slam is in forty-eight hours.

Kids come into English class fast and take out their notebooks and push their desks together and don't even wait for Mrs. Baldwin to announce that today is another workday before the poetry slam and to use our time well.

"Eeny meeny miney mo," one girl chants while tapping each of her four poems. "Catch a tiger by the—"

Then Mrs. Baldwin claps her hands three times fast and counts down from five to get our attention.

"Elena's rendition of *Eeny Meeny* just reminded me that maybe I could share a hint about how to choose which of your four poems you'll share out loud with the class," Mrs. Baldwin announces. Everyone laughs and starts to *eeny meeny miney mo* their own poems, joking along with Ms. Baldwin.

Elena calls back, "Should I pick out of a hat instead? I like all my poems."

"I don't like any of mine," a boy grumbles from the back of the class.

Mrs. Baldwin quiets everyone down again and says, "When you're choosing, I want you to pick the one that makes you feel comfortable, but also makes you feel brave. We are all agreeing to be the best, most kind, and generous audience there ever was, so now is the time to do something brave."

"Definitely going with *meeny*, then," Elena says, tapping the second poem in her notebook, and Mrs. Baldwin gives her a high five.

"Now back to work."

Kids break off into partners and keep erasing and jotting and erasing and jotting and reading beneath their breath and erasing again.

I'm not the kind of person to procrastinate because I know that's just the brain's way of trying to minimize uncertainty and the feeling of danger, but really it doesn't make any of that feeling go away, and that's a fact because my mom used to talk to Guthrie about waiting until the last minute all the time. But reading any poem in front of anyone feels a little dangerous, and I agreed to read Amelia's too, so I just start counting the lines on my blank notebook page instead of working.

I can hear Elena reading her poem to the girl sitting next to her. She stumbles over the first line and stops and sighs and says, "Can I start again?"

Her partner nods her head and says, "You got this."

Mrs. Baldwin is sitting with the boy in the back who said he didn't like any of his poems and she's running her finger down a page of his notebook and he doesn't look like he hates the one Mrs. Baldwin has just picked out and says is beautiful. He shrugs his shoulders and says, "I guess so," and the second she moves on to another desk group, he starts reading under his breath to himself and I'm 89 percent certain he smiles at the end.

"H-here," Amelia says, and pushes a piece of loose-leaf paper to me. "I-if you d-don't w-want to do it anymore—"

"I want to."

First I read it to myself. It's a short poem, only eight lines, and it's about her fifth-grade graduation. She does a lot of what Mrs. Baldwin taught us about imagery, using colors and sounds and feelings so we can really feel like we're there.

"It's good," I tell her.

"It's only OK," she says.

I spend the rest of the class practicing reading

Amelia's poem because it feels less scary than working on my own. By the end of the period, I have it almost memorized. And when the bell rings, everyone walks out standing one inch taller, like Mrs. Baldwin watered them overnight and planted them in just the right light.

CHAPTER 32

Memory Games

Today I can't go to Dacie's because I'm at the hospital in my mom's office. She's free on Wednesdays at four thirty, which is perfect because it's right after practice, and we need more copies of the fliers for the fund-raiser. Mom says I can use her machine for free and she'll even get colored paper. I choose neon green and she teaches me how to stack the paper in the trays and send our hand-written flier into the machine. It chugs and spits out perfect neon green versions with Frankie's handwriting on top in Spanish, and mine on the bottom in English.

As the machine works and green papers pile up I look around the office. There are diagrams and posters of the brain, binders and plastic-covered reports on her wide wooden desk, and plants growing in the windowsill.

Mom catches my eye, points a finger at me, and says, "Pants. Go!"

It might sound random to anyone else, but I know exactly what we're doing. Playing a memory game.

"Pants," I repeat, and in less than one second my brain makes one hundred clicks and connects *pants* to different memories back and back and back. "Pants. Buying navy pants for the school uniform . . . when I ripped my pants in third grade and you had to come bring me a new pair . . . sneaking Guthrie's pants out of his bottom drawer before he was ready to hand them down."

Then my brain just stops and my eyes just fill and Mom gets up to check the copy machine. She brings over a stack of neon green fliers and tells me that she'll help me fold them. And I know what she's doing. She's keeping my hands busy because physical activity helps your brain focus. That's why she got Guthrie a guitar when he was four years old and why she marched into his middle school and told the principal her son *would* be chewing gum and doodling all over his notebook while the teacher talked, and maybe the teacher shouldn't be talking so long to a group of thirteen-year-olds anyway, and if she had any questions about why he would be chewing gum and doodling, she would be happy to explain about the neurotransmitters in the brain that control focus and attention and how keeping your hands busy increases those levels. Then she hustled right out of the office.

So we fold and fold the fliers between the Spanish and English and my brain starts to click again.

"Sneaking Guthrie's pants out of his bottom drawer before he was ready to hand them down and rolling them up and up until they didn't drag on the ground . . . wishing on my sixth birthday cake that I could wear pants every day and never have to wear a dress again . . . pulling a denim dress over my head, getting stuck, then running to the garden. Dirt beneath my fingernails."

"It always ends there," Mom says. "Your first memory."

We fold in silence for forty-five seconds before she tries a new word. "Light."

My brain makes its clicks. "Running home after practice with Frankie, Amelia, and Ana, watching the white and red blink on the walk signals." Then red lights flash with the beat of sirens in my head, and that remembering rises on up and tightens my throat.

Mom hands me another flier to fold, so I get my hands busy. "What's next?" she asks.

"Guthrie's ambulance."

Mom folds two fliers fast and puts them in the done pile, and my brain tries to hustle past that night and on to the next memory.

"Turning on our flashlight every Christmas Eve when we creaked down the stairs and tried to catch Santa coming down the chimney . . . Izzy climbing up the tree house ladder, her headlamp bouncing light through the door and across the wall . . . The flash of the camera when Guthrie took my picture crying at the garden. The dirt beneath my nails."

Mom and I smile.

"I know I'm the queen of hustle," she says. We're out of fliers, so she straightens out the pile again and again, tapping the edges against her desk. "But you don't have to hustle past your memories with him. He's part of who you are."

The first thing I think is that she still hasn't said his name, but then two seconds later I'm thinking about my mom being "the queen of hustle" and my brain's picturing her goofy dancing across our kitchen floors like she used to.

It feels wrong to laugh right now because this is only the third time Mom's talked about Guthrie in 363 days, but I can feel it starting in my stomach and I can't erase the image of Mom sliding across the floor in her socks.

"Queen of hustle?" I say, and a little laugh escapes.

She looks up and even though her eyes are full of tears that look like they could spill out at any second, she laughs too. "You've seen my moves," she says. And now I can tell that we're both picturing her goofy dance.

She does a little chair dance, jolting her shoulders and jutting her chin, and we both laugh.

"But it's true," she says. "I'd benefit from slowing down every once in a while."

And I'm hoping she slows down enough to realize that she doesn't want to live away from Dad. If she slows down a little and Dad picks up the pace, like he has been at Dacie's and getting ready for the fund-raiser, maybe they'll be running at the same speed again. And maybe it's not too late to be one in four.

CHAPTER 33

Poems

I have four poems due in seventeen hours, but really nine hours because I'm not the kind of person to sneak and do their English homework in other classes just because English isn't until the end of the day, and really three hours because I'm not the kind of person who can sleep if they haven't finished all their home-work before bed.

It's not that I don't have four poems. I have eighteen if you count the ones that are just six words and don't sing or punch, nineteen if you count Nestor's poem that he scribbled in my notebook. I just don't have any that I want to read out loud to my whole class.

Dad knocks on my bedroom door and comes in. He's

wearing a dirty flannel, but the good kind of dirty, the kind that comes from working in the actual dirt, not from wearing the same shirt every day and never getting out of bed to change.

"You're busy," he says, pointing to the poems in my notebook. "But I just wanted to say that you and your friends have done a great job organizing this fund-raiser for Dacie, and even if it doesn't work, it'll be a great day, and a great tribute to her."

"It'll work—" I start.

"But it might not. She's losing a lot of funding, Rain. I just don't want your hopes soaring." He rubs the little beard growing on his face. "I can promise you one thing, though. Those gardens will be beautiful on Saturday."

I smile.

"Now, write some poems," he says, and closes my door.

It takes me forever, even though for the first three poems I pretty much use what I already wrote in my notebook, except I add a little or change a little. I especially add to "Poem 3" because when Ms. Dacie read it this week she said she loved how some words meant two different things and how that feels like poetry to her. I think

about the word *hard* and how it can mean hard like the
floor of Izzy's tree fort, but also hard like difficult, and I
think I can make that a poem.

Poem 1
When you feel all jumbled, go for a run.
It's more than just exercise and fun.
It empties your brain,
At least if you're Rain.

Poem 2
We'll need the whole neighborhood.
We'll fill the space.
And we'll make change for good.
Everyone needs Ms. Dacie's place.

Poem 3
Best place to sleep is
a tall tree fort with your friend.
Hard can be OK.

Ivan's past was hard.
Even though his life's good now,
he's from that hard past.

Find a friend who will
go high above the ground where
hard can be OK.

There aren't any other poems in my notebook that I really like except the one Nestor scribbled in there in the café, and I can't use that one because that's called plagiarism and I could get in big trouble for pretending I wrote it instead.

So I start over, and this time I try no rules, even though it makes me feel kind of lost and uncomfortable. But I fill it with what I know—facts.

Poem 4
363 days gone
1 Christmas
4 gardening seasons
3 report cards
55 ski runs
51 Friday family dinners
3 pairs of worn-out sneakers,
that have run through, run away, run to erase
the length of 130,680 songs that I've counted
out in my head,
wondering,

if maybe you could just still be there,
at the concert,
listening.
The number of our memories together between now
and the dirt is
a big who-knows.
But I won't let those sneak off and out.
And if they try, I promise. Promise. I'll say no. Stay.

CHAPTER 34

Slam

My heart rate is one hundred thirty, which is seventy beats per minute faster than usual. At least twenty-five of those extra beats are because tomorrow is June fifteenth, the worst day ever, and the track championships, and Mom is skipping work and she and Dad are going to meet us there to watch and cheer, and we have to win because maybe they'll jump in the air and high-five and end up in a hug right as the first-ever all-sixth-grade relay team crosses the finish line.

Another twenty-five of those beats is because Saturday is Dacie's fund-raiser and ever since Dad popped his head in my door and said that he doesn't want my hopes to soar, my brain has been clicking with a hundred questions about what will happen if there is no Ms. Dacie's house. What will happen to Ms. Dacie? Will Slick Suit buy her house and what will he turn it into, and who will go there instead of all the kids who need that living room, and that kitchen stocked with cookie ingredients, and that door that's always open?

The other twenty beats per minute is because I'm sitting in Mrs. Baldwin's class and she's pulling numbers out of a hat, one through thirty-four, and when she pulls out the number that's next to our name on the library card chart, it's our turn to read a poem out loud.

Even though I'm reading "Poem 1," which is short and easy to read, and not about anything that makes my heart hurt, my notebook is still shaking in my hands as I sit and wait for her to call my number.

Four kids have already read, so I have about a 3 percent chance that I'll be called next, and what's worse, if I don't get called, my chances go up and up and up.

I'm number thirty-four.

"Seventeen," she calls, and most of the class sighs and a few kids cheer and José hides his face.

José's poem is about his dad. It's five lines long and each line starts with the letters that spell out *DADDY*. Mrs. Baldwin makes him put it up on the SMART board so we can see how he wrote *DADDY* down the page. It's really good. It's a singing kind of poem right up to the last line.

"You aren't always here, but you're never far from me."

The class claps, and I'm 70 percent certain if José stays standing up there for two more seconds his eyes will fill up. He returns to his seat fast and the kids around him lean over and pat his shoulders.

I wish I had written a poem about Izzy with the letters of her name down the page like that. Though I can't think of one line that starts with *Z*, and I definitely can't think of two.

Mrs. Baldwin calls number three, then twenty-four and eleven.

One poem is Elena's, and it's about moving to the United States and how much she misses her home. And even though I've never been to the Dominican Republic, she's so good at imagery I feel like I'm there every second she's reading.

The next reader is the boy from the back row who said he didn't like any of his poems. His name is Sam and it takes everyone saying *You can do it* and *Come on, Sam* to get him to stand up and walk slowly to the front of the room.

"Fine," he says. "But only so I can pass English, because I'm not doing this all over again."

Everyone laughs with him and chants, "For the grade! For the grade!" He wrote about missing his grandma who passed away last year. I can see Mrs. Baldwin catch his eye and nod like he can do this, and even though we can tell he's nervous, he doesn't stop once, and as soon as he reads his last word, he walks fast back to his seat in the last row as everyone claps and says, "Wow."

The next poem is from Anthony, who everyone thought might really actually read a *roses are red* poem, but instead he reads one about how hard school is, and it sings and punches in all the right places.

The class cheers after each one, and I calculate that Mrs. Baldwin will go through two and a half boxes of tissues at this rate. She wipes her eyes and blows her nose and passes the box around. I've only been here for ten school days, but I feel like I'm getting little secret messages from everyone in the room, that it's OK to share something hard if you want, and that everyone has everyone else's back.

Every time someone else goes up, my own poem seems smaller and smaller, and after hearing about José's dad, and how much Elena misses her home, reading a short poem about running seems stupid, even if that's a word I'm not supposed to use.

Ms. Dacie calls number ten. Frankie.

She stands there in front of the class, her hands shaking her paper so much I'm not sure she'll be able to read the words, and I remember when I first saw her sitting on the stoop when we were moving into apartment thirty-one. Even though she's shaking and taking deep breaths before she starts her first line, she still looks as tough as she did then, tying her Flyknit Racers and glaring up at me.

Then she starts, and her voice doesn't shake like her paper does, not at all. She's as confident as she is when she's sprinting toward the finish line, and her poem sings as loud and deep as church music.

The class is silent until the last stanza.

"Reggie.

She helped me be me.

From Franchesca, who fears who she is

To Frankie, who's free."

Kids are clapping and cheering, maybe because it sounds so good with all those *f*s flying, or maybe because they knew Reggie too.

"Beautiful," Mrs. Baldwin says.

Frankie sits back down in the desk next to me, and kids from the row behind are patting her shoulders and saying that they miss Reggie, but they know she and Reggie are best friends forever. And it seems like there are thirty-three voices in Spanish and English that are telling little stories about Reggie. *Remember when . . .* and laughter. Even Amelia pipes up and says, "And the f-f-faucet in science c-class. Mr. R-Roberts's f-face!"

Everyone cracks up, and I wish I knew the whole story.

I pat Frankie's shoulder too and smile. She smiles back, even though I live in apartment thirty-one.

Then Mrs. Baldwin calls number thirty. No one jumps up to read, and Mrs. Baldwin calls it again.

"Who is thirty?"

But before I remember that number thirty is Amelia, and it's my turn to read her poem, Amelia leans over and whispers, "I g-got this."

"Amelia, I'll read—"

"I w-w-want t-to."

The whole class hushes, and Mrs. Baldwin nods her head.

From the first word, I know that Amelia isn't reading about her fifth-grade graduation anymore. She switched, and that's a fact because I have her fifth-grade graduation poem memorized.

The one she's reading is a series of rhyming punches that makes the class go "Ohhhh," and she has to wait until everyone quiets down to continue on. She stutters through each line, but somehow that makes it better because the whole poem is about her voice.

"And j-just b-b-because I
D-don't say it s-s-smooth
Doesn't mean y-y-y-you have to be r-rude

And j-just b-because my b-brain and t-tongue fight
w-wars

D-doesn't mean m-my voice is l-l-less than yours."

The class goes wild, and Amelia is half laughing and crying all at the same time and she holds up her hand to quiet us down because she's not done.

"Yes, I w-wish I s-sounded slick l-like butter,
B-but alas, I h-have a st-st-stutter."

The class whoops and hollers again and Amelia takes her seat, and three girls hug her and say that she is such a good poet, and she is. Even the boys who laughed at her ten days ago are clapping for her, and something tells me that they won't ever laugh at someone else like that again.

I'm about to lean over and pat Amelia on the shoulder too, but Mrs. Baldwin calls number thirty-four.

"Rain! Rain! Rain!" Frankie starts chanting, and before I even know how I got there I'm standing in front of the whole class, my heart beating one hundred forty beats per minute, and all the extra beats are for this moment, and even though I want to start reading, it's like my voice doesn't work, and instead of reading, I'm wondering if this is how Amelia feels all the time.

I stand there silent for twenty seconds, holding my notebook tighter and tighter, and every second I'm standing there I'm receiving secret little messages, everyone rooting for me, saying it's OK. And I remember what Mrs. Baldwin said about which poem to read aloud. Something that makes you feel brave.

My fingers flip a few pages forward in my notebook, past "Poem 1," and I start.

"'Poem Four,'" I say.

I read each line slowly, and the whole class is silent. I don't look up from the page at all until I say the last line.

"And if they try, I promise. Promise. I'll say no. Stay."

No one cheers right away or whoops and hollers like they did for Amelia, and I think I'm such an idiot and I should have forgotten about being brave and just read "Poem 1" and I don't know what I was thinking, and now I have tears running fast down my cheeks and everyone is staring.

Then all at once I hear clapping, lots, and when I look up I see Amelia standing and then Frankie. Then others stand and clap loud and cheer and Mrs. Baldwin blows her nose and passes the tissue box around the class. I'm not the only one with tears falling off my chin.

The clapping doesn't stop when I sit back down. I feel

hands on my shoulders and Frankie sneaks me a secret team handshake.

And in this minute, I don't feel so much like a one-and-only.

CHAPTER 35

June Fifteenth

From where our team is gathered and huddled on the outside of the track, I count nineteen different team uniforms, and that's just what I can see from here. I know there are more teams around the back of the bleachers, which reach up and up almost as high as the buildings around them.

One team has matching maroon-and-white warm-up suits and gym bags and water bottles and even their maroon-and-white sneakers all match, and they're those fancy track shoes that have a low profile and probably weigh 6.3 ounces. And I'm wondering if every runner on the team really wanted that exact pair, because I'm 100 percent certain that Frankie wouldn't race in anything but her Nike Flyknit Racers, and I wouldn't trade in my

Ultraboosts for anything. But they look fast, matching like that. Really fast.

I'm also 100 percent certain that our uniforms aren't even new, because when Coach Okeke handed me one on the day I joined there were no tags and he told me I should probably wash it first. I wonder if it was Reggie's.

I wiggle my toes and feel Guthrie's guitar pick, which I slid into my shoe this morning.

I watch my mom and dad step up and up the bleacher stairs and sit down halfway to the top, right in the middle. They don't leave a seat between them, and I'm thinking that's a good sign. Plus, my mom's wearing white and my dad's wearing navy, and I know they planned it that way because those are my school's colors, and they look like a team. And I'm thinking that's another good sign too because today is June fifteenth, and to get through a day like today, you're going to need a team. At least that's what Dr. Cyn says.

"I have to warm up," Frankie says, and she bounces off toward the far gate, bringing her knees high to her chest and varying fast steps with slow steps. Ana joins her.

Our relay is the last event of the whole meet, but Frankie and Ana are both running the 100m before then, so Coach Okeke is talking them through a visualization technique as they stretch.

Because Amelia and I are just last-minute substitutes

for the relay, we couldn't register for other races, but I wish we could have because waiting through thousands of meters of races and dozens of long-jump flights and shot-put grunts until the girls' 4x100m relay feels like watching seeds grow as soon as you cover them with soil.

My brain is running sprints between my parents, trying to read their lips and their faces to see what they're talking about, and Ms. Dacie, and if we'll raise enough money at the fund-raiser tomorrow. And exactly what I was doing at this time last year, before that night.

It was a regular day of school. We were reading *The Bridge to Terabithia* in Ms. Jenna's class, and she cried at the end. Ms. Jenna cried at every book we read that year, but this cry wasn't a happy cry, it was a sad, life-is-not-fair-and-we-can't-always-fix-it cry, and I remember thinking this isn't how things are supposed to go in books. Jess and Leslie were supposed to be friends until they were ninety-two and magical places are supposed to keep you safe forever and kids aren't supposed to die.

Before my brain can replay 10:43 and the flares sparking up from the blacktop of that night, I get up from my spot in the grass next to Amelia and join Frankie and Ana warming up, running easy between two cones beside the bleachers.

But Coach Okeke says, "Rest your legs, Rain," and

points back to where I was sitting next to Amelia.

"I'm good—"

"Rest your legs, Rain." He points again and looks at me like he means it.

I sit back down next to Amelia. "T-t-trying to erase your-b-brain?" she asks. "It's J-June fifteenth. Y-you said—"

"I know what I said."

It takes one second for me to feel bad. Amelia's just trying to talk to me because it must be obvious that I need it, and she wrote this whole powerful poem about her voice and here I am shutting her down, but her asking me anything isn't helping me erase my brain.

"Sorry," I say. "Yeah. Trying to erase my brain."

Frankie and Ana are lining up behind their lanes for the 100m, and our whole team stands up to cheer.

There are two girls next to them from the maroon-and-white matching school, and four girls from other schools in the next lanes. The maroon-and-white matching girls stretch and bounce on the toes of their fancy track shoes, and their ponytails bob up and down. Frankie and Ana stretch and bounce too, but before they take their mark they give each other the secret team handshake. The matching maroon girls don't have one. They just crouch into position and look straight ahead.

The gun goes off and the runners shoot from their starts and turn stride over stride down the straightaway. Frankie, Ana, and the two matching girls are leading. Frankie pulls ahead by half a stride and crosses the line first. Then matching girl one and matching girl two, then Ana, and the final four stumble across after her.

Frankie whoops and cheers and all the parents from our school in the crowd are on their feet, including my mom and dad, who are yelling, "Yeah, Frankie! Number one!" and "Go, Ana!" And I'm thinking my plan might already be working because they certainly don't look like they need space with their hands cupped over their mouths hooting and hollering like that.

Frankie and Ana hug and walk slowly back toward all our cheers and chants. Coach Okeke gives them handshakes and calls Frankie "Champ," and says, "You know, those girls are eighth graders." We glance over and it looks like their coach, whose jacket matches their uniforms, is giving them pointers. He gestures to the track and makes quick moves with his hands. The girls hang their heads and put on their warm-ups and drink from their water bottles and shake out their legs as they listen.

Frankie and Ana pull on their sweatshirts and sit with Amelia and me in the grass while they reach out over their legs to stretch their hamstrings. We're all still giddy that Frankie won the 100m as a sixth grader, and that Ana came in fourth.

"I can't wait for the relay," Frankie says.

"That's a fact," I say.

On the lawn in the middle of the track, girls are throwing shot put and a small section of the crowd erupts in cheers, the gun blasts, and a heat of eight boys takes off down the track and curves around the bend for a 200m. Parts of the crowd cheer, and the gun goes off again. Girls are now lining up for the long jump and Coach Okeke is talking our star jumper through a last-minute visualization.

And that's when it happens.

The whole crowd gasps.

One boy lies on the track, holding his ankle and screaming.

Everything is still except one mom running from the bleachers to the track.

Then someone with a first aid kit from the medic tent hustles over.

Then there's a slow, flashing light of an ambulance that has arrived at the entrance. The medic waves his hand from the track to the driver. It's not an emergency. No need to rush.

His coach and the medic carry the boy off and all his

teammates huddle around and one by one everyone in the crowd stands and applauds.

It's the slow, silent rotation of the ambulance lights.

I can't stop watching them revolve red and blue and white.

Each flash fills me with that night.

And before I can stand and hop off with high knees to the gate and warm up my muscles and try to erase my brain with each step, I can feel my chest heave hard like it did that night, like it did that night when the ambulance arrived too slowly, too silently, like someone had waved their hand to say it's not an emergency. Not anymore.

And I can feel the gravel beneath my knees and I can see my parents in the crowd, standing and clapping for the boy, but I can also see the tears on their faces glisten from here, and I can almost feel their arms wrapped tight around me, keeping me back from the *Do Not Cross* tape and in a heap on the ground.

I lean back on my hands in the grass and jam my foot into the ground over and over until I can feel Guthrie's guitar pick under my heel.

Then Amelia lays her hand on top of mine, and Ana's on top of hers, and Frankie looks right at me and I hear her secret message loud and clear. That it's OK, my team is here if I need to run, and my team is here if I need to talk. She adds her hand to the pile, like we did at La Cocina, when we had a plan, when we were all in, and I pick a piece of grass to busy my hands and try to imagine the neurotransmitters increasing in my brain, helping me to focus.

I tie four blades together in a knotted chain and I roll the knots between my thumb and forefinger, and before my brain can start playing memory games on its own, remembering back and back, past the baby quilt that Guthrie rubbed all the knots out of before it could become mine, I keep my eyes on the grass and say, "I've never told anyone everything that happened that night."

CHAPTER 36

That Night

"Hey, sleepyhead."

I pressed the light on my digital watch. 10:43.

He held his finger to his lips and whispered, "There's a band playing at the Basement that I want to see. I have it all planned out. I just need your help. One favor."

"OK," I agreed fast, happy my big brother needed me for something, and our pinkies met in a pact.

"When will you be . . ."

But he held a finger to his lips.

"I'm not going to tell you when," he whispered. "Because I know you, and you'll start counting. No counting, Rain. No worrying."

He explained how he would walk quietly down the stairs, and right as he was opening the door to sneak out, I would have my big job.

"You'll flush the toilet so Mom and Dad won't hear the door squeak open and close shut." I nodded my head as we practiced counting out one, two, three silently on our fingers.

"Flush on three," he said.

Then he rustled my already bed-headed hair. "Thanks."

He carried his shoes in his hands so they wouldn't make noise against the wood floors, and I wondered how he knew to do that. Probably the same way he knew how to get in to see a band at the Basement when you had to be twenty-one to enter.

I walked to the bathroom up on the balls of my feet and laid one finger on the toilet handle. Then I looked down the staircase to the front door and locked eyes with Guthrie.

We counted out together silently. One, two, three.

Flush.

And he was gone before the water swirled down the bowl.

And I helped him go.

I crawled back in bed, straining to make out his truck tires on the gravel driveway, but all I could hear was the toilet bowl filling back up and running loud before it faded away and the house was silent again.

I tried not to think of all the things that could happen when you break the rules, in the dark, past curfew. I tried not to worry. And I tried not to count. I tried not to press the light on my digital watch for four minutes. Then another four. I counted out perfect seconds in my head. One-one-thousand, two-one-thousand, three-one-thousand, and wondered how long a concert goes. The average length of a song is four minutes, and that's a fact because I used to sneak into my brother's room and study the labels of all the records in his collection so that I would know all the names of the songs too. But I didn't know how many songs a band played at a concert, or how long it would take him to drive there and home since all the stoplights in town were blinking yellow at this hour.

I pressed the light on my watch again. Four minutes. Another song.

12:34 . . . 12:38 . . . 1:02 . . . 1:06 . . . 1:10 . . .

At 2:41, the phone rang four long rings. I could hear my dad clear his voice through my bedroom wall.

Then panic.

Mom's voice. And drawers slamming and, "What about Rain?"

"Call the neighbors."

But I had already pulled on my hand-me-down jeans and Guthrie's worn hooded sweatshirt and I stood in their bedroom doorway. "I want to go with you."

"Rain," Mom started. "Honey—"

"I'm going."

Dad tried too. "It's really best if—"

"I'm going."

I slid my bare feet into my Adidas Ultraboosts, and we all ran to the car. I laced my shoes in the back seat while Dad reversed down the driveway and sped off at fifty miles per hour down our dirt road. The speed limit is thirty-five, and Mom and Dad always complained that thirty-five was too high for a dirt road with so many dips and curves, but right then, it wasn't fast enough. And when the dirt turned to pavement, the needle on the speedometer got close to sixty and we whizzed right through the first blinking light and the new stop sign in town that everyone missed anyway because they just weren't used to it yet.

Then I saw the lights and an ambulance and three cop cars. And my brother's truck. And I didn't want to think about what could make a truck look like that. Crushed so hard from the side that it looked like half a truck, pushed into the median, with dirt and grass dug up in two streaks behind it. I squinted my eyes against the lights and looked for Guthrie in the driver's seat, but there was no more driver's seat, just squished metal, and broken glass glinting in the red lights.

I thought he must be sitting on the edge of the ambulance with a blanket over his shoulders. That's what happens in books. The family looks and looks and just when it seems too terrible to be true, they find him, sitting on the back of an ambulance with a nasty cut above his eye and all the EMTs saying that he's going to be OK, and everyone hugs.

I squinted my eyes again, but the lights were too bright and we were stopped and couldn't go any farther because of barricades and *Do Not Cross* tape and a cop asking Dad to roll down his window, but I had to find Guthrie, so I flung open my door and took off running.

I counted each stride until that was all I could hear. The one, two, three of my sneakers against the pavement drowned out the policemen shouting after me. They waved their arms and tried to cut me off, but they weren't as fast as I was. Not even close. I ducked under a barricade and stretched the yellow tape over my head, running toward the flashing lights of the ambulance. The lights were slowly rotating, no big whoop-whoops that you hear when they're driving like crazy to save someone's life because every second matters. And the lights were too slow. Everyone was too slow. No one was rushing like I was.

I was trying to keep count of my strides, but my legs were losing pace until I stopped because I didn't know which direction to turn. Then I felt a hand on my shoulder and another. Mom and Dad. And even though I'd only run twenty-eight strides, my muscles were shaking and I was feeling heavy and I collapsed on the pavement into a big heap with Mom and Dad's arms wrapped around me and each other, and I thought maybe, maybe if we just stayed like this forever and didn't look up, we wouldn't see the ambulance door close and see it drive off slowly. We wouldn't hear the officers asking us to come with them so they could tell us that an eighteen-wheeler lost its brakes on the interstate ramp and soared through a red light and right into Guthrie. And we could just squeeze our eyes closed and make it all untrue.

But no amount of pretending ever brought anyone back. And that's a fact.

CHAPTER 37

Flying

By the time I tell them the whole story of that night, my knotted grass chain has twenty-four blades and is long enough for a necklace.

I don't look up because it feels too hard to see their faces. But I can see that their hands are busy making grass chains too, which makes me think they were really listening and heard every word I told them. And before Coach Okeke comes over and tells us it's time to get warmed up for the relay, I can feel their secret messages rise up and up in that same place that the remembering rises up—that they are right here, even though there isn't anything to say, they are right here.

We take off our sweatshirts and stand up and Coach

Okeke tells us, "High knees to the gate." Before I can throw my first knee to my chest, Frankie looks at me and her eyes are a little red and her nose a little runny and she ties her grass chain around her neck and nods. Amelia and Ana tie theirs too and so do I, and even though no grass chain necklace ever brought anyone back, it makes me feel lighter, like I could fly.

And we have a relay to win.

My hand is tight around the baton as I bounce at the start line. I can see my parents in the bleachers. My dad's pointing at me and waving, and Mom's hand is cupped around her mouth and chanting, "Rain! Rain! Rain!" And even though it sends a rush of embarrassment straight up to my cheeks, I'm glad they're smiling and cheering and happy and maybe not thinking about 365 days ago.

Then I see the white of Ms. Dacie's hair. She's making her way up the bleachers to an empty seat at the top. And when I scan the crowd up and down I see Mrs. Baldwin clapping and cheering too, which means school is out now, and that's a fact because a bunch of other teachers and kids from our school are rushing through the entrance to catch the last race.

Then I focus ahead and see Amelia one hundred meters ahead of me on the track, shaking out her legs and arms and rolling her neck, getting loose, and Ana one hundred meters from her, then Frankie. Together we'll make one loop around the track.

In the lane next to ours is the all-eighth-grade maroon-and-white relay team. Their coach is yelling something about the handoff and the girls watch him and nod.

Amelia, Ana, Frankie, and I all look to Coach Okeke for last-minute advice, and when he's sure he's got all our attention he raises his fist in the air and slowly starts bopping it once, twice, three times and we all join him and start our secret team handshake even though we're all one hundred meters apart. We do the spin turn at the end, and even if we feel a little silly doing a handshake to the empty air in front of us, it feels like we're already closer to each other than the one hundred meters we have to run.

"Those are my sixth graders!" Coach Okeke yells. The rest of our track team is standing with him and the whole crowd is on their feet and the gun hasn't even gone off yet.

Then the official lifts the bullhorn to his mouth and says, "Runners! Take your mark!" I crouch down next to the maroon-team eighth grader.

"Set!"

Then the gun blasts and I explode forward.

I can hear Coach Okeke and the team and Mrs. Baldwin and the other kids from MS 423 and Dacie and Mom and Dad and all the parents in the bleachers. Coach Scottie's voice is loud in my head. *Hut! Hut! Hut!* And I swear for one second I can hear Izzy shout, *Look at her go!* And Guthrie, and the way he used to cheer me on at my meets in Vermont. *Rain, Rain, feel no pain!*

My feet are turning over fast, and I'm flying, and even though my brain isn't emptying like it's supposed to, it's filling up. Filling up with all the voices cheering me on.

Hut! Hut! Hut!

My little Raindrop!

Rain, Rain, feel no pain!

I clutch the baton and dig hard and keep my eyes focused on Amelia in front of me.

She's looking over her shoulder and getting set for our handoff. I can feel Guthrie's guitar pick with each stride, and can see the knotted grass chain bounce off my chest each time I pull my arms through the air.

Look at her go!

Rain, Rain, feel no pain!

I see Amelia's back-stretched, open hand, reaching for me, and I reach for her and pass the baton. As soon as she feels it safe in her hand, she takes off, and she's flying too. I slow my legs and gulp the air and watch

Amelia round the curve toward Ana. Their handoff is perfect too, and Ana is neck and neck with the maroon-team runner, but she holds with her stride for stride. Frankie cheers her on and reaches back. Ana stretches forward and the pass is perfect and Frankie digs deep and pumps her arms and it looks like her Flyknit Racers aren't even touching the track she's going so fast. I watch her sprint to the finish line, her knotted grass chain bouncing on her chest too, and I reach for mine and rub the knots and cheer and cheer until she strides across the line.

Before I can even look to see if my parents are hugging, I'm in a falling heap of arms and legs and the rough rubber of the track is digging into my knees and it's the same kind of heap that I wish I could hold on to forever, like maybe if we did, just stayed in a tangled web of sixth-grade relay team, I wouldn't ever have to feel the prick of Guthrie's guitar pick again, or see a closed door, or calculate the amount of space between my parents, or miss Izzy.

"W-we d-did it!"

"Made history!"

Then the whole team is surrounding us, and I can't hear any singular voices anymore because they're all blended together into a roar of applause and cheers, but I know that in that roar is Amelia, Ana, and Frankie, and

Mrs. Baldwin, and Coach Okeke, and Dacie, and Mom and Dad, and Coach Scottie, and Izzy. And Guthrie.

On the way home we all wear our medals around our necks with our knotted grass chains, which are still holding strong even after the run, and the big heaping pile of cheering, and the award ceremony. We walk side by side by side by side linked at the elbows, and everyone on the sidewalk smiles at our first-place medals and weaves around us. Mom and Dad, and Frankie's dad, and Amelia's mom, and Ana's mom follow behind us and I can hear Mom trying out little phrases in Spanish, and it doesn't even embarrass me as much.

Ana's mom wears her hair pulled up in two tight buns on the top of her head, just like Ana does, and it reminds me of Ana's comic strip, the superhero woman with the Dominican flag cape. My brain doesn't even need to make one hundred clicks before I'm 100 percent certain that Ana's superhero is her mom, and that Ana is the little girl she's carrying through the dark sky.

We stop at La Cocina, and it's the same waitress we had before. As soon as she sees our medals, she pushes the little tables together and we pull all the chairs around until our knees all touch underneath. Then the waitress disappears and comes out with a big tray of hot chocolate mugs with huge scoops of melty vanilla ice cream floating on top. There are enough mugs for everyone, even the parents.

"*Felicidades*," she says, and points to our gold medals. Then she returns to the counter to refill the coffee mugs of everyone sitting and chatting.

At first we can't stop replaying every tenth of a second of the whole relay race.

"I r-really th-thought that g-girl was going to c-catch me!"

"I could hear her footsteps right behind me the whole way!"

I take a slurp of hot chocolate around the mound of ice cream and say, "The crowd was so loud. I've never run in front of that many people!"

"We were going crazy up there!" Ana's mom puts her arm around Ana. "Stomping our feet. Screaming at the top of our lungs. I don't know if I'll have a voice all weekend!"

Then we all start talking about tomorrow's fundraiser. Dad is telling everyone about the tomato plants he transferred in yesterday and how it took two days and all the kids at Ms. Dacie's to pull out the weeds and mix in good soil. "A real team effort."

Amelia's mom and my mom are having a little side conversation about her new job at the hospital, and Amelia's mom is telling her that she's a high school teacher and maybe my mom might want to come up to the school next year for a career fair.

"I'd love to do that," she responds.

Even though my mom and dad aren't sitting next to each other, and there's a whole long table of space between them, I'm thinking they both sound good, like they used to sound when everything was normal. Their voices lift at the right times and they're leaning in and laughing along. And I'm hoping that tomorrow, even if there's space between them, they'll sound the same. Like they're OK, like they're getting out and putting one foot down and then the next, even if it doesn't erase their brain.

The waitress comes back with refills we didn't even order, and we all cheer, maybe because it's the best hot chocolate in the whole world, and maybe because we're happy for more time, all nine of us, squished around the pushed-together tables in La Cocina.

And when we're all walking home, with chocolate mustaches, linked arm in arm in arm in arm, it feels like I'm still flying.

CHAPTER 38

Twice as Tall

I wake up at exactly 10:43 because my brain knows that time, and instead of flying, I'm crashing. The race and the medals and the hot chocolate with ice cream and Mom and Dad cheering feels four hundred miles away, and all I can feel is Guthrie's guitar pick against my ear through my pillowcase and my heart beating one hundred twenty beats per minute wishing I hadn't told Frankie and Amelia and Ana everything about that night because now when I see them tomorrow without our shiny gold medals and the crowd cheering behind us, they'll look at me with sad eyes, or blaming eyes.

Hey, sleepyhead.

I need a favor.

I try to erase my brain and play memory games, but

they're all leading back to that night, and even when I try counting, it comes out in four minutes, four minutes, four minutes, and I wonder how many songs Guthrie listened to before he got back in his truck to come home and why he couldn't have stayed for just one more song, one more four minutes, so that eighteen-wheeler could have lost its brakes and zoomed through an empty intersection.

I hear a door open and close, and when I press the light on my digital watch I'm surprised it's already 2:41. I pull back the comforter and walk up on my toes slowly and open my door too. Dad is sitting on the couch.

"Rain?"

"I'm just—"

"It's OK. Come sit." He pats the cushion next to him, and I crawl up and sit with my feet tucked under me.

"Can't sleep?"

I shake my head.

He pushes the light on his digital watch. "2:41 was when the phone rang," he says.

"Four rings," I say.

He nods.

Then a light turns on and Mom opens the bedroom door and shushes her slippers across the wood floors, tying her bathrobe.

"Can't sleep?" she asks.

I pat the cushion on the other side of me and she sits.

Then my brain makes one hundred clicks and I realize that *this* is the anniversary, and I was so busy trying to fill the day with cheer and winning and gold medals and chocolate and forgetting, that I wasn't thinking about the whole night and how there isn't anything Dr. Cyn could say that could get us through the night.

"Tonight sucks," Mom says.

And because that's a word I'm not supposed to say and it sounds so funny coming out of my mom's mouth, it makes me laugh a little at first, but in three seconds I'm tasting salty tears reach my lips.

Mom grabs my hand and Dad grabs my other one and it makes me think of the knots in the grass chain necklaces.

"It's not your fault that your dad and I are taking a little space."

My heart feels like it drops right out of my chest. Winning the relay and cheering and secret team handshakes and hot chocolate and walking and laughing with Frankie and Amelia and Ana and their parents and meeting Dacie and getting the gardens ready for today didn't push them back together.

And they don't even know the facts. That it is. It is my fault.

"Yes, it is." I sniff.

"No—" Dad starts.

But I don't let him finish because I have to tell them how I know. How I know it's my fault. I tell them about 10:43 and saying OK and our pinkie pact and flushing on three.

And they're both sobbing by the time I tell them that I couldn't even hear Guthrie drive out of the driveway because the water was still running in the toilet bowl and I can't erase it and no amount of counting or secret messages or shovels of snow ever brought anyone back.

And if he hadn't gone, he would be alive, and Mom wouldn't have wanted a fresh start, a new job, a new city, and we wouldn't be here in the Muñozes' apartment and Dad would have his backyard garden and I would have Izzy and we would all have each other just like always.

Then I stop because there's nothing more to say and Mom's and Dad's shoulders are shaking, they're crying so hard, but they're both holding on to me so tight in a big heaping pile of limbs and tears.

Then Mom holds me out at arm's length and looks right at me and instead of keeping me there, she pulls me in again and whispers right in my ear. "No, my little Raindrop. It's not your fault. I'm his mom. It's my job to protect him."

Then Dad sniffs and clears his throat and says, "It's no one's fault."

We're still shaking, all three of us.

"Guthrie went to that concert because he loved music and hated curfew."

And that makes me laugh a little but not enough to stop crying and quivering and sniffing.

"And that stupid eighteen-wheeler lost its stupid brakes that very stupid moment," Dad continues. "And no one made that happen. And no one could have made that not happen."

I say Dad's words over and over again in my brain so I can't forget them.

Mom snorts tears. "He really did hate curfew."

Then she unwraps herself from our heap and for one minute I think she's hustling off to the bedroom like Dad does, but she reemerges with the photo albums that disappeared 365 days ago.

We look through them picture by picture, all three of us. And because memories stick best when we tell them into stories with feelings and smells and colors, we tell the story of each one.

And when we get to the one of three-year-old naked me, crying in the dress-strewn garden, Mom puts her arm around me.

"You tell this one," she says.

And so I do.

"I'd wait until you two weren't looking . . ." I start, and I add every detail I know and I don't stop until I get to the dirt beneath my fingernails.

Then I turn to Mom. "And you told me, *When you bury things deep, they grow up twice as tall.*"

She smiles at me and squeezes my shoulder and pulls me close. "Yes, I did."

And I'm 98 percent certain that we're sharing a secret message right then, all three of us.

CHAPTER 39

Something Great

We wake up in a heap on the couch and Dad says, "We have to hurry!"

We skip breakfast, which is fine because I plan on buying at least two dozen cookies today just for myself, and no one showers, which is also fine because I plan on having dirt under my nails all day too.

We meet Frankie and her dad outside the building and all walk over together and when Frankie first sees me she doesn't look at me with sad eyes or blaming eyes. She just says, "Ready to kick butt again?" and it makes us all laugh.

"Ready," I say.

And now I'm glad that I told her and Amelia and Ana and Mom and Dad about that night because the way it's making me feel reminds me of what Dad taught me about weight-bearing walls when you're doing a house renovation. If you take down a weight-bearing wall without setting up a system of support beams, the whole weight of the house will collapse down on you. But if you build up a strong system of support beams, you can take that weight right off. And it feels good to take that weight right off, knowing that I've got a whole team of beams holding strong.

When we get to Dacie's, I help Alia carry a table outside for the cookies and lemonade. The kitchen already smells like peanut butter and melty chocolate, and Jer and Trevor are in the living room taping a sign to the big plastic donation jar.

When Amelia and Ana get there, they give me a team handshake and say, "What can we do?"

"A menu for the bake sale," I say, and Ana runs inside for art supplies.

Ms. Dacie is hugging everyone when they arrive and saying, "Thank you, thank you, thank you," just like that, three times each for everyone, like she means something so much more but there just isn't a way to say it.

Mom and Dad have all the garden plots sectioned off, and no one can believe how healthy they look. The soil is dark and watered and the rows are labeled with little pictures of vegetables and all the weeds are long gone.

"Beautiful," Dacie says.

"Really happy to do it," Dad tells her.

I help him plant the final seeds before everyone starts to show up, and he reminds me to give each one a little space to grow. I count out the inches with my fingers and place the seeds in the dark soil and I can already feel that they'll grow up and up into something healthy.

Then I wait until Mom and Dad aren't looking and sneak Guthrie's guitar pick from my jeans pocket deep down in the dirt by the tomato plant roots. And I know what my mom says, I know it'll just grow up twice as tall, and that's OK. I want Guthrie to grow up twice as tall. All the details and stories of him.

Sixty-seven people come. Yasmin and Cris throw open the front windows and put on one of Ms. Dacie's records and turn it up to full volume. Matthew runs down the three steps to the basement apartment, where an older couple lives, and asks if we can use their oven too because people are buying cookies faster than we can bake them.

Dad is giving everyone tours of the gardens and explaining when the vegetables will come up and how if they decide to rent a plot he'll help them get the best produce they can. Frankie follows him, translating his words into Spanish. Mom and Frankie's dad are squeezing lemons with Casey, who needs to keep his hands busy because sixty-seven people is a lot, and Ms. Dacie is welcoming everyone walking by on the street.

Amelia's mom is there too, and Ana's, and so is Claudia from the church, and the waitress from La Cocina and her boyfriend and their little daughter, who is running circles around the raised garden beds. Three kids from our class are there, and I recognize another kid from school with his grandpa, and Mrs. Baldwin comes too and congratulates us on a great relay race. She also tells my parents that I'm *quite* a poet, which makes my cheeks feel hot, and now I'm 99 percent certain that they're going to make me read them a poem tonight, which doesn't actually feel too terrible anymore now that I kind of like poetry.

"Ms. Dacie helped me," I say.

One person I recognize from sitting in the café passes by with a laptop bag over her shoulder, and she stops in too and buys some cookies and tours the gardens and leaves a twenty-dollar bill in the donations jar.

And then, right before we start the sale of the garden plots, Nestor comes limping around the corner on his sore feet and worn shoes.

He takes a break at the gate and looks through the

crowd from the sidewalk. I wave and he smiles when he sees me. "New Rain."

Ms. Dacie welcomes him in, and I bring him a lemonade and chocolate chip cookie and help him sit down on the front stoop. When he's not looking, I sneak four dollars for him in the cash box. Some people look at him a little long at first, but then because Ms. Dacie's house is always sending out the secret message that everyone is welcome and everyone belongs, people just go on with eating cookies and listening to music and asking Dad questions about the gardens.

Then Dad and Ms. Dacie get up on the top step of the stoop, turn down the music, and call out, "Gather around!"

He explains about the garden plots and how there are sixteen currently for rent. He tells them what kind of vegetables each will produce in the next few months and the type of care it will require until next planting season. He says that today, if they're interested, they can register to rent a plot, and if Ms. Dacie raises enough money to keep her doors open for the year, monthly garden plot rent payments will begin July first.

Then Frankie stands up, and she looks just as brave and proud as when she read her poem in class. "I just want to say Ms. Dacie means a lot to us." She points to

Jer and Ana and Casey and Trevor and me, and anyone else she can find in the crowd. "She lets us come after school any day, helps us with our homework, teaches us how to bake, encourages our art, and lets us use her computers." She looks at Ms. Dacie. "Ms. Dacie belongs here."

"W-w n-need Ms. Dacie!" Amelia shouts.

Everyone starts cheering and chanting, and Ms. Dacie waves and covers her eyes because I'm 96 percent certain she's about to cry.

Ana's mom puts her arm around Ms. Dacie and speaks up. "This place is home to more than just Ms. Dacie. What she gives to our children, and to us, is more than we can repay."

I'm watching the people in the crowd nod their heads and whisper with their families and friends, and they start pointing at the garden plots.

Then my dad speaks up again. "If you are interested in renting a plot for the year, please form a line to speak with Ms. Dacie, or me, or Maggie." And he points to my mom, and she waves.

In less than two minutes, the line is long enough that we have to open the gate so it can curve down the sidewalk.

Trevor and I carry plates of cookies outside to sell while people stand in line, and almost everyone buys one for the wait, and no one even asks for change.

My heart is beating one hundred beats per minute because the donation jar is stuffed full and so is the cash box, and everyone is excited about the transplanted tomatoes, which are growing tall and red, and I'm thinking this just might work. We just might save Ms. Dacie's place.

Each time someone registers to rent a plot, Ana makes a cool sign with the new renter's name on it, attaches it to a garden stake, and sticks it deep into their new soil.

By the end of the day, there are only cookie crumbs and lemon rinds left and all the plots have been rented and everyone starts hugging Ms. Dacie goodbye and leaving. And Ms. Dacie reminds everyone that her door is always open.

Frankie, Amelia, Ana, and I stay to count the money in the cash box and the donation box, but I keep losing count because Nestor is still here and I'm watching him make slow laps around the new garden beds. Each section has a sign.

Claudia y Roberto
La familia Rodolis
Heather and Andy
Héctor y Frankie
Ortiz
La Cocina Restaurante

Pamela Baldwin

And on and on, the names of people from our neighborhood all stuck in the same soil.

I go over to walk with Nestor and tell him thanks for coming.

"New Rain," he says. "This"—he points to the growing gardens and all the names—"*this* is something great."

I remember his haiku in my notebook, but before I figure out what to say, I see a sign I didn't see before.

The Andrews Family.

And it makes a warm hot-chocolate-and-cookies feeling rise on up where the remembering usually does, because it doesn't just say *Henry Andrews* or *Maggie Andrews* and it doesn't say *Henry, Maggie, and Rain.* It says *The Andrews Family*, and I'm thinking that even though I know Dad will be moving to another apartment in fourteen days, and no matter where we ever live there will always be a big hole where Guthrie should be, at least here we are *The Andrews Family*, and we'll come and plant and water and see what we can make grow up and up, and leave with dirt beneath our fingernails.

And I'm already thinking that maybe we could bring some of the vegetables to the church on Sundays and give them to Nestor and Natasha and her mom.

Nestor circles the gardens again. "Really," he says. "Something great."

Then Frankie and Amelia and Ana squeal and they're jumping up in a hug and Ms. Dacie is dancing and crying and my mom and dad are pumping their fists and high-fiving.

"What? What?"

"We did it!"

It takes me 1.2 seconds to run over and jump into their hugs and celebration.

"We've raised enough money for the year. We rented all the garden plots," Dad says.

"And p-people ate lots of c-cookies!"

Then Mom says, "And Ms. Claudia organized the church congregation for a generous donation too. All of that together will sustain the house for the year." I think of Ms. Claudia and her crow's-feet wrinkles, and now I'm 100 percent certain that's what those mean, a life of kindness. And I can't wait to hug her tomorrow morning in the little church basement kitchen.

After a quadruple high five, Frankie, Amelia, and Ana leave with their parents, and Nestor follows down the street not long after them. I wonder where he's going and if he'll eat again before tomorrow. And I just keep replaying his deep rumble voice in my brain. *Something great.*

Mom and Dad and I help Ms. Dacie clean up and wash the last dishes and Dad makes sure the plots are watered before we leave. When we walk down the steps, through the gate, and turn onto the sidewalk to wave goodbye to Ms. Dacie, I look back at *The Andrews Family* plot and even though I'm too old now to think that a plant of guitar picks will grow up in its place, I *feel* something growing tall, rising up and up and up, taller than the buildings in Washington Heights.

And I think there's a poem singing in me right now, so I tell my brain to remember it so I can write it down with my others when I get home.

Poem 5
And even though 365 days from now is a big who-knows,
 if Ms. Dacie's door will still be open,
 if Dad's will be closed,
 if they'll still need space,
 or need more,
 whether they'll be that one out of four.
And even if you never know
 if the seeds you plant and water
 will grow up tall,
 I at least know that I've got a team.
Frankie, Amelia, and Ana.

Coach Okeke and Mrs. Baldwin.
Nestor.
Izzy and Coach Scottie.
Ms. Dacie, the kids from her house, and Claudia.
Mom and Dad.
Guthrie.
And they're cheering for me.

And that's a fact.

ACKNOWLEDGMENTS

It takes a team to write a book, and I am so grateful to have such an incredible group of smart, supportive people on my side.

I am especially appreciative to have the parents I do—who encouraged my childhood dream to be a writer, and are celebrating every moment of it with me. They, themselves, are an excellent team and have taught me the importance of picking great teammates.

My agent, Stephen Barbara, cheered Rain from the beginning. His confidence in me and in this story, and his excited phone calls and quick responses, have given me that extra bit of courage that a writer needs. Plus, after twenty-six emails back and forth, he came up with the perfect title.

I am beyond lucky to have a teammate in my editor, Erica Sussman. At each stage she armed me with an extraordinary guide to tighten this story into a stronger version. She is so smart and insightful and has made me a better writer.

A writer's manuscript passes through many hands that make it into a beautiful book. Thank you to the whole crew at HarperCollins for the care you've taken with *Right as Rain*.

Writing can sometimes make you feel, as Rain would say, like a one-and-only, because when it really comes down to it, you just have to write. You. Pen. Notebook. Laptop. Write. I cannot tell you how grateful I am to have someone who shares in the process with me daily.

Kamahnie, you are my home team. You have allowed all my characters to live right there with us in our apartment. You talk about them like they're old friends, like they're family, and really care how they're faring at the end of each day. You have been there, cheering and listening, and following me paragraph by daily paragraph, through the exciting beginning, and murky middle, and all the way to the finish line. I'm so happy I get to share all this, side by side, with you. And that's a fact.

And to Miles and Paige—I have done my very best writing heartbeat to heartbeat with you. And your hearts will always be the inspiration for me to be my very best.

Books by
LINDSEY STODDARD

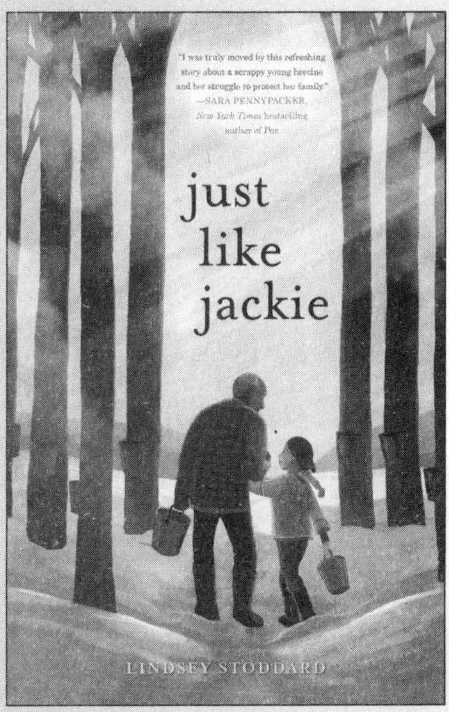
"I was truly moved by this refreshing story about a scrappy young heroine and her struggle to protect her family."
—SARA PENNYPACKER, New York Times bestselling author of Pax
just like jackie
LINDSEY STODDARD

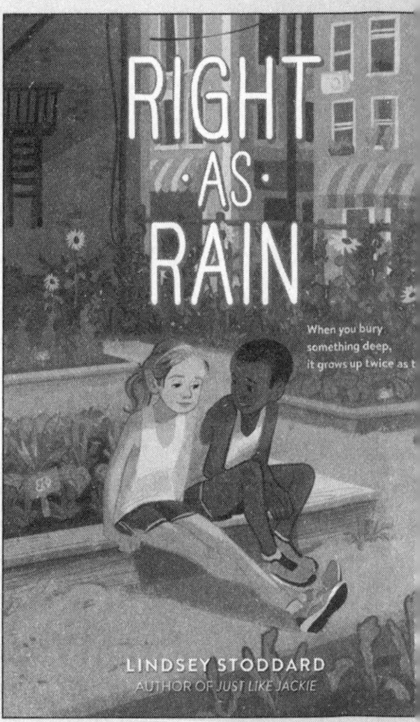
RIGHT AS RAIN
When you bury something deep, it grows up twice as t
LINDSEY STODDARD
AUTHOR OF JUST LIKE JACKIE